The Transnational Illegal Adoption Market

The Transnational Illegal Adoption Market

A Criminological Study of the German and Dutch Intercountry Adoption Systems

Elvira Loibl

eleven
international publishing

Published, sold and distributed by Eleven International Publishing
P.O. Box 85576
2508 CG The Hague
The Netherlands
Tel.: +31 70 33 070 33
Fax: +31 70 33 070 30
email: sales@elevenpub.nl
www.elevenpub.com

Sold and distributed in USA and Canada
Independent Publishers Group
814 N. Franklin Street
Chicago, IL 60610, USA
Order Placement: +1 800 888 4741
Fax: +1 312 337 5985
orders@ipgbook.com
www.ipgbook.com

Eleven International Publishing is an imprint of Boom uitgevers Den Haag.

ISBN 978-94-6236-916-0
ISBN 978-94-6274-050-1 (e-book)

Cover photograph: Nicholas Poussin, The Judgment of Solomon (Musée du Louvre, 1649).

This book is dedicated to my parents, Martha and Werner, and to all birth, adoptive and foster parents, who do the best they can for their children.

Preface

The cover of this book features King Solomon of Israel who rules between two women both claiming to be the mother of an infant son. 1 Kings 3:16-28 recounts that two women living in the same house, each the mother of a baby boy, came to Solomon. The child belonging to one woman had smothered, and its mother had exchanged it for the living one, putting her own dead child in the other woman's bed as she laid sleeping, and taking the living child to herself. In the morning, the mother of the living child had discovered that the child was not hers, but the woman whose child was dead would not give up the one that she had stolen. The two women stood before the king, each one claiming that the living child was hers, and that the dead child belonged to the other. Solomon called for a sword and declared his judgment: "Cut the living child in two and give half to one and half to the other". One mother did not contest the ruling, declaring that if she could not have the baby then neither of them should, but the other begged Solomon, "Give the baby to her, just don't kill him!" The king declared the second woman the true mother, as a mother would even give up her baby if that was necessary to save its life.

How is the story of King Solomon's judgment relevant for the intercountry adoption system? Just like the woman's vulnerable state was taken advantage of (being asleep meant that she was unable to protect her child), the extreme powerlessness of numerous birth parents that face poverty and/or discrimination is often being exploited. As several reports have shown, not only children that were given up freely by their parents enter the adoption system, but also children who have been purchased, kidnapped or abducted from their vulnerable families. Also the stealing mother's role does share some parallels with the role of adoptive parents: Just like the woman in the story, many adopters are driven by the desperate desire to have a child of their own. And although they would not kidnap anybody else's baby, some might at least facilitate the illegal removal of a child by ignoring the significance of their money in the adoption system and by turning a blind eye to signs of irregular practices by other stakeholders involved in adoptions.

The judgment of Solomon is often referred to as an example of profound wisdom. The king's verdict has revealed the truth and solved the dispute between the two women in the best interests of the child. In the current intercountry adoption system, such a Solomonic judgement is difficult to render. The different stakeholders involved in international adoptions have to face a myriad of complex questions and dilemmas: Who should care for the numerous children worldwide who have to live and work on the streets? Would it be in the best interests of the child to be placed for adoption if he or she has birth parents that want to keep their child but do not have the financial means to provide proper care? What do `the best interests of the child' and `proper care' mean in the first place? Would it be right to interpret these terms according to Western standards or would it ultimately lead to an imperialist, neo-colonial outcome? What should happen to children who live in child care institutions? Should a child's right to identity preservation trump the possibility to be placed into a loving adoptive family abroad? Is it legitimate for a Western adoption agency or adopters to donate money or goods to the birth family or the orphanage to help care for the rest of the children, or would it constitute payment for a child? What should a judge decide when it turns out that a child, who has lived with his or her new adoptive family for already quite some time, had actually been obtained illegally from the birth parents? Would it be right to leave the child with the adoptive family or to send him or her back to the country of origin in order to be reunited with the birth family? The present book sheds light on these questions and unearths the factors in the intercountry adoption system which impede a wise judgement by the different stakeholders involved that actually serve the best interest of the children.

Table of Contents

Acknowledgements

One of the great delights of finishing a PhD is finally being able to publicly express feelings of gratitude to the people who have supported me in completing this book. First and foremost, I would like to express my sincerest thanks to my supervisors, André Klip, Susan Rutten and Lies Wesseling, for their inspiration, encouragement, trust and patience. You carefully accompanied me throughout my PhD journey and your constructive feedback and constant support greatly benefitted my research. You not only cared for me as a PhD student but also as a person. Special thanks also go to René de Groot who was member in the PhD selection committee and who regularly sent me interesting articles and reports on intercountry adoption.

My gratitude also goes to Hans Nelen who encouraged me to apply for this PhD position, who contributed his criminological expertise and valueable ideas, and who helped me to publish my first academic article.

I would like to thank all experts who agreed to share their insights and expierences with me, most notably Wolfgang Weitzel and Jörg Reinhardt who patiently responded to numerous inquiries. Many thanks to David Smolin who encouraged me to explore the issue of child trafficking for adoption purposes and with whom I discussed some avenues of research at the early stage of my PhD project. I am also grateful to Arun Dohle whose enthusiasm, and yes, sometimes annoying, persistency greatly helped me to explore the dark underside of the adoption industry. He provided me with crucial information and showed me new ways of thinking about intercountry adoption. The numerous heated debates we have helped me a lot to think outside the box.

I am indebted to Marlies Lijten who saved me a lot of time by transcribing numerous interviews with great professionalism. Special thanks also to Paul Adriaans who provided me with technical support for my interviews and who had to witness my rage attack when I realized I had lost the recording of an interview.

I want to express my sincerest thanks to Hannah Brodersen and Anna Pivaty, who supported me throughout my PhD journey from the beginning and who agreed to serve as my paranymphs. Thanks also to other colleagues and friends within the faculty with whom I could share ideas, feelings of joy and insecurities, including but not limited to: my office mates Benedicta Deogratias, Naina Khanna and Vanessa Thünsmeyer, Natassa Athanasiadou, Constantijn van Aartsen, Kim Geurtjens, Anna Goldberg, Johannes Keiler, Christina Peristeridou, David Roef, Zvezda Vankova and Antonia Waltermann. Special thanks go to Claire Boost who patiently clarified my language related questions and offered to read some parts of the final manuscript when I suddenly lost all confidence in my English.

Thanks also to my dear friends in Austria who supported me from afar, most notably Hanna Kastner and Simone Schill who carefully listened to my ideas and problems and always support me in what I do.

I wish to express my deepest gratitude to my family who contributed to the succesful accomplishment of this book. Thanks to my sisters Cynthia, Olivia and Verena and to my dear cousin Andrea who were always there for me. Special thanks go to my parents whose undefatigle emotional and financial support made my personal and academic development possible. I would not be where I am right now if it was not for you. My heartfelt gratitude also goes to Erika Loibl and Lambert Cipek who deeply care for me and what I do as if I was their own daugther. I would also like to thank Sabine Hofmann who always makes me feel home far away from home.

This book would never have been written without the love and unique support of Robin Hofmann, my partner in crime, who inspired and encouraged me to pursue a PhD and who always believed in me and my ability to complete this book, also at times when I did not. You were the rock during my writing process and I am deeply grateful for that.

Maastricht,
6 Janurary 2019

I Introduction

1 Central Focus and Scope

Intercountry adoption has provided many parentless children with a loving family and a nurturing home that they would otherwise not have had in their native countries. In many societies, extreme poverty, wars, cultural norms, social policies or epidemics produce children that are not wanted or cannot be cared for. For instance, in China, the one-child policy that was introduced in the 1980s, combined with the cultural preference for sons, resulted in numerous abandoned baby girls in the 1990s.[1] In India and South Korea, unwed motherhood is still stigmatized and leaves many desperate young women relinquishing their children so as to avoid social exclusion.[2] In many African countries, AIDS has disrupted extended family networks, leaving children in institutions or on the streets.[3] Furthermore, numerous special-needs children, meaning children that are mentally or physically disabled (e.g. because they have a cleft lip or a club foot), are unwanted by their families, who are overwhelmed by their child's disability. For many of these children, intercountry adoption was probably the best solution as it spared them a life without a stable home and an attachment figure. It has also brought great joy for numerous couples and individuals, many of which were unable to have their own children. Without a doubt, in a number of cases, intercountry adoption has constituted a win-win situation for all involved parties.

However, intercountry adoption also has a dark underside. The social practice has not only produced good for children and their adoptive parents, but at the same time also great harm.Within the last couple of years, numerous cases have been uncovered whereby illicit practices were employed to generate 'adoptable' children in order to meet the high demand for adoption among Western couples and individuals. Children were purchased from their impoverished families, or abducted from their homes, the streets or from orphanages where they were placed temporarily by their parents for the purpose of education and care.[4] Birth mothers were fooled into thinking that their newborn children were stillborn

1 K. A. Johnson (2004). "Wanting a Daugther, Needing a Son." Yeong & Yeong, Minneapolis.

2 P. Bos (2007). "Once a Mother: Relinquishment and Adoption From the Perspective of Unmarried Mothers in South India." PhD thesis, University of Amsterdam; K. Joyce (2013). "The Child Catchers: Rescue, Trafficking, and the New Gospel of Adoption." Public Affairs, New York, pp. 284-288.

3 See, for example, W. C. Chirwa (2002). "Social Exclusion and Inclusion: Challenges to Orphan Care in Malawi." Nordic Journal of African Studies, 11, 1, 93-113.

4 UNICEF International Child Development Centre (1998). "Intercountry adoption." UNICEF, Florence (Innocenti Digest no. 4), p. 6; D. M. Smolin (2006). "Child Laundering: How the Intercountry Adoption

or died shortly after birth, while in reality the babies were being abducted from the hospitals or maternity clinics.[5] Vulnerable birth parents were coerced or provided with misleading information on the consequences of an adoption in order to obtain their consent for an adoption.[6] Birth certificates and other documents that are necessary for an adoption were falsified so as to hide the children's origin and background and to identify them as legally abandoned.[7] Government officials or judges in the sending countries were being bribed to secure or approve a fraudulent intercountry adoption.[8] All of these practices have left numerous parents desperately searching for their children or grieving over their loss, and adoptees growing up far from their native countries with the false idea that their families did not want them or had died. They also left numerous adoptive parents believing that they 'saved' an orphan from a life without a family in their native country.

The illegal and abusive practices within the intercountry adoption system have so far largely escaped the attention of criminologists. Within the last couple of years, a great body of criminological research has focused on transnational crime, and human trafficking for the purpose of sexual and labour exploitation in particular.[9] Yet, the issue of child trafficking for the purposes of adoption has so far been neglected by criminologists.[10] The present research aims to fill this gap.

The objectives of the study are twofold. First, it aims to identify the organization and operation of the illegal transnational adoption market in children from a criminological perspective and it seeks to outline the similarities and main differences in terms of structure and functioning between conventional forms of human trafficking (meaning human traf-

---

System Legitimizes and Incentivizes the Practices of Buying, Trafficking, Kidnapping, and Stealing Children." The Wayne Law Review, 52, 1, 113-200, pp. 119-124.

5 UNICEF International Child Development Centre (1998). "Intercountry adoption." UNICEF, Florence (Innocenti Digest no. 4), p. 6.

6 *Ibid.*

7 N. Cantwell (2005). "Is intercountry adoption linked with trafficking for exploitation?" International Social Service, Nr. 11-12, pp. 1-2.

8 *Ibid.*

9 See, for instance, J. Winterdyk, et al. (2010). "Introduction to Special Issue: Human Trafficking." European Journal of Criminology, 7, 1, 5-10; B. C. Oude Breuil, et al. (2011). "Human Trafficking Revisited: Legal, Enforcement and Ethnographic Narratives on Sex Trafficking to Western Europe." Trends in Organized Crime, 14, 1, 30-46; T. O. Mahmoud and C. Trebesch (2010). "The economics of human trafficking and labour migration: Micro-evidence from Eastern Europe." Journal of Comparative Economics, 38, 2, 173-188.

10 A great deal of research on child trafficking for adoption purposes has been conducted by Smolin, professor of law at Cumberland School of Law in Birmingham, Alabama. Even though he is not a criminologist, he had published many articles about crime in the intercountry adoption system which addressed questions that are criminological in nature, see, for example, D. M. Smolin (2004). "The Two Faces of Intercountry Adoption: The Significance of the Indian Adoption Scandals." Seton Hall Law Review, 35, 403-493; D. M. Smolin (2006). "Child Laundering: How the Intercountry Adoption System Legitimizes and Incentivizes the Practices of Buying, Trafficking, Kidnapping, and Stealing Children." The Wayne Law Review, 52, 1, 113-200.

ficking for the purpose of, for instance, sexual and labour exploitation), and child trafficking for adoption purposes.

Some readers might be struck by the study's focus on the 'illegal adoption market', wondering whether anything such as a 'legal adoption market' exists. This book will explain that the last half-century has indeed witnessed the emergence of a transnational market in adoptable children. The international adoption community agrees that the costs of adopting a child internationally have soared over the last years. Couples and individuals wishing to adopt a child from abroad must pay considerable adoption fees, depending on the adoption agency as well as the sending country they choose to adopt from. For instance, couples and individuals adopting a child from Russia *via* the German adoption agency *Zukunft für Kinder* must pay almost €17,300 for adoption services rendered in Germany and abroad.[11] An adoption from Kyrgyzstan arranged by the Dutch agency *Kind en Toekomst* costs around €29,500.[12] Financial transactions, including fees paid to the adoption agencies, family courts, government officials, orphanages, embassies etc. make international adoption a lucrative business. Such financial exchanges, although characterized as 'service costs' or 'administrative fees', resemble payments that take place in most other economic spheres.[13] Spar notes: "When parents choose a child to adopt [...] they are doing business. Firms are making money, customers are making choices, and children – for better or worse – are being sold".[14]

The adoption market has both a legitimate and an illegitimate side.[15] At one end of the spectrum are legal intercountry adoptions that involve the payment of large sums of money. At the other end of the market spectrum are illicit practices that are employed to generate adoptable children that are not legitimately available for intercountry adoption. These practices include, as outlined above, purchasing or abducting children from their families and deceiving birth parents in order to obtain their consent to adoption, but also circumventing the subsidiarity principle which provides that an international adoption may be considered only if no domestic child care option can be found. The present study focusses on the illegal dimension of the transnational adoption market.

Second, this study aims at detecting and explaining the weaknesses of the intercountry adoption systems of two European receiving countries – meaning countries to which children are adopted – namely Germany and the Netherlands. The main research question

---

11 https://www.zukunftfuerkinder.de/kosten (last accessed on 07.08.2018).

12 http://www.kindentoekomst.nl/30/adoptie/adoptiekosten/30.html (last accessed on 07.08.2018).

13 M. Goodwin (2010). "Baby Markets: Money and the New Politics of Creating Families." Cambridge University Press, pp. 4-5.

14 D. L. Spar (2006). "The baby business: How money, science, and politics drive the commerce of conception." Harvard Business School Press, Boston, p. xi.

15 M. Freundlich (2000). "Adoption and Ethics, The Market Forces in Adoption." Child Welfare League of America, Washington, p. 41; S. Marijnen and J. Doomernik (2015). "Baby Migration." AEMI Journal, 13, 133-149, p. 147.

that will be dealt with is: What are the systems' structural features that encourage and facilitate the trafficking of children into Germany and the Netherlands for the purpose of adoption? This question reflects developments in the study of crime that focus on the *criminogenic* factors in a given organizational system that compel or facilitate criminal activities, rather than on the individual perpetrators themselves.[16] The aim of the present study is therefore not to identify individual scapegoats in the German and Dutch adoption systems and to hold them responsible for illegal adoption practices in the sending countries. Rather, this research seeks to expose systemic weaknesses in both adoption systems that are conducive to the trafficking in children for adoption purposes.

Generally speaking, an intercountry adoption system is a set of stakeholders and procedures that are in place to carry out and supervise intercountry adoptions. In the receiving countries, the stakeholders not only include the adopters and adoption agencies, which co-operate with the sending countries and carry out the placement of children, but also state authorities that accredit and supervise the agencies, assess the adopters' suitability and eligibility, recognize foreign adoption decisions and process visas or passports for the adoptees. The present study scrutinizes the roles of the stakeholders and the procedures in both the German and Dutch adoption system for potential weaknesses and conditions that might work to encourage the trafficking for adoption purposes. A particular focus will be placed on the systems' following features: (a) access to private adoptions that adopters pursue without the involvement of state authorities, (b) the accreditation requirements for German and Dutch adoption agencies, as well as their financial status, (c) the co-operation of the adoption agencies with the sending countries, particularly the agencies' supervision of their foreign representatives and partner organizations, as well as the transfer of money (in the form of fees and donations) abroad, (d) the monitoring and control of the adoption agencies and of adoption placements by the German and Dutch authorities and (e) the criminal liability of German and Dutch adopters and adoption agencies.

National adoption systems are strongly shaped by international legal instruments, most notably the 1989 United Nations Convention on the Rights of the Child and the 1993 Hague Convention on Protection of Children and Co-Operation in Respect of Intercountry Adoption. Together, both treaties set forth the guiding standards and principles from

16 M.L. Needleman and C. Needleman (1979). "Organizational Crime: Two Models of Criminogenesis." The Sociological Quarterly, 20, 517-528; H. A. Faberman (1975). "A Criminogenic Market Structure: the Automobile Industry." The Sociological Quarterly, 16, 438-457; W. N. Leonard and M. G. Weber (1970). "Automakers and Dealers: A Study of Criminogenic Market Forces." Law & Society Review, 4, 407-424; H. Nelen and L. Ritzen (2013). "How They Still Try to get Away With It: Crime in the Dutch Real Estate Sector Before and After The Crisis." In S. Will et al. (eds), "How They Got Away With It: White Collar Criminals and The Financial Meltdown." Colombia University Press, New York, 223-245.

which all adoption laws and practices of their Contracting States should flow.[17] They aim to safeguard the rights of children that are involved in intercountry adoptions and to prevent their abduction, sale or trafficking. The present study also critically analyses these two Conventions with a view to uncovering and explaining their pitfalls and weaknesses. Both Germany and the Netherlands have ratified the treaties referred to above. Thus, any of the Conventions' limitations and potential weaknesses will probably also be reflected in the German and Dutch adoption systems.

Adopters, meaning couples and individuals who (wish to) adopt a child, are particularly crucial stakeholders in the adoption system due to their privileged, and thus powerful, position therein. International adopters are usually well-educated and belong to the higher or middle social class.[18] In many receiving countries, they are organized into interest groups which seek to influence laws and policies on intercountry adoption, at both the national and international level. There is, thus, much to suggest that not only their interests and wishes, but also their values and beliefs, strongly influence and shape the adoption systems. The present study therefore also seeks to unearth the German and Dutch adopters' perceptions of intercountry adoption, parenthood, children, and the countries they adopt from as well as the role they play in the adoption system. It particularly aims at exploring how (prospective) adoptive parents manage the mingling of what is culturally considered to be incompatible: parenthood and consumption, love and money.

In intercountry adoption, parenting a child – culturally relegated to the intimate, private sphere and thus understood as non-economic in scope – is complexly intertwined with commodification and consumption.[19] As was explained above, foreign adopters must pay considerable sums of money for a child to love. It is well-established that the money paid by foreign adopters is the main driving force behind the transnational illegal adoption market.[20] However, it is less evident how the adopters' hidden cultural assumptions, beliefs and attitudes influence and shape the illegal market in children. This study thus aims at illuminating the adopters' invisible expectations, values and perceptions that underlay their actions and reasoning, and explains how they might work to facilitate child trafficking for adoption purposes.

---

17 R. Rios-Kohn (1998). "Intercountry adoption: An international perspective on the practice and standards." Adoption Quarterly, 1, 4, 3-32, p. 15.

18 See, for example, R. A. C. Hoksbergen (2011). "Kinderen die niet konden blijven: zestig jaar adoptie in beeld." Aspekt, Soesterberg; J. A. Welsh et al. (2008). "Ready to Adopt: Characteristics and Expectations of Preadoptive Families Pursuing International Adoptions." Adoption Quarterly, 11, 3, 176-203, p. 197.

19 M. Homans (2013). "The Imprint of Another Life: Adoption Narratives and Human Possibility." University of Michigan Press, Ann Arbor, p. 26.

20 R. Post (2007). "Romania–for Export Only: The Untold Story of the Romanian 'Orphans'." Netherlands: EuroComment Diffusion; D. M. Smolin (2006). "Child Laundering: How the Intercountry Adoption System Legitimizes and Incentivizes the Practices of Buying, Trafficking, Kidnapping, and Stealing Children." The Wayne Law Review, 52, 1, 113-200, p. 175; H. Bochéat et al. (2012). "Investigating the Grey Zones of Intercountry Adoption." International Social Service, p. 36.

Several studies have dealt with the adoption systems of the sending countries, highlighting their corrupt systems and limited or ineffective administrative and enforcement capacities as being responsible for illegal and abusive practices.[21] Yet, considerably less attention has been paid to the adoption systems of the receiving states.[22] The present research switches the focus to the countries where children are moved to for mainly two reasons. First, it is primarily the Western adults' demand for adoptable children and their willingness to pay large amounts of money that are the driving forces behind the illegal transnational adoption market.[23] Second, child trafficking for adoption purposes can only be tackled if the criminogenic conditions in the adoption systems of both the sending and receiving countries are identified and then removed or circumvented. The intercountry adoption system can only be made more sustainable and ethical if we are able to understand the organization and functioning of the illegal transnational adoption market – that involves both supply as well as demand countries –, and if we are fully aware of all the conditions

21 See, for example, J. Dickens (2002). "The paradox of inter-country adoption: analysing Romania's experience as a sending country." International Journal of Social Welfare, 11, 1, 76-83, p. 76; J. L. Roby and J. Ife (2009). "Human rights, politics and intercountry adoption: An examination of two sending countries." International Social Work, 52, 5, 661-671; M. Breuning and J. Ishiyama (2009). "The Politics of Intercountry Adoption: Explaining Variation in the Legal Requirements of Sub-Saharan African Countries." Perspectives on Politics 7, 1, 89-101; A. Dohle (2008). "Inside Story of an Adoption Scandal." Cumberland Law Review, 39, 131-185; P. J. Meier and Z. Xiaole (2008). "Sold into Adoption: The Hunan Baby Trafficking Scandal Exposes Vulnerabilities in the Chinese Adoptions to the United States." Cumberland Law Review, 39, 1, 87-130; T. Maskew (2004). "Child Trafficking and Intercountry Adoption: The Cambodian Experience." Cumberland Law Review, 35, 619-638; S. Hoelgaard (1998). "Cultural determinants of adoption policy: A Colombian case study." International Journal of Law, Policy and the Family 12, 2, 202-241, pp. 217-218; V. Tadler (2010). "Child Trafficking for the Purpose of Inter-country Adoption, With a Case Study on Guatemala." PhD Thesis, University of Vienna; A. Cardarello (2009). "The Movement of the Mothers of the Courthouse Square: "Legal Child Trafficking," Adoption and Poverty in Brazil." Journal of Latin American and Caribbean Anthropology, 14, 1, 140-161; A. Cardarello (2012). "The Right to have a Family: 'Legal Trafficking of Children', Adoption and Birth Control in Brazil." Anthropology & Medicine, 19, 2, 225-240; J. L. Roby and T. Maskew (2012). "Human Rights Considerations in Intercountry Adoption: The Children and Families of Cambodia and Marshall Islands." In Gibbons and K. Smith Rotabi (eds), "Intercountry Adoption: Policies, Practices, and Outcomes." Ashgate, Farnham, 55-66.

22 See, for example, D. M. Smolin (2006). "Child Laundering: How the Intercountry Adoption System Legitimizes and Incentivizes the Practices of Buying, Trafficking, Kidnapping, and Stealing Children." The Wayne Law Review, 52, 1, 113-200; D. M. Smolin (2004). "The Two Faces of Intercountry Adoption: The Significance of the Indian Adoption Scandals." Seton Hall Law Review, 35, 403-493; P. J. Meier (2008). "Small commodities: How child traffickers exploit children and families in intercountry adoption and what the United States must do to stop them." The Journal of Gender, Race & Justice, 12, 185-224; I. Lammerant and M. Hofstetter (2008). "Adoption: at what cost? For an ethical responsibility of receiving countries in intercountry adoption." Terre des hommes, Lausanne.

23 K. P. Nelson (2006). "Shopping for children in the international marketplace." In J. J. Trenka et al. (eds), "Outsiders Within: Writing on transracial adoption." South End Press, Cambridge, 89-104; N. B. Graff (2000). "Intercountry Adoption and the Convention on the Rights of the Child: Can the Free Market in Children be Controlled?" Syracuse Journal of International Law & Commerce, 27, 405-430; E. B. Kapstein (2003). "The baby trade." Foreign Affairs, 82, 6, 115-125; R. Högbacka (2008). "The quest for a child of one's own: Parents, markets and transnational adoption." Journal of Comparative Family Studies, 39, 3, 311-330.

that are present on both sides of the adoption market which are conducive to the trafficking in children for adoption purposes.

The present study only deals with trafficking in children for the purpose of adoption and not with trafficking in children through adoption for (other) exploitation purposes, such as prostitution or forced labour.[24] Furthermore, it only focusses on international adoptions from non-Western countries. Thus, it does not deal with the placement of children from, for instance, the United States, which is not only the most significant recipient of adoptees but also an important provider of children (mostly of African descent) to same-sex couples in Europe.[25] This is because the forces and conditions that are present in the adoption market involving children from Western-countries are arguably different from the ones that are present in the market that has emerged between Western and non-Western states. For the same reasons, the research mainly focusses on stranger adoptions. Finally, the study does not deal with the adoption of surrogate children, meaning children that were born as a result of a surrogacy agreement. Surrogacy and intercountry adoptions are strongly linked to each other and distinguish themselves through several similarities. Both are (in some countries prohibited) means for involuntarily childless couples and individuals to form a family, and both are driven by socio-political inequalities.[26] Since more and more previously important sending states limited the number of adoptees to be sent abroad, a shift has been observed from intercountry adoption to surrogacy.[27] However, dealing with the issue of surrogacy as well would go beyond the scope of this research.

Some readers may not be pleased with the way this book is written. They may claim that it is a one-sided account which puts all the attention on the illegal practices within the intercountry adoption system, to the exclusion of the many positive things it has brought to children and their adoptive parents. Braithwaite, the famous Australian criminologist who conducted research on corporate crime within the pharmaceutical industry, explains this one-sided nature of criminological studies as follows:

> Unfortunately, it is the job of criminologists to explore the seamy side of human existence. If a criminologist undertakes a study of mugging or murder, no one

24 See T. W. Brown and J. Roby (2016). "Exploitation of Intercoumtry Adoption: Toward a Common Understanding and Action." Adoption Quarterly, 19, 2, 63-80, distinguishing between child trafficking and the sale of children.

25 D. Marre and L. Briggs (2009). "International Adoption: Global Inequalities and the Circulation of Children." New York University Press, p. 9.

26 R. Scherman et al. (2016). "Global commercial surrogacy and international adoption: parallels and differences." Adoption & Fostering, 40, 1, 20-35; J. Bhabha (2004). "Moving Babies: Globalization, Markets and Transnational Adoption." The Fletcher Forum of World Affairs, 28, Summer, 181-198, p. 185.

27 K. S. Rotabi and N. F. Bromfield (2012). "The Decline in Intercountry Adoptions and New Practices of Global Surrogacy: Global Exploitation and Human Rights Concerns." Affilia: Journal of Women and Social Work, 27, 2, 129-141.

> expects a 'balanced' account which gives due credit to the fact that many muggers are good family men, loving fathers who provide their children with a Christian upbringing, or perhaps generous people which have shown a willingness to help neighbours in trouble. Yet criminologists are expected to provide such 'balance' when they study corporate criminals.[28]

The fact that the present study does not emphasize the good that this social practice has brought does not mean it is not acknowledged and appreciated. An extensive body of psychological, behavioural and sociological research exists that points to the positive effects that intercountry adoption has on individual children, thus on a micro level.[29] Yet, this criminological study primarily focuses on intercountry adoption on a macro level. It uncovers and explains the structural weaknesses of the adoption system and addresses the harm that illegal and abusive practices create for adoptees, their birth parents and families, as well as the child welfare system in the sending countries.

Of course, when considering policies on intercountry adoption, for instance, the question, which is was debated in the Dutch parliament in 2016 and 2017, whether or not to ban this social practice altogether, both the positive effects for individual children on a micro level, as well as the structural weaknesses on a macro level, need to be taken into account and carefully weighed against each other. This criminological study should therefore inform policymakers dealing with intercountry adoption about the latter.

2 METHODOLOGICAL FRAMEWORK

2.1 *Interdisciplinary Approach*

This book presents an interdisciplinary study of child trafficking for adoption purposes. Intercountry adoption, and the abusive practices connected thereto, is an enigmatic phenomenon that is strongly influenced and shaped by international laws, global demographics and economic conditions, societal changes as well as cultural perceptions of children and childhood. It is thus appropriate if not necessary to employ an interdisciplinary approach to studying the dark underside of this complex phenomenon. This approach generally

28 J. Braithwaite (1984). "Corporate Crime in the Pharmaceutical Industry." Routledge, London, pp. vii-viii.

29 See, for example, C. Schoenmaker, et al. (2014). "From infancy to young adulthood: The Leiden longitudinal adoption study." Leiden University, available at https://openaccess.leidenuniv.nl/bitstream/handle/1887/25253/04.pdf?sequence=8; F. Juffer, et al. (2008). "Adoptie als interventie (2)." Kind en Adolescent, 29, 1, 31-49; F. Juffer, et al. (2008). "Adoptie als interventie (1)." Kind en Adolescent, 29, 1, 17-30; Van den Dries, et al. (2009). "Fostering security? A meta-analysis of attachment in adopted children." Children and Youth Services Review, 31, 3, 410-421.

reflects the interdisciplinary nature of criminology, a field that seeks to understand and explain crime in a holistic way by drawing knowledge from a variety of disciplines. The present criminological research studies the illegal transnational adoption market in children and the criminogenic conditions of the German and Dutch adoption systems by borrowing ideas and theories from criminology, sociology and cultural anthropology, most notably, the routine activities theory,[30] the prism of crime,[31] the concept of denial (Chapter II),[32] the idea of Western (neo-) imperialism[33] (Chapter III), the theory of neutralization (Chapter IV),[34] as well as the concept of individualization[35] (Chapter VI).

The present study combines a normative legal analysis with empirical legal research. It not only analyses international and national laws and policies on intercountry adoption, but it also examines how these laws and policies are put into practice in Germany and the Netherlands, as well as the challenges and pitfalls they create. Legal research explores the legal framework of adoption and how it operates in practice. Yet, it does not capture and explain the underlying cultural values that shape and influence the actions of the stakeholders within the adoption system. The 'blindness' of legal research is compensated for by the insights afforded by another approach: cultural studies. By using a narrative analysis, the present study seeks to unearth the views, beliefs and perceptions of the adoption system's stakeholders. It aims to unveil the reasoning underlying their actions with regard to intercountry adoption and its procedures.

2.2 *Comparative Approach*

The present research employs a comparative approach. Germany and the Netherlands have been selected as the two receiving countries whose adoption systems are analysed and compared throughout this book. Such a comparative approach has the advantage of providing a broader picture of the possible weaknesses that may be encountered in a recipient state's adoption system. It furthermore offers policy makers in Germany and the Netherlands, but also in other receiving countries, the opportunity to learn from each

30 L. E. Cohen and M. Felson (1979). "Social Change and Crime Rate Trends: A Routine Activity Approach." American Sociological Review, 44, 4, 588-608.

31 S. Henry and M. M. Lanier (1998). "The Prism of Crime: Arguments for an Integrated Definition of Crime." Justice Quarterly, 15, 4, 609-627.

32 S. Cohen (1993). "Human Rights and Crimes of the State: The Culture of Denial." Australian and New Zealand Journal of Criminology, 26, 2, 97-115.

33 E. W. Said (1993). "Culture and imperialism." Vintage, New York; E. W. Said (1979). "Orientalism." Vintage, New York.

34 G. M. Sykes and D Matza (1957). "Techniques of Neutralization: A Theory of Delinquency." American Sociological Review, 22, 664-670.

35 U. Beck (2002). "Individualization: Institutionalized Individualism and Its Social and Political Consequences." Sage, London.

other's systems' weaknesses as well as strengths and to adopt or reform policies in order to address such weaknesses accordingly.

The two countries share similarities, but also differences, that make them interesting subjects for a comparative study. Both Germany and the Netherlands have ratified the 1989 United Nations Convention on the Rights of the Child as well as the 1993 Hague Convention on Protection of Children and Co-Operation in Respect of Intercountry Adoption. Since both countries are thus Hague receiving countries, it is to be expected that their adoption laws and policies are similar. Furthermore, considering their geographical proximity, they also share cultural similarities.

Yet, the two countries have experienced a different history of intercountry adoption. Whereas the Netherlands began moving children from other countries in the early 1950s,[36] Germany only emerged as a receiving country some 20 years later.[37] Up until the late 1960s/early 1970s, Germany was itself a sending country. The anti-Semitism that was witnessed during World War II, as well as the economic hardship and reservations towards so-called 'brown babies' following the war were reasons why Germany transferred thousands of its children to other countries for adoption, including to the Netherlands.[38]

Both countries also differ in terms of significance as recipients of adoptees. Between 2002 and 2017, Dutch couples and individuals adopted some 11,000 children from abroad.[39] In Germany, more than 13,000 international adoptions were officially registered.[40] Since

---

36 R. A. C. Hoksbergen (1991). "Intercountry Adoption Coming of Age in The Netherlands: Basic Issues, Trends, and Developments." In H. Altstein and R. J. Simon (eds), "Intercountry Adoption: A Multinational Perspective." Praeger, New York, 141-158, p. 142.

37 M. Guelich (2006). "Adoptionen aus dem nicht-europäischen Ausland." BIS-Verlag der Carl-von-Ossietzky-Universität.

38 R. Göpfert (1999). "Der jüdische Kindertransport von Deutschland nach England 1938/39. Geschichte und Erinnerung." Campus, Frankfurt; G. Lilienthal (1993). "Der "Lebensborn e.V." Ein Instrument nationalsozialistischer Rassenpolitik." Fischer, Frankfurt; M. Guelich (2006). "Adoptionen aus dem nicht-europäischen Ausland." BIS-Verlag der Carl-von-Ossietzky-Universität; M. R. Textor (1991). "International Adoption in West Germany: A private Affair." In H. Altstein and R. J. Simon (eds), "Intercountry Adoption: A Multinational Perspective." Praeger, New York, 109-126; Y.-C. Lemke Muniz de Faria (2003). "Germany's 'Brown Babies' Must Be Helped! Will You?: US Adoption Plans for Afro-German Children, 1950-1955." Callaloo 26, 2, 342-362.

39 Ministerie van Justitie en Veiligheid (2010). "Adoptie, Trends en Analyse, Statistisch overzicht interlandelijke adoptie over de jaren 2005 tot en met 2009." (on file with author); Ministerie van Justitie en Veiligheid (2013). "Adoptie, Trends en Analyse, Statistisch overzicht interlandelijke adoptie over de jaren 2008 tot en met 2012." Available at https://adoptie.nl/wp-content/uploads/2017/03/Adoptie_trends_en_analyse_2013.pdf; Ministerie van Justitie en Veiligheid (2016). "Adoptie, Trends en Analyse, Statistisch overzicht interlandelijke adoptie over de jaren 2011 tot en met 2015." Available at https://adoptie.nl/wp-content/uploads/2017/03/2011_tm_2015_Trends_en_analyse_interlandelijke_adoptie.pdf; Ministerie van Justitie en Veiligheid (2017). "Adoptie, Trends en Analyse, Statistisch overzicht interlandelijke adoptie over de jaren 2012 tot en met 2016." Available https://adoptie.nl/wp-content/uploads/2017/03/2012-2016-Trends-en-analyse-interlandelijke-adoptie.pdf; Ministerie van Justitie en Veiligheid (2018). "Adoptie, Trends en Analyse, Statistisch overzicht interlandelijke adoptie over de jaren 2013 tot en met 2017." Available https://www.rijksoverheid.nl/documenten/rapporten/2018/03/07/adoptie-trends-en-analyse.

40 Bundeszentralstelle für Auslandsadoption (2018). "Gesamtsumme – 2002-2017." Bonn (on file with author).

it is estimated that in Germany a considerable number of international adoptions take place privately, i.e. without the involvement of the official authorities (about 50%),[41] which are not in turn included in the official adoption statistics, the actual numbers might be higher. Yet still, considering Germany's population of 82.5 million, the number of children moved from abroad is low compared to the numbers in the Netherlands, which has a population of only 17 million.

Germany and the Netherlands also contrast with regard to the sending countries they move children from. For the Netherlands, China was and still is the most significant sending state, even though the number of children placed for adoption has dramatically decreased over the last couple of years. Between 2002 and 2017, almost 5,000 adoptions involved Chinese children.[42] Adoptions from China thus made up approximately 50% of all intercountry adoptions to the Netherlands. In Germany, only 130 adoptions took place from China within the given time frame.[43] The vast majority of children placed for adoption in Germany came from Russia (2,405), followed by Kazakhstan (751) and Thailand (736).[44] Interestingly, the number of Russian children sent to the Netherlands is very low (only 4),[45] which is surprising given that Russia was, and still is, one of the most significant sending states in the intercountry adoption system.[46]

Furthermore, both receiving countries differ as to the way they deal with private international adoptions. In Germany, privately pursued adoptions are tolerated, which

41 S. Schlauss (2007). "Die Anerkennung von Auslandsadoptionen in der vormundschaftsgerichtlichen Praxis." FamRZ, 20, 1699-1702.

42 Ministerie van Justitie en Veiligheid (2010). "Adoptie, Trends en Analyse, Statistisch overzicht interlandelijke adoptie over de jaren 2005 tot en met 2009." (on file with author); Ministerie van Justitie en Veiligheid (2013). "Adoptie, Trends en Analyse, Statistisch overzicht interlandelijke adoptie over de jaren 2008 tot en met 2012." Available at https://adoptie.nl/wp-content/uploads/2017/03/Adoptie_trends_en_analyse_2013.pdf; Ministerie van Justitie en Veiligheid (2016). "Adoptie, Trends en Analyse, Statistisch overzicht interlandelijke adoptie over de jaren 2011 tot en met 2015." Available at https://adoptie.nl/wp-content/uploads/2017/03/2011_tm_2015_Trends_en_analyse_interlandelijke_adoptie.pdf; Ministerie van Justitie en Veiligheid (2017). "Adoptie, Trends en Analyse, Statistisch overzicht interlandelijke adoptie over de jaren 2012 tot en met 2016." Available https://adoptie.nl/wp-content/uploads/2017/03/2012-2016-Trends-en-analyse-interlandelijke-adoptie.pdf; Ministerie van Justitie en Veiligheid (2018). "Adoptie, Trends en Analyse, Statistisch overzicht interlandelijke adoptie over de jaren 2013 tot en met 2017." Available https://www.rijksoverheid.nl/documenten/rapporten/2018/03/07/adoptie-trends-en-analyse.

43 Bundeszentralstelle für Auslandsadoption (2018). "Gesamtsumme – 2002-2017." Bonn (on file with author).

44 *Ibid.*

45 Ministerie van Justitie en Veiligheid (2010). "Adoptie, Trends en Analyse, Statistisch overzicht interlandelijke adoptie over de jaren 2005 tot en met 2009." (on file with author); Ministerie van Justitie en Veiligheid (2013). "Adoptie, Trends en Analyse, Statistisch overzicht interlandelijke adoptie over de jaren 2008 tot en met 2012." Available at https://adoptie.nl/wp-content/uploads/2017/03/Adoptie_trends_en_analyse_2013.pdf; Ministerie van Justitie en Veiligheid (2016). "Adoptie, Trends en Analyse, Statistisch overzicht interlandelijke adoptie over de jaren 2011 tot en met 2015." Available at https://adoptie.nl/wp-content/uploads/2017/03/2011_tm_2015_Trends_en_analyse_interlandelijke_adoptie.pdf.

46 P. Selman (2018). "Global Statistics for Intercountry Adoption: Receiving States and States of Origin 2004-2016." 03.05.2018, The Hague Conference on Private International Law, p. 3.

might be one of the reasons why such a high number thereof can be observed. The Netherlands, by way of contrast, explicitly prohibits adopters from adopting without the involvement of the Dutch authorities.

2.3 *Case Study Approach*

This research also undertakes two case studies. A case study is an empirical study that examines a phenomenon within its real-life context.[47] It aims to provide an understanding of a phenomenon by examining an event or a situation as well as the interpretations and explanations that the stakeholders involved attach to the (social) processes underlying this event or situation.[48]

The present study conducts an in-depth analysis of two incidences of child trafficking for adoption purposes, and the way the stakeholders in Germany and the Netherlands responded to them and the reasoning underlying their responses. First, it describes the irregular and abusive practices that were uncovered in the Ethiopian adoption system around 2009 and zooms in on how a German adoption agency, moving children from Ethiopia, reacted to allegations of abuses by an orphanage it co-operated with. Second, it gives a detailed account of the child trafficking incidences in China, by far the most significant supply country for the Netherlands, which have been exposed as of 2005, and illustrates how the Dutch stakeholders (primarily the Dutch Ministry of Justice and Security) responded to them. The case studies do not only analyze as to how the German and Dutch stakeholders dealt with the reports about irregular and abusive practices in the two sending states, but also tries to explain their responses.

Case studies have been criticized for being context-dependent. Individual cases, critics claim, cannot form the basis for generalizations and can therefore not contribute to scientific knowledge.[49] Yet, even though the results from case studies cannot be formally generalised, they have "the potential to contribute to the process of knowledge accumulation in a given field or in a society".[50] The two case studies conducted in the present research illustrate and explain the attitudes and actions of the adoption system's stakeholders that might work to encourage the trafficking of children into Germany and the Netherlands. Even though the studies only dealt with individual events and stakeholders, and do therefore not yield any generalizable findings, they provide valuable theoretical and practical lessons about possible criminogenic conditions in the intercountry adoption system.

47 R. Yin (2003). "Case Study Research: Design and Methods." Sage, London.
48 F. L. Leeuw and H. Schmeets (2016). "Empirical Legal Research, A Guidance Book for Lawyers, Legislators and Regulators." Edward Elgar, Cheltenham, p. 112.
49 B. Flyvbjerg (2006). "Five Misunderstanding About Case-Study Research." Qualitative Inquiry, 12, 2, 219-245.
50 *Ibid.*, p. 227.

2.4 Data Sources and Analysis

This research uses multiple data sources and mixed methods of data analysis in order to provide a more nuanced understanding of the criminogenic factors in the German and Dutch adoption systems.[51] It employs legal, policy, academic and media sources, semi-structured interviews conducted with key informants in the field of international adoptions, as well as autobiographic stories that have been written by German and Dutch adoptive parents. These data sources were analysed using content, narrative and discourse analysis methods.

2.4.1 Legal sources

The present study gathered and analysed German and Dutch laws and policies on inter-country adoption and studied the relevant case law which was made publicly available.[52] A particular focus was placed on court decisions dealing with private intercountry adoptions that were pursued without the involvement of state authorities and with criminal actions by adopters and adoption agencies. The relevant case law of the European Court of Human Rights was also considered in the analysis.

Since the German and Dutch laws and policies on intercountry adoption, as well as the jurisdiction in both countries, are strongly influenced and shaped by both the 1989 United Nations Convention on the Rights of the Child and the 1993 Hague Convention on Protection of Children and Co-Operation in Respect of Intercountry Adoption, these two international legal instruments were also critically scrutinized. The study sought to uncover and explain the pitfalls and limitations of the two treaties that may consequently result in weaknesses in the national adoption systems.

In addition, international legal instruments dealing with the issue of trafficking in children were scrutinized so as to assess whether or not they cover child trafficking for adoption purposes, including the 2000 Protocol to Prevent, Suppress and Punish Trafficking in Persons, Especially Women and Children, supplementing the United Nations Convention Against Transnational Organized Crime, the 2005 Council of Europe Convention on Action against Trafficking in Human Beings, Directive 2011/36/EU on preventing and combating trafficking in human beings and protecting its victims and the 2000 Optional Protocol to the United Nations Convention on the Rights of the Child on the Sale of Children, Child Prostitution and Child Pornography.

---

51 L.B. Nielsen (2010). "The Need for Multi-Method Approaches in Empirical Legal Research." In P. Cane and H.M. Kritzer (eds) "The Oxford Handbook of Empirical Legal Research." Oxford University Press, Oxford, p. 955.

52 In Germany https://beck-online.beck.de/Home; in the Netherlands: https://www.rechtspraak.nl/.

2.4.2 Policy, academic and media sources

Policy documents at the national and international level were also used as data sources in this book. In particular, policy documents recording Dutch parliamentary debates on intercountry adoption were employed. Unlike in Germany, intercountry adoption has become a highly controversial political topic in the Netherlands, and the numerous adoption scandals (especially in India, China, Haiti, and Sri Lanka) that have been exposed by Dutch media investigations were the subject of heated debates in the Second Chamber of the Dutch parliament. A total of 108 parliamentary documents dealing with intercountry adoption in the period after the Netherlands ratified the 1993 Hague Convention in 1998 were sourced through the official digital databases[53] and their content, discourse, and narratives were analysed. A special focus was placed on the way in which the Dutch Ministry of Justice and Security responded to reports about abusive practices in the Chinese adoption system as well as on the reasoning underlying its responses.

Moreover, other documents published by national institutions were used, including official statistics on intercountry adoption, reports and working papers. In the Netherlands especially, numerous reports about intercountry adoption were drawn up, examining incidences of adoption irregularities and proposing policy recommendations. Thus, this study employs several reports that were set up by the Dutch Ministry of Justice and Security (more specifically by the *Raad voor de Strafrechtstoepassing en Jeugdbescherming* and the *Wetenschappelijk Onderzoek- en Documentatiecentrum*), the Dutch Youth Inspectorate, the Dutch Committee on Lesbian Parenthood and Intercountry Adoption and Dutch consulting agencies (Van Montfoort, Cap Gemini and Andersson Elffers Felix), as well as documents produced by the Dutch adoption placement agencies.

In addition, the relevant academic literature as well as reports published by international organizations were relied upon, including documents published by the Permanent Bureau of the Hague Conference on Private International Law, the Human Rights Commission, the Committee on the Rights of the Child, The United Nations Children's Fund (UNICEF), Defence for Children, International Social Service (ISS), Save the Children International, Terre des hommes, Against Child Trafficking (ACT), the United Nations Office on Drugs and Crime (UNODC) and the World Bank.

National and international newspaper articles and documentaries dealing with intercountry adoption and abusive adoption practices constituted a crucial source of data for the present study. As will be explained later on in this book, illegal adoptions often remain invisible, and numerous incidences of child trafficking for adoption purposes would not have come to light if it was not for the media uncovering and investigating them. Finally, the websites of the German and Dutch adoption agencies and their reports, but also pictures published online, were accessed for information.

53 https://zoek.officielebekendmakingen.nl; https://www.tweedekamer.nl.

2.4.3 Semi-structured interviews

In order to gather more information on the practice of intercountry adoption in both Germany and the Netherlands, in-depth interviews were conducted with national stakeholders, academic experts as well as experts from national and international organizations. This research method is extensively employed in empirical legal research because interviews are an effective means of gathering data on individual's perceptions, views and reasoning behind their responses.[54] The study uses semi-structured interviews, including both close-ended questions, formulated on the basis of the analysis of the other data sources, and open-ended questions that allowed the interviewees to reflect on the topic on the basis of their own experiences and perceptions. Between March 2014 and March 2018, at total of 29 interviews took place with 34 respondents, including:

- nine staff members of seven intercountry adoption placement agencies (five German and two Dutch agencies);
- I. Hut, director of the Dutch adoption placement agency *Wereldkinderen* between 2003 and 2009;
- B. Wacker, staff member of the former German adoption placement agency *Terre des hommes between* 2000 and 2010;
- M. Holz, staff member of the former German adoption placement agency *Terre des hommes* between 1978 and 2014,
- W. Weitzel, head of the German Federal Central Office for International Adoption at the German Federal Office of Justice between 2002 and 2017;
- B. Siebert and K. Meissner, head and, respectively, social worker of the Joint Central Adoption Office for Hamburg, Bremen, Lower-Saxony, and Schleswig-Holstein;
- I. Egger-Otholt, head of the Central Adoption Office Rhineland-Pfalz and Hessen;
- U. Möller-Bierth, head of the Central Adoption Office North-Rhine-Westphalia/Rhineland;
- C. Flynn, head of the Central Adoption Office Bavaria;
- J. Reinhardt, international adoption law scholar and head of the Central Adoption Office Bavaria between 2001 until 2008;
- J. Kouwenhoven, head of and a policy advisor at the Dutch Central Authority;
- M. Kroon, official of the Youth Department at the Dutch Ministry of Justice and Security;
- A. van Leur, policy advisor at the Dutch Central Authority;
- Two advisors at the Dutch Immigration and Naturalisation Service (IND);
- Two policy officers at the Dutch Ministry of Foreign Affairs;

---

54 L. Webley (2010). "Qualitative Approaches to Empirical Legal Research." In P. Cane and H.M. Kritzer (eds), "The Oxford Handbook of Empirical Legal Research." Oxford University Press, Oxford, 926-950, p. 937.

- L. Mártinez-Mora, the Principal Officer at the Permanent Bureau of the Hague Conference on Private International Law, responsible for intercountry adoptions;
- R. Post, official at the European Commission in Brussels and founder of the organization *Against Child Trafficking (ACT)*;
- A. Dohle, executive director of the organization *Against Child Trafficking (ACT)*;
- H. Westra, former chairman of the organization *United Adoptees International*;
- L. Bosch, legal adviser at *Defence for Children Netherlands*;
- R. A. C. Hoksbergen, Emeritus Professor specializing in national and international adoption at Utrecht University, and
- P. Vlaardingerbroek, Emeritus Professor of Family Law at Tilburg University.

Several semi-structured questioning guides were used for the interviews that were specifically tailored to the expertise of the respondents. The questioning guides for the adoption agencies included a set of standard questions, addressing the agency's personnel, financial situation, co-operation with representatives, partner organizations and authorities in the sending countries, and adoption costs the adopters have to pay, as well as specific questions relating to their experiences with adoption irregularities in the sending countries. Moreover, the questioning guides for the German and Dutch state authorities involved standard questions about the monitoring and control structure, and specific questions with regard to reports about illegal or irregular adoption practices.

The interviews lasted between 60 and 120 minutes, were audio-recorded and transcribed in a literal, verbatim manner. The interviews with the German respondents were conducted in German; the other interviews took place mainly in English. The Dutch interviewees were given the opportunity to answer (parts of) the questions in Dutch if they had difficulties expressing themselves in English. A follow-up interview was conducted with one respondent using a specific questioning guide. Three interviews took place *via* telephone; all of the others were conducted face-to-face.

In a few cases, the respondents were asked follow-up questions *via* e-mail with the aim of gathering additional information or seeking clarification. An A. Hartung, an official at the German Federal Foreign Office, and the personnel of one Dutch adoption placement agency agreed to provide written answers to a set of questions sent *via* e-mail but refused to participate in an interview.

The interview transcripts were analysed using codes linked to the adoption system's particular features listed in section 1. The study did not only analyse the content of the interviews but also the respondents' narratives. Thus, it examined how they described experiences (for instance, with incidences of irregular or abusive practices in the sending country) and how they interpreted them.[55] Narratives help individuals make sense of past events as well as of themselves. The process of telling a narrative is thus not only an act of recalling and retelling experiences, but also an act of constructing them.[56] The way a past episode is described by the adoption system's stakeholders therefore reveals a lot about their underlying values, beliefs and attitudes[57] which might constitute but another criminogenic factor in the adoption system.

The use of semi-structured interviews as data sources generally has several limitations, however. Most notably, the findings might not be generalized to a greater population.[58] In the present study, a number of important stakeholders that were contacted did not respond at all. Others declined to participate in an interview, claiming that they have had negative experiences with researchers and journalists investigating child trafficking for adoption purposes in the past or explaining that they would only place legal adoptions. Thus, out of the nine adoption placement agencies that were active in Germany at the time this study was conducted, only five were willing to participate in an interview. And out of the four Dutch adoption agencies that were contacted, only two agreed to be interviewed; another one was only willing to give written answers to questions sent *via* e-mail, which were rather short and did not provide much content. Furthermore, only four out of the 12 German Central Adoption Offices could be interviewed for this study. The perspectives and experiences of these respondents might thus not necessarily be representative for all German and Dutch adoption agencies or the Central Adoption Offices in both countries.

Another general disadvantage of interviews is that the respondents may distort information through recall error or answer questions in what they perceive to be a socially desirable manner.[59] Arguably, the risk of a social desirability bias is particularly high within the field of intercountry adoption, which has been subject to lot of scrutiny and pressure in recent years, also due to numerous reports about illegal adoption practices. It is thus expected that experts that work within this field, and whose jobs are may be dependent on this social practice, have the tendency to give answers that present their activities in the best possible light. A social desirability bias of the respondents is a limitation for the data collection through content analysis, as it might lead to distorted information about

55 J. R Herbert and I.S. Rubin (2012). "Qualitative Interviewing, The Art of Hearing Data." (3rd ed.) Sage, London, pp. 28-29.

56 A. Shankar et al. (2009). "Identity, Consumption and Narratives of Socialization." Marketing Theory, 9, 1, 75-94, p. 79.

57 J. R Herbert and I.S. Rubin (2012). "Qualitative Interviewing, The Art of Hearing Data." (3rd ed.) Sage, London, p. 29.

58 S. Kvale (2007). "Doing Interviews." In U. Flick (ed) "The SAGE Qualitative Research Kit." Sage, London, p. 87.

59 F. L. Leeuw and H. Schmeets (2016). "Empirical Legal Research, A Guidance Book for Lawyers, Legislators and Regulators." Edward Elgar, Cheltenham, pp. 140-141.

the adoption system. Yet, for the narrative analysis, such a bias is arguably not a restriction. As was explained, the way the interviewees portray themselves and their experiences reveals a lot about their underlying beliefs and attitudes, which are in turn an important factor to be considered when analysing the intercountry adoption system. Thus, the interviewees' efforts to describe past events and their activities in a favourable manner are interesting aspects to look at.

2.4.4 Adopters' autobiographic stories

The present study also conducts a narrative analysis of 15 autobiographical stories that were written by German and Dutch adopters in which they explain how they came to adopt a child from a foreign country and describe their transition to adoptive parenthood.[60] The aim is to identify recurring tropes and commonplaces that the authors mobilize in their stories to resolve the moral tension between the cultural conception of children as being priceless and their paying considerable sums of money in the adoption process for a child to love.

A narrative analysis of the autobiographic stories written by adopters does not only provide the opportunity to detect and understand the recurring linguistic choices that adopters use to manage the tension between consumption and parenthood. More importantly, it helps to unearth their tacit and invisible values and beliefs, which are shaped by the authors' culture and which they unwittingly take for granted. As was mentioned above, narratives help individuals to make sense of events and situations that they have experienced. They therefore reveal a lot about the narrator's underlying attitudes and perceptions. By analysing them, therefore, the researcher can gain insights into the way in which the narrator understands the world and his or her experiences.[61]

60 German books: M. Gaedicke (2009). "Wunschkind, Geschichte einer Adoption." Hoffmann und Campe, Hamburg; A. Michaela (2014). "Neun Monate Sommer, Tagebuch einer Adoptionsschwangerschaft in Kenia." Tausendschlau Olga Bien, Munich; A. Palm-Hensel (2008). "Stella, Unser Stern aus Indien, Die Geschichte einer glücklichen Adoption." Kleine Schritte, Trier; B. Schulz (2005). "Tochter Indira, Die Geschichte einer Adoption aus Indien." Ullstein, Berlin; T. Schumann (2012). "Faith - Adoption in Kenia, Ein Vater erzählt." Norderstedt, Books on Demand; T. Schumann (2014). "Hope - Adoption in Haiti, Ein Vater erzählt." Books on Demand, Norderstedt; A. Wenzek-Grüneberg (2005). "Das Regenbogenkind, Die Geschichte einer Auslandsadoption." Books on Demand, Norderstedt; R. Vollmer (2004). "Mein Kind aus der Fremde." Rowohlt, Reinbek bei Hamburg. Dutch books: M. & K. Van der Staaij (2004). "Liefs uit Bogotá, Ons verhaal over adoptie." Uitgeverij Boekencentrum, Zoetermeer; G. Bakker (2008). "Het Adoptieboek, Stap voor Stap, Stress Tijdens de Adoptie Periode." Uitgeverij Aspekt, Soesterberg; D. Michielsen (2005). "Dochters van ver, belevenissen van een adoptiemoeder." Archipel, Amsterdam; I. Holla (2005). "Mijn droom van een kind, Waargebeurd verhaal van een vrouw die haar wens om moeder te worden niet opgeeft." Uitgeverij Sirene, Amsterdam; M. & I. Koolen (2009). "Moeders mooiste, vaders trots, Een bijzonder verslag van de lange weg naar adoptie." The house of books, Antwerpen; I. Andersson (2006). "Bloem van China, Dochter in Nederland." Free Musketeers, Woerden; I. Andersson (2009). "Dochters van China, Zusjes in Nederland." Free Musketeers, Zoetermeer.

61 M. Sandelowski (1991). "Telling Stories: Narrative Approaches in Qualitative Research." Image: Journal of Nursing Scholarship, 23, 3, 161-166, p. 163

Autobiographic books rather than individual interviews with the adopters were chosen as a data source in this thesis. They allow the researcher to observe how adopters deal with the issue of consumption and money in intercountry adoption, without the potential of researcher contamination that could arise in interviews. This is particularly important given the delicate nature of the present study's topic. The adopters do not perform for the researcher by giving answers to specific questions, but rather they write freely about their experiences. Whereas an interview is about the interviewer, a narrative is about the narrator. Narratives thus provide the researcher with the unique opportunity to explore the adoptive parents' unmasked views, opinions and attitudes vis-à-vis intercountry adoption.

The findings of the narrative analysis presented in this book cannot be considered representative of international adopters as a whole. Each adoption story is different, and the individual experiences of the authors are context-dependent. In addition, not all international adopters write stories about their transition to adoptive parenthood. Arguably, the very fact that some craft autobiographies already distinguishes them from those adoptive parents who do not. Thus, the collected results may have only limited application to other adopters and cannot be generalized to the population of adoptive parents as a whole. Yet having said that, the narratives that the adopters employ to tell their stories do not arise in a vacuum, but are influenced and shaped by a wider cultural stock[62] that is shared by other Western individuals that pursue an international adoption. Thus, it is likely that the narrator's attitudes and beliefs can also be observed in other adopters.

2.5 *Ethical Considerations*

The experts were asked for an interview *via* e-mail, which contained information about the research project (thus, about the research subject, the overall purpose of the investigation and the main features of the design) and the purpose of the interview. Once they agreed to participate in the study, an interview was scheduled. At the beginning of the interview, the information about the research project was provided again and further questions were answered (if the respondents had any).

All interview respondents consented to the audio-recording of the interviews. Three interviewees wished to remain anonymous; all the others gave their consent to be cited with their full names. At the end of the study, it was decided to keep some respondents anonymous in this book, even though they agreed to have their names included in the study. This was done in order to avoid any negative consequences for the respondents themselves or their institutions that they had probably not anticipated. Thus, this book does not disclose the names of the Dutch and German adoption agencies and their personnel

62 D. E. Polkinghorne (1991). "Narrative and Self-Concept." Journal of Narrative and Life History, 1, 2 & 3, 135-153, p. 148.

when quoting their interview statements. Rather, it refers to them as 'German adoption placement agency A, B, C, D, and E' and 'Dutch adoption agency X and Y'.

Several respondents agreed to participate in the interview on the condition that they would be given the opportunity to review the transcribed version of the interview. Some of them added information to the transcription in order to clarify statements they made or deleted statements which they did not want to have included in the study because they considered them to be too sensitive. Statements that the respondents deleted from the transcription are not considered in this study.

3 Structure of the Book

This book is composed of eight Chapters. After this introduction, *Chapter II* seeks to identify the organization and operation of the illegal transnational adoption market in children by applying the basic logic of the routine activity theory, which was developed by Felson and Cohen. It explains that in the context of extreme demographic as well as economic inequalities between the sending and the receiving countries ('criminogenic asymmetries'), demand, supply and weak public and private sector social control mechanisms have contributed to the nature and size of the illegal adoption market. Furthermore, the main differences between the conventional forms of human trafficking and child trafficking for adoption purposes will be addressed. The Chapter outlines the international legal framework on child trafficking and shows that the 2000 Protocol to Prevent, Suppress and Punish Trafficking in Persons, Especially Women and Children - the first global legally binding instrument with an agreed definition on human trafficking - but also other human trafficking instruments neglect to cover kidnapping, purchasing and selling children for the purposes of adoption. Finally, it seeks to shed light on the different dimensions of child trafficking for adoption purposes by applying Henry and Lanier's crime prism.

Chapter III takes a closer look at the rights of the child and the principle of 'the child's best interests' in intercountry adoption. It outlines the three value positions in the current debate about the legitimacy of intercountry adoption that all substantiate their positions by referring to the children's rights and the principle of the best interests of the child. The Chapter then identifies those provisions of the 1989 United Nations Convention on the Rights of the Child, as well as other human rights instruments that are most relevant with regard to intercountry adoption. It explains the rights which children deprived of their family environment have and under which circumstances they may be placed for intercountry adoption, according to the UNCRC, and it exposes the myth of a 'global orphan crisis'. The Chapter finally scrutinizes the 'child's best interests' principle, the cornerstone of the adoption system, and illustrates how it may actually facilitate abusive adoption practices.

Chapter IV examines the pitfalls and weaknesses of the 1993 Hague Convention on Protection of Children and Co-Operation in Respect of Intercountry Adoption. The Convention was drafted with the aim of tackling illegal and abusive practices in the international adoption system. Yet today, some 20 years after the treaty came into force, children are still kidnapped, bought and sold for the purposes of adoption. The Chapter takes a closer look at the treaty's pitfalls and limitations and claims that it might even work to facilitate the trafficking of children for adoption purposes by having created mutual trust between its Contracting States.

Chapters V and VI both uncover and explain the weaknesses of the German and Dutch intercountry adoption systems. Both chapters are structured according to the system's five features that were outlined in section 1. Firstly, they examine how adoptions that are pursued in circumvention of the official adoption placement procedure are dealt with in both jurisdictions. How are private adoptions regulated in Germany and the Netherlands? What are their actual consequences? Particularly, are the children being removed from their private adopters? Secondly, the Chapters take a closer look at the requirements that German and Dutch adoption agencies, especially their personnel, must comply with, as well as the way in which they finance their activities. Thirdly, the co-operation of the adoption agencies with the sending countries will be scrutinized. Are the monies that are being paid for the adoption steps in the sending countries (in the form of fees, donations, and contributions) transparent and reasonable? How do German and Dutch adoption agencies monitor the activities of their foreign representatives and partner organizations? And how do they deal with and respond to reports of illegal practices abroad? Fourthly, the Chapters analyse and assess the monitoring and control by the German and Dutch authorities. How are adoption agencies being supervised in Germany and the Netherlands? And what possibilities do the state authorities have to monitor the activities and developments in the sending countries? Finally, the Chapter zooms in on the criminal liability of German and Dutch adopters and adoption agencies. Are adopters and adoption agencies that pay money to the orphanages, the child's birth parents, government officials or court in the sending countries criminally liable? If they are convicted at all, what are the sentences that they receive for their crimes?

Both Chapters also provide a case study analysis which highlights the way in which the adoption system's stakeholders deal with allegations of child trafficking incidences in the sending countries. *Chapter V* scrutinizes a German adoption agency's response to reports about abusive practices by its Ethiopian co-operation partner. *Chapter VI* examines how the Dutch authorities have reacted to the irregularities uncovered in the Chinese adoption system.

Chapter VII then focusses on German and Dutch adoptive parents. It aims at unearthing and explaining the German and Dutch adopters' interests as well as their beliefs and perceptions about intercountry adoption, children, and the countries they adopt from, as well as the role which they and their money plays in the adoption system. It does so by analysing their autobiographic stories. The Chapter uncovers the adopters' selfish and self-centred motives and explains which narratives they use to resolve the moral tension between, on the one hand, the moral imperative to save a child that urgently needs loving parents and, on the other hand, their own desires and preferences: adopting a healthy baby, as well as the moral tension between the cultural perception of children as being priceless and them paying large sums of money in the adoption process.

Chapter VIII concludes this book. It summarizes the main findings of the present study, compares the German and Dutch adoption systems and gives policy recommendations.

4 Terminology

In this book, the term 'adoption' refers to both legal and *de facto* adoption. A legal adoption is a judicial process whereby a couple or individual ('adopter') that is taking care of a child ('adoptee') permanently assumes the rights and responsibilities from the child's biological parents. Whereas in a 'simple or limited adoption' the pre-existing legal child-parent relationship is only restricted, in a 'full adoption' the ties between the adopted child and his or her birth parents are severed completely. In a *de facto* adoption, a couple or individual takes someone else's child into their home for an indefinite period of time for the purpose of care, without having followed an official adoption procedure. A *de facto* adoption would thus also refer to a situation whereby a couple or individual passes off someone else's child as their biological child in order to avoid the legal adoption act, for instance because they do not meet the requirements for adopting a child or fear that the adoption would not be granted due to their involvement in illegal or irregular adoption practices. In a kinship adoption, the child is adopted by a relative, whereas in a stranger adoption no connection between the adoptee and the adopters exists.

An intercountry, international or transnational adoption takes place where someone else's child is permanently transferred from his or her state of residence ('sending country', 'supply country', 'source country', 'country of origin' or 'the child's native country') to another state ('receiving country', 'demand country', or 'recipient country') for the purposes of adoption by a couple or individual that havetheir permanent residency in that state. 'Hague countries' are countries that have ratified the 1993 Hague Convention on Protection of Children and Co-Operation in Respect of Intercountry Adoption. 'Non-Hague countries' are states that have not done so at the time of writing this thesis.

The term 'adoption placement' refers to the union or matching of a child with a couple or individual who wants to adopt that child. An 'adoption placement office or agency' is a state body or a private body that is located in the adopters' state of residence or in the sending country, which has been accredited by the state authorities and authorized to carry out intercountry adoption placements.

In an 'agency adoption', the intercountry adoption placement is carried out with the involvement of an adoption placement office or agency in the receiving country. This agency would either assess the adopters' suitability to adopt itself or have a youth welfare office conduct such an assessment, and then carry out the adoption placement *via* its permitted representative or co-operation partner in the sending country (for example, an orphanage, authorized by the sending countries' authorities to place children for intercountry adoption, or an adoption placement agency), or the foreign competent authority (Central Authority). An agency adoption takes place under the supervision of the competent authorities in both the sending and receiving country.

In this book, the terms 'independent adoption', 'private adoption', or 'do-it-yourself adoption' are used to refer to an adoption that is directly arranged between the adopters and the birth parents or the organisation caring for the child (e.g. an orphanage). It takes place without the involvement of an adoption placement office in the recipient state. Individuals and couples who pursue an independent adoption often use an unauthorized private contact, such as a foreign social worker, priest, doctor or attorney, who acts as an intermediary. The latter would identify and locate an attractive child, secure the necessary consent to adoption and handle the adoption paperwork. In a private adoption, the official adoption placement procedure is circumvented. The authorities in the receiving country, if at all, only gain knowledge of the international adoption placement when the child has been transferred to the receiving country: if the adopters want to register the child, apply for an adoption or want an adoption judgment recognized which had been rendered in the child's country of origin. In the Netherlands, a privately pursued international adoption is regarded as an 'illegal adoption'.

A 'partial do-it-yourself adoption', which is a permitted form of adoption in the Netherlands (*deelbemiddeling*), takes place when a Dutch couple or individual pursues an international adoption *via* a foreign private contact (an authority, institution or individual in the sending country which is not the representative or co-operation partner of a Dutch adoption agency) that has been assessed by a Dutch adoption agency and approved by the Dutch Ministry of Justice and Security.

In this book, 'child trafficking' refers to a situation whereby a child is obtained illegally and then transferred to another country for the purposes of adoption. The term trafficking applies if a child was brought into the intercountry adoption system illegitimately, through purchase, abduction, coercion or circumvention of the subsidiarity principle. It does not apply to illegal activities that facilitate the adoption of a child that is in the intercountry adoption system legitimately (e.g. bribery, falsification of the child's paperwork to make the child appear more attractive for adopters).

'Illegal or irregular adoption practices' include adoption activities that violate the standards and principles laid down in the relevant international legal instruments, most notably the 1993 Hague Convention on Protection of Children and Co-Operation in

Respect of Intercountry Adoption and the 1989 United Nations Convention on the Rights of the Child, or national legal provisions adopted by the sending or the receiving country.

'Child laundering' refers to the process of falsifying or fabricating documents (e.g. the child's birth certificate, documents containing the child's parents' consent to adoption, death certificates of the child's parents) in order to hide the illegal conduct in the sending country and to identify the illegally obtained child as the adopters' biological child or as an actual orphan. Children whose paperwork falsely declares them as orphans are referred to as 'paper orphans' or 'manufactured orphans'.

An intercountry adoption procedure is typically composed of the following steps: the adoption placement procedure involving the matching of the child with the adopters; the judicial adoption procedure in which a judge decides whether or not to grant the adoption; the child's immigration to the receiving country and – if the adoption was granted in the sending country – the adoption recognition procedure, whereby a family court in the receiving country determines the recognition of the foreign adoption judgment as well as the effects of the adoption in the receiving country.

The 'intercountry adoption system' is the set of stakeholders and procedures in place to carry out an intercountry adoption. In this book, the term either refers to the set of stakeholders and procedures established in both the sending and the receiving country (the 'intercountry adoption system' as a whole) or only those set up in the receiving countries (the German or Dutch intercountry adoption system). Naturally, the German and Dutch intercountry adoption systems must be understood as a part of the intercountry adoption system as a whole.

II Child Trafficking for Adoption Purposes – A Criminological Analysis of the Illegal Adoption Market[1]

1 Introduction

Globalization and changes in international relations have caused an increase in integrated markets and resulted in the transnational movement of people, capital, goods, and services. Transnational crime is one negative consequence of this interconnectedness and the global character of our life.[2] Crime is now, more than ever, less constrained by national boundaries. In addition to exerting a broader geographic influence, the scope of transnational criminal activities has also broadened.[3] Although traditional transnational criminal activities remain the same (e.g. trafficking in drugs or persons), criminals have learned to increase their profits by diversifying their spheres of illicit activity to include, for instance, cybercrime, trade in human organs, trafficking in flora and fauna and the theft of art.[4] Also, child trafficking for the purposes of adoption is a form of transnational crime,[5] as it involves the illegal obtaining and export of children from sending countries, which supplies the demand in the receiving countries.

The issue of transnational crime, especially trafficking in human beings, has attracted considerable academic and political attention in recent years. Criminological research on human trafficking for the purposes of sexual and labour exploitation has been extensive[6]

---

1 Parts of this Chapter were published in E. Loibl (2016). "Crime in the Intercountry Adoption Industry: Towards a Broader Definition of Child Trafficking." in R. Moerland and H. Nelen, "Denialism and Human Rights." Intersentia, Cambridge, 119-134, and will be published in E. Loibl (upcoming). "Trafficking in Children for Adoption Purposes: A Criminological Analysis of the Illegal Adoption Market." In J.A. Winterdyk and J. Jones (eds), "The Palgrave International Handbook of Human Trafficking." Palgrave Macmillan, London.

2 N. Passas (2002). "Cross-border crime and the interface between legal and illegal actors." In P. van Duyne et al. (eds.), "Upperworld and underworld in cross-border crime." Wolf Legal Publishers, Nijmegen, 11-41.

3 N. Passas and B. Bowman Proulx (2011). "Overview of Crimes and Antiquities." In S. Manacorda and D. Chappell (eds), "Crime in the Art and Antiquities World, Illegal Trafficking in Cultural Property." Springer, New York, 51-67.

4 *Ibid.*

5 See also T. Feltes and R. Hofmann (2016). "Transnational Organised Crime and its Impacts on States and Societies." In P. Hauck and S. Peterke (eds), "International Law and Transnational Organised Crime." Oxford University Press, 42-62.

6 See, for instance, J. Winterdyk, et al. (2010). "Introduction to Special Issue: Human Trafficking." European Journal of Criminology, 7, 1, 5-10; B. C. Oude Breuil, et al. (2011). "Human Trafficking Revisited: Legal, Enforcement and Ethnographic Narratives on Sex Trafficking to Western Europe." Trends in Organized

and the issue has been high on the political agendas, resulting in a number of international legal instruments and new criminal laws that are designed to react and combat one of the fastest growing forms of transnational organized crime worldwide.[7] Yet, in criminological research, as well as in the political arena, much less attention has been paid to the phenomenon of trafficking in children for adoption purposes.

This Chapter examines the phenomenon of child trafficking for adoption purposes from a criminological perspective. Section 2 identifies the organization and operation of the illegal transnational adoption market in children by applying the basic logic of routine activity theory developed by Felson and Cohen. It explains that in the context of extreme demographic and economic inequalities between the sending and the receiving countries ('criminogenic asymmetries'), demand, supply and weak public and private sector social control mechanisms have contributed to the nature and size of the illegal adoption market. Furthermore, it outlines the difference between the conventional forms of human trafficking and child trafficking for adoption purposes.

Section 3 provides an overview of the international legal framework on child trafficking. It shows that neither the 2000 Protocol to Prevent, Suppress and Punish Trafficking in Persons, Especially Women and Children, the first global legally binding instrument with an agreed definition on trafficking in persons, nor other international legal instruments on human trafficking (fully) cover the kidnapping, purchasing and selling of children for the purposes of adoption.

Section 4 attempts to shed light on the different dimensions of child trafficking for adoption purposes, applying the crime prism: a framework developed by Henry and Lanier that brings together the multiple dimensions of crime. It illustrates that child trafficking for adoption purposes causes serious individual, as well as social, harm and it seeks to explain why the issue receives far less attention by politicians and academics than conventional forms of human trafficking.

Crime, 14, 1, 30-46; T. O. Mahmoud and C. Trebesch (2010). "The economics of human trafficking and labour migration: Micro-evidence from Eastern Europe." Journal of Comparative Economics, 38, 2, 173-188.

7 C. Friesendorf (2007). "Pathologies of Security Governance: Efforts Against Human Trafficking in Europe." Security Dialogue, 38, 3, 379-402.

2 The Structural Components of the Transnational Illegal Adoption Market

2.1 The Basic Logic of Routine Activity Theory

In order to understand the organization of the transnational illegal market in children, it is important to identify its structural components. The basic logic of routine activity theory offers a means to conceptualize this market. Routine activity theory was developed by Cohen and Felson so as to explain the behaviour of individuals engaged in predatory street crimes (e.g. robbery, burglaries, larcenies or murders).[8] Routine activities refer to the "recurrent and prevalent" activities of individuals in everyday life (e.g. work, leisure, social interaction).[9] The premise of the theory is that crime is the product of three minimum elements that converge in space and time in the course of the population's routine activities: (1) motivated offenders, (2) suitable targets and (3) the absence of capable guardians.[10] The first element refers to offenders with both criminal inclinations and the ability to carry out the crime. Target suitability refers to a target's qualities, such as the value of a person or property, physical visibility, access to them as well as resistance capability.[11] A capable guardian is someone with the capacity to stop or impede a crime, one in whose presence the crime is not committed, and whose absence makes it more probable. This definition includes formal third parties (e.g. police or security guards) as well as informal ones (any private person who in the performance of his or her routine activities can, through presence or activity, prevent or impede a crime).[12] Routine activity theory seeks to explain criminal activities and their patterns on a macro level. By way of contrast to micro-level theories of criminality, which are centred on the criminal and the biological, psychological or social factors that motivate criminal actions, routine activity theory focusses on crime as an event, by highlighting its relation to space and time.[13]

Criminologists have already applied the theory's basic logic so as to structurally analyse illegal markets. For instance, Lane et al. have transposed the theory's three components into structural equivalents to analyse the market in illegal art and antiquities.[14] According to them, this market is a patterned system of economic exchange that consists of three

8 L. E. Cohen and M. Felson (1979). "Social Change and Crime Rate Trends: A Routine Activity Approach." American Sociological Review, 44, 4, 588-608.
9 *Ibid.*, p. 593.
10 *Ibid.*, p. 589.
11 *Ibid.*, p. 591.
12 F. Miro (2014). "Routine Activity Theory." In J. M. Miller (ed), "The Encyclopedia of Theoretical Criminology." Whiley Blackwell, Oxford, 735-742.
13 *Ibid.*
14 D. C. Lane, et al. (2008). "Time Crime: The Transnational Organization of Art and Antiquities Theft." Journal of Contemporary Criminal Justice, 24, 3, 243-262.

factors: demand, supply and regulation. Thus, from a structural market perspective, motivated offenders constitute the demand component, whereas suitable targets constitute the supply component of the illegal market. The absence of capable guardians then involves both weak public sector as well as private sector social control mechanisms that establish the link between the demand and the illegal supply component.[15]

In the following paragraphs, the basic logic of routine activity theory will be applied to structurally analyse the transnational illegal market in adoptable children. It will be explained that the adopters and adoption agencies in Western countries constitute the demand component, whereas a large number of poor families and orphanages caring for children in the developing countries form the supply component. To meet the high demand for adoptable children, children are illegally obtained from their birth families or from orphanages caring for them. Demand and illegal supply are then being connected by individuals and organizations from both the public and private sector that ought to serve as legal guardians in the adoption system, but who misuse their function to launder children through legitimate channels.

2.2 *Demand Component*

2.2.1 From a humanitarian deed to a remedy for involuntary childlessness

The transfer of children within national borders for the purposes of care or adoption has a relatively long history. For instance, in the late 19th and early 20th century, more than 100,000 children were transported *via* so-called 'orphan trains' from the overcrowded and poor cities in the East of the United States to foster families in the rural areas of the Mid-west.[16] In the 1950s and 1960s, the United States, Canada, and Australia began to forcefully remove Native children from their families and they began placing them into institutions and later white foster or adoptive families.[17]

Yet, intercountry adoption – meaning the transnational movement of children for purposes of adoption – is a fairly recent phenomenon that has only developed in the second half of the 20th century as a humanitarian response to massive devastation in war-torn countries.[18] During World War II, intercountry adoption became an important measure

15 *Ibid.*

16 See generally M. I. Holt (1992). "The Orphan Trains: Placing Out In America." University Of Nebraska Press, Lincoln and London.

17 See Chapter III, section 6.4 where these 'forced' removals and the principle of the child's best interests revolving around them will be discussed in more depth.

18 K. Lovelock (2000). "Intercountry Adoptions as a Migratory Practice: A Comparative Analysis of Intercountry Adoption and Immigration Policy and Practice in the United States, Canada and New Zealand in the Post W.W. II Period." International Migration Review, 34, 3, 907-949, p. 908.

to rescue European children from war atrocities.[19] Moreover, in the two decades following the war, thousands of children from Germany, Austria, Italy, Greece and Japan were sent to the United States, Scandinavian countries, the Netherlands and Belgium for the purposes of adoption. Some of them were illegitimate children fathered by black soldiers of the Allied Forces (so-called 'brown babies') who were expected to face major difficulties with societal acceptance.[20] Other children had been orphaned by war, or their parents were unable to feed and house them due to widespread destruction and poverty.[21]

European countries were the main source of adoptees for families in the United States right up until the late 70s.[22] Yet, as they were being rebuilt and their economy was being stabilized, the number of European orphans decreased dramatically. Adoptions from Korea and Vietnam became increasingly important, not only for the United States but also for many European countries, which had all experienced an economic upsurge after World War II and which later became important receiving countries as well.[23]

Initially, the motivation to adopt a child from abroad has revolved mainly around an altruistic core. Television broadcasts about the wars in Korea and Vietnam as well as about extreme poverty in 'Third-World' countries, showed the suffering of thousands of children. Pictures of this misery prompted many couples in Western countries to offer themselves as adoptive families for these children.[24] Rescue missions, such as the infamous 'Operation Babylift' in Vietnam, were initiated so as to evacuate thousands of children from war countries and to fly them to the United States, Europe, and Australia where they have since been adopted.[25] Hoksbergen describes the generation of adoptive parents from 1956 to 1970 as being open and idealistic. They perceived intercountry adoption as a concrete

---

19 D. Marre and L. Briggs (2009). "International Adoption: Global Inequalities and the Circulation of Children." New York University Press, p. 3.

20 Y.-C. Lemke Muniz de Faria (2003). "Germany's 'Brown Babies' Must Be Helped! Will You?: US Adoption Plans for Afro-German Children, 1950-1955." Callaloo 26, 2, 342-362.

21 M. R. Textor (1991). "International adoption in West Germany: A private affair." in H. Altstein and R. J. Simon "Intercountry adoption: A multinational perspective." Greenwood Publishing Group, New York, 109-126, p. 109.

22 P. Selman (2002). "Intercountry adoption in the new millennium; the "quiet migration" revisited." Population Research and Policy Review, 21, 3, 205-225, p. 209.

23 H. Altstein and R. J. Simon (1991). "Intercountry adoption: A multinational perspective." New York, Greenwood Publishing Group, p. 4.

24 R. A. C. Hoksbergen (2011). "Kinderen die niet konden blijven: zestig jaar adoptie in beeld." Aspekt, Soesterberg, pp. 71-72; M. Quartly, et al. (2013). "The Market In Babies: Stories of Australian Adoption." Monash University Publishing, Clayton, p. 107.

25 H. Altstein and R. J. Simon (1991). "Intercountry adoption: A multinational perspective." New York, Greenwood Publishing Group, p. 3. P. J. Meier (2008). "Small commodities: How child traffickers exploit children and families in intercountry adoption and what the United States must do to stop them." The Journal of Gender, Race & Justice 12, 185-224, p. 194; M. Rupprecht (2012). "Intercountry Adoption: ensuring that the best interests of the child are upheld." Parlamentary Assembly of the Council of Europe, Committee on Social Affairs, Health and Sustainable Development, 19.10.2012, Doc. 12597, p. 6; J. L. Carro (1994). "Regulation of Intercountry Adoption: Can the Abuses Come to an End?" Hastings International & Comparative Law Review, 18, 121-155, p. 125.

form of development aid as well as an acceptable way to form or enlarge a family that already included biological children.[26] It was at this time that the first adoption agencies were founded in Western countries, often by motivated adoptive parents who wanted to help as many needy children as possible.[27]

Since the mid-70s, the interests and needs of adopters began to play a more prominent role in the intercountry adoption system.[28] Intercountry adoptions were still shaped by humanitarian concerns for children living in war zones or in poverty. However, they were also driven by declining infertility rates and the decreasing number of children available for domestic adoption in the West.[29] In the industrialized developed countries, the proportion of couples who wanted to become parents but who could not have their own biological children has risen since the 1970s.[30] Women's increased level of education, their higher occupational status as well as processes of individualization have resulted in patterns of delayed motherhood. The proportion of women having their first child above age 30 has increased significantly. However, since the possibility of bearing a healthy baby starts to decline after the age of 30,[31] the number of couples who have tried, but failed, to have children has increased in most Western societies.[32] Many involuntarily childless couples and individuals therefore sought to create their own families through adoption – some after having undergone infertility treatments without success. For instance, in the United States, two million couples and one million single individuals wanted to adopt a child in 1989.[33] Also in other Western countries the pressure to adopt has intensified. For instance,

26 R. A. C. Hoksbergen (2011). "Kinderen die niet konden blijven: zestig jaar adoptie in beeld." Aspekt, Soesterberg, p. 72; R. A. C. Hoksbergen (1998). "Changes in Motivation for Adoption, Value Orientations and Behavior in Three Generations of Adoptive Parents." Adoption Quarterly, 2, 2, 37-55, p. 45.

27 In Germany the organization *terre des hommes* was established by a group of adoptive parents in 1967. In the Netherlands two years later, the *Nederlandse Stichting voor Interlandelijke Adoptie* and in 1971 *Wereldkinderen* were set up by adopters.

28 S. King (2008). "Challenging Monohumanism: An Argument for Changing the Way We Think About Intercountry Adoption." Michigan Journal of International Law, 30, 413-470, p. 423; M. Holz et al. (2013). ""Wir suchen Eltern für Kinder" Die Geschichte der Adoptionsarbeit von terre des hommes." Terre des hommes e.V., Osnabrück, available at https://www.tdh.de/fileadmin/user_upload/inhalte/04_Was_wir_tun/Themen/Weitere_Themen/Ado/2013-05_Geschichte-der-Adoptionsarbeit.pdf, p. 28; J. Triseliotis (2000). "Intercountry adoption: Global trade or global gift?" Adoption and Fostering, 24, 2, 45-54, p. 48.

29 K. Lovelock (2000). "Intercountry Adoptions as a Migratory Practice: A Comparative Analysis of Intercountry Adoption and Immigration Policy and Practice in the United States, Canada and New Zealand in the Post W.W. II Period." International Migration Review, 34, 3, 907-949, p. 908.

30 E. Te Velde et al. (2012). "The effect of postponement of first motherhood on permanent involuntary childlessness and total fertility rate in six European countries since the 1970s." Human Reproduction, 27, 4, 1179-1183, pp. 1179-1180.

31 *Ibid.*

32 R. Högbacka (2008). "The quest for a child of one's own: Parents, markets and transnational adoption." Journal of Comparative Family Studies, 39, 3, 311-330, p. 313.

33 H. Altstein and R. J. Simon (1991). "Intercountry adoption: A multinational perspective." New York, Greenwood Publishing Group, p. 8.

in Germany, the number of adoption applicants increased to some 21,000 in 1984.[34] Whereas the number of involuntarily childless couples and individuals that applied for an adoption was on the rise, the number of applicants who already had biological children was decreasing.[35]

At the same time, infertility rates were declining, meaning that the proportion of (attractive) children available for domestic adoption in Western countries fell due to liberal abortion politics, widespread contraception use, and the increasing acceptance of unwed motherhood.[36] Hence, the adoption of a child from a foreign country has become an attractive (and often last resort) alternative for many involuntary childless couples.[37] In fact, the decrease in the number of domestic adoptions strongly correlates with the increasing number of intercountry adoptions in all Western countries.[38]

From the 90s, intercountry adoptions were almost entirely driven by the adopters' need for children and therefore were less driven by humanitarian considerations.[39] Hoksbergen describes the generation of adoptive parents from 1991 to 2005 as particularly materialistic and demanding.[40] Many individuals or couples wished to adopt a child that was younger than two years and they were less willing to accept an orphan with medical risks. Young and healthy girls were particularly 'high in demand'. Whereas in the past adoptive parents could always have found a child in need, children that were already older and/or suffered from mental or physical diseases became increasingly difficult to place.[41] The adopters' demanding attitude can also be observed in the following generations of adoptive parents.[42] International adopters do not only wish to adopt children that are as young and healthy as possible, but they also want to do this more speedily and in a less a bureaucratic way.

Yet, infertility is not the only reason why the new generation of Western couples and individuals pursue an intercountry adoption. Rather, humanitarian convictions and religious

---

34 R. P. Bach (1986). "Gekaufte Kinder, Babyhandel mit der Dritten Welt." Rowohlt, Hamburg, p. 17.

35 R. A. C. Hoksbergen (1998). "Changes in Motivation for Adoption, Value Orientations and Behavior in Three Generations of Adoptive Parents." Adoption Quarterly, 2, 2, 37-55, pp. 50-51.

36 A. Fleisher (2003). "The Decline of Domestic Adoption: Intercountry Adoption as a Response to Local Adoption Laws and Proposals to Foster Domestic Adoption." Review of Law and Women's Studies, 13, 1, 171-197, p. 175; R. Rios-Kohn (1998). "Intercountry adoption: An international perspective on the practice and standards." Adoption Quarterly, 1, 4, 3-32, p. 7; R. Högbacka (2008). "The quest for a child of one's own: Parents, markets and transnational adoption." Journal of Comparative Family Studies, 39, 3, 311-330, p. 312; E. L. Kleiman (1996). "Caring for our own: why American adoption law and policy must change." Columbia Journal of Law and Social Problems, 30, 327-368, pp. 333-341.

37 *Ibid.*

38 *Ibid.*

39 A. Young (2012). "Developments in intercountry adoption - From humanitarian aid to market-driven policy and beyond." Adoption and Fostering, 36, 2, 67-78.

40 R. A. C. Hoksbergen (2011). "Kinderen die niet konden blijven: zestig jaar adoptie in beeld." Aspekt, Soesterberg, p. 255.

41 *Ibid.*

42 Interview with R. A. C. Hoksbergen, Emeritus Professor specializing in national and international adoption at Utrecht University, The Netherlands, 25.05.2017.

faith coexists alongside the desire for a child. Whereas a large number of adopters consider intercountry adoption as a way of forming a family, others are primarily motivated by the call to 'save a child' and to mitigate the global orphan crisis.[43] Regardless of their individual motivation, the adopters' demand exerts an inexorable pull on the healthy babies located in the poor countries.[44]

2.2.2 The role of adoption agencies

Some prospective adoptive parents choose to adopt privately or independently. A private adoption is arranged directly between the adopters and the birth parents or the child care institution, often with the help of independent agents in the sending countrie, such as foreign social workers, doctors or attorneys, who act as intermediaries. Others use the services of adoption placement agencies in the receiving countries in order to pursue an intercountry adoption.[45]

Adoption agencies, too, play an important role on the demand side of the adoption market by channeling the adopters' pressure on the sending countries. Although they repeatedly stress that their main mission is to find parents for children and that they exclusively serve the best interests of the child,[46] they effectively act as representatives of the adopters which seek to find suitable children for their paying clients. Adoption agencies typically let the applicants fill out a check-list indicating their preferences in relation to the child's age, origin, health status and sometimes gender, which in turn serves the agencies as a basis for their placement services. They seek out 'attractive' source countries, negotiate placement quotas with the local institutions and organizations and make sure that the proposed children actually comply with their clients' preferences.

The pressure on the sending countries does not only originate from the adoptive parents who seek to adopt a suitable child as quickly as possible. As will be shown in the subsequent chapters on the German and Dutch adoption system, the pressure to place children also emanates from the adoption agencies themselves.[47] In both countries, adoption agencies do not receive any subsidies, and they must cover their expenses exclusively with the fees paid by the adopters. This means that the agencies' very existence is dependent on the number of intercountry adoptions they place. Due to this dependency, agencies feel forced to put the pressure on the sending countries to fulfil their needs. This pressure has arguably

43 M. Breuning (2013). "Samaritans, Family Builders, and the Politics of Intercountry Adoption." International Studies Perspectives, 14, 4, 417-435; K. Joyce (2013). "The Child Catchers: Rescue, Trafficking, and the New Gospel of Adoption." Public Affairs, New York.

44 S. Marijnen and J. Doomernik (2015). "Baby Migration." AEMI Journal, 13, 133-149, p. 141. See also Chapter VII, section 4.2.

45 See Chapter IV, section 5.1 and Chapter V, section 4.1 that explain the difference between agency adoptions and private adoptions and the risks involved in the latter.

46 See Chapter V, section 5.2 and Chapter VI, section 5.2.

47 *Ibid.*

increased as the number of international adoptions has been on a constant decline since 2004. In addition, the agencies are also ideologically motivated to keep children moving for adoption purposes.[48]

2.3 *Supply Component*

2.3.1 **Source countries**

Whereas adopters and adoption agencies in the wealthy Global North (primarily in North America and Western European countries) constitute the demand component, large numbers of poor families and orphanages caring for children in low-income countries of the Global South (including post-communist Eastern Europe) form the supply component of the adoption market. The reasons why there are children in need of a family or care in these countries are basically exogenous to the demand: wars, natural disasters, extreme poverty, AIDS, religious and cultural traditions (e.g. stigmatizing unwed mothers) and changes in economic and social policies.[49] Typically, a combination of these factors as well as expedient and bureaucratic adoption procedures makes a state an attractive source of children for the purposes of intercountry adoption.

When intercountry adoption first became popular in the second half of the last century, war-torn countries were significant suppliers of adoptees. During and after World War II, thousands of children from European countries and Japan were sent abroad for the purpose of adoption and care. As the European countries were recovering from the war, however, they gradually became the recipients of adoptees themselves. In the 50s and 60s, Korea and Vietnam emerged as important providers of children for the United States and Western Europe. South Korea remained the main source of healthy infants – the majority of them were mixed race offspring of Korean women and allied soldiers – until the late 80s, with more than 6,000 children placed for adoption between 1980 and 1989.[50] However, the flow of children out of the country did not end after the mixed-race children found families in the West. Until 2006, South Korea ranked among the top five most significant suppliers of children,[51] which often came from impoverish and broken families or unwed mothers who would face stigmatization if they decided to keep their children.[52]

48 See Chapter V, section 7.2.

49 R. Högbacka (2008). "The quest for a child of one's own: Parents, markets and transnational adoption." Journal of Comparative Family Studies, 39, 3, 311-330, p. 313.

50 P. Selman (2002). "Intercountry adoption in the new millennium; the "quiet migration" revisited." Population Research and Policy Review, 21, 3, 205-225, p. 214.

51 P. Selman (2009). "The rise and fall of intercountry adoption in the 21st century." International Social Work, 52, 5, 575-594, p. 580.

52 K. Joyce (2013). "The Child Catchers: Rescue, Trafficking, and the New Gospel of Adoption." Public Affairs, New York, p. 273.

In the 80s, India and Colombia emerged as important sending states, each sending some 1,500 children abroad between 1980 and 1989. This was followed by Brazil, Sri Lanka, Chile and the Philippines.[53] Extreme poverty made these countries strong suppliers of adoptable children during the late 80s and early 90s.

In the 90s, the end of the Cold War opened a number of Eastern European countries up for the adoption market. For a short period of time in the early 90s, Romania became the largest source of children for international adoption.[54] The country that allowed only 30 intercountry adoptions in 1989[55] became "almost synonymous with intercountry adoption" in the year after the Ceausescu's demise.[56] With the end of the Cold War and the fall of the 'Iron Curtain' in the early 90s, market-driven economics were ushered into Central and Eastern Europe, causing the collapse of communist-era welfare systems and a surge in the number of abandoned children.[57] After the distressing conditions in Romanian child care institutions became known internationally, thousands of foreigners from the United States, as well as Western Europe, flocked to the country to "save the children".[58] The exact number of adoptions from Romania in the months following the fall of Ceausescu remains uncertain. According to estimates, however, more than 10,000 Romanian children were adopted internationally between March 1990 and July 1991, when Romania temporarily banned international adoptions due to reports of abusive practices.[59]

A similar development can be observed in Russia which did not allow intercountry adoptions prior to 1990, but which quickly became one of the most significant supply countries.[60] The number of children sent from Russia abroad rose sharply from 324 in 1992 to 4,491 in 1998[61] and constitutes one of the most significant sending countries even since.[62]

Additionally, China – which refused on giving up its children for international adoption in the late 80s – later became a significant sending country in the 90s. Since the mid-90s,

53 P. Selman (2002). "Intercountry adoption in the new millennium; the "quiet migration" revisited." Population Research and Policy Review, 21, 3, 205-225, p. 214.

54 *Ibid.*, p. 213.

55 E. B. Kapstein (2003). "The baby trade." Foreign Affairs, 82, 6, 115-125, p. 116.

56 J. Dickens (2002). "The paradox of inter-country adoption: analysing Romania's experience as a sending country." International Journal of Social Welfare, 11, 1, 76-83, p. 76.

57 *Ibid.*

58 *Ibid.*, p. 77.

59 P. Selman (2002). "Intercountry adoption in the new millennium; the "quiet migration" revisited." Population Research and Policy Review, 21, 3, 205-225, p. 213.

60 E. B. Kapstein (2003). "The baby trade." Foreign Affairs, 82, 6, 115-125, p. 116.

61 P. Selman (2002). "Intercountry adoption in the new millennium; the "quiet migration" revisited." Population Research and Policy Review, 21, 3, 205-225, p. 215.

62 P. Selman (2006). "Trends in intercountry adoption: Analysis of data from 20 receiving countries, 1998-2004." Journal of Population Research, 23, 2, 183-204, p. 191; P. Selman (2018). "Global Statistics for Intercountry Adoption: Receiving States and States of Origin 2004-2016." 03.05.2018, The Hague Conference on Private International Law, p. 3.

the country is ranked as one of the strongest supply states.[63] Its one-child policy, combined with the cultural status of boys, has resulted in many abandoned Chinese girls. Since China could not or did not want to afford the immense costs of the growing number of abandoned children in institutions, many of them were sent to the United States and Europe for the purposes of adoption.[64] After China had established an intercountry adoption programme in the 90s, the number of foreign adoptions increased each year, peaking in 2005 where some 14,500 children were sent abroad.[65] China was a particularly attractive source country as it offered the kind of children that most Western adopters were looking for: relatively young and healthy girls.[66]

At the end of the 1990s, beginning of the millennium, Guatemala, Haiti, Cambodia Kazakhstan, and Ukraine also emerged as sending countries.[67] Guatemala in particular became a significant supplier of adoptable children. Between 2003 and 2008, the country placed some 23,000 children for adoption and therefore constituted the third most significant sending state after China (65,000) and Russia (41,000).[68] This number is remarkably high considering Guatemala's population of only about 13 million (at that time). In comparison, China and Russia had a population of 1.3 billion and 143 million respectively. The number of adoptions from Guatemala fell dramatically after the country banned international adoptions in 2008 for almost two years.[69]

Haiti also emerged as a strong supply country with the number of foreign adoptions rising to more than 1,300 in 2008.[70] In 2010, after Haiti was rocked by an earthquake that destroyed about 25,000 homes and left more than a million Haitians homeless, the number of adoptions increased dramatically.[71] It is estimated that in the aftermath of the earthquake,

---

63 P. Selman (2009). "The rise and fall of intercountry adoption in the 21st century." International Social Work, 52, 5, 575-594, p. 582; P. Selman (2018). "Global Statistics for Intercountry Adoption: Receiving States and States of Origin 2004-2016." 03.05.2018, The Hague Conference on Private International Law, p. 3.

64 E. B. Kapstein (2003). "The baby trade." Foreign Affairs, 82, 6, 115-125, p. 116.

65 P. Selman (2012). "The Global Decline of Intercountry Adoption: What Lies Ahead?" Social Policy and Society, 11, 03, 381-397, p. 384.

66 P. J. Meier and Z. Xiaole (2008). "Sold into Adoption: The Hunan Baby Trafficking Scandal Exposes Vulnerabilities in the Chinese Adoptions to the United States." Cumberland Law Review, 39, 1, 87-130, p. 97; K. Johnson (2002). "Politics of International and Domestic Adoption in China." Law & Society Review, 36, 2, 379-396, p. 389.

67 P. Selman (2006). "Trends in intercountry adoption: Analysis of data from 20 receiving countries, 1998–2004." Journal of Population Research, 23, 2, 183-204, p. 190.

68 P. Selman (2012). "The Global Decline of Intercountry Adoption: What Lies Ahead?" Social Policy and Society, 11, 03, 381-397, p. 384.

69 *Ibid.*

70 P. Selman (2011). "Intercountry adoption after the Haiti earthquake: Rescue or robbery?" Adoption & Fostering, 35, 4, 41-49, p. 42.

71 K. Joyce (2013). "The Child Catchers: Rescue, Trafficking, and the New Gospel of Adoption." Public Affairs, New York, p. 1.

some 2,000 children were sent to the United States, Canada, France, Germany, the Netherlands, and other European countries for adoption purposes.[72]

Since the 90s, the number of intercountry adoptions has been constantly rising, peaking at more than 45,000 placements in 2004.[73] This rise, Selman explains, "seems in many ways to have been driven by an increasing 'demand' for children, fuelled by the apparent steady increase in the number of children available in China, Russia, and Guatemala and the opening up of possibilities for adoption by single individuals".[74] Since 2004, however, the number of intercountry adoptions fell to about 29,000 in 2010 and to 11,000 in 2016.[75] This decline is particularly attributable to the suspension of intercountry adoptions by Guatemala in 2008, as well as the restriction in the number of children sent by China and Russia. Whereas in 2005, more than 14,000 Chinese children were placed for international adoption, the number had fallen to less than 3,500 by 2013.[76] Similar declines could also be observed in Russia which placed over 9,000 children in 2004 but less than 2,000 in 2013.[77] In other important sending states, most notably in South Korea, India, Haiti, Cambodia and Nepal, the number of children sent abroad fell dramatically.[78]

Several factors have caused the drop in intercountry adoptions from these countries, which include, but are not restricted to, economic developments, doubts as to whether intercountry adoption was a proper child care measure, stronger reliance on domestic adoption, reports about illegal practices and concerns over adoptions by singles and same-sex couples.[79] In several sending countries, these factors resulted in stricter adoption laws which made adoptions by foreigners more difficult to execute. For instance, in 2007, China prohibited adoptions by single adults and tightened the application process for families who wished to adopt a healthy child.[80] Russia banned adoptions to the United States in

---

72 M. Dambach and C. Baglietto (2010). ""Expediting" intercountry adoptions in the aftermath of a natural disaster...preventing future harm." International Social Service, p. 22.

73 P. Selman (2016). "The Rise and Fall of Intercountry Adoption in the 21st Century: Global Trends from 2001 to 2010." In J. L. Gibbons and K. S. Rotabi (eds), "Intercountry Adopion: Policies, Practices and Outcomes." Ashgate, Farnham, 2-27, p. 8.

74 *Ibid.*, p. 24.

75 P. Selman (2018). "Global Statistics for Intercountry Adoption: Receiving States and States of Origin 2004-2016." 03.05.2018, The Hague Conference on Private International Law, p.3.

76 *Ibid.*

77 *Ibid.*

78 *Ibid.*

79 D. M. Smolin (2010). "Child Laundering and the Hague Convention on Intercountry Adoption: The Future and Past of Intercountry Adoption." University of Louisville Law Review, 48, 441-498, p. 471; P. Selman (2012). "The Global Decline of Intercountry Adoption: What Lies Ahead?" Social Policy and Society, 11, 03, 381-397, p. 385.

80 E. Poncz (2007). "China's Proposed International Adoption Law: The Likely Impact on Single U.S. Citizens Seeking to Adopt from China and the Available Alternatives." Harvard International Law Journal, 48, 74-82.

2012 due to the deteriorating diplomatic relations between the two countries,[81] and in 2014 it stopped sending children to countries that allowed same-sex couples to adopt.[82]

As the number of adoptions from China and Russia decreased, African states became an attractive supplier of adoptees.[83] In 2004, 7% of international adoptions took place from Africa, whereas by 2013 the numbers had risen to 27%.[84] Particularly, reports about actress Angelina Jolie's adoption of an Ethiopian child in 2005 and pop-singer Madonna's adoption from Malawi one year later have drawn attention to the possibility of adopting from Africa (experts refer to this as the 'Madonna effect').[85] The rise in intercountry adoptions from this continent mostly consists of adoptions from Ethiopia. Between 2003 and 2013, this country placed more than 30,000 children up for adoption.[86] Within this time period, South Africa, Republic of the Congo, Nigeria, Madagascar, Liberia, Mali, Uganda, Ghana, Burkina Faso, Morocco and Kenya collectively sent more than 20,000 children abroad.[87] Yet, even though intercountry adoptions from Africa were on the rise, the overall figure continued to fall. Ethiopia and other African countries could never make up for the declining significance of China, Russia and Guatemala.

The number of African children sent abroad for adoption purposes fell in 2009 after some countries began to either restrict or ban intercountry adoptions altogether. For instance, Liberia suspended intercountry adoptions in 2009,[88] Rwanda did so in until 2017[89] and Kenya followed suit in 2014.[90] Ethiopia suspended adoptions by foreigners in May

81 M. Lipman (2012). "What's behind the Russian Adoption Ban?" The New Yorker, 21.12.2012, available at https://www.newyorker.com/news/news-desk/whats-behind-the-russian-adoption-ban.

82 P. Black and A. Eshchenko (2014). "Russia enacts anti-gay adoption ban." CNN, 14.2.2014, available at https://edition.cnn.com/2014/02/13/world/europe/russia-same-sex-marriage-adoption-ban/index.html.

83 K. S. Rotabi (2010). "From Guatemala to Ethiopia: Shifts in Intercountry Adoption Leaves Ethiopia Vulnerable for Child Sales and Other Unethical Practices." The Social Work and Society Online News Magazine, available at https://www.uni-vechta.de/fileadmin/user_upload/Soziale_Arbeit/Dokumenten/Kutscher/Socmag_Archiv/June2010/June2010-Rotabi__Kara_Smith-_From_Guatemala_to_Ethiopia__Shifts_in_intercountry_adoption_leaves_ethopia_vunerable_for_child_sales_and_other_unethical_practies.pdf; M. A. Davis (2011). "Intercountry Adoption Flows from Africa to the U.S.: A Fifth Wave of Intercountry Adoptions?" International Migration Review, 45, 4, 784-811.

84 P. Selman (2015). "AFRICA: The 'new frontier' in international adoption." Paper Presented at 2015 SPA Conference, Belfast, available at http://www.adoptionhoksbergen.com/index.php/nl/2-algemeen/87-africa-the-new-frontier-in-international-adoption.

85 B. D. Mezmur (2008). "Intercountry Adoption as a Measure of Last Resort in Africa: Advancing the Rights of a Child rather than a Right to a Child." International Journal of Human Rights, 6, 10, 82-103.

86 P. Selman (2015). "AFRICA: The 'new frontier' in international adoption." Paper Presented at 2015 SPA Conference, Belfast, available at http://www.adoptionhoksbergen.com/index.php/nl/2-algemeen/87-africa-the-new-frontier-in-international-adoption.

87 *Ibid.*

88 See https://travel.state.gov/content/adoptionsabroad/en/country-information/alerts-and-notices/liberia10-04-26.html (last accessed on 03.08.2018).

89 P. Tumwebaze (2017). "Govt lifts ban on foreign adoption of Rwandan kids." The New Times, 21.09.2017, available at http://www.newtimes.co.rw/section/read/220313/.

90 See https://travel.state.gov/content/adoptionsabroad/en/country-information/alerts-and-notices/kenya14-12-12.html (last accessed on 03.08.2018).

2017[91] and ceased them altogether in January 2018, after the Ethiopian Parliament passed new legislation banning intercountry adoptions.[92]

2.3.2 Illegal practices to secure adoptable children

War, natural disasters, extreme poverty and AIDS leave numerous children worldwide extremely vulnerable. However, contrary to the common Western belief of an 'orphan crisis', only a small fraction of these children are deprived of their family environment and are therefore legitimately available for intercountry adoption. Those children who are in need of an adoption do not often have the characteristics that international adopters are looking for as they are sick and /or older.[93] For several years, China has been an exception in this respect. The country's one-child policy, combined with the cultural preference for sons, created an unprecedented number of abandoned female infants available for intercountry adoption in the 80s and 90s. But this situation changed in the early 2000s as sex-selective abortions replaced sex-selective abandonment and the number of institutionalized children decreased as a consequence.[94]

In order to meet the high Western demand for babies, actors in the sending countries employ a variety of illegal means to generate 'adoptable' children. Real cases are typically a combination of these methods.[95] In some sending countries, citizens - including independent agents, attorneys, orphanage directors and others - establish a system for *purchasing* children from their birth parents. According to Smolin,

> [t]hese systems usually involve persons at the head of the conspiracy who possess the language and literacy skills, and the financial and social position, to interact with first-world adoption agencies and prospective adoptive parents. These persons usually send out intermediaries, generally of a lower social station, to serve as scouts or recruiters. The targets of this recruiting are generally the poor of poor societies, who earn less than one dollar per day.[96]

Impoverished families and potentially vulnerable pregnant women or birth mothers – often young and impoverished unmarried mothers – are approached and incited to give

91 See https://travel.state.gov/content/adoptionsabroad/en/country-information/alerts-and-notices/AdoptionAlertSuspensionofAdoptionsfromEthiopia.html (last accessed on 03.08.2018).

92 See https://travel.state.gov/content/travel/en/News/Intercountry-Adoption-News/ethiopia-adoption-notice--ethiopia-passes-legislation-banning-in.html (last accessed on 03.08.2018).

93 See Chapter III, section 5.3.

94 See Chapter VI, section 7.4.1.

95 D. M. Smolin (2006). "Child Laundering: How the Intercountry Adoption System Legitimizes and Incentivizes the Practices of Buying, Trafficking, Kidnapping, and Stealing Children." The Wayne Law Review, 52, 1, 113-200, p. 118.

96 *Ibid.*

up their future or newborn child.[97] Consent to relinquishment is hardly given freely, but rather it is induced by psychological pressure and financial or material rewards. The parents may be told that they are not the most suitable person to properly bring up a child and that they should give their future or newborn children the opportunity to have a better life than themselves.[98] Such pressure is often reinforced by rewards of money or goods, thereby resulting in an actual purchase of the child.[99] In other incidences, parents are forced to give up their baby in order to settle their debts.[100] Some involve women who are not able to pay for the costs of childbirth; others involve money lenders who indebt vulnerable women and then propose or prompt them to place their child in an orphanage.[101]

Another method that is used to illegally obtain children is the *deception of biological parents to obtain their consent to adoption*. Biological parents are intentionally provided with false information about the consequences of an adoption in order to obtain their consent.[102] They may be told that their child is only going away for educational purposes and on a temporary basis. Or they may be promised that they can keep contact with their child, receive payments and letters from the adoptive parents or will be allowed to follow their child to the Western nation once the child has grown up.[103] This makes them believe that they are maintaining the parental connection with their child.[104] In other cases, birth parents are urged to sign paperwork relinquishing their parental rights without properly understanding the concept of 'relinquishment' that is based on a culturally foreign, exclusivist nuclear (than extended family) model.[105]

Furthermore, there are cases where children are obtained through *kidnapping or abduction*. The children are kidnapped either from the streets, hospitals or their homes[106]

97 *Ibid.*

98 UNICEF International Child Development Centre (1998). "Intercountry adoption." UNICEF, Florence (Innocenti Digest no. 4), p. 6.

99 *Ibid.*

100 D. M. Smolin (2006). "Child Laundering: How the Intercountry Adoption System Legitimizes and Incentivizes the Practices of Buying, Trafficking, Kidnapping, and Stealing Children." The Wayne Law Review, 52, 1, 113-200, p. 124.

101 *Ibid.*

102 UNICEF International Child Development Centre (1998). "Intercountry adoption." UNICEF, Florence (Innocenti Digest no. 4), p. 6; D. M. Smolin (2006). "Child Laundering: How the Intercountry Adoption System Legitimizes and Incentivizes the Practices of Buying, Trafficking, Kidnapping, and Stealing Children." The Wayne Law Review, 52, 1, 113-200, p. 121.

103 D. M. Smolin (2006). "Child Laundering: How the Intercountry Adoption System Legitimizes and Incentivizes the Practices of Buying, Trafficking, Kidnapping, and Stealing Children." The Wayne Law Review, 52, 1, 113-200, p. 121.

104 *Ibid.*

105 D. M. Smolin (2007). "Intercountry Adoption and Poverty: A Human Rights Analysis." Capital University Law Review, 36, 413-453, p. 443.

106 D. M. Smolin (2006). "Child Laundering: How the Intercountry Adoption System Legitimizes and Incentivizes the Practices of Buying, Trafficking, Kidnapping, and Stealing Children." The Wayne Law Review, 52, 1, 113-200, p. 122.

or they are abducted from orphanages, hostels or schools where they have been placed temporarily by their parents for the purposes of education or care.[107] Poor families often use these child care institutions as a safety net without ever intending to sever their parental rights or ties. They either place their children into the institution on their own initiative for a period of time during which they are not able to care for them due to financial or other reasons,[108] or the children are deliberately recruited into such an institution on the basis of false pretenses and then sent abroad for adoption.[109]

In other incidences, birth mothers are duped into thinking that their newborn child was stillborn or that the child died shortly after birth, while in reality the babies are being abducted from the hospitals or maternity clinics.[110] Finally, there is the scenario of child abduction in the aftermath of a natural disaster or in a conflict situation where 'lost' or 'missing' children are placed for intercountry adoption without any efforts having been made to find their birth parents or relatives.[111]

Another method of illegally obtaining children is by *subverting or bribing someone to subvert the subsidiarity principle*. Both the 1989 United Nations Convention for the Rights of the Child (hereinafter UNCRC) and the 1993 Hague Convention on Protection of Children and Co-Operation in Respect of Intercountry Adoption (hereinafter Hague Convention) stipulate that intercountry adoption should only be considered for a child that has been deprived of his or her family environment and if no child care solution can be found in the child's native country.[112] Even though the two legal instruments suggest different hierarchies of child care options (the UNCRC has been interpreted as giving priority to any conceivable domestic solution – institutionalization and foster care – over intercountry adoption, whereas the Hague Convention favours international adoption over institutionalization and foster care), they both prioritize domestic over international adoption.[113] This is because they acknowledge the importance of continuity in the child's upbringing, as well as of the child's ethnic, religious, cultural and linguistic background.[114]

In practice, however, the subsidiarity principle is often violated in the sending countries. It is not uncommon for staff members of child care institutions or government officials –

107 *Ibid.*, p. 119.

108 See Chapter III, section 5.3.

109 D. M. Smolin (2006). "Child Laundering: How the Intercountry Adoption System Legitimizes and Incentivizes the Practices of Buying, Trafficking, Kidnapping, and Stealing Children." The Wayne Law Review, 52, 1, 113-200, p. 120.

110 UNICEF International Child Development Centre (1998). "Intercountry adoption." UNICEF, Florence (Innocenti Digest no. 4), p. 6.

111 D. M. Smolin (2006). "Child Laundering: How the Intercountry Adoption System Legitimizes and Incentivizes the Practices of Buying, Trafficking, Kidnapping, and Stealing Children." The Wayne Law Review, 52, 1, 113-200, p. 121.

112 Art. 21(b), Art. 20(3) UNCRC, Art. 4(b) Hague Convention.

113 See Chapter III, section 5.2 and Chapter IV, section 4.2.

114 Art. 20(3) UNCRC, see Chapter III, sections 4.7 and 5.1.

bribed by adopters and adoption agencies – to approve an intercountry adoption, even though not all domestic childcare solutions have been exhausted or explored. This leads to the paradox that children are placed for international adoption even when waiting lists for domestic adoptive or foster families are lengthening.[115]

The foregoing methods of obtaining adoptable children are undoubtedly illegal. They either constitute criminal offences (e.g. child abduction, bribery) or they violate provisions of relevant international legal instruments, most notably the subsidiarity principle,[116] the standards concerning the consent to adoption laid down in the Hague Convention[117] and the principle that no improper financial or other gain should be derived from an activity related to intercountry adoption,[118] as well as the human rights of the children and their parents (see section 4.2.1).

2.4 *Social Control Component*

2.4.1 Child laundering – connecting demand and illegal supply

In order to sustain an illegal transnational market in adoptable children, a diverse set of demand and supply sources is necessary. However, demand and supply sources alone are not sufficient; it is equally important to ensure that these sources are linked. Connecting buyers and sellers with each other is crucial, and this is organized differently than in conventional forms of human trafficking.

There is at least one important feature that immediately distinguishes the trafficking in children for the purposes of adoption from other forms of human trafficking. Whereas the purpose of conventional forms of human trafficking is illegal (e.g. sexual exploitation, organ removal, slavery), adopting a child is perfectly legal at the demand end of the system. An adoption only becomes illegal when the child has been obtained illegally. Therefore, the illicit means by which children are obtained must be disguised: a laundering process is therefore crucial here. Just as crime proceeds and 'dirty money' are laundered, illegally secured children must be purified in order for them to be profitable.[119] Yet, whereas the damage caused by money laundering can be repaired (by ordering the convicted offender to pay back the laundered money), this is not usually the case with regard to the harm

115 D. M. Smolin (2004). "The Two Faces of Intercountry Adoption: The Significance of the Indian Adoption Scandals." Seton Hall Law Review, 35, 403-493, p. 474.

116 See Chapter III, section 5.2 and Chapter IV, section 4.2.

117 See Chapter IV, section 4.5.

118 Chapter IV, section 4.4.

119 D. M. Smolin (2006). "Child Laundering: How the Intercountry Adoption System Legitimizes and Incentivizes the Practices of Buying, Trafficking, Kidnapping, and Stealing Children." The Wayne Law Review, 52, 1, 113-200, p. 115.

caused by child laundering. As we will see, the child's best interests, the guiding principle in intercountry adoptions, often legitimizes the child's illegal origin.[120]

There are two ways to launder a child. The first one involves the adopters who bypass the intercountry adoption system by trafficking the illegally obtained child as their biological child, after either having the child's birth certificate falsified or fabricated. These adoptions are commonly referred to as 'illegal adoptions'. In these scenarios, the adopters circumvent the adoption procedure because they do not fulfil the adoption requirements or because they are not willing to endure the long waiting times and bureaucratic hurdles that are redolent of the adoption process. They often use a private contact as an intermediary who has located the child for them and who then assists them in the laundering process. Adoptive mothers may have the child's birth certificate issued with their name as the biological mother or adoptive fathers may wrongfully acknowledge the paternity of the allegedly 'illegitimate' child (in Germany, this illegal method is referred to as '*Vaterschaftstrick*').[121] Sometimes, this approach has already been prearranged prior to the children's birth, thereby involving psychological pressures and/or payments to the pregnant mother.[122] The latter may also be involved in the laundering process by registering the name of the adoptive mother at a maternity clinic. In other cases, birth certificates are issued with the names of the adoptive parents, while the biological mothers are told that their newborn baby was stillborn or died shortly after birth.[123] The adopters may not necessarily be aware of the illegal origin of the child that is presented to them. Their intermediary may tell them that the baby was legally abandoned by the mother or orphaned. Adopters may also circumvent the intercountry adoption system by bringing the child to the receiving country as a foster child with the intention to pursue a domestic adoption.[124]

The second means to launder an illegally obtained child is by passing the child through the adoption system. Again, the child's birth certificates and other necessary documents (e.g. maternity and paternity certificates, documents containing the birth parents' consent to adoption, death certificates of the birth parents, rejection letter from domestic adoption applicants etc.) need to be falsified or fabricated in order to mask the illegal conduct, as well as to identify the illegally obtained child as legally abandoned and for which no domestic child care solution could be found.[125] As a final step in this laundering process,

120 See Chapter III, section 6.4.

121 UNICEF International Child Development Centre (1998). "Intercountry adoption." UNICEF, Florence (Innocenti Digest no. 4), p. 6; UN Commission on Human Rights (2000). "Report of the Special Rapporteur on the Sale of Children, Child Prostitution and Child Pornography." 27.01.2000, E/CN.4/2000/73/Add.2, para. 61.

122 G. Wuttke (1996). "Ein Kind um jeden Preis? Eine Studie zum Adoptionskinderhandel "terre des hommes Deutschland e.V., Osnabrück, p. 36-38.

123 *Ibid.*, p. 38.

124 International Social Service (2007). "From respite care abroad... to adoption?" Geneva, Nr. 2.

125 H. Bochéat et al. (2012). "Investigating the Grey Zones of Intercountry Adoption." International Social Service, p. 81.

an illegal decision on an adoption is rendered by a court of law that bears all the hallmarks of a perfectly legal adoption procedure.[126] Cantwell explains:

> The 'illegality' of that decision could [...] result from situations where, variously, the required procedures have not been followed, documents have been falsified, the child has been declared adoptable without due cause or as a result of manipulation, money has changed hands... but if it is truly an adoption, rather than some other form of transfer or removal, it will necessarily and by definition have been approved by a judge. It follows that all events and acts that would make it "illegal" must therefore have taken place up to and including, but not after, the judgement. "Illegal international adoptions", therefore, are not the same as "illegally moving children abroad": in cases of the former, children are moved abroad legally following an adoption process that contains illegal elements.[127]

All traces of the illegal adoption will, in most cases, be wiped out by the time the child arrives in the receiving country and the adoptive parents, the adoption agencies and the government authorities might plausibly deny any knowledge of illegal practices overseas and therefore will adhere to the idea that the intercountry adoption was a humanitarian deed which saved a child from the terrible circumstances in the country of origin. It is only because of the possibility of laundering children that a lively adoption industry can actually exist. This need for transforming the status of human beings trafficked is not found in the traditional forms of human trafficking. Since the very purpose of human trafficking is illegal, there is no need to 'clean' the status of the trafficked persons.

The process of laundering is usually facilitated by legitimate individuals and organizations from both the public and the private sector. For instance, in cases where children are passed off as the adopters' biological parents, a nurse or doctor may issue the child's false birth certificate. In cases where children are channelled through the adoption system as 'orphans', the laundering process is commonly facilitated by actors who actually ought to serve as guardians in the adoption system. Basically, the adoption system's integrity relies on capable guardians in the form of effective regulatory institutions, which effectively monitor and control the adoption process and make sure that only those children that are truly suited for international adoption can enter the system. The drafters of 1993 Hague Convention on Protection and Co-operation in Respect of Intercountry Adoption believed that illegal and abusive adoption practices can best be prevented by increasing capable

126 UNICEF International Child Development Centre (1998). "Intercountry adoption." UNICEF, Florence (Innocenti Digest no. 4), p. 6.

127 N. Cantwell (2005). "Is intercountry adoption linked with trafficking for exploitation?" International Social Service, Nr. 11-12, p. 1-2.

guardians in the adoption system. Hence, the treaty obliges its Contracting States to designate a Central Authority[128] to act as a gatekeeper through which all intercountry adoptions have to be channelled.[129] The Central Authority must fulfill the tasks that are outlined in the Convention, some of which may be delegated to public authorities (e.g. youth welfare offices, family courts) or to private bodies that must be accredited by the state (e.g. child care institutions, adoption placement agencies).[130]

Yet, as uncovered cases of illegal adoptions have shown, these public and private sector institutions do often not serve as guardians in the adoption system, but rather they misuse their knowledge and status so as to pass the children through their organization. They thereby create the necessary linkage between demand and illegal supply sources by converting illegally obtained children into 'orphans' first and then into 'adoptees'. These institutions might not only serve to connect buyers and sellers, but they may also have been involved in illegally sourcing the children for adoption in the first place. For instance, a child care institution might illicitly secure adoptable children (e.g. by circumventing the subsidiarity principle or by sending out scouts) and then falsify the necessary paperwork to hide both, the illegal conduct as well as the children's true origin and history.[131]

The limited effectiveness of regulatory institutions facilitating the child laundering process can also be traced to corruption and unwillingness to enforce the existing laws. A high incidence of corruption in the sending countries is a significant reason for the occurrence of illicit practices within the intercountry adoption system.[132] Public officials are accustomed to demanding and receiving payoffs to provide not only legitimate, but also illegitimate, approvals and services.[133] As Smolin explains, generous (by sending nations standards) fees and payments from Western adopters and adoption agencies therefore provide ample means for creating an intercountry adoption system that is 'greased by bribery'.[134] Corruption is the lubricant that enables child laundering to flourish, as it covers up illegal adoption practices, skews the decision-making process, and diverts law enforcement resources. Arguably, the issue of child laundering will not be tackled for as long as there is widespread corruption in the sending countries.

---

128 Art. 6 Hague Convention.

129 C. E. Kimball (2005). "Barriers to the Successful Implementation of the Hague Convention on Protection of Children and Co-Operation in Respect of Intercountry Adoption." Denver Journal of International Law and Policy, 33, 4, 561-584, p. 570.

130 See Chapter IV, section 3.4.

131 See, for example, P. J. Meier and Z. Xiaole (2008). "Sold into Adoption: The Hunan Baby Trafficking Scandal Exposes Vulnerabilities in the Chinese Adoptions to the United States." Cumberland Law Review, 39, 1, 87-130.

132 D. M. Smolin (2006). "Child Laundering: How the Intercountry Adoption System Legitimizes and Incentivizes the Practices of Buying, Trafficking, Kidnapping, and Stealing Children." The Wayne Law Review, 52, 1, 113-200, p. 129.

133 *Ibid.*

134 *Ibid.*, pp. 129-130.

2.4.2 Adoption agencies' representatives and cooperation partners in the sending countries

The foreign representatives and co-operation partners of the adoption agencies in the receiving states play a particularly crucial role at the demand-supply nexus. Generally speaking, there are different forms of cooperation between German and Dutch adoption agencies and the countries from which they place children up for adoption.[135] These forms of co-operation depend on the laws as well as the structures in the sending states. Kazakh law, for instance, obliges foreign international adoption placement offices to establish a representative office in Kazakhstan, which must in turn be accredited by the Central Authority in Astana. The staff members of the representative offices are in close contact with the child care institutions as well as the local official authorities.[136]

In other sending countries, adoption agencies have established cooperation with local partner organizations. Sometimes these partner organizations are orphanages that are accredited by the sending countries' authorities to place children for international adoption. In other cases, the partner organizations operate as adoption placement agencies with strong links to the local child care institutions.

Then there are sending states where the German and Dutch adoption agencies have not established a collaboration with a partner organization, but cooperate directly with the competent authorities who place the adoption applicants on a 'waiting list' and also do the matching with a child that becomes available for intercountry adoption. For instance, in China, adoption agencies collaborate exclusively with the Chinese Central Authority, the CCAA. They may have representatives which mediate between them and the CCAA, but which are not in direct contact with the Chinese child care institutions from which the adoptees are placed.[137]

Many German and Dutch adoption agencies have representatives in the sending countries – in some states of origin, this is even required by law or in established procedures.[138] The representatives manage the agencies' representative office or mediate between the agencies and their foreign partner organizations and/or the competent authorities. Often, they are locals who know the language and who are familiar with the adoption laws and procedures in the sending country. The representatives' qualifications and the range of functions to be performed basically differ from body to body, as well as from country

135 § 2(1)(1) and (4) AdVermiStAnKoV.

136 Interview with a staff member of German adoption agency D, Germany, 02.09.2015.

137 Interview with I. Hut, director of the Dutch adoption placement agency Wereldkinderen between 2003 and 2009, The Netherlands, 06.07.2017.

138 Burkina Faso, Chile, Colombia, Ecuador, Hungary, Lithuania, Mexico and Peru require foreign adoption agencies to have a representative in the sending country (The Permanent Bureau of the Hague Conference on International Private Law (2012). "Accreditation and Adoption Accredited Bodies: Guide to Good Practice No. 2." The Hague, para. 241).

to country.[139] Some representatives, like for instance those in China, only handle bureaucratic matters by translating documents and accompanying the adoption applicants to the official authorities and court hearings. Others play a more proactive role in the adoption process. They have strong contacts with the local child care institutions, which they visit on a regular basis in order to inquire if there are children in need of an adoption. Also, they may be required to undertake certain functions and duties for the authorities in the sending countries. In such cases, they commonly have to fulfil certain requirements and qualifications.[140]

Some states of origin do not allow foreign adoption agencies to use representatives in the sending countries. They prefer their Central Authority to provide the adoption applicants with the necessary information and assistance, or they require the foreign adoption agencies to cooperate with an accredited body in the sending country in order to perform these tasks.[141] In other cases, it may not be necessary for the adoption agencies to appoint a representative since the cooperation partner in the state of origin is already taking care of the bureaucratic matters and is guiding the adoption applicants through the adoption proceedings.

The adoption placement agencies' foreign co-operation partners and representatives play an important role in the adoption procedure, as they are involved in the most crucial phase of the child placement process: the phase beginning with the abandonment or relinquishment of the child by his/her birth parents and ending with the actual adoption in a court, where most illegal and abusive practices occur. They are important 'cogs' in the adoption system as their working method, ethical stance, as well as understanding of the child's best interests, have a significant influence on the subsequent processes and, ultimately, the resulting adoption. On the one hand, they could – and actually should – serve as guardians which only let those children pass through the adoption system, that are eligible for intercountry adoption in the first place. On the other hand, they may allow illegally obtained children to be laundered through the system.

As uncovered cases of child trafficking have shown, adoption agencies' partners and representatives in the sending countries are often involved in abusive adoption practices. They either illegally secure children for intercountry adoption themselves (like, for instance, the Indian child care institution *Missionaries of Charity*, the cooperation partner of the German adoption agency *pro infant action: Kind in Not*), launder illegally obtained children through the system or facilitate abusive practices by other actors and organizations by simply looking the other way.

139 *Ibid.*, para. 240.
140 *Ibid.*, para. 241.
141 Philippines, Czech Republic, and Lativa (*Ibid.*, para 242).

2.5 Criminogenic Asymmetries between Demand and Source Countries

The high demand for and the illegal supply of adoptable children, as well as the reduced ability of legal guardians to control the intercountry adoption system, are caused by demographic as well as economic asymmetries between the sending and the receiving countries. Passas argues that transnational crime is the product of 'criminogenic asymmetries', which he defines as "structural discrepancies, mismatches and inequalities in the realm of economy, law, politics, and culture".[142] Such asymmetries are produced in the course of interactions between unequal actors or systems with distinctive features.[143] They cause crime in three ways:

1. by fuelling the demand for illegal goods and services;
2. by generating incentives for people and organizations to engage in illegal practices; and
3. by reducing the ability of authorities to control crime.[144]

The dynamics of globalization, Passas claims, have further intensified the existing criminogenic asymmetries.[145] Globalization has brought into closer contact, interaction and interdependence countries with unequal power and diverse cultures, legal traditions, economic and political outlooks. This reinforces the inequalities of both power and wealth within nation states and among them respectively, and this intensifies the global hierarchies of privilege, wealth and control.[146] As criminogenic asymmetries are multiplied by these dynamics, rates of criminal activities naturally increase unless effective control systems are in place. Yet, Passas argues, official controls become weakened by processes leading to dysnomie, which is constituted by "(1) the absence of a widely accepted transnational normative framework to regulate cross-border activities, and (2) the existence of many different, inconsistent and often conflicting legal frameworks".[147]

With regard to the intercountry adoption market, economic and demographic asymmetries between the sending and the receiving countries have fuelled the demand and the illegal supply of adoptable children. Whereas the rich Western countries are struggling with low birth rates and decreasing numbers of children available for domestic adoption, birth rates are increasing in the poor countries located in the Global South. These asym-

142 N. Passas (1999). "Globalization, Criminogenic Asymmetries and Economic Crime." European Journal of Law Reform, 1, 4, 399-423, p. 402.

143 N. Passas (2000). "Global Anomie, Dysnomie, and Economic Crime: Hidden Consequences of Neoliberalism and Globalization in Russia and Around the World." Social Justice, 27, 2, 16-44, p. 18.

144 N. Passas (1999). "Globalization, Criminogenic Asymmetries and Economic Crime." European Journal of Law Reform, 1, 4, 399-423, p. 402.

145 *Ibid.*, p. 404.

146 *Ibid.*

147 *Ibid.*, p. 410.

metries have been intensified by the processes of globalization, which has further increased the wealth in industrialized Western countries, leading to reduced birth rates, while simultaneously aggravating poverty in other parts of the world, which in turn is linked with population growth.[148] The bifurcation between wealthy child-poor countries exerting the demand for adoptable healthy babies and poor child-rich countries that are the source of the highly valued children is evident in the statistics on intercountry adoption, which clearly refer to industrialized countries as receiving nations and developing countries as sending states.[149] An exception is the United States which is both the most significant recipient, as well as an important provider, of children (mostly of African descent) to same-sex couples in Europe, particularly to the United Kingdom as well as the Netherlands.[150]

The economic and demographic asymmetries between the sending and receiving states have fuelled the demand for adoptable children and have shaped the motivation of actors in the source countries to illegally obtain them. A large proportion of the population in attractive supply states live in poverty. In societies with very low per capita incomes, country fees and other costs that may seem reasonable from a Western perspective are sufficient to create an incentive to illicitly source children and then launder them through the adoption system.[151] As Smolin stresses,

> [m]oney is the primary motivation in most cases of child laundering in the intercountry adoption system. The transfer of Western wealth into sending nations is the primary vulnerability of the intercountry adoption system. Western funds provide an incentive to engage in child laundering which attracts unscrupulous persons into the system while tempting even charitable child welfare institutions into unscrupulous conduct.[152]

An example of the enormous sums of money that can be earned from an international adoption is Guatemala, a country that emerged as a significant supplier of children between 2003 and 2008 and which has become almost synonymous with illegal adoption practices. Although Guatemala is a developing country where about 38% of the population live below

148 See generally A. Harrison (2007). "Globalization and Poverty." University of Chicago Press.

149 P. Selman (2018). "Global Statistics for Intercountry Adoption: Receiving States and States of Origin 2004-2016." 03.05.2018, The Hague Conference on Private International Law.

150 D. Marre and L. Briggs (2009). "International Adoption: Global Inequalities and the Circulation of Children." New York University Press, p. 9.

151 See also G. Marquez (2000). "Transnational Adoption: The Creation and Ill Effects of an International Black Market Baby Trade." Journal of Juvenile Law, 21, 25-39, pp. 28-29.

152 D. M. Smolin (2006). "Child Laundering: How the Intercountry Adoption System Legitimizes and Incentivizes the Practices of Buying, Trafficking, Kidnapping, and Stealing Children." The Wayne Law Review, 52, 1, 113-200, p. 175.

$2 a day,[153] the fees for international adoptions paid to Guatemalan attorneys handling international adoptions ranged from anything between $18,000 and $19,000.[154] The attorneys would "use middlemen to seek out pregnant women who, because of poverty or prostitution, might be willing to give up their children or to sell them"[155] and who would "resort to threats or even baby-stealing" if the mother could not be persuaded.[156]

Even charitable organizations may be financially motivated to generate and supply 'adoptable' children. They may subvert the subsidiarity principlelaid down in the UNCRC and the Hague Convention, as more money can be made from international placements rather than from domestic childcare solutions. Or they may even place children whose families have not actually relinquished their parental rights. Orphanage directors may engage in these illegal practices out of the necessity to cover the institutions' expenses or in order to profit financially. Hoelgaard explains how the large sums of money involved in intercountry adoption has resulted in foreign adoption applicants being prioritized over domestic adoptive families in Colombia:

> Although payments for adoption are now legally banned, money still changes hands [...]. The casas, which are the chief suppliers of Colombian children going abroad [...], expect adopters and referring agencies abroad to make 'donaciones'. Since donations are used to maintain the superior, sometimes luxurious casa facilities and expand services and as these donations are likely to be most generous from well-to-do foreigners, the directors are naturally motivated to keep up the flow of children to their sponsors. [...] Apart from these more or less legitimate activities, some practitioners, including institute officers, allegedly profit personally from adoptions and elicit money from unsuspecting foreigners, sometimes under the pretext of recovering expenses incurred for the child. Thus financial feedback from overseas agencies coupled with individual gain has generated a self-perpetuating system of interests and reciprocities, which may be inflating the supply of children and directing them towards foreign homes.[157]

153 The World Bank (2013). "World Development Indicators." Available at http://databank.worldbank.org/data/download/wdi-2013-ebook.pdf, p. 28.

154 D. M. Smolin (2006). "Child Laundering: How the Intercountry Adoption System Legitimizes and Incentivizes the Practices of Buying, Trafficking, Kidnapping, and Stealing Children." The Wayne Law Review, 52, 113-200, p. 164.

155 UN Commission on Human Rights (2000). "Report of the Special Rapporteur on the Sale of Children, Child Prostitution and Child Pornography." 27.01.2000, E/CN.4/2000/73/Add.2, para. 36.

156 *Ibid.*, para. 38.

157 S. Hoelgaard (1998). "Cultural determinants of adoption policy: A Colombian case study." International Journal of Law, Policy and the Family 12, 2, 202-241, pp. 217-218.

The criminogenic asymmetries have also reduced the number of capable guardians in the adoption system. Basically, the Hague Convention sought to establish an effective control system with a view to reducing incidences of illegal adoption practices. Yet, as will be explained in Chapter IV, the treaty does not provide for an overseeing international body that would ensure that intercountry adoptions comply with its principles and standards. Rather, it leaves regulatory enforcement functions in the hands of national bodies. Yet, widespread corruption in the sending countries, which both were caused by and further increased existing asymmetries, have weakened official controls. Individuals and organizations from both the public and private sector that ought to monitor and control the adoption system consequently abuse their functions so as to connect demand and illegal supply by laundering children through their organization.

Profit is not the only reason why actors have become involved in illegally sourcing children and then laundering them through the adoption system. Also the idea that children are better off growing up in a wealthy Western state than staying with their impoverished families in their poor native countries, and the view that international adoption is in any case in the child's best interests may incite actors in the adoption system to engage in abusive adoption practices. In countries where children and their families live in extreme poverty and who cannot afford shelter and food, let alone education, trafficking the child for adoption purposes may be perceived as a necessary evil toward a greater good.

2.6 *Displacements Effects of Supply Reduction and 'Cycles of Abuse'*

China and Russia can be described as 'persistent supply countries'. Both countries emerged as sending states in the 90s and they have remained among the top suppliers of children ever since, even though the number of children sent abroad has significantly decreased over the past several years. This cannot be said about most other countries that would emerge as significant providers for a couple of years only and then shut down intercountry adoptions after serious incidents of abuse. The decreasing significance or entire drop-out of an important supply country would then result in a displacement effect, whereby the Western demand for adoptable children would shift to another vulnerable source that would quickly rise as an adoption hotspot until illegal practices emerge.

'Temporary supply countries' usually follow a common pattern: a 'cycle of abuse'[158] that consists of three phases.[159] In the first phase, only a relatively small number of intercountry adoptions take place that are considered as a humanitarian measure for only a

158 D. M. Smolin (2006). "Child Laundering: How the Intercountry Adoption System Legitimizes and Incentivizes the Practices of Buying, Trafficking, Kidnapping, and Stealing Children." The Wayne Law Review, 52, 113-200, pp. 132-135.

159 E. J. Graff (2014). "They Steal Babies, Don't They?" Pacific Standard, 24.11.2014, available at https://psmag.com/news/they-steal-babies-dont-they-international-adoption-schuster-institute-95027.

few needy children. The number of foreign adoption agencies working in this county is limited. The adoption system can effectively manage foreign adoptions, which are considered as a last resort measure for children that cannot be placed into domestic families. However, once word spreads among Western parents and agencies that children are coming quickly out of a particular channel, more and more people then sign up for adoptions. As has just been explained, the explosive growth is often caused by the entire dropout of a significant supplier. The number of foreign adoption agencies is increasing dramatically, as is the number of children sent abroad. The sending country would then reach the second phase: the 'gold rush',[160] where demand begins to outstrip supply, resulting in abuse and irregularities. The local authorities, overwhelmed by the Western run on children, are unable or unwilling to properly control each adoption case and to prevent manufactured orphans from entering the system. As more and more reports about abuses and irregularities emerge, the supply country reaches the third phase of recession, where the authorities decide to cut down on or entirely ban intercountry adoptions.[161]

In the past, 'cycles of abuse' and the resulting market shifts to other source countries have been observed often. For instance, a number of Latin American countries, which were important supply states for a couple of years, have tightened their adoption procedures after reports of illegal adoption practices that occurred in the 90s (most notably in Brazil,[162] Chile, Peru and El Salvador).[163] As a result, the number of adoptees sent from these countries has decreased significantly,[164] and many of those children were older or had special needs.[165] This has led many adopters to look for other source countries. The end of the Cold War opened Eastern European states up for the adoption market in the early 90s, whose child care institutions seemed to provide an unlimited supply of adoptees. After Ceausescu was overthrown, Romania rose to become a sending country of unusual significance for a few years, only to shut down intercountry adoptions after serious adoption abuses were disclosed.[166]

A market shift also took place after Guatemala, which quickly emerged as an important supply country between 2003 and 2008, banned foreign adoptions due to illegal practices,

160 *Ibid.*

161 *Ibid.*

162 C. Fonseca (2009). "Transnational Connections and Dissenting Views, The Evolution of Child Placement Policies in Brazil." In D. Marre and L. Briggs (eds), "International Adoption: Global Inequalities and the Circulation of Children." New York University Press, 154-173.

163 P. Selman (2009). "The rise and fall of intercountry adoption in the 21st century." International Social Work, 52, 5, 575-594, pp. 582-583.

164 P. Selman (2006). "Trends in intercountry adoption: Analysis of data from 20 receiving countries, 1998–2004." Journal of Population Research, 23, 2, 183-204, pp. 190-191.

165 D. M. Smolin (2006). "Child Laundering: How the Intercountry Adoption System Legitimizes and Incentivizes the Practices of Buying, Trafficking, Kidnapping, and Stealing Children." The Wayne Law Review, 52, 113-200, p. 133.

166 See Chapter IV, section 5.1.1.

and after China and Russia decided to limit the number of adoptees sent abroad. Particularly African states, most notably Ethiopia, which had not ratified the Hague Convention and was believed to putting fewer barriers between adopters and children, became an attractive supply country, where the cycle of abuse repeated itself.[167] Between 2003 and 2013, Ethiopia sent some 33,500 children abroad,[168] and only decided to limit and then suspend foreign adoptions after reports of serious abuses emerged.[169]

The restriction of supply in adoptable healthy babies has led not only to geographical, but also a functional, displacement. As more and more sending countries limit the number of (young and healthy) children sent abroad by enforcing tighter adoption laws and procedures (this often happens in the course of ratifying the Hague Convention), the international adoption market slowly dries out and a shift takes place from intercountry adoption to surrogacy.[170] Compared to intercountry adoption practices, surrogacy is less visible, less regulated and even more difficult to control. This therefore makes it a particularly attractive remedy to involuntary childlessness in Western countries.

3 The International Legal Framework on Child Trafficking

There are a number of international legal instruments which deal with the issue of trafficking in children. However, as will be shown in this section, most of them only cover 'conventional' forms of child trafficking, meaning trafficking for the purposes of sexual exploitation, slavery, forced labour or organ removal, but not the trafficking in children for the purposes of adoption.

The *2000 Protocol to Prevent, Suppress and Punish Trafficking in Persons, Especially Women and Children, supplementing the United Nations Convention Against Transnational Organized Crime*[171] (hereinafter, Trafficking Protocol), was the first global legally binding instrument with an agreed definition on trafficking in persons, especially in women and children. The intention behind this definition is to facilitate the harmonization of national legislation against trafficking in human beings and to establish the parameters of judicial

167 International Social Service (2008). "Diversification of countries of origin and an increase in the age of adopted children against a background of inter-country adoption that continues to be tense." Geneva, Nr. 7-8.

168 P. Selman (2015). "AFRICA: The 'new frontier' in international adoption." Paper Presented at 2015 SPA Conference, Belfast, available at http://www.adoptionhoksbergen.com/index.php/nl/2-algemeen/87-africa-the-new-frontier-in-international-adoption.

169 See Chapter V, section 7.1.

170 K. S. Rotabi and N. F. Bromfield (2012). "The Decline in Intercountry Adoptions and New Practices of Global Surrogacy: Global Exploitation and Human Rights Concerns." Affilia: Journal of Women and Social Work, 27, 2, 129-141.

171 UN General Assembly, Protocol to Prevent, Suppress and Punish Trafficking in Persons, Especially Women and Children, Supplementing the United Nations Convention against Transnational Organized Crime, 15 November 2000, A/RES/55/25.

cooperation and exchanges of information among countries.[172] In Article 3(a) of the Protocol 'trafficking in persons' is defined as

> the recruitment, transportation, transfer, harbouring or receipt of persons, by means of the threat or use of force or other forms of coercion, of abduction, of fraud, of deception, of the abuse of power or of a position of vulnerability or of the giving or receiving of payments or benefits to achieve the consent of a person having control over another person, for the purpose of exploitation. Exploitation shall include, at a minimum, the exploitation of the prostitution of others or other forms of sexual exploitation, forced labour or services, slavery or practices similar to slavery, servitude or the removal of organs.[173]

According to this definition, trafficking in persons has three constituent elements: (1) the recruitment, transfer and receipt of the person, (2) by the use of fraudulent means, including threats or the use of force, coercion, abduction, fraud, deception, abuse of power or vulnerability, giving payments or benefits to a person in control of the victim, (3) for an exploitative purpose. In cases where children under the age of 18 are recruited, transferred and received for the purpose of exploitation, no fraudulent means need to be involved in order for the practice to be regarded as trafficking in persons.[174] Whereas the first two elements of the definition can be viewed as the *actus reus*, the last element provides the basis for identifying the *mens rea* of the offence.[175]

The Trafficking Protocol does not provide a definition of the term 'exploitation', but lists specific forms of it in Article 3(a) thereof, namely: prostitution, sexual exploitation, forced labour, slavery and the removal of organs. Adoption is not included in the list of exploitative forms, however, the phrasing "at a minimum" basically indicates that the list is to be understood as non-exhaustive, allowing the addition of unnamed or new forms of exploitation.[176] The drafters of the Trafficking Protocol considered suggestions for including 'forced adoption', 'illegal adoption' and the 'purchase or sale of children' within the list of exploitative purposes, but these did not make it into the final text.[177] The *travaux préparatoires* to the Trafficking Protocol attempts to clarify when illegal adoption is to be

---

172 J. G. Raymond (2002). "The New UN Trafficking Protocol." Women's Studies International Forum 25, 5, 491.

173 Art 3(a) Trafficking Protocol.

174 Art 3(c) *leg. cit.*

175 UNODC (2015). "Issue Paper, The Concept of "Exploitation" in the Trafficking in Person Protocol." Available at http://www.unodc.org/documents/human-trafficking/2015/UNODC_IP_Exploitation_2015.pdf, pp. 23-24.

176 A. T. Gallagher (2010). "The International Law of Human Trafficking." Cambridge University Press, p. 40.

177 UNODC (2015). "Issue Paper, The Concept of "Exploitation" in the Trafficking in Person Protocol." Available at http://www.unodc.org/documents/human-trafficking/2015/UNODC_IP_Exploitation_2015.pdf, p. 38.

considered a form of exploitation. They state that: "[w]here illegal adoption amounts to a practice similar to slavery as defined in article 1, paragraph (d), of the Supplementary Convention on the Abolition of Slavery, the Slave Trade, and Institutions and Practices Similar to Slavery it will also fall within the scope of the protocol".[178]

According to Article 1(d) of the Supplementary Convention on the Abolition of Slavery, the Slave Trade, and Institutions and Practices Similar to Slavery (1956) (hereinafter Supplementary Slavery Convention),[179] the term "institutions or practices similar to slavery" include *inter alia* "[a]ny institution or practice whereby a child or young person under the age of 18 years, is delivered by either or both of his natural parents or by his guardian to another person, whether for reward or not, with a view to the exploitation of the child or young person or of his labour". Hence, just as with the Trafficking Protocol, the Supplementary Slavery Convention requires an exploitation of the child, but it neither defines the term 'exploitation' nor does it clarify whether the parents, an intermediary or the legal guardian must intend to exploit the child.[180] The Trafficking Protocol's reference to the Supplementary Slavery Convention, as Smolin claims, creates "a problem of circular definitions": the Trafficking Protocol defines illegal adoption as a form of exploitation when it amounts to a practice that is similar to slavery, whereas the Supplementary Convention defines practices similar to slavery as the transfer of a child for the purposes of exploitation.[181]

Some scholars claim that intercountry adoption does not *per se* amount to exploitation which would occur primarily on an affective level.[182] As will be explained in Chapter VII, in Western societies children fulfill a number of crucial functions for their parents. In an increasingly individualized society, children serve to compensate for the decreasing chances of finding a loving relationship that lasts, as well as to avoid loneliness in old age. Furthermore, they help their parents to build social and cultural capital. Notwithstanding the numerous role options that are afforded to women and men in individualized Western societies, there is still an intense cultural pressure to have children.[183] Achieving parenthood,

178 UNODC (2006). "Travaux Préparatoires of the negotiations for the elaboration of the United Nations Convention against Transnational Organized Crime and the Protocols thereto." New York, p. 347.

179 UN Economic and Social Council (ECOSOC), Supplementary Convention on the Abolition of Slavery, the Slave Trade, and Institutions and Practices Similar to Slavery, 7 September 1956, Res. 608(XXI).

180 A. T. Gallagher (2010). "The International Law of Human Trafficking." Cambridge University Press, p. 40.

181 D. M. Smolin (2004). "Intercountry adoption as child trafficking." Valparasio University Law Review, 39, 2, 281-325, p. 296.

182 D. L. Eng (2006). "Political Economics of Passion: Transnational Adoption and Global Woman: Roundtable on Global Woman." Studies in Gender and Sexuality, 7, 1, 49–59; R. Lilith (2000). "Buying a Wife but Saving a Child: A Deconstruction of Popular Rhetoric and Legal Analysis of Mail-Order Brides and Intercountry Adoptions." Buffalo Women's Law Journal, 9, 225-262.

183 K. P. Nelson (2006). "Shopping for children in the international marketplace." In J. J. Trenka et al. (eds), "Outsiders Within: Writing on transracial adoption." South End Press, Cambridge, 89-104, p. 89.

Anagnost argues, is necessary in order to become a "fully realized citizen".[184] For some involuntarily childless couples and individuals, intercountry adoption is a viable (and also often last) resort in order to have their own child. The international adoptee, Eng suggests, thus functions as an unconsenting emotional labourer for his or her adoptive parents' access to full recognition in their community.[185] This labour, he claims, would remain invisible as "discourses on globalization have largely been examined under the lens of political rather than affective economies. Emotions, affects, and passions, though clearly commodified in the New Economy, are difficult to quantify".[186] Hübinette even goes as far as to assimilate international adoptees with slaves, which were "brought over only to satisfy the needs and desires of other well-to-do-acquirers".[187]

Nonetheless, there is much to suggest that adoption cannot be added to the Trafficking Protocol's open-ended list of exploitation forms that is found in Article 3(a) thereof. Even if the children have been purchased, kidnapped or abducted from their parents, the ultimate objective is to place them into families who wish to care for them. Unlike forced prostitution, sexual exploitation, forced labour and organ removal, intercountry adoption is perfectly legal and it is commonly considered as absolutely contrary to the concept of exploitation and slavery. Illegally obtaining a child and then transferring him or her to the receiving country for the purpose of adoption is, therefore, most probably not considered to be a form of human trafficking according to the Trafficking Protocol.[188]

On the European level, both the *2005 Council of Europe Convention on Action against Trafficking in Human Being*[189] (hereinafter CoE Trafficking Convention) and *Directive 2011/36/EU on preventing and combating trafficking in human beings and protecting its victims*[190] (hereinafter EU Trafficking Directive) provide a definition of human trafficking that is identical to the one set out in the Trafficking Protocol.[191] The Explanatory Report of the CoE Trafficking Convention clarifies that illegal adoptions only fall within the

184 A. Anagnost (2000). "Scenes of Misrecognition: Maternal Citizenship in the Age of Transnational Adoption." Positions: east asia cultures critique, 8, 2, 389-421, p. 392.

185 D. L. Eng (2006). "Political Economics of Passion: Transnational Adoption and Global Woman: Roundtable on Global Woman." Studies in Gender and Sexuality, 7, 1, 49–59, p. 57.

186 *Ibid.*, p. 53.

187 T. Hübinette (2006). "From Orphan Trains to Babylifts: Colonial Trafficking, Empire Building, and Social Engineering." In J. J. Trenka et al. (eds), "Outsiders Within: Writing on Transracial Adoption." South End Press, Cambridge, 139-149, p. 143.

188 See also D. M. Smolin (2004). "Intercountry adoption as child trafficking." Valparasio University Law Review, 39, 2, 281-325, p. 296.

189 Council of Europe, Council of Europe Convention on Action Against Trafficking in Human Beings, 16 May 2005, CETS 197.

190 Council of the European Union, Directive 2011/36/EU of the European Parliament and of the Council of 5 April 2011 on preventing and combating trafficking in human beings and protecting its victims, and replacing Council Framework Decision 2002/629/JHA, 15 April 2011, OJ L. 101/1-101/11; 15.4.2011, 2011/36/EU.

191 EU Trafficking Directive, Art 2; CoE Trafficking Convention, Art 4.

Convention's scope if they amount to "practices similar to slavery".[192] Like the *travaux préparatoires* to the Trafficking Protocol, the Explanatory Report refers to Article 1(d) of the Supplementary Slavery Convention, suggesting that adoption is not *per se* an exploitative purpose. The CoE Trafficking Convention does therefore not acknowledge kidnapping or purchasing and selling a child as a form of trafficking in cases where the purpose is to place the child up for adoption. The same is true for the EU Trafficking Directive. In the preamble thereof, the directive specifically mentions the issue of illegal adoption and clarifies when it amounts to trafficking: "The definition also covers trafficking in human beings for the purpose of [...] other behaviour such as illegal adoption [...] in so far as they fulfil the constitutive elements of trafficking in human beings".

The *1989 United Nations Convention on the Rights of the Child*[193] (hereinafter UNCRC) is the first binding international legal instrument to address the issue of child trafficking for the purposes of adoption. Article 35 thereof calls for its States Parties to "take all appropriate national, bilateral and multilateral measures to prevent the abduction of, the sale of or traffic in children for any purpose or in any form". The Article does not elaborate on what is to be understood by the term "sale of or traffic in children". However, the wording "for any purpose or in any form" indicates that the term is to be broadly interpreted, thereby allowing for the inclusion of child trafficking for the purpose of adoption.[194] The Committee on the Rights of the Child has regularly raised child trafficking issues in its concluding observations on the States Parties' reports. As Gallagher observes: "While the emphasis has been firmly on trafficking for sexual exploitation, the Committee has also (and increasingly) recognized the phenomenon of trafficking for economic exploitation, including [...] trafficking for adoption".[195]

The *2000 Optional Protocol to the United Nations Convention on the Rights of the Child on the Sale of Children, Child Prostitution and Child Pornography*[196] (hereinafter Optional Protocol to the UNCRC) adopts a criminal justice approach to the sale of and traffic in children.[197] The protocol obliges its States Parties to criminalize and appropriately punish

192 Explanatory Report to the Council of Europe Convention on Action against Trafficking in Human Beings (2005), para. 94.

193 UN General Assembly, Convention on the Rights of the Child, 20 November 1989, Res. 44/25.

194 V. Tadler (2010). "Child Trafficking for the Purpose of Inter-country Adoption, With a Case Study on Guatemala." PhD Thesis, University of Vienna, p. 54.

195 A. T. Gallagher (2010). "The international law of human trafficking." Cambridge University Press, p. 66. See, e.g., UN Committee on the Rights of the Child (2009). "Report on the 50th session: Concluding observations on the Democratic Republic of Congo." 10.02.2009, CRC/C/COD/CO/2, para. 82-83; UN Committee on the Rights of the Child (2009). "Report on the 50th session: Concluding observations on the Republic of Moldova." 20.02.2009, CRC/C/MDA/CO/3, para. 68; UN Committee on the Rights of the Child (2007). "Report on the 44th session: Concluding Observations on Malaysia." 25.06.2007, CRC/C/MYS/CO/1, para. 95.

196 UN General Assembly, Optional Protocol to the Convention on the Rights of the Child on the Sale of Children, Child Prostitution and Child Pornography, 16 March 2001, A/RES/54/263.

197 A. T. Gallagher (2010). "The international law of human trafficking." Cambridge University Press, p. 67.

the offences that it lists,[198] as well as to establish jurisdiction over them.[199] Its preamble expresses concern at "the significant and increasing international traffic in children for the purpose of the sale of children, child prostitution and child pornography". Yet, apart from its preamble, the Optional Protocol to the UNCRC does not expressly mention or define the term "trafficking". Article 2(a) thereof only provides a definition for the term "sale of children" as being "any act or transaction whereby a child is transferred by any person or group of persons to another for remuneration or any other consideration". In Article 3(1)(a) thereof, the Protocol requires ratifying States to prohibit an exhaustive list of acts and activities made in the context of the sale of children. With regard to adoption, Article 3(1)(a)(ii) of the Protocol obliges its States Parties to criminalize and appropriately punish "improperly inducing consent, as an intermediary, for the adoption of a child".

Article 3(1)(a)(ii) of the Optional Protocol to the UNCRC acknowledges an alarming form of an illegal adoption practice, but it does not address all forms of illegal activities listed above. It requires the criminalization of only certain actors (intermediaries between adoptive parents and birth parents) and of a limited scope of illegal adoption practices (inducing consent by offering financial or material rewards, exerting psychological pressure or by providing false information about the consequences of an adoption). However, it does not cover situations where adoptive parents induce the birth parents' relinquishment of the child themselves, without the intervention of an intermediary, or purchase a child from an orphanage. Nor does it cover the abduction or kidnapping of children from their birth families, hospitals or child care institutions.[200] At the time of writing, 173 states have ratified the Protocol, including all receiving countries and almost all significant sending countries, with the exception of Liberia, Nigeria, Ghana and Kenya.[201]

The 1993 Hague Convention on Protection and Co-operation in Respect of Intercountry Adoption[202] (hereinafter The Hague Convention) was established in order to tackle illegal practices in the adoption system. The treaty seems to adopt the broad definition of child trafficking as enshrined in Article 35 of the UNCRC. According to Article 1(b) thereof, the primary object of the Hague Convention is to prevent "the abduction, the sale of, or traffic in children", directly referring to the wrongs listed in the UNCRC. The broad interpretation of the term "trafficking" is also reflected in the Convention's Guide to Good Practice No. 1:

198 Optional Protocol to the CRC, Preamble, Art 1, 3.

199 Art 4. *leg. cit.*

200 D. M. Smolin (2004). "Intercountry adoption as child trafficking." Valparasio University Law Review, 39, 2, 281-325, p. 300.

201 See http://indicators.ohchr.org/ (last accessed on 03.08.2018).

202 The Hague Conference on Private International Law, The Hague Convention on the Protection of Children and Co-operation in Respect of Intercountry Adoption, 29 May 1993, 32 I.L.M. 1134.

> 'the demand for children by industrialised nations and the availability of many homeless children in developing nations, has in addition to regular and legal intercountry adoptions, led to practices of international child trafficking either for purposes of adoption abroad, or under the cloak of adoption, for other – usually illegal – purposes.' The traffic in children in this context may lead to an illegal adoption. The abduction or sale of a child for adoption could occur as a single event. The abduction or sale of children which amounts to trafficking in children for adoption is likely to be done as a systematic organised operation. The term trafficking refers to the payment of money or other compensation to facilitate the illegal movement of children for the purposes of illegal adoption or other forms of exploitation.[203]

From the phrase "for the purpose of illegal adoption or other forms of exploitation", it can be inferred that the Hague Convention acknowledges illegal adoption *per se* as a form of exploitation. This is substantiated by the Report on Intercountry Adoption in which Van Loon claims that "[international child trafficking] may serve the purpose of adoption abroad, but may also be carried out for purposes of prostitution, pornography, cheap labour and other forms of exploitation abroad".[204] Purchasing or abducting a child from his or her birth family or from another person or institution whose consent is required for an adoption (e.g. orphanage, child care institution) is thus acknowledged as child trafficking by the Hague Convention.

The UNCRC and the Hague Convention both acknowledge that illegally obtaining a child and transferring him or her to a receiving country for the purpose of adoption is a form of child trafficking. Yet, none of these international legal instruments oblige their Contracting States to criminalize and appropriately punish these acts. The Optional Protocol to the UNCRC has basically addresses this gap. However, it does not cover all illegal adoption practices listed above, nor does it cover the practice of adoptive parents inducing the birth parents to give up their child or actually purchasing a child from an orphanage. It also fails to address the abduction or kidnapping of children.

Most importantly, the Trafficking Protocol, the CoE Trafficking Convention and the EU Trafficking Directive do not consider kidnapping or purchasing and selling a child as a form of trafficking in cases where the purpose is to place the child for adoption, since they do not consider adoption *per se* as a form of exploitation. Arguably, the concept of exploitation that is included in the international legal instruments is strongly influenced

203 The Permanent Bureau of the Hague Conference on Private International Law (2008). "The Implementation and Operation of the 1993 Hague Intercountry Adoption Convention: Guide to Good Practice No. 1." The Hague, para. 74.

204 J. H. A. Van Loon (1990). "Report on Intercountry Adoption." The Hague Conference on Private International Law, April 1990, Prel. Doc. No. 1, p. 51.

by cultural values and beliefs. The following section illustrates the Western conception of intercountry adoption, the sending countries and the children' parents and it seeks to explain why kidnapping, selling and trafficking children for the purposes of adoption is not considered exploitative and why it is thus not recognized as a form of human trafficking.

4 The Prism of Child Trafficking for Adoption Purposes

4.1 *The Crime Prism*

Criminologists strongly disagree over the concept of crime.[205] Some define crime as acts or omissions that are violate the criminal law.[206] Others, however, criticize this strict legal definition of crime for being too value-laden, arguing that the criminal law is shaped by the interests of powerful groups with the ability to influence legislation which does not cover all socially injurious actions.[207] Critical criminologists therefore suggest that the conception of crime should not rely on the criminal law, but rather it should focus on the harm an act causes. Hence, the definition of crime should be expanded so as to include offenses of powerful groups against the powerless that are socially injurious,[208] as well as to behaviour that violates basic human rights.[209] In an attempt to bring all of these differing definitions of crime together, Henry and Lanier conceptualize crime as a prism, taking into account the multiple dimensions of crime:

> We use the term prism not only because of its visual appearance, but also because, just as a prism is used to analyze a continuous spectrum, so in our case it is used to analyze the spectrum of dimensions that constitute 'crime'. Furthermore, light is refracted in a prism to reveal various colors; likewise, through our crime prism, people may view the same criminal act in different

205 S. Henry and M. Lanier (2001). "What is Crime? Controversies over the Nature of Crime and What to Do about It." Rowman & Littlefield Publishers, Lanham.

206 Most notably, P. Tappan, W. (1947). "Who is the Criminal?" American Sociological Review, 12, 1, 96-102.

207 E. H. Sutherland (1940). "White-Collar Criminality." American Sociological Review, 5, 1, 1-12; G. Barak (1998). "Integrating criminologies." Allyn and Bacon, Boston.

208 R. J. Michalowski (1985). "Order, Law, and Crime: An Introduction to Criminology." Random House, New York; H. Bianchi (1956). "Position and Subject-Matter of Criminology: Inquiry Concerning Theoretical Criminology." North Holland Pub., Amsterdam; S. Cohen (1993). "Human Rights and Crimes of the State: The Culture of Denial." Australian and New Zealand Journal of Criminology, 26, 2, 97-115.

209 H. Schwendinger and J. Schwendinger (1970). "Defenders of Order or Guardians of Human Rights?" Issues in Criminology, 5, 2, 123-157.

contextual terms depending on their prior experiences, socialization, and worldview.[210]

The first dimension of crime is the *individual or social harm* that an act inflicts. It refers to direct individual harm that is suffered by the victims, but also less direct social harm and injuries by offences of powerful groups against the powerless.[211]

The second dimension of crime is the *degree of social agreement about the wrongfulness of an act* that can vary from great agreement, through moderate agreement, apathy or disinterest, to high disagreement or extreme conflict.[212]

The third dimension is the *probability of severe social response* that refers to the likelihood that a convicted offender will actually receive a severe response that is provided in the law. This dimension may range from "high probability of severe sanctions for convicted offenders (e.g., death penalty or life imprisonment), through moderate sanctions (e.g., short-term sentences, fines, or probation), to a high probability of mild sanctions (e.g., community service, counselling, or public condemnation)".[213]

Another dimension of crime, according to Henry and Lanier, is the *extensiveness of victimisation*.[214] The number of victims of a criminal act influences the public's perception of its seriousness. Thus, a crime that only harms one person is somehow qualitatively different from acts of violence that harm many people. Yet, the perception of a crime's seriousness is not only shaped by the absolute number of victims, but also by the victims' social and political status.[215]

The last dimension is the *visibility of crime*, which is linked to the public's awareness that a particular behaviour is harmful and thus needs to be criminalized.[216] Some crimes may be extremely harmful, yet victims might never, or only after a long time has passed, realize that they have actually been harmed (e.g. government or corporate crime). Crime

210 S. Henry and M. Lanier (2001). "The Prism of Crime: Toward an Integrated Definition of Crime." In S. Henry and M. Lanier (eds), "What is Crime? Controversies over the Nature of Crime and What to Do about It." Rowman & Littlefield Publishers, Lanham, 227-243, p. 229.

211 H. Schwendinger and J. Schwendinger (1970). "Defenders of Order or Guardians of Human Rights?" Issues in Criminology, 5, 2, 123-157; S. Cohen (1993). "Human Rights and Crimes of the State: The Culture of Denial." Australian and New Zealand Journal of Criminology, 26, 2, 97-115; R. J. Michalowski (1985). "Order, Law, and Crime: An Introduction to Criminology." Random House, New York; A. von Hirsch and N. Jareborg (1991). "Gauging Criminal Harm: A Living-Standard Analysis." Oxford Journal of Legal Studies, 11, 1, 1-38.

212 S. Henry and M. Lanier (2001). "The Prism of Crime: Toward an Integrated Definition of Crime." In S. Henry and M. Lanier (eds), "What is Crime? Controversies over the Nature of Crime and What to Do about It." Rowman & Littlefield Publishers, Lanham, 227-243.

213 *Ibid*, p. 231.

214 S. Henry and M. M. Lanier (1998). "The Prism of Crime: Arguments for an Integrated Definition of Crime." Justice Quarterly, 15, 4, 609-627, 620.

215 *Ibid*.

216 *Ibid*, p. 619.

may, therefore "range from 'being obvious' or 'readily apparent' to 'relatively hidden' and, finally, so 'obscure' that it is accepted by many as normal, even though it harms its victims (e.g. environmental crimes, racism, and patriarchy)".[217]

Henry and Lanier designed the 'prism of crime' in order to visualise the continuous spectrum of the five dimensions of crime. The upper half of the prism represents the highly visible crime, typically committed in public by the powerless and including acts that are widely agreed as wrongful and that are likely to receive a severe societal response. Its lower half represents the less visible crimes. These include a variety of crimes by the powerful and are often met with apathy and disinterest or disagreement about their wrongfulness and they are therefore likely to be moderately or mildly sanctioned.[218]

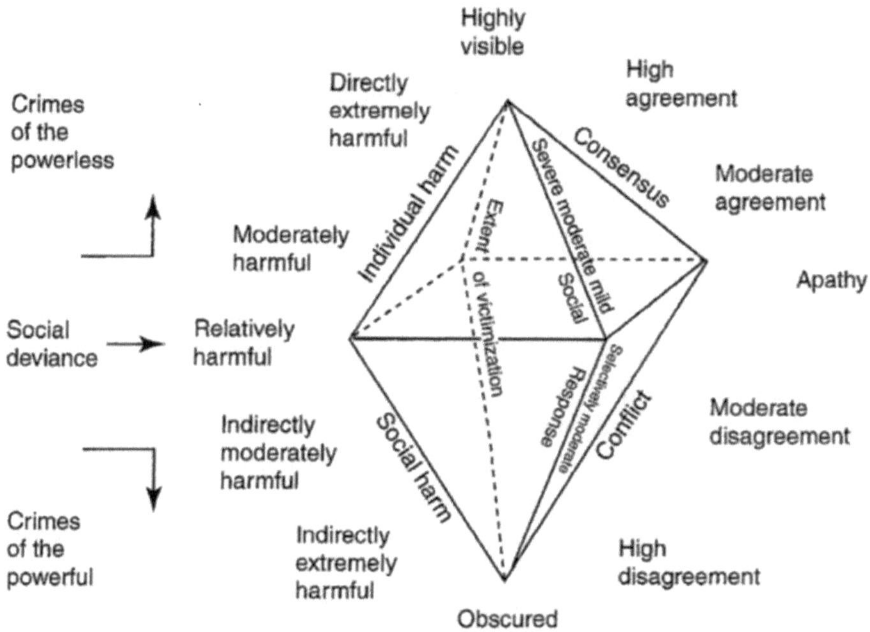

Source: Lanier and Henry (1998:28).

4.2 *The Prismatic Analysis of Child Trafficking for Adoption Purposes*

Like Henry and Lanier's concept of crime, the phenomenon of child trafficking for adoption purposes can be conceptualized as a prism that is composed of multiple dimensions.

217 S. Henry and M. Lanier (2001). "The Prism of Crime: Toward an Integrated Definition of Crime." In S. Henry and M. Lanier (eds), "What is Crime? Controversies over the Nature of Crime and What to Do about It." Rowman & Littlefield Publishers, Lanham, 227-243, p. 228.

218 *Ibid*, p. 229.

Shedding light on these dimensions will help the author to highlight and better comprehend this social phenomenon. It will also aid in understanding as to why it is not generally considered a form of human trafficking in the strict legal sense.

4.2.1 Individual and social harm

Trafficking children for the purpose of adoption appears to be a victimless crime. The children, who do often not realize that they have been obtained illegally, are placed in loving families in wealthy countries where they have access to food, clean water, advanced medical care and educational opportunities that they would likely not receive in their native countries. The children's birth parents are either totally left out of the picture or, as will be explained below, are perceived as unable to properly care for their offspring. In those cases, where the trafficked children were really orphans who were placed for intercountry adoption in violation of the subsidiarity principle, the harm might even more difficult to acknowledge. However, stripped off all humanitarian and charitable justification, child trafficking causes deep individual harm to both the children and their birth parents whose human rights are seriously violated.

Basically, every legitimate intercountry adoption involves an interference with the adoptee's rights. The child that is being transferred to another country for the purpose of adoption is permanently removed from the culture and community of his or her native country and severed from his or her ethnic, religious, cultural and linguistic background. Being placed with an adoptive family of a different race, with a different culture and in a different country, the child has his or her right to identity preservation, as laid down in Article 8 of the UNCRC, impeded.[219] Arguably, the interference with the child's right to identity preservation can be justified by the purpose of placing him or her into a permanent family environment, after no suitable child care solutions were found in the child's country of origin (subsidiarity principle)[220] and where intercountry adoption was considered to be in the best interests of the child.[221]

The practice of child trafficking for adoption purposes, however, results in an interference with the child's fundamental rights that cannot be justified. Contrary to a legitimate intercountry adoption, in which the child's interests were the paramount consideration, an illegal adoption does not primarily serve the interests of the child. In cases of child trafficking, the institution of intercountry adoption is abused by the powerful stakeholders within the system – adopters, adoption agencies, orphanage directors, lawyers, government officials etc. – in order to serve their own interests. The intercountry adoption's primary purpose is not to place an unparented child in a permanent family environment. Rather,

219 See Chapter III, section 4.7.
220 See Chapter III, section 5.2.
221 See Chapter III, section 6.3.

intercountry adoption is misused as a remedy by involuntarily childless couples in Western societies who wish to have their own child as well as a source of capital by those involved in the system. The child is not seen as a unique human being with needs, interests and basic human rights. Rather, the child is denied humanity and reduced to a marketable commodity. His or her characteristics as healthy and young are exploited by adoptive parents who want to have 'their own child', regardless of the price,[222] as well as by the individuals and organizations involved in the adoption system who wish to gain financially from intercountry adoption.[223] The child is not placed for international adoption because he or she was in need of a family and – after the individual circumstances of the case as well as the available domestic child care options have been examined carefully – intercountry adoption was considered to be in the child's best interests. The child is adopted internationally primarily because monies or goods were provided or expected by the stakeholders involved in the international adoption system.

Child trafficking for adoption purposes does not only violate the child's right to identity preservation but – in those cases where he or she is removed from his or her parents through purchase, abduction or deception – also the right to be cared for by his or her parents as laid down in Article 7 UNCRC.[224] Furthermore, the child is violated in his or her right to privacy and family life as enshrined in Article 16 UNCRC (as well as Article 17 ICCPR, Article 12 UDHR and Article 8 ECHR) which provides the child the right to be protected by law against arbitrary or unlawful interference with, *inter alia*, his or her family.[225] In addition, the child's right to know his or her origin and identity is violated, which is laid down in Article 8 of the UNCRC and derived from Articles 17 and 24 of the ICCPR and Article 8 ECHR, as well as his or her right not to be subjected to forced disappearance as laid down in Article 1 of the (ICPPED).[226]

Removing a child from his or her intact family through purchase, abduction or deception of the parents does not only deeply harm the child, but it also harms his or her birth family by violating their parental rights. According to Article 5 UNCRC, the State is obliged "to respect the responsibilities, rights and duties of parents or, where applicable, the members of the extended family or community as provided for by local custom [...]". Furthermore, Article 18(1) and Article 27(2) lay down the primary responsibilities of the parents for their child's upbringing and development.[227] These provisions aim to protect

222 See Chapter VII, section 4.1.
223 K. Herrmann (2010). "Reestablishing the humanitarian approach to adoption: The legal and social change necessary to end the commodification of children." Family Law Quarterly, 44, 3, 409-428, p. 421; D. M. Smolin (2007). "Child laundering as exploitation: applying anti-trafficking norms to intercountry adoption under the coming Hague regime." Vermont Law Review, 32, 1-55, p. 33.
224 See Chapter III, section 4.2.
225 See Chapter III, section 4.5.
226 See Chapter III, section 4.7.
227 See Chapter III, section 4.3.

parents against excessive intervention by the state as well as social structures in which the role of parents may be diminished.

In many sending countries, families are discriminated and marginalized on the basis of their status, including poverty, race, religion, sex, mental and physical disabilities, HIV/AIDS or other serious illnesses, birth out of wedlock and other socio-economic stigmas. Impoverished birth parents, ethnic minorities and unmarried mothers are often considered as inferior and unworthy of keeping their children that are deemed, by way of contrast, highly valuable. In cases of child trafficking, their status as the child's family, their responsibilities and capacities for the upbringing and development of their child are systematically denied. By illegally taking their children, marginalized birth parents are misused as a 'breeding unit' whose fertility, but also extreme powerlessness, is being exploited.[228] In an intercountry adoption system that is shaped and influenced by the powerful, discriminated and often uneducated birth parents neither have a voice nor the capacity to effectively defend themselves against the illegal removal of their children.

The illegal adoption activities do not only cause individual harm to the children and their birth families. Providing monies or goods to the director of a childcare institution or to a government official also causes indirect social harm by disrupting the child protection and welfare system in the sending country.[229] Generally speaking, the proper implementation of the subsidiarity principle that is laid down in the UNCRC, as well as in the Hague Convention, costs the state of origin a lot of effort and money. They are required to establish a child welfare system that assists families in keeping their children during times of crisis or in regaining custody of children from whom they were previously separated, or to reunite children with members of the extended family. In cases where such assistance is not possible or unsuccessful, efforts should be made to place the child within a domestic adoptive family before even considering an intercountry adoption.[230] However, the extraordinary large sums of money that are paid by foreign adoptive parents or adoption agencies make international adoption more lucrative than domestic adoptions, which usually yield much less money,[231] and which are obviously more attractive than family preservation or reunification and foster care programmes, which would require sufficient

---

228 P. J. Meier (2008). "Small commodities: How child traffickers exploit children and families in intercountry adoption and what the United States must do to stop them." The Journal of Gender, Race & Justice, 12, 185-224, p. 217; D. M. Smolin (2007). "Child laundering as exploitation: applying anti-trafficking norms to intercountry adoption under the coming Hague regime." Vermont Law Review, 32, 1-55, p. 14.

229 D. M. Smolin (2004). "The Two Faces of Intercountry Adoption: The Significance of the Indian Adoption Scandals." Seton Hall Law Review, 35, 403-493, pp. 447-448; R. Post (2007). "Romania–for Export Only: The Untold Story of the Romanian 'Orphans'." Netherlands: EuroComment Diffusion; S. Hoelgaard (1998). "Cultural determinants of adoption policy: A Colombian case study." International Journal of Law, Policy and the Family 12, 2, 202-241.

230 See Chapter III, section 5.2. and Chapter IV, section 4.2.

231 D. M. Smolin (2010). "Child Laundering and the Hague Convention on Intercountry Adoption: The Future and Past of Intercountry Adoption." University of Louisville Law Review, 48, 441-498, p. 489.

financial means. Directors of childcare institutions and government officials in the sending countries thus often prefer to place the children for adoption internationally, rather than to invest in the local child welfare system. The generous payments made in connection with the intercountry adoption of an orphaned child, therefore, undermine the subsidiarity principle that is laid down in the UNCRC and the Hague Convention which prioritizes reintegrating the child into her (extended) family or finding a domestic childcare solution.[232]

4.2.2 Invisibility

As has been shown, the illegal practices that are employed to generate adoptable children engender profound individual and social harm. Yet, the harm often remains invisible to the victims, the wider public, or both, for a variety of reasons.

First, the link between the causes (payments, contributions) and the effects (consent to adoption, circumvention of the subsidiarity principle) are in many cases obscure. Monies or goods are usually not granted as explicit considerations for the child. Rather, financial or material means are changing hands that might seem legitimate, even honorable, at first glance, but actually cause deep harm. Adopers may provide money or gifts to the birth parents in order to enable them to properly care for the rest of the family.[233] In developing countries, many families live in extreme poverty, facing severe struggles to obtain food, water, clothing, housing, medical care and education. Adopting a child without providing some assistance to the rest of the family to improve their living conditions would understandably seem ruthless and cruel to many adopters.[234]

Moreover, it is not uncommon that adopters or adoption agencies donate money or goods to the orphanage that provided the child for adoption. Childcare institutions in developing countries often lack the sufficient resources to provide their children with the very barest necessities. Adopters may feel urged to help the orphanage cover its expenses and to improve the living conditions for the children 'left behind' that will never be adopted. Also, adoption agencies often make generous donations to the orphanages which they co-operate with, or they cover the costs of raising the children that they place.

When does such well-intentioned assistance to birth families or donations to childcare institutions transcend into the illicit sale of children? In the majority of cases, assistance to birth parents is arguably not given due to pure compassion or kindness, but it is implicitly conditioned on the relinquishment of the child.[235] If assistance would be given for the mere sake of compassion or kindness, many families would not need to relinquish

232 Preamble of the Hague Convention on Intercountry Adoption; Article 21(b) UNCRC.
233 D. M. Smolin (2004). "Intercountry adoption as child trafficking." Valparasio University Law Review, 39, 2, 281-325, p. 312.
234 *Ibid.*, p. 311.
235 *Ibid.*

their children, thereby making intercountry adoptions unnecessary in most cases.[236] For extremely poor families, small financial or material support that is conditioned on the relinquishment of their children will have the effect of actually inducing relinquishment.[237] Even assistance provided after consent was given could be seen as the fulfilment of an expectation that in itself induced the relinquishment in the first place.[238] The difference between a donation and an actual payment for a child then becomes only a theoretical one.

The same basically applies to monies and goods that are donated to childcare institutions. In developing countries, many orphanages heavily rely on donations from receiving states. Donations commonly serve the purpose of assisting the orphanage to improve the living conditions of the children, particularly those that are ineligible for adoption or that cannot be placed as they are older and/or sick. However, monies or goods which are donated not independently, but which are linked to intercountry adoption (as they are provided by adoptive parents adopting from or adoption agencies cooperating with the child care institution), create an incentive for childcare institutions to secure a steady supply of children for intercountry adoption.[239] They may be incited to subvert the subsidiarity principle by placing orphans for adoption internationally without having exhausted the domestic childcare solutions or children whose families have not relinquished their parental rights, in order to cover its necessary expenses or even profit.[240] In practice, it is virtually impossible to establish whether donations actually cause such harmful activities.

A second reason why the harm caused by the illegal adoption practices remains hidden is the fact that many victims either do not realize their victimization or they do not have

236 Some experts criticize intercountry adoption for that reason, arguing that huge amounts of money are paid for the international adoption process under the pretext of saving children, whereas a small amount of financial support would already suffice to keep the child with his or her family [see, for example, D. M. Smolin (2007). "Intercountry Adoption and Poverty: A Human Rights Analysis." Capital University Law Review, 36, 413-453].

237 D. M. Smolin (2004). "Intercountry adoption as child trafficking." Valparasio University Law Review, 39, 2, 281-325, p. 312.

238 D. M. Smolin (2007). "Intercountry Adoption and Poverty: A Human Rights Analysis." Capital University Law Review, 36, 413-453, p. 434.

239 Hague Conference on Private International Law. Accreditation and Adoption Accredited Bodies: General Principles and Guide to Good Practice, Guide No 2 under the Hague Convention of 29 May 1993 on Protection of Children and Co-operation in Respect of Intercountry Adoption, para. 418.

240 See also R. Post (2007). "Romania–for Export Only: The Untold Story of the Romanian 'Orphans'." Netherlands: EuroComment Diffusion; and R. Post (2008). "De perverse effecten van het Haags Adoptieverdrag." Justitiële Verkenningen, 7, 25-37, who describes how the Romanian 'point system' established in 1997, that required foreign adoption agencies to support the local child protection system with money or other contributions in return for points on the basis of which adoptable children would be allocated, dramatically increased the number of children placed for intercountry adoption; see also Hague Conference on Private International Law (2012). Accreditation and Adoption Accredited Bodies: General Principles and Guide to Good Practice, Guide No 2 under the Hague Convention of 29 May 1993 on Protection of Children and Co-operation in Respect of Intercountry Adoption, pp. 90 – 97.

the means or capacity to report it. The majority of adoptive children that are taken from their families are infants that do not conceive the illegal circumstances of their placements and, therefore, do not realize that they have been victimized in the first place.[241] Moreover, the child's birth mothers might not notice that they have been harmed in cases where they were falsely told that their newborn children were stillborn or died shortly after birth. Yet, even if birth parents realized that they have been victimized, the harm caused by the illegal practices often remains invisible to the wider public in the majority of cases. Due to their extreme powerlessness, vulnerable birth parents usually lack the voice as well as the capacity to report the purchase or abduction of their children and therefore to ultimately seek justice.[242]

The victims' invisibility is further exacerbated by the fact that intercountry adoptions commonly include a 'clean break' from the biological parents. According to the national laws of most countries, an adoption has the effect of terminating a pre-existing legal parent-child relationship. Legally, the adoptee ceases to be the child of his or her biological parents and becomes the child of the adoptive parents 'as if' he or she was born to them. This 'clean break' approach is the reason why the identity of the birth parents is not disclosed to the adoptive parents, and vice versa. In some countries, the child's birth certificate would not even indicate the birth mothers' name but would be issued with the name of the adoptive mother appearing thereon.[243] Some scholars claim that the exclusivity of adoptive parenthood is a Western construction which works to protect the nuclear family from outside interference.[244] As Högbacka notes: "a family can only have one mother and one father, and all 'other' parents are understood as a threat with the new parent automatically cancelling out the previous one".[245] The concept of a 'clean break' adoption often contrasts with child care arrangements in many countries of origin, in which children are traditionally brought up in extended family networks and in which the circulation of children would not imply a severance of ties with their biological parents.[246] Given the fact that the Western conception of adoption and the exclusivity of parenthood is culturally unknown in many

241 D. M. Smolin (2006). "Child Laundering: How the Intercountry Adoption System Legitimizes and Incentivizes the Practices of Buying, Trafficking, Kidnapping, and Stealing Children." The Wayne Law Review, 52, 1, 113-200, p. 160.

242 D. M. Smolin (2007). "Child laundering as exploitation: applying anti-trafficking norms to intercountry adoption under the coming Hague regime." Vermont Law Review, 32, 1-55, p. 3.

243 See, for example, UNICEF (2009). "Guidance Note on Intercountry Adoption in the CEE/CIS Region." (on file with author).

244 J. S. Modell (1994). "Kinship with Strangers: Adoption and Interpretations of Kinship in American Culture." University of California Press, Berkley.

245 R. Högbacka (2014). "Intercountry Adoption, Countries of Origin, and Biological Families, Report for Thematic Area 2 International Forum on Intercountry Adoption and Global Surrogacy 11-13 August 2014." Working Paper No. 598, International Institute of Social Studies, pp. 7-9; R. Högbacka (2011). "Exclusivity and Inclusivity in Transnational Adoption." In R. Jallinoja and E. D. Widmer (eds), "Families and Kinship in Contemporary Europe: Rules and Practices of Relatedness." Palgrave MacMillan, Basingstoke, 129–144.

246 Chapter III, section 4.1.

sending countries, parents would often agree to give up their child for adoption, without really understanding the consequences thereof.[247] The general and widespread acceptance of a clean-break linear adoption and the resulting birth parents' anonymity in the adoption documents makes them totally invisible to the adoptees and adoptive parents and it further reduces the chances of detecting the children's illegal origin.

Furthermore, and most importantly, illegal adoption activities remain invisible because, as was explained above (see section 2.4.1), they are embedded within a legitimate system. Illegally obtained children are not traded clandestinely, but they are passed through the same legal channels as children that are legally declared eligible for intercountry adoption. As a result, illegal and legal adoptions become hopelessly mixed up in the adoption system. The children can therefore not easily be identified and construed as illegally obtained. The stakeholders in the receiving countries may only detect the illegal origin of the child if the child was not laundered 'properly'. This is the case if the adoption documents provide contradictory information on the familial status of the child; for instance, if the affidavits issued by the orphanage state that the child was abandoned by the mother, whereas the court decision says that the child was an orphan whose mother passed away.[248]

As will be explained in Chapters IV, V and VI, also the Hague Convention works to further increase the invisibility of illegal adoption practices in the countries of origin. The treaty has distributed the responsibility for fulfilling the requirements of an international adoption between the sending and receiving countries and has created mutual trust between its contracting states, which often leads the authorities in the receiving countries to readily accept the information provided about the adoptees without assessing its reliability. Furthermore, the Convention has increased the level of bureaucracy as well as the wealth of paperwork within the adoption system, which ultimately reinforces an intercountry adoption's appearance of legitimacy and which therefore obscures any illegal and abusive practices that might have taken place in the state of origin.[249]

Arguably, also cases where children are passed off as the adopters' biological children often remain invisible. They would not even appear in the official adoption statistics and they may only be detected if there is reasonable suspicion to start an investigation into the child's actual origin.

Finally, also the current mindset and rhetoric surrounding intercountry adoption may serve as a layer of insularity. As will be explained in Chapter VII, in Western countries, intercountry adoption is commonly perceived and portrayed as the ultimate humanitarian

247 K. E. Cheney and K. S. Rotabi (2015). "Addicted to Orphans: How the Global Orphan Industrial Complex Jeopardizes Local Child Protection Systems." In C. Harker et al. (eds) "Conflict, Violence and Peace." Springer, Singapore, 89-107.

248 See, for instance, B. Wacker (1994). "Verbrechen und andere Kleinigkeiten." terre des hommes, Osnabrück.

249 See also R. Post (2008). "De perverse effecten van het Haags Adoptieverdrag." Justitiële Verkenningen, 7, 25-37.

deed that always rescues and never harms children.[250] This romanticized conception of intercountry adoption may blind adopters and adoption agencies to the potential risks of illegal practices and the harm that their actions might cause to the children, their birth parents and the welfare systems in the sending countries.

4.2.3 Extent of victimization

No comprehensive study of the number of children purchased, kidnapped and sold for the purpose of intercountry adoption has ever been undertaken. Since children are passed off as the adopters' biological parents or laundered through the legitimate adoption system, most cases of illegal adoption remain invisible, thereby making it impossible to present official statistics on their incidence. The actual nature and extent of the illegal adoption practices do, therefore, remain largely invisible. Nonetheless, prominent adoption scandals in, for example, Brazil,[251] Colombia,[252] Romania,[253] Sri Lanka,[254] Nepal,[255] Guatemala,[256] Vietnam,[257] India,[258] Haiti,[259] China,[260] Ethiopia[261] and Cambodia[262] have thrown light on

250 See Chapter VII, section 4.2.

251 C. Fonseca (2009). "Transnational Connections and Dissenting Views, The Evolution of Child Placement Policies in Brazil." In D. Marre and L. Briggs (eds), "International Adoption: Global Inequalities and the Circulation of Children." New York University Press, 154-173.

252 S. Hoelgaard (1998). "Cultural determinants of adoption policy: A Colombian case study." International Journal of Law, Policy and the Family 12, 2, 202-241.

253 J. L. Carro (1994). "Regulation of Intercountry Adoption: Can the Abuses Come to an End?" Hastings International & Comparative Law Review, 18, 121-155, pp. 131-140.

254 S. Bom and H. Van Zon (2017). "Sri Lanka erkent handel in sjoemelbaby's." Algemeen Dagblad, 20.09.2017, available at https://www.ad.nl/buitenland/sri-lanka-erkent-handel-in-sjoemelbaby-s~a5687b0c/.

255 UNICEF and Terre des Hommes (2008). "Adopting the Rights of the Child, A Study on Intercountry Adoption and Its Influence on Child Protection in Nepal." available at http://www.bettercarenetwork.org/sites/default/files/attachments/Adopting%20the%20Rights%20of%20the%20Child.pdf.

256 D. M. Smolin (2006). "Child Laundering: How the Intercountry Adoption System Legitimizes and Incentivizes the Practices of Buying, Trafficking, Kidnapping, and Stealing Children." The Wayne Law Review, 52, 1, 113-200, p. 163; K. Smith Rotabi (2012). "Fraud in Intercountry Adoption: Child Sales and Abduction in Vietnam, Cambodia, and Guatemala." In J. L. Gibbons and K. Smith Rotabi, "Intercountry Adoption: Policies, Practices, and Outcomes." Ashgate, Farnham, 67-66, pp. 73-75.

257 E. J. Graff (2010). "Anatomy of an Adoption Crisis." Foreign Policy, 12.09.2010, available at https://foreignpolicy.com/2010/09/12/anatomy-of-an-adoption-crisis/.

258 D. M. Smolin (2004). "The Two Faces of Intercountry Adoption: The Significance of the Indian Adoption Scandals." Seton Hall Law Review, 35, 403-493.

259 S. King (2012). "Owning Laura Silsby's Shame: How the Haitian Child Trafficking Scheme Embodies the Western Disregard for the Integrity of Poor Families." Harvard Human Rights Journal 25, 1-47.

260 B. H. Stuy (2014). "Open Secret: Cash and Coercion in China's International Adoption Programm." Cumberland Law Review, 44, 3, 355-422.

261 Wereldkinderen and Against Child Trafficking (2009). "Fruits of Ethiopia. Intercountry Adoption: The Rights of the Child, or the "Harvesting" of Children? A Study on Intercountry Adoption in Ethiopia." available at http://www.againstchildtrafficking.org/wp-content/uploads/Second-Interim-Report-FINAL-redacted-for-distribution+annexures.pdf.

262 T. Maskew (2004). "Child Trafficking and Intercountry Adoption: The Cambodian Experience." Cumberland Law Review, 35, 619-638.

the widespread existence of child trafficking for adoption purposes. Given the intrinsically criminogenic character of the international adoption system, which results from the high demand for adoptable children from wealthy Western countries, the vulnerability of the supply nations, as well as a financial motivation to exploit them, there is much to suggest that the exposed and publicized adoption scandals only represent the tip of the iceberg.[263]

4.2.4 Lack of public agreement on seriousness

Despite the wealth of information that exists on illegal and irregular adoption practices, we will never know just how many children have been obtained illegally and laundered through the adoption system. This is significant because it is due to this uncertainty that many people – adoptive parents, adoption agencies as well as commentators – insist that the prevalence of these practices is greatly exaggerated.

Over the last couple of years, several critics of intercountry adoption have emerged who have voiced their concern about the system's widespread abuses. Some promote restrictive state regulations to limit the number of intercountry adoptions and to eliminate illicit adoption practices (*regulationists*).[264] Others favour a total ban on international adoptions. They claim that due to the high demand for adoptable children, as well as the large sums of monies involved, the system cannot be effectively safeguarded against profiteering and corruption and hence needs to be abolished altogether (*abolitionists*).[265] Critics of intercountry adoption are facing a powerful pro-adoption lobby, including politicians, adopters, conservative think tanks as well as legal scholars who deny the seriousness and scope of the illegal and abusive adoption practices.[266]

King has analysed the discourse on intercountry adoption in law review articles in the United States and illustrates the recurrent tropes and commonplaces that proponents of intercountry adoption use to downplay the incidence of illegal adoption practices: "reports of child trafficking from sending countries are often qualified in law review articles as "rumors of," "scandals of," "tales of," and at times are explicitly described as misrepresentations or exaggerations by the media of sending countries that hurt children who need adoption".[267] Wardle, for example, claims:

263 See also B. Wacker (1994). "Verbrechen und andere Kleinigkeiten." terre des hommes, Osnabrück, p. 13; D. M. Smolin (2006). "Child Laundering: How the Intercountry Adoption System Legitimizes and Incentivizes the Practices of Buying, Trafficking, Kidnapping, and Stealing Children." The Wayne Law Review, 52, 1, 113-200, p. 160.

264 See Chapter III, section 2.3.

265 See Chapter III, section 2.1.

266 R. Post (2007). "Romania–for Export Only: The Untold Story of the Romanian 'Orphans'." Netherlands: EuroComment Diffusion; see Chapter III, section 2.2.

267 S. King (2008). "Challenging Monohumanism: An Argument for Changing the Way We Think About Intercountry Adoption." Michigan Journal of International Law 30, 413-470, p. 438.

> Concerns about baby-selling are exaggerated… [S]tories of baby-selling, baby-napping, and "black market adoptions," are given greatly exaggerated air time by the sensationalizing media. They sell newspapers and attract viewers, and thus are given excessive attention by profit-seeking media producers.[268]

Similarly, Chadwick downplays adoption scandals by arguing that: "Pre-existing suspicion, coupled with the large sums of money exchanged in an international adoption, have fuelled the rumor mills which continue to churn out allegations of baby-selling rings."[269] Berger asserts that "the media has found some instances of baby-selling and made the most of them".[270]

Opponents of intercountry adoption are often demonized and their responses to abusive adoption practices are depicted as an overreaction and a threat to the children's best interests. Decisions by sending countries to restrict or oppose intercountry adoption due to serious incidents of child trafficking are described as irrational and disproportional responses "due to public shame, fear of imperialism, nationalistic pride, or xenophobic attitudes toward Westerners" and therefore as severe infringements of children's rights.[271] Chadwick, for instance, claims that

> stoic national pride has led countries such as the Ukraine and Georgia to impose bans on intercountry adoptions. These moratoriums are almost entirely economical and political decisions that neglect the best interests of the children.[272]

Liu dismisses developing countries' opposition to intercountry adoption "as a result of their history of colonialism. […] They do not see the practice as being one of love for the child, but one used to satisfy the greediness and selfishness of others".[273] McMillan criticizes Latin American countries for often being "reluctant to allow foreign adoption because of their own ethnocentric bias, […they…] do not want to appear to the rest of the world as

268 L. D. Wardle (2005). "Parentlessness: Adoption Problems, Paradigms, Policies, and Parameters." Whittier Journal of Child & Family Advocacy, 4, 2, 323-373, p. 347.

269 K. A. Chadwick (1999). "The Politics and Economics of Intercountry Adoption in Eastern Europe." Journal of International Legal Studies, 5, 113-144, p. 121.

270 D. Berger (1995). "Improving the Safety and Efficiency of Foreign Adoptions: US Domestic Adoption Programs and Adoption Programs in Other Countries Provide Lessons for INS Reform." Cornell Journal of Law and Public Policy, 5, 33-65, pp. 38-39.

271 S. King (2008). "Challenging Monohumanism: An Argument for Changing the Way We Think About Intercountry Adoption." Michigan Journal of International Law 30, 413-470, p. 434.

272 K. A. Chadwick (1999). "The Politics and Economics of Intercountry Adoption in Eastern Europe." Journal of International Legal Studies, 5, 113-144, p. 114.

273 M. Liu (1994). "International Adoptions: An Overview." Temple International & Comparative Law Journal, 8, 187-213, pp. 194-195.

unable or unwilling to care for their own children".[274] Marx portrays Romania's ban on all international adoptions after reports of illegal practices as "overly sweeping and restrictive [...it] is a blatantly self-serving move aimed at achieving its own political and economic goals. Sadly, this comes at the expense of the children's best interests. Romania is hiding behind the best interest standard promulgated in international treaties and using is it to justify its own narcissistic policies".[275]

Proponents of intercountry adoption do not only deny the frequency of adoption scandals, they also downplay the harm inflicted upon the children and their birth parents. Bartholet, one of the most visible advocates of intercountry adoption, provides a particularly explicit example. Talking about stealing and selling children, she claims:

> [...] if we really care about children, we should be prepared to see even these evils in perspective. They are by no means the worst things that are happening to children or their parents today, and they occur relatively rarely.[276]

She also denies the harmful consequences that the monies involved in intercountry adoptions have on the welfare systems in the sending countries by qualifying them as "significant new funds to poor orphanages in sending countries"[277] that relieves the children's home countries of the burden of support.[278] Bartholet's blindness to the profound individual and social injuries that are caused by abusive adoption practices leads her to propose that restrictive state regulations and bureaucratic hurdles should be lifted as they would only delay the speedy rescue of needy children. She also promotes the facilitation of private adoptions – i.e. adoptions directly arranged between the adoptive and birth parents which are often criticized for being linked to abusive practices – so as to ensure that as many children as possible can be placed for international adoption.[279]

What are the reasons for the lack of public conviction about the seriousness of the illegal adoption practices? Why do legal scholars that ought to be advocates of justice and guardians of human rights deny the existence of illegal adoption practices and their harmful consequences? Arguably, this denial stems from the Western cultural mindset of developing countries in general and about intercountry adoptions in particular that enable

274 M. A. C. McMillan (1993). "International Adoption: A Step Towards a Uniform Process." Pace International Law Review, 5, 1, 137-164, p. 140.

275 M. S. Marx (2007). "Whose best interests does it really serve? A critical examination of Romania's recent self-serving international adoption policies." Emory International Law Review, 21, 373-412, p. 411.

276 E. Bartholet (1993). "Family Bonds. Adoption and the Politics of Parenting." Houghton Mifflin, Boston, pp. 154-155.

277 E. Bartholet (2007). "International Adoption: Thoughts on the Human Rights Issue." Buffalo Human Rights Law Review, 13, 151-203, p. 186.

278 *Ibid.*, p. 185.

279 E. Bartholet (2007). "International Adoption: The Child's Story." Georgia State University Law Review, 24, 333-379, pp. 355-356.

promoters of intercountry adoption to perceive this social practice as the ultimate humanitarian act. Western societies, post-colonialist critics claim, tend to identify themselves, their culture and their knowledge as superior in comparison to non-Western people and their cultures.[280] In contrast, the non-Westerns, particularly people from countries in which the United States or European countries previously had colonies, are identified as "the others" and their culture, knowledge, and discourse are excluded or debased. The narratives in Western literature, films, legal practices, jurisprudence, and political discourse, critics claim, reflect this post-colonialist mindset and allow individuals to subscribe universality to the Western culture and knowledge and its "supporting institutions, vocabulary, scholarship, imagery, [and] doctrines".[281] King refers to the post-colonial way of thinking about intercountry adoption as MonoHumanism in which

> children are not seen in the context of their family, community, and culture, but instead, narrowly as the potential children of Western adults. In other words, children are seen through a narrative of identity in the United States, which I am calling *MonoHumanism*, to the exclusion of knowledge and discourse with its origins in the lives, cultures, and vocabulary of the children themselves.[282]

This conception of intercountry adoption, King believes, does not only exist in legal scholarship, but also in other scholarship on adoption, in the media and in reports of governmental and non-governmental organizations. MonoHumanism is generally prevalent in public discourse on intercountry adoption. Western society has painted a picture of intercountry adoption that is shaped by their own view of themselves and on non-Western people that suits their own interests and needs.[283] In this picture, the children's native countries and their birth families are portrayed as inferior and degenerated, and intercountry adoption is depicted as the only viable childcare option serving the best interests of the children.

The children's countries of origin – many of them formerly colonized by the West – are described as suffering from impregnable conditions, such as economic collapses, political instability, civil wars, natural disasters, diseases, over-population and widespread poverty from which children need to be rescued as soon as possible.[284] If the birth parents

280 E. W. Said (1993). "Culture and imperialism." Vintage, New York.; E. W. Said (1979). "Orientalism." Vintage, New York.

281 E. W. Said (1979). "Orientalism." Vintage, New York, p. 2.

282 S. King (2008). "Challenging Monohumanism: An Argument for Changing the Way We Think About Intercountry Adoption." Michigan Journal of International Law 30, 413-470, p. 415.

283 *Ibid.*, p. 425.

284 *Ibid.*, p. 432. See also D. M. Hoffman (2011). "Saving children, saving Haiti? Child vulnerability and narratives of the nation." Childhood, 1-14.

are acknowledged at all in the legal literature, they are commonly described as "dead, sick, incapacitated, impoverished, desperate, neglected, addicted to drugs and alcohol, or shamed into abandoning their children".[285] Western societies portray them as inferior, unworthy of keeping their children, or selfish as they deliberately relinquish their rights for a small amount of money.[286]

Intercountry adoption is conceptualized as the best solution, a charitable, humanitarian deed that saves children from their immediate circumstances and their neglectful families and offers them a 'better life' in a Western country with advanced medicine, better educational institutions, and so-called Western conveniences.[287] The concept of 'best interest of the child' is interpreted as meaning growing up in a Western family environment, whereas any child not living in such an ideal family environment is identified as an 'orphan' according to these narratives.[288] Kind explains, "[l]aw review articles create this narrative by freely interchanging the word 'orphan' with 'abandoned', 'street', 'homeless', and 'needy'. The dominant narrative in law review suggests that an expanding discourse of who is adoptable has broadened the concept of who is adoptable".[289] The idea that intercountry adoption might cause harm to the children is fundamentally contrary to the Western conception of this social practice as the ultimate humanitarian deed.[290]

The denial of the harm inflicted upon the birth families might be the result of an 'othering process' that people in non-Western countries undergo.[291] In Western societies, the abduction or purchase of children, e.g. by a parent/guardian or by a stranger usually shocks the common conscience and produces moral outrage in people. For instance, the alleged kidnapping of the three-year-old British girl Maddie MacCann has attracted sustained attention and triggered a great wave of sympathy for the girl's parents in Europe as well as other Western countries. Yet, comparable incidences in, for instance, India or Cambodia would offend the Western consciousness considerably less so.

As Henry and Lanier explain, "[t]his distinction is related to differences in the importance attached to human life, based on people's social and political status in a hierarchically ordered society and on the social distance and divisions that complex societies create between human beings. In short, it pertains to socially constructed differences created

285 S. King (2008). "Challenging Monohumanism: An Argument for Changing the Way We Think About Intercountry Adoption." Michigan Journal of International Law 30, 413-470, p. 443.

286 *Ibid.*, p. 443.

287 *Ibid.*

288 See Chapter III, section 6.4.

289 S. King (2008). "Challenging Monohumanism: An Argument for Changing the Way We Think About Intercountry Adoption." Michigan Journal of International Law 30, 413-470, p. 443, pp. 444-445.

290 See also D. M. Smolin (2007). "Child laundering as exploitation: applying anti-trafficking norms to intercountry adoption under the coming Hague regime." Vermont Law Review, 32, 1-55, p. 27.

291 S. King (2008). "Challenging Monohumanism: An Argument for Changing the Way We Think About Intercountry Adoption." Michigan Journal of International Law 30, 413-470, p. 443.

between those with whom we can identify and 'others' with whom we cannot".[292] The material division between the rich (industrialized) and poor (developing) countries has constructed social distance between the Western people and the non-Western people. We, the Western society, define ourselves as superior and attach primary importance to the pursuance of our needs and interests. On the contrary, the non-Western people are considered as the lesser 'others' with whom we cannot identify. This detachment allows us to ruthlessly exploit their resources, their labour, their bodies and their fertility. Whereas we are appalled when cases emerge where 'our' children or families are harmed, we disavow or deny the harm that our practices cause to the 'others'.

4.2.5 Low probability of severe social response

The profits to be gained from laundering children are substantial while the risks of detection are rather low. Even if cases of kidnapping, purchasing and selling children for purposes of adoption are uncovered, the probability that the actors involved receive a serious official response that is designed to punish the unjustness involved in their illegal practices is very low. The actors in the sending countries who engage in illegal adoption practices do not fear harsh consequences for their activities, given the weak and corrupt enforcement mechanisms that exist in their countries.[293] And the adoption placement agencies in the receiving countries, that will claim that they had no knowledge whatsoever of the irregular practices abroad, can usually not be held accountable for the activities of the cooperation partners in the sending countries.

If the adopters are involved in laundering the child, they may be held criminally liable for human smuggling and forgery of documents.[294] In the Netherlands, adopters may also be held responsible for violating the adoption regulations if they bypassed the adoption system. Yet, even if adopters are convicted for their illegal actions, they commonly receive relatively mild sentences, such as a fine, probation or community work as they do usually not have a criminal record.[295] Most importantly, they in many cases get to keep the illegally adopted child as removing the child from his or her new family is not considered to be in the child's best interests.[296]

292 S. Henry and M. Lanier (1998). "The Prism of Crime: Arguments for an Integrated Definition of Crime." Justice Quarterly 15, 609-627, p. 620.

293 D. M. Smolin (2006). "Child Laundering: How the Intercountry Adoption System Legitimizes and Incentivizes the Practices of Buying, Trafficking, Kidnapping, and Stealing Children." The Wayne Law Review, 52, 1, 113-200, p. 194.

294 See Chapter V, section 9 and Chapter VI, section 8.

295 See Chapter V, section 9.1.1 and Chapter VI, section 8.1.

296 See Chapter V, section 4.3 and Chapter VI, section 4.3.

5 Conclusion and Discussion

The last half-century has witnessed the emergence of a transnational adoption market in illegally obtained children. The basic logic of routine activity theory offers a means of conceptualizing this market and identifying its structural components: demand, supply and regulation. Adopters and adoption agencies, especially in the United States and Europe, constitute the demand component. In Western countries, the number of children available for adoption has decreased since the 70s due to liberal abortion politics, contraception and the increasing acceptance of unwed motherhood. Hence, the adoption of a child from a foreign country has become an attractive (and often last resort) alternative for many involuntary childless couples.[297] Their demand for easily adoptable healthy babies exerts an inexorable pull on child-rich poor countries. The pressure on these countries not only originates from the adoptive parents, but also from adoption agencies whose very existence is dependent on the number of intercountry adoptions they place.[298]

Whereas Western countries constitute the demand states, child-countries of the Global South, particularly China, Russia, Guatemala and more recently some African countries, form the source countries for adoptable children. However, most children that are actually available for intercountry adoption in these states are already older and/or have special needs and are therefore not the attractive adoptees that Western couples are looking for. In order to meet the high Western demand for babies, actors in the sending countries employ a variety of illegal means to generate adoptable children. Children are purchased or abducted from their families, hospitals or orphanages. Vulnerable birth parents are coerced or provided with misleading information on the consequence of an adoption in order to obtain their consent. Directors of child care institutions and government officials are paid to subvert the subsidiarity principle that is laid down in the Hague Convention and the UNCRC so as to increase the supply of adoptable children. From a supply perspective, the magnitude of the current illegal adoption market is the product of a large number of poor families struggling to provide for their children, as well as orphanages caring for many parentless children.

In order to sustain an illegal market in adoptable children, demand and illegal supply sources need to be securely linked. Connecting buyers and sellers with each other is necessary, which is organized differently than in conventional forms of human trafficking.

297 A. Fleisher (2003). "The Decline of Domestic Adoption: Intercountry Adoption as a Response to Local Adoption Laws and Proposals to Foster Domestic Adoption." Review of Law and Women's Studies, 13, 1, 171-197, p. 175; R. Rios-Kohn (1998). "Intercountry adoption: An international perspective on the practice and standards." Adoption Quarterly, 1, 4, 3-32, p. 7; R. Högbacka (2008). "The quest for a child of one's own: Parents, markets and transnational adoption." Journal of Comparative Family Studies, 39, 3, 311-330, p. 312.

298 See Chapter V, section 5.2. and Chapter VI, section 5.2.

Whereas the purpose of conventional forms of human trafficking is illegal (e.g. sexual exploitation, organ removal, slavery), adopting a child is perfectly legal on the demand end of the system. An adoption only becomes illegal when the child has been obtained illegally. Therefore, the illicit means by which the children were obtained must be disguised: a laundering process is crucial here. This process is facilitated by individuals and organizations from both the public and private sector that ought to serve as legal guardians in the adoption system but who misuse their function to convert illegally obtained children into 'orphans' and then 'adoptees'. They would falsify or fabricate necessary documents in order to hide the illegal conduct as well as to identify the illegally obtained children as legally abandoned orphans for which no domestic children care solution could be found.[299]

The high demand for and the illegal supply of adoptable children as well as the reduced ability of legal guardians to control the adoption system are caused by demographic as well as economic asymmetries between the sending and the receiving countries. Whereas the rich Western countries are struggling with low birth rates and decreasing numbers of children available for domestic adoption, birth rates are increasing in the poor countries of the Global South. These asymmetries shape the motivation of actors in the source countries to illegally obtain adoptable children. The adoption costs that may seem reasonable from a Western perspective are sufficient to create an incentive for orphanage directors, government officials and others to illicitly source adoptable children. The criminogenic asymmetries have also reduced capable guardians in the intercountry adoption system. Widespread corruption in the sending countries, which were both caused by and further increased these existing asymmetries, have weakened official controls. Individuals and organizations from both the public and private sector that ought to monitor and control the adoption system misuse their function in order to connect demand and illegal supply by laundering children through their organization.

There is widespread consensus among people within and across cultures that child trafficking for the purposes of prostitution, pornography, organ removal and forced labour is a serious crime which creates profound harm. Societal responses and moral outrage to uncovered child trafficking cases are immediate and pointed. In recent years, the issue has climbed the political agenda, resulting in a number of international and regional treaties as well as national criminal laws which are designed to react to and combat one of the fastest growing forms of transnational organized crime. Law enforcement agencies commonly devote all their available resources and assemble specific task forces so as to deal with this particular crime. People involved in running the trafficking network are usually punished severely. Therefore, child trafficking for the purpose of prostitution, forced labour and organ removal would be placed on the top of Henry and Lanier's 'prism of crime'.

---

299 H. Bochéat et al. (2012). "Investigating the Grey Zones of Intercountry Adoption." International Social Service, p. 81.

In contrast, there seems to be social disagreement on the seriousness of purchasing, kidnapping and selling children for the purpose of adoption. Proponents of intercountry adoption downplay the significance of the illegal adoption practices as well as the harm caused by them. Reports of stealing and selling children are interpreted as exaggerations by the sensationalizing and profit-seeking media. Sending countries' decision to ban or restrict intercountry adoption due to incidents of child trafficking is construed as irrational responses due to public shame, ethnocentric bias, narcissism or xenophobic attitudes. With regards to the harm that is caused by the illegal adoption practices, proponents either literally deny or justify them by claiming that there are far worse things happening to children and their birth parents.

The lack of public conviction about the seriousness of the illegal adoption practices might be due to the Western cultural mindset about intercountry adoption which identifies this social practice as the ultimate humanitarian deed that always saves children from poverty and starvation in the developing countries. The idea that intercountry adoption might cause harm to children is absolutely contrary to our post- way of thinking about intercountry adoptions. This cultural mindset seems to be reflected in the Trafficking Protocol, the first and most important international legal instrument with an agreed definition on the trafficking of persons, especially women and children. This Protocol does not consider the purchasing, kidnapping and selling of children for the purpose of adoption as a form of human trafficking, because adoption *per se* does not amount to exploitation: the third constituent element of human trafficking. The Trafficking Protocol's definition of child trafficking is, in turn, mirrored in the national criminal laws that themselves fail to provide the necessary criminal prohibitions and responses designed to punish the kinds of wrongs involved in the purchasing, kidnapping and selling of children for the purposes of adoption. Even when cases of illegal adoption practices are detected, the probability that the criminal actors receive a serious official response is low. The people in the criminal network usually either go unpunished or are only convicted of relatively minor criminal offences.

This chapter has demonstrated how the illegal adoption practices employed to serve the market in children create profound individual and social harm. Removing a child from her intact family through purchase, abduction or deception of the parents exploits the child and her birth family and severely violates their fundamental human rights. The institution of intercountry adoption is therefore stripped of its humanitarian *rationale* and is being abused by the powerful in the system – adopters, orphanage directors, lawyers and government officials – in order to serve their interests. The child is not seen as a unique person with needs, interests and basic rights. Rather, the child is denied humanity and reduced to a marketable commodity. His or her characteristics as healthy and young are exploited by adoptive parents who want to fulfil their desire for a child at any price and by individuals and organizations that want to financially gain from intercountry adoption.

Additionally, the child's birth parents are denied humanity and the status of the child's family. They are degraded to a breeding unit whose fertility, and also extreme powerlessness, is exploited. Illicit payments made to facilitate the intercountry adoption of an orphaned child also create profound social harm by disrupting and destroying the social welfare system in the child's country of origin and by inciting childcare institutions or other organisations or individuals to secure 'adoptable children'.

The harm that is caused by illegal adoption practices is difficult to trace and therefore it often remains invisible to the victims or the wider public, or both. The majority of adoptive children who are taken from their families are infants who cannot conceive of the illegal circumstances of their placement. Their vulnerable birth parents usually lack the voice and the capacity to effectively report the purchase or abduction of their children. After the child has been obtained illicitly, the child is either passed off as the adopters' biological child or channelled through the legitimate adoption system as an 'orphan' and then adoptee. The general and widespread acceptance of a clean-break adoption and the resulting birth parents' anonymity in the adoption documents reduces the chance of detecting the child's illegal origin. Purchasing, kidnapping and selling children for the purpose of adoption would, therefore, be located in the lower half of the 'prism of crime'.

III The Rights of the Child and the 'Best Interests' Principle in Intercountry Adoption

1 Introduction

The rights of the child, as well as the overarching principle of 'the child's best interests', that are laid down in several international legal instruments, most notably The UN Convention on the Rights of the Child[1] (hereinafter UNCRC), form the basis of the intercountry adoption system, from which all adoption laws and practices should flow. They have also substantially shaped the heated debate on the legitimacy of intercountry adoption, lending support to arguments on either side of the controversy. Proponents argue that placing children for intercountry adoption would serve their interests best, as it would protect many of the rights laid down in the UNCRC – most notably the right to grow up in a family environment, the right to enjoy the highest attainable standard of health, the right to an adequate standard of living, the right to education and the right to enjoy rest, leisure and recreational activities. Opponents of intercountry adoption, however, argue that this social practice is intrinsically harmful to children. They consider it as a purely commercial and post-colonial act which unnecessarily severs children from their ethnic, religious, cultural and linguistic background and therefore violates the child's right to identity.

The present Chapter identifies those provisions of the UNCRC which are most relevant with regard to intercountry adoption. Although this treaty is the most comprehensive international instrument concerning the rights of the child, other human rights treaties will also be dealt with insofar as their provisions are of special relevance in matters of intercountry adoption or where they contribute to a better understanding of the rights laid down in the UNCRC. These instruments, many of which are expressly referred to in the Preamble of the Convention, include: the 1959 Declaration of the Rights of the Child,[2] the 1948 Universal Declaration of Human Rights[3] (hereinafter UDHR), the 1966 International Covenant on Civil and Political Rights[4] (hereinafter ICCPR), the European Convention on Human Rights[5] (hereinafter ECHR), the 1986 Declaration on Social and Legal Principles relating to the Protection and Welfare of Children, with Special Reference to

1 UN General Assembly, Convention on the Rights of the Child, 20 November 1989, Res. 44/25.

2 UN General Assembly, Declaration of the Rights of the Child, 20 November 1959, A/RES/1386(XIV).

3 UN General Assembly, Universal Declaration of Human Rights, 10 December 1948, 217 A (III).

4 UN General Assembly, International Covenant on Civil and Political Rights, 16 December 1966, United Nations, Treaty Series, vol. 999, p. 171.

5 Council of Europe, European Convention for the Protection of Human Rights and Fundamental Freedoms, as amended by Protocols Nos. 11 and 14, 4 November 1950, ETS 5.

Foster Placement and Adoption Nationally and Internationally[6] and the 2006 International Convention for the Protection of All Persons from Enforced Disappearance[7] (ICPPED).

The Chapter seeks to throw light on the debate surrounding the legitimacy of intercountry adoption by clarifying as to when children are eligible for intercountry adoption under the current human rights law framework. Furthermore, it explains that the indeterminate concept of 'the best interests of the child', which should be the paramount consideration in all adoption decisions, is a criminogenic factor in the adoption system as it constitutes a breeding ground for misconception and manipulation and is a suitable device to justify and legitimize adoption practices that are actually harmful to children.

Section 2 takes a closer look at the three value positions in the current debate surrounding the legitimacy of intercountry adoption. Section 3 briefly outlines the historical background and the development of the UNCRC. Section 4 focuses in on the rights that the Convention grants to children and their parents and families. Section 5 then explains the rights of children that are deprived of their family environment and under which circumstances they may be placed for intercountry adoption according to the UNCRC. It exposes the myth of a 'global orphan crisis' and clarifies that, contrary to common conceptions, only a small fraction of children living in institutions or on the streets may actually be considered for adoption. Section 6 scrutinizes the 'child's best interests' principle and explains why this vague concept is a criminogenic factor in the intercountry adoption system. Section 7 then concludes this Chapter.

2 Positions on the Legitimacy of Intercountry Adoption

For several years, a fierce debate on the legitimacy of international adoption has been waged and continues to be waged by politicians, in academia as well as in the wider public sphere. In this academic debate, three value camps can be identified that all substantiate their positions by referring to the child's rights and the principle of the best interests of the child: (1) *abolitionists* who condemn intercountry adoptions altogether as a commercial and imperial act that violates the child's right to preserve his or her cultural heritage and identity, (2) *promoters* who consider intercountry adoption to be the preferred option for homeless children that needs to be encouraged and facilitated as it serves the child's right to a family and (3) *regulationists* who promote the idea of reforming the intercountry

6 UN General Assembly, Declaration on Social and Legal Principles relating to the Protection and Welfare of Children, with Special Reference to Foster Placement and Adoption Nationally and Internationally, 3 December 1986, A/RES/41/85.

7 UN General Assembly, International Convention for the Protection of All Persons from Enforced Disappearance, 20 December 2006, A/RES/61/177.

adoption system as a way of limiting the number of intercountry adoptions and preventing abusive practices.

2.1 Abolitionists

Abolitionists see little difference between legal and illegal intercountry adoptions, but condemn this practice altogether as they regard it as purely commercial and imperial. Stripped of its humanitarian justification, they claim that this practice is, or has at least become, a business in which the rich from powerful Western countries buy the children from their poor families in developing countries. The child is not seen in the context of his or her family, community or culture, but is perceived in a narrow sense as a potential adoptee for Western adults.[8] Altstein and Simon observe: "what the West has generally viewed as charitable, humane – even noble – behavior, developing countries have come to define as imperialistic, self-serving, and a return to a form of colonialism in which whites exploit and steal natural resources".[9] Hübinette illustrates the colonial and imperial character of intercountry adoption. Employing the lens of anthropology and migration history, he draws attention to the striking parallels that exist between intercountry adoption and the Atlantic slave trade:

> Both practices are driven by insatiable consumer demand, private market interests, and cynical profit making, and both utilize a highly advanced system of pricing where the young, the healthy, and the light-skinned are the most valued. Both are dependent on the existence of native intermediaries in the form of slave hunters and adoption agencies as well as a reliable and efficient global transportation system of shipping routes. Both the enslaves and the adopted are separated from their parents, siblings, relatives, and significant others at an early age; stripped of their original cultures and languages; reborn at harbors and airports; Christianized, rebaptized, and bestowed with the names of their masters; and in the end only retaining racialized nonwhite bodies that have been branded or given case numbers. The so-called house or servant slaves must have been the closest parallels to international adoptees as both live permanently together with their masters and are legally defined as belonging to their household and their family. Furthermore, both practices have been legitimized by the same shallow argument that when moved to their new homes,

8 S. King (2008). "Challenging Monohumanism: An Argument for Changing the Way We Think About Intercountry Adoption." Michigan Journal of International Law 30, 413-470, p. 415.

9 H. Altstein and R. J. Simon (1991). "Intercountry adoption: A multinational perspective." Greenwood Publishing Group, New York, p. 2.

> the material solutions of the slaves and the adoptees are unquestionably greatly bettered as both are benefiting from the wealth and civilization of the West. Finally, both groups are brought over only to satisfy the needs and desires of their well-to-do acquirers.[10]

Lilith juxtaposes intercountry adoptions with mail-ordering brides, focusing on the transactions between the United States and Asia.[11] She stresses that both practices are abusive and exploitative by-products of imperial activities and criticizes popular and legal writing for drawing a distinction between them. Differentiating between mail-ordering brides and adopting a child internationally, Lilith argues, obscures the commercialism and imperialism that is implicit in intercountry adoption.[12] She argues:

> The double standard of condemning mail-order brides as prostitutes, while uncritically supporting intercountry adoptions must be reconsidered, for when the historical notions and modern constructions that enable mail-order brides and intercountry adoptions to be considered discrete practices are removed, what remains in both cases is the essential fact that white Americans, who cannot satisfy their desires for wives and children in the U.S., are paying billions of dollars to enable Asian women and children to immigrate to the U.S. in order to join these Americans' families.[13]

Abolitionists claim that intercountry adoption violates the rights that are enshrined in the UNCRC. They argue that the children's right to identity preservation presupposes the right to grow up and be cared for in the country within which they were born – a right which is profoundly violated when the children are sent abroad for intercountry adoption purposes.[14] The UNCRC provides the child separated from one or both parents the right "to maintain personal relations and direct contact with both parents on a regular basis, except if it is contrary to the child's best interests". This right, abolitionists claim, is violated

10 T. Hübinette (2006). "From Orphan Trains to Babylifts: Colonial Trafficking, Empire Building, and Social Engineering." In J. J. Trenka et al. (eds), "Outsiders Within: Writing on Transracial Adoption." South End Press, Cambridge, 139-149, p. 143.

11 R. Lilith (2000). "Buying a Wife but Saving a Child: A Deconstruction of Popular Rhetoric and Legal Analysis of Mail-Order Brides and Intercountry Adoptions." Buffalo Women's Law Journal, 9, 225-262.

12 *Ibid.*, p. 229.

13 *Ibid.*, p. 262.

14 A. Bainham (2003). "International adoption from Romania–why the moratorium should not be ended." Child and Family Law Quarterly 15, 3, 223-236, p. 231.

by an international adoption that reflects the modern Western understanding of adoption as involving a total severance of the link between the adopted child and the birth parents.[15]

Abolitionists promote domestic childcare arrangements, including foster care or institutional care, that enable the children to maintain the relationship with their families and to enjoy their cultural heritage. Instead of providing some assistance to help the children remain in their native countries, critics claim, inordinate sums of money are spent in order to strip the children of their national identity and to place them with a family of a different ethnic origin in foreign culture.[16] These inordinate sums of money encourage a preference for intercountry adoption over domestic childcare solutions, and it provides an opportunity for profiteering by the actors involved in the adoption system.

Due to the high demand for adoptable healthy children, as well as the large sums of monies involved in intercountry adoptions, abolitionists claim that the system cannot be effectively safeguarded against profiteering.[17] Carro, having analysed the changes in intercountry adoption laws and the efforts to curb abusive practices between 1989 and 1994, came to a despondent conclusion in this regard:

> It is apparent that as long as the demand for adoptable children increases, and the supply decreases, abuses in intercountry adoptions will abound. [...] efforts have been made at all levels to curb the abuses, but expectations of success cannot be very high. While the efforts taken by individual countries are laudable, their efficacy is questionable. The prospects are no better at the inter-national level. The 1993 Hague Convention on Protection of Children and Co-operation in Respect of Intercountry Adoption will set uniform, minimum standards which every contracting country must meet, yet will still allow countries the flexibility to shape adoption procedures to meet their needs.[18]

Consequently, many opponents of intercountry adoption promote the abolition of this harmful and intrinsically abusive social practice.

15 T. Hübinette (2006). "From Orphan Trains to Babylifts: Colonial Trafficking, Empire Building, and Social Engineering." In J. J. Trenka et al. (eds), "Outsiders Within: Writing on Transracial Adoption." South End Press, Cambridge, 139-149, p. 140.

16 D. M. Smolin (2004). "Intercountry adoption as child trafficking." Valparasio University Law Review, 39, 2, 281-325, p. 283.

17 See, for example, J. Dickens (2002). "The paradox of inter-country adoption: analysing Romania's experience as a sending country." International Journal of Social Welfare, 11, 1, 76-83.

18 J. L. Carro (1994). "Regulation of Intercountry Adoption: Can the Abuses Come to an End?" Hastings International & Comparative Law Review, 18, 121-155, p. 155.

2.2 Promoters

Promoters of intercountry adoption point to the numerous orphaned children worldwide that are in need of nurturing homes.[19] They often rely on statistics or estimates of orphans and children living in institutions or on the streets so as to highlight the urgency to intervene and help the most vulnerable members of society (see section 5.3).

Promoters reject foster care arrangements due to its lack of permanency[20] as well as institutional care for being profoundly damaging to children.[21] Instead, intercountry adoption, they claim, should be deemed the preferred childcare option for parentless children.[22] It provides an immediate solution for thousands of children who lack basic human rights, such as a loving family, food, healthcare and education. Placing these children with adoptive families would protect many of the rights that are laid down in the UNCRC – most notably the right to grow up in a family environment, the right to enjoy the highest attainable standard of health, the right to an adequate standard of living, the right to education and the right to enjoy rest, leisure and recreational activities – and it fulfils the guiding principle of the UNCRC, namely to protect and promote the best interests of the child.[23] Bartholet, one of the most visible proponents of intercountry adoption claims:

> Many of us who support international adoption see it as serving the most fundamental human rights of the most helpless of humans – the rights of children to the kind of family love and care that will enable them to grow up with a decent chance of living a healthy and fulfilling life.[24]

Similarly, Dillon argues that institutional care violates the child's right to a family and the corresponding right to be protected against the adverse psychological and social effects of institutionalization. These rights, she claims, cannot be trumped by the child's right to identity preservation:

19 E. Bartholet (2007). "International Adoption: Thoughts on the Human Rights Issue." Buffalo Human Rights Law Review, 13, 151-203, p.183.
20 Ibid.
21 E. Bartholet (2007). "International Adoption: The Child's Story." Georgia State University Law Review, 24, 333-379, p. 347.
22 H. E. Bogard (1991). "Who are the Orphans?: Defining Orphan Status and the Need for an International Convention on Intercountry Adoption." Emory International Law Review, 5, 571-616, pp. 574-580.
23 L. McKinney (2007). "International Adoption and the Hague Convention: Does Implementation of the Convention Protect the Best Interests of Children?" Whittier Journal of Child & Family Advocacy, 6, 2, 361-412, p. 378.
24 E. Bartholet (2007). "International Adoption: Thoughts on the Human Rights Issue." Buffalo Human Rights Law Review, 13, 151-203, pp. 151-152.

> It is certainly true that the UNCRC articulates an important right to identity, but this can hardly be taken so far as to suggest that remaining in institutional care in the country of origin is to be preferred to intercountry adoption, though this is what many appear to conclude.[25]

Promoters claim that the regulations which delay or even prohibit intercountry adoption violate the child's fundamental rights.[26] Restrictive state regulations and bureaucratic hurdles should, therefore, be lifted and private adoptions facilitated so as to ensure that as many children as possible can be placed up for international adoption.[27]

Proponents of intercountry adoption acknowledge incidences of stealing and selling children, but consider such abuses as individual rather than systemic problems. They endorse the need to eliminate irregularities but urge observers to keep the focus on the bigger picture: ensuring that homeless children receive permanent nurturing homes as early in life as possible.[28] Promoters often criticize the media and academia for paying too much attention to illegal adoption practices, whereas the evils of neglect and institutionalization of children are addressed comparatively less so in their analysis.[29] Some do not acknowledge the harmful consequences of large sums of Western money that are involved in the intercountry adoption system but rather consider them as "significant new funds to poor orphanages in sending countries"[30] that relieves the children's home countries of the burden of support.[31]

2.3 Regulationists

Regulationists advance the view that seems to lie somewhere in the middle of the abolitionists' and promoters' positions. They are concerned about the commercial character of the intercountry adoption system and its vulnerability to abusive practices. Unlike the aboli-

25 *Ibid.*, p. 223.

26 E. Bartholet (2007). "International Adoption: The Child's Story." Georgia State University Law Review, 24, 333-379, pp. 355-356.

27 *Ibid.*

28 S. Dillon (2003). "Making Legal Regimes for Intercountry Adoption Reflect Human Rights Principles: Transforming the United Nations Convention on the Rights of the Child with the Hague Convention on Intercountry Adoption." Boston University International Law Journal, 21, 179-257, pp. 233-234; E. Bartholet (2007). "International Adoption: Thoughts on the Human Rights Issue." Buffalo Human Rights Law Review, 13, 151-203, p. 186.

29 S. Dillon (2003). "Making Legal Regimes for Intercountry Adoption Reflect Human Rights Principles: Transforming the United Nations Convention on the Rights of the Child with the Hague Convention on Intercountry Adoption." Boston University International Law Journal, 21, 179-257, p. 196.

30 E. Bartholet (2007). "International Adoption: Thoughts on the Human Rights Issue." Buffalo Human Rights Law Review, 13, 151-203, p. 184.

31 *Ibid.*, p. 185.

tionists, however, limiters claim that prohibiting intercountry adoption would not be an appropriate response to the irregularities.[32] Kapstein explains the negative consequences of a ban:

> Moratoriums have been imposed on adoptions from Cambodia and Romania, for example, but they only succeeded in denying orphans there a chance to find families while shifting the demand to new suppliers such as Russia and China.[33]

Instead, regulationists point to the need to reform the system as a means of eliminating illicit adoption practices.[34] They recognize intercountry adoption as a possible childcare solution for parentless children. Yet, contrary to the view of promoters, many limiters do not categorically reject foster and institutional care solutions for parentless children, but rather they assert that it might be a viable childcare option in individual cases. Carlson, for example, claims that:

> There may be some children for whom intercountry adoption is inadvisable. Older children who have acquired a deep sense of cultural and community identity might be poorly suited for intercountry adoption. For such children, institutionalization or other local alternatives, such as foster care or some other variant, might be the preferred method of care.[35]

The acceptance of intercountry adoption in limited cases, as well as the belief that abusive adoption practices can be effectively prevented, led to the resolution of the Hague Conven-

---

32 For example, D. M. Smolin (2006). "Child Laundering: How the Intercountry Adoption System Legitimizes and Incentivizes the Practices of Buying, Trafficking, Kidnapping, and Stealing Children." The Wayne Law Review, 52, 1, 113-200, p. 117; E. J. Graff (2008). "The lie we love." Foreign Policy, November/December, 58-66, available at http://www.brandeis.edu/investigate/adoption/docs/FPFinalTheLieWeLove.pdf, p. 66; N. B. Graff (2000). "Intercountry Adoption and the Convention on the Rights of the Child: Can the Free Market in Children be Controlled?" Syracuse Journal of International Law & Commerce, 27, 405-430; E. B. Kapstein (2003). "The baby trade." Foreign Affairs, 82, 6, 115-125.

33 E. B. Kapstein (2003). "The baby trade." Foreign Affairs, 82, 6, 115-125, p. 115.

34 See, for example, D. M. Smolin (2006). "Child Laundering: How the Intercountry Adoption System Legitimizes and Incentivizes the Practices of Buying, Trafficking, Kidnapping, and Stealing Children." The Wayne Law Review, 52, 1, 113-200, p. 117; E. J. Graff (2008). "The lie we love." Foreign Policy, November/December, 58-66, available at http://www.brandeis.edu/investigate/adoption/docs/FPFinalTheLieWeLove.pdf, p. 66; N. B. Graff (2000). "Intercountry Adoption and the Convention on the Rights of the Child: Can the Free Market in Children be Controlled?" Syracuse Journal of International Law & Commerce, 27, 405-430.

35 R. R. Carlson (1994). "The Emerging Law of Introductory Adoptions: An Analysis of the Hague Conference on Intercountry Adoption." Tulsa Law Journal, 30, 243-304, p. 258.

tion on Protection and Co-operation in Respect of Intercountry Adoption in 1993 (hereinafter Hague Convention).[36]

3 Background and Development of the UNCRC

On 20 November 1989, after nearly a decade of preparatory work, the United Nations General Assembly unanimously adopted the Convention on the Rights of the Child which came into force on 2 September 1990. The Convention is not the first international instrument on the rights of children.[37] In 1924, the Assembly of the League of Nations endorsed the Declaration of the Rights of the Child in reaction to World War I, which caused considerable suffering to many children. After World War II, which, too, caused enormous pain to numerous children, the General Assembly of the newly established United Nations took immediate efforts to set up a revised Declaration of the Right of the Child that was finally adopted on 20 November 1959.[38]

The UNCRC goes further than the preceding children's rights instruments. It creates new rights under international law for children, including the child's right to preserve his or her identity and the right of indigenous children to practice their own culture.[39] Furthermore, it lays down rights in a global treaty which had hitherto only been acknowledged in case law under regional human rights treaties, for example, the child's right to be heard in any proceedings affecting the child and to have his or her views taken into account.[40] Finally, the Convention creates binding standards in areas where previously there were only non-binding recommendations, notably the safeguards in adoption procedures.[41]

The UNCRC is based on four core principles: non-discrimination, the child's best interests, the right to life, survival, and development and the respect for the views of the child. These principles provide the foundation for the recognition and protection of a number of civil, social, economic, cultural and political rights that are to be enjoyed by children everywhere: the right to survival, to develop to the fullest, to protection from harmful influences, abuse and exploitation and to participate fully in family, cultural and social life. The Convention sets out these rights in 54 articles as well as in two Optional

36 Hague Convention on Protection of Children and Co-Operation in Respect of Intercountry Adoption, May 29, 1993, 32 I.L.M. 1134, Art

37 D. McGoldrick (1991). "The United Nations Convention on the Rights of the Child." International Journal of Law and the Family, 5, 132-169, p. 132.

38 S. Detrick (1999). "A Commentary on the United Nations Convention on the Rights of the Child." Martinus Nijhoff Publishers, Leiden, pp. 13-14.

39 Art. 8 and 30 UNCRC.

40 Art. 12 *leg. cit.*

41 Art. 21; G. Van Bueren (1998). "The International Law on the Rights of the Child." Martinus Nijhoff Publishers, The Hague, p. 16.

Protocols: the Optional Protocol on the Involvement of Children in Armed Conflict[42] and the Optional Protocol on the Sale of Children, Child Prostitution and Child Pornography.[43] The UNCRC views children's rights through the lens of shared and mutually dependent state and parental responsibilities, which are meant to ensure that all children are provided with the basic necessities and have the best opportunity to fulfil their potential.

The UNCRC has received unprecedented support by many states. This is shown by the speed at which it has been ratified. Alston and Parker have noted, for example, that no other treaty, especially in the field of human rights law, has "been ratified by so many states in such an extraordinarily short periode of time".[44] Another indication of support is the number of countries that have become States Parties to this Convention. To date, 196 countries have ratified the UNCRC,[45] making it one of the most widely accepted international treaties. Due to the universal ratification of the Convention, there appears to be a consensus within the international community as to the need to acknowledge and protect children's rights. Yet, this universal normative agreement is called into question by the number and nature of reservations that were made by states upon their ratification. Many of the 58 reservations to the Convention are very broad in nature as is illustrated, for instance, by the reservation expressed by Kuwait "on all provisions of the Convention that are incompatible with the laws of Islamic Shari'a and the local statutes in effect". Furthermore, although the UNCRC has been ratified by nearly every nation in the world, many states lack the resources that are necessary to implement its provisions effectively. Millions of children are denied their basic rights laid down in the treaty: e.g. they do not have access to education, food, clean drinking water or medical care.

4 FAMILY AND THE RIGHTS OF THE CHILD

In the Preamble to the UNCRC, the family is acknowledged as "the fundamental group of society and the natural environment for the growth and well-being of all its members and particularly children". The Committee on the Rights of the Child (hereinafter Committee) views the family as "the basic institution in society for the survival, protection and development of the child"[46] and as crucial to the realization of the child's rights and needs.

42 Optional Protocol to the Convention on the Rights of the Child on the involvement of children in armed conflict, G. A. Res. A/RES/54/263 of 25 May 2000.

43 Optional Protocol to the United Nations Convention on the Rights of the Child on the Sale of Children, Child Prostitution and Child Pornography, G.A. Res. 263, U.N. GAOR, 54th Sess., Supp. No. 49, U.N. Doc. A/RES/54/263 (2000).

44 P. Alston and S. Parker (1992). "Children, Rights and The Law." Oxford University Press, p. viii.

45 See http://indicators.ohchr.org/ (last accessed on 03.08.2018). The United States of America is the only country that has signed but has not ratified the UNCRC.

46 Committee on the Rights of the Child, Report on the 7th Session: Role of the Family in the Promotion of the Rights of the Child. Excerpted from UN Doc CRC/C/24 (Oct. 10th, 1994), para. 2.1.

In the Report on the 5th session, the Committee stated: "The civil rights of the child begin within the family [...]. The family is an essential agent for creating awareness and preservation of human rights, and respect for human values, cultural identity and heritage, and other civilisation".[47] Articles 3(2), 5, 7(1), 9, 18 and 27 of the UNCRC provide a framework for the relationship between the child, his or her parents and family and the State. They emphasize the primacy of the child's parents and family, and they oblige the State to support the family whenever it is in need. Article 9 thereof places strict limits on state intervention and any separation of the child from his or her parents or other primary caregivers.

4.1 *The Definition of the Family*

The UNCRC defines the term 'child' in Article 1 thereof, but it lacks a definition of the term 'family'. This is for cultural-anthropological reasons. The concept of the family varies over time and between different cultures.[48] Throughout the world, children are brought up in a variety of family arrangements: in nuclear families, single-parent families, polygamous families or extended families.

The nuclear family (composed of mother, father, and children) is a comparatively recent family structure that emerged after the Industrial Revolution in Western countries.[49] Due to the development of an industrialised society, members of the family began working separately and moving away from the family home for the purposes of obtaining work. The modal structure of families has consequently changed from extended to nuclear, and its primary functions have shifted from social-institutional to emotional-supportive.[50]

Yet, in many African, South American and Asian societies, children are raised in extended families which extend beyond the nuclear family, including relatives and close friends of the family with whom the child has a family-like relationship (also referred to as fictive kin).[51] In many societies, there is a sense that the children 'belong' to their community.[52] Child care is, therefore, a communal affair, whereby all members of the extended

47 UN Committee on the Rights of the Child (1994). "Report on the 5th Session." 08.03.1994, CRC/C/24, para. 2.2.

48 R. Hodgkin and P. Newell (2007). "Implementation Handbook for the Convention on the Rights of the Child." UNICEF (3rd ed.), p. 77; International Social Service (2014). "The concept of 'family': The challenge of protecting children in and out of families." Geneva, Nr. 187 November – December.

49 V. L. Bengtson (2001). "The Burgess Award Lecture: Beyond the Nuclear Family: The Increasing Importance of Multigenerational Bond." Journal of Marriage and Family, 63, 1, 1-16.

50 *Ibid.*

51 B. Broad (2007). "Kinship Care: Providing Positive and Safe Care for Children Living Away from Home." Save the Children UK, p. 2; R. Högbacka (2014). "Intercountry Adoption, Countries of Origin, and Biological Families, Report for Thematic Area 2 International Forum on Intercountry Adoption and Global Surrogacy 11-13 August 2014." Working Paper No. 598, International Institute of Social Studies, pp. 4-5.

52 UNICEF (2006). "Alternative Care for Children in Without Primary caregivers in Tsunami-affected countries: Indonesia, Malaysia, Myanmar and Thailand." Available at https://www.unicef.org/eapro/Alterna-

family, tribe or clan share child-rearing responsibilities, especially in crisis times. Because of this shared responsibility, in some African societies, for instance, there is no terminological distinction between a 'father' and an 'uncle' or a 'brother' and a 'cousin'.[53] Individual members of an extended family other than the biological parents can, therefore, be as important to a child for the simple reason that they are or have been involved in the child's development. Child care by members of the extended family is the most common form of out-of-home care option in the world.[54] Children may live with kinship carers because their parents have to work (abroad) and cannot take care of them or because they have lost their parents. In cases where a child's parents have died, care is in many times automatically provided by members of the extended family or community.[55] In many regions in Africa, the notion of an 'orphan' did therefore not exist before Western humanitarian interventions which aimed to save orphans, as there were always extended kin and community networks absorbing such children.[56]

The UNCRC does not seek to impose a universal definition of the concept of 'family' that is to apply to all cultures at all times. According to the Implementation Handbook for the UNCRC, the term 'family' is to be understood broadly, "reflect[ing] the wide variety of kinship and community arrangements within which children are brought up around the world".[57] In its General Comment No. 7 on 'Implementing child rights in early childhood', the Committee recognized that "'family' [...] refers to a variety of arrangements that can provide for young children's care, nurturance, and development, including the nuclear family, the extended family, and other traditional and modern community-based arrangements, provided these are consistent with the children's rights and best interests".[58]

---

tive_care_for_children.pdf, p. 68; A. Ansah-Koi (2006). "Care of orphans: Fostering interventions for children whose parents die of AIDS in Ghana." Families in Society: The Journal of Contemporary Social Services, 87, 4, 555-564; see also J. L. Roby (2004). "Understanding Sending Country's Traditions and Policies In International Adoptions: Avoiding Legal and Cultural Pitfalls." Journal of Law & Family Studies, 6, 2, 303-322.

53 J.A.M. Cobbah (1987). "African Values and the Human Rights Debate: An African Perspective." Human Rights Quarterly, 9, 309-331, p. 320.

54 D. Tolfree (2006). "A Sense of Belonging: Case studies in positive care options for children." Save the Children UK, pp. 14; UNICEF and International Social Service (2004). "Improving Protection for Children Without Parental Care - Kinship Care, An Issue for International Standards." Available at https://better-carenetwork.org/sites/default/files/Improving%20Protection%20for%20Children%20Without%20Parental%20Care%20-%20Kinship%20Care%20-%20An%20Issue%20for%20International%20Standards.pdf.

55 *Ibid.*

56 K. E. Cheney (2014). "Conflicting Protectionist and Participation Models of Children's Rights: Their Consequences for Uganda's Orphans and Vulnerable Children", in A. Twum-Danso and N. Ansell (eds.), *Children's Lives in an Era of Children's Rights: The Progress of the Convention on the Rights of the Child in Africa*. Routledge, New York, 17-33.

57 R. Hodgkin and P. Newell (2007). "Implementation Handbook for the Convention on the Rights of the Child." UNICEF (3rd ed.), p. 76.

58 Committee on the Rights of the Child. General Comment No. 7: Implementing child rights in early childhood. UN Doc CRC/C/GC/7/Rev.1 (Sep. 20th, 2006), para. 15.

The term 'family' in the UNCRC therefore not only refers to the parents and others who are legally responsible for the child (the nuclear family), but it also covers to the extended family or community where they are recognized by local custom.

4.2 *The Child's Right to be Cared for by His or Her Parents*

Article 7(1) provides the child, *inter alia*, the right "to be cared for by his or her parents" as far as this is possible. According to the Implementation Handbook for the UNCRC, the definition of 'parents' does not only include genetic or birth parents – that is the mother who gave birth and the father who claimed paternity of the child through partnership with the mother at the time of birth (or whatever the social definition of father is within the culture)[59] – but also the child's psychological parents who act as the child's primary care-givers throughout infancy and childhood, such as adoptive of foster parents.[60]

The exercise of this right may not be possible if the parents are dead, or where they have rejected or abandoned the child or if the separation of the child from his or her parents was necessary for the child's best interests. Article 7(1) is strongly related to Article 9(1) which requires "that a child shall not be separated from his or her parents against their will, except when [...] such separation is necessary for the best interests of the child" (see section 4.6 for more details in this regard).

4.3 *The Primacy of the Child's Family and Parents*

Whereas Article 7(1) refers to the child's right, Article 5 is framed in terms of the rights and duties of the child's family.[61] It obliges States Parties "to respect the responsibilities, rights, and duties of parents or, where applicable, the members of the extended family or community as provided for by local custom, legal guardians or other persons legally responsible for the child, to provide [...] appropriate direction and guidance in the exercise by the child of the rights recognized in the present Convention". The clear intent of Article 5 is to protect whoever is primarily responsible for the child, irrespective of the nature of their exact legal relationship to the child. The wording 'extended family or community as provided for by local custom' was inserted in order to accord adequate recognition to the role of extended family and community members when parental care is not available, taking into consideration that cultures, traditions and customs in many countries and areas provide for such a role. The qualifying phrase 'as provided for by local custom' infers

59 R. Hodgkin and P. Newell (2007). "Implementation Handbook for the Convention on the Rights of the Child." UNICEF (3rd ed.), pp. 105-106.

60 *Ibid.*

61 *Ibid.*, p. 108.

that Article 5 would not be applicable in a situation in which the notion of the responsibility of the extended family or of the community for a child is not recognized by local custom (see also above, section 4.1).[62]

Article 5 is closely related to Article 18(1) which provides that "[p]arents or, as the case may be, legal guardians have the primary responsibility for the upbringing and development of the child" as well as to Article 27(2) which states that "parent(s) or others responsible for the child have the primary responsibility to secure, within their abilities and financial capacities, the conditions of living necessary for the child's development". Whereas Article 5 makes a clear statement supporting the primacy of the *family*, Articles 18(1) and 27(2) recognize the primacy of the *parents*.

The aim of the latter two provisions was to protect parents or legal guardians against excessive intervention by the State,[63] as well as against social structures in which the role of parents may be diminished to the detriment of children.[64] Furthermore, they are meant to indicate that parents could not expect the state to always intervene because the upbringing and development of their children was primarily their responsibility.[65] The use of the term "primary responsibility" suggests a "secondary responsibility" of the state to secure the child's needs and rights if their parents and families cannot manage this themselves.[66]

4.4 *The State's Responsibility to Support the Child's Family and Parents*

The "secondary responsibility" of the state is explicated in Article 18(2), Article 3(2) as well as in Article 27(3). Article 18(2) obliges States Parties to "render appropriate assistance to parents and legal guardians in the performance of their child-rearing responsibilities". This provision reflects Article 3(2)[67] which obliges States Parties to take all appropriate legislative and administrative measures, taking into account the rights and duties of the child's parents, legal guardians, or other individuals who are legally responsible for him or her, to ensure the child such protection and care as is necessary for his or her wellbeing.

---

62 S. Detrick (1999). "A Commentary on the United Nations Convention on the Rights of the Child." Martinus Nijhoff Publishers, Leiden, p. 122.

63 *Ibid.*, p. 459.

64 For example, the Committee has expressed concern about social structures in the Democratic Republic of the Congo: "The Committee [...] is concerned [...] at the increasing practice of ‚bi-linear' families under which a community leader assumes parental responsibilities for children and that this practice is replacing parents and has a negative impact on children".

65 S. Detrick (1999). "A Commentary on the United Nations Convention on the Rights of the Child." Martinus Nijhoff Publishers, Leiden, p. 459.

66 D. McGoldrick (1991). "The United Nations Convention on the Rights of the Child." International Journal of Law and the Family, 5, 132-169, p. 143.

67 S. Detrick (1999). "A Commentary on the United Nations Convention on the Rights of the Child." Martinus Nijhoff Publishers, Leiden, p. 94.

Similarly, Article 27(3) requires States Parties to take appropriate measures to assist parents and others responsible for the child to implement the child's right to a standard of living that is adequate for his or her development. If they lack the requisite resources, states must provide "material assistance and support programmes, particularly with regard to nutrition, clothing and housing". The UN Guidelines for the Alternative Care of Children emphasizes that:

> States should pursue politics that ensure support for families in meeting their responsibilities towards the child and promote the right of the child to have a relationship with both parents. These policies should address the root causes of child abandonment, relinquishment and separation of the child from his/her family by ensuring, inter alia, the right to birth registration [provided by Article 7(1)] and access to adequate housing and to basic health, education and social welfare services [...]. States should develop and implement consistent and mutually reinforcing family-oriented policies designed to promote and strengthen parent's ability to care for their children.[68]

The phrase "in accordance with the national conditions and within their means" in Article 27(3) thereof implies that the obligations imposed on States Parties are subject to the general obligations clause that is contained in the second sentence of Article 4. According to this provision, States Parties are obliged to take all appropriate legislative, administrative and other measures to implement the rights that are recognized in the UNCRC. However, the second sentence suggests a distinction between civil and political rights and economic, social and cultural rights by providing that: "With regard to economic, social and cultural rights, States Parties shall undertake such measures to the maximum extent of their available resources and, where needed, within the framework of international cooperation". In its General Comment No. 5, the Committee explains that:

> The second sentence of article 4 reflects a realistic acceptance that lack of resources – financial and other resources – can hamper the full implementation of economic, social and cultural rights in some States; this introduces the concept of "progressive realization" of such rights: States need to be able to demonstrate that they have implemented "to the maximum extent of their available resources" and, where necessary, have sought international cooperation. When States ratify the Convention, they take upon themselves obligations not only to implement it within their jurisdiction, but also to contribute, through international cooperation, to global implementation. [...] Whatever their eco-

68 Guidelines for the Alternative Care of Children. UN Doc A/Res/64/142 (Feb. 24th, 2010), para. 32-33.

> nomic circumstances, States are required to undertake all possible measures towards the realization of the rights of the child, paying special attention to the most disadvantaged groups.[69]

The concept of 'progressive realization' of economic, social and cultural rights is reflected in Article 2(1) of the International Covenant on Economic, Social and Cultural Rights (ICESCR). The wording used in this provision is similar to the second sentence of Article 4.[70] The Committee on the Rights of the Child entirely concurs with the Committee on Economic, Social and Cultural Rights in asserting that "even where the available resources are demonstrably inadequate, the obligation remains for a State party to strive to ensure the widest possible enjoyment of the relevant rights under the prevailing circumstances [...]". Whatever their economic circumstances, states are required to undertake all possible measures towards the realization of the rights of the child, paying special attention to the most disadvantaged groups.[71]

4.5 *The Child's Right to Privacy and Family Life*

Article 16 provides the child with the right to be protected by law against arbitrary or unlawful interference with his or her privacy, family, home or correspondence or unlawful attacks on his or her honour and reputation. This provision mirrors Article 17 of the International Covenant on Civil and Political Rights (hereinafter ICCPR),[72] and Article 8 of the European Convention on Human Rights, and is similar to the wording found in Article 12 of the Universal Declaration of Human Rights (hereinafter UDHR).[73] In the context of intercountry adoption, the child's right to protection against arbitrary interference with her family is of particular importance.

---

69 UN Committee on the Rights of the Child (2003). "General Comment No. 5: General Measures of Implementation of the Convention on the Rights of the Child (arts. 4, 42 and 44, para. 6)." 27.11.2003, CRC/GC/2003/5, para. 7-8.

70 Art. 2(1) ICESCR: "Each State Party to the present Covenant undertakes to take steps, individually and through international assistance and cooperation, especially economic and technical, to the maximum of its available resources, with a view to achieving progressively the full realization of the rights recognized in the present Covenant by all appropriate means, including particularly the adoption of legislative measures."

71 R. Hodgkin and P. Newell (2007). "Implementation Handbook for the Convention on the Rights of the Child." UNICEF (3rd ed.), p. 52.

72 Art. 17 ICCPR: "1. No one shall be subjected to arbitrary or unlawful interference with his privacy, family, home or correspondence, nor to unlawful attacks on his honour and reputation. 2. Everyone has the right to the protection of the law against such interference or attacks."

73 Art. 12 UDHR: "No one shall be subjected to arbitrary interference with his privacy, family, home or correspondence, nor to attacks upon his honour and reputation. Everyone has the right to the protection of the law against such interference or attacks".

The term 'family' is interpreted widely by both the UNCRC[74] and the Human Rights Committee.[75] According to the Human Rights Committee, the term 'unlawful' in Article 17 of the ICCPR means that no interference can take place except in cases envisaged by the law.[76] Interference that is authorized by states can only take place on the basis of law, which itself must comply with the provisions, aims and objectives of the ICCPR.[77]

The expression 'arbitrary' is intended to guarantee that even interference provided for by law should be in accordance with the provisions, aims and objectives of the Covenant and they should be, in any event, reasonable in the particular circumstances.[78] The relevant legislation must specify, in detail, the precise circumstances in which interference is to be permitted. A decision to make use of such authorized interference must only be made by the authority that is designated under the law and on a case-by-case basis.[79]

The Human Rights Committee has emphasized that States Parties are under a duty themselves not to engage in interferences which are inconsistent with Article 17 of the ICCPR and to provide the legislative framework prohibiting such acts by natural or legal persons.[80]

4.6 *Separation of the Child from His or Her Parents*

Article 16 strongly relates to Article 9(1) which provides the child the right not be separated from his or her *parents* against their will. According to Hodgkin and Newell, the words 'against their will' refer either to the parents' will or to the parents' and the child's will together.[81] The exercise of this right may be restricted, namely when "such separation is necessary for the best interests of the child". This complies with the general principle of the best interests of the child embodied in Article 3(1) (see section 6.2). Article 9(1), sentence 2, suggests two examples of when separation may be necessary for the child's best interests: if the parents are abusive or neglectful, or when the parents are living separately and a

74 Art. 5 UNCRC clarifies that "family" includes "parents or, where applicable, the members of the extended family or community as provided for by local custom, legal guardians or other persons legally responsible for the child".

75 UN Commission on Human Rights (1988). "CCPR General Comment No. 16: Article 17 (Right to Privacy), The Right to Respect of Privacy, Family, Home and Correspondence, and Protection of Honour and Reputation." Adopted at the 32nd Session of the Human Rights Committee on 08.04.1988, para. 5 states: "Regarding the term "family", the objectives of the Covenant require that for purposes of article 17 this term be given a broad interpretation to include all those comprising the family as understood in the society of the State party concerned."

76 *Ibid.*, para. 3.

77 *Ibid.*

78 *Ibid.*, para. 4.

79 *Ibid.*, para. 8.

80 *Ibid.*, para. 9.

81 R. Hodgkin and P. Newell (2007). "Implementation Handbook for the Convention on the Rights of the Child." UNICEF (3rd ed.), p. 122.

decision must be made as to the child's principal place of residence. The removal of a child from his or her parents should be considered as an *ultima ratio* measure and should, whenever possible, be temporary and for the shortest possible duration.[82]

The decision to separate the child from her parents must be made by the "competent authorities, subject to judicial review, in accordance with applicable laws and procedures". The reference to 'competent authorities' indicates that States Parties are required to have public authorities that are specially designated as competent to make decisions pertaining to the separation of a child from her parents.[83] Such authorities must have the skills to determine, on the basis of the relevant evidence, what is in the child's best interest.[84]

The phrase 'subject to judicial review' carries with it expectations about the principles of natural justice and fair hearings. According to Hodgkin and Newell, these principles include that: (a) the judges have no personal interest in the case, (b) they are as well informed as possible about all the circumstances of the case, (c) they provide reasons for their rulings and (d) all parties are given access to all relevant evidence and are being heard.[85]

The reference to 'applicable law and procedures' infers that States Parties are obliged to enact laws specifying the grounds on which children can be removed from their parents and to lay down a separation procedure.[86] If laws leave the criteria for separation open to judicial discretion, the judge must render an objective decision about what is in the child's best interests.[87] All laws and procedures must be free from "discrimination of any kind, irrespective of the child's or his or her parent's [...] race, colour, sex, language, religion, political or other opinion, national, ethnic or social origin, property, disability, birth or other status" (Article 2(1)). Therefore, homelessness or poverty of the child's parents cannot be grounds in themselves to remove the child against their will.[88] Rather, Article 18(2), Article 3(2) as well as in Article 27(3) oblige States Parties to provide appropriate assistance to disadvantaged families so as to help them keep and adequately care for their children. This is emphasized in the UN Guidelines for the Alternative Care of Children as follows: "Financial and material poverty alone, or conditions directly and uniquely imputable to such poverty, should never be a justification for the removal of a child from

---

82 Resolution adopted by the General Assembly. 64/142. Guidelines for the Alternative Care of Children. UN Doc A/Res/64/142 (Feb. 24th, 2010), para. 14.

83 S. Detrick (1999). "A Commentary on the United Nations Convention on the Rights of the Child." Martinus Nijhoff Publishers, Leiden, p. 171.

84 R. Hodgkin and P. Newell (2007). "Implementation Handbook for the Convention on the Rights of the Child." UNICEF (3rd ed.), p. 127.

85 *Ibid.*, p. 128.

86 S. Detrick (1999). "A Commentary on the United Nations Convention on the Rights of the Child." Martinus Nijhoff Publishers, Leiden, p. 171.

87 R. Hodgkin and P. Newell (2007). "Implementation Handbook for the Convention on the Rights of the Child." UNICEF (3rd ed.), 129.

88 *Ibid.*, p. 123.

parental care, for receiving a child into alternative care, or for preventing his/her reintegration, but should be seen as a signal for the need to provide appropriate support to the family".[89] This is why the Committee recommends that "States parties take all necessary measures to raise the standard of living among families living in poverty, inter alia, through implementing poverty reduction strategies and community development [...]".[90]

Article 9(2) provides for a procedural right, asserting that all "interested parties shall be given an opportunity to participate in the proceedings and make their views known". 'Interested parties' includes any child affected by the proceedings pursuant to Article 9(1) (this right can be derived from Article 12(2), providing that the child is given the opportunity to be heard in any judicial and administrative proceedings affecting the child, either directly or through a representative or an appropriate body, in a manner that is consistent with the procedural rules of national law), both parents as well as members of the child's extended family, or professionals with specialist knowledge of the child.[91]

If the child has to be separated from his or her parents, the state should first seek placement within the child's wider family, as it is defined in Article 5,[92] before looking for alternative childcare solutions (section Article 5(1)). Article 4 of the 1986 Declaration on Social and Legal Principles relating to the Protection and Welfare of Children, with Special Reference to Foster Placement and Adoption Nationally and Internationally states that: "When care by the child's own parents is unavailable or inappropriate, care by relatives of the child's parents, by another substitute – foster or adoptive – family or, if necessary, by an appropriate institution should be considered".

As per Article 9(3), a child that is separated from one or both parents has the right to maintain personal relations and direct contact with both parents on a regular basis, except if it is contrary to the child's best interests. This provision is reflected in Article 18(1) which provides that both parents have the primary responsibility for the upbringing and development of the child.[93] Failure to keep children in contact with their parents may occur when the state makes arrangements for them to live far away from home, for example in institutions, specialist schools, street children projects, foster care, or where they are placed with an adoptive family living in another city or even in another country.[94]

89 Resolution adopted by the General Assembly. 64/142. Guidelines for the Alternative Care of Children. UN Doc A/Res/64/142 (Feb. 24th, 2010), para. 15.

90 UN Committee on the Rights of the Child (2006). "Report on the 40th session." 17.03.2006, CRC/C/153, para. 659.

91 R. Hodgkin and P. Newell (2007). "Implementation Handbook for the Convention on the Rights of the Child (3rd edition)." UNICEF, p. 129.

92 Resolution adopted by the General Assembly. 64/142. Guidelines for the Alternative Care of Children. UN Doc A/Res/64/142 (Feb. 24th, 2010), para. 18.

93 R. Hodgkin and P. Newell (2007). "Implementation Handbook for the Convention on the Rights of the Child (3rd edition)." UNICEF, p. 130.

94 *Ibid.*, p. 123.

4.7 The Child's Right to know His or Her Origin and Identity

Article 7 also provides the child the right to know of his or her origin. This right is to be understood in relation to the more general right to preserve one's identity that is laid down in Article 8.[95] The UNCRC does not define the term 'identity', but it provides a non-exhaustive list of elements that are fundamental to its preservation, namely "nationality, name and family relations". According to Hodgkin and Newell, these include the child's personal history since birth (life place, caregivers, the reasons why crucial decisions were taken), the child's culture, religion and language (reflecting Article 30), as well as the child's physical appearance, abilities, gender identity and sexual orientation.[96]

The right to identity preservation is of particular importance when the child is separated from the parents.[97] Article 8(2) provides that where children are "illegally deprived of some or all of the elements of their identity States Parties will be obliged to provide appropriate assistance and protection with a view to speedily re-establishing their identities". The concept of 'illegality' is key to this paragraph. 'Illegally' applies both when the deprivation is illegal under domestic law and when the deprivation of identity is contrary to international law. According to Van Bueren, interpreting Article 8 as to only include the former would open up a dangerous loophole.[98]

The child's right to know his or her origin is also derived from Article 17 ICCPR, which guarantees the right to privacy and which is complemented by Article 24(2) and (3) thereof which provides that every child shall be registered immediately after birth. This right is also provided by Article 8 ECHR which protects the right to respect for one's family and privacy (see section 4.5). According to the European Court of Human Rights (hereinafter ECtHR), Article 8 ECHR covers the right to know one's parent's identity, as well as the circumstances of one's birth.[99]

The ICPPED also deals with the preservation of the child's identity. Article 1 thereof lays down that "no one shall be subjected to enforced disappearance", and Article 25 thereof obliges its Contracting States to criminalize "the wrongful removal of children who are subjected to enforced disappearance, children whose father, mother or legal guardian is subjected to enforced disappearance or children born during the captivity of a mother

95 S. Besson (2007). "Enforcing the Child's Right to know her Origins: Contrasting Approaches under the Convention on the Rights of the Child and the European Convention on Human Rights." International Journal of Law, Policy, and the Family, 21, 137-159, p. 141.

96 R. Hodgkin and P. Newell (2007). "Implementation Handbook for the Convention on the Rights of the Child (3rd edition)." UNICEF, p. 115.

97 See UN Committee on the Rights of the Child (2006). "Report on the 40th session." 17.03.2006, CRC/C/153, para. 680.

98 G. Van Bueren (1998). "The International Law on the Rights of the Child." Martinus Nijhoff Publishers, The Hague, p. 119.

99 See Odièvre vs. France, 13.02.2003, No. 42326/98; Jäggi vs. Switzerland, 13.07.2007, No. 58757/00.

subjected to enforced disappearance", and "the falsification, concealment or destruction of documents attesting to the true identity" of these children.

5 Children Deprived of Their Family Environment

Article 20 obliges States Parties to provide a child who is temporarily or permanently unable to live with her family "special protection and assistance" and to "ensure alternative care". It is worth noting that this provision refers to *family* in the wider sense, as defined in Article 5 (i.e. "parents or, where applicable, the members of the extended family or community as provided for by local custom, legal guardians or other persons legally responsible for the child"), and not to *parents*. Consequently, a child is only deprived of her family environment if (a) the child's wider family is dead or (b) has rejected or abandoned the child or (c) if the state authorities have decided that separating the child from her parents was necessary for the child's best interests, according to Article 9(1), and the child cannot be allowed to remain in the wider family as this would, too, be contrary to her best interests. Only then may alternative childcare solutions, as laid down in Article 20(2) as well as Article 21, be considered.

5.1 Alternative Child Care Solutions

Where the child's own family is unwilling or unable – even with appropriate support (!) – to provide adequate care for the child, the state ensure an alternative childcare solution must in accordance with its national laws (Article 20(2)).[100] This could include, *inter alia*, foster placement, *Kafalah* of Islamic Law, adoption or, if necessary, placement in a suitable institution (Article 20(3)). It was not felt appropriate to impose on States Parties legal institutions such as foster placement or adoption. The method of care will partly depend on national traditions. For example, Islamic law does not recognize adoption but has developed instead the concept of *kafalah* – a permanent form of foster care that generally stops short of the child taking the family name or having inheritance rights.[101] This led to the insertion of the phrase "in accordance with their national laws".[102]

Commentators agree that the order of the alternative childcare solutions listed in Article 20(3) as well as the qualifying phrase "if necessary" reflects the UNCRC's preference

100 Guidelines for the Alternative Care of Children. UN Doc A/Res/64/142 (Feb. 24th, 2010), para. 5.

101 Declaration on Social and Legal Principles relating to the Protection and Welfare of Children, with Special Reference to Foster Placement and Adoption Nationally and Internationally. UN Doc A/RES/41/85 (Dec. 3rd 1986), Preamble.

102 S. Detrick (1999). "A Commentary on the United Nations Convention on the Rights of the Child." Martinus Nijhoff Publishers, Leiden, pp. 335-336.

for placement within a substitute family over institutional care.[103] The UNCRC's Preamble also stresses the need for a child to grow up in a family environment,[104] which is considered to be one of the cornerstones of the Convention. Accordingly, the Committee has repeatedly stressed that the family environment provides the best possibilities for the harmonious development of a child and that placement in an institution should be a measure of last resort.[105] Institutional care may be necessary and in the child's best interests in exceptional cases, for example, if the child has suffered multiple foster care breakdowns already, or when large families of siblings wish to remain together, or if the child is already older, nearing independence.[106] Yet, institutional care is particularly inappropriate for younger children whose developmental needs require a permanent adult caregiver.

Promoters of intercountry adoption often stress that a child has a right to a family, referring to the UNCRC's Preamble which lays down that children "for the full and harmonious development of his or her personality, should grow up in a family environment, in an atmosphere of happiness, love, and understanding". Yet, whereas the UNCRC generally supports family-based child care solutions,[107] it does not lay down a child's right to a family. Van Bueren notes:

> [a]lthough children have a right under a variety of treaties to respect for family life, and to protection against unlawful interference with the family, children, as with adults, understandably, do not have a right to a family per se under international law.[108]

As a consequence, children do not have a right to be adopted.[109] Their family-related rights only concern their existing family.

---

103 G. Van Bueren (1998). "The International Law on the Rights of the Child." Martinus Nijhoff Publishers, The Hague, p. 94; S. Detrick (1999). "A Commentary on the United Nations Convention on the Rights of the Child." Martinus Nijhoff Publishers, Leiden, p. 336; R. Hodgkin and P. Newell (2007). "Implementation Handbook for the Convention on the Rights of the Child." UNICEF (3rd ed.), p. 284.

104 "Recognizing that the child, for the full and harmonious development of his or her personality, should grow up in a family environment, in an atmosphere of happiness, love and understanding."

105 UN Committee on the Rights of the Child (2000). "Report on the 24th Session: Concluding Observations on Kyrgyzstan." 09.08.2000, CRC/C/15/Add. 127, para. 36; UN Committee on the Rights of the Child (2006). "Report on the 40th session." 17.03.2006, CRC/C/153, para. 665-666; UN Committee on the Rights of the Child (2000). "Report on the 25th Session." 14.11.2000, CRC/C/100, para. 676.

106 See J. L. Roby (2007). "From Rhetoric to Best Practice: Children's Rights in Intercountry Adoption." Children's Legal Rights Journal, 27, 3, 48-71, p. 58, claiming that nations should provide children with the right to be adopted.

107 R. Hodgkin and P. Newell (2007). "Implementation Handbook for the Convention on the Rights of the Child." UNICEF (3rd ed.), p. 282.

108 G. Van Bueren (1998). "The International Law on the Rights of the Child." Martinus Nijhoff Publishers, The Hague, p. 93.

109 *Ibid.*, p. 95.

It follows that "When considering the available childcare solutions, due regard shall be paid to the desirability of continuity in a child's upbringing and to the child's ethnic, religious, cultural and linguistic background", as per to Article 20(3). 'Continuity of upbringing' implies continuity of contact between the child and his or her parents, family and the wider community, whenever this is possible.[110] It also means that the state should avoid multiple placements of the children in its care.[111] Finally, it denotes finding a foster or adoptive family from the same cultural background or ensuring that all or some staff members in an institution are from the same culture and speak the child's language.[112] Article 20(3) relates to Article 8 which grants the child the right identity preservation (see section 4.7).

5.2 *Adoption*

Article 21, which is closely related to Article 20, addresses the rights of children who are being adopted. It obliges the Contracting States to ensure that in all adoption arrangements, the best interests of the child are the paramount consideration (rather than only the primary consideration as in Article 3, see section 6.2).[113]

Article 21(a) entails minimum requirements for an adoption procedure. It obliges States Parties to "ensure that the adoption of a child is authorized only by competent authorities [...] in accordance with applicable law and procedures" (competent authorities' principle). The term 'Competent authorities' includes both judicial and professional authorities, such as trained social workers, as well as licensed and approved agencies. They shall render an adoption decision exclusively based upon existing laws and procedures that the state is obliged to enforce.[114]

Article 21(a) furthermore determines that the competent authorities shall determine "on the basis of all pertinent and reliable information, that the adoption is permissible in view of the child's status concerning parents, relatives and legal guardians". As was already explicated above (section 4.2.), the child's parents and family have the primary responsibility for the upbringing and development of the child and, if need be, they are entitled to assistance and support by the state. Accordingly, an adoption is only "permissible" if, (a)

110 *Ibid.*, p. 289.

111 *Ibid.*

112 *Ibid.*

113 Similarly, Article 5 of the 1986 UN Declaration on Social and Legal Principles relating to the Protection and Welfare of Children, with Special Reference to Foster Placement and Adoption Nationally and Internationally provides: "In all matters relating to the placement of the child outside the care of the child's own parents, the best interests of the child, particularly his or her need for affection and right to security and continuing care, should be the paramount consideration."

114 R. Hodgkin and P. Newell (2007). "Implementation Handbook for the Convention on the Rights of the Child." UNICEF (3rd ed.), p. 297.

the child's wider family is dead or (b) is unwilling – even with appropriate support – to care for the child or (c) if the state authorities have decided that separation of the child from her parents is necessary for the child's best interests, according to Article 9(1), and the child cannot be placed with other family members. If the child's parents and family are unwilling to care for the child, the competent authorities must establish that they "have given their informed consent to the adoption on the basis of such counselling as may be necessary". Consent must be given freely, without pressure and it should be free from financial or material compensation and not before birth or during the first week after delivery.[115] The child's views are not explicitly mentioned in the requirements relating to consent to an adoption; however, proper consideration of them is required according to Article 12.

Article 21(b) to (e) relate specifically to intercountry adoptions.[116] Article 21(b) provides that States Parties shall recognize "that intercountry adoption may be considered as an alternative means of child's care if the child cannot be placed in a foster or an adoptive family or cannot in any suitable manner be cared for in the child's country of origin".[117] Intercountry adoption must, therefore, be considered as a measure of last resort, placed behind all suitable domestic child care arrangements. Article 21(b) corresponds with Article 20(3), requiring that due regard be paid to "the desirability of continuity in a child's upbringing and to the child's ethnic, religious, cultural and linguistic background", as well as with Article 8(1) which grants the child the right "to preserve his or her identity" (see section 4.7). Together, these provisions establish the 'subsidiarity principle' for intercountry adoptions, which is also provided in the Hague Convention, whereby Article 4(b) thereof states that intercountry adoption should only take place "after possibilities for placement of the child within the State of origin have been given due consideration".

Scholars generally agree that priority should be given to finding a suitable family in the child's country of origin. However, the question as to what should happen with a child if a domestic family cannot be found is disputed. Is institutional care in the child's country of origin a childcare measure that can be considered as "suitable" according to Article 21(b) and that should be preferred over intercountry adoption? This question is closely linked to the question as to which rights laid down in the UNCRC are to be prioritized if

---

115 International Social Service (1999). The Rights of the Child in Internal and Intercountry Adoption: Ethics and Principles - Guidelines for Practice, para. 6.

116 N. B. Graff (2000). "Intercountry Adoption and the Convention on the Rights of the Child: Can the Free Market in Children be Controlled?" Syracuse Journal of International Law & Commerce, 27, 405-430, p. 416.

117 Similarly, Article 17 of the 1986 UN Declaration on Social and Legal Principles relating to the Protection and Welfare of Children, with Special Reference to Foster Placement and Adoption Nationally and Internationally, provides that "[i]f a child cannot be placed in a foster or an adoptive family or cannot in any suitable manner be cared for in the country of origin, intercountry adoption may be considered as an alternative means of providing the child with a family."

a state is unable to satisfy them. Does a child's right to identity preservation outweigh the right to an adequate standard of living and healthcare? Does a child's right to maintain personal relations and direct contact with both parents on a regular basis trump the basic human rights to access clean drinking water, food, medical care and shelter and education?[118] Neither the UNCRC nor the Implementation Handbook provide for clear answers to these questions. The disputed hierarchy of children's rights forms the basis of the debate about the legitimacy of intercountry adoption (see section 2).

Abolitionists interpret Article 21(c) in conjunction with Article 20(3) and Article 8(1) and argue that the UNCRC puts the possibility of intercountry adoption behind every conceivable childcare solution available in the child's country of origin, including foster arrangements and even institutional care.[119]

Promoters of intercountry adoption argue that intercountry adoption should generally be prioritized over institutional care which, they claim, has harmful consequences for the children as is shown by several studies.[120] They refer to the order of alternative childcare solutions that are listed in Article 20(3) and the qualifying phrase 'if necessary', which reflects the UNCRC's general preference for placement within a substitute family over institutional care.[121] Furthermore, they argue that a child has a right to a family (see section 5.1), which, they argue, trumps the child's right to identity preservation.[122]

Regulationists claim that each case requires a careful examination of the individual child and the available childcare options, in which the child's interests are to be given paramount consideration.[123] Carlson, for instance, suggests that:

---

118 L. McKinney (2007). "International Adoption and the Hague Convention: Does Implementation of the Convention Protect the Best Interests of Children?" Whittier Journal of Child & Family Advocacy, 6, 2, 361-412, p. 382.

119 N. B. Graff (2000). "Intercountry Adoption and the Convention on the Rights of the Child: Can the Free Market in Children be Controlled?" Syracuse Journal of International Law & Commerce, 27, 405-430, p. 417.

120 See, for instance, C. A. Nelson et al. (2007). "Cognitive Recovery in Socially Deprived Young Children: The Bucharest Early Intervention Project." Science, 318, 1937-1940; M. Van IJzendoorn et al. (2008). "IQ of Children Growing Up in Children's Homes: A Meta-Analysis on IQ Delays in Orphanages." Merrill-Palmer Quarterly, 54, 3, 341–366; C. H. Zeanah et al. (2005). "Attachment in Institutionalized and Community Children in Romania." Child Development, 76, 5, 1015-1028.

121 R. Rios-Kohn (1998). "Intercountry adoption: An international perspective on the practice and standards." Adoption Quarterly, 1, 4, 3-32, pp. 19-20; S. Detrick (1999). "A Commentary on the United Nations Convention on the Rights of the Child." Martinus Nijhoff Publishers, Leiden, p. 336.

122 S. Dillon (2003). "Making Legal Regimes for Intercountry Adoption Reflect Human Rights Principles: Transforming the United Nations Convention on the Rights of the Child with the Hague Convention on Intercountry Adoption." Boston University International Law Journal, 21, 179-257.

123 D. M. Smolin (2007). "Intercountry Adoption and Poverty: A Human Rights Analysis." Capital University Law Review, 36, 413-453, p. 424, arguing that this approach is reflected by Article 3(1) UNCRC which asserts that "all actions concerning children [...] the best interests of the child shall be a primary consideration." The UNCRC "child's best interest" standard is also mirrored in Article 4(b) of the Hague Convention on Protection and Co-Operation in Respect of Intercountry Adoption (1993) that asserts that an intercountry

> Every child and his situation are unique. A statement that intercountry adoption is better than in-country institutionalization can only be a generalization. There may be some children for whom intercountry adoption is inadvisable. Older children who have acquired a deep sense of cultural and community identity might be poorly suited for intercountry adoption. For such children, institutionalization or other local alternatives, such as foster care or some other variant, might be the preferred method of care.[124]

Article 21 provides further guidelines for intercountry adoptions which aim to regulate the system and to tackle its abuses.[125] Article 21(c) requires the States Parties to "ensure that the child concerned by intercountry adoption enjoys safeguards and standards equivalent to those existing in the case of national adoption". Read in conjunction with Article 21(a), every intercountry adoption must be authorized by a competent authority, on the basis of all pertinent and reliable information, with the informed consent of all persons concerned having been obtained and the best interests of the child being the paramount consideration.[126]

Article 21(d) specifically aims to prevent trafficking in children. It obliges the UNCRC's States Parties to take all appropriate measures to ensure that, in intercountry adoption situations, the placement of a child does not result in an improper financial gain for those involved therein.[127] In the context of intercountry adoption, this provision strongly relates to Article 35 which obliges States Parties to take measures in order "to prevent the abduction of, the sale of or traffic in children for any purpose or in any form" as well as Article 36 under which States Parties assume the obligation to "protect the child against all other forms of exploitation prejudicial to any aspects of the child's welfare". Chapter 3 (The

---

adoption shall take place only if the competent authorities have determined, after considering the childcare possibilities in the country of origin, that an intercountry adoption is in the child's best interests.

124 R. R. Carlson (1994). "The Emerging Law of Introductory Adoptions: An Analysis of the Hague Conference on Intercountry Adoption." Tulsa Law Journal, 30, 243-304, p. 258.

125 *Ibid.*

126 R. Hodgkin and P. Newell (2007). "Implementation Handbook for the Convention on the Rights of the Child." UNICEF (3rd ed.), pp. 299-300.

127 Similarly, Article 20 of the 1986 UN Declaration on Social and Legal Principles relating to the Protection and Welfare of Children, with Special Reference to Foster Placement and Adoption Nationally and Internationally, provides: "In intercountry adoption, placement should, as a rule, be made through competent authorities or agencies with application of safeguards and standards equivalent to those existing in respect of national adoption. In no case should the placement result in improper financial gain for those involved in it." As regards the distinction between "improper" and "proper", Article 32 of the 1993 Hague Convention on Protection of Children and Co-operation in Respect of Intercountry Adoption states: "1. No one shall derive improper financial or other gain from an activity related to intercountry adoption. 2. Only costs and expenses, including reasonable professional fees of persons involved in the adoption, may be charged or paid. 3. The directors, administrators and employees of bodies involved in an adoption shall not receive remuneration which is unreasonably high in relation to services rendered."

Underbelly of Intercountry Adoption as a Form of Child Trafficking) will deal extensively with these two latter provisions.

Finally, Article 21(e) encourages States Parties to promote the objectives of Article 21 by concluding bilateral and multilateral arrangements or agreements. On the basis of this provision, a number of international treaties regarding intercountry adoption have been adopted in the areas of private international law and of the unification of substantive law and procedure, most notably the Hague Convention, as well as the 1967 European Convention on Adoption of Children Furthermore (see Chapter IV). Article 21(e) furthermore seeks to prevent private agencies and individuals from profiteering from intercountry adoptions by emphasising that intercountry adoptions must be carried out by the competent authorities.[128]

5.3 *The Myth of a Global 'Orphan Crisis'*

War, natural disasters, extreme poverty and AIDS have left numerous children worldwide vulnerable. Many children lack proper food, shelter, medical care and education and may be separated from their parents. Only a small fraction of these children are deprived of their family environment according to Article 22(1) and as such are legitimately available for adoption. This reality runs contrary to the common Western belief that there are millions of children around the world who desperately need parents.[129] This perception is created by estimates of orphans, institutionalized children and street children that are published by international organizations, which are often misinterpreted and then appropriated by adoption advocates to stress the legitimacy of intercountry adoption.[130]

For instance, in one of her articles, Bartholet, one of the most visible promoters of intercountry adoption, refers to a report published by UNICEF, USAID and UNAIDS in 2004 which estimated that there are 12.3 million AIDS orphans out of 43.4 million total orphans in Africa.[131] In another article, she noted that there were 143 million orphans worldwide, a figure which also came from the aforementioned report.[132] What she failed

128 N. B. Graff (2000). "Intercountry Adoption and the Convention on the Rights of the Child: Can the Free Market in Children be Controlled?" Syracuse Journal of International Law & Commerce, 27, 405-430, p. 417.

129 International Social Service (2008). "Exposing myths about the number of adoptable children and the need for more precision when defining who is adoptable." Geneva, Nr. 10.

130 *Ibid.* See also N. Cantwell (2003). "Intercountry Adoption. A Comment on the Number of "Adoptable" Children and the Number of Persons Seeking to Adopt Internationally." The Hague Conference on Private International Law, International Child Protection, The Judges' Newsletter, V.

131 E. Bartholet (2007). "International Adoption: Thoughts on the Human Rights Issue." Buffalo Human Rights Law Review, 13, 151-203, p. 163; UNICEF et al. (2004). "Children on the Brink 2004: A Joint Report of New Orphan Estimates and a Framework of Action."

132 E. Bartholet and D. M. Smolin (2012). "The Debate." In J. L. Gibbons and K. Smith Rotabi, "Intercountry Adoption: Policies, Practices, and Outcomes." Ashgate, Farnham, 232-251, p. 232.

to mention, however, is that the report defines 'orphans' as children under the age of 18 who had lost one or both parents. International organizations adopted the broad definition of 'orphanhood' in the mid-1990s in order to draw development aid's attention to the growing AIDS crisis which was causing the death of millions of people worldwide and leaving an increasing number of children growing up without one or two parents to any cause of death.[133] Their reports on (AIDS) orphans are often misunderstood as meaning that millions of children are in need of a new family or care.[134] However, only a limited number of the millions of children defined as 'orphans' by international organizations fall within the scope of Article 22 and can therefore be considered for adoption.

In 2016, UNICEF estimated that out of the 140 million orphans in Sub-Saharan Africa, Asia, Latin America, and the Caribbean, 'only' 15.1 million had lost both parents.[135] As numerous studies have suggested, the majority of double-orphans live in kinship care arrangements and are therefore not deprived of their family environment. For instance, one of the broadest studies covering households in 51 countries using nationally representative samples found that at least 90% of children that had lost both parents lived with relatives.[136] Another study on Sub-Saharan Africa showed that in 13 countries, about 90% double orphans and children not living with a surviving parent were cared for by extended family networks.[137] Similar results were yielded by a study conducted by UNICEF using data from Burkina Faso, Cameroon, Ethiopia, Ghana, Kenya, Malawi, Mozambique, Nigeria and Uganda.[138] As was explained above, in many cultures, children who have lost their parents are automatically absorbed by their extended family and are often not even considered as orphans. UNICEF furthermore estimates that about 95% of all children that have lost both their parents are already older than five.[139] Hence, UNICEF's and other international organization's 'millions of orphans' are not healthy babies and toddlers in need of parents, but they are mostly older children living with extended families who need financial support.

---

133 K. E. Cheney and K. S. Rotabi (2015). "Addicted to Orphans: How the Global Orphan Industrial Complex Jeopardizes Local Child Protection Systems." In C. Harker et al. (eds) "Conflict, Violence and Peace." Springer, Singapore, 89-107, p. 91.

134 K. Joyce (2013). "The Child Catchers: Rescue, Trafficking, and the New Gospel of Adoption." Public Affairs, New York, p. 62.

135 UNICEF (2016). "The State of the World's Children 2016: A fair chance for every child", p. 121.

136 M. Ainsworth and D. Filmer (2006). "Inequalities in Children's Schooling: AIDS, Orphanhood, Poverty, and Gender." World Development, 34, 6, 1099–1128.

137 R. Monasch and J. T. Boerma (2004). "Orphanhood and childcare patterns in sub-Saharan Africa: an analysis of national surveys from 40 countries." AIDS, 18, 2, 55-65.

138 USAID and UNICEF (2008). "The evidence base for programming for children affected by HIV/AIDS in low prevalence and concentrated epidemic countries." Available at https://www.unicef.org/aids/files/OVC_final.pdf.

139 See UNICEF's Statement about "Orphans", available at https://www.unicef.org/media/media_45279.html (last accessed on 03.08.2018).

The statistics on orphans give little account of the number of children falling within the scope of Article 22. On the one hand, they include many children that are not actually deprived of their family environment. On the other hand, they do *not* include children that were abandoned by their parents, are living in institutions or on the streets, and are in need of alternative care. Furthermore, the studies estimating that 90% of the orphaned children are living within extended family networks are based on data from household surveys only. This means that institutionalized orphans or orphaned children living on the streets were not included in the analyses. The number of orphans deprived of a family environment is, therefore, higher than these studies seem to suggest.

Moreover, statistics on children living in institutions hardly give an indication of the number of children for which adoption may be considered. UNICEF estimates that 2 million children are institutionalized worldwide,[140] stressing that the figure is likely to be severely underestimated given the lack of available data from many countries and the large proportion of unregistered institutions.[141] Some institutionalized children were relinquished by their parents due to stigma, poverty or disease. They are thus without a family environment and in need of alternative care. However, the vast majority of children living in institutions – estimates range from 80% to more than 90% – are not orphans but have a living parent that is known to the authorities.[142] Cantwell notes: "This reality has generated the highly dubious term 'social orphans' to describe the status of these children, in an attempt to legitimize a view of them as being in a similar situation to that of genuine orphans".[143] In many developing countries, it is common for poor families to place their children in institutions for purposes of food, shelter, and education, without ever intending to sever their parental rights. These institutions – be they called orphanages, crèches, schools, children's homes or hostels – serve as a safety net or an extended family resource in times when parents face difficulty in feeding their children or have no one to care for them while they are at work.[144] The children are not relinquished by their parents and cannot thus be considered for adoption.

Cheney et al. claim that in some developing countries, the number of institutionalized children has increased dramatically as a result of UNICEF's and other international orga-

---

140 UNICEF (2009). "Progress for Children: A Report Card on Child Protection." Available at https://www.unicef.org/publications/files/Progress_for_Children-No.8_EN_081309.pdf, p. 19.

141 *Ibid.*

142 K. Browne (2009). "The Risk of Harm to Young Children in Institutional Care." Save the Children UK, p. 2.

143 N. Cantwell (2014). "The Best Interests of the Child in Intercountry Adoption." UNICEF, Office of Research, Florence, p. 75.

144 D. M. Smolin (2006). "Child Laundering: How the Intercountry Adoption System Legitimizes and Incentivizes the Practices of Buying, Trafficking, Kidnapping, and Stealing Children." The Wayne Law Review, 52, 1, 113-200, p. 119.

nizations' inflated orphan statistics.[145] These statistics, they argue, have led to the myth of a global 'orphan crisis'. The persistent belief that there are millions of orphans has driven the building of orphanages, especially in poor communities, attracting the children of numerous vulnerable families. For instance, in Uganda, the number of children living in institutions rose from 2,900 in 1992 to 50,000 in 2013.[146] Cheney and Rotabi explain that: "as orphanages spring up around the country, so do children to fill them. Though many people assume that orphanages are being established to meet the increase in orphans due to child abandonment, it is more likely the other way around".[147] Most children, they note, are in these institutions for education purposes and not because they require alternative care.[148]

Those institutionalized children that do in fact fall within the scope of Article 22 often do not have the characteristics that international adopters are looking for. This was, for instance, revealed in a survey conducted by the Guatemalan government together with UNICEF and Holt International Children's Services in 2007. The report estimated that around 5,600 children and adolescents were placed in Guatemalan institutions[149] the majority of which – namely 4,600 – were age 4 or older. Only 7% of the institutionalized children, thus fewer than 400, were under one-year-old[150] and only 8% of them were declared to be adoptable.[151] Yet in 2006, more than 270 Guatemalan babies, all younger than 12 months, were sent to the United States each month.[152] The vast majority of those children did not come from an institution. In 2007, 98% of Guatemalan children that were placed to the United States were relinquished, meaning that they were signed over directly to a private attorney without ever having been in an institution that approved the international adoption and therefore without any review by a judge or social service agency.[153] In most intercountry adoption cases, illegal methods were employed to obtain the children who had the characteristics which were desired by adopters.[154]

In short, the vast majority of children living in institutions are not orphans but actually have families. Some of them use these institutions as a safety net in times of poverty or

145 K. E. Cheney and K. S. Rotabi (2015). "Addicted to Orphans: How the Global Orphan Industrial Complex Jeopardizes Local Child Protection Systems." In C. Harker et al. (eds) "Conflict, Violence and Peace." Springer, Singapore, 89-107.

146 *Ibid.*

147 *Ibid.*, p. 97.

148 *Ibid.*

149 L. Méndez Pérez (2008). "Situation faced by institutionalized children and adolescents in shelters in Guatemala." SBS, La Secretaría de Bienestar Social de la Presidencia de la República, Charcas, p. 48.

150 *Ibid.*, p. 49.

151 *Ibid.*, p. 10.

152 E. J. Graff (2008). "The lie we love." Foreign Policy, November/December, 58-66, available at http://www.brandeis.edu/investigate/adoption/docs/FPFinalTheLieWeLove.pdf, p. 62.

153 *Ibid.*

154 See Chapter IV, section 5.1.1.

when they have to work and require somebody to look after their children. They come to visit their children regularly and they do not ever intend to relinquish their parental rights. Other parents have abandoned their children due to poverty or other reasons. Only orphaned children as well as abandoned children living in institutions are actually deprived of a family environment and may therefore be considered for adoption. However, these children do not typically fall within the parameters of what adoptive parents are looking for. They are not healthy babies or infants but are older, have diseases and/or are severely traumatized. Nonetheless, the statistics on children living in institutions are often appropriated by adoption advocates in order to stress the urgency of intercountry adoption.[155]

Moreover, contrary to popular belief, many street children do not fall within the scope of Article 22 and are not eligible for adoption. Basically, the exact number of children living and working on the streets is difficult to quantify. This is due to the lack of an exclusive definition of 'street children' as well as the hidden and isolated nature of this phenomenon which makes it difficult to ascertain accurate statistics. Yet, the latest estimates put the number of children working and living on the streets as high as 100 million.[156] As the global population grows and urbanization continues apace, it is likely that this number will increase further.[157] Many of the children living on the streets do not fall within the scope of Article 20 UNCRC because they are not actually deprived of their family environment.[158] For example, a study on street children in New Delhi that was conducted in 2010 revealed that approximately 36% of these children were children from street families, about 29% worked on the streets and returned to their families on a regular basis, whereas some 28% of the total street children population were street-living children that ran away from their families and lived alone on the streets.[159] In most of these cases, economic hardship drove

155 See, for instance, S. Dillon (2003). "Making Legal Regimes for Intercountry Adoption Reflect Human Rights Principles: Transforming the United Nations Convention on the Rights of the Child with the Hague Convention on Intercountry Adoption." Boston University International Law Journal, 21, 179-257, pp. 183-184, referring to statistical data submitted to the Second International Conference in Stockholm on Children and Residential Care according to which, "in Uganda there are 88 residential institutions for 4,788 orphaned children; in Ukraine there are 102 residential homes, 91 orphanages and 47 child homes for 100,000 children; in the Serbian Republic there are 25 institutions for 5,000 children deprived of parental care; in Russia there are 246 children's homes and 156 boarding homes for 110,900 orphaned children (excluding children in specialized institutions); and in the Philippines there are 197 residential care facilities catering to abandoned, neglected, and abused children.

156 UNICEF (2002). "The State of the World's Children 2003." Available at https://www.unicef.org/publications/index_4810.html, p. 37.

157 UNICEF (2006). "Excluded and Invisible, The State of the World's Children 2006." Available at https://www.unicef.org/sowc06/pdfs/sowc06_fullreport.pdf, pp. 40-41.

158 R. Hodgkin and P. Newell (2007). "Implementation Handbook for the Convention on the Rights of the Child." UNICEF (3rd ed.), p. 288.

159 R. Bhaskaran and M. Balwant (2011). "Surviving the Streets: A Census of Street Children in Delhi." Institute for Human Development and Save the Children, p. 27.

the children on to the streets, rather than rejection, abuse or neglect within the family unit.[160]

Nonetheless, a significant proportion of children that live on the streets are orphans because they have been abandoned or because they ran away from abuse at home.[161] Many of them are not attractive adoptees as they are older, sick or more damaged from trauma than most families are willing to accept. Yet, some promoters of intercountry adoption appropriate statistics on street children to further their cause.[162]

The plight of orphans is also often wrongfully assumed in developing countries that are hit by war or natural catastrophes. In many incidents in the past, numerous children that were not orphans were airlifted from disaster zones and then adopted in the United States and Europe. For instance, the infamous 'Operation Babylift' that took place in 1975 and which has historically been portrayed as heroic act that saved the lives of numerous Vietnamese children, transported many infants who were neither orphans nor available for adoption.[163] Many other disaster-related mass-evacuations of children have taken place that are reminiscent of 'Operation Babylift'.[164] In 2010, after an earthquake rocked Haiti, some 2,000 children were flown out and then adopted in the United States, Canada, France, Germany, the Netherlands and other European countries.[165] Many international organizations warned that international adoption should not take place in the immediate aftermath of the earthquake, as it was impossible to verify the family situations of the children.[166] Notwithstanding these warnings, numerous charitable individuals and organizations from Western countries flocked to Haiti to 'save' orphaned children.[167] Some of them had already been approved for intercountry adoption and were in the process of being adopted before

160 R. Hodgkin and P. Newell (2007). "Implementation Handbook for the Convention on the Rights of the Child." UNICEF (3rd ed.), p. 288.

161 *Ibid.*

162 See, for instance, S. Dillon (2003). "Making Legal Regimes for Intercountry Adoption Reflect Human Rights Principles: Transforming the United Nations Convention on the Rights of the Child with the Hague Convention on Intercountry Adoption." Boston University International Law Journal, 21, 179-257, p. 184, claiming: "Childhope and Casa Alianza, both advocacy groups for street children, agree that there are approximately 100 million street children worldwide, with 40 million in Latin America alone. According to estimates, approximately 25% of these children truly live on the streets and without meaningful family ties."

163 K. J. S. Bergquist (2009). "Operation Babylift or Baby Abduction?: Implications of the Hague Convention on the Humanitarian Evacuation and 'Rescue' of Children." International Social Work, 52, 5, 621-633; P. Fronek and D. Cuthbert (2012). "History Repeating...Disaster-Related Intercountry Adoption and the Psychosocial Care of Children." Social Policy and Society, 11, 03, 429-442;

164 *Ibid.*

165 M. Dambach and C. Baglietto (2010). ""Expediting" intercountry adoptions in the aftermath of a natural disaster...preventing future harm." International Social Service, p. 22.

166 P. Selman (2011). "Intercountry adoption after the Haiti earthquake: Rescue or robbery?" Adoption & Fostering, 35, 4, 41-49.

167 M. Dambach and C. Baglietto (2010). ""Expediting" intercountry adoptions in the aftermath of a natural disaster...preventing future harm." International Social Service, p. 39.

the disaster struck.[168] Others were transported abroad without any reasonable efforts having been made to trace the child's surviving family and, as it later transpired, many children were not real orphans but had family members who were desperately looking for them.[169]

Millions of children worldwide do not have their basic needs fulfilled. They are placed in institutions by their desperate parents who are unable to feed or care for them or they live and starve on the streets, often together with their families. Sometimes natural disasters or war have separated them from their families, thereby leaving parentless. This is naturally a tragic situation. Yet, intercountry adoption is, in many cases, not the solution to this tragedy as the vast majority of these children are not without a family environment according to Article 22 UNCRC and therefore they are not eligible for adoption. As Joyce explains: "the crisis at hand isn't so much an orphan crisis as a crisis of poverty, food insecurity, conflict, and a host of other, less sensational development issues that have rendered children especially vulnerable".[170] And all these conditions are not grounds in themselves to remove a child from his or her family against their will, according to the UNCRC (see section 4.6).

Those children that are actually deprived of their family environment according to Article 22 may only be considered for intercountry adoption if they cannot be placed in a domestic foster or adoptive family or cannot in any suitable manner be cared for in their country of origin. In many sending countries (like, for instance, China), the number of couples interested in a domestic adoption (particularly where it involves a healthy baby) is on the rise. Hence, contrary to the general Western belief, the number of young and healthy children in need of intercountry adoption is considerably low.

6 The Best Interests of the Child

6.1 *Meaning and Historical Background of the Concept*

Article 3(1) provides the child with the right to have his or her best interests assessed and taken into account as a primary consideration in all actions that concern his or her public and private sphere respectively. The 'child's best interests' came to be a key concept in the UNCRC. It is not only to be understood as a *substantive right*. In its General Comment No. 14, the Committee on the Rights of the Child also identified the concept as one of the four *general principles* of the UNCRC, guiding the implementation and interpretation of

168 *Ibid.*

169 K. Joyce (2013). "The Child Catchers: Rescue, Trafficking, and the New Gospel of Adoption." Public Affairs, New York, p. 5.

170 K. Joyce (2016). "The Trouble With the Christian Adoption Movement." New Republic, 11.01.2016, available at https://newrepublic.com/article/127311/trouble-christian-adoption-movement.

all rights of the child set out in the subsequent articles.[171] It serves as a mediating device which can assist in resolving conflicts between different rights that may arise within the overall framework of the UNCRC. Furthermore, it also serves as an interpretive aid. If a legal provision can be interpreted in different ways, the interpretation which most effectively serves the child's best interests should be chosen. Finally, it is a *rule of procedure*. Whenever a decision is to be made concerning a specific child, an identified group of children or children in general, the decision-making process must include assessing and determining the decision's possible impact on the best interests of the child or children concerned.[172]

The concept of the child's best interests is not new. It preceded the development of international human rights and was designed to compensate for the absence of rights.[173] In domestic jurisprudence, the concept has long served as a basis to justify decisions about people that were deemed incapable of making rational decisions for themselves, particularly persons with disabilities and children.[174] With the development of human rights instruments, the concept of the best interests vis-à-vis adults has become something of an anathema. Cantwell explains that: "The very fact of having human rights has been viewed as negating the need and justification for using best interests as a basis for decision-making".[175] The notion of the best interests has therefore been retained in international human rights law solely in relation to children. Thus, the UNCRC as well as the two international instruments on children's rights preceding the UNCRC – the 1959 Declaration of the Rights of the Child and the 1986 Declaration on Social and Legal Principles Relating to the Protection and Welfare of Children, with Special Reference to Foster Placement and Adoption Nationally and Internationally – still refer to the child's best interests.[176] Cantwell

171 UN Committee on the Rights of the Child (2003). "General Comment No. 5: General Measures of Implementation of the Convention on the Rights of the Child (arts. 4, 42 and 44, para. 6)." 27.11.2003, CRC/GC/2003/5, para. 12. The other three general principles of the UNCRC are the obligation of States to respect and ensure the rights set forth in the Convention to each child within their jurisdiction without discrimination of any kind (Article 2), the child's inherent right to life and States parties' obligation to ensure to the maximum extent possible the survival and development of the child (Article 6), and the child's right to express his or her views freely in "all matters affecting the child", those views being given due weight (Article 12).

172 UN Committee on the Rights of the Children (2013). "General Comment No. 14 on the right of the child to have his or her interests taken as a primary consideration (art. 3, para. 1)." 29.05.2013, CRC/C/GB/14, para. 6.

173 N. Cantwell (2014). "The Best Interests of the Child in Intercountry Adoption." UNICEF, Office of Research, Florence, p. 9.

174 *Ibid.*, p. 6.

175 *Ibid.*, p. 9.

176 Principle 2 of the 1959 Declaration of the Rights of the Child: "The child shall enjoy special protection, and shall be given opportunities and facilities, by law and by other means, to enable him to develop physically, mentally, morally, spiritually and socially in a healthy and normal manner and in conditions of freedom and dignity. In the enactment of laws for this purpose, the best interests of the child shall be the paramount consideration." Article 5 of the 1986 Declaration on Social and Legal Principles Relating to the Protection and Welfare of Children, with Special Reference to Foster Placement and Adoption Nationally and Internationally: "In all matters relating to the placement of a child outside the care of the child's own parents,

notes that: "This is certainly, in part, a legacy of the charitable approach to children's issues that prevailed in the nineteenth and twentieth centuries – a legacy that continues to make itself felt in any and all decisions concerning children".[177]

Within the UNCRC, the best interests' principle is not only referred to in Article 3 but is also mentioned in other articles that are particularly relevant with regard to adoptions. According to Article 9(1) the child shall not be separated from his or her parents against their will unless such separation is "necessary for the best interest of the child" (see section 4.6). Furthermore, Article 20 provides the child that is temporarily or permanently deprived of her family environment, or "in whose own best interests cannot be allowed to remain in that environment", special protection and assistance by the state (see section 5.1). Finally, pursuant to Article 21, "the best interests of the child shall be the paramount consideration" in all adoption decisions (see sections 5.2 and 6.3).

6.2 *Analysis of Article 3(1) UNCRC*

The concept of 'the best interests of the child' was left deliberately undefined by the drafters of the UNCRC so as to allow a sufficiently flexible application to diverse individual situations. This, however, has led to a notable disagreement on what, precisely, the principle actually entails and it has also led to diverse interpretations in different historical as well as ideological contexts. What is considered to be in a child's best interests will naturally vary between societies "depending on culture and values, laws, customary practices, and the facts presented in each situation"[178] (see section 6.4). It was only about two decades after the UNCRC came into force that the Committee on the Rights of the Child sought to clarify this vague concept in its General Comment No. 14 as follows:

> The concept of the child's best interests is complex and its content must be determined on a case-by-case basis. [...] It should be adjusted and defined on an individual basis, according to the specific situation of the child or children concerned, taking into consideration their personal context, situation and needs. For individual decisions, the child's best interests must be assessed and determined in light of the specific circumstances of the particular child. For collective decisions – such as by the legislator – the best interests of children

---

the best interests of the child, particularly his or her need for affection and right to security and continuing care, should be the paramount consideration."

177 N. Cantwell (2014). "The Best Interests of the Child in Intercountry Adoption." UNICEF, Office of Research, Florence, p. 9.

178 R. Rios-Kohn (1998). "Intercountry adoption: An international perspective on the practice and standards." Adoption Quarterly, 1, 4, 3-32, p. 12.

in general must be assessed and determined in the light of the circumstances of the particular group and/or children in general.[179]

Article 3(1) uses the indefinite phrase '*a* primary consideration' instead of '*the* primary consideration'. This wording indicates that the consideration of the best interests of the child is of primary importance among other considerations, but that the child's best interests do not have absolute priority, overriding other interests (e.g. of other children, the parents, the family, the extended family, the local community, the society and the State) that might be equal or even superior in some cases, e.g. in medical emergencies during childbirth.[180] Article 3(1) is an umbrella provision that covers a wide range of situations in which numerous competing considerations may be appropriate. An approach that gives the best interests of the child the primary consideration might not be justified in all situations in which this article is invoked.[181] The child's best interests must be the subject of active consideration. It needs to be demonstrated that all aspects of the child's best interests have been explored and taken into account as a primary consideration.[182]

The phrase "all actions concerning children" in Article 3(1) is designed to emphasize a wide-ranging application of the principle of the child's best interests. Indeed, Article 3(1) makes no specific reference to the rights that are recognized in the UNCRC. It may, therefore, be assumed that it is applicable only in conjunction with each of the UNCRC's substantive rights as well as with respect to actions that are not covered by express obligations pursuant to the UNCRC.[183] The word 'actions' not only includes "decisions, [...] all acts, conduct, proposals services, procedures and other measures",[184] but also omissions, meaning decisions not to intervene.[185] The use of the phrase 'concerning children', rather

179 UN Committee on the Rights of the Children (2013). "General Comment No. 14 on the right of the child to have his or her interests taken as a primary consideration (art. 3, para. 1)." 29.05.2013, CRC/C/GB/14, para. 32.

180 UN Commission on Human Rights (1981). "Report of the Working Group on a Draft Convention on the Rights of the Child." 17.02.1981, UN Doc. E/CN.4/L.1575, para. 24; UN Commission on Human Rights (1989). "Report of the Working Group on a Draft Convention on the Rights of the Child." 02.03.1989, UN Doc. E/CN. 4/1989/48, para. 121.

181 P. Alston and B. Gimour-Walsh (1996). "The Best Interests of the Child, Towards a Synthesis of Children's Right and Cultural Values." UNICEF, Innocenti Studies, p. 11.

182 R. Hodgkin and P. Newell (2007). "Implementation Handbook for the Convention on the Rights of the Child." UNICEF (3rd ed.), p. 38.

183 S. Detrick (1999). "A Commentary on the United Nations Convention on the Rights of the Child." Martinus Nijhoff Publishers, Leiden, p. 90.

184 UN Committee on the Rights of the Children (2013). "General Comment No. 14 on the right of the child to have his or her interests taken as a primary consideration (art. 3, para. 1)." 29.05.2013, CRC/C/GB/14, para. 17.

185 J. Zermatten (2010). "The Best Interests of the Child: Literal Analysis, Function and Implementation." Institute International Des Droits De L'Enfant, p. 9; P. Alston (1994). "The Best Interests Principle: Towards a Reconciliation of Culture and Human Rights." International Journal of Law and the Family, 8, 1-25, pp. 13-14.

than the singular 'child', implies that the word 'concerning' is to be understood in a very broad sense.[186] It refers not only to actions directly concerning a child, children as a group or children in general but also to other actions which indirectly affect children.[187] Yet, when actions can be considered "too general in nature, or too indirect in focus", then the child's best interests do not need to be a primary consideration.[188] The Committee on the Rights of the Child explains as follows that:

> Indeed, all actions taken by a State affect children in one way or another. This does not mean that every action taken by the State need to incorporate a full and formal process of assessing and determining the best interests of the child. However, where a decision will have a major impact on a child or children, a great level of protection and detailed procedures to consider their best interests is appropriate.[189]

The wording "whether undertaken by public or private social welfare institutions, courts of law, administrative authorities or legislative bodies" emphasizes the principle's wide scope, covering not only acts of public officials but also acts of private bodies, if they can be classified as 'social welfare institutions'. Parents are not explicitly mentioned, yet according to Article 18(1), the child's best interests shall be their basic concern. In its General Comment No. 14, the Committee clarified that "public or private social welfare institutions" are to be understood widely, including all institutions whose work and decisions have an impact on children and on the realization of their rights.[190] Whether the 'social welfare institutions' also include extended family arrangements is, however, not clarified by the Committee.[191]

---

186 S. Detrick (1999). "A Commentary on the United Nations Convention on the Rights of the Child." Martinus Nijhoff Publishers, Leiden, p. 90.

187 UN Committee on the Rights of the Children (2013). "General Comment No. 14 on the right of the child to have his or her interests taken as a primary consideration (art. 3, para. 1)." 29.05.2013, CRC/C/GB/14, para. 19.

188 P. Alston (1994). "The Best Interests Principle: Towards a Reconciliation of Culture and Human Rights." International Journal of Law and the Family, 8, 1-25, p. 14.

189 UN Committee on the Rights of the Children (2013). "General Comment No. 14 on the right of the child to have his or her interests taken as a primary consideration (art. 3, para. 1)." 29.05.2013, CRC/C/GB/14, para. 20.

190 *Ibid.*, para. 26.

191 P. Alston (1994). "The Best Interests Principle: Towards a Reconciliation of Culture and Human Rights." International Journal of Law and the Family, 8, 1-25, p. 15.

6.3 *The Child's Best Interests in Adoption Arrangements*

As was explained above, the general provision of Article 3(1), which covers a broad range of situations, states that "the best interests of the child shall be *a primary* consideration" in all actions concerning the child. Yet, in the specific case of adoption, which represents one of the most far-reaching and definitive decisions that could be made about a child's future, Article 21 provides a stronger formulation of the 'best interests' principle. It obliges States Parties to "ensure that the best interests of the child shall be *the paramount consideration*" and not only a primary consideration. This means that the interests of the child have absolute priority, overriding any other interests, whether economic, political, state security or those of adoptive parents.[192] The best interests of the child become automatically and explicitly the determining factor for adoptions.

The requirement to 'ensure' is one of the strongest in human rights law, obliging the state to take active measures to fulfil a right, rather than to merely respect it (refrain from interfering with the right) or protect it (prevent violations of the right by any party, including the state itself and its agents).[193] The implications of this obligation are even greater in the context of an intercountry adoption, which involves the removal of a child from his or her country of origin and cultural background.[194]

In private international law, the Hague Convention refers to the UNCRC's concept of the child's best interests as a guiding principle in several of its provisions.[195] In the Hague Convention too, the implications for ensuring the child's best interests are left relatively vague, although its substantive provisions indicate, albeit implicitly, how 'best interests' should be interpreted.[196] The Hague Convention stipulates the procedural requirements for an intercountry adoption, and the Guide to Good Practice sets out clear guidance on how to implement the best interests of the child principle throughout the adoption process.[197]

6.4 *The Vague Concept of 'The Child's Best Interests' – A Criminogenic Factor in the Intercountry Adoption System?*

Although the concept of the child's best interests is the cornerstone of the UNCRC and is generally recognized as the determining factor in adoption decisions, it does not have a

192 R. Hodgkin and P. Newell (2007). "Implementation Handbook for the Convention on the Rights of the Child." UNICEF (3rd ed.), p. 289. *Ibid.*, p. 296.

193 *Ibid.*

194 *Ibid.*, p. 1.

195 See Chapter IV, section 4.1.

196 N. Cantwell (2014). "The Best Interests of the Child in Intercountry Adoption." UNICEF, Office of Research, Florence, p. 14.

197 See Chapter IV.

universally agreed-upon content or meaning.[198] As was already mentioned above, the notion was deliberately left undefined by the drafters of the Convention in order to take account of diverse individual situations and different socio-cultural contexts. Generally, this openness is a distinctive feature of international human rights law which, according to Alston, is characterized by the following paradox:

> [O]n the one hand, the norms must be sufficiently clear, comprehensive and inflexible to provide the international community with some basis on which it might seek to constrain a government which undermines or circumvents minimum standards of decent behaviour. On the other hand, any enterprise which is avowedly universalist in its aspirations and aims to address a very wide range of issues involving, inter alia, the relationship between the state, the family and the child, must be characterised by a significant degree of flexibility and adaptability. As the European Court of Human Rights has observed in upholding a degree of indeterminacy even in laws at the national level: '[W]hile certainty is highly desirable, it may bring in its train excessive rigidity and the law must be able to keep pace with changing circumstances. Accordingly, many laws are inevitably couched in terms which, to a greater or lesser extent, are vague and whose interpretations and application are questions of practice. [...] If international human rights norms in general can be said to be inherently indeterminate, the 'best interests' principle is located by most of its critics at the most indeterminate outer margins even of that body of norms.[199]

Some promote the open-endedness of the 'best interests' principle as it would allow it to respond to advances in knowledge, changing societal attitudes and different socio-cultural settings. Yet, others strongly criticize the inclusion of the 'best interests' concept in the UNCRC as it is too vague and inherently subjective.[200] Its meaning ultimately depends on localized conventions and understandings, as well as the value systems of the individual decision makers which will naturally vary over time. What is considered to be in the best interests of the child in one society, by one judge or at one point in time, may be regarded

198 P. Alston (1994). "The Best Interests Principle: Towards a Reconciliation of Culture and Human Rights." International Journal of Law and the Family, 8, 1-25, p. 4.

199 *Ibid.*, pp. 17-18.

200 K. E. Cheney (2016). "Preventing Exploitation, Promoting Equity: Findings from the International Forum on Intercountry Adoption and Global Surrogacy 2014." Adoption & Fostering, 40, 1, 6-19, p. 10; R. Högbacka (2014). "Intercountry Adoption, Countries of Origin, and Biological Families, Report for Thematic Area 2 International Forum on Intercountry Adoption and Global Surrogacy 11-13 August 2014." Working Paper No. 598, International Institute of Social Studies, pp. 9-10.

as harmful in another society, by another decision-maker or in another time.[201] Moreover, there is a real danger that the concept 'best interests of the child' merely reflects the (class-based and gendered) notions and values of the powerful.[202]

An example of a practice that was once considered as being in the child's best interests and that is now universally condemned as an outright human rights abuse is the 'forced removal' of children from parental care that took place in numerous Western countries throughout the 19th and 20th centuries. For instance, in Australia between the late 1940s and the early 1980s, an estimated 150,000 children were removed from their unwed mothers and placed into adoptive families (these children are now referred to as the 'Stolen White Generation') – the result of a government policy that was sanctioned by churches and charities. The report of the Australian Senate Committee, set up in 2012 to examine these harmful practices, describes the prevailing mindset about unmarried mothers and poor families that time and explains how the 'child's best interests' principle served as a justification for the removal of their children:

> Collectively, attitudes during the 1950s and 1960s towards adoptions, young single mothers and impoverished families indicate a general intolerance of individuals and families who did not fit the idealised family unit. This intolerance appears to have coalesced with a general entitlement mentality advocating the 'right' of all legitimate couples to have children. This powerful mix of intolerance and sense of entitlement appears to have partly manifested itself in the adoption practices of the era, encapsulated by the belief that if children were born to people of 'low moral standard' or poverty, they should be adopted by infertile couples of better social standing so as to ensure the best interests of the child were being looked after.[203]

A similar development also took place in the United States and Europe, whereby unwed pregnant mothers were systematically forced to give up their newborn babies for adoption as this was considered to be in the child's best interests. The time period when these practices took place began with the end of World War II and lasted until the early 1970 and is referred to as the 'Baby Scoop Era'.

The best interests of the child also served as a leitmotif behind the forced removals of indigenous children from their families that took placed in the United States, Australia

201 S. Parker (1994). "The Best Interests of the Child - Principles and Problems." International Journal of Law and the Family, 8, 26-41, p. 36.

202 R. Högbacka (2014). "Intercountry Adoption, Countries of Origin, and Biological Families, Report for Thematic Area 2 International Forum on Intercountry Adoption and Global Surrogacy 11-13 August 2014." Working Paper No. 598, International Institute of Social Studies, p. 10.

203 R. Siewert et al. (2012). "Commonwealth Contribution to Former Forced Adoption Policies and Practices." Community Affairs References Committee Australia, Canberra, para. 2.21.

and Canada (the so-called 'Stolen Generations'). In the 19th and 20th centuries, government authorities in the United States and Australia systematically separated children from their Indigenous families and placed them into the care of the child welfare system and later into white middle-class foster and adoptive families.[204] Haskins and Jacobs explain that:

> Using the rhetoric of protecting and saving indigenous children, reformers and government officials touted child removal as a means to 'uplift' and 'civilize' indigenous children.[205]

In the United States, the removal of Indian children as a systematic state policy began in the 1880s as a central component of the assimilation agenda.[206] Children were separated from their Native families and placed into boarding schools with the purpose of assimilating and remoulding them.[207] After World War II, the United States government revived the assimilation policy under a new name: termination and relocation. The aim was to solve the 'Indian child welfare crisis'.[208] Jacobs explains that:

> Government authorities and social workers asserted that Indian families and communities exhibited such a degree of social dysfunction that it was necessary to apprehend large numbers of Indian children in order to protect them from neglect and a grim future. These officials claimed they were making necessary interventions to uphold 'the best interests of the child'.[209]

Numerous American Indian families experienced heartbreak and trauma and mourned the loss of their children. By the late 1960s, an estimated 25% to 35% of Indian children were separated from their families.[210]

In Australia, indigenous people endured similar practices in the context of the government's absorption plans. Child removal was brought in under the auspices of 'Protection' in the 1870s.[211] Children were separated from their families and then placed in institutions

204 V. Haskins and M. D. Jacobs (2002). "Stolen Generation and Vanishing Indians: The Removal of Indigenous Children as a Weapon of War in the United States and Australia." In J. Marten (ed), "Children and War: A historical anthropology." New York University Press, 227-241.

205 *Ibid.*, p. 227.

206 *Ibid.*, p. 228.

207 *Ibid.*

208 *Ibid.*, p. 229.

209 M. D. Jacobs (2014). "A Generation Removed, The Fostering & Adoption of Indigenous Children in the Postwar World." University of Nebraska Press, Lincoln and London, p. xxxvi.

210 *Ibid.*, p. xxvi.

211 V. Haskins and M. D. Jacobs (2002). "Stolen Generation and Vanishing Indians: The Removal of Indigenous Children as a Weapon of War in the United States and Australia." In J. Marten (ed), "Children and War: A historical anthropology." New York University Press, 227-241, p. 229.

and 'training homes' for the purposes of assimilating them to a non-native society. As Haskins and Jacobs explain, this practice of

> [c]hild removal was aimed ostensibly at making Aboriginal children into 'decent and useful members of the community' and couched in the language of benevolent welfare policy. Thus, the New South Wales (NSW) Aborigines Protection Board had the power to secure custody and control of any Aboriginal child 'if it is satisfied that such a course is in the interest of the moral or physical welfare of such child'.[212]

Just as in the United States, after World War II, these policies were renamed as 'Assimilation'.[213] In 1995, the Australian government launched an inquiry into the practice of forced child removal. The report which was delivered before the Australian parliament estimated that between 1910 and 1970, between 10% and 33% of all Indigenous children were separated from their families.[214]

Also in Canada, a government programme forcibly separated indigenous children from their families and then put them into non-indigenous foster homes and adoptive families around the world between the 1960s and 1980s – a practice that became known as the 'Sixties Scoop'. In the early 1980s, the Manitoba government established a Review Committee on Indian and Métis Adoptions and Placements which investigated the forced removal of indigenous children in detail. The Committee's report concluded as follows:

> An abysmal lack of sensitivity to children and families was revealed. Families approached agencies for help and found that what was described as being in the child's 'best interest' resulted in their families being torn asunder and siblings separated. Social workers grappled with cultural patterns far different than their own with no preparation and no opportunity to gain understanding.[215]

The best interests of the child were also advanced in the practice of 'forced migration'. Between the 1920s and 1970s, around 150,000 British children from deprived backgrounds and who were already in some form of social or charitable care were sent to Canada, Aus-

212 *Ibid.*

213 *Ibid.*, pp. 229-230.

214 Human Rights and Equal Opportunity Commission (1997). "Report of the National Inquiry into the Separation of Aboriginal and Torres Strait Islander Children from Their Families." Sydney.

215 E. C. Kimelman (1985). "No quiet place: final report to the Honourable Muriel Smith, Minister of Community Services." Review Committee on Indian and Métis Adoptions and Placements, Manitoba, p. 274.

tralia, New Zealand and other British colonies.[216] According to the report of the UK Parliamentary Selection Committee on Health, which was established to investigate this practice in depth, the child's best interests did not only serve as the main motive for such forced migration but also as a disguise for the underlying economic intentions:[217]

> The motivation underlying child migration policy was mixed. On the one hand, there was a genuine philanthropic desire to rescue children from destitution and neglect in Britain and send them to a better life in the Colonies. This went hand in hand with a wish to protect children from 'moral danger' arising from their home circumstances—for instance, if their mothers were prostitutes. [...] Child migration was also seen to be of economic benefit both to Britain (because it relieved the burden on public finances of looking after these children) and to the receiving countries (because child migrants were seen as being potential members of a healthy and well-trained workforce). Evidence shows that they were actually used as cheap labour. Demand for child labour in Canada and Australia often exceeded supply.[218]

Also in the present practice of intercountry adoption, the concept of the child's best interests plays a key role. As we will see in Chapter VII, the wish to 'save a child' from an underprivileged part of the world is a crucial motive behind many adopters' decision to adopt internationally.[219] Also, the Western adoption agencies' primary motivation is to serve the best interests of the child by finding loving homes for needy orphans.[220] The commonplace of a global orphan crisis (see section 5.3) helps adopters and adoption agencies to stress the urgency of intercountry adoption. This conviction of 'saving children' might lead them to engaging in harmful practices. Adopters might pursue a faster adoption without the involvement of the authorities, pay large sums of money to the orphanage they adopt from or bribe government officials to accelerate the adoption process. Adoption agencies might continue to place children from a sending country in which systemic abuses had become apparent for the sake of rescuing orphans.

216 See generally, E. Boucher (2014). "Empire's Children: Child Emigration, Welfare, and the Decline of the British World, 1869-1967." Cambridge University Press; R. Parker (2010). "Uprooted: The shipment of poor children to Canada, 1867-1917." Policy Press, Bristol.

217 N. Cantwell (2014). "The Best Interests of the Child in Intercountry Adoption." UNICEF, Office of Research, Florence, p. 9.

218 UK Parliament Selection Committee on Health. "Th Welfare of Former British Child Migrants." 23.07.1998, 3rd report, available at https://publications.parliament.uk/pa/cm199798/cmselect/cmhealth/755/75502.htm, para. 15-16.

219 See Chapter VII, section 4.2.

220 See Chapter V, section 4.2.

The logic of 'saving a child' does not only serve as a motive in itself, but at the same time also as a cloak for adopters' own wishes and desires, as well as for the adoption agencies' economic interests. Furthermore, it may even serve as a justification for their harmful, unethical or blatantly illegal practices.

Most international adopters are involuntarily childless, who have often already spent quite some effort and money on reproductive treatments so as to have a child of their own. In individualized Western societies, children fulfil important affective functions for their parents. They help to countervail the eroding chances of having a partner relationship that lasts as well as to avoid loneliness in old age.[221] Furthermore, children serve their parents in building social and cultural capital. Parenting has been increasingly marked as a measure of value, self-worth and citizenship. Achieving parenthood is thus necessary in order to become a 'fully realized' citizen.[222] This is not only the case for heterosexual couples but, increasingly, also for same-sex couples as well as singles who seek recognition in their own community.[223] For many couples and individuals who are unable to have their own biological child, intercountry adoption is a measure of last resort to ultimately accomplish parenthood. The logic of 'saving a child' from a poor country thereby helps them to come to terms with their decision to form a family by adopting internationally,[224] as well as to downplay or justify any harmful practices.

The logic of 'saving children' also serves as a cloak for the adoption agencies' economic interests. Adoption agencies' placement activities do not only serve the best interests of the children, but also the interests of their staff members whose jobs are reliant on the number of intercountry adoptions. As we will see, in Germany and the Netherlands, adoption agencies do not receive any government subsidies. They, therefore, have to finance themselves exclusively with the 'administrative' fees that are paid by their adoption applicants. This means that they are financially dependent on adoption placements.[225] Given the decreasing number of intercountry adoptions, both German and Dutch adoption agencies face difficulties in keeping their business up and running. This financial strain might lead them to cut ethical corners, for instance, by placing children from a sending country in which abuses and irregularities occur on a regular basis, by holding on to a shady foreign cooperation partner or by accepting child proposals that do not include sufficient information about the child.[226] The best interests of the child may then serve the adoption agencies as an important neutralization and then justification for such decisions.[227]

221 See Chapter VII, section 4.1.

222 *Ibid.*

223 *Ibid.*

224 See Chapter VII, section 4.2.

225 See Chapter V, section 5.2. and Chapter VI, section 5.2.

226 See Chapter V, section 7.2.

227 See Chapter V, section 7.3.

The vague concept of the child's best interests is open to an interpretation that ultimately serves the desires and interests of the adopters and adoption agencies and that differs greatly from the cultural understandings in the child's native countries.[228] The cultural relativism inherent in the 'best interests' principle creates the danger of ethnocentric colonialism or, as King calls it, MonoHumanism.[229] Padilla explains:

> What it means to be a good parent in Bangladesh differs from what it means to be a good parent in the United States. Against this backdrop, it is easy for adoptive parents to rationalize that their adoptive child will 'be better off' living with them because from their cultural viewpoint, their family better fits their definition of 'the best interests of the child'. The rationalization is further supported by the adoptive parents' ability to offer the child better economic conditions than what the child would have been afforded in the country of origin.[230]

In more traditional societies, where the links to kinship and the local community are regarded as being of great importance, it may be argued that the best interests of the child requires the child to grow up in his or her (extended) family network and her community, even when it lacks the necessary recourses to send the child to school or to provide him or her with access to advanced medical care.

In industrialized Western societies, by way of contrast, the child's interests are considered to be best served by policies and practices that encourage material prosperity and education. Furthermore, the concept of the 'child's best interests' is based on a liberal and individualistic notion of childhood.[231] It implies that all children should be treated the same without regard to their different social backgrounds and that their interests are independent of those of their parents or wider community.[232] It is due to this Western conception of the 'child's best interests' that the actors in the receiving countries tend to focus on the child as an individual, abstracted from his or her community and cultural context. Since the child's community or culture is often conceived as inferior or even harmful – as it cannot properly provide for their children – the imperative of 'saving the child' emerges as a result. Against this backdrop, extracting the child from his or her web of social relations and cultural background appears to be natural and legitimate, even

228 See also K. E. Cheney (2014). "Executive Summary of the International Forum on Intercountry Adoption and Global Surrogacy 11-13 August 2014." Working Paper No. 596, International Institute of Social Studies.

229 See Chapter III, section 6.4.

230 S. S. Padilla "Adoption of Alien Orphan Children: How United States Immigration Law Defines Family." Georgetown Immigration Law Journal, 7, 817-844, p. 839.

231 B. Rwezaura (1994). "The Concept of the Child's Best Interests in the Changing Economic and Social Context of Sub-Saharan Africa." International Journal of Law and the Family, 8, 82-114, p. 100.

232 U. Beck (2002). "Individualization: Institutionalized Individualism and Its Social and Political Consequences." Sage, London, p. 392.

honourable.[233] Arguably, this individualistic and liberal notion of childhood, on which the concept of the best interests is based, is also the reason why the belief of a global orphan crisis is so persistent and difficult to tackle, despite numerous estimates and statistics that suggest otherwise.

Arguably, the Western conception of the 'child's best interests' principle is mirrored in the UNCRC which provides that in all adoption decisions, "the best interests of the child shall be the paramount consideration".[234] This means that the interests of the child basically trump those of all others involved in an adoption, including the child's biological parents and his or her wide family network.

The vague and open-ended concept of the child's best interests constitutes a breeding ground for misconception and manipulation and is a suitable device to justify and legitimize adoption practices that are harmful to children, most notably illegally obtaining children from their parents. Even worse, it might blind actors involved in intercountry adoption towards the harmful consequences of their practices – like the government officials and social workers in the 'Baby Scoop Era' or during the 19th and 20th century in the United States, Australia and Canada.

The 'child's best interests' principle may not only serve adopters and adoption agencies to neutralize and justify their irresponsible actions. The principle is also often advanced by the courts in the receiving countries to *ex post* legitimize a private adoption. As we will see in Chapters V and VI, German and Dutch courts have to deal quite regularly with private intercountry adoptions. Such adoptions are particularly risky as they provide a breeding ground for illegal and commercial adoption practices.[235] Nevertheless, the German and Dutch courts regularly tolerate them, arguing that it would not be in the interests of the individual child to refuse declaring a foreign adoption decision as being recognizable[236] or to remove him or her from the new family.[237]

This line of argumentation may also be advanced in cases where the child was obtained illegally from his or her biological parents, like in the adoption involving the boy Indian Rahul who was stolen from his parents, laundered through the intercountry adoption system and then adopted by a Dutch couple who was told that Rahul was an orphan.[238] Rahul's case was one of at least 350 illegal adoptions that led to criminal investigations in India. After Rahul's Indian parents managed to track down their supposed son, they went to the Netherlands and requested a DNA examination to verify that they were Rahul's real parents. This is extraordinary considering that most cases of child laundering remain

233 See also M. Kline (1992). "Child Welfare Law, "Best Interests of the Child" Ideology, and First Nations." Osgoode Hall Law Journal, 30, 2, 376-425.

234 Art. 21 UNCRC.

235 See Chapter V, section 4.1.

236 See Chapter V, section 4.3.

237 See Chapter VI, section 4.3.

238 See Chapter VI, section 6.3.

invisible, also because the birth parents do often not have the capacity to seek justice for the illegal removal of their children.[239] The *Rechtbank Zwolle-Lelystad*, however, rejected their request. It argued that the best interests of the child Rahul, who refused to participate in the DNA examination as he feared being sent back to India in case of positive results, outweighed the interests of the alleged biological parents as well as the public interests in the criminal investigations in India.[240] The Dutch court even ordered the Indian couple to pay the process costs of €4,763.

Basically Article 8 of the UNCRC, which lays down the child's right to identity preservation, asserts that "[w]here a child is illegally deprived of some or all of the elements of his or her identity, States Parties shall provide appropriate assistance and protection, with a view to re-establishing speedily his or her identity". According to this provision, the Dutch court would have been obliged to take an active role in investigating the serious allegations, by allowing a DNA test to be taken in order to establish Rahul's original identity. Yet, the overarching principle of the child's best interests allows Article 8 to be annulled altogether. It basically permits the UNCRC to be interpreted as meaning that a stolen child's identity should not be established, if doing so would be contrary to the child's best interests. As Smolin rightly claims: "The subjective nature of the 'best interests of the child' standard renders disputable the proper outcome in virtually any difficult case, including instances of children illegally adopted".[241]

7 Conclusion and Discussion

The UNCRC provides important guidelines and principles for intercountry adoptions. Based on the child's right to be cared for by his or her parents (Article 7) and the primacy of the child's parents and family (Article 5), the treaty obliges its Contracting States to appropriately support families in the performance of their child-rearing responsibilities, if they are in need (Articles 18 and 27). The term 'family' is thus to be understood broadly, not only including the parents and others legally responsible for the child (the nuclear family) but also to the extended family or community where they are recognized by local custom. Article 9 places strict limits on state intervention and any separation of the child from his or her parents or other primary caregivers. It provides that a child must not be separated from his or her parents against their will, except when the competent authorities subject to judicial review determine, in accordance with applicable law and procedures, that such separation is necessary for the best interests of the child. Such laws and procedures

239 See Chapter II, section 4.2.2.

240 *Rechtbank Zwolle-Lelystad*, 04.03.2011, 170085 / FA RK 10-1401, ECLI:NL:RBZLY:2011:BP6936.

241 D. M. Smolin (2004). "The Two Faces of Intercountry Adoption: The Significance of the Indian Adoption Scandals." Seton Hall Law Review, 35, 403-493, p. 412.

must be free from discrimination of any kind, irrespective of the child's or his or her parent's race, colour, sex, language, religion, political or other opinion, national, ethnic or social origin, property, disability, birth or other status (Article 2(1)). Therefore, homelessness or poverty of the child's parents cannot be grounds in themselves to remove the child against his or her parents' will.

Only children that are deprived of their family environment may be considered for intercountry adoption. Basically, a child is deprived of his or her family environment only if (a) the child's wider family is dead or (b) has rejected or abandoned the child or (c) if the state authorities have decided that separation of the child from her parents was necessary for the child's best interests, according to Article 9(1), and the child cannot be allowed to remain in the wider family as this would, too, be contrary to his or her best interests. Many children have lost a parent due to AIDS, live in institutions or on the streets. But only a small fraction of them are deprived of their family environment according to the UNCRC. And those who are deprived of their family environment may only be considered for intercountry adoption if they cannot be placed in a domestic foster or an adoptive family or cannot in any suitable manner be cared for in their country of origin. In many sending countries (like, for instance, China), the number of couples interested in a domestic adoption (particularly when it concerns a healthy baby) is on the rise. Therefore, contrary to the general Western belief, the number of young and healthy children in need of intercountry adoption is considerably low.

The UNCRC provides that in all decisions concerning a child, the child's best interests need to be taken into account as a primary consideration. In all adoption decisions, the child's best interests shall be the paramount and not only a primary consideration, meaning that the child's interests override the interests of any others involved in adoption. Although the concept of the child's best interests lies at the cornerstone of the UNCRC and is generally recognized as the determining factor in adoption decisions, it does not have a universally agreed-upon content or meaning. Hence, what is considered to be in the best interests of the child in one society, by one judge or at one point in time, may be perceived as harmful in another society, by another decision maker or at another point in time.

In industrialized Western societies, the child's interests are considered to be best served by policies and practices that encourage material prosperity and education. Furthermore, the concept of the 'child's best interests' is based on a liberal and individualistic notion of childhood. It implies that all children should be treated the same without regard to their different social backgrounds and that their interests are independent of those of their parents or wider community. Since the child's community or culture is often conceived as inferior or even harmful, the imperative to 'save the child' emerges. Against this backdrop, extracting the child from his or her web of social relations and cultural background appears to be natural and legitimate, even honourable.

The vague and open-ended concept of the child's best interests constitutes a breeding ground for misconception and manipulation. As was explained, in the 19th and 20th centuries, governmental officials and social workers in the United States, Australia and Canada advanced the principle to justify and legitimize the forced removal of children from their unwed mothers or their indigenous families. In the current intercountry adoption system, the 'child's best interests' principle not only serves adopters and adoption agencies as a motive in itself, but at the same time also as a cloak for their selfish desires and economic interests, and furthermore even as a justification for irresponsible or clearly illegal practices (e.g. paying large sums of money to the orphanage, bribing government officials to accelerate the adoption or continue co-operating with a shady partner organization in the sending country). Finally, the principle is often advanced by the courts in the receiving countries to legitimize an illegal adoption or even the adoption of a stolen child.

IV The 1993 Hague Convention – A Trojan Horse in the Intercountry Adoption System?

1 Introduction

Since the 1960s, international adoptions have occurred to such an extent that "intercountry adoption had become a worldwide phenomenon involving migration of children over long geographical distances and from one society and culture to another very different environment".[1] For decades, the intercountry adoption system had been a 'Wild West' where children were being transferred across borders without there being any meaningful regulations and oversight.[2] It became noticeable that intercountry adoptions would not always take place in the best interests of children and with respect for their rights. Adopters had not been screened properly and it became doubtful whether the high number of adoptees that were removed from their native countries was really in need of families. Furthermore, numerous reports of illegal adoptions emerged suggesting that the large sums of money involved in the system were conducive to all sorts of commercial and abusive practices. As a result, both sending and receiving countries demanded to regulate the system and tackle irregularities and abuses.

In 1988, when the number of intercountry adoptions peaked at over 19,000[3] and it was obvious that previous international legal instruments proved insufficient to eliminate abusive practices, the Permanent Bureau of the Hague Conference proposed to draft a 'convention on adoption of children coming from abroad' in 1988.[4] In 1993, the Hague Convention on Protection of Children and Co-operation in Respect of Intercountry Adoption (hereinafter Hague Convention)[5] was drafted, the result of a long and heated debate about the protection of children's rights in intercountry adoptions.

With its 98 Contracting States, the treaty is one of the most successful instruments of private international law. The Convention, its two Guides to Good Practice as well as

1 J. H. A. Van Loon (1990). "Report on Intercountry Adoption." The Hague Conference on Private International Law, April 1990, Prel. Doc. No. 1, p. 17.

2 E. J. Graff (2010). "The Baby Business." Democracy Journal, Summer No. 17, available at https://democracyjournal.org/magazine/17/the-baby-business/.

3 P. Selman (2002). "Intercountry adoption in the new millennium; the "quiet migration" revisited." Population Research and Policy Review, 21, 3, 205-225, p. 210.

4 J. H. A. Van Loon (1990). "Report on Intercountry Adoption." The Hague Conference on Private International Law, April 1990, Prel. Doc. No. 1, p. 15; J. H A Van Loon (1993). "International Co-operation and Protection of Children with Regard to Intercountry Adoption." 244 Recueil des cours, 195-456.

5 The Hague Conference on Private International Law, The Hague Convention on the Protection of Children and Co-operation in Respect of Intercountry Adoption, 29 May 1993, 32 I.L.M. 1134.

numerous recommendations drawn up by the Permanent Bureau of the Hague Conference on Private International Law (hereinafter HCCH) have set the standards for ethical and sustainable adoptions which respect the rights of children as well as of their birth parents. Without a doubt, the treaty represents the most significant attempt to tackle illegal and commercial practices in the international adoption system. Yet, today, approximately 20 years after the treaty came into force, children are still being bought and trafficked for the purposes of adoption. Several adoption scandals that have occurred in Contracting States to the Hague Convention, such as Colombia, China, Romania, and India, suggest that the ratification of the treaty does not *ipso eo* prevent "the abduction, the sale of, or traffic in children", one of the treaty's main objectives.[6]

This Chapter examines the pitfalls and weaknesses of the Convention and investigates as to whether the treaty might even work to facilitate the laundering of kidnapped, stolen and purchased children through the intercountry adoption system. Numerous experts have criticized the Hague Convention for its limitations, arguing that the provisions do not go far enough and do not constitute an appropriate tool to tackle abuses.[7] Yet, stakeholders in Germany and the Netherlands often seem to consider the treaty as a sound warrant against illegal and abusive adoption practices. This conception is dangerous as it might lead to less scrutiny towards child proposals from sending countries that are Contracting States to the Convention, thereby ultimately removing the hurdles for the trafficking of children for adoption purposes.

Section 2 briefly analyses the international legal instruments on intercountry adoption that preceded the 1993 Hague Convention. Section 3 outlines the Convention's provisions and Section 4 explains the minimum set of standards and principles that the treaty provides. Section 5 then takes a look at the Convention's pitfalls and limitations. It shows that the treaty has left states with much leeway to create adoption systems as they see it fit and in which violations of the Convention's provisions will go unpunished. Furthermore, it explains how the Convention, notwithstanding its limitations, has made adoption procedures in Hague countries appear legitimate and created blind trust between its Contracting States which might facilitate the process of laundering children. Section 6 then concludes this Chapter.

---

6 Art. 1(b) Hague Convention.

7 See, for example, K. S. Rotabi and J. L. Gibbons (2011). "Does the Hague Convention on Intercountry Adoption Adequately Protect Orphaned and Vulnerable Children and Their Families?" Journal of Child and Family Studies, 21, 1, 106-119; N. S. Thompson (2004). "Hague is Enough?: A Call for More Protective, Uniform Law Guiding International Adoptions." Wisconsin International Law Journal, 22, 2, 441-469; E. J. Ryan (2006). "For the Best Interests of the Children: Why the Hague Convention of Intercountry Adoption Needs to Go Farther, as Evidenced by Implementation in Romania and the United States." Boston College International and Comparative Law Review, 29, 2, 353-383; R. Worthington (2009). "The Road to Parentless Children is Paved with Good Intentions: How the Hague Convention and recent Intercountry Adoption Rules are Affecting Potential Parents and the Best Interests of Children." Duke Journal of Comparative & International Law, 19, 559-586.

2 Background and Development of the Hague Convention

The *1965 Hague Convention on Jurisdiction, Applicable Law and Recognition of Decrees Relating to Adoption*[8] was the first attempt to regulate intercountry adoptions. The treaty addresses rules of jurisdiction,[9] choice of law[10] as well as mutual recognition of adoption decrees.[11] Furthermore, it determines that an adoption should only be granted if it was in the child's best interests and if it was preceded by "a thorough inquiry relating to the adopter or adopters, the child and his family".[12] The Convention primarily addresses private international law aspects of intercountry adoption but does not provide any practical guidelines for the procedures to be executed in relation thereto. This is probably the reason why it did not receive much support: it was ratified only by three nations (Austria, Sweden and the UK).[13]

The next effort to regulate intercountry adoptions was the *1967 European Convention on the Adoption of Children* that the Member States of the Council of Europe adopted.[14] This Convention attempted to harmonize the substantive adoption laws among the Member States of the Council of Europe. Thus, it includes provisions about the granting of an adoption[15] and its conditions,[16] the consent to an adoption,[17] the adopters' minimum age,[18] the effects of an adoption,[19] the adopted child's nationality,[20] the revocation of an adoption[21] as well as access and disclosure of information.[22] Moreover, the treaty provides some procedural guidelines that aim at preventing illegal practices. It states that an international adoption must be granted by a competent authority,[23] specifies the persons whose consent is necessary for an adoption as well as the circumstances under which their consent shall not be accepted,[24] sets forth that an adoption shall be granted only if appropriate

8 The Hague Conference on Private International Law, The Hague Convention on Jurisdiction, Applicable Law and Recognition of Decrees Relating to Adoption, 15 November 1965.
9 Art. 3 and 7 *leg. cit.*
10 Art. 4-5 *leg. cit.*
11 Art. 8 *leg. cit.*
12 Art. 6 *leg. cit.*
13 L. M. Katz (1995). "A Modest Proposal? The Convention on Protection of Children and Cooperation in Respect of Intercountry Adoption." Emory International Law Review, 9, 283-328, p. 289.
14 Council of Europe, European Convention on the Adoption of Children, 24 April 1967, ETS No. 058.
15 Art. 4, 8, 9 and 17 *leg. cit.*
16 Art. 6 *leg. cit.*
17 Art. 5 *leg. cit.*
18 Art. 7 *leg. cit.*
19 Art. 10 *leg. cit.*
20 Art. 11 *leg. cit.*
21 Art. 13 *leg. cit.*
22 Art. 20 *leg. cit.*
23 Art. 4 *leg. cit.*
24 Art. 5 *leg. cit.*

inquiries into child and his family have been made,[25] and requires its Contracting States to prohibit any improper financial advantage arising from an adoption.[26] The 1967 European Convention was ratified by 16 Member States of the Council of Europe.[27]

In 2011, a revised version of the European Convention on the Adoption of Children came into force[28] which *inter alia* allows for international adoptions by same-sex couples[29] and modifies the provisions on access to an disclosure of information.[30] The instrument was ratified by 10 Member States.[31] The two Conventions did not have a significant impact: they only regulated intercountry adoptions in European countries (and not on a global level) and were mainly ratified by traditional receiving states.

In 1986, the United Nations General Assembly adopted the *Declaration on Social and Legal Principles Relating to the Protection and Welfare of Children with Special Reference to Foster Placement and Adoption Nationally and Internationally*.[32] One of the drafters' main intentions was to decrease the issue of baby selling and trafficking.[33] The Declaration stresses the first priority of the child to be cared for by his or her own parents and encourages the States to place a high priority on family and child welfare. It provides that intercountry adoption should be considered as an alternative childcare solution only if the child "cannot be placed in a foster or an adoptive family or cannot in any suitable manner be cared for in the country of origin".[34] Furthermore, it stresses that "the best interests of the child should be the paramount consideration", meaning that the interests of the child have absolute priority, overriding any other interests, whether economic, political, state security or those of adoptive parents.[35] It sets forth that the placement of a child should

25 Art. 9 *leg. cit.*

26 Art. 15 *leg. cit.*

27 See Chart of signatures and ratifications to the 1968 European Convention on the Adoption of Children, available at http://www.coe.int/en/web/conventions/full-list/-/conventions/treaty/058/signatures (last visited on Dec. 13th, 2016).

28 Council of Europe, European Convention on the Adoption of Children (revised), 27 November 2008, ETS No. 202.

29 Art. 7 *leg. cit.*

30 Art. 22 *leg. cit.*

31 See Chart of signatures and ratifications to the 2011 European Convention on the Adoption of Children, available at https://www.coe.int/en/web/conventions/full-list/-/conventions/treaty/202/signatures?p_auth=lLZ-dokQf (last visited on Dec. 13th, 2016).

32 UN General Assembly, Declaration on Social and Legal Principles relating to the Protection and Welfare of Children, with Special Reference to Foster Placement and Adoption Nationally and Internationally, 3 December 1986, A/RES/41/85.

33 J. G. Stein (2001). "A Call to End Baby Selling: Why the Hague Convention on Intercountry Adoption Should be Modified to Include the Consent Provisions of the Uniform Adoption Act." Thomas Jefferson Law Review, 24, 39-82, p. 71.

34 Art. 17 UN General Assembly, Declaration on Social and Legal Principles relating to the Protection and Welfare of Children, with Special Reference to Foster Placement and Adoption Nationally and Internationally, 3 December 1986, A/RES/41/85.

35 R. Hodgkin and P. Newell (2007). "Implementation Handbook for the Convention on the Rights of the Child." UNICEF (3rd ed.), p. 289.

not result in an improper financial gain for those involved therein[36] and encourages the tates to establish policies and enact laws prohibiting the "abduction and any other act for illicit placement of children".[37] The Declaration was the first international legal instrument that promoted the subsidiarity principle and urged the States to take active measures to tackle illegal adoption practices. However, it fails to lay down specific measures directed at reducing trafficking in children and is not legally binding.[38]

In 1989, the *United Nations Convention on the Rights of the Child* (hereinafter UNCRC) was adopted that entered into force in 1990.[39] It addresses adoption and other forms of alternative care, including intercountry adoption, in Articles 20 and 21 thereof (see Chapter III). The Convention enshrines the guiding principles of the human rights of children, which underpin intercountry adoption and from which all adoption laws and practices should flow. It lays down that an intercountry adoption must be authorized by the competent authorities,[40] provides that an international adoption may be considered as an alternative childcare measure only if the child cannot be cared for in his or her native country (subsidiarity principle),[41] obliges the States to ensure that the same standards and safeguards existing for international adoptions are applied on intercountry adoptions,[42] and finally requires them to take all appropriate measures to ensure that the placement of the child does not result in improper financial gain for those involved.[43] Yet, like the Declaration on Social and Legal Principles Relating to the Protection and Welfare of Children with Special Reference to Foster Placement and Adoption Nationally and Internationally, the UNCRC does not contain any specific measures to regulate and control intercountry adoption.[44]

Recognizing that prior efforts to standardize intercountry adoption and tackle the system's abuses proved insufficient, the members of the Hague Conference on Private International Law, and other non-members who were invited to participate,[45] drafted *the*

36 Art. 20 UN General Assembly, Declaration on Social and Legal Principles relating to the Protection and Welfare of Children, with Special Reference to Foster Placement and Adoption Nationally and Internationally, 3 December 1986, A/RES/41/85.

37 Art. 19 *leg. cit.*

38 M. Van Leeuwen (1999). "The Politics of Adoption Across Borders: Whose Interests are Served? (A Look at the Emerging Market of Infants from China)." Pacific Rim Law & Policy Journal, 8, 189-218, p. 204.

39 United Nations Convention on the Rights of the Child, G.A. Res. 44/25, U.N. GAOR, 44th Sess., Supp. No. 49, at 166, U.N. Doc. A/44/736 (1989).

40 Art. 21(a) *leg. cit.*

41 Art. 21(b) *leg. cit.*

42 Art. 21(c) *leg. cit.*

43 Art. 21(d) *leg. cit.*

44 L. K. Carlberg (2007). "The Agreement Between The United States and Vietnam Regarding Cooperation on the Adoption of Children: A More Effective and Efficient Solution to the Implementation of the Hague Convention on Intercountry Adoption or Just Another Road to Nowhere Paved With Good Intentions?" Indiana International & Comparative Law Review, 17, 1, 119-153, p.122.

45 The Hague Conference's members include mainly Western nations – the world's receiving countries – whereas significant sending countries are not members of the Hague Conference. To allow representation

Hague Convention on the Protection of Children and Co-Operation in Respect of Intercountry Adoption in 1993 that entered into force in 1995.[46] The Hague Convention was specifically designed with the purpose of implementing Article 21(e) of the UNCRC, which requests its State Parties to conclude multilateral agreements to ensure that the placement of the child in another country is carried out by "competent authorities or organs".[47] According to Article 1 thereof, the Hague Convention has three main objectives:

a. to establish safeguards to ensure that intercountry adoptions take place in the best interests of the child and with respect for his or her fundamental rights as recognised in international law;
b. to establish a system of close co-operation amongst Contracting States to ensure that those safeguards are respected and thereby prevent the abduction, the sale of, or traffic in children;
c. to secure the recognition in Contracting States of adoptions, made in accordance with the Convention.[48]

The Hague Convention provides a minimum set of standards and procedures ('safeguards') for its Contracting States to follow which are allowed to maintain or add additional guidelines and restrictions as they deem fit.[49] These standards and procedures aim to harmonize – and thereby also simplify – the adoption process as well as to protect the best

of these countries' interests, the Conference invited many of these non-member sending countries to participate in the Hague Convention drafting process as well (R. R. Carlson (1994). "The Emerging Law of Introductory Adoptions: An Analysis of the Hague Conference on Intercountry Adoption." Tulsa Law Journal, 30, 243-304, p. 248). The resulting deliberative body involved representatives of 66 countries that played or continue to play a significant role – either as sending or receiving countries – in the intercountry adoption system. The following member countries were present during the discussion: Argentina, Australia, Austria, Belgium, Canada, Chile, China, Cyprus, the Czech Republic, Denmark, Egypt, Finland, France, Germany, Greece, Hungary, Ireland, Israel, Italy, Japan, Luxembourg, Mexico, The Netherlands, Norway, Poland, Portugal, Romania, Slovenia, Spain, Sweden, Switzerland, Turkey, the United Kingdom of Great Britain and Northern Ireland, the United States of America, Uruguay, and Venezuela. In addition, the following non-member countries were invited: Albania, Belarus, Benin, Bolivia, Brazil, Bulgaria, Burkina Faso, Colombia, Costa Rica, El Salvador, Ecuador, Haiti, the Holy See, Honduras, India, Indonesia, Kenya, the Republic of Korea, Lebanon, Madagascar, Mauritius, Nepal, Panama, Peru, the Philippines, the Russian Federation, Senegal, Sri Lanka, Thailand, and Vietnam. J. G. Stein (2001). "A Call to End Baby Selling: Why the Hague Convention on Intercountry Adoption Should be Modified to Include the Consent Provisions of the Uniform Adoption Act." Thomas Jefferson Law Review, 24, 39-82, pp. 73-74.)

46 R. Rios-Kohn (1998). "Intercountry adoption: An international perspective on the practice and standards." Adoption Quarterly, 1, 4, 3-32, p. 15.

47 N. B. Graff (2000). "Intercountry Adoption and the Convention on the Rights of the Child: Can the Free Market in Children be Controlled?" Syracuse Journal of International Law & Commerce, 27, 405-430, p. 420.

48 Art. 1 Hague Convention.

49 P. Pfund (1993). "Hague Convention on Intercountry Adoption." Women Lawyers Journal, 79, 3, 6-8, p. 7.

interests and rights of the child. To ensure that the rules of the Hague Convention are followed, and to "prevent the abduction, the sale of, or traffic in children", the treaty places special emphasis on close cooperation between the States Parties.[50] Finally, the Hague Convention aims to ensure mutual recognition of foreign judgments in intercountry adoption cases that were promulgated in accordance with its provisions.

3 Provisions of the Hague Convention

3.1 *Preamble*

The Preamble to the Hague Convention sets forth the principles that should serve as "a guidance for the interpreter when applying the Convention to particular situations".[51] It recognizes that "the child, for the full and harmonious development of his or her personality, should grow up in a family environment" and encourages States Parties to take "appropriate measures to enable the child to remain in the care of his or her family of origin". The Preamble further acknowledges "that intercountry adoption may offer the advantage of a permanent family to a child for whom a suitable family cannot be found in his or her State of origin" and stresses the "necessity to take measures to ensure that intercountry adoptions are made in the best interests of the child and with respect for his or her fundamental rights, and to prevent the abduction, the sale of, or traffic in children".

3.2 *Scope of Application*

Chapter I explains the Convention's scope of application. According to Article 2 thereof, the Convention applies when a child under the age of eighteen that is habitually resident in one Contracting State ('sending State') has been, is being, or is to be moved to another Contracting State ('receiving State') either after he or she has been adopted in the sending state by a spouse or a single person that is habitually resident in the receiving State, or for the purposes of such an adoption in the receiving or sending state.[52] The transfer of the child's habitual residence from one country to another is decisive and not the nationality of the child or of the adoptive parents.[53] This transfer of the child must correlate with an

50 Parra-Aranguren (1994). "Explanatory Report on the Convention on Protection of Children and Co-operation in Respect of Intercountry Adoption." para. 66.

51 G. Parra-Aranguren (1994). "Explanatory Report on the Convention on Protection of Children and Co-operation in Respect of Intercountry Adoption." The Hague Conference on Private International Law, para. 36.

52 Art. 2(1) Hague Convention.

53 J. Reinhardt (2012), Adoptionsübereinkommens-Ausführungsgesetz, Nomoskommentar, Baden, Rn. 4-6.

adoption that has been carried out in the child's country of origin or with an adoption that is intended to be carried in the receiving State. The Convention's regulations do not apply to temporary childcare solutions (such as foster care).[54]

3.3 *Requirements of Intercountry Adoptions, Distribution of Responsibility*

In its Chapter II, the Hague Convention lists the minimum substantive requirements that an intercountry adoption must fulfil and distributes the responsibility for their fulfilment between the competent authorities of the sending and receiving countries.[55] According to Article 4, the *sending countries* are obliged (1) to verify – according to its laws and procedures[56] – that the child is adoptable;[57] (2) to carefully consider possible domestic childcare arrangements before determining that an intercountry adoption is in the best interests of the specific child;[58] (3) to ensure that the consents necessary for an adoption have been given[59] and meet the requirements,[60] as well as to ensure (4) that the wishes, opinions, and consent of the child have been verified.[61] Pursuant to Article 5, it is the responsibility of the *receiving countries* (1) to determine the prospective adoptive parents' eligibility and suitability;[62] (2) to ensure that they have been counselled as may be necessary[63] and to (3) guarantee that the child is authorized "to enter and reside permanently in that State".[64]

---

54 Art. 2(2) Hague Convention.

55 It is up to each Contracting State to determine the competent authorities. They might either be administrative, juridical or even the Central Authority (Parra-Aranguren (1994). "Explanatory Report on the Convention on Protection of Children and Co-operation in Respect of Intercountry Adoption.", para. 111, 176).

56 The Permanent Bureau of the Hague Conference on Private International Law (2008). "The Implementation and Operation of the 1993 Hague Intercountry Adoption Convention: Guide to Good Practice No. 1." The Hague, para. 324.

57 Art. 4(a) Hague Convention.

58 Art. 4(b) *leg. cit.*

59 The persons whose consent to an adoption is necessary are determined by the applicable national law. It usually includes not only the child's biological parents, but also his or her relatives or legal guardians. (G. Parra-Aranguren (1994). "Explanatory Report on the Convention on Protection of Children and Co-operation in Respect of Intercountry Adoption." The Hague Conference on Private International Law, para. 129).

60 Art. 4(c) Hague Convention.

61 Art. 4(d) *leg. cit.*

62 Art. 5(a) *leg. cit.*, to be read in conjunction with Article 16(b) which requires information about the child's adoptability in the report.

63 Art. 5(b) *leg. cit.*, confirming the principle of subsidiarity of an intercountry adoption already included in the third paragraph of the Preamble.

64 Art. 5(c) *leg. cit.*

3.4 *Central Authorities and Accredited Bodies*

Chapter III concerns the creation and tasks of Central Authorities and accredited bodies that must ensure that the proper investigations and tasks are performed. Article 6 obliges its Contracting States to designate a Central Authority in their country,[65] which must oversee every step in the international adoption process.[66] Central Authorities must fulfil non-delegable and delegable tasks.[67] The non-delegable duties include: co-operating with the Central Authorities in other countries and promoting co-operation amongst national authorities involved in intercountry adoption;[68] providing information as to their national adoption laws and other general information;[69] eliminating any obstacles to the Convention's application[70] as well as ensuring that appropriate measures are taken when a provision of the Convention has not been or is at serious risk of not being respected.[71]

Duties which the Central Authority may delegate to public authorities or accredited bodies include: taking "all appropriate measures to prevent improper financial or other gain in connection with an adoption and to deter all practices contrary to the objects of the Convention";[72] collecting, preserving and exchanging "information about the situation of the child and the prospective adoptive parents";[73] facilitating, following and expediting adoption proceedings;[74] promoting "the development of adoption counselling and post-adoption services";[75] providing "each other with general evaluation reports about experience with intercountry adoption"[76] and replying to requests from other Central Authorities for information about a particular adoption case.[77] Also, the functions listed in Chapter IV (Articles 14 to 22) may be assigned.

Articles 10 and 11(a) and (b) set forth minimum requirements for the accreditation of private bodies and Article 11(c) provides certain minimum standards for their supervision by competent authorities. Finally, Article 12 provides that an accredited body in one

65 According to Art. 6(2) *leg. cit.*, "Federal States, States with more than one system of law or States having autonomous territorial units shall be free to appoint more than one Central Authority".
66 C. E. Kimball (2005). "Barriers to the Successful Implementation of the Hague Convention on Protection of Children and Co-Operation in Respect of Intercountry Adoption." Denver Journal of International Law and Policy, 33, 4, 561-584, p. 570.
67 J. M. Lippold (1995). "Transnational Adoption from an American Perspective: The Need for Universal Uniformity." Case Western Reserve Journal of International Law, 27, 465-503, p. 494.
68 Art. 7(1) Hague Convention.
69 Art. 7(2)(a) *leg. cit.*
70 Art. 7(2)(b) *leg. cit.*
71 Art. 33 *leg. cit.*
72 Art. 8 *leg. cit.*
73 Art. 9(a) *leg. cit.*
74 Art. 9(b) *leg. cit.*
75 Art. 9(c) *leg. cit.*
76 Art. 9(d) *leg. cit.*
77 Art. 9(e) *leg. cit.*

Contracting States may only act in another state if it was permitted by the competent authorities in both states.

3.5 *Procedural Requirements of Intercountry Adoptions*

Chapter IV describes the procedural requirements of intercountry adoptions. Prospective adoptive parents must apply to the Central Authority in the state in which they habitually reside.[78] They are not allowed to pursue their application directly with the Central Authority, or any other competent authority or accredited body of the sending state.[79] If the Central Authority in the *receiving state* is satisfied that the prospective adoptive parents are eligible and suited to adopt internationally, it must draw up a report to be transmitted to the Central Authority in the sending state, including information about their identity, eligibility and suitability to adopt, their familial, social and medical background, reasons for adopting and the characteristics of the children for whom they would be qualified to care.[80]

If the Central Authority in the *sending state* is satisfied that the child is adoptable, it must prepare a similar report which provides information about the child's identity adoptability background, social environment, family and medical history and any special needs.[81] Furthermore, the Central Authority in the sending state must give due consideration to the child's upbringing and to his or her ethnic, religious and cultural background, ensure that consent has been obtained pursuant to Article 4, and to determine, on the basis of the reports relating to the child and the prospective adoptive parents, whether the international placement is in the child's best interests.[82] The report must then be sent to the Central Authority in the receiving state together with proof that the consent necessary for an adoption have been obtained and the reasons for its determination on the placement, "taking care not to reveal the identity of the mother and the father if, in the State of origin, these identities may not be disclosed".[83]

If the Central Authorities in both states agree that the adoption may proceed and all conditions have been met, the prospective adoptive parents will be allowed to adopt the child.[84] Where the adoption takes place in the receiving state after the child has arrived and it appears to the Central Authority in the receiving state that the continued placement

78 Art. 14 *leg. cit.*

79 G. Parra-Aranguren (1994). "Explanatory Report on the Convention on Protection of Children and Co-operation in Respect of Intercountry Adoption." The Hague Conference on Private International Law, para. 291.

80 Art. 15 Hague Convention.

81 Art. 16(1)(a) *leg. cit.*

82 Art. 16(1)(b)-(d) *leg. cit.*

83 Art. 16(2) *leg. cit.*

84 Art. 17 *leg. cit.*

of the child is not in his or her best interests, it must stop the adoption and provide alternative care.[85]

The Central Authorities may delegate the tasks listed in Chapter IV (Articles 14 to 21) to public authorities and accredited bodies.[86] The duties that are listed in Articles 15 to 21 may be assigned to non-accredited bodies, such as agencies, lawyers, or social workers under specific requirements and limitations.[87]

3.6 *Recognition and Effects of Intercountry Adoptions*

Chapter V regulates the recognition and effects of an intercountry adoption. According to Article 23, an adoption that was certified by the competent authority of the state of the adoption as having been made in accordance with the Convention must be recognized *ex lege*, in the other Contracting States, without a judicial or administrative decision being required. Pursuant Article 24, a Contracting State may refuse to recognize an adoption only if the adoption is "manifestly contrary to its public policy, taking into account the best interests of the child". An *ex lege* recognition should prevent adopters from having to seek a re-adoption in the receiving country.[88] Chapter V furthermore explains the implications of such recognition[89] and regulates the conversion of a weak into a full adoption.[90]

3.7 *General Provisions and Final Clauses*

Chapter VI includes general provisions. Particularly, Article 29 prohibits contact between the prospective adoptive parents and the birth parents or the persons actually caring for the child before certain requirements are met. Articles 30 and 31 address the preservation of information concerning the identity of the child and his or her parents and the use of personal data that are gathered or transmitted under the auspices of the Convention. Article 32 forbids deriving "improper financial or other gain" from an intercountry adoption. Article 33 concerns violations of the treaty's provisions. Articles 36 to 38 address the issue of Contracting States having two or more systems of law. Article 40 prohibits

85 Art. 21 *leg. cit.*
86 Art. 22(1) *leg. cit.*
87 Art. 22(2) *leg. cit.*
88 G. Parra-Aranguren (1994). "Explanatory Report on the Convention on Protection of Children and Co-operation in Respect of Intercountry Adoption." The Hague Conference on Private International Law, para. 402.
89 Art. 26 Hague Convention.
90 Art. 27 *leg. cit.*

reservations to the Convention to ensure that ratifying States are bound by all its provisions.[91]

According to Article 42, the Secretary General of the Hague Conference on Private International Law shall regularly review and convene a Special Commission to review the practical operation of the Convention. In practice, the Special Commission, composed of representatives of the Contracting States and states that are interested in becoming parties, meets up in a 5-year interval. Within one week, the specific issues and challenges countries are facing are discussed (e.g. financial aspects, abuses, the principle of subsidiarity, support for birth families, adoptability etc.). The results of the discussions are then published in the Guides to Good Practice as well as in the reports and recommendations which provide guidelines for the implementation of the Hague Convention's safeguards and procedures.[92]

Chapter VII includes the final clauses concerning signature, accession, entry into force and denunciation of the Convention. Article 44(3) provides the Contracting States with the option to raise an objection to the accession of a state which was not a Member State of the Hague Conference at the time the Convention was adopted and which did also not participate in the drafting process thereof.

4 THE STANDARDS AND PRINCIPLES OF THE HAGUE CONVENTION

The Hague Convention was the first international legal instrument to deal with intercountry adoption in a significant manner. The drafters' intention was to establish a sustainable and ethical intercountry adoption system in which the best interests of unparented children would be served and their fundamental rights protected.[93] They believed that intercountry adoptions would best be safeguarded against illegal and abusive practices if they were adequately regulated and controlled. To this end, the Convention sets forth principles mirroring the children's rights' principles laid down in the UNCRC and it provides a minimum set of standards and procedures for its Contracting States to follow.

91 R. Rios-Kohn (1998). "Intercountry adoption: An international perspective on the practice and standards." Adoption Quarterly, 1, 4, 3-32, p. 21.

92 Interview with L. Mártinez-Mora, the Principal Officer at the Permanent Bureau of the Hague Conference on Private International Law, responsible for intercountry adoptions, The Netherlands, 24.02.2017.

93 Preamble: "Convinced of the necessity to take measures to ensure that intercountry adoptions are made in the best interests of the child and with respect for his or her fundamental rights [...]"

The Explanatory Report,[94] the two Guides to Good Practice[95] as well as numerous reports and recommendations adopted by the Special Commissions,[96] its Experts Group[97] and Working Groups[98] as well as by the International Social Service, an NGO that assists with the implementation of the Convention, explain and elaborate on these fundamental principles and standards and serve the Contracting States as a guide on the proper implementation of the treaty. They respond to developments in the adoption system, address important questions that the Convention itself leaves unanswered (e.g. the regulation of adoption costs, donations and contributions to child protection services in the sending countries) and generally constitute the primary source of what are to be considered as mandatory good practices.

4.1 *The Best Interests of the Child*

The concept of the best interests of the child is the most fundamental principle of the Hague Convention, referred to in several of its articles. The treaty's Preamble and Article 1(a) thereof both emphasize that intercountry adoptions must "take place in the best interests of the child and with respect for his or her fundamental rights". Particularly, Article 4(b) obliges the competent authorities in the sending countries to determine, after the possibilities for domestic childcare arrangements have been given due consideration, "that an intercountry adoption is in the child's best interests". If it is satisfied that the child is adoptable, it shall determine whether the envisaged placement is in the best interests of the child, according to Article 16(1)(d). Pursuant to Article 21, the competent authorities of the receiving countries, on the other hand, are authorized to take the child out of the care of the prospective adoptive parents or to cancel an adoption, if they consider one of those actions to be in the child's best interests.[99] The latter may furthermore refuse to recognize an intercountry adoption according to Article 24, if it is manifestly contrary to its public policy, "taking into account the best interests of the child".

---

94 G. Parra-Aranguren (1994). "Explanatory Report on the Convention on Protection of Children and Co-operation in Respect of Intercountry Adoption." The Hague Conference on Private International Law.

95 The Permanent Bureau of the Hague Conference on Private International Law (2008). "The Implementation and Operation of the 1993 Hague Intercountry Adoption Convention: Guide to Good Practice No. 1." The Hague; The Permanent Bureau of the Hague Conference on International Private Law (2012). "Accreditation and Adoption Accredited Bodies: Guide to Good Practice No. 2." The Hague.

96 Available at https://www.hcch.net/en/instruments/conventions/publications1/?dtid=57&cid=69 (last visited on Jan. 19th, 2017).

97 Reports drawn up by the Experts Group on the Financial Aspects of Intercountry Adoption available at https://www.hcch.net/en/publications-and-studies/details4/?pid=6310&dtid=63.

98 Reports drawn up by the Working Group, available at https://www.hcch.net/en/instruments/conventions/publications1/?dtid=62&cid=69.

99 M. Van Leeuwen (1999). "The Politics of Adoptions Across Borders: Whose Interests are Served? (A Look at the Emerging Market of Infants from China)." Pacific Rim Law & Policy Journal, 8, 1, 189-218, p. 207.

4.2 The Subsidiarity Principle

One of the drafters' aims was to prevent intercountry adoption from becoming a preferred child care measure, by encouraging its Contracting States to invest in family welfare and to prioritize domestic adoption over international adoption. Thus, similar to the Declaration on Social and Legal Principles Relating to the Protection and Welfare of Children with Special Reference to Foster Placement and Adoption Nationally and Internationally as well as the UNCRC, the Hague Convention embraces the subsidiarity principle, which basically states that intercountry adoption should be considered as an *ultimate ratio* child care measure. Compared to the UNCRC, the Convention provides a hierarchy of alternative care solutions that shows a higher propensity towards intercountry adoption.

During the negotiations that led to the creation of the Hague treaty, there was disagreement among the drafters as to when an intercountry adoption would be appropriate.[100] Some participating countries argued that the Convention should adopt the UNCRC's preference for domestic child care measures, while others, especially the United States delegation, supported a more positive stance on intercountry adoption.[101] The final version of the Hague Convention clearly prioritizes national adoption over international adoption, but seems to favour international adoption over institutionalization.[102]

In its Preamble, the treaty states that a child "should grow up in a family environment". In order to accomplish this objective, the Contracting States "should take, as a matter of priority, appropriate measures to enable the child to remain in the care of his or her family of origin". Just like the UNCRC, the Hague Convention encourages family preservation and reunification efforts. The Convention's Guide to Good Practice No. 1 stresses that "States should examine the most common reasons families relinquish or abandon children [and] [t]o the extent possible, [...] should provide funding for family preservation programmes and develop programmes to meet the needs of relinquishing families".[103] Yet, it is worth noting that nowhere in its objectives or operational sections does the Convention explicitly require such efforts to be made as a prerequisite for international adoption.[104]

The Preamble continues to recognize that "intercountry adoption may offer the advantage of a permanent family to a child for whom a suitable family cannot be found in his or her State of origin". Unlike the UNCRC,[105] the Hague Convention, therefore,

100 R. R. Carlson (1994). "The Emerging Law of Introductory Adoptions: An Analysis of the Hague Conference on Intercountry Adoption." Tulsa Law Journal, 30, 243-304, pp. 261-262.

101 *Ibid.*

102 *Ibid.*

103 The Permanent Bureau of the Hague Conference on Private International Law (2008). "The Implementation and Operation of the 1993 Hague Intercountry Adoption Convention: Guide to Good Practice No. 1." The Hague, para. 273.

104 D. M. Smolin (2010). "Child Laundering and the Hague Convention on Intercountry Adoption: The Future and Past of Intercountry Adoption." University of Louisville Law Review, 48, 441-498, p. 448.

105 See Chapter III, section 5.2.

explicitly prioritizes intercountry adoption over institutionalization (a child "should grow up in a family environment") and even foster care ("intercountry adoption may offer the advantage of a *permanent* family"). The Convention's Guide to Good Practice No. 1 clarifies that: "National solutions for children such as remaining permanently in an institution, or having many temporary foster homes, cannot, in the majority of cases, be considered as preferred solutions ahead of intercountry adoption. In this context, institutionalisation is considered as 'a last resort'".[106] Yet, notwithstanding the principle that a child should grow up in a family environment, the Hague Convention does not in any way mandate that its Contracting States place their children up for intercountry adoption, if no family is available in the child's country of origin ("intercountry adoption *may* offer the advantage of a permanent family").[107]

The subsidiarity principle, as it is set forth in the Convention's Preamble, is further elaborated upon in Article 4(b) which states that "possibilities for placement of the child within the State of origin" must be given due consideration before considering an intercountry adoption. The principle is not absolute, as it does not require the competent authorities of the Contracting States to exhaust all local adoption alternatives before allowing an intercountry adoption to go ahead.[108] Rather, they only need to give "possibilities" for the placement of the child within the state of origin "due consideration".[109]

The relationship between the UNCRC and the Hague Convention has for a long time been subject to debate. Some experts argue that the Hague Convention should be accepted as the guiding law, as it was adopted subsequent to the UNCRC and because it is far more specific to intercountry adoption.[110] The UN Committee on the Rights of the Child, UNICEF and many other organizations believe, however, that the Hague Convention makes no change to the subsidiarity principle that is found in the UNCRC and they therefore treat the UNCRC provisions as the governing law in this area.[111]

---

106 The Permanent Bureau of the Hague Conference on Private International Law (2008). "The Implementation and Operation of the 1993 Hague Intercountry Adoption Convention: Guide to Good Practice No. 1." The Hague, para. 53.

107 D. M. Smolin (2010). "Child Laundering and the Hague Convention on Intercountry Adoption: The Future and Past of Intercountry Adoption." University of Louisville Law Review, 48, 441-498, p. 448.

108 R. R. Carlson (1994). "The Emerging Law of Introductory Adoptions: An Analysis of the Hague Conference on Intercountry Adoption." Tulsa Law Journal, 30, 243-304, p. 264.

109 The Permanent Bureau of the Hague Conference on Private International Law (2008). "The Implementation and Operation of the 1993 Hague Intercountry Adoption Convention: Guide to Good Practice No. 1." The Hague, para. 50.

110 F. J. Earls (2011). "The child as citizen." Los Angeles, SAGE, p. 97.

111 *Ibid.*

4.3 Competent Authorities Principle

The Hague Convention seeks to curtail the free market in children by withdrawing intercountry adoptions from private dispositions. Similar to the UNCRC,[112] it provides that international adoptions must be undertaken or approved by the competent authorities in order to guarantee that all safeguards and standards have been followed. The treaty establishes a system of close cooperation between its Contracting States. It obliges each state to designate a Central Authority which acts as a gatekeeper through which all intercountry adoptions must be channelled. States are permitted to allow private bodies to perform the functions of the Central Authority[113] only, however, if they have been duly accredited by the Central Authority or a competent authority and are subject to its supervision. Independent individuals or bodies that do not qualify for accreditation are also allowed to operate under certain requirements and under the strict supervision of the authorities.[114]

The drafters of the Hague Convention have recognized that the lax licensing and regulation of adoption agencies makes the intercountry adoption system conducive to illegal and abusive practices as it allows inexperienced and gullible individuals, who are either ill-equipped to identify risk factors in the adoption process or who place their own interests (e.g. financial, religious) over the interests of the child, to operate.[115] Hence, in order to ensure that intercountry adoptions that are handled by private bodies take place in an ethical manner and with respect for the rights of the child and his or her parents, the Convention provides a set of minimum requirements[116] for their accreditation. First, they must demonstrate their competence to carry out their tasks and duties properly.[117] Second, they must not pursue profit objectives,[118] meaning that profit-making should not form any part of the decision-making process.[119] Nevertheless, it is permitted to charge prospective adoptive parents costs and expenses, including reasonable fees for professional services,[120] and to remunerate its directors, administrators and employees with a salary that is reasonably high in relation to the services rendered.[121] Third, the accredited bodies'

112 Art. 21(a) UNCRC.
113 Art. 8 and 9 Hague Convention.
114 Art. 22(2) *leg. cit.*
115 D. M. Smolin (2006). "Child Laundering: How the Intercountry Adoption System Legitimizes and Incentivizes the Practices of Buying, Trafficking, Kidnapping, and Stealing Children." The Wayne Law Review, 52, 1, 113-200, pp. 180-184.
116 The Contracting States may impose additional criteria or obligations on private bodies seeking accreditation.
117 Art. 10 Hague Convention.
118 Art. 11(a) *leg. cit.*
119 The Permanent Bureau of the Hague Conference on International Private Law (2012). "Accreditation and Adoption Accredited Bodies: Guide to Good Practice No. 2." The Hague, para. 64.
120 Art. 32(2) Hague Convention.
121 Art. 32 (3) *leg. cit.*

directors and staff need to be "qualified by their ethical standards and by training or experience to work in the field of intercountry adoption".[122]

The Convention furthermore provides minimum standards for the control of the accredited bodies and submits them to the periodical supervision. The Central Authority or the competent authorities of the state must, at the very least, monitor the adoption agencies' composition to verify that their directors and staff actually meet the ethical and professional requirements. They are furthermore required to control their operation in order to check whether they pursue only non-profit objectives, as well as to monitor their financial situation in order to avoid any improper practices in their actual operation.[123] If accredited bodies do not perform their functions according to the standards of the Convention or if they cease to fulfil the accreditation requirements, their license should be withdrawn or its renewal should be rejected.[124]

4.4 *Principle of Preventing Improper (Financial) Gain*

The drafters of the Hague Convention acknowledged the fact that money constitutes a primary motivation in many cases of illegal and abusive adoptions.[125] The importance of preventing improper financial gain was strongly emphasized during the negotiations that led up to the drafting of the Hague Convention, where it was recalled that "it is not only the intermediary bodies [adoption agencies] that are attracted by improper financial gain", "but as it has sometimes happened that lawyers, notaries, public servants, even judges and university professors, have either requested or accepted excessive amounts of money or lavish gifts from prospective adoptive parents".[126] The treaty, therefore, provides the principle that "no one shall derive improper financial or other gain from an activity related to an intercountry adoption".[127] Furthermore, it clarifies that only costs and expenses, including the professional fees for persons involved in the adoption (directors, administrators, and employees of bodies) that are reasonably high in relation to services rendered, may be charged or paid.[128]

---

122 Art. 11(b) *leg. cit.*

123 G. Parra-Aranguren (1994). "Explanatory Report on the Convention on Protection of Children and Co-operation in Respect of Intercountry Adoption." The Hague Conference on Private International Law, para. 266.

124 The Permanent Bureau of the Hague Conference on Private International Law (2008). "The Implementation and Operation of the 1993 Hague Intercountry Adoption Convention: Guide to Good Practice No. 1." The Hague, para. 209.

125 See Chapter II, section 2.5.

126 G. Parra-Aranguren (1994). "Explanatory Report on the Convention on Protection of Children and Co-operation in Respect of Intercountry Adoption." The Hague Conference on Private International Law, para. 527.

127 Art. 32(1) Hague Convention.

128 Art. 32(2) and (3) *leg. cit.*

The Convention leaves it up to the Contracting State to determine as to when remuneration will be considered unreasonably high.[129] Yet, the treaty's Guide to Good Practice No. 2 specifies the situations in which improper financial gain could commonly arise as follows: "when the salary of the accredited body's representative in the State of origin is too high compared to the average wage of workers in that country doing the same type of job; professional services offered by certain persons in the receiving State or State of origin are too expensive compared to the same type of service outside of the adoption context; administration costs of the accredited body are too high in comparison with the services rendered; donations and contributions required of prospective parents are used for the personal enrichment of the recipient".[130] Moreover, it lists the factors that need to be considered in order to assess whether costs charged by adoption agencies are reasonably high.[131]

The Hague Convention obliges the Central Authorities to take, directly or through public authorities, all appropriate measures to prevent improper financial or other gain derived from an intercountry adoption-related activity.[132] According to the Guide to Good Practice No. 1, such measures shall include: "regulat[ing] the non-profit objectives of accredited bodies; ensur[ing] compliance with the general prohibition on improper financial gain; verify[ing] that only fees of persons involved in the adoption, are charged or paid; establish[ing] safeguards to prevent directors, administrators and employees of bodies involved in an adoption from receiving remuneration which is unreasonably high in relation to services rendered; establish[ing] safeguards to prevent consents of persons, institutions or bodies [or the child] from being induced by payment or compensation of any kind; require[ing] an accredited body or approved (non-accredited) person to provide a list of their fees and costs, for publication on a website or in brochures".[133] All other stakeholders that are involved in the intercountry adoption process, particularly accredited bodies, have a responsibility to support and comply with any such measures.[134]

4.2 *Standards for the Consent to Adoption*

The Convention's drafters have recognized that an intercountry adoption can only be made in the child's best interests and with respect to his or her fundamental rights if the

129 The Permanent Bureau of the Hague Conference on International Private Law (2012). "Accreditation and Adoption Accredited Bodies: Guide to Good Practice No. 2." The Hague, para. 73.

130 *Ibid.*, para. 74.

131 *Ibid.*, para. 401.

132 Art. 8 Hague Convention.

133 The Permanent Bureau of the Hague Conference on Private International Law (2008). "The Implementation and Operation of the 1993 Hague Intercountry Adoption Convention: Guide to Good Practice No. 1." The Hague, para. 177.

134 The Permanent Bureau of the Hague Conference on International Private Law (2012). "Accreditation and Adoption Accredited Bodies: Guide to Good Practice No. 2." The Hague, para. 358.

decision of the birth parents or the person or institution that is legally responsible for the child has not been influenced. Therefore, the treaty provides specific guidelines and requirements for their consent to an adoption, which are stricter than those contained in the previous international legal instruments on intercountry adoption. Consent to adoption is to be considered valid only if it meets the following criteria.

First, the persons, institutions and authorities, whose consent is necessary for the adoption, need to be *counselled* as may be necessary and *duly informed* of the effects of their consent.[135] In particular, it must be explained whether or not an adoption will result in the termination of the legal relationship between the child and his or her family of origin. Counselling must not be given in cases where institutions or authorities intervene, as it is generally assumed that they do not need it.[136] It is, however, required in cases where the child's birth parents' consent is necessary for the adoption, as they might be unfamiliar with the concept of 'relinquishment' which is based on a culturally foreign, exclusivist nuclear (rather than extended family) model.[137]

Second, the Hague Convention requires consent to be given *freely*, in the required legal form, and expressed or evidenced in writing.[138] This means that it must not be affected by, for instance, "fraud, misrepresentation, duress, undue influence or mistake".[139] The treaty thereby responds to cases where consent to relinquishment is induced by psychological pressure. For example, incidences have emerged whereby pregnant women or birth mothers – often young, unmarried and impoverished – were told that they were not the most suitable person to bring up their child properly and that they should give their future or newborn children the opportunity to have a better life than themselves.[140] The Hague Convention also sought to prevent those cases where parents are deceived about the consequences of an adoption, by being told that, for example, their child is only going away for educational purposes or on a temporary basis or by being promised that they can keep contact with their child, receive payments and letters from the adoptive parents or will be allowed to follow their child to the Western nation once the child has grown up.[141]

---

135 Art. 4(c)(1) Hague Convention.

136 G. Parra-Aranguren (1994). "Explanatory Report on the Convention on Protection of Children and Co-operation in Respect of Intercountry Adoption." The Hague Conference on Private International Law, para. 130-131.

137 D. M. Smolin (2007). "Intercountry Adoption and Poverty: A Human Rights Analysis." Capital University Law Review, 36, 413-453, p. 443.

138 Art. 4(c)(2) Hague Convention.

139 G. Parra-Aranguren (1994). "Explanatory Report on the Convention on Protection of Children and Co-operation in Respect of Intercountry Adoption." The Hague Conference on Private International Law, para. 141.

140 UNICEF International Child Development Centre (1998). "Intercountry adoption." UNICEF, Florence (Innocenti Digest no. 4), p. 6.

141 D. M. Smolin (2006). "Child Laundering: How the Intercountry Adoption System Legitimizes and Incentivizes the Practices of Buying, Trafficking, Kidnapping, and Stealing Children." The Wayne Law Review, 52, 1, 113-200, p. 121.

Third, the consent to the adoption must *not be induced* by payment or other compensation of any kind and must not be *withdrawn*. This requirement responds to the reported practice of solicitation, whereby intermediaries actively approach vulnerable families (isolated mother and impoverished parents) and incited them to give up their future or newborn child for adoption in return for money or goods.[142] It also prohibits donations that are made to birth families by adoptive parents, as they might influence or bring about the decision to relinquish a child for adoption.[143] This is supported by Article 29 which prohibits any contact between the prospective adoptive parents and the birth parents. The Hague Convention leaves open the possibility for birth parents to withdraw their consent if they change their mind. Basically, it is up to the Contracting States to specify the period after the child's birth in which the parents may revoke their consent to adoption.[144]

Finally, the Hague Convention provides that the mother's consent to adoption *was given after* her child's *birth.*[145] The drafters' aim was to prevent unmarried mothers "from making hurried decisions caused by strain, anxiety or pressures to give their consent".[146] Clearly, with the high standards and requirements for the consents to adoption, the treaty does not only aim to protect the rights of the child, but also those of his or her birth parents or family.

4.6 *Principle of Co-operation and Co-responsibility*

One of the Hague Convention's main objectives is "to establish a system of co-operation amongst Contracting States" to ensure that the treaty's standards are respected and to thereby prevent the abduction, the sale of, or traffic in children.[147] Article 7, therefore, requires the Central Authorities of both countries to co-operate with each other. In particular, they shall exchange information about their adoption laws, statistics and standard forms and information about the practical operation of the Hague Convention. This duty cannot be delegated. Nonetheless, the Guide to Good Practice No. 2 stresses that the accredited bodies, too, have the responsibility to cooperate in order to achieve the objectives

142 See Chapter II, section 2.3.2.

143 The Permanent Bureau of the Hague Conference on Private International Law (2014). "Note on the Financial Aspects of Intercountry Adoption", para. 145.

144 G. Parra-Aranguren (1994). "Explanatory Report on the Convention on Protection of Children and Co-operation in Respect of Intercountry Adoption." The Hague Conference on Private International Law, para. 154.

145 Art. 4(c) Hague Convention.

146 G. Parra-Aranguren (1994). "Explanatory Report on the Convention on Protection of Children and Co-operation in Respect of Intercountry Adoption." The Hague Conference on Private International Law, para. 153.

147 Art. 1(b) Hague Convention.

of the treaty.[148] Also, the procedural requirements that are laid down in Articles 14 to 21 require cooperation between the competent authorities and the accredited bodies in both the sending and receiving countries.[149]

The sending and receiving states have a co-responsibility to ensure that intercountry adoptions are compliant with the standards and safeguards stipulated in the Hague Convention. The treaty itself does not specify how the obligation of co-responsibility is to be met. Yet, the Guides to Good Practice give some guidance in this regard. They particularly encourage the recipient countries, which are the primary source of demand and have greater resources, to assist the countries of origin to improve their child welfare and adoption systems. They are advised to refrain from exerting pressure on the sending countries in order to maintain a 'supply' of children (e.g. by sending an unreasonable number of adoption applications or by providing financial inducements), to respect the state of origin's requirements regarding the profile and number of accredited agencies, to actively respond to abuses or irregularities in the sending countries (e.g. by eliminating risk factors or discontinuing cooperation with shady partner organizations or underperforming sending states), to properly prepare adoption applicants by sensitizing them to the risks and pitfalls of an international adoption and by managing their expectations.[150]

5 Limitations and Pitfalls of the Hague Convention

Without a doubt, the Hague Convention constitutes the most comprehensive attempt to tackle abuses in the intercountry adoption system. It does not intend to do that directly by providing criminal law responses to such illegal practices. In fact, the Optional Protocol to the Convention on the Rights of the Child on the Sale of Children, Child Prostitution and Child Pornography (2000) addresses this need by adopting an "explicitly criminal justice approach" to the issue of child trafficking[151] by requiring its States Parties to criminalize and appropriately punish the relevant acts[152] and to establish jurisdiction over its offenses (Article 4).[153] Rather, the Hague Convention aims to indirectly prevent illegal and abusive adoption practices by providing for a minimum set of standards and procedures which ought to be implemented through a system of cooperation between Contracting

148 The Permanent Bureau of the Hague Conference on International Private Law (2012). "Accreditation and Adoption Accredited Bodies: Guide to Good Practice No. 2." The Hague, para. 550.

149 *Ibid.*

150 *Ibid.*, para. 553.

151 A. T. Gallagher (2010). "The international law of human trafficking." Cambridge University Press, p. 67.

152 Optional Protocol to the CRC, Preamble, Art 1, 3.

153 *Ibid.*

States, "because it is expected that the observance of the Convention's rules will bring about the avoidance of such abuses".[154]

This approach was strongly supported by Interpol, the International Criminal Police Organization, which commented that "the establishment of strict international civil and administrative procedures would make it much more difficult for people to use intercountry adoption procedures as a means of trafficking in children, from one country to another".[155] Particularly, it was believed that "the system of Central Authorities would offer the possibility of reporting offenses against criminal law 'to the appropriate department so that international police or judicial co-operation may begin, if necessary'".[156]

Unfortunately, several adoption scandals that have occurred in the Contracting States to the Hague Convention, such as in Colombia, Romania and India, suggest that the ratification of the treaty does not *ipso eo* prevent illegal and abusive practices. In the following paragraphs, the weaknesses and limitations of the treaty will be analysed and evaluated. Some of them are the result of necessary compromises that every international legal instrument, created by numerous State delegations with different cultural backgrounds, reflects. Others relate to the practical pitfalls of the Convention. One of the major weaknesses is the receiving countries' trust in the integrity of the adoption process in the sending countries that have ratified the treaty.

5.1 *Private Adoptions*

5.1.1 Private adoptions and illegal practices

Private or independent adoptions are those which are directly arranged between the adopters and the birth parents or the organisation caring for the child (e.g. orphanage). They take place without the involvement of a permitted adoption placement office in the sending or the receiving country.[157] The adopters often use an unauthorized private contact, such as a foreign social worker, priest, nurse, doctor or attorney, acting as an intermediary. Such an intermediary or independent adoption agent usually offers a shortening or circumvention of the otherwise very time-consuming official adoption placement procedure.[158] They identify and locate an attractive child, secure the necessary consent to adoption and handle the adoption paperwork.

154 Parra-Aranguren (1994). "Explanatory Report on the Convention on Protection of Children and Co-operation in Respect of Intercountry Adoption.", para. 52.

155 *Ibid.*, para. 54.

156 *Ibid.*

157 See, for example, International Social Service (2007). "Adoption 'on holiday'." Geneva, Nr. 1.

158 H. C. Kennard (1993). "Curtailing the Sale and Trafficking of Children: A Discussion of the Hague Conference Convention in Respect to Intercountry Adoptions." University of Pennsylvania Journal of International Business Law, 14, 4, 623-649, p. 627.

Two studies were conducted with a view to examining the correlation between private adoptions and illegal practices. An investigation carried out by the organizations Defence for Children International, International Social Service and Terre des Hommes sought to identify "the degree to which 'independent inter-country adoptions [...] are constant with the rights and interests of the children concerned".[159] It considered responses from 12 receiving countries and 11 sending countries which "indicated that questionable and/or illicit adoption practices in the process of inter-country adoption are numerous",[160] including 'fait accompli adoptions',[161] unprincipled selection of adoptive parents,[162] improper pressure on biological parents,[163] falsification of documents,[164] charging unreasonably high fees as well as the trafficking and sale of children. The investigations' results were inconclusive:[165] "According to the receiving countries reports, [questionable and/or illicit adoptions practices] are often linked to independent adoptions; in contrast, there is no agreement among country of origin reports, some of which associate them with agencies, independent adoptions or both".[166] Thus, whereas the receiving countries reported that illegal practices would often occur in independently pursued adoptions, the sending countries observed that both private and agency adoptions were linked to illegal practices.

A study that was conducted in Germany in the late 80s shows a more distinctive link between private adoptions and illegal practices.[167] It evaluated data about intercountry adoptions carried out between 1984 and 1987 in four Western German states – Bremen, Hamburg, Lower Saxony and Schleswig-Holstein. In total, 1,046 cases were registered of

---

159 Defence for Children International, Terre des Hommes, International Social Service (1991). "Preliminary Findings of a Joint Investigation on Independent Intercountry Adoptions." (on file with author), p. 3.

160 *Ibid.*, p. 14.

161 In cases of "fait accompli adoptions", adopters would approach the immigration or other authority in their home country together with the child that they want to adopt in the receiving country without having first obtained the necessary authorization (e.g. home study, visa) to do so (*Ibid.*).

162 Prospective adoptive parents would be selected only on the basis of their wealth or religious affiliation (*Ibid.*, p. 15).

163 "Examples included the soliciting of biological parents, providing biological parents with little if any time for their relinquishment decision (reflection), offering services to pregnant women in return for their promise to relinquish their child for adoption and misleading biological parents about the destiny of their children". (*Ibid.*)

164 "Many examples of falsification of documents were mentioned including: false declarations of paternity, maternity, relinquishment and abandon; falsification of birth certificates and falsifying documents related to the purpose of entry in to the receiving country." (*Ibid.*, p. 16.)

165 P. Hayes (2011). "The Legality and Ethics of Independent Intercountry Adoption Under the Hague Convention." International Journal of Law, Policy and the Family, 25, 3, 288-317, p. 3.

166 Defence for Children International, Terre des Hommes, International Social Service (1991). "Preliminary Findings of a Joint Investigation on Independent Intercountry Adoptions." (on file with author), p. 18.

167 R. P. Bach (1988). "Daten und soziale Hintergründe der Adoption von Kindern aus der Dritten Welt. Eine Untersuchung der Gemeinsamen Zentralen Adoptionsstelle der vier norddeutschen Bundesländer in Hamburg." Zentralblatt für Jugendrecht, 75, 328-333; M. R. Textor (1991). "International Adoption in West Germany: A private Affair." in H. Altstein and R. J. Simon, "Intercountry Adoption: A Multinational Perspective." Praeger, New York, providing an English summary of Bach's study.

which 638, thus about 61%, involved the adoption of children from a "Third World" country.[168] The study presented more detailed information – with regard to the adoptive parents, the children as well as the placement – about 300 of these 638 adoption cases.[169] Only 134, thus approximately 45%, took place *via* a German international adoption placement office. As for the other 55%, parents obtained their children through personal contacts or with the help of commercial organizations or individuals.[170]

In 70 of these 300 cases "clear indications of commercial, illegal or criminal practices" could be found, meaning that "23 % of all adoptions of children from the Third World or 42% of all private adoptions are violating the adoption laws of the Federal Republic of Germany and – in general – those of the sending countries".[171] Moreover, in a great number of private adoption cases, the required documents, such as the relinquishment decree, the child's birth and health certificate, the social report and the administrative or judicial decisions deviated significantly from the documents in authority adoptions. They were often incomplete, doubtful and would not comply with the sending countries' laws.[172]

In addition, experiences in, for instance, Romania and Guatemala have shown that private adoptions are closely connected to illegal and abusive practices. In the early 1990s, after the distressing conditions in Romanian child care institutions became known internationally, thousands of foreigners from the United States, as well as Western Europe, came to the country and arranged private adoptions to 'save the children'.[173] It soon became clear, however, that the majority of these children were actually not orphans – and hence not available for adoption – but had been placed in these institutions by their families on a temporary basis due to economic hardship or illness. Other children were suffering from severe mental or physical disabilities and were therefore not attractive to prospective adoptive partens.[174] Foreigners soon started to look outside the institutions for suitable children to adopt.[175] Maternity clinics were a primary source of adoptable children, where pregnant or new mothers would be approached and induced into relinquishing their

168 R. P. Bach (1988). "Daten und soziale Hintergründe der Adoption von Kindern aus der Dritten Welt. Eine Untersuchung der Gemeinsamen Zentralen Adoptionsstelle der vier norddeutschen Bundesländer in Hamburg." Zentralblatt für Jugendrecht, 75, 328-333, p. 330.

169 *Ibid.*, pp. 331-333.

170 *Ibid.*, p. 332.

171 *Ibid.* According to Bach, an adoption is considered *commercial* when financial rewards are granted to a person having the care and custody of a child (birth parent, warden or director of an orphanage) in exchange for the required consent to the adoption (deed of relinquishment). Adoptions are *illegal* when they violate civil or administrative legal provisions and they are *criminal* when they constitute a criminal offence, such as child abduction, falsification of documents or child trafficking.

172 *Ibid.*

173 J. Dickens (2002). "The paradox of inter-country adoption: analysing Romania's experience as a sending country." International Journal of Social Welfare, 11, 1, 76-83, p. 77.

174 *Ibid.*

175 *Ibid.*

child.[176] According to estimates, more than 10,000 Romanian children were adopted internationally between March 1990 and July 1991, after which Romania finally decided to ban international adoptions.[177]

Also in Guatemala, private adoptions took place on a large scale. In this sending country, international adoptions were generally processed under a 'notarial system' which operated to facilitate the swift adoption of young infants.[178] Adopters would hire a private attorney for around $15,000-20,000 who would then represent the prospective adoptive parents, the birth parents as well as the child. The primary review of the adoption case was then conducted by the Guatemalan Solicitor General's Office.[179] Although Guatemala was and still is a developing country where about 39% of the population live below $2 a day,[180] the fees for international adoptions paid to Guatemalan attorneys were extraordinarily high, ranging between $18,000 and $19,000.[181] Between 2003 and 2010, this country placed some 24,000 children up for international adoption, constituting the third most significant sending state after China (75,000) and Russia (47,000).[182] This number is remarkably high when one considers Guatemala's population of only 13 million. In comparison, China and Russia had a population of 1.3 billion and 143 million respectively at that time.

It soon became apparent that "legal adoption appears to be the exception rather than the rule".[183] In her report on the mission to Guatemala, the Special Rapporteur on the sale of children, child prostitution and child pornography concluded that: "In the majority of cases, intercountry adoption involves a variety of criminal offences including the buying and selling of children, the falsifying of documents, the kidnapping of children, and the housing of babies awaiting private adoptions in homes and nurseries set up for that purpose".[184] Attorneys would, for instance, "buy babies while they are still in the mother womb",[185] "trick[ing] or drug[ging] illiterate birth mothers into putting their thumbprint on blank pieces of legal paper which are subsequently filled in to read as a consent to

176 *Ibid.*
177 P. Selman (2002). "Intercountry adoption in the new millennium; the "quiet migration" revisited." Population Research and Policy Review, 21, 3, 205-225, p. 213.
178 D. M. Smolin (2006). "Child Laundering: How the Intercountry Adoption System Legitimizes and Incentivizes the Practices of Buying, Trafficking, Kidnapping, and Stealing Children." The Wayne Law Review, 52, 113-200, p. 165.
179 *Ibid.*
180 The World Bank (2013). "World Development Indicators." Available at http://databank.worldbank.org/data/download/wdi-2013-ebook.pdf, p. 28.
181 D. M. Smolin (2006). "Child Laundering: How the Intercountry Adoption System Legitimizes and Incentivizes the Practices of Buying, Trafficking, Kidnapping, and Stealing Children." The Wayne Law Review, 52, 113-200, p. 164.
182 P. Selman (2012). "The Global Decline of Intercountry Adoption: What Lies Ahead?" Social Policy and Society, 11, 03, 381-397, p. 384.
183 UN Commission on Human Rights (2000). "Report of the Special Rapporteur on the Sale of Children, Child Prostitution and Child Pornography." 27.01.2000, E/CN.4/2000/73/Add.2, para. 13.
184 *Ibid.*
185 *Ibid.*, para. 33.

adoption of the baby",[186] "use middlemen to seek out pregnant women who, because of poverty or prostitution, might be willing to give up their children or to sell them"[187] and who would "resort to threats or even baby-stealing" if the mother could not be persuaded.[188]

5.1.2 The Hague Convention's compromise in Article 22(2)

The Hague Convention admits "a limited possibility of 'independent' or 'private' adoptions".[189] As was mentioned in section 3.5, the Central Authority may allocate its functions listed in Chapter IV of the Convention to public authorities or accredited bodies.[190] Independent agents or bodies that do not qualify for accreditation are also allowed to operate in certain circumstances. Article 22(2) permits the Contracting States to declare to the depositary of the Hague Convention that non-accredited bodies or persons are permitted to operate to the extent permitted by local law.[191] However, they may only perform the duties listed in Articles 15 to 21. The functions they are allowed to perform are more limited than those of the accredited bodies. Article 22(5) furthermore limits their scope of action by asserting that the reports provided for in Articles 15 and 16 shall, in any case, be prepared under the responsibility of the Central Authority. Contracting States are free to impose additional restrictions on the activities that are carried out by approved (non-accredited) persons and bodies.[192]

Sending States have the option to declare that adoptions of children habitually resident in their territory may only take place if the functions assigned to the Central Authority in the receiving state are performed by the Central Authority, either by public authorities or accredited bodies.[193] Yet, receiving states do not have such an option. They cannot declare that adoptions may not be carried out if the functions assigned to the Central Authority in the sending countries are performed by private agents and bodies.

The Hague Convention sets forth minimum standards that non-accredited bodies or persons must comply with (each Contracting State may establish additional criteria).[194] Pursuant to Article 22(2)(a) and (b), they must "meet the requirements of integrity, pro-

186 *Ibid.*, para. 35.

187 *Ibid.*, para. 36.

188 *Ibid.*, para. 38.

189 G. Parra-Aranguren (1994). "Explanatory Report on the Convention on Protection of Children and Co-operation in Respect of Intercountry Adoption." The Hague Conference on Private International Law, para. 378.

190 Art. 22(1) Hague Convention.

191 Silence by a Contracting State is thus to be interpreted as an objection to the operation of non-accredited bodies and agents in its adoption system.

192 The Permanent Bureau of the Hague Conference on International Private Law (2012). "Accreditation and Adoption Accredited Bodies: Guide to Good Practice No. 2." The Hague, para. 631.

193 Art. 22(4) Hague Convention.

194 G. Parra-Aranguren (1994). "Explanatory Report on the Convention on Protection of Children and Co-operation in Respect of Intercountry Adoption." The Hague Conference on Private International Law, para. 383.

fessional competence, experience and accountability" and must be "qualified by their ethical standards and by training or experience to work in the field of intercountry adoption". These requirements are similar to the minimum criteria which accredited bodies must fulfil according to Articles 10 and 11. Unlike the latter, non-accredited persons and agencies are generally allowed to pursue profit objectives.[195] However, Article 32 prohibits them from deriving improper financial or other gain from their intercountry adoption-related activities. They must therefore not charge fees that are unreasonably high in relation to the services they render.[196] Approved non-accredited bodies and agents are subject to the supervision of the competent authorities of the State that made the declaration according to Article 22(2). Such supervision will cover the requirements of Article 22(2)(a) and (b), as well as compliance with the rules and standards of the Convention, particularly the prohibition contained in Article 32.[197]

Article 22(2) was a compromise that came about after a heated discussion over the type of legal framework that should be established to regulate intercountry adoptions.[198] The delegates from numerous countries participating in the preparatory work – notably many continental European nations – promoted a 'social democratic approach' towards adoption policy.[199] They advocated a state-regulated system in which the adoption procedure would rely on Central Authorities and accredited bodies and from which private, independent and for-profit individuals and organizations would be excluded. They "*perceive[d]* private adoptions to be more prone to abuses, such as occurred in Romania a few years ago, than adoptions for which licensed agencies provide adoption services".[200] They feared that permitting private adoptions would give way to a marketplace in children where profits override concerns for the best interests and rights of the child and where the poor would not be adequately protected from exploitation.[201]

The United States delegation, on the other hand, favoured a more 'liberal approach' and strongly lobbied to allow for-profit individuals and organizations to act as intermediaries.[202] In the United States, independent agents have long dominated domestic as well

195 *Ibid.*, para. 389.

196 H. C. Kennard (1993). "Curtailing the Sale and Trafficking of Children: A Discussion of the Hague Conference Convention in Respect to Intercountry Adoptions." University of Pennsylvania Journal of International Business Law, 14, 4, 623-649, p. 640.

197 G. Parra-Aranguren (1994). "Explanatory Report on the Convention on Protection of Children and Co-operation in Respect of Intercountry Adoption." The Hague Conference on Private International Law, para. 384.

198 P. Hayes (2011). "The Legality and Ethics of Independent Intercountry Adoption Under the Hague Convention." International Journal of Law, Policy and the Family, 25, 3, 288-317, p. 1.

199 *Ibid.*, p. 15.

200 P. Pfund (1993). "Hague Convention on Intercountry Adoption." Women Lawyers Journal, 79, 3, 6-8, p. 7.

201 P. Hayes (2011). "The Legality and Ethics of Independent Intercountry Adoption Under the Hague Convention." International Journal of Law, Policy and the Family, 25, 3, 288-317, p. 16.

202 *Ibid.*, p. 15.

as intercountry adoptions, whereas agency-facilitated adoptions were generally viewed sceptically. Granting monopoly to the state, proponents of private adoptions argue, would lead to the abuse of power, needless bureaucracy and inefficiencies that are likely to harm children by slowing down the adoption process and by failing to reach out to as many children in need of an adoption as possible.[203] Private adoptions, on the other hand, are considered to be a good practice as they empower the individuals involved in the adoption process, allowing them to make an arrangement that best suits their interests and wishes.[204] The prospective adoptive parents have quicker access to the adoptable children they like, probably get more information about their social and medical status and would not be subject to a seemingly subjective, discriminatory and arbitrary agency selection procedure. Furthermore, the birth parents would play a more active role in selecting the 'right' adoptive parents for their child.[205]

During the negotiations, the United States delegation made it clear that the United States would not ratify the Hague Convention if it did not allow private adoptions.[206] Pfund, the Drafting Committee's chief negotiator of the United States "consistently sought [...] to ensure that the convention remains sufficiently flexible and capable of support by the various elements of the U.S. adoption community to permit the United States to become a party. The delegation supported and achieved a decision that the convention would permit and set standards for independent adoptions".[207] The delegates finally settled on Article 22(2), leaving it at the discretion of each individual Contracting State to allow for-profit organizations and individuals to operate as intermediaries when particular conditions are fulfilled.

5.1.3 The no contact rule in Article 29

Moreover, Article 29 is decisive for private adoptions. This provision generally prohibits contact between prospective adoptive parents and the child's parents or any other person

203 *Ibid.*, p. 16; N. C. Baker (1978). "Baby Selling: The Scandal of Black-Market Adoption." The Vanguard Press, New York, p. 135; P. Hayes (2011). "The Legality and Ethics of Independent Intercountry Adoption Under the Hague Convention." International Journal of Law, Policy and the Family, 25, 3, 288-317, p. 23; E. Bartholet (2007). "International Adoption: Thoughts on the Human Rights Issue." Buffalo Human Rights Law Review, 13, 151-203, pp. 189-191.

204 D. M. Smolin (2013). "The Corrupting Influence of the United States on a Vulnerable Intercountry Adoption System: A Guide for Stakeholders, Hague and Non-Hague Nations, NGOs, and Concerned Parties." Utah Law Review, Journal of Law & Family Studies, 15, 81-209, p. 112; J. B. Singer (1992). "The Privatization of Family Law." Wisconsin Law Review, 1444-1567, pp. 1481-1485; E. Bartholet (2007). "International Adoption: The Child's Story." Georgia State University Law Review, 24, 333-379, p. 340.

205 *Ibid.*

206 P. Pfund (1994). "Intercountry Adoption: The 1993 Hague Convention: Its Purpose, Implementation, and Promise." Family Law Quarterly, 28, 1, 53-88, p. 80

207 P. Pfund (1993). "Hague Convention on Intercountry Adoption." Women Lawyers Journal, 79, 3, 6-8, pp. 7-8.

who has actual care of the child (e.g. the director of an orphanage, a child care institution)[208] in the most sensitive phase of the adoption process, namely *before* it has been established that (1) the child is adoptable, (2) intercountry adoption is in his or her best interests, (3) the required consent have been obtained[209] and (4) the prospective adoptive parents are suited and eligible to adopt internationally.[210] According to the Convention's Explanatory Report, Article 29 aims to "prevent trafficking and any other kind of practices that may be contrary to the purposes of the Convention, in particular, to avoid that the consents required for the granting of the adoption are induced by payment or compensation, as is expressly forbidden by Article 4, sub-paragraph c(3)".[211]

The prohibition contained in Article 29 is not absolute but has far-reaching exemptions. First, contacts are not restricted in cases of intra-family adoptions since prospective adoptive parents usually already know the child's birth parents. Second, contact with the child is allowed, as it "does not have the potential for abuse that contact with the parents has, and may normally be both desirable and unavoidable".[212] Third, the prohibition contained in Article 29 does not extend to "the representative of the prospective adoptive parents", including bodies or persons who are allowed to perform functions under the Convention according to Article 22(2).[213] Finally, each sending country may individually decide whether or not to allow contact between the adopters and child's parents or legal guardians and if so, under which conditions.[214] It may do so "either in general terms, by the legislator, or on a case-by-case basis, i.e. by the administrative or judicial authority, taking into account the particularities of the situation".[215] Hence, a sending country is free

208 G. Parra-Aranguren (1994). "Explanatory Report on the Convention on Protection of Children and Co-operation in Respect of Intercountry Adoption." The Hague Conference on Private International Law, para. 500.

209 Art. 4(a)-(c) Hague Convention.

210 Art. 5(a) *leg. cit.*

211 G. Parra-Aranguren (1994). "Explanatory Report on the Convention on Protection of Children and Co-operation in Respect of Intercountry Adoption." The Hague Conference on Private International Law, para. 495; see also International Social Service (2005). "In the spirit of article 29 of THC-1993, any contact between prospective adoptive parents (PAPs) and the child's parents or carer, should be prohibited until the matching decision." Geneva, Nr. 6.

212 G. Parra-Aranguren (1994). "Explanatory Report on the Convention on Protection of Children and Co-operation in Respect of Intercountry Adoption." The Hague Conference on Private International Law, para. 499.

213 *Ibid.*, para. 501.

214 R. R. Carlson (1994). "The Emerging Law of Introductory Adoptions: An Analysis of the Hague Conference on Intercountry Adoption." Tulsa Law Journal, 30, 243-304, p. 267.

215 G. Parra-Aranguren (1994). "Explanatory Report on the Convention on Protection of Children and Co-operation in Respect of Intercountry Adoption." The Hague Conference on Private International Law, para. 503.

to permit direct contact without any restraints whatsoever, thereby annulling Article 29 altogether.[216]

The Convention's Guide to Good Practice No. 1 emphasizes that "adoptions arranged directly between birth parents and adoptive parents" (which it refers to as 'private adoptions') "are not compatible with the Convention" and "could *never* [emphasis added] be certified by Article 23".[217] The same applies to 'independent adoption' which the Guide to Good Practice describes as "those cases where prospective adoptive parents, after being approved by their Central Authority or accredited body, go to the State of origin and find a child to adopt, without the assistance of the Central Authority or an accredited body or approved (non-accredited) person in the State of origin".[218] The Guide stresses that such independent adoptions would "undermine the system of safeguards put in place by the Convention, in particular Article 29".[219]

5.1.4 The Hague Convention's regulation on private adoptions – a limitation?

The Hague Convention adopts a clear stance on privately organized intercountry adoptions. The treaty establishes the competent authorities' principle (see section 4.3), which clearly forbids prospective adoptive parents from directly arranging an adoption with the birth parents or the person or organisation actually caring for the child, without the involvement of a competent authority, an accredited body or approved (non-accredited) person or agency in the state of origin.

Article 29 generally prohibits contact between prospective adoptive parents and the child's parents or the person caring for the child before the official matching took place. However, it permits sending countries to annul this rule by allowing direct contact without any limitations. This permission is problematic as it basically erodes the system of safeguards that the Hague Convention has put in place. By allowing the members of the adoption triad to get in touch with each other, it becomes virtually impossible to prevent adopters from influencing the birth parents' or the legal guardian's decision to give up the child for adoption. Adopters may provide assistance in form of money or goods or exert (probably even unintentionally) psychological pressure on them and thereby induce their consent to adoption.[220]

With regard to intercountry adoptions arranged privately with the help of independent agencies or individuals, such as lawyers, doctors, social workers, the Convention also takes

---

216 R. R. Carlson (1994). "The Emerging Law of Introductory Adoptions: An Analysis of the Hague Conference on Intercountry Adoption." Tulsa Law Journal, 30, 243-304, p. 267.

217 The Permanent Bureau of the Hague Conference on Private International Law (2008). "The Implementation and Operation of the 1993 Hague Intercountry Adoption Convention: Guide to Good Practice No. 1." The Hague, p. 16.

218 *Ibid.*, para. 191.

219 *Ibid.*

220 See Chapter II, section 4.2.2.

a liberal stance. Article 22(2) permits the Contracting States to allow non-accredited persons and bodies to handle intercountry adoptions under certain requirements and limitations. They are permitted to mediate between the adopters and the birth parents or the institution caring for the child (the prohibition of Article 29 does not apply to them) and to arrange the adoption placement.

The treaty has been strongly criticized for the compromise on private adoptions.[221] Experts argue that Article 22(2) would provide fertile ground for illegal practices as it allows non-accredited agents, who account for the greatest abuses in the adoption system, to flourish.[222] Indeed, the study conducted by Bach as well as the incidences observed in Romania and Guatemala do suggest that privately arranged adoptions are closely linked to illegal and abusive practices. However, it is worth noting that this evidence stems from a time *before* the Hague Convention came into force.

The Hague Convention does establish significant limitations on private adoptions. Non-accredited persons and bodies must meet the ethical and professional standards which are quite similar to those that the accredited bodies have to fulfil. Although they are not required to have a non-profit status, they must not derive improper financial or other gain from their intercountry adoption-related activities, by charging fees that are unreasonably high in relation to the services they render. Moreover, just like the accredited bodies, they are subject to the supervision of the competent authorities.

In addition, the treaty limits approved non-accredited persons' and organizations' scope of action. Unlike accredited bodies, they are only allowed to perform the duties that are listed in Articles 15 to 21. They are, for instance, not permitted to collect, preserve and exchange information about the child and the prospective adoptive parents and to facilitate, follow and expedite proceedings with a view to bringing about the adoption (Article 9). Furthermore, prospective adoptive parents cannot submit an adoption application through them but have to apply at the Central Authority, a public authority or an accredited body (Article 14). The Convention permits its Contracting States to allow approved non-accredited persons and organizations to draw up the report about the applicants' eligibility and suitability to adopt (Article 15) or the child proposal (Article 16). These reports must be prepared under the responsibility of the Central Authority, a public authority or an accredited body. Only these bodies are permitted to establish communication with the

221 H. C. Kennard (1993). "Curtailing the Sale and Trafficking of Children: A Discussion of the Hague Conference Convention in Respect to Intercountry Adoptions." University of Pennsylvania Journal of International Business Law, 14, 4, 623-649, pp. 636-640; J. G. Stein (2001). "A Call to End Baby Selling: Why the Hague Convention on Intercountry Adoption Should be Modified to Include the Consent Provisions of the Uniform Adoption Act." Thomas Jefferson Law Review, 24, 39-82, p. 76; M. Farid (2012). "International Adoption: The Economics of the Baby Industry." Whittier Journal of Child and Family Advocacy, 12, 1, 81-103, p. 95.

222 See, for instance, H. C. Kennard (1993). "Curtailing the Sale and Trafficking of Children: A Discussion of the Hague Conference Convention in Respect to Intercountry Adoptions." University of Pennsylvania Journal of International Business Law, 14, 4, 623-649, p. 637.

sending country.[223] Each intercountry adoption must therefore be channelled through them.

Private adoptions that are permitted under the Hague Convention, therefore, differ significantly from those that were observed in the *pre*-Hague era. It would be wrong to claim that Article 22(2) is conducive to illegal and abusive practices by pointing to the private adoptions that took place in the 80s and 90s and in those countries that have not ratified the Convention, which were arranged without any state regulation and supervision whatsoever. Critics seem to assume that there is no qualitative difference between an intercountry adoption pursued privately, meaning without the involvement of an accredited or approved (non-accredited) agent or body, and an independent adoption according to Article 22(2) of the Convention. However, the empirical basis for this argument is somewhat lacking. There is no evidence to suggest that private adoptions as permitted by the Hague Convention are any riskier than agency adoptions, or – put differently – that agency adoptions are any safer than private adoptions pursuant to Article 22(2).

Critics also note that the risk of illegal and abusive adoption practices is particularly acute in cases where approved non-accredited agents are professionals, such as doctors, lawyers, or social workers.[224] This is, they argue, because professionals can hide illicit payments more easily than non-professionals as it is difficult to distinguish such payments from the permissible reasonable fees and compensation.[225] Yet, arguably, the difficulty of drawing the line between permitted reasonable remuneration for services and improper financial gain by illegal payments is a general problem in the intercountry adoption system and not one that can particularly be observed in adoptions arranged by independent agents or bodies which are professionals.

5.2 *Much Latitude for the Contracting States*

The Hague Convention lays down a set of principles that must be respected and complied with in an intercountry adoption procedure. However, it still leaves its Contracting States latitude to define and regulate individually specific aspects of the international adoption process. Hence, some terms in the treaty were deliberately left vague by the treaty itself as well as by its supporting documents. It is up to each Contracting State to determine as to

223 L. M. Katz (1995). "A Modest Proposal? The Convention on Protection of Children and Cooperation in Respect of Intercountry Adoption." Emory International Law Review, 9, 283-328, p. 315.

224 H. C. Kennard (1993). "Curtailing the Sale and Trafficking of Children: A Discussion of the Hague Conference Convention in Respect to Intercountry Adoptions." University of Pennsylvania Journal of International Business Law, 14, 4, 623-649, pp. 637-638; J. G. Stein (2001). "A Call to End Baby Selling: Why the Hague Convention on Intercountry Adoption Should be Modified to Include the Consent Provisions of the Uniform Adoption Act." Thomas Jefferson Law Review, 24, 39-82, pp.76-77.

225 *Ibid.*

when a child is considered 'adoptable' and to interpret the terms 'child's best interests' as well as 'contrary to public policy'.

According to Article 4(a), the competent authorities of the sending country are required to ensure that the child that is being considered for adoption is adoptable. The Convention does not define *'adoptable'* but leaves it up to the Contracting States to determine this term.[226] Usually, a child is adoptable if he or she was relinquished or abandoned by the birth parents or legal guardians or if the state authorities decided that separation of the child from her parents was necessary for the child's best interests. The Hague Convention provides some requirements for the consent to adoption that is given by the child's birth parents or legal guardians. For instance, it lays down that the consent of the mother is only valid if it was given after the birth of her child. However, the treaty does not say when the consent has to be given: it could be either 2 hours or two weeks after birth. Furthermore, it does not establish any guidelines for separating the child from his or her family. The sending countries are given great leeway to determine when a child is to be considered adoptable, which could lead to abuses and exploitation of vulnerable families and their children.

The concept of *'the best interests of the child'* was also left undefined. Like the UNCRC, the Hague Convention, its Explanatory Report as well as its two Guides to Good Practice deliberately left vague the concept of the 'child's best interests'. It is up to the Contracting States to define and interpret this term, taking into account the diverse situations and different social-cultural contexts. As was already explained in Chapter III, this open-ended principle is problematic as it is too biased and subjective.[227] Contracting States may use it to justify decisions on an adoption that are actually condemnable from a human rights perspective.[228]

Finally, the Convention includes the broad term *'contrary to public policy'*. According to Articles 23 and 24, an adoption granted in one Contracting State (and certified by its competent authorities as having been made in accordance with the Convention) must be automatically recognized in the other Contracting States, unless "the adoption is manifestly contrary to its public policy, taking into account the best interests of the child". The Convention does not provide any guidelines for interpreting the notion of "manifestly contrary to public policy" and it fails to explain as to when the recognition of an international adoption is definitely to be refused. Particularly, the treaty does not mandate its Contracting States to refuse the recognition of an international adoption which was made in violation

226 N. S. Thompson (2004). "Hague is Enough?: A Call for More Protective, Uniform Law Guiding International Adoptions." Wisconsin International Law Journal, 22, 2, 441-469, p. 460.

227 See Chapter III, section 6.4.

228 Also the UNCRC left the notion of 'the child's best interests' undefined, see Chapter IV, section 5.2.

of its provisions.[229] Rather, as the Explanatory Reports explains, the question of recognition is outside of the scope of the treaty and must be answered by the applicable law of the recognizing state.[230] The treaty's Guide to Good Practice No. 1 only clarifies that "[a]s a matter of public policy, adoptions procured through abduction of children should not be recognised".[231] In all other cases of illegally procured intercountry adoptions, it is up to the individual (receiving) state to decide on their compatibility with its public policy.

The treaty seeks to limit the Contracting States' wide latitude in this respect by acknowledging the child's best interests as the overriding concern.[232] Yet, as has just been shown, this concept is equally ambiguous and may be used to legitimize an illegal adoption. The competent authorities in a receiving country might, therefore, acknowledge the international adoption of a child that was bought from his or her birth parents or an orphanage (as "donations" or unreasonably high adoption fees were paid) as being in accordance with its public policy. They may argue that leaving the child in the new adoptive family, which is able to provide the child with 'a better life', is in his or her best interests.

As with most international legal instruments, the Hague Convention has to be ratified by numerous Contracting States with different socio-cultural backgrounds. On the one hand, some of the treaty's terms need to be sufficiently broad and indeterminate so as to allow for a flexible application.[233] On the other hand, too much discretion placed in the hands of the Contracting States to define and interpret key terms might not only undermine uniformity upon which the treaty is based[234] but may also lead to illegal or abusive adoption practices.

5.3 *Poor Implementation and Lacking Monitoring and Enforcing Mechanisms*

The provisions of the Hague Convention require its Contracting States to make substantial changes in their adoption systems. They must designate a Central Authority that is responsible for overseeing all international adoptions and that needs to ensure that the

229 G. Parra-Aranguren (1994). "Explanatory Report on the Convention on Protection of Children and Co-operation in Respect of Intercountry Adoption." The Hague Conference on Private International Law, para. 411.

230 *Ibid.*

231 The Permanent Bureau of the Hague Conference on Private International Law (2008). "The Implementation and Operation of the 1993 Hague Intercountry Adoption Convention: Guide to Good Practice No. 1." The Hague, para. 75.

232 J. M. Lippold (1995). "Transnational Adoption from an American Perspective: The Need for Universal Uniformity." Case Western Reserve Journal of International Law, 27, 465-503, p. 498.

233 N. S. Thompson (2004). "Hague is Enough?: A Call for More Protective, Uniform Law Guiding International Adoptions." Wisconsin International Law Journal, 22, 2, 441-469, p. 462.

234 J. M. Lippold (1995). "Transnational Adoption from an American Perspective: The Need for Universal Uniformity." Case Western Reserve Journal of International Law, 27, 465-503, p. 498.

adoption procedures comply with the Convention's minimum set of standards. The Permanent Bureau of the Hague Conference provides states, which have officially requested help (usually the sending countries), with technical assistance to implement the treaty. This might include conducting fact-finding missions in order to assess the situation in the country, training the Central Authorities, reviewing draft legislation and giving recommendations. Technical assistance is funded by the receiving countries and is either provided by the Permanent Bureau itself or (as would usually be the case) by external consultants, such as UNICEF or people who have previously worked in a Central Authority. For instance, experts from Chile and Colombia went to Guatemala to share their experiences and to help the country overcome certain challenges.[235]

The implementation of and the compliance with the Convention's standards and procedures obviously require ample financial and personal resources that many sending countries do not have.[236] States of origin often face extreme poverty – a significant cause for child abandonment or relinquishment in the first place[237] – and lack an established governmental structure to create and maintain a well-functioning, effective and professional Central Authority that is able to fulfil the tasks and responsibilities of the Hague Convention.[238] In addition, they often do not have the political will to invest in revamping a system that does not only save them a lot of money – by relieving them from the responsibility to invest in family welfare and to take care of unparented children – but which also generates millions of dollars per year.[239]

In particular, the determination of the child's adoptability requires ample time and financial resources. In most countries, a child is considered adoptable only if he or she was abandoned or relinquished by the biological parents. According to the Guide to Good Practice, in the case of abandonment, "an investigation of the child's background and circumstances should be made to the extent possible, with every attempt made to locate the family and relatives of the child, and effect a reunification. A similar process should be followed for orphaned children".[240] If the child is relinquished by his or her parents or

235 Interview with L. Mártinez-Mora, the Principal Officer at the Permanent Bureau of the Hague Conference on Private International Law, responsible for intercountry adoptions, The Netherlands, 24.02.2017.

236 L. McKinney (2007). "International Adoption and the Hague Convention: Does Implementation of the Convention Protect the Best Interests of Children?" Whittier Journal of Child & Family Advocacy, 6, 2, 361-412, p. 392.

237 D. M. Smolin (2006). "Child Laundering: How the Intercountry Adoption System Legitimizes and Incentivizes the Practices of Buying, Trafficking, Kidnapping, and Stealing Children." The Wayne Law Review, 52, 113-200, p. 127.

238 N. S. Thompson (2004). "Hague is Enough?: A Call for More Protective, Uniform Law Guiding International Adoptions." Wisconsin International Law Journal, 22, 2, 441-469, p. 459.

239 J. Dickens (2002). "The paradox of inter-country adoption: analysing Romania's experience as a sending country." International Journal of Social Welfare, 11, 1, 76-83, p. 78.

240 The Permanent Bureau of the Hague Conference on Private International Law (2008). "The Implementation and Operation of the 1993 Hague Intercountry Adoption Convention: Guide to Good Practice No. 1." The Hague, para. 326.

legal guardian, the competent authorities of the sending country must ensure that their consent to adoption has been given after "appropriate counselling".[241] In order to facilitate compliance with this requirement, Article 9(c) obliges the Central Authorities to take, directly or through public authorities or accredited bodies, all appropriate measures to "promote the development of adoption counselling [...] in their States". Such counselling should be carried out "by skilled and experienced social workers and professionals, preferably those who are specialised in working with birth mothers and relatives".[242]

Also, the proper implementation of the subsidiarity principle that is laid down in the Preamble to the Hague Convention, as well as in its Article 4(b), costs the states of origin a lot of effort and money. According to the Guide to Good Practice, this principle implies, "that efforts should be made to assist families in remaining intact or in being reunited, or to ensure that a child has the opportunity to be adopted or cared for nationally. The principle also implies that intercountry adoption procedures should be set within an integrated child protection and care system, which maintains these priorities".[243] This means that sending countries are required to establish a child welfare system that assists families in keeping their children during times of crisis or in regaining custody of children from whom they were previously separated, or to reunite children with members of their extended family.[244] In cases where such assistance is not possible or unsuccessful, efforts should be made to place the child within a domestic adoptive family before considering an intercountry adoption.[245] But the high fees and donations that foreign adoptive parents are willing to pay, make international adoptions more lucrative than national adoptions which usually generate far less money[246] and obviously more attractive than family preservation or reunification foster care programmes which would obviously require sufficient funding.

Due to the financial implications of implementing the Hague Convention, several sending countries have long refused to sign or ratify the treaty at all.[247] Other states did

241 G. Parra-Aranguren (1994). "Explanatory Report on the Convention on Protection of Children and Co-operation in Respect of Intercountry Adoption." The Hague Conference on Private International Law, para. 130.

242 The Permanent Bureau of the Hague Conference on International Private Law (2012). "Accreditation and Adoption Accredited Bodies: Guide to Good Practice No. 2." The Hague, para. 474.

243 The Permanent Bureau of the Hague Conference on Private International Law (2008). "The Implementation and Operation of the 1993 Hague Intercountry Adoption Convention: Guide to Good Practice No. 1." The Hague, para. 48.

244 *Ibid.*, para. 271.

245 *Ibid.*, para. 292.

246 D. M. Smolin (2010). "Child Laundering and the Hague Convention on Intercountry Adoption: The Future and Past of Intercountry Adoption." University of Louisville Law Review, 48, 441-498, p. 489.

247 Vietnam, for instance, was for a long time unwilling and unable to undertake the responsibilities imposed by the Hague Convention. As an underdeveloped country, it has long considered the costly implementation of the treaty as impossible to attain. [L. K. Carlberg (2007). "The Agreement Between The United States and Vietnam Regarding Cooperation on the Adoption of Children: A More Effective and Efficient Solution to the Implementation of the Hague Convention on Intercountry Adoption or Just Another Road to Nowhere Paved With Good Intentions?" Indiana International & Comparative Law Review, 17, 1, 119-153, pp. 146-

but have failed to adequately implement the treaty's procedures and safeguards due to a lack of financial and personal resources and/or the necessary political will.[248] Moreover, a high incidence of corruption often impedes the creation of a Hague compliant adoption system in many countries of origin.

The Hague Convention is based on the premise that illegal and abusive adoption practices can best be prevented by withdrawing intercountry adoptions from private dispositions and by increasing capable guardians in the form of regulatory institutions that are responsible for monitoring and controlling the adoption process. It obliges each state to designate a Central Authority which acts as a gatekeeper through which all intercountry adoptions must be channelled (competent authorities' principle, section 4.3). The Central Authorities have to fulfil the tasks that are outlined in the treaty, some of which may be delegated to public authorities (e.g. youth welfare offices or family courts) or to private bodies that must be accredited by the state (e.g. child care institutions, adoption placement agencies).[249] Independent individuals or bodies that do not qualify for accreditation are only allowed to operate under strict requirements and are subject to supervision by the competent authorities.

However, in sending countries that suffer from high levels of corruption, the effectiveness of these regulatory institutions is limited. Instead of serving as guardians in the adoption system that monitor the adoption process and make sure that only children that are truly suited for international adoption enter the system, they might abuse their knowledge and status to illegally secure adoptable children and/or pass them through their organization. This can be illustrated by the Indian adoption system. Already before India ratified the Hague Convention in 2003,[250] it created an adoption system that could be considered as well-regulated. It involves numerous regulatory institutions that all have to approve each international adoption[251] and that seem to constitute multiple layers of

---

147] Vietnam signed the treaty only in 2010 and ratified it one year later [status table of the Hague Convention available at https://www.hcch.net/en/instruments/conventions/status-table/?cid=69 (last accessed on 03.08.2018)].

248 The Permanent Bureau of the Hague Conference on Private International Law (2015). "20 Years of the 1993 Hague Convention: Assessing the Impact of the Convention on Laws and Practices Relating to Intercountry Adoption and the Protection of Children." The Hague, para. 25.

249 See Chapter IV, section 3.5.

250 See https://www.hcch.net/en/instruments/conventions/status-table/?cid=69 (last accessed on 03.08.2018).

251 The Central Adoption Agency (CARA) was established as the Central Authority, and is responsible for determining the rules and procedures for international adoptions and for accrediting national as well as foreign adoption agencies. The Department of Women and Child Welfare in each Indian state is in charge of licensing and monitoring orphanages and for recommending the licensing of an Indian adoption agency. The Child Welfare Committee (CWC) was constituted to process abandonment reports from orphanages, the Adoption Coordinating Agency (ACA) was set up to collect and register information about Indian prospective adoptive parents and adoptable children as well as to promote domestic adoptions. The Adoption Scrutiny Agency (ASA) is involved in guardianship processes in court, responsible for determining whether the adoption is in the child's best interests and if all guidelines have been complied with. Based on the recommendation of the ASA, the Indian court may then transfer guardianship to the prospective

capable guardians against illegal and abusive practices.[252] Nonetheless, as numerous adoption scandals have shown, the system was being used extensively to launder children.[253] The regulatory institutions in the Indian adoption system did not prevent illegal adoption practices but actually facilitated the laundering process. Smolin, who analysed the Indian adoption system in light of the uncovered adoption scandals in Andhra Pradesh, explains that:

> By creating a system where multiple institutions must approve each adoption, within the context of a system often suffering from corruption through bribery and personal connections, safeguards can instead become opportunities for abuse.[254]

The Hague Convention, its two Guides to Good Practices as well as numerous recommendations that have been drawn up by the Permanent Bureau of the HCCH have set the standards for ethical and sustainable adoptions that respect the rights of children as well as of their birth parents. Nonetheless, the treaty does not adequately address the structural root cause of the illegal adoption market: the economic and demographic asymmetries between the sending and the receiving states that have fuelled the demand for adoptable children, created the motivation of actors in the source countries to illegally obtain them and further increased corruption.[255] In the end, the Convention is no more than a set of principles and procedures, which are only as good as their implementation. As with most international agreements, ratification alone does not guarantee that the Contracting States will actually comply with the treaty.[256]

The Hague Convention does not designate an overseeing international body that ensures that the Contracting States' laws and practices are actually in compliance with its

---

adoptive parents and allow the child to be transferred to the receiving country where he or she has to be adopted within 2 years. On the basis of the court order and other documents, the Regional Passport Office (RPO) issues an Indian passport for the child and the Embassy a visa. (A. Dohle (2008). "Inside Story of an Adoption Scandal." Cumberland Law Review, 39, 131-185, pp. 136-142).

252 D. M. Smolin (2004). "The Two Faces of Intercountry Adoption: The Significance of the Indian Adoption Scandals." Seton Hall Law Review, 35, 403-493, p. 446.

253 D. M. Smolin (2006). "Child Laundering: How the Intercountry Adoption System Legitimizes and Incentivizes the Practices of Buying, Trafficking, Kidnapping, and Stealing Children." The Wayne Law Review, 52, 113-200, pp. 154-158, describing the adoption scandals that were uncovered in Maharashtra and Tamil Nudu; A. Dohle (2008). "Inside Story of an Adoption Scandal." Cumberland Law Review, 39, 131-185, pp. 143-177, illustrating the adoption scandal surrounding the Indian adoption agency Preet Mandir in Maharashtra.

254 D. M. Smolin (2004). "The Two Faces of Intercountry Adoption: The Significance of the Indian Adoption Scandals." Seton Hall Law Review, 35, 403-493, p. 446.

255 See also J. Bhabha (2004). "Moving Babies: Globalization, Markets and Transnational Adoption." The Fletcher Forum of World Affairs, 28, Summer, 181-198, p. 184.

256 B. H. Stuy (2014). "Open Secret: Cash and Coercion in China's International Adoption Programm." Cumberland Law Review, 44, 3, 355-422, p. 358.

standards and procedures. The Permanent Bureau of the HCCH observes the developments in the Contracting States. Yet, it does not have the resources to closely monitor the proper implementation of the treaty.[257] Furthermore, the Convention does not provide any measures to hold the participating countries accountable for violating its provisions.[258] States parties to the Hague Convention that face irregular or abusive adoption practices can request technical assistance from the Permanent Bureau of the HCCH. However, the HCCH does not have the role, nor the mandate, to impose sanctions on a particular country. Martínez-Mora, the Principal Legal Official at the Permanent Bureau responsible for the work related to the 1993 Hague Convention, explains that it is not the role of the HCCH to admonish Contracting States that violate the standards of the Hague Convention:

> That is the difference between [the Permanent Bureau] and an NGO, for example, that has more liberty to go [to a country of origin] and point out things [that are not going well]. [...] As we are an intergovernmental organization, we only visit a country after receiving an official invitation from the government [...]. Receiving an official invitation is important as it shows the commitment from the government to discuss issues and allows us to meet with high-level ranking officials, who can make changes more easily.[259]

The Permanent Bureau encourages authorities and important stakeholders to enforce the treaty's safeguards and procedures in their countries. It is ultimately, however, the Contracting States' responsibility and choice to do so, as they have sovereignty over their own adoption laws.[260] According to Article 6, it is the Central Authorities that have the duty to enforce conformance with the treaty's provisions.[261] Pursuant Article 33, the competent authorities are required to immediately inform the Central Authority about any violations of the Hague Convention. The latter is then "responsible for ensuring that appropriate measures are taken". The Hague Convention does not clarify as to what is to be considered

257 Interview with L. Mártinez-Mora, the Principal Officer at the Permanent Bureau of the Hague Conference on Private International Law, responsible for intercountry adoptions, The Netherlands, 24.02.2017.

258 C. E. Kimball (2005). "Barriers to the Successful Implementation of the Hague Convention on Protection of Children and Co-Operation in Respect of Intercountry Adoption." Denver Journal of International Law and Policy, 33, 4, 561-584, p. 572.

259 Interview with L. Mártinez-Mora, the Principal Officer at the Permanent Bureau of the Hague Conference on Private International Law, responsible for intercountry adoptions, The Netherlands, 24.02.2017.

260 E. Briscoe (2009). "Comment, The Hague Convention on Protection of Children and Co-operation in Respect of Intercountry Adoption: Are Its Benefits Overshadowed by Its Shortcomings?" Journal of the American Academy of Matrimonial Lawyers, 22, 437-460, p. 450.

261 Art. 6(1) Hague Convention: "A Contracting State shall designate a Central Authority to discharge the duties which are imposed by the Convention upon such authorities."

as "appropriate measures".[262] Particularly, the treaty does not provide any concrete remedies for cases in which children have been kidnapped or purchased and are trafficked abroad for the purposes of an adoption.[263] This system of self-regulation is problematic because, as Thompson convincingly argues:

> it essentially allows each country to continue policing international adoption as it sees fit despite the Hague Convention's intentions to provide for and protect children based on 'the child's best interest' guidelines. When each country's Central Authority is essentially its own judge, it is highly unlikely to admit to its own faults and failures with regard to international adoption procedures and harmful consequences, and instead may justify its acts as being in line with their understanding of 'public policy' or 'in the best interests of the child'.[264]

Much latitude is given to the Contracting States to establish their own intercountry adoption system in which violations of the Convention's provisions – if ever uncovered at all – will go unpunished. For instance, Romania, one of the first Contracting States to the Hague Convention, set up and maintained a child welfare and adoption system which operated fundamentally against to the treaty's objectives and principles,[265] without there being any

262 J. M. Lippold (1995). "Transnational Adoption from an American Perspective: The Need for Universal Uniformity." Case Western Reserve Journal of International Law, 27, 465-503, p. 497.

263 D. M. Smolin (2013). "The Corrupting Influence of the United States on a Vulnerable Intercountry Adoption System: A Guide for Stakeholders, Hague and Non-Hague Nations, NGOs, and Concerned Parties." Utah Law Review, Journal of Law & Family Studies, 15, 81-209, p. 90.

264 N. S. Thompson (2004). "Hague is Enough?: A Call for More Protective, Uniform Law Guiding International Adoptions." Wisconsin International Law Journal, 22, 2, 441-469, p. 466.

265 Romania adoption law provided procedures which would relieve the government from its obligation to invest into the child welfare system and thereby *de facto* nullify the subsidiarity principle. Foreign adoption agencies were required to support the development of domestic child care solutions such as family support, foster care and residential care. The amount of support was then translated into points on the basis of which adoptable children would be allotted. The foreign money involved in the Romanian child protection system created a market in adoptable children in which adopters would pay fees ranging from $ 6,000 to $ 30,000. Since adoptions by Romanian families involved much lower fees, corrupt local officials would commonly prefer international adoptions, which soon came to be considered as a routine child care solution rather than a 'last resort' measure. Thus, the number of intercountry adoptions increased significantly from 851 in 1997 to 3,035 in 2000, more than double the number of national adoptions (1,219). Hundreds of agencies were operating in Romania and even though thousands of children were leaving the country, the number of children in institutions continued to increase. Not all of these children were actual orphans. As a matter of fact, the majority of them had one or more living parents who were often persuaded or financially induced to relinquish their children and/or not appropriately counselled about the consequences of an international adoption. If they wanted to reclaim their children did not have the possibilities to do so [J. Dickens (2002). "The paradox of inter-country adoption: analysing Romania's experience as a sending country." International Journal of Social Welfare, 11, 1, 76-83; W. Jacoby, et al. (2009). "Success in Slow Motion: The Europeanization of Romanian Child Policy." Review of International Organizations, 4, 111-133; R. Post (2008). "De perverse effecten van het Haags Adoptieverdrag." Justitiële Verkenningen, 7, 25-37].

consequences from The Hague. Only in 2001 did the Romanian government place a moratorium on intercountry adoptions due to increased pressure from the European Union, to which the country wanted to accede.[266]

5.4 *Trust in the Sending Countries and Appearance of Legitimacy*

Also the stakeholders in Germany and the Netherlands (the adoption agencies and the authorities) are often reluctant to check whether the adoption procedure in the states of origin is actually compliant with the Hague Convention and to suspend intercountry adoptions altogether if irregularities keep occurring. As we will see in Chapters V and VI, they often trust the integrity of the authorities and the adoption procedures in sending countries that have ratified the Hague Convention. For instance, after child laundering incidents were uncovered in China, the Dutch Ministry of Justice and Security, the Central Authority in the Netherlands, accepted quite uncritically the explanations and reassurances of the Chinese authorities, notwithstanding recurring reports about irregular adoption practices and several studies signalling systemic abuses in the Chinese adoption system. In several statements, the Minister explained that the responsibility to control whether an adoption complies with the Hague Convention's requirements rests with the sending country and that the Netherlands needs to have trust in the foreign authorities' integrity as well as the reliability of the information provided about the children.

Indeed, the Hague Convention distributes the responsibility for fulfilling the requirements of an international adoption between the sending and the receiving countries. The competent authorities in the sending countries are in charge of verifying the child's adoptability, ensuring that the necessary consent for an adoption have been given freely, fully informed, counselled, without any financial inducement and in the required form and determining that the subsidiarity principle is complied with.[267] The States of Origin are therefore responsible for the most delicate phase of the adoption procedure in which most abusive or illegal practices commonly take place. The authorities in the receiving countries, on the other hand, are only required to examine the prospective adoptive parents' eligibility and suitability to adopt internationally, to properly counsel them and to make sure that the child is allowed to enter and reside permanently in the receiving state[268] (see

266 Due to the international media coverage of Romania's institutionalized children as well as numerous reports of illegal adoption practices, child protection became a formal EU accession criterion. The EU mandated Romania to reform its child protection system by developing small 'group home alternatives', replacing the large old-style child care institutions, and by banning intercountry adoptions which were not considered to be a proper child care solution in EU Member States (I. Iusmen (2013). "The EU and International Adoption from Romania." International Journal of Law, Policy and the Family, 27, 1, 1-27, pp. 8-9).

267 Art. 4 Hague Convention.

268 Art. 5 *leg. cit.*

section 3.3). The Convention allocates the lion share of responsibility to the states of origin.[269] This basically makes sense as the competent authorities in the child's native country are in a better position than foreign authorities to clarify the child's adoptability and determine whether or not an intercountry adoption is in his or her best interests.

Moreover, a relationship of trust between the authorities in the sending country and the receiving country forms the basis of the Hague Convention. One of the treaty's main objectives is to establish a system of close cooperation amongst the Contracting States which shall work together to prevent abuses and to ensure the protection of children. The authorities, therefore, are required to exchange information about their adoption laws and the practical operation of the Hague Convention, as well as statistics and standard forms (see section 4.6). Such close cooperation should help to promote confidence between the states. The Explanatory Report to the Convention lists one of the needs the treaty's drafters aimed to address:

> a need for co-operation between the countries of origin and of destination (an effective working relationship, based on mutual respect and on the observance of high professional and ethical standards, would *help to promote confidence between such countries, it being reminded that such forms of co-operation already exist between certain countries with results which are satisfactory to both sides* [emphasis added]).[270]

Based on this idea of mutual trust, Article 23 of the Hague Convention provides that adoptions certified by the competent authority in the sending country as having been made in accordance with the Convention shall be automatically recognized in the receiving country (section 3.6.), unless they are manifestly contrary to Dutch public policy, taking into account the best interests of the child (Article 24). The *ex lege* recognition of the adoption superseded the traditional two-step process, where the adoption procedure in the country of origin was practically replicated in the receiving country.[271] The two-step process was often perceived as cumbersome by international adopters who had to go through two judicial adoption proceedings. However, it constituted an important safeguard in the adoption system, as the courts in the receiving countries had to assess the adoptability of the child independently of the courts' findings in the sending country.

269 R. Rios-Kohn (1998). "Intercountry adoption: An international perspective on the practice and standards." Adoption Quarterly, 1, 4, 3-32, p. 27.

270 G. Parra-Aranguren (1994). "Explanatory Report on the Convention on Protection of Children and Co-operation in Respect of Intercountry Adoption." The Hague Conference on Private International Law, para. 7.

271 *Ibid.*, para. 402.

Despite the Hague Convention' allocation of the most important duties to the sending countries and the idea of mutual trust between its Contacting states, the receiving nations are still required to make their own assessments regarding the integrity of the sending countries' intercountry adoption system and the reliability of the information provided about the children.[272] As was just explained, there are sending countries that have ratified the Hague Convention but are either unwilling or unable to adequately implement the treaty's procedures and safeguards. The authorities in the receiving states can therefore *not* necessarily trust that their foreign counterparts properly fulfil the tasks and responsibilities assigned to them by the Convention and that the proposed children are legitimately available for intercountry adoption.[273] This is why the Convention's Guide to Good Practice No. 2 emphasizes a mandate of 'joint responsibility' or 'co-responsibility':

> The Contracting States must not only assume their own specific responsibilities, but also share certain others. In essence, receiving States and States of origin have a collective responsibility to make the Convention work as it was intended, and they must work together to ensure the effective regulation of intercountry adoptions.[274]

This also means, as the Guide explains further, that "receiving countries need to take proactive steps when systemic abuses occur, by trying to eliminate them, if necessary, by discontinuing or refusing adoptions from an underperforming sending state".[275] Finally, co-responsibility arguably also implies that receiving countries must refuse the recognition of an adoption according to the treaty's Article 24 if the adoption procedure took place in violation of the standards and guidelines of the Convention.

Yet, as we will see in Chapter VI, the Dutch Central Authority interprets the treaty's allocation of duties as relieving the Netherlands from any responsibility for the adoption steps taken in the sending countries and seems to understand the idea of mutual trust as a mandate of deference or bar against scrutiny.[276] Also, the stakeholders in the German adoption system seem to consider the Convention as a sound warrant against abuses and irregularities. Whereas German adoption agencies and the official authorities are often more suspicious when it comes to intercountry adoptions from non-Hague countries, they commonly have faith in the integrity of the adoption procedure in those states that have

272 B. H. Stuy (2014). "Open Secret: Cash and Coercion in China's International Adoption Programm." Cumberland Law Review, 44, 3, 355-422, p. 358.

273 See Chapter IV, sections 5.3. and 5.4.

274 The Permanent Bureau of the Hague Conference on International Private Law (2012). "Accreditation and Adoption Accredited Bodies: Guide to Good Practice No. 2." The Hague, para. 551.

275 *Ibid.*, para. 553.

276 See Chapter VI, section 7.4.2.

ratified the Convention.[277] Confidence in the procedures in Hague sending countries can also be observed with adopters. For example, in her adoption narrative Michaela, a German woman who adopted a boy from Kenya, assures other adopters of the safety of adoptions from Hague countries:

> Since Kenya ratified the Hague Convention, the process is completely official and carried out according to the strict rules of the Convention. This guarantees that international adoptions are safe. Child trafficking, for example, is thus excluded.[278]

On the occasion of the treaty's ratification by the United States in 2007, Van Loon, the former Secretary General of the HCCH, praised the Hague Convention for having established mutual confidence between its Contacting States. He claimed: "[t]he Convention has created a global framework that provides stability by giving countries the control they need to trust their partners."[279] It is doubtful whether the treaty has really given its Contracting States more control over the adoption process. The following Chapters will show that the adoption agencies and authorities in Germany and the Netherlands often lack the necessary insight into the developments and processes in the countries they co-operate with. This is particularly the case if the adoption system is entirely state-run, like in China, where foreign adoption agencies do not co-operate with Chinese partner organizations but directly and conclusively with state authorities.

The Central Authorities in the states of origin often refuse to share information with foreign adoption agencies as they do not consider them as their official counterpart.[280] Also, the exchange of information between the Competent Authorities is often not working well either as the authorities in the sending countries would not respond to inquiries or do not share the requested information.[281] Particularly, they are often reluctant to provide insight into the financial aspects of intercountry adoption.[282] The authorities in the receiving countries would accept this poor level of cooperation. Rather than putting pressure on the foreign authorities or, where necessary, suspending intercountry adoptions altogether if they see that the Central Authority refuses to share information or to co-operate, they

277 See Chapter V, sections 6.2. and 8.3.

278 A. Michaela (2014). "Neun Monate Sommer, Tagebuch einer Adoptionsschwangerschaft in Kenia." Tausendschlau Olga Bien, Munich, p. 151.

279 J. H. A. Van Loon (2007). "Statement on the Occasion of the Deposit of the Instrument of Ratification of the Hague Convention of 29 May 1993 on Protection of Children and Co-operation in Respect of Intercountry Adoption, by the United States of America." The Hague Conference on Private International Law, 12.12.2007.

280 P. Vlaardingerbroek (2012). "Interlandelijke adoptie, bezien vanuit het perspectief van het vertrouwensbeginsel." Beleidsdoorlichting interlandelijke adoptie, 15.03.2012, Kamerstukken II 2011-2012, 33199, Nr. 1, Bijlage V, p. 25.

281 See Chapter V, section 8.3.

282 See Chapter VI, section 7.3.

stress the sending countries' responsibility for the adoption process' integrity as well as the principle of mutual trust that the Hague Convention is based on.[283]

The creation of mutual trust between the Contracting States is probably one of the Hague Convention's major pitfalls as it has lowered the level of scrutiny and control towards the adoption steps taken in the sending countries. The treaty has created an appearance of legitimacy which leads stakeholders in the receiving countries to blind out signals of illegal and abusive practices in the states of origin.[284] They are quick to assume the reliability of the adoption system simply because the sending country has ratified the Hague Convention. Accordingly, Bos, a Dutch anthropologist who examined the relinquishing of children by their unmarried mothers in India, concluded that regulations and guidelines have actually obscured the adoption process and mystified the underlying reality:

> I am convinced that these Conventions, Regulations and Guidelines are not the appropriate instruments because they do not address the main concerns. The controlling and monitoring policy implies that the business component is under control. But in practice, the formal controlling process is counter-productive. Instead of taking away threats, it takes away transparency and causes a mystification of reality. The more adoption is regulated and monitored, the more politically correct objectives get distanced from daily practices.[285]

In the backdrop of continuing adoption scandals in the post-Hague era, the trust of the receiving States in the sending countries' adoption processes and the integrity of their official documents is dangerous. As was explained, some states of origin have ratified the Convention but fail to adequately implement its procedures and safeguards as they are unable or unwilling to do so. Yet, these countries would still be labelled as 'Hague states' by the authorities in the receiving countries. A country that wants to ratify or accede to the Hague Convention can do so, even if it has not yet established the necessary structures that would ensure compliance with the treaty's standards and procedures, in fact, it does not even need to have set up a Central Authority. The depository of the Convention, the Ministry of Foreign Affairs in The Netherlands, with which the instrument of ratification or accession is being deposited,[286] cannot and will not reject a state that wants to become a member of the Hague Convention but that does not meet the minimum standards and

283 See Chapter VI, section 7.4.2.

284 See also R. Post (2008). "De perverse effecten van het Haags Adoptieverdrag." Justitiële Verkenningen, 7, 25-37.

285 P. Bos (2007). "Once a Mother: Relinquishment and Adoption From the Perspective of Unmarried Mothers in South India." PhD thesis, University of Amsterdam, p. 241.

286 Art. 43 and 44 Hague Convention.

principles laid down in the treaty.[287] Furthermore, even if a sending country has established a Central Authority and formally enforced adoption laws that are in compliance with the treaty, a high incidence of corruption may prevent the intercountry adoption system from *actually* working according to the treaty.

Yet, stakeholders in Germany and the Netherlands do not seem to differentiate between Hague-countries that actually comply with the treaty's standards and safeguards and those that do not, either because they lack the necessary knowledge to make this distinction or because they think that they are not the ones who should make this distinction. They trust or claim that they need to trust that the sending countries have established an adoption system that is in compliance with the Hague Convention.

With regard to intercountry adoptions from Hague countries that fail to properly implement the Convention's safeguards, the treaty, or rather the paperwork of an adoption certified according to Article 23 of the treaty, might work as a Trojan Horse: the placement of a child that was in the international adoption system illegitimately (because it was kidnapped, stolen or purchased or could have been cared for domestically) appears to be perfectly legal as it formally complies with the procedures of the treaty. In that way, the Convention further facilitates and encourages the laundering of paper orphans through the adoption system.

6 Conclusion

The Hague Convention, its two Guides to Good Practices and numerous reports and recommendations drawn up by the Permanent Bureau of the HCCH set the standards and procedures which aim to ensure that intercountry adoptions take place in an ethical manner and with respect for the rights of children and their birth parents. Without a doubt, the treaty represents the most significant attempt to tackle illegal and abusive adoption practices. However, the treaty has limitations and pitfalls.

First, it still leaves its Contracting States with much latitude to continue policing their international adoption system as they see it fit. The treaty permits the states of origin to nullify the no contact rule established in Article 29 by allowing prospective adoptive parents to get in touch with the birth family or the legal guardian actually caring for the child without any restrictions. This permission makes it impossible to prevent adopters from inducing the birth parents' or legal guardian's decision to give the child up for adoption and therefore hollows out the system of safeguards put in place by the Hague Convention. Furthermore, it includes broad key terms, such as 'adoptable', 'the child's best interests' and 'contrary to public policy' that must be determined by the Contracting States, giving

287 Interview with L. Mártinez-Mora, the Principal Officer at the Permanent Bureau of the Hague Conference on Private International Law, responsible for intercountry adoptions, The Netherlands, 24.02.2017.

them much leeway in designing an adoption system according to their own ideas and interests that might have harmful consequences for the children and their parents.

Second, the Hague Convention has created an appearance of legitimacy which leads stakeholders in the receiving countries to assume the reliability of the Hague countries' adoption system. The Convention is basically only as good as its implementation. Sending countries often lack the sufficient financial and human resources to effectively administer and enforce the standards and procedures of the Hague Convention. In addition, many of them face major issues of corruption and bribery which in turn make a proper implementation of the treaty almost impossible. Some do also not have the political will to change a system that not only saves them a lot of costs but also generates huge amounts of money. They ratify the Hague Convention but establish an intercountry adoption system that *de facto* runs contrary to the treaty's objectives and principles. The Convention does not provide an international body – for instance, comparable to the Committee on the Rights of the Child, the official monitoring body of the UNCRC – which would examine whether the laws and practices of the Contracting States actually comply with the treaty's provisions and which hold them accountable for any violations.

Numerous experts have criticized the Hague Convention for its weaknesses and limitations and claim that the treaty could not effectively prevent illegal and abusive practices in the adoption system. However, many practitioners in the receiving countries seem to consider the Convention as a sound warrant against abuses and irregularities. They often trust that states which have ratified or acceded to the treaty have assigned a functioning Central Authority and that they have established proper safeguards and procedures that would prevent illegal and abusive practices. This faith is dangerous when it is placed in States Parties to the Convention that have failed to properly implement the treaty's regulations. With regard to these countries, the Convention might then work as a 'Trojan horse': the illegal placement of a child appears to be perfectly legal as it formally complies with the procedures of the treaty. In that way, the treaty helps to facilitate and encourage the laundering of paper orphans through the adoption system.

V The German Intercountry Adoption System

1 Introduction

In the 1980s, it became apparent in Germany that international adoptions would not always serve the best interests of children in need of parents. It was exactly 30 years ago that Bach, former head of the Central Adoption Office in Hamburg, published the book 'Purchased Children, Baby Trade with the Third World' in which he pointed to the illegal and criminal practices in the international adoption system.[1] He observed that dealers in the Global South would kidnap children, pressure young and unmarried pregnant women to give up their babies or purchase children from their impoverished birth parents. After the necessary adoption documents were falsified, the children would then be trafficked to countries in the Global North, including Germany, in order to be adopted by families willing to pay the price. Bach concluded: "Over the years, it became obvious that only a small part of international adoptions from Asia and South America would take place in a legal and responsible manner, where 'parents would actually be sought for children'".[2]

Initially, it was the adopters who engaged in questionable unsupervised activities to obtain a child from abroad. They would use their personal contacts with orphanages, priests, lawyers or commercial organizations in the developing countries to adopt a child, without the involvement of a German adoption placement office. Bach's evaluation of intercountry adoption cases registered between 1986 and 1987 at the Joint Central Adoption Office in Hamburg illustrates the scale of the problem of private adoptions and shows a clear link between these adoptions and commercial and illegal practices.[3] Only 134 of the 300 adoptions of children from 'Third World' countries, thus approximately 45%, took place *via* a German international adoption placement office. In the other 55% of these intercountry adoption cases, parents obtained their children independently.[4] In 70 of 300 cases that involved the adoption of a child from a 'Third World' country "clear indications of commercial, illegal or criminal practices" could be found, meaning that "23 % of all adoptions of children from the Third World or 42% of all private adoptions are violating

1 R. P. Bach (1986). "Gekaufte Kinder, Babyhandel mit der Dritten Welt." Rowohlt, Hamburg.

2 *Ibid.*, p. 7.

3 R. P. Bach (1988). "Daten und soziale Hintergründe der Adoption von Kindern aus der Dritten Welt. Eine Untersuchung der Gemeinsamen Zentralen Adoptionsstelle der vier norddeutschen Bundesländer in Hamburg." Zentralblatt für Jugendrecht, 75, 328-333, p. 332.

4 *Ibid.*

the adoption laws of the Federal Republic of Germany and – in general – those of the sending countries".[5]

Whereas initially commercial and illegal practices were observed exclusively in intercountry adoption cases pursued by adoptive parents on a private basis, German accredited adoption agencies gradually became involved in international adoption scandals in the 1990s. This indicated that the intervention of an accredited agency as well as of the German state authorities would *ipso eo* not rule out irregular activities in the intercountry adoption system.[6] In 1999, the organisation *terre des hommes* published a study into the shady practices of a prominent German adoption agency (*pro infante. action: Kind in not*) that carried out several international adoption placements from India, in cooperation with the Indian organization *Missionaries of Charity*, which ran an orphanage in Delhi and which was authorized to place children for intercountry adoption.[7] The study by *terre des hommes* investigated and substantiated five intercountry adoption cases in which *Missionaries of Charity* obtained the children from their birth mothers for temporary care or schooling and then processed them through the adoption system to Germany as orphans.[8]

The children involved in these cases were already older, realized the illegal circumstances of their placements and challenged the false histories of their background and origin. Upon closer examination, *terre des hommes* found that the adoption documents provided contradictory information on the familial status of these children. Whereas in the affidavits issued by the head of the organization *Missionaries of Charity* the children were "born of unknown persons [...] and abandoned with the Missionaries of Charity", they were referred to as 'orphans' in the forms of appointment issued by the High Court in Delhi. The German agency ignored the apparent inconsistencies in the adoption documents and nevertheless finalized the child placements.[9] Even after these child laundering cases were uncovered, the agency was not willing to help clarify the true circumstances of the cases. It maintained that the children's birth mothers relinquished their parental rights but could not present the deeds of relinquishments.[10]

In 2001, Germany ratified the Hague Convention. It was hoped that illegal adoption practices would be tackled by enforcing the treaty's minimum standards and principles.

5 *Ibid.* According to Bach, an adoption is considered *commercial* when financial rewards are being granted to a person having the care and custody of a child (birth parent, warden or director of an orphanage) in exchange for the required consent to the adoption (deed of relinquishment). Adoptions are *illegal* when they violate civil or administrative legal provisions and they are *criminal* when they constitute a criminal offence, such as child abduction, falsification of documents or child trafficking.

6 G. Wuttke (1996). "Ein Kind um jeden Preis? Eine Studie zum Adoptionskinderhandel "terre des hommes Deutschland e.V., Osnabrück.

7 B. Wacker (1994). "Verbrechen und andere Kleinigkeiten. Der Fall „pro infante. Action: kind in not e.v." und seine Konsequenzen." terre des hommes Deutschland e.V., Osnabrück.

8 *Ibid.*

9 *Ibid.*

10 *Ibid.*, p. 8.

However, in 2010, another adoption scandal involving the German adoption agency *International Child Care Organization (ICCO)* shocked the adoption community. For several years, the agency carried out numerous adoption placements in cooperation with the Indian organization *Preet Mandir*, a child care organization located in Pune, which, as it turned out, was involved in illegal and criminal adoption practices.[11] Furthermore, from 2004 until 2006, *ICCO* placed a number of Russian children up for adoption in Germany *via* the U.S. agency *AMREX*, a non-accredited commercial adoption agency that charged fees for its services depending on the age of the children.[12] The German agency sent the applicants' home study reports to its U.S. partner which then arranged adoption placements to Germany with the authorities in Russia.[13] The German agency did not only cooperate with commercial organizations or shady partners in the sending countries, but it also profited from its adoption placements activities.[14]

This Chapter seeks to identify and explain the structural features of the German adoption system that encourage and facilitate the trafficking of children to Germany. Section 2 gives a brief overview of the history, development and current trends of intercountry adoption in Germany. Section 3 describes the German legal framework of intercountry adoption. It outlines the relevant German adoption laws and policies, identifies the system's stakeholders, and describes the steps that are typically involved in the official intercountry adoption procedure.

Section 4 focusses on private intercountry adoptions. It explains why adoptions that are carried without the involvement of an adoption agency in the receiving country are particularly prone to illegal practices and why adopters would choose to circumvent the adoption placement procedure that are is provided for under German law. This section shows that the German adoption system fails to provide mechanisms for preventing adopters from pursuing an independent adoption. It illustrates how the German adoption law and the jurisprudence on the recognition of foreign adoption decisions invite adopters to bypass the official adoption placement procedure and to pursue an adoption without the involvement of a German adoption placement office.

The subsequent five sections deal with agency adoptions and illustrate why they, too, are not immune from abusive or irregular practices. Section 5 takes a close look at the German adoption placement agencies' accreditation and authorization requirements as well as their financial situation. It explains that the demanding requirements that German adoption agencies have to fulfil, their financial dependency on the number of placements and the decreasing numbers of adoptions combined with the increasing competition among

11 A. Dohle (2008). "Inside Story of an Adoption Scandal." Cumberland Law Review, 39, 131-185.
12 Verwaltungsgericht Hamburg, 4 Bs/224/06, 13 E 2153/06.
13 *Ibid.*
14 *Ibid.*

the adoption placement offices are reasons why German agencies find themselves being caught up in a tension between integrity and money.

Section 6 focuses on the German adoption agencies' cooperation with the sending countries. It analyses how German agencies remunerate their foreign representatives and partner organizations in the states of origin, and how they supervise their activities. The section shows that some German agencies accept the fees that their cooperation partners require for their services without knowing as to how they are being used exactly. And even if the fees are made transparent, not all German adoption agencies scrutinize the individual items to see if they are reasonably high. Since controlling the representatives and partner organizations is hardly possible over distance, trust and confidence in them and their working methods play an important role in the cooperation between the German adoption placement office and the sending countries.

Section 7 then zooms in on the Ethiopian child trafficking incidences which involved a German adoption agency's cooperation partner. It seeks to explain why the German agency decided to continue moving children from Ethiopia even after signs of systemic irregularities became apparent and why it decided to hold on to its foreign cooperation partner, a child care institution that was exposed to have been engaged in illegally securing children for adoption. It will be argued that the adoption agency had both an ideological and financial motivation to keep children moving from Ethiopia to Germany. The section then uncovers and explains the various techniques of rationalization that the agency personnel advanced to reject criticism and to protect the agency's image as a child welfare organization abiding by ethical norms and obligations.

Section 8 scrutinizes the monitoring system that Germany established when it ratified the Hague Convention. It shows that the control structure does not go far enough as it does not extend to the agencies' activities in the sending countries and is furthermore too fragmented and cumbersome to effectively prevent the trafficking of children to Germany. It explains how the lack of control is being compensated by trust in the competent authorities in the sending countries, particularly if they have ratified the Hague Convention. Section 9 explains why the fact that the Central Adoption Offices which are responsible for monitoring the adoption agencies and also permitted to carry out adoption placements is a weakness in the German adoption system.

Section 10 discusses the criminal liability of German actors involved in child trafficking. It explains that the German Criminal Code does basically not cover irregular practices by adopters and adoption agencies. It does neither cover German adopters providing money or goods to the orphanage or the child's birth parents facing extreme financial hardship, nor German adoption agencies which carry out adoption placements for consideration or with the intention of enrichment or which provide money or goods to the orphanage in the sending countries they place children from.

Section 11 concludes this Chapter by summarizing the weaknesses, or criminogenic factors, of the German adoption system.

2 History, Development and Current Trends

In Germany, intercountry adoption is a relatively recent phenomenon that only came about in the middle of the 20th century.[15] In 1938 and 1939, anti-Semitism forced numerous desperate Jewish families in the 'Third Reich' to send their children to foster families in Switzerland, France and England in order to protect them from the Holocaust. In many cases, these children were adopted after their birth parents were murdered in concentration camps.[16] Intercountry adoption was also employed by the National Socialists as a political means. In the context of the *'Eindeutschungspolitik'*, several hundreds of children born to 'Aryan' women in occupied countries, such as Norway, Poland, Czechoslovakia, and Yugoslavia, and fathered by German soldiers were separated from their families by the organization *Lebensborn* and brought to the 'fatherland' where they were adopted by German families, particularly by SS-members.[17]

During the two decades following the end of World War II, thousands of German children were transferred to other countries for the purposes of adoption.[18] The number of German children adopted by foreigners increased from 489 in 1950 to a peak of 2,628 in 1957.[19] Most of these children were sent to the United States, Scandinavia, the Netherlands, Belgium and other Western countries. Some of them were illegitimate children fathered by black soldiers of the Allied Forces (so-called 'brown babies').[20] Others had been orphaned by war or were relinquished by their parents who were unable to feed and house them due to widespread destruction and poverty.[21]

15 M. Guelich (2006). "Adoptionen aus dem nicht-europäischen Ausland." BIS-Verlag der Carl-von-Ossietzky-Universität, p. 18.

16 R. Göpfert (1999). "Der jüdische Kindertransport von Deutschland nach England 1938/39. Geschichte und Erinnerung." Campus, Frankfurt.

17 G. Lilienthal (1993). "Der "Lebensborn e.V." Ein Instrument nationalsozialistischer Rassenpolitik." Fischer, Frankfurt.

18 M. Guelich (2006). "Adoptionen aus dem nicht-europäischen Ausland." BIS-Verlag der Carl-von-Ossietzky-Universität, p. 19.

19 M. R. Textor (1991). "International adoption in West Germany: A private affair." in H. Altstein and R. J. Simon "Intercountry adoption: A multinational perspective." Greenwood Publishing Group, New York, 109-126, p. 109.

20 Y.-C. Lemke Muniz de Faria (2003). "Germany's 'Brown Babies' Must Be Helped! Will You?: US Adoption Plans for Afro-German Children, 1950-1955." Callaloo 26, 2, 342-362.

21 M. R. Textor (1991). "International adoption in West Germany: A private affair." in H. Altstein and R. J. Simon "Intercountry adoption: A multinational perspective." Greenwood Publishing Group, New York, 109-126, p. 109.

In the late 1950s, the number of children sent abroad for the purposes of adoption began to fall. Whereas in 1959, 2,307 children were placed, the number was only 743 in 1969 and 247 in 1985. Due to the economic revival in Germany, the number of children relinquished for adoption decreased, whereas the number of German couples interested in adopting rose rapidly.[22] It was right up until the late 1960s that American and Scandinavian couples were still seeking adoptees from Germany. In German newspaper advertisements, they offered young, unwed women to finance the secret births of their illegitimate children in the prospective adoptive parents' home countries. Often considerable amounts of money, as well as material goods, were promised.[23]

The number of couples in Germany wishing to adopt a young and healthy child steadily increased from the 1950s. In 1950, more than 4,000 domestic adoptions were completed, whereas adoptive parents could still not be found for 4,000 children. From 1955 until the mid-1970s, about 8,000 domestic adoptions were recorded per year. At the same time, the number of couples wishing to adopt a child increased from 2,500 to 15,000 annually. As in other industrialized Western countries, the number of children available for domestic adoption in Germany has decreased since the 1980s, whereas the number of applicants wishing to adopt a child continued to increase to 21,000 in 1984, resulting in waiting periods of three or more years.[24]

In the late 1960s/early 1970s, Germany finally made the transition from a sending to a recipient country.[25] The military conflicts in Korea (1950-1953), as well as the Vietnam War (1964-1975), prompted the foundation of German humanitarian organizations with the goal of helping children affected by these conflicts. *Terre des hommes*, founded in 1967, as well as the *Internationaler Sozialdienst*, founded in 1978 – back then the two largest children's aid organizations – were the first institutions involved with finding suitable German adoptive parents for orphaned Korean and Vietnamese children and later also for orphans from other countries.[26]

The generation of German adoptive parents from the early 70s pursued an international adoption mainly as a result of their idealistic and altruistic motives.[27] However, as in other

---

22 *Ibid.*

23 R. P. Bach (1986). "Gekaufte Kinder. Babyhandel mit der Dritten Welt." Rowohlt, Hamburg, p. 15.

24 *Ibid.*, pp. 16-18.

25 M. Guelich (2006). "Adoptionen aus dem nicht-europäischen Ausland." BIS-Verlag der Carl-von-Ossietzky-Universität, p. 19.

26 M. Holz et al. (2013). ""Wir suchen Eltern für Kinder" Die Geschichte der Adoptionsarbeit von terre des hommes." Terre des hommes e.V., Osnabrück, available at https://www.tdh.de/fileadmin/user_upload/inhalte/04_Was_wir_tun/Themen/Weitere_Themen/Ado/2013-05_Geschichte-der-Adoptionsarbeit.pdf.

27 See, for instance, E. M. Weinwurm (1976). "Mutter-Kind-Interaktion bei asiatischen Kindern in Deutschen Adoptivfamilien. Begleitende Verhaltsbeobachtung von Terre des Hommes Kindern hinsichtlich des Deprivationssyndroms." PhD thesis, Universität Münster, which studied 71 German couples who had adopted children from Korea and Vietnam *via terre des hommes,* finding that the most common motive

receiving countries, their own interests and needs started to play an increasingly important role from the 1980s onwards.[28] Increasing numbers of couples who were unable to produce biological children sought to become parents by means of adoption. Since the number of children available for adoption in Germany was decreasing,[29] many considered intercountry adoption as a last resort means of having a child.[30]

Official statistics on intercountry adoptions to Germany are only available as of 2002, as this is when the Federal Central Office responsible for managing the central adoption database was established.[31] As the graph below illustrates, the number of foreign children adopted by German adopters peaked in 2003 with 1,204 adoption placements. Between 2003 and 2017, however, intercountry adoptions fell to 957 in 2009 and to 313 in 2017.[32] The official statistics do not give a complete account of international adoptions to Germany. They only include adoptions that were pursued with the knowledge and/or involvement of a German adoption placement office, but not private adoptions which are estimated to constitute around 50% of all international adoptions. The reasons why the numbers of intercountry adoptions are decreasing worldwide are discussed in Chapter II.

---

for adoption was the wish to help children that suffered from the consequences of war, natural disasters and starvation and that did not have any prospective of a healthy childhood in their own countries, followed by the wish for a child and the feeling of responsibility for children of the developing countries.)

28 M. Holz (2005). "Die Situation in den Herkunftsländern, Auslandsadoptionen bei terre des hommes Deutschland e.V." Forum für Politik, Gesellschaft und Kultur, Nr. 247, 35-38, available at https://www.forum.lu/wp-content/uploads/2015/11/5308_247_248_Holz.pdf, p. 35; G. Lange (2003). "Auslandsadoption - Wissenswertes zu einem aktuellen Thema." Schulz-Kirchner, Idstein, p. 12.

29 R. P. Bach (1986). "Gekaufte Kinder, Babyhandel mit der Dritten Welt." Rowohlt, Hamburg, pp. 16-18.

30 R. P. Bach (2002). "Internationaler Kinderhandel aus der Sicht des Aufnahmelandes Bundesrepublik Deutschland." In K. Holm and U. Schulz (eds) "Kindheit in Armut weltweit." Leske & Budrich, Opladen, 241-252, p. 248; R. P. Bach (1986). "Gekaufte Kinder. Babyhandel mit der Dritten Welt." Rowohlt, Hamburg, pp. 15-18.

31 Bundeszentralstelle für Auslandsadoption (2018). "Gesamtsumme – 2002-2017." Bonn (on file with author).

32 *Ibid.*

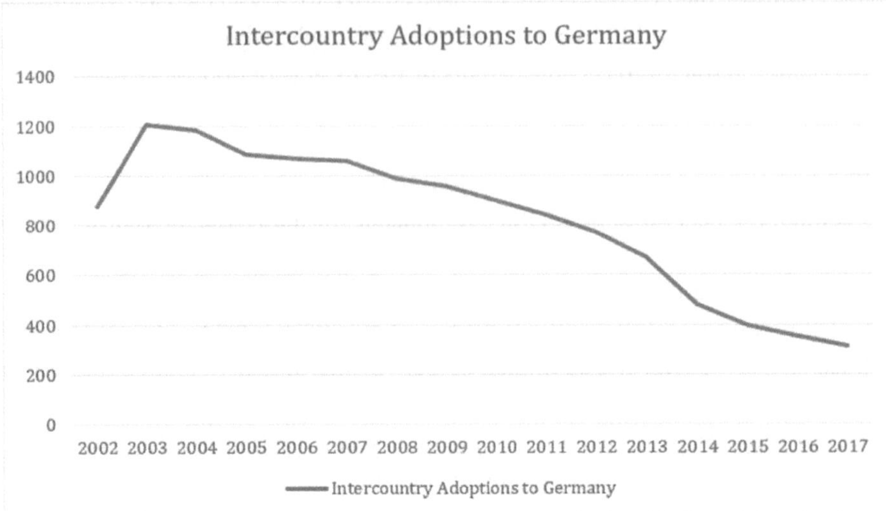

3 The German Legal Framework of Intercountry Adoption

Germany signed the Hague Convention in 1997 and ratified the treaty in 2001 by introducing the Act on the Regulation of Legal Issues Regarding Intercountry Adoptions and on the Advancement of the Adoption Placement Law,[33] which came into effect on 1 January 2002. The Act implemented several fundamental changes in the German intercountry adoption law. It is composed of the following acts:

- Adoption Convention Implementation Statute (Article 1)[34] (hereinafter AdÜbAG);
- Act on the Effects of the Adoption According to Foreign Law (Article 2)[35] (hereinafter AdWirkG);
- amendments to the Act on Adoption Placement (Article 3)[36] (hereinafter AdVermiG); and

33 *Gesetz zur Regelung von Rechtsfragen auf dem Gebiet der internationalen Adoption und zur Weiterentwicklung des Adoptionsvermittlungsrechts vom 5. November 2001 (BGBl. I S. 2950).*

34 *Adoptionsübereinkommens-Ausführungsgesetz vom 5. November 2001 (BGBl. I S. 2950), das zuletzt durch Artikel 4 Absatz 17 des Gesetzes vom 17. Dezember 2006 (BGBl. I S. 3171) geändert worden ist.*

35 *Gesetz über Wirkungen der Annahme als Kind nach ausländischem Recht vom 5.11.2001 (BGBl. I S. 2950, 2953), das zuletzt durch Artikel 22 des Gesetzes vom 20.11.2015 (BGBl. I S. 2010) geändert worden ist.*

36 *Gesetz über die Vermittlung der Annahme als Kind und über das Verbot der Vermittlung von Ersatzmüttern in der Fassung der Bekanntmachung vom 22. Dezember 2001 (BGBl. 2002 I S. 354), das zuletzt durch Artikel 21 des Gesetzes vom 20. November 2015 (BGBl. I S. 2010) geändert worden ist.*

- amendments to the Act on Voluntary Jurisdiction,[37] which was later repealed by the Act on Proceedings in Family Matters and in Matters of Non-Contentious Jurisdiction in 2009[38] (hereinafter FamFG), and amendments to the Introductory Act to the Civil Code (Article 4)[39] (hereinafter EGBGB).

With the exception of the AdÜbAG, all of the listed acts are applicable to intercountry adoptions from both Hague as well as non-Hague countries.

3.1 *Stakeholders in the German Adoption System*

Germany has not established one Central Authority within the meaning of Article 6(1) and (2) of the Hague Convention. Rather, since Germany is a federal state, it has assigned
- a Federal Central Office for International Adoption at the Federal Office of Justice (*Bundeszentralstelle für Auslandsadoptionen*) at federal level and
- twelve Central Adoption Offices of the Land youth welfare offices (*Zentrale Adoptionsstellen der Landesjugendämter*) at state level.[40]

Public authorities and accredited bodies within the meaning of Articles 9 and 22(1) of the Hague Convention are:
- the adoption placement offices of the youth welfare offices (*Adoptionsstellen der örtlichen Jugendämter*) insofar as the competent Central Adoption Office has authorized the adoption placement activities relative to one or several sending countries in general or in an individual case, and
- accredited international adoption placement agencies (*anerkannte Auslandsvermittlungsstellen*) within the scope of the authorization issued by the competent German Central Adoption Office in relation to one or several sending countries.[41]

Except for the Federal Central Office, only the listed offices are admitted as international adoption placement offices in Germany.[42] Private bodies that have not been accredited or

37 *Gesetz über die Angelegenheiten der freiwilligen Gerichtsbarkeit vom 12. März 2009 (BGBl. I S. 470), außer Kraft getreten am 01.09.2009 aufgrund Gesetzes vom 17. Dezember 2008 (BGBl. I S. 2586).*

38 *Gesetz über das Verfahren in Familiensachen und in den Angelegenheiten der freiwilligen Gerichtsbarkeit vom 17. Dezember 2008 (BGBl. I S. 2586, 2587), das zuletzt durch Artikel 7 des Gesetzes vom 20. Juli 2017 (BGBl. I S. 2780) geändert worden ist.*

39 *Einführungsgesetz zum Bürgerlichen Gesetzbuche in der Fassung der Bekanntmachung vom 21. September 1994 (BGBl. I S. 2494; 1997 I S. 1061), das zuletzt durch Artikel 2 Absatz 4 des Gesetzes vom 20. Juli 2017 (BGBl. I S. 2787) geändert worden ist.*

40 § 1(1) AdÜbAG.

41 § 1(2) and (3) *leg. cit.*

42 § 2a(3) AdVermiG.

independent agents, such as social workers or lawyers, are prohibited from operating in the German adoption system.[43] Germany does therefore not use the limited possibility of independent adoptions provided for by Article 22(2) of the Hague Convention. In practice, the youth welfare offices do not place international adoptions as they lack the necessary know-how as well as cooperation partners in the sending countries. Yet, they must be involved in every adoption placement.[44]

The Central Adoption Offices are not only permitted to handle international adoption placement procedures (from both Hague as well as non-Hague countries), they are also responsible for accrediting and approving private international adoption agencies and to monitor them.[45] They are involved in the adoption placement procedure right from the beginning and verify the reports and documents that are issued by the competent authorities in the sending country.[46]

The Federal Central Office is responsible for cooperating with the Central Authorities in the receiving countries and for promoting cooperation among the German international placement offices. It has must take all appropriate measures to provide information about German adoption law and other general information, such as statistics and standard forms, as well as to keep one another informed about the operation of the Convention and, as far as possible, eliminate any obstacles to its application.[47] The Federal Central Office manages a central database in which all intercountry adoptions (from both Hague and non-Hague countries) to Germany are recorded.[48] Furthermore, it must be involved in the adoption recognition procedure where it submits a statement on the question as to whether it should approve or refuse the recognition of a foreign adoption decision.[49] The Federal Central Office is neither permitted to carry out international adoption placements,[50] nor does it have any monitoring or control functions with regard to the German adoption agencies.

3.2 *International Adoption Placement Procedure*

As far as the adoption placement procedure is concerned, German law basically distinguishes between adoptions falling within and those falling outside the scope of the Hague Convention. The placement of a child from a non-Hague country is regulated exclusively by the AdVermiG. With regard to adoption placements from a sending country which has

43 § 5(1) *leg cit.*
44 § 7(2) *leg. cit.*
45 § 2a(3)(2.) and (3.); § 4(1) to (4) *leg. cit.*
46 § 11(1) and (2) *leg. cit.*
47 § 2(2) AdÜbAG; Art. 7 Hague Convention.
48 § 2a(5)(1.) and (6) *leg. cit.*
49 § 5(3) AdWirkG.
50 § 1(4)(1) *leg. cit.*

ratified the Hague Convention, the AdÜbAG, which basically regulates the implementation of the Convention's standards and principles in German adoption law, as well as the relevant provisions of the Act on the AdVermiG, are applicable. However, practitioners do not generally differentiate between Hague and non-Hague procedures but rather they apply the treaty's standards to all adoption placements. Thus, in the following sections, only the Hague adoption placement procedure will be delineated and any differences between Hague and non-Hague procedures will only be pointed out briefly.

Couples wishing to adopt a foreign child must apply at an admitted international adoption placement office, either to the competent Central Adoption Office or an accredited international adoption agency.[51] The adoption placement office evaluates the applicants' eligibility and suitability to adopt, either itself or by the competent youth welfare office.[52] In case of a positive evaluation, it prepares a report ('home study') about the adoption applicants including information about their identity, eligibility and suitability to adopt, background, family and medical history, social environment, reasons for adoption, ability to undertake an intercountry adoption, as well as the characteristics of the children they would be qualified to care for.[53] This report, together with the requested application documents, is sent to the Central Authority or another competent authority in the sending country which usually does the 'matching'.[54] In order to prevent private adoptions, the report is not handed to the adoption applicants or their representatives.[55]

After the competent authority in the sending state has accepted the adoption application, it sets up a placement proposal by transmitting a report about a child ('child proposal'). The child proposal needs to be approved by the German international adoption placement office, which examines whether the adoption is in the best interests of the child and whether an adoption judgment is probable in Germany[56] by assessing the criteria determined by German adoption law (see section 3.3). In case the adoption decision is rendered in the child's country of origin, the German adoption placement office must examine if such an adoption would be consistent with German public policy, in particular with the fundamental rights.[57]

---

51 § 2a(3) leg. cit.; § 4(1) AdÜbAG.

52 In those cases, where a Central Adoption Office carries out the adoption placement, the competent youth welfare office has to counsel the adoption applicants (§ 9(1) AdVermiG) and evaluate their eligibility and suitability to adopt a foreign child. If an accredited agency is handling the international adoption application, the agency might request the youth welfare office to evaluate the adoption applicants (§ 7(2) and (3) AdVermiG; § 4(4) AdÜbAG). However, in any case the youth welfare office has to be involved in the adoption placement procedure.

53 § 7(3) AdVermiG; The Hague Convention, Art. 15(1).

54 § 7(3) sentence 6 AdVermiG; § 4(5) AdÜbAG; A.rt 15(2) Hague Convention.

55 *Verwaltungsgerichtshof München, 24.4.2010, M 18 K 09.4652.*

56 § 5(1)(1) AdÜbAG.

57 § 5(1)(2) *leg. cit.*

If an accredited adoption agency carries out the adoption placement, it is obliged to present all child proposals and their supporting documents they have received from the official authorities or the accredited bodies in the sending country to the Central Adoptions Office in whose jurisdiction the agency is located.[58] In case the adoption applicants reside in a state other than the one in which the agency is located, the child proposal also has to be forwarded to the Central Adoption Office in whose jurisdiction the adoption applicants have their residency.[59] For instance, if a couple living in Baden-Württemberg decides to adopt a child from South Africa *via* an adoption agency located in Bavaria, the child proposal has to be presented to both the Central Adoption Office in Baden-Württemberg, that is responsible for supervising the agency, and the Central Adoption Office in Bavaria.

The German adoption placement office approves the child proposal after having heard the competent youth welfare office[60] and after having presented it together with the necessary adoption documents to the competent Central Adoption Office.[61] It then informs the adoption applicants about its content.[62] If the adoption applicants accept the child proposal, the German adoption placement office agrees that the adoption may proceed, according to Article 17(c) of the Hague Convention.[63] This must then be reported to the Federal Central Office.[64]

3.3 *Judicial Adoption Procedure*

After the child has been matched with a German couple or individual, a judgment on the adoption has to be rendered by a competent court either in the child's country of origin or in Germany. In the majority of cases, the adoption is granted in the sending country[65] which needs to be recognized in Germany (see section 3.4). If the adoption judgment is rendered in Germany, the judicial adoption procedure is governed by the provisions of the FamFG (§§ 186-199).

The competent German guardianship court (*Vormundschaftsgericht*) first has to examine whether it has international jurisdiction according to § 101 FamFG. This is the case if at least one of the adopters has the German nationality or their main residence in Germany. If the German court has jurisdiction, it must assess whether the adoption law

58 § 11(1) and (2) AdVermiG.

59 E-mail from J. Reinhardt, international adoption law scholar and head of the Central Adoption Office Bavaria between 2001 until 2008, 21.02.2017.

60 § 2(3) AdVermiG; § 5(4) AdÜbAG.

61 § 11 AdVermiG.

62 § 5(1) and (2) *leg. cit.*

63 § 5(3) AdÜbAG; Art. 17(c) Hague Convention.

64 § 2a(5)(1) AdVermiG, § 9c(1)(1) AdVermiG and § 2(1)(2) AuslAdMV.

65 E-mail from Weitzel, head of the German Federal Central Office for International Adoption at the German Federal Office of Justice between 2002 and 2017, 05.04.2017.

of the sending country or of Germany is applicable, according to the rules of German international private law laid down in the EGBGB. If the adoptive parents have the German nationality, German adoption law applies.[66] §§ 1741-1766 of the German Civil Code[67] (hereinafter BGB) lay down the requirements that an adoption has to meet in order to be granted according to German adoption law:

- the adoptive parent(s) must have reached the age of twenty-five;[68] (German law only provides for a minimum but not a maximum age requirement; however, in practice, it is generally accepted that the age difference between the adopters and the child should not exceed 40 years)[69];
- a notarized declaration of consent of the child's biological parents or legal representative;[70] the consent of the child's biological parents is not necessary if they are permanently not in a position to make a declaration or their abode is unknown,[71] it can be substituted by the court in cases where this is necessary for the child's best interests;[72]
- the adoptive parent(s) has had the child in foster care for a reasonable period of time;[73]

66 Art. 22(1) EGBGB.

67 *Bürgerliches Gesetzbuch in der Fassung der Bekanntmachung vom 2. Januar 2002 (BGBl. I S. 42, 2909; 2003 I S. 738), das zuletzt durch Artikel 1 des Gesetzes vom 20. Juli 2017 (BGBl. I S. 2787) geändert worden ist.*

68 § 1743 BGB.

69 Bundesarbeitsgemeinschaft Landesjugendaemter (2014). "Empfehlungen zur Adoptionsvermittlung - 7., neu bearbeitete Fassung." 117. Arbeitstagung der Bundesarbeitsgemeinschaft Landesjugendaemter, available at http://www.bagljae.de/downloads/120_empfehlungen-zur-adoptionsvermittlung_2014.pdf, p. 53.

70 §§ 1746, 1748, 1750 BGB.

71 § 1747(4) *leg. cit.*

72 § 1748 *leg. cit.*: "(1) The family court, on the application of the child, must substitute the consent of one parent where that parent has persistently grossly violated his duties to the child or has shown through his conduct that he is indifferent to the child, and where it would be disproportionately disadvantageous to the child if the adoption did not take place. The consent may also be substituted if the violation of duty, although not persistent, is particularly serious and it is probable that it will permanently not be possible to entrust the child to the care of the parent. (2) The consent may not be substituted on account of indifference that is not at the same time a persistent gross breach of duty until the parent has been instructed by the youth welfare office on the possibility of its substitution and advised under section 51 (2) of Book Eight of the Social Security Code (*Sozialgesetzbuch*) and at least three months have passed since the instruction; the instruction should point out the limitation period. No instruction is necessary if the parent has changed his residence without leaving his new address and the residence cannot be determined by the youth welfare office within a period of three months despite appropriate research; in this case, the period commences on the first action of the youth welfare office directed towards instruction and advice or towards determining the residence. The periods expire at the earliest five months after the birth of the child. (3) The consent of a parent may also be substituted where he is permanently incapable of caring for and bringing up the child as the result of a particularly serious psychological illness or a particularly serious mental or psychological handicap and where the child, if the adoption does not take place, could not grow up in a family and the child's development would as a result be seriously endangered."

73 § 1744 *leg. cit.*

- it is to be expected that a parent-child relationship will arise between the adoptive parent and the child;[74] and
- the adoption serves the best interests of the child.[75]

In order to determine whether an adoption serves the best interests of the child, the German court has to ask the adoption placement office that handled the adoption placement to make a statement on whether it believes that the adopters and the child are suited for the international adoption.[76] In the case of an independent adoption, the competent youth welfare office must give such a statement.[77] Adopters who were involved in illegal or immoral adoption placement can adopt the child only if the adoption is necessary for the best interests of the child.[78]

An adoption is granted by a German court if the requirements laid down in §§ 1741-1766 BGB are met and if the necessary consent to adoption required by the law of the child's country of origin are available (consent of the child, his or her biological parents and other family members).[79] If the law of the child's country of origin does not provide for an adoption or only provides for a simple adoption, the required consent to adoption cannot be given.[80]

According to Article 23 EGBGB, only German adoption law (§§ 1741-1766 BGB) shall apply if this is necessary for (instead of only serving) the child's best interests.[81] This is, for instance, the case if the child's parents' consent to the adoption cannot be obtained or can only be obtained with great difficulty, but a speedy adoption is required for the child who would otherwise face serious harm.[82] In such an instance, §§ 1747 and 1748 BGB, which allow for an adoption without the required consents, are applicable, and the law of the child's country of origin, which does not provide for an adoption when the consent cannot be obtained, would not apply.[83] According to § 1747(4) BGB, the parents' consent to adoption is not required if they are unable to give consent or if their residence is unknown (for instance, because they abandoned the child anonymously). Pursuant to § 1748 BGB, the parents' consent to adoption can be substituted if they have seriously violated their duties to care for the child, have shown through this conduct that they are indifferent to

74 § 1741 *leg. cit.*
75 § 1741 *leg. cit.*
76 § 189 FamFG.
77 *Leg. cit.*
78 § 1741(1) sentence 2 BGB.
79 Art. 23 EGBGB.
80 Heiderhoff (2017). "Art. 23 EGBGB." In Bamberger et al. (eds) "Kommentar zum Bürgerlichen Gesetzbuch." 45. edition, C.H Beck, München, Rn. 14.
81 Art. 23 EGBGB.
82 T. Helms (2018). "Art. 23 EGBGB." In Säcker et al. (eds) "Münchner Kommentar zum Bürgerlichen Gesetzbuch." 7. Edition, C.H. Beck, München, Rn. 28-29.
83 *Ibid.*

the child, or if they are permanently incapable of caring for and bringing up the child due to a serious psychological illness and where it would be disproportionately disadvantageous to the child if the adoption were not to take place.

3.4 *Adoption Recognition and Conversion Procedure*

In the vast majority of cases, the judicial decision about an intercountry adoption is rendered in the child's country of origin. The question is therefore whether or not this foreign decision is to be recognized in Germany. An adoption granted in a sending country which *is* a State Party to the Hague Convention is to be recognized *ex lege*, according to Articles 23 and 24. If the adoption is certified by the foreign competent authority as having been made in accordance with the Convention then it must be recognized automatically, without a German judicial or administrative decision being required.[84] German courts and authorities must recognize "[a]n adoption certified by the competent authority of the State of the adoption as having been made in accordance with the Convention" (Article 23), unless "the adoption is manifestly contrary to its public policy, taking into account the best interests of the child" (Article 24).

An adoption decision rendered in a sending country which is *not* a State Party to the Hague Convention, or an adoption decision that was not certified as having been made in accordance with the treaty (Article 23(1)) is to be recognized according to § 108(1) FamFG. Pursuant to this regulation, a foreign judgment is to be recognized *ex lege*, unless one of the grounds for exclusion listed in § 109 FamFG applies:

- The court of the sending country did not have jurisdiction according to German law;[85]
- Persons whose interests are directly affected by the decision (the child, the birth parents, and the adoptive parents)[86] claim that they were not given the opportunity to express their opinions before the court or that they were not notified in good time so that they could properly exercise their rights;[87]
- The foreign judgment is incompatible with a judgment issued or recognized earlier in Germany, or the proceedings are incompatible with proceedings that were previously pending in Germany.[88] The recognition of an intercountry adoption may, therefore, be refused if the adoption applicants' application with regard to the same child has

84 § 97(1)FamFG.

85 § 109(1)(1) *leg. cit.*

86 T. Steiger (2002). "Das neue Recht der internationalen Adoption und Adoptionsvermittlung: Einführung-Erläuterung-Materialien." Bundesanzeiger-Verlag, Köln, Rn. 330.

87 § 109(1)(2) FamFG.

88 § 109(1)(3) *leg. cit.*

already been rejected either by a German decision or a previous foreign decision that has been recognized by German law; and[89]

- The recognition of the foreign adoption decision would lead to a result that is manifestly contrary to the German public policy (*ordre public*), thus incompatible with the general principles of German (adoption) law.[90]

An important general principle of German law is that the adoption takes place in the best interests of the child (§ 1741(1) BGB). However, it is widely disputed as to when the recognition of a foreign adoption decision would violate the child's best interests. Particularly, German case law is inconsistent on the question as to whether the lack of an assessment of the adopters by a German international adoption placement office is manifestly contrary to German public policy (see section 3.4).

The AdWirkG provides for an optional judicial procedure in which a German court renders a declaratory decision on the recognition of a foreign adoption judgment and its legal effects. It is applicable to both adoptions from Hague countries as well as non-Hague countries and seeks to safeguard legal clarity and certainty for the child and the adoptive parents with regard to their relationship. Before the AdWirkG was adopted, the German courts and authorities who had to rule on issues for which the foreign adoption decision was relevant (e.g. registering the child, granting child benefits, issuing a passport) had to determine independently and for themselves whether the foreign adoption judgment was to be recognized *ex lege*. Their decision was not legally binding on other courts and authorities.[91] Another problem was the legal effects of an adoption that varied from jurisdiction to jurisdiction. For instance, the adoption laws of some sending countries only provide for simple adoptions that restrict but not terminate the pre-existing legal child-parent relationship and it was therefore uncertain as to which legal effects such an adoption had on the relationship between the child and the adoptive parents.[92] This was the reason why many adopters sought a re-adoption in Germany, meaning an additional adoption decision rendered by a German court according to German adoption law.[93]

The AdWirkG was adopted with the aim of countering these problems. It provides an optional judicial procedure in which a family court – upon receiving an application – renders a declaratory decision on the recognition of a foreign adoption judgment and on its legal effects, which is binding for all other German courts and authorities.[94] According to § 2(1) AdWirkG, the family court determines whether a foreign adoption judgment is

89 T. Steiger (2002). "Das neue Recht der internationalen Adoption und Adoptionsvermittlung: Einführung-Erläuterung-Materialien." Bundesanzeiger-Verlag, Köln, Rn. 331.

90 § 109(1)(4) FamFG.

91 W. Weitzel (2013). "Adoptionswirkungsgesetz." 2. edition, Nomos Bundesrecht Erläuterungen, Rn. 2.

92 *Ibid.*, Rn. 1.

93 *Ibid.*, Rn. 2.

94 *Ibid.*, Rn. 5.

to be recognized *erga omnes* according to §§ 108, 109 FamFG or Articles 23, 24 of the Hague Convention. In case the adoption is recognized, the family court must furthermore establish which legal effects the adoption based on a foreign judgment has with regard to the existing parent-child relationship, pursuant to § 2(2) AdWirkG. The Federal Central Office must participate in the judicial proceeding according to § 2 AdWirkG.[95]

If an adoption granted by a foreign judgment does not terminate a pre-existing legal parent-child relationship ('simple adoption'), § 3 AdWirkG provides that the family court may convert this adoption into a 'full adoption' within the meaning of German adoption law, if this is in the best interests of the child, and if the child's parents give their consent thereto.[96] In a conversion procedure, both the competent Central Adoption Office as well as the youth welfare office have to be involved.[97] § 3 AdWirkG basically corresponds to Article 27(1) of the Hague Convention, which regulates the conversion of adoptions from Hague countries.

3.5 *The Child's Entry into Germany*

If a full adoption is granted in the sending country which is to be recognized (according to Articles 23 and 24 Hague Convention or §§ 108, 109 FamFG) and if at least one of the adoptive parents is a German national, then the child acquires German nationality *ex lege* and can enter Germany with a German passport.[98] If the German embassy in the sending country which is responsible for processing the passport refuses to recognize the foreign adoption decision, the adopters have the option to start an adoption recognition procedure according to AdWirkG (see section 3.4).

If an adoption decision is still to be rendered by a court in Germany (for instance after a particular period of foster care expired) or if the court in the sending country only granted a simple adoption, the child does not acquire German nationality and might require a visa to be able to enter Germany. A visa is not required if the child comes from a visa-free state, such as, for instance, an EU country, Brazil, Colombia, Argentina, Guatemala, South Korea or the United States.[99]

95 § 5(3) AdWirkG.

96 W. Weitzel (2013). "Adoptionswirkungsgesetz." 2. edition, Nomos Bundesrecht Erläuterungen, § 3 AdWirkG, Rn. 2.

97 § 5(3) AdWirkG.

98 § 6 *Staatsangehörigkeitsgesetz in der im Bundesgesetzblatt Teil III, Gliederungsnummer 102-1, veröffentlichten bereinigten Fassung, das zuletzt durch Artikel 3 des Gesetzes vom 11. Oktober 2016 (BGBl. I S. 2218) geändert worden ist.*

99 See https://www.auswaertiges-amt.de/de/einreiseundaufenthalt/visabestimmungen-node/staatenlistevisumpflicht-node (last accessed on 04.08.2018).

In case the child is resident in a Hague country, the special regulations on the subsequent immigration of children (§ 32 of the Residence Act[100], hereinafter AufenthG) are applicable, according to § 6(1) AdÜbAG. Thus, after the German adoption placement office has approved the child proposal and the adoption applicants have accepted it, the child obtains the legal status of the adopters' child already before the adoption is granted by a German court. As a consequence, the child is permitted to enter Germany if the adopters' biological child were also permitted to do so, according to § 32 AufenthG. If the child is from a non-Hague sending country, he or she might require a visa according to § 4(1)(1) and § 6 AufenthG.

The German embassy in the sending country decides on processing the visa for the child after the German Foreigners Office (*Auslaenderbehoerde*), in whose jurisdiction the adoptee will have his or her permanent residency, has given its pre-consent thereto (§ 31 AufenthV).[101], [102] In cases where the child comes from a Hague sending country, both the Foreigners Office's pre-consent and the visa have to be granted upon the request of the German adoption placement agency, after the child proposal has been approved by the agency and accepted by the adopters.[103] In adoptions from Hague sending countries, thus, the German adoption placement office ultimately has the power to decide on the child's entry into Germany.[104] Neither the German embassy nor the Foreigners Office has any discretion to deny processing a visa or providing pre-consent thereto.

4 Tolerance towards Private Adoptions

4.1 *International Adoptions in Germany – Often a 'Private Affair'*

The Hague Convention seeks to withdraw international adoption from private dispositions. It provides that intercountry adoptions must be channelled through the Central Authorities in the sending and receiving country (competent authorities' principle). Their purpose is to serve as gatekeepers overseeing the adoption process and making sure that it complies with the treaty's minimum standards and safeguards.[105] Adopters must not go to the

100 *Gesetz über den Aufenthalt, die Erwerbstätigkeit und die Integration von Ausländern im Bundesgebiet, in der Fassung der Bekanntmachung vom 25.02.2008 (BGBl. I S. 162), das zuletzt durch Gesetz vom 08.03.2018 (BGBl. I S. 342) geändert worden ist.*

101 *Aufenthaltsverordnung vom 25. November 2004 (BGBl. I S. 2945), die zuletzt durch Artikel 1 der Verordnung vom 1. August 2017 (BGBl. I S. 3066) geändert worden ist.*

102 As will be explained in section 4.1, a visa cannot be processed if the adoption placement procedure laid down in the AdVermiG has not been followed, that is if the adopters pursued a private adoption.

103 § 6(1) AdÜbAG.

104 H. Bienentreu und M. Busch (2003). "Stiefkind- und Verwandtenadoptionen im Recht der internationalen Adoptionsvermittlung." Das Jugendamt, 6, 273-278.

105 See Chapter IV, section 4.3.

sending country themselves in order to locate an adoptable child. Rather, they have to apply to the Central Authority, a public authority or an accredited body in the receiving country who then handles the adoption placement in cooperation with the Central Authority, a public authority or an accredited body in the sending country.[106] In Germany, the intercountry adoption placement procedure provided by the Hague Convention is regulated in the AdÜbAG and in the AdVermiG respectively. As has already been mentioned, there are no major differences between adoption placements from Hague and non-Hague countries as the standards and procedures are basically applied to both (see section 3.2).

A high number of private adoptions can be observed where the adoption placement procedure provided by German law has been bypassed.[107] In 2007, Schlauss examined international adoption cases that were brought before a German court between 2005 and 2006 so as to be recognized according to § 2 AdWirkG. He found that approximately 50% of these cases were pursued *without* the involvement of a German adoption placement office.[108] Interestingly, this percentage applies to both adoptions from non-Hague countries as well as from states that have ratified the Convention.[109] Experts estimate that the number of private adoptions is still as high today.[110]

The German immigration authorities are not equipped to prevent private adopters from bringing the child to Germany. Generally, the child either needs a German passport or a visa to be able to enter Germany, depending on whether or not the adoption has already been granted in the sending country (section 3.4). According to a judgement of the German Federal Administrative Court from 2010, a visa cannot be processed if the adoption placement procedure laid down in the AdVermiG has not been followed (thus if the adopters pursued a private adoption).[111] However, the immigration law does not constitute an obstacle for private adopters if the child originates from a visa-free country. And even if the child does require a visa, adopters might simply apply for a tourist visa to

106 Art. 15, 17 Hague Convention.

107 S. Schlauss (2007). "Die Anerkennung von Auslandsadoptionen in der vormundschaftsgerichtlichen Praxis." FamRZ, 20, 1699-1702; M. Rupprecht (2012). "Intercountry Adoption: ensuring that the best interests of the child are upheld." Parlamentary Assembly of the Council of Europe, Committee on Social Affairs, Health and Sustainable Development, 19.10.2012, Doc. 12597, p. 11; R. P. Bach (1988). "Daten und soziale Hintergründe der Adoption von Kindern aus der Dritten Welt. Eine Untersuchung der Gemeinsamen Zentralen Adoptionsstelle der vier norddeutschen Bundesländer in Hamburg." Zentralblatt für Jugendrecht, 75, 328-333.

108 S. Schlauss (2007). "Die Anerkennung von Auslandsadoptionen in der vormundschaftsgerichtlichen Praxis." FamRZ, 20, 1699-1702, p. 1701.

109 *Ibid.*

110 M. Rupprecht (2012). "Intercountry Adoption: ensuring that the best interests of the child are upheld." Parlamentary Assembly of the Council of Europe, Committee on Social Affairs, Health and Sustainable Development, 19.10.2012, Doc. 12597, p. 11.

111 Bundesverwaltungsgerichtshof, 26.10.2010, 1 C 16.09.

be able to bring the child to Germany.[112] And, as we will see, once the child is in Germany, the adopters often do not have to face any negative consequences.

The official adoption placement procedure is not a warrant against illegal adoption practices. As was illustrated at the beginning of this chapter, incidents of child trafficking were even uncovered in adoptions that were pursued with the involvement of a German adoption placement agency. However, as Bach's study from 1988 suggests, private international adoptions are more prone to commercial and illegal practices than agency adoptions are. One might now counter that given the intrinsically criminogenic nature of the intercountry adoption system, private adoptions are just as risky as those that take place with the involvement of an agency; but that in the latter, illegal practices would remain more invisible as the agency's representatives and cooperation partners involved in the placement potentially provide an opportunity for laundering the child and thus obscuring the child's illegal origin.

Yet, even if – as the following sections will show – agency adoptions are risky, private adoptions are arguably more prone to illegal practices as they take place without there being any opportunity for supervision and control whatsoever.[113] In an agency adoption, the adoption placement office is able to regulate the payments made for an intercountry adoption. It can make sure that the costs which adopters are required to pay for the adoption services in the sending country are reasonably high and admonish them in order to refrain from paying any extra fees or donations to families, orphanages or officials. In an agency adoption, all payments made by the adopters are channelled through the adoption placement office which enables them to control the flow of money into the states of origin. Furthermore, an adoption placement office can try to eliminate adopters' common beliefs about intercountry adoption, manage their expectations by informing them about the prospects of adopting a young and healthy child and the waiting times as well as to sensitize them to the risks in an intercountry adoption procedure. In the sending countries, the adopters are assisted by the agency's foreign representative or cooperation partner, which can make sure that the adopters do not directly contact the child's birth parents or make generous donations to the orphanage they wish to adopt from. Finally, in an agency adoption, the German authorities have to be involved which could serve as another layer of safety in the adoption system. The adoption placement office is obliged to present the child proposal and the supporting documents it has received from the sending country to the youth welfare office and the competent Central Adoption Office (see section 8.2). The latter have the opportunity to scrutinize the documents and can advise the agency to reject

112 J. Reinhardt (2006). "Gewollt oder nicht? Die private Adoption von Kindern aus dem Ausland." Zeitschrift für Rechtspolitik, 8, 241-272, p. 246.

113 See, for example, International Social Service (2005). "Benefits of compulsory participation of adoption accredited bodies in the receiving countries under the supervision of the Central Authorities." Geneva, Nr. 70, September.

the child proposal if it notices any sign of irregularities or inconsistent information about the child's origin.

Private adopters, on the contrary, are completely left to their own devices in the sending country. They might fall into the hands of shady adoption agents that promise them a quick and unbureaucratic adoption placement procedure, directly contact the child's parents and be inclined to make donations to families and orphanages, unaware of the harms they create as a consequence. The German authorities, if at all, only gain knowledge of the international adoption placement *after* the child has been transferred to Germany: if the adopters want to register the child, apply for an adoption or want an adoption judgment recognized which was rendered in the child's country of origin. They therefore do not have the opportunity to examine the adoption documents and to prevent the child from immigrating to Germany in case they suspect any irregularities in the adoption placement procedure. Given the lack of supervision and control exercised by the adoption placement office and the German authorities, privately pursued intercountry adoptions are arguably riskier than agency adoptions.

4.2 *Adopters' Motivation to Pursue a Do-It-Yourself Adoption*

Intercountry adoptions are pursued privately for a variety of reasons. Some people are unaware of the fact that they adopt internationally and that a German local youth welfare office and/or an international adoption placement office are to be involved in the adoption proceedings. Intercountry adoptions by relatives or step-parents, particularly of children from Turkey or the former parts of Yugoslavia, are in many cases pursued on a private basis.[114] Also, in many cases where foreign people with a permanent residence in Germany adopt a child from their country of origin, no adoption placement office is consulted, often due to a lack of knowledge.[115]

Yet, other people maliciously bypass the adoption placement procedure as described in section 3.2. Many adopters perceive this procedure as too bureaucratic, time-consuming and invasive. The preparation of the prospective adoptive parents, including the evaluation of their suitability to adopt, might take up to nine months or even a year. Applicants need to attend intensive preparatory courses, group meetings as well as personal interviews and must go through thorough medical and psychological check-ups. This preparation phase might even last longer if the adoption applicants are involuntarily childless, as they must first deal with the inability to have their own child – which is often associated with psychological pressure as well as high expectations – before they can be considered as suited to

114 Interview with J. Reinhardt, international adoption law scholar and head of the Central Adoption Office Bavaria between 2001 until 2008, Germany, 16.03.2015.

115 *Ibid.*

adopt.[116] Yet, even after the applicants have been 'approved' to adopt, they face long waiting times until they finally receive a child proposal. Waiting times might amount to several years if the applicants wish to adopt a healthy baby.

The cumbersome and tedious adoption placement procedures, the thorough check-ups that many applicants perceive as intrusive or even humiliating, as well as the poor prospects of adopting a young and healthy child incite some adopters to seek for alternative, and more facile, ways to adopt. Impatient adopters or adopters that were considered unsuited to adopt a child, for instance, because they were too old, would use their private contact to a child care institution or hire an unauthorized agent in the sending country that would identify and locate an attractive child and help them with the adoption procedure.

4.3 No Ban, No Negative Consequences

§ 2a AdVermiG lists those public and private bodies that are admitted as international adoption placement offices in Germany (see section 3.1). Individuals (e.g. doctors, midwives, nurses, pastors) and organizations that have not been accredited as an adoption placement office and authorized to place intercountry adoptions are prohibited by § 5 AdVermiG to carry out adoption placements.[117] Individuals who violate the placement ban of § 5 AdVermiG commit a misdemeanour (§ 14 AdVermiG), or – if they act with consideration or the intent of enrichment – a criminal offence (§ 236 StGB, see section 9.1).

However, German law does not explicitly prohibit adoption applicants from adopting without the involvement of an admitted German placement office.[118] Steiger argues that Germany has accepted a ban on independent adoptions by ratifying the Hague Convention, of which Article 5(a) obliges the competent authorities in the receiving countries to determine the prospective adoptive parents' eligibility and suitability to adopt. Thus, intercountry adoptions which are privately pursued, Steiger argues, are illegal in Germany.[119] Indeed, several provisions in the AdÜbAG and the AdVermiG may be interpreted as providing that intercountry adoptions can only take place with the involvement of a German

116 *Ibid.*

117 The placement ban in § 5(1) AdVermiG is not absolute but has exceptions provided in § 5(2) AdVermiG: it does not extend to kinship adoptions and adoptions that are arranged with close friends of parents who, for instance, died in an accident unexpectedly, as long as an adoption placement office or youth welfare office is informed thereof immediately.

118 R. Reinhardt (2017). "§ 2a AdVermiG." In J. Reinhardt (ed) "Adoptionsvermittlungsgesetz." 4. Edition, Nomos Bundesrecht, Erläuterungen, Rn. 27.

119 T. Steiger (2002). "Das neue Recht der internationalen Adoption und Adoptionsvermittlung: Einführung-Erläuterung-Materialien." Bundesanzeiger-Verlag, Köln, Rn 334.

adoption placement office.[120] With regard to adoptions from Hague countries, § 4 AdÜbAG provides that adoption applicants must consult with the competent adoption placement office in Germany and §§ 4 and 5 AdÜbAG concretize the required intercountry adoption placement procedure. As far as adoptions from non-Hague countries are concerned, § 7(3) AdVermiG provides that the adoption placement office has to send the 'home study report' only to an accredited adoption placement office in Germany or abroad and must not hand it out to the adoption applicants themselves or to their independent agents.[121] That way an independent adoption should be prevented. However, German adoption law does not *expressis verbis* prohibit private international adoptions. In fact, the explanatory memorandum on the AdVermiG states that the adopters' eligibility and suitability to adopt a child should 'generally' be assessed by an adoption placement office,[122] which could be interpreted as meaning that international adoptions that are pursued independently are not generally excluded and therefore not illegal.[123]

In 2011, the *Bundestag* requested that private adoptions be prohibited by German law, referring to Schlauss' study which showed that in Germany about 50% of all intercountry adoptions were pursued in circumvention of the official adoption placement procedure and claiming that such adoptions were incompatible with the standards and principles of the Hague Convention.[124] Hitherto, this request has fallen on deaf ears.[125]

The German legislator has not only failed to prohibit private intercountry adoptions, but also to provide for negative consequences. § 1741(1) sentence 2 BGB, which is applicable if the adoption is granted in Germany (see section 3.3), stipulates that adopters who were involved in an illegal or an immoral adoption placement can adopt the child only if this is necessary for the child's best interests. An adoption placement is illegal if it violates German law.[126] This is the case if it is undertaken by someone who is not permitted to do so according to § 2a AdVermiG (§ 5(1) AdVermiG), if it is carried out with the aim of bypassing the adoption system (§ 5(4) AdVermiG) (see section 9.1) or if it involves a criminal offence (see section 9.2).[127] As was just explained, German law does not explicitly

---

120 J. Reinhardt (2006). "Gewollt oder nicht? Die private Adoption von Kindern aus dem Ausland." Zeitschrift für Rechtspolitik, 8, 241-272, p. 245.

121 *Ibid.*

122 *Begründung des Entwurfs eines Gesetzes zur Regelung von Rechtsfragen auf dem Gebiet der internationalen Adoption und zur Weiterentwicklung des Adoptionsvermittlungsrechts vom 10.05.2001, Deutscher Bundestag, 14. Wahlperiode, Drucksache 14/6011*, p. 29.

123 *Oberlandesgericht Celle*, 12.10.2011, 17 UF 98/11.

124 *Entwurf eines Gesetzes zur Stärkung eines aktiven Schutzes von Kindern und Jugendlichen vom 22.06.2011, Deutscher Bundestag, 17. Wahlperiode, Drucksache 17/6256*, p. 45.

125 *Antwort der Bundesregierung auf die Kleine Anfrage der Abgeordneten Cornelia Pieper, Ina Lenke, Klaus Haupt, weiterer Abgeordneter und der Fraktion der FDP vom 19.11.2014, Deutscher Bundestag, 15. Wahlperiode, Drucksache 15/4240*, p. 7.

126 M. Pöcker (2018). "BGB § 1741 Zulässigkeit der Annahme." In Bamberger et al. (eds) "Kommentar zum Bürgerlichen Gesetzbuch." 46. edition, C.H Beck, München, Rn. 25.

127 *Ibid.*

prohibit private adoptions; an adoption placement is thus not illegal if it took place without the involvement of a German adoption placement office. § 5 AdVermiG only applies to adoption placement activities that take place in Germany.[128] Thus, if an individual in the sending country carries out the adoption placement without being permitted to doing so, no violation of § 5 AdVermiG takes place that would render the adoption placement illegal.

Yet, the adopters can still be considered as having been involved in an immoral adoption placement, according to § 1741 sentence 2 BGB. An adoption placement is immoral if, for instance, it involves the payment of unreasonably high sums of money,[129] an act which does not necessarily constitute a criminal offence (see section 9.1). However, even if the adopters were involved in an unmoral adoption placement, they can nevertheless adopt the child if this is *necessary* for the child's best interests (§ 1741(1) sentence 2 BGB). It does not suffice that the adoption only *serves* the best interests of the child.[130] The German legislator thus raised the adoption requirement in order to prevent adopters from getting involved in illegal or immoral placement practices.[131] An adoption can be considered necessary for the best interests of the child if an intensive relationship has emerged between the child and the adopters, which should not be disrupted, or if there are no other possibilities to find a suitable family for the child.[132] Once the child has lived with the adopters for a particular period of time, the refusal to grant an adoption might be contrary to the child's best interests. In addition, it might violate the child's and the adopters' right to family life as laid down in Article 8 of the ECHR.[133]

Basically, Article 8 ECHR does not involve the right to adopt a child. Already in 1996, the European Commission of Human Rights held that "the right to adopt is not as such included among the rights and freedoms guaranteed by the Convention, and that there is no positive obligation for the Contracting States under article 8 of the Convention to grant a person the status of adoptive parent or adoptive child".[134] This has been confirmed by the ECtHR in several subsequent judgments.[135] However, the right to family life according

128 R. Reinhardt (2017). "§ 5 AdVermiG." In J. Reinhardt (ed) "Adoptionsvermittlungsgesetz." 4. edition, Nomos Bundesrecht, Erläuterungen, Rn. 2.

129 P. Kunkel et al. (2006). "Adoptionsverfahren und Verwaltungsrecht." In H. Paulitz and R. P. Bach (eds), "Adoption: Positionen, Impulse, Perspektiven." (2nd edition) C. H. Beck, München, 181-241, p. 223.

130 M. Pöcker (2018). "BGB § 1741 Zulässigkeit der Annahme." In Bamberger et al. (eds) "Kommentar zum Bürgerlichen Gesetzbuch." 46. edition, C.H Beck, München, Rn. 25.

131 *Beschlußempfehlung und Bericht des Rechtsausschusses (6. Ausschuß) vom 12.09.1997, Deutscher Bundestag, 13. Wahleriode, Bundesdrucksache 13/8511,* p. 75.

132 M. Pöcker (2018). "BGB § 1741 Zulässigkeit der Annahme." In Bamberger et al. (eds) "Kommentar zum Bürgerlichen Gesetzbuch." 46. edition, C.H Beck, München, Rn. 27.

133 See Chapter III, section 5.3.

134 Di Lazzaro vs. Italy, 10.07.1997, No. 31924/96, p. 139; see also Akin vs. The Netherlands (1998), 01.07.1998, No. 34986/97, para. 2.

135 Fretté vs. France, 26.02.2002, no. 36515/97; Pini and Others vs. Romania, 22.06.2004, No. 78028/01 and 78030/01.

to Article 8 ECHR may nevertheless be violated if a request for adoption or guardianship is rejected by the court.

Family life does not only exist between married parents and their biological or *de jure* (adopted) children. Article 8 ECHR also protects 'sufficiently close de facto ties' between family members who are legally and biologically unrelated.[136] Family life may thus also exist between a couple or individual and an unrelated child they have cared for and already bonded with. If family life according to Article 8 ECHR exists, any interference, such as the refusal to grant adoption or guardianship, must be justified. This is only the case if it is in accordance with the law and necessary in a democratic society in the interests of national security, public safety or the economic well-being of the country, for the prevention of disorder or crime, for the protection of health or morals or for the protection of the rights and freedoms of others. Therefore, a child may be removed from caretakers, with whom he or she already has close *de facto* ties only if this is necessary to protect the child's best interests. If this is not the case, the right to family life according to Article 8 ECHR is violated by the removal of the child from the family. Thus, in order to accomplish an adoption according to § 1741(1) sentence 2 BGB, adopters that were involved in an illegal or unmoral adoption placement better hide the child from the German authorities for several months before seeking an adoption.[137] Because the closer the tie between them and the child has become, the harder it is for the court to establish that removing the child from the adopters is in his or her best interests.

The majority of adoptions are already granted in the child's country of origin.[138] Thus, the question arises as to whether the foreign adoption judgment is to be recognized in Germany, according to Article 23 of the Hague Convention or § 108 FamFG (see section 3.4), if no German adoption placement office was involved in the placement procedure. The German legislator does not provide a clear answer to that question. The explanatory memorandum on the AdVermiG only states that the lack of an assessment of the adopters' suitability by a German adoption placement office would "give rise to doubts" as to whether the foreign adoption decision is compatible with German public policy.[139] Consequently, commentators and courts disagree on whether or not an adoption that was pursued independently is manifestly contrary to German public policy.

Some German courts argue that the recognition of a foreign adoption decision violates the principle of the child's best interests, and is thus contrary to German public policy, if

136 X, Y and Z vs. the United Kingdom (no. 21830/93); Pini vs. Romania (2004), no. 78028/01 and 78030/01.

137 P. Kunkel et al. (2006). "Adoptionsverfahren und Verwaltungsrecht." In H. Paulitz and R. P. Bach (eds), "Adoption: Positionen, Impulse, Perspektiven." (2nd edition) C. H. Beck, München, 181-241, p. 223.

138 E-mail from Weitzel, head of the German Federal Central Office for International Adoption at the German Federal Office of Justice between 2002 and 2017, 05.04.2017.

139 *Begründung des Entwurfs eines Gesetzes zur Regelung von Rechtsfragen auf dem Gebiet der internationalen Adoption und zur Weiterentwicklung des Adoptionsvermittlungsrechts vom 10.05.2001, Deutscher Bundestag, 14. Wahlperiode, Drucksache 14/6011*, p. 27.

the court in the sending country did not (properly) assess whether the child was suitable for an intercountry adoption (Article 2(1) and Article 6(2) German Constitution, Article 21b UNCRC, Article 4 Hague Convention)[140] and if the adopters' eligibility and suitability to adopt has not been evaluated by a German adoption placement office (Article 5 of the Hague Convention).[141] Most commentators agree with this jurisdiction.[142] They claim that the involvement of a German adoption placement office which assesses the adopters and draws up a home study report that it is required to send to the competent authorities in the sending country (§ 7(3) AdVermiG and Article 15(1) Hague Convention) aims to ensure that the adoption takes place in the child's best interests.[143] Hence, recognizing a foreign decision on an adoption that is not based on such a home study report would be manifestly contrary to German public policy, according to Article 24 Hague Convention or § 109(1)(4) FamFG.[144] The formal recognition procedure provided by the AdWirkG, many courts and commentators argue, is furthermore not intended and designed for the German courts to conduct an *ex post* assessment of the child's adoptability and the adopters' suitability to adopt.[145] Thus, the foreign adoption decision must not be recognized. The adopters have to seek re-adoption in Germany (see section 3.3), which will only be granted if the child's parents' consent to the adoption can be obtained again (their former consent which referred to the adoption granted by foreign law is generally not recognized by judges).[146]

---

140 This is the case if the adopters bypass such an assessment by concealing the international nature of the adoption (*Amtsgericht Hamm, 30.12.2009 - XVI 82/09; Amtsgericht Hamm, 26.04.2010 - XV I 15/09; Oberlandesgericht Düsseldorf, 22.06.2010 - 25 Wx 15/10; Oberlandesgericht Celle, 12.10.2011 - 17 UF 98/11; Oberlandesgericht Düsseldorf, 27.07.2012 - II-1 UF 82/11; Oberlandesgericht Hamm, 21.01.2014 - 11 UF 127/13*), if the child has been removed from a socially intact family only because he or she is considered to be better off growing up in Germany (*Oberlandesgericht Köln, 29.05.2009 - 16 Wx 16/09; Oberlandesgericht Karlsruhe, 08.07.2010 - 11 Wx 113/09*) or if the foreign court did not assess whether a suitable domestic child care option could have been found in the child's country of origin (*Oberlandesgericht Düsseldorf, 18.01.2011 - I-25 Wx 28/10*).

141 *Amtsgericht Hamm, 26.04.2010, XV I 15/09; Amtsgericht Düsseldorf 02.10.2009, 98 XVI 16/08.*

142 T. Steiger (2002). "Das neue Recht der internationalen Adoption und Adoptionsvermittlung: Einführung-Erläuterung-Materialien." Bundesanzeiger-Verlag, Köln, Rn. 334; W. Weitzel (2006). "Anerkennung einer Auslandsadoption nach deutschem Recht trotz schwerwiegender Mängel der ausländischen Entscheidung?" Das Jugendamt, 8, 333-336, p. 334; J. Reinhardt (2006). "Die Praxis der Anerkennung ausländischer Adoptionsentscheidungen aus der Sicht der Adoptionsvermittlung." Das Jugendamt, 8, 325-329, p. 325.

143 T. Steiger (2002). "Das neue Recht der internationalen Adoption und Adoptionsvermittlung: Einführung-Erläuterung-Materialien." Bundesanzeiger-Verlag, Köln, Rn. 334.

144 *Ibid.*

145 See, for example, *Oberlandesgericht Koeln, 29.05.2009 - 16 Wx 251/08; Oberlandesgericht Karlsruhe, 08.07.2010 - 11 Wx 113/09; Oberlandesgericht Celle, 12.10.2011 - 17 UF 98/11; KG 23.12.2011 - 17 UF 177/11; Oberlandesgericht Frankfurt, 19.01.2012 - 20 W 93/11; Begründung des Entwurfs eines Gesetzes zur Regelung von Rechtsfragen auf dem Gebiet der internationalen Adoption und zur Weiterentwicklung des Adoptionsvermittlungsrechts vom 10.05.2001, Deutscher Bundestag, 14. Wahlperiode, Drucksache 14/6011,* p. 32.

146 Majer (2015). "Die Anerkennung ausländischer Adoptionsentscheidungen." Neue Zeitschrift für Familienrecht, 1138-1142, p. 1138.

Other German courts and scholars, however, argue that the lack of involvement of a German adoption placement office in the adoption procedure would not *per se* be manifestly contrary to German public policy; rather it is decisive whether the international adoption can ultimately be considered as being in the best interests of the child.[147] They often refer to a judgment by the German Supreme Court from 1989 which pointed out that the question as to whether or not the recognition of a foreign adoption decision is contrary to public policy has to be assessed at the time of the recognition procedure and not at the time when the foreign adoption decision was rendered.[148] Thus, many German courts assess themselves as to whether the adopters are 'actually' (*tatsächlich*) suited to adopt the child at the time of the recognition procedure and – after a positive evaluation – determine that the foreign adoption judgment is to be recognized.[149] That way the formal recognition procedure of § 2 AdWirkG is turned into a procedure in which the foreign adoption decision is *de facto* annulled in Germany and a new decision on the adoption is rendered.[150]

Some German commentators advocate this line of jurisdiction. Beyer, for instance, argues that the lack of an assessment of the adopters' suitability by a German adoption placement office constitutes a violation of a procedural regulation that, according to the German legislator, would only "give rise to doubts" as to whether the foreign adoption decision is compatible with German public policy.[151] Thus, Beyer claims, the German court has to refuse the recognition only in those cases where it finds – after having assessed the adopters' suitability itself – that the adoption would violate the substantive requirement of being in the child's best interests.[152] Similarly, Majer claims that Article 8 ECHR (which provides the child with the right to family life) as well as Article 3 UNCRC require the German courts to assess, during the adoption recognition procedure, whether the intercountry adoption serves the best interests of the child.[153] He argues that refusing to recognize a foreign decision on an adoption only because it was not pursued with the involvement of a German adoption placement office would often be manifestly contrary to the best interests of the child. The adopters would need to seek re-adoption according to German law which requires that the child's parents' consent to adoption be obtained once again.

147 *Amtsgericht Hamm, 17.04.2006 – XVI 44/05; Landesgericht Potsdam, 11.11.2010, 5 T 447/10; Oberlandesgericht Hamm, 17/02.2015 – 11 UF 222/14; Oberlandesgericht Brandenburg, 28.04.2016 – 15 UF 184/15; Oberlandesgericht Celle, 20.02.2017 – 17 UF 131/16.*

148 *Bundesgerichtshof, 14.12.1988, Iva ZR 231/87.*

149 W. Weitzel (2006). "Anerkennung einer Auslandsadoption nach deutschem Recht trotz schwerwiegender Mängel der ausländischen Entscheidung?" Das Jugendamt, 8, 333-336, p. 335.

150 *Ibid.*, p. 336.

151 M. Beyer (2006). "Zur Frage der ordre public-Widrigkeit ausländischer Adoptionsentscheidungen wegen unzureichender Elterneignungs- und Kindeswohlprüfung." Das Jugendamt, 8, 329-332, p. 330.

152 *Ibid.*, p. 331.

153 Majer (2015). "Die Anerkennung ausländischer Adoptionsentscheidungen." Neue Zeitschrift für Familienrecht, 1138-1142, pp. 1139-1140.

This, however, would often prove to be difficult in practice, meaning that the child is left without (legal) parents and might even be forced to go back to the sending country.[154]

Other legal scholars, however, criticize this line of case law for two reasons. First, they argue that it lowers the high child protection standards that are provided for in the German law.[155] Once the child has lived with his or her new family for a certain period of time, the question that the court is confronted with in its *ex post* assessment of the adoptive parents' suitability changes from "Are the adoption applicants suited to adopt a child?" to "Are the adoption applicants unsuited to such an extent that the child has to be removed from the family?".[156] This is what Reinhardt refers to as the 'adopters' post-adoption assessment light'.[157] Second, commentators claim that this jurisdiction would undermine the strict international adoption placement procedure that is laid down in the AdVermiG and the AdÜbAG as it would invite adopters to circumvent the typically very time-consuming involvement of a German adoption placement office and to pursue a more rapid and less bureaucratic private intercountry adoption.[158]

The study conducted by Schlauss in 2007 illustrates that the German courts were rather reluctant to refuse the recognition of intercountry adoptions that were privately pursued.[159] Although only about 50% of the intercountry adoptions registered between 2005 and 2006 were pursued with the involvement of a German adoption placement office, approximately 90% of them were recognized by the German courts.[160] In only 4% of the cases was recognition refused and in 6% the applications for recognition were – in some cases upon instruction of the court itself – withdrawn.[161] Schlauss claims that the fact that those intercountry adoptions that were not recognized were – with only one exception – private adoptions, underlines the importance of the involvement of a German adoption placement office.[162]

Some experts estimate that the rate of intercountry adoptions that are pursued privately still amounts to about 50% today, some 10 years after Schlauss' study was conducted.[163] Arguably, a recent judgment by the German Federal Court of Justice[164] could further

154 *Ibid.*, p. 1138.
155 *Ibid.*
156 *Ibid.*
157 J. Reinhardt (2006). "Gewollt oder nicht? Die private Adoption von Kindern aus dem Ausland." Zeitschrift für Rechtspolitik, 8, 241-272, p. 247.
158 H. Bienentreu (2008). "Grenzüberschreitende Adoptionen – Eine Bestandsaufnahme." Das Jugendamt, 2, 57-62, p. 60.
159 S. Schlauss (2007). "Die Anerkennung von Auslandsadoptionen in der vormundschaftsgerichtlichen Praxis." FamRZ, 20, 1699-1702.
160 *Ibid.*, p. 1702.
161 *Ibid.*
162 *Ibid.*
163 Interview with J. Reinhardt, international adoption law scholar and head of the Central Adoption Office Bavaria between 2001 until 2008, Germany, 16.03.2015.
164 *Bundesgerichtshof, 10.12.2014, XII ZB 463/13.*

increase the family courts' readiness to recognize foreign adoption decisions. Even though the judgment dealt with surrogacy, its observations on the child's best interests have important implications for the intercountry adoption system as well.[165]

In this case, a German homosexual couple entered into a surrogacy agreement with a woman from California. Whereas one of the men was the child's biological father, the egg came from an anonymous donor. After the child was born, a court in California declared the German couple to be the child's legal parents. The German Federal Court of Justice then dealt with the question as to whether this foreign court judgment had to be recognized according to § 108 FamFG. Even though it had been settled case law that foreign decisions granting parenthood to the intended parents (and not to the surrogate mother) were manifestly contrary to German public policy,[166] the Federal Court of Justice found that the Californian decision had to be recognized.[167]

It stated that the recognition of foreign decisions generally seeks to ensure a harmonization of international judgements as well as to avoid "limping legal relationships". § 109(1)(4) FamFG must therefore be interpreted restrictively, meaning that the recognition of foreign decisions may only be refused in exceptional cases.[168] The German Federal Court of Justice ruled that the child's right to family life laid down in Article 8 ECHR would be violated if the Californian court decision were not recognized in Germany. This is because refusing the recognition would mean that the child, who was after all given up by the surrogate mother, only had one legal parent: the biological father.[169] Furthermore, the Court stated that both Article 8 ECHR and the principle of the child's best interests would generally preclude that the recognition of a foreign decision is refused "only due to the general preventive consideration that (further) circumventions of the ban on surrogacy agreements can thereby be prevented".[170] In other words: the recognition of the legal parenthood cannot be rejected only because this might prevent others from pursuing a surrogacy agreement that is prohibited in Germany.

165 Majer (2015). "Die Anerkennung ausländischer Adoptionsentscheidungen." Neue Zeitschrift für Familienrecht, 1138-1142, pp. 1139-1140.

166 In Germany, surrogacy agreements are illegal according to § 1 I Nr. 7 ESchG. However, neither the surrogate mother nor the intended parents are punished for entering into such an agreement, according to § 1 III Nr. 2 ESchG. § 1591 BGB provides that the woman who gave birth to the child is to be considered as the child's mother, even if the woman is not genetically related to the child, because the egg came from another woman. German law does not allow the parenthood of two men acknowledging a child's fatherhood. Thus, according to established German case law, the surrogate woman and the biological father, acknowledging fatherhood of the child, would have been the child's legal parents in that case. The German man that was genetically unrelated to the child would only have become the child's legal parent by way of adoption.

167 *Bundesgerichtshof, 10.12.2014 – XII ZB 463/13.*

168 *Ibid.*, para. 29.

169 *Ibid.*

170 *Ibid.*, para. 56.

The German Supreme Court's considerations in its judgment from 2014 are also relevant for intercountry adoptions.[171] Even if adopters have circumvented the adoption placement procedure laid down in the AdVermiG and the AdÜbAG, the foreign adoption decision must nonetheless be recognized if this ultimately serves the best interests of the particular child involved. General preventive considerations, namely the consideration that the best interests of the children *in abstracto* can best be served by refusing the recognition and thereby preventing further private intercountry adoption, cannot justify a violation of the best interests of the child *in concreto*.

A number of German family courts that have had to decide on the recognition of foreign adoption decisions have referred to the judgment of the German Supreme Court from 2014. For instance, the *Oberlandesgericht Brandenburg* had to deal with the question as to whether a Chinese adoption decision had to be recognized, even though the intercountry adoption placement procedure laid down in the Hague Convention had been circumvented.[172] The adopters concealed the international nature of the adoption, which is why the court in China granted a domestic adoption and failed to assess whether the child was suitable for an intercountry adoption according to Article 4 of the Convention, particularly whether there were domestic child care options available. Furthermore, the adopters' suitability to adopt was not assessed, neither by a German adoption placement office nor a Chinese authority. Notwithstanding these deficiencies, the *Oberlandesgericht Brandenburg* decided to recognize the Chinese adoption decision. It argued that the lack of an assessment of the adopters and of the question as to whether the child was suitable for an intercountry adoption would "give rise to doubts" as to whether the Chinese adoption decision was compatible with German public policy. However, these doubts, the court stated, would not justify refusing the recognition as the adoption granted by the Chinese authority could ultimately be considered as being in the best interests of the child at the time of the recognition procedure.[173] In this judgment, the principle of the child's best interests is thus not only advanced to remedy the lack of an evaluation of the adopter's suitability to adopt, but also the lack of an assessment of the child's adoptability by the authorities in the sending country.

In addition, the *Oberlandesgericht Celle* referred to the German Supreme Court's judgment from 2014 in its decision on the recognition of a private intercountry adoption.[174] In this case, the adopters and the biological parents agreed on the adoption of the child "during a festive adoption ceremony". Even though the adopters' suitability to adopt had not been assessed (neither by a German adoption placement office nor an authority in the

171 Majer (2015). "Die Anerkennung ausländischer Adoptionsentscheidungen." Neue Zeitschrift für Familienrecht, 1138-1142, pp. 1140-1141.

172 *Oberlandesgericht Brandenburg, 28.04.2016 – 15 UF 184/15.*

173 *Ibid.*, para. 20.

174 *Oberlandesgericht Celle*, 20.02.2017, 17 UF 131/16.

sending country), the German Court decided to recognize the foreign adoption decision. It stated that a violation of the standards of the Hague Convention would not *per se* justify refusing the recognition of a foreign adoption decision. Referring to the judgement of the German Supreme Court, the *Oberlandesgericht Celle* established that

> General preventative considerations referring to the objective of the Hague Convention to ensure that, by an advanced co-operation amongst the Contracting States and agreed up procedural standard, intercountry adoptions are made in the best interests of the child and with respect for his or her fundamental rights, and to prevent the abduction, the sale of, or traffic in children, cannot justify a violation of the best interests of the particular child involved. [...] It must not be to the detriment of the individual child that the biological parents and the adopters – intentionally or unintentionally – circumvented the procedure provided by the Hague Convention.[175]

According to the court, the recognition of a foreign adoption decision must only be refused if the recognition would lead to a result that was manifestly contrary to the rights or best interests of the child at the time of the recognition procedure. The *Oberlandesgericht Celle* argued that the child's right to family life according to Article 8 ECHR, as well as his or her best interests, would be violated if the foreign adoption decision were not to be recognized.[176] This is because refusing to recognize the foreign adoption decision would leave the child in 'legal limbo': on the one hand, he is denied a legal relationship with the new family in Germany, that he had already bonded with, and might even have to leave the country as he would lose his residency status; in his native country, on the other hand, he could not simply return to his biological parents as they had given up their parental rights and responsibilities.[177] The child would be left without (legal) parents, which cannot be considered to be in his best interests.

The family court's decision on the recognition of a foreign adoption decision is not subject to appeal, even by the Federal Central Office. According to § 5(3) AdWirkG, the Federal Central Office has to be involved in the judicial recognition procedures. It submits a statement in which it assesses the facts of the case and issues an opinion on whether the intercountry adoption is manifestly contrary to German public policy and if it would approve or refuse its recognition. But ultimately it is up to the court to decide on the recognition of an independent intercountry adoption and, as Schlauss' survey suggests,

175 *Ibid.*, para. 21.
176 *Ibid.*, para. 29.
177 *Ibid.*, para. 43-44.

many do so on a large scale. The former head of the Federal Central Office criticizes the limited possibilities that his institution has in that respect:

> If our task is to ensure uniformity of jurisprudence, we should have the legal means to bring those cases where we say that the decision of the judge is not acceptable to the court of appeal. Because – I don't want to presume bad faith, but – for a judge, it is of course always easy to recognize and this decision cannot be contested by anybody: the parents have what they want and we cannot do anything.[178]

This means, that the Federal Central Office's hands are also tied in cases where a judge decides to recognize a (private) adoption, where clear indications of commercial and illegal practices can be found. The former head of the Federal Central Office argues that the German courts' reluctance to refuse foreign adoption decisions is attributable to the emotional nature of adoptions:

> For us it is, of course, easy: we see the files and write our statements. However, the judge calls the parents who appear in the courtroom with their child who is rollicking on their laps and kissing and hugging them. He would then say: my God, they did this or that wrong, the heck with it, isn't it nice? We do not have this emotional element. I think that many judges render gut decisions that are not legally correct.[179]

The tendency of the German courts to recognize foreign decisions on an adoption that have taken place without the involvement of a German adoption placement office undermines the strict legal procedures that are laid down in the AdVermiG and the AdÜbAG, which seek to protect not only the best interests of the individual child but also the best interests of children in general. By advancing the best interests of the individual child to legitimize adoptions that were carried out without any supervision by the German authorities (and which may even have been based on an improper assessment of the child's adoptability), the German courts essentially create a situation that is contrary to the best interests of children in general. After all, prospective adopters might be encouraged by this case law to pursue an independent adoption which is much riskier than agency adoptions. As will be explained in section 9, private adoptions may even have criminal legal consequences.

---

178 Interview with W. Weitzel, head of the German Federal Central Office for International Adoption at the German Federal Office of Justice between 2002 and 2017, Germany, 21.04.2015.

179 *Ibid.*

5 German Adoption Agencies Caught in a Tension between Integrity and Money

5.1 Accreditation and Authorization Requirements

A private agency is only admitted as an international adoption placement office if (1) it has been accredited by its competent Central Adoption Office as an adoption placement office[180] and (2) is authorized to place intercountry adoptions from one or several particular sending countries. Unlike in the Netherlands, a general authorization for placing international adoptions is not provided for in Germany.[181] In the course of ratifying the Hague Convention, the German legislator has tightened the accreditation and authorization requirements for adoption placement offices.

In order to be accredited as an adoption placement office, a private agency has to meet *strict personnel requirements* that correspond to those set forth in Article 11(b) of the Hague Convention.[182] In order to guarantee a high level of expertise, they are required to employ at least two full-time staff members or a corresponding number of part-time staff members.[183] Engaging staff members who only work on a voluntary or freelance basis is not permitted any longer. The personnel must be qualified as social workers, psychologists or pedagogues[184] and they need to have gained work experience in the field of intercountry adoption for at least one year.[185]

In addition to the professional qualifications, the agency's staff members are required to have the *personal competencies* to carry out adoption placement activities, such as empathy, communication skills, trustworthiness and reliability.[186] Of particular importance is their integrity since extraneous considerations and influences are to be suspected in the delicate field of intercountry adoption.[187] According to the German case law, the personnel are expected to be able to disregard their own feelings as well as to cope with frustration and powerlessness.[188]

180 § 4(1) AdVermiG.

181 § 4(2) *leg. cit.*

182 § 4(1)(1), § 3 *leg. cit.*

183 § 3(2) *leg. cit.*

184 R. Reinhardt (2017). "§ 3 AdVermiG." In J. Reinhardt (ed) "Adoptionsvermittlungsgesetz." 4. edition, Nomos Bundesrecht, Erläuterungen, Rn. 4.

185 *Ibid.*, Rn. 5.

186 *Ibid.*, Rn. 3.

187 R. Reinhardt (2017). "§ 4 AdVermiG." In J. Reinhardt (ed) "Adoptionsvermittlungsgesetz." 4. edition, Nomos Bundesrecht, Erläuterungen, Rn. 7.

188 *Oberverwaltungsgericht Hamburg, 18.10.2006, 4 Bs 224/06.*

Furthermore, the desire to help must not become an end in itself as this may obstruct the view on the complex problems that are redolent of an international child adoption.[189] The staff members are, thus, required to keep a professional distance and to be robust against subjective considerations, such as a wrong understanding of the child's best interests or any influences from adoption applicants.[190] These professional and personal requirements also have to be met by persons who give functional instructions to the staff members that carry out adoption placement activities.[191]

Furthermore, a private agency seeking an accreditation as an adoption placement office must be able *to carry out properly its tasks and duties.* This *inter alia* means that the agency's existence must not be dependent on the number of adoption placements, but that it needs to be able to operate without deriving any income from adoption placements over a particular period of time.[192] Hence, it is required to have sufficient financial resources to cover its personnel's salaries and other running costs during a period of six months (this means about €100,000).[193]

Finally, an adoption agency must *only pursue non-profit objectives.*[194] This does not mean that cost-covering incomes or reasonable financial contributions from adoption applicants are excluded. However, deriving improper financial or other gain or charging fees that are unreasonably high is strictly prohibited.[195] This requirement basically corresponds with Article 11(a) of the Hague Convention, asserting that an accredited body must not pursue profit, as well as with Article 32, which provides that "no one shall derive improper financial or other gain from an activity related to an intercountry adoption"[196] and that "only costs and expenses, including reasonable professional fees of persons involved in the adoption, may be charged or paid".[197]

An accredited adoption agency is given the authorization to place intercountry adoptions only if it meets the accreditation requirements for a special degree required for the work in the field of intercountry adoption.[198] Furthermore, it needs to have a *sound cooperation with the sending countries* it wants to place children from.[199] It must establish a collaboration

189 *Verwaltungsgericht Hamburg, 20.2.2006 – 13 E 3690/05.*

190 R. Reinhardt (2017). "§ 4 AdVermiG." In J. Reinhardt (ed) "Adoptionsvermittlungsgesetz." 4. edition, Nomos Bundesrecht, Erläuterungen, Rn. 8.

191 R. Reinhardt (2017). "§ 3 AdVermiG." In J. Reinhardt (ed) "Adoptionsvermittlungsgesetz." 4. edition, Nomos Bundesrecht, Erläuterungen, Rn. 4.

192 R. Reinhardt (2017). "§ 4 AdVermiG." In J. Reinhardt (ed) "Adoptionsvermittlungsgesetz." 4. edition, Nomos Bundesrecht, Erläuterungen, Rn. 2.

193 *Ibid.*

194 § 4(1)(3) AdVermiG.

195 R. Reinhardt (2017). "§ 3 AdVermiG." In J. Reinhardt (ed) "Adoptionsvermittlungsgesetz." 4. edition, Nomos Bundesrecht, Erläuterungen, Rn. 2.

196 Art. 32(1) Hague Convention.

197 Art. 32(2) *leg. cit.*

198 § 4(2) AdVermiG.

199 § 2(1) Nr. 1-4 AdVermiStAnKoV.

with the Central Authority and/or a foreign accredited partner organization, appoint a legal representative if necessary or set up a representative office that might need to be accredited in the country of origin.

5.2 *Financial Strain*

In Germany, eight international adoption placement agencies are accredited at the time of writing: *AdA Adoptionsberatung e.V., Eltern-Kind-Brücke e.V., Eltern für Afrika e.V., Eltern für Kinder e.V., Evangelischer Verein für Adoption und Pflegekinderhilfe (EVAP), familie international frankfurt (fif) e.V., HELP a child e.V.*, and *Zukunft für Kinder e.V.* As was shown in the previous section, the requirements that these agencies must fulfil in order to become accredited and to get the authorization to place intercountry adoptions are considerably high. The personnel need to have personnel and professional competencies and the agency may not operate on a for-profit basis.

All agencies openly endorse the standards and principles of the Hague Convention as well as the UNCRC. They routinely claim that they exist to serve the best interests of the child and to find parents for children, not children for parents.[200] Many assert to promote the subsidiarity principle by supporting aid projects in the sending states that are aimed at helping children to grow up in their own ethnic and cultural environment, and they emphasize that they only place parentless children that cannot be cared for in their native countries.[201] Some clarify on their websites that it is therefore not healthy infants they are placing for adoption, but primarily children with special needs (e.g. with mental or physical diseases, or a social stigma) for whom no domestic childcare solution can be found.[202] In an interview, the head of a German adoption agency emphasized that:

200 See, for example, *Eltern für Kinder*: "Parents for Children: The name speaks for itself. *Eltern für Kinder e.V.* is finding parents for children and not the other way round." Available at https://www.efk-adoptionen.de/adoption/ (last accessed on 27.07.2018); *Eltern für Afrika*: "We have our focus on the needs and interests of the individual child." Available at "http://www.elternfuerafrika.de/startseite.html (last accessed on 27.07.2018); *Evangelischer Verein für Adoption und Pflegekinderhilfe*: "The objective of an adoption is to find new parents for a child that cannot be cared for by his/her biological parents." Available at http://www.evangelische-adoption.de/node/69 (last accessed on 27.07.2018).

201 See, for example, *Zukunft für Kinder*: "Unfortunately, despite numerous social projects, there are many abandoned children that cannot find a family in their own country and whose last chance of a humane future is an 'international adoption'. Zukunft für Kinder e.V. is looking for parents for these children." Available at http://www.zukunftfuerkinder.de/ (last accessed on 27.07.2018).

202 See, for example, *Eltern für Kinder*: "Eltern für Kinder e.V. places children [...] who cannot find parents in their native countries due to their skin colour, age, illness or mental retardation, or other reasons, who are handicapped and need medical care that is not available in their native countries." Available at https://www.efk-adoptionen.de/adoption/verlassene-kinder/ (last accessed on 27.07.2018).

> It is important not to facilitate adoptions, meaning the relinquishment of children by their parents, but to offer adoption for those only that do not have a chance of returning to their birth families.[203]

Yet, in practice, the high standards and principles, that the agencies regularly claim to give high priority to, are prone to be undermined, as in Germany almost all adoption placement offices lack the sufficient capital. The strict legal requirements that the adoption agencies have to meet presuppose considerable financial resources. They have to pay the staff members' salaries, the rent for their offices as well as the costs that incur by establishing and maintaining the cooperation with the sending countries. The director estimates the running costs of his agency:

> If I hire a proper full-time social worker, I have monthly costs between €4,000 and €5,000 including ancillary wage costs. I thus have to spend €10,000 per month for social workers alone. Add to this [the costs for] the contacts with the sending countries. All in all, at least €150,000 are required to keep the adoption agency up and running.[204]

In Germany, adoption agencies must cover all of their personal and material expenses themselves as they are not provided with any financial support through subsidies.[205] This is arguably because in Germany there is no public interest in international adoptions.[206] This means that the agencies have to finance themselves exclusively with 'administration fees' (*Verwaltungsgebühren*) that are paid by their adoption applicants. This fee is calculated on the basis of the running costs that the adoption placement office incurs annually, regardless of the office's volume of placement activity, and currently varies between €5,000 and €9,600. In addition to the administration fee, the adoption applicants have to pay a 'country fee' (*Ländergebühr*), a fixed fee that is charged for the services rendered by the adoption agency's partner organisation or representatives in the sending country (see section 6.2).

---

203 Interview with the director of German adoption agency A, Germany, 09.06.2015.

204 *Ibid.*

205 H. Paulitz, et al. (2000). "Interstaatliche Adoptionsvermittlungsstellen in Deutschland, Vermittlungspraxis, Kinderhandel." In H. Paulitz et al. (eds), "Adoption: Positionen, Impulse, Perspektiven." C. H. Beck, München, 185-231, p. 187.

206 C. Tribowski (2015). "Kinder kauft man nicht. Die politische Ökonomie von Auslandsadoptionen in Deutschland und den Vereinigten Staaten von Amerika." PhD Thesis, Universität zu Köln, p. 253.

Since the administration fee constitutes the adoption agency's sole source of revenue, the agency's existence is reliant on a particular number of international adoptions.[207] If the annual running costs of the adoption agency amount to, say, €200,000 and the administration fee is €5,000, then about 40 adoptions need to be handled each year to keep the agency up and running. Many placement offices, however, face difficulties getting to this figure. As was explained above, intercountry adoptions are on the decrease in Germany. Within the last couples of years, numerous cooperations between German adoption agencies and sending states had to be terminated. In some countries, the social-economic situation improved and sufficient domestic adoptive families were found for the unparented children. As a consequence, German adoption agencies ceased to place children from Brazil and several Eastern European states. In other countries, agencies simply stopped processing international adoptions because the placement procedures became too opaque or irregular,[208] the competition with other foreign adoption agencies became too harsh (see section 5.3) or because the government in the sending country decided to ban intercountry adoptions due to reports of illegal adoption practices.[209]

As a result, only 313 intercountry adoptions were placed by German adoption agencies in 2017. This number is low, considering that nine private adoption placement offices were accredited at that time.[210] The declining number of intercountry adoption placements has increased the pressure on the adoption placement offices. A social worker of an agency explains:

> The problem is that we have too few adoption placements [...] but that's a matter of perspective. I mean for us it is problematic because we make a living out of it.[211]

Commonly, adoption agencies respond to the drop in international adoptions by raising the administration fee that the adoption applicants need to pay to cover their running expenses. This has often led to a lack of understanding on the part of the adoption applicants and the general impression that the placement offices are profiting from intercountry

207 See also H. Paulitz, et al. (2000). "Interstaatliche Adoptionsvermittlungsstellen in Deutschland, Vermittlungspraxis, Kinderhandel." In H. Paulitz et al. (eds), "Adoption: Positionen, Impulse, Perspektiven." C. H. Beck, München, 185-231, p. 227.

208 German adoption agencies stopped placing children from, for example, India, Nepal, Ethiopia, Ukraine and Mali.

209 For example, due to major adoption scandals, Romania, Kenia and Nepal had issued a total ban on intercountry adoptions.

210 The adoption agency Children and Parent e.V. had its accreditation withdrawn in February 2018, see https://www.bundesjustizamt.de/DE/Themen/Buergerdienste/BZAA/Aktuelles/Aktuelles_node.html (last accessed on 04.08.2018).

211 Interview with a staff member of German adoption agency C, Germany, 10.09.2015.

adoptions.[212] Other agencies found themselves forced to reduce the number of employees or to shut down their business completely.[213]

The dependency of the adoption placement office's existence on the number of adoptions is problematic for two reasons. First, an adoption agency cannot simply afford to decline adoption applicants that are actually not suited to adopt a child, which obviously undermines the principles of the Hague Convention as well as the UNCRC.[214] Some adoption agencies accept more adoption applicants that they can realistically find a child for.[215] This practice is not only unfair towards the adoption applicants that are strung along in the belief that they actually have a chance to adopt. It is also dangerous as it may make the prospective adoptive parents feel entitled to a child. After they have been accepted as eligible and suitable to adopt and already paid a considerable amount of money for preparation workshops, they might increase the pressure on the agency to get a child proposal in return. The German agencies, in turn, then might pass on the pressure on the states of origin by overwhelming them with adoption applications.[216]

Second, the placement office cannot easily afford to discontinue the cooperation with a sending country. The establishment of collaborations with foreign partner organisations commonly requires a lot of effort, time and money: contacts need to be established, cooperation agreements must be made and suitable and qualified representatives have to be found and trained. The termination of such a collaboration would frustrate the several months or years of work and it would cause a reduction in the number of adoptions that the adoption placement agency so desperately relies on. For agencies that have numerous cooperation partners in the sending countries, the loss of one partnership might be economically viable. However, if an adoption agency collaborates with only one or two organizations, terminating a cooperation agreement could spell the end of the agency's existence. Adoption placement agencies might thus be financially motivated to accept or turn a blind eye to irregularities in the sending countries or on the abusive practices of their foreign partner organisations or representatives[217] (see section 7).

The German adoption law seeks to prevent the adoption agencies' financial dependence. It requires placement offices to prove, during the accreditation procedure, that their exis-

212 See, for instance, complaints of adoption applicants on an online forum available at http://www.eltern-foren.com/threads/austausch-adoption-ueber-zukunft-fuer-kinder.38510/ (last accessed on 04.08.2018).

213 In 2015, *Global Adoption Germany – Help for Kids*, authorized to place children from Bulgaria, Hungary, Russia and Kasachstan, shut down and in 2016 *Zentrum für Adoptionen*, authorized for the countries Russia and Kazakhstan, had to quit due to the increasing number of adoptions.

214 C. Tribowski (2015). "Kinder kauft man nicht. Die politische Ökonomie von Auslandsadoptionen in Deutschland und den Vereinigten Staaten von Amerika." PhD Thesis, Universität zu Köln, p. 255.

215 *Ibid.*

216 See Chapter II, section 2.2.2.

217 H. Paulitz, et al. (2000). "Interstaatliche Adoptionsvermittlungsstellen in Deutschland, Vermittlungspraxis, Kinderhandel." In H. Paulitz et al. (eds), "Adoption: Positionen, Impulse, Perspektiven." C. H. Beck, München, 185-231, p. 227.

tence is not reliant on the number of adoptions they place and that they are able to operate without deriving any income from adoption placements over a certain period of time.[218] Thus, they must provide evidence that they have sufficient financial resources to cover their personnel's salaries as well as other running costs during a six month period (generally this would mean about €100,000).[219] These financial reserves are certainly a safety net when the number of international adoptions is temporarily low. However, they do not rule out the agencies' reliance on adoption placements if the fees paid by the adoption applicants constitute the agency's sole source of revenue.

In order to avoid the adoption placement office's reliance on the number of adoptions, one agency charges the adoption applicants not only administrative fees of €4,000 but also urges them to become agency members with a monthly membership fee of €20/person or €30/couple. Currently, the adoption agency has 800 members whose contributions account for between 40% and 60% of the agency's running expenses.[220] The fact that adoption applicants, including those that have been declined, can become agency members is problematic: from the moment that they become a member, they have the right to vote and can get their way in the agency's policy. That way, an adoption agency can easily become an association of involuntarily childless couples whose primary motivation is to adopt a child as quickly as possible.[221]

The strict requirements that adoption agencies have to meet in order to be accredited and to get an authorization to place intercountry adoptions do not necessarily guarantee the absence of illicit activities. Even the most benevolent of adoption placement office might feel forced to turn a blind eye to signs of questionable practices by its foreign partners, if it derives its funds exclusively from adoption placements. As Tribowski notes, "[t]he lack of sufficient financial resources in the German distribution system for international adoptions can lead to a conflicting and, thus, *[morally]* tense situation for the agencies: they find themselves standing between the standards of the best interests of the child [...], on the one hand, and a cost-benefit calculation, on the other hand".[222]

218 R. Reinhardt (2017). "§ 4 AdVermiG." In J. Reinhardt (ed) "Adoptionsvermittlungsgesetz." 4. edition, Nomos Bundesrecht, Erläuterungen, Rn. 2.

219 *Ibid.*

220 Interview with the director of German adoption agency A, Germany, 09.06.2015.

221 H. Paulitz, et al. (2000). "Interstaatliche Adoptionsvermittlungsstellen in Deutschland, Vermittlungspraxis, Kinderhandel." In H. Paulitz et al. (eds), "Adoption: Positionen, Impulse, Perspektiven." C. H. Beck, München, 185-231, pp. 227-228.

222 C. Tribowski (2015). "Kinder kauft man nicht. Die politische Ökonomie von Auslandsadoptionen in Deutschland und den Vereinigten Staaten von Amerika." PhD Thesis, Universität zu Köln, p. 256.

5.3 *Competition among Helpers*

Adding to the decreasing number of international adoptions is the competition among the adoption placement agencies. In Germany, currently eight international adoption placement offices are accredited (section 5.1). They are authorized by the competent Central Adoption Office to carry out adoptions placements from 33 countries in total, most of which have ratified the Hague Convention: Chile, Honduras, Colombia, Peru, Haiti, Vietnam, Hong Kong, Taiwan, Sri Lanka, Mongolia, Thailand, Philippines, Indonesia, Madagascar, Togo, South Africa, Burkina Faso, Mali, Czech Republic, Bulgaria, Latvia, Poland, Bosnia and Herzegovina, Croatia, Macedonia, Montenegro, Serbia, Slovakia, Slovenia, Turkey, Ukraine, Kazakhstan and Russia. From some of these countries, only kinship and step-parent adoptions are carried out (for example in, the Czech Republic, Slovenia, the Western Balkans, and Turkey).

In some of these countries, more than one German adoption agency is active. German adoption law neither prohibits nor regulates multiple agency authorizations for one sending state. The Central Adoption Office must deny the authorization relative to a specific sending country if competition between several adoption agencies in the sending country is expected to hinder efficient cooperation or where it may decrease the quality of the placement activities.[223] However, it is up to the Central Adoption Office to decide when this is the case. Currently, two German adoption placement agencies are cooperating with Bulgaria, Russia, Haiti and Thailand, which could potentially result in them competing for adoptable children, especially considering the fact that the number of adoptions from these countries has decreased in recent years.[224]

German adoption agencies not only compete with each other, but also with other foreign placement offices in the sending countries. Particularly, adoption agencies from the United States and France which commonly contribute a lot of money into adoption programmes are considered as major competitors, whose work has already forced a number of German agencies to shut down their adoption programmes in some states. Head of German adoption agency A explains:

> I think the situation changed in those places where the Americans are represented strongly and attract with their money. There, people start thinking: Why not? Why should we give a child to the Germans that are not prepared to give so much money? In most countries where Americans are very active, we quit

223 R. Reinhardt (2017). "§ 4 AdVermiG." In J. Reinhardt (ed) "Adoptionsvermittlungsgesetz." 4. edition, Nomos Bundesrecht, Erläuterungen, Rn.17.

224 B. Wacker, et al. (2006). "Interstaatliche Adoptionsvermittlungsstellen in Deutschland, Vermittlungspraxis, Kinderhandel." In H. Paulitz et al. (eds), "Adoption: Positionen, Impulse, Perspektiven." (2nd edition) C. H. Beck, München, 327-369, p. 340.

– not only [*German adoption agency A*] but all German adoption agencies – because we are not able to participate anymore. In Africa, France is bidding for adoptions very strongly and aggressively.[225]

Also, the Central Adoption Offices can be competitors if they are placing children from countries for which one or more private adoption agencies has been authorized.[226] In Germany, all 12 Central Adoption Offices of the State Youth Welfare Offices are allowed to carry out international adoption placements (see section 8.4). Some refer adoption applicants to the private agencies and only carry out international adoptions from Hague countries for which no agency has been authorized. Other Central Adoption Offices, however, do not give the accredited agencies primacy but are very active stakeholders in the intercountry adoption placement system themselves. For example, the Central Adoption Office in Baden-Württemberg has placed some 127 children from Asia, South America and Eastern Europe between 2002 and 2014[227] and is, therefore, a serious competitor for those agencies that also co-operate with countries from these regions.

Many German adoption agencies complain that the Central Adoption Offices are luring away potential adoption applicants by offering their services for seemingly lower adoption costs. Adoption applicants who adopt with the involvement of a private adoption agency have to pay between €20,000 and €30,000 in fees. This amount is composed of the administration fee invoiced for the work of the agency in Germany (see section 5.2) as well as a country fee that is charged for the services rendered by the agency's cooperation partners in the sending country (see section 6.2). Central Adoption Offices charge adoption applicants around €2,000-€1,200 for assessing the applicants' suitability to adopt and €800 for carrying out the international adoption placement.[228] This fee is significantly lower than the costs that are charged by the private agencies as the Central Adoption Offices do not render any services in the sending countries. They have not established any cooperation with foreign partner organizations nor do they have local representatives who would assist the adoption applicants in the adoption procedure (see section 8.4).

Their relatively low adoption fee appeals to many adoption applicants who do often not bear in mind that they need to hire and pay an interpreter and a lawyer in the sending country who will assist them in handling the adoption process. The difference in costs that are incurred by adopting with the involvement of a Central Adoption Office, on the one

225 Interview with the director of German adoption agency A, Germany, 09.06.2015.

226 B. Wacker, et al. (2006). "Interstaatliche Adoptionsvermittlungsstellen in Deutschland, Vermittlungspraxis, Kinderhandel." In H. Paulitz et al. (eds), "Adoption: Positionen, Impulse, Perspektiven." (2nd edition) C. H. Beck, München, 327-369, p. 341.

227 Kommunalverband für Jugend und Soziales Baden-Württemberg (KVJS) (2014). "Auslandsadoptionen: Beratung, Unterstützung und Vermittlung durch den KVJS." Stuttgart, available at https://www.kvjs.de/fileadmin/publikationen/spezial/Spezial-Adoption.pdf, p. 7.

228 § 5(1) AdVermiStAnKoV.

hand, and by adopting *via* a private agency, on the other hand, is only an ostensible one. Nonetheless, the Central Adoption Office in Baden-Württemberg stresses the cost difference on its website.[229] The Director of *German adoption agency A* claims: "It is an unfair comparison. [...] It would be the same as if you said that at BMW the car costs €33,000 but I am offering the wheel for only €2,000. Every company in Germany would be sued as it is an unfair competition".[230]

6 Cooperation with the Sending Countries – A Matter of Trust

6.1 Foreign Partners, the Cogs in the Adoption System

As was explained in Chapter II, the adoption agencies' foreign representatives and partner organizations play a crucial role in the adoption placement procedure as they constitute the link between the sending and the receiving country.[231] They are important cogs in the adoption system. On the one hand, they may serve as guardians who only let those children pass the adoption system that are legitimately available for adoption. On the other hand, they may illegally obtain children and/or launder them through the system themselves or turn a blind eye to the illegal practices of other actors.

One factor that influences the cooperation partners' and representatives' actions is the amount of money involved. Financial inducements may lead them to illegally procure children for intercountry adoption or turn a blind eye to unethical or illegal activities by others. Thus, Article 32(2) and (3) of the Hague Convention clarify that "[o]nly costs and expenses, including reasonable professional fees of persons involved in the adoption, may be charged or paid" and that "[t]he directors, administrators and employees of bodies involved in an adoption shall not receive remuneration which is unreasonably high in relation to services rendered".

6.2 Adoption Costs – Don't Ask, Don't Tell

Internationally adopting a child is a costly enterprise: numerous procedural steps have to be taken by different actors in both the sending as well as the receiving country that need to be reimbursed. In addition to the 'administrative fee' that is paid for the German adoption agency's work (see section 5.2), the adoption applicants also need to pay a fee

229 Kommunalverband für Jugend und Soziales Baden-Württemberg (KVJS) (2014). "Auslandsadoptionen: Beratung, Unterstützung und Vermittlung durch den KVJS." Stuttgart, available at https://www.kvjs.de/fileadmin/publikationen/spezial/Spezial-Adoption.pdf, p. 6.

230 Interview with the director of German adoption agency A, Germany, 09.06.2015.

231 See Chapter II, section 2.4.2.

for the services rendered by the adoption agency's cooperation partners and representatives in the sending country. This fee is often called a 'country fee' and is a fixed fee that is composed of indirect costs as well as direct costs.

Indirect costs are operating costs that the cooperation partners or representatives incur, such as salaries, rent, office equipment, insurance and electricity, that are to be shared among all the adoption cases carried out during the year. Direct costs are costs directly connected with the processing of an individual adoption case and include expenses for, for instance, the translation and legalization of documents, communication costs, lawyers' fees, court fees, medical fees and 'child maintenance costs' that an orphanage may charge for the care of the adoptive child.[232] In order to avoid creating financial inducements for the actors involved in the adoption process, the country fee should be reasonable. Thus, it must be determined by comparison with local procedures and services requiring a similar type and amount of work.[233] Yet, it can only be determined if the fees are reasonably high and if they are made transparent.

The country fees vary greatly between cooperation partners and sending countries, based on the services provided as well as the applicable national laws and regulations.[234] Often they are determined individually by the German adoption agencies' representative or partner organization which estimates the indirect adoption costs that they incur as well as the costs of an individual adoption case. In some sending countries, however, the country fees are determined by the official authorities and do not vary between individual organizations. For instance, in Haiti and Bulgaria, all adoption applicants have to pay a standardized fee of €8,500 and €9,500 respectively.[235]

The country fee that the German adoption agency is presented with by its co-worker or partner organization is a fixed sum that is broken down into fixed items. German law does not explicitly require adoption agencies to disclose the detailed categories of the adoption costs to the adoption applicants. Hence, some placement offices pass on the country fee that their partner organization or representative estimated to their adoption applicants without clearly itemizing it. For example, one agency charges its adoption applicants an all-encompassing country fee of more than €15,000 - for both Kazakhstan and Russia - without specifying the costs for each service that is to be rendered during the

232 The Permanent Bureau of the Hague Conference on International Private Law (2012). "Accreditation and Adoption Accredited Bodies: Guide to Good Practice No. 2." The Hague, p. 86.

233 G. Parra-Aranguren (1994). "Explanatory Report on the Convention on Protection of Children and Co-operation in Respect of Intercountry Adoption." The Hague Conference on Private International Law, para. 384.

234 In Thailand, for example, the country fee is relatively low. The adoption applicants only have to pay the fees for the court hearings, amounting to €500, as well as the 'child maintenance costs' to the orphanage they are adopting from. In Bulgaria, by way of contrast, the fee to be paid amounts to €9,000 and in Russia it may be up to €15,000, depending on the foreign partner.

235 Interview with the director of the German adoption agency A, Germany, 09.06.2015; interview with a staff member of the German adoption agency D, Germany, 02.09.2015.

adoption process.[236] The adoption applicants know which procedural steps are being covered with the country fee. Yet, they do not know exactly which persons and organizations are involved in the adoption process and how much they are getting paid for their services. Due to the lack of transparency vis-à-vis the adoption costs, adoption applicants often complain in online forums that they are being ripped off by their agencies.[237]

In some sending states, the standardized country fee is not even itemized for the German adoption agencies, which makes it impossible for them to know exactly what it is that their adoption applicants are paying for. For instance, *German adoption agency A* is placing children from Haiti where the country fee of €8,500 is determined by the official authorities. The director of the agency only vaguely knows where the money goes: "We now have an agreement with the Central Authority and the child care institutions that our adoption applicants need to pay €8,500 in total for the time the child has spent in the child care institution, the lawyer who is to be involved in the adoption process, and other costs that incur for the services of official authority, excluding the adoption applicants".[238] However, he does not know how much the lawyer is being remunerated for his/her services and how much is being paid to the child care institution.

The lack of transparency of the adoption fee makes it impossible for the German agencies to examine if they are reasonable or if they actually include hidden contributions or donations that might facilitate unethical or illegal practices. For the agency's director, the Haiti fee seems exaggerated, but since Haiti is a State Party to the Hague Convention, his agency has decided to accept the fee after all:

> The Hague Conference wrote down in the Convention that nobody should profit from an adoption and that no unreasonably high fees must be charged. It approved Haiti as a States Party to the Convention, so I cannot say that their fees are unreasonably high but must accept them as they are. However, for me personally, it is difficult to understand [the country fee] because I know how child care institutions work and I also see that the Thai orphanage manages to cover its expenses with €150 that is to be spent for each month the child has spent in the institution.[239]

The agency assumes that the adoption fee established by the Haitian authorities must be accepted as reasonable simply because Haiti has ratified the Hague Convention. As has been shown in the previous Chapter, general trust in 'Hague countries' is not justified.

236 Interview with the director of the German adoption agency E, Germany, 08.07.2015.

237 See, for instance, http://forum.gofeminin.de/forum/adoption/__f1004_adoption-Hat-jemand-Erfahrungen-mit-dem-EVAP.html (last accessed on 03.08.2018).

238 Interview with the director of German adoption agency A, Germany, 09.06.2015.

239 *Ibid.*

The treaty leaves its Contracting States with much leeway to continue policing international adoption as they deem fit. The Guides to Good Practice basically clarify as to when improper financial gain could commonly arise and which measures should be taken to prevent that. Yet, ultimately it is up to the individual Contracting State to determine the reasonableness of the adoption fees and many have done so in a very generous manner without this having had any negative consequences from The Hague. Haiti is one of the poorest countries in the world, where the gross national income per capita is about €1,600.[240] Against this backdrop, an all-in adoption fee of €8,500 can hardly be justified as reasonable. Numerous reports claim that the standards in Haitian child care institutions are absent or not compliant with the UNCRC,[241] suggesting that this fee probably does not include donations which would be invested in the Haitian child protection system. Hence, it is to be assumed that Haitian stakeholders involved in an international adoption gain financially from their activities which, in turn, increases the risk of illegal and abusive practices.

Even if the country fee is made transparent by the representative or cooperation partner, not all German adoption agencies scrutinize the individual items to see if they are actually reasonable. As s staff member at one German adoption agency was asked how the agency checks if the country fees were adequate, she replied: "Checking? I wonder how one can check that…well, if it seemed strange and we had the feeling that there is something fishy, then we would of course investigate".[242] Often it is believed that the representatives and partner organization that are familiar with the adoption process and the local conditions have a better overview of the costs that are incurred during the proceedings as well as a better understanding of their reasonableness. The staff of the German adoption agency would only intervene if they had, as the social worker explained, a 'feeling' that the costs were not appropriate.

Arguably, an adoption agency's motivation to carefully examine the reasonableness of the country fee and its actual use is only limited, as doing so might open a can of worms. If the agency detects that the costs established by its partner organization are actually unreasonably high, it would need to press for them to lower their fees. However, German adoption agencies know that they are only small fish in a big pond. They are well aware of the fact that their foreign partners are not reliant on them, as there are thousand other agencies from other receiving countries, particularly from the United States and France that are willing to pay whatever price they give. The chances are therefore high that a German agency's attempt to push for lower costs will not be successful, which would cause a dilemma for the agency: it either terminates the cooperation agreement with its partner

240 The World Bank (2016). "Gross national income per capita 2015, Atlas method and PPP." Available at https://astrofizyka.files.wordpress.com/2016/09/pnb-na-gc582owc499-wg-ppp-2015.pdf.

241 P. L. A. Ken (2007). "Children without Parental Care in the Caribbean Systems of Protection." UNICEF, available at https://www.unicef.org/easterncaribbean/cao_resources_children_without_parental_care.pdf.

242 Interview with a staff member of German adoption agency C, Germany, 10.09.2015.

organisation which could potentially spell the end of its existence; or it accepts the unreasonably high costs which would contradict the high standards and principles that it wishes to accord high priority to. To avoid this dilemma, an agency would be best to avoid asking too many questions and taking a closer look at the country fee.

The adoption agencies' *laissez-faire* approach to adoption costs is being supported by German law which fails to establish financial limits or guidelines on intercountry adoptions. According to Article 8 of the Hague Convention, "Central Authorities shall take [...] all appropriate measures to prevent improper financial or other gain in connection with an adoption and to deter all practices contrary to the objects of the Convention". German adoption law does not restrict the amount of country fees that German agencies should pay to their foreign cooperation partners, for instance, through providing guidelines for reasonable fees and remuneration. Also, the German Central Adoption Offices have not specified which adoption costs should be considered as 'reasonable'. They commonly leave it up to the Central Authority of the sending countries to establish the relevant standards for fees and remunerations. The German adoption system, therefore, allows inordinate sums of money to be introduced into the international adoption system, which might in turn facilitate and encourage abusive and illegal practices. As will be shown in the following section, this does not only apply to the country fees but also to other contributions and donations.

6.3 *Incentive Fees and Donations*

Not only unreasonably high adoption costs, but also extra 'contingency fees' paid to representatives or donations and contributions offered to cooperation partners in the sending countries, might induce 'generating' children that are actually not in need of an intercountry adoption. In Germany, standards and guidelines for salaries paid to co-workers in the sending countries are absent. German adoption agencies, therefore, remunerate their foreign representatives differently. Some agencies pay them a fixed salary that is not dependent on the actual number of adoptions to avoid spurring them. For example, the head of *German adoption agency A* has stated that:

> All our representatives get a monthly salary, meaning that they are not being paid for actual adoption placements...because it would create problems if I told them they would only get their money if they placed a child...there would be some kind of inducement. However, we want that they are in the position to say that a child is better off in his or her native country and that they do not want to place this child for an intercountry adoption and still get their wage. That is important to us.[243]

243 Interview with the director of German adoption agency A, Germany, 09.06.2015.

Other adoption agencies compensate their representatives on a per case basis. For example, *German adoption agency D* which places children from Russia does not pay its foreign representatives a monthly wage but only compensates them for the hours that the employees have actually worked on a case.[244] This is because the services provided by the representatives are very irregular due to the low number of adoptions from Russia. *German adoption agency E* which places children from Russia and Kazakhstan pays their representatives a fixed monthly salary but also rewards them with a contingency fee for each child placed for intercountry adoption.[245]

German law also lacks specific provisions that regulate donations and contributions to sending countries. Many German adoption agencies have set up or support aid projects in the sending states from which they place children for adoption. Some donate material goods (e.g. vehicle, playground, stove) to the orphanage they are collaborating with or help finance special aid projects (e.g. building up a well, contribute to the medical treatment of a sick child). They may do this with the intention of helping to improve the living conditions of the children, forgetting that such contributions could potentially influence the orphanages' decision concerning the placement of their children. After all, they may feel forced to secure a steady supply of children for intercountry adoption.[246]

Other adoption agencies deliberately do not donate to the orphanages they are cooperating with and also tell their adoption applicants to refrain from doing so before the adoption is finalized. Instead, they support aid projects that are not related to intercountry adoption – at least not directly. For example, *German adoption agency A* supports *AGERTO*, a project that provides young adults professional training to become carpenters, hairdressers, wood carvers etc. According to the information provided on the project's website, it particularly helps 'young mothers'[247] and seems to have ties to a nearby orphanage that it has donated benches and beds to.[248] While there is no actual evidence of wrongdoing, such a link between a project helping young mothers and an orphanage could become problematic, especially if one of the project's funder is a foreign adoption agency.

In the authorization procedure, German adoption agencies are required to describe the aid projects in the sending countries that they are running or supporting (see section 8.3). In addition, they need to disclose any donations in the financial statement that they have to submit to their supervising Central Adoption Office annually (see section 8.1). Yet, German adoption law neither specifies the control of these donations nor does it set

244 Interview with a staff member of German adoption agency D, Germany, 02.09.2015.

245 Interview with the director of German adoption agency E, Germany, 08.07.2015.

246 Hague Conference on Private International Law. Accreditation and Adoption Accredited Bodies: General Principles and Guide to Good Practice, Guide No 2 under the Hague Convention of 29 May 1993 on Protection of Children and Co-operation in Respect of Intercountry Adoption, para. 418.

247 See http://agerto.jimdo.com/welcome/what-is-agerto/ (last accessed on 03.08.2018).

248 See http://agerto.jimdo.com/welcome/what-do-we-do/ (last accessed on 03.08.2018).

up any limitations.[249] Adoption agencies are only prohibited from providing donations with regard to a specific adoption.[250] It is therefore up to each individual Central Adoption Office to decide to what extent it monitors its agency's contributions to charity organizations and when to intervene if the latter is too closely connected to an intercountry adoption. Most importantly, however, neither the agencies nor the Central Adoption Offices conduct any spot-checks on how exactly the donations are being used for in the sending countries.

6.4 *Supervision of Representatives and Cooperation Partners*

Paying reasonable service fees as well as fixed salaries and refraining from providing partner organizations donations contributions help to minimize the inducement to engage in unethical or illegal practices, but it cannot abolish them altogether. This is because the jobs of the representatives and the existence of the partner organizations ultimately depend on intercountry adoptions who might, therefore, feel incited to resort to irregular means in order to sustain the flow of adoptable children.

A representative knows that his or her collaboration agreement with a German adoption agency ultimately depends on the number of children that is placed for an intercountry adoption. If this number is too low, renting a local office in the sending country and/or paying a monthly salary to the representative would not be economically worthwhile for the German adoption agency.

Also, a child care institution may be financially dependent on intercountry adoptions if it gets very little funding from the government and has to finance the lion's share of its expenses with adoption fees. Orphanages often get the costs that are incurred by caring for the child that is being placed for an intercountry adoption covered. In some sending countries, adoption applicants are also required by law to pay 'child maintenance' fees to the orphanage they are adopting from.

Sometimes the sending countries' entire child protection systems are largely financed by donations and contributions that are provided by accredited adoption agencies of the receiving countries. In some states, foreign adoption offices are only allowed to place children if they donate a certain amount of money to local aid projects (that are not necessarily related to adoptions).[251] These mandatory donations are often justified by the sending countries on two grounds. First, they would assist the government in caring for the children that will not be placed for intercountry adoption because they are older and/or sick. Second, it is argued, they would help the country to apply the subsidiarity principle more effectively,

249 W. Weitzel et al. (2006). "Rechtslage und Verfahrensgang bei Auslandsadoptionen." In H. Paulitz et al. (eds) "Adoption: Positionen, Impulse, Perspektiven." C. H. Beck, München, 271-326, p. 302.

250 C. Grünewald and T. Nunez (2017). "Zentralbehörden nach dem HAÜ und deren Aufgaben." In R. Behrentin (ed), "Handbuch Adoptionsrecht." C.H. Beck, München, 76-87, p. 84.

251 See Chapter VI, section 7.4.1.

since they would also be used to support programmes for the prevention of child abandonment.[252] Yet, these contributions often have the exact opposite effect: they are stimulating the state to provide children for intercountry adoption in order to keep their child protection systems up and running.[253]

The dependency of representatives, partner organizations, child care institutions or even entire child protection systems on intercountry adoptions is a structural problem in the adoption system, and it one that is difficult to resolve. As long as individuals and organizations earn their living with adoptions, child care institutions heavily rely on the income deriving from intercountry adoptions and entire child protection systems are financed by foreign adoption agencies, there will inevitably be unethical and illegal practices. This is one of the reasons why some critics promote abolishing international adoption as a child care measure altogether. Others believe that a tight control and monitoring system will help to prevent abusive adoption practices.[254]

German law obliges the Central Adoption Offices to supervise the German adoption agencies and provides them with a number of supervisory competencies (see section 8.1). These competencies do not extend to the German agencies' co-workers and partner organizations that are licensed or accredited in the sending countries. It is mainly the foreign competent authorities that are responsible for monitoring and controlling the organizations in their state. But also the adoption agencies in the receiving countries have a responsibility to closely supervise their foreign representatives and cooperation partners. German law does not provide general guidelines and standards for the supervision of the cooperation partners by the German adoption agencies. The latter have developed different methods of control that they usually combine. For one, they strongly rely on the information provided by the adoption applicants. As the staff member of *German adoption agency D* was asked how the agency would supervise its representatives in the sending countries, she explained:

252 The Permanent Bureau of the Hague Conference on Private International Law (2008). "The Implementation and Operation of the 1993 Hague Intercountry Adoption Convention: Guide to Good Practice No. 1." The Hague, para. 228.

253 See, for instance, R. Post (2007). "Romania–for Export Only: The Untold Story of the Romanian 'Orphans'." Netherlands: EuroComment Diffusion; and R. Post (2008). "De perverse effecten van het Haags Adoptieverdrag." Justitiële Verkenningen, 7, 25-37, who describes how the Romanian 'point system' established in 1997, required foreign adoption agencies to support the local child protection system with money or other contributions in return for points on the basis of which adoptable children would be allocated. This had the effect of dramatically increasing the number of children placed for intercountry adoption; see also Hague Conference on Private International Law (2012). Accreditation and Adoption Accredited Bodies: General Principles and Guide to Good Practice, Guide No 2 under the Hague Convention of 29 May 1993 on Protection of Children and Co-operation in Respect of Intercountry Adoption, pp. 90-97.

254 See Chapter III, section 2.1.

> Well, I have to say that this is almost impossible. When we are in Germany, it is difficult to monitor the actions of your staff members in the sending countries. We ask our couples to draw up travel reports. They ought to describe in great detail what they did where and with whom and attach pictures...also who they remunerated for what and so on. We then take a look at that and examine if everything went well or if they had to make any payments that haven't been agreed upon in advance or if there was anything else that went wrong.[255]

Basically, there is nothing wrong with sensitizing adoption applicants to be careful in the sending country and asking them to report any irregularities that they may have become aware of during the adoption process. Indeed, many adoption scandals were uncovered with the help of some very dedicated adoptive parents.[256] Yet, it would go too far to consider them as an adoption agency's extended arm or as reliable controlling agents in the sending country. First, their main motivation is to become parents and their wish to 'bring home their child'[257] might be so intense that they easily accept shady practices. Towards the adoption agency, they might conceal that they donated money or goods to the child care institution they adopted from or that they paid some extra fees to accelerate services or authorizations by official authorities. Second, even the most trustworthy and careful adoption applicants are arguably not in the position to discover and prevent illegal adoption practices. They often do not speak the local language, have little insight into the adoption procedure and lack the necessary know-how to uncover the pitfalls and weaknesses of a foreign adoption system. Usually, they rely on the facilitators in the sending state whom they believe to know best how things work in their country.

It is also common for the staff members of German adoption placement offices to travel regularly to the sending countries in order to inspect the local conditions and the working methods of their representatives and partner organizations. But since financial resources are scarce, many adoption agencies do not do that more than once or twice a year. Usually these visits are announced, so the co-workers and partner organizations have enough time to 'prepare' for such inspections. When the head of *German adoption agency A* was asked how his agency controls the representatives and cooperation partners in the sending countries, he stated:

255 Interview with a staff member of German adoption agency D, Germany, 02.09.2015.

256 See, for instance, http://www.adoptionsopfer.de/www/ (last accessed on 03.08.2018), a website that was set up by adoptive parents. The couples had all adopted children from India with the involvement of the German agency *pro infante. Aktion: Kind in Not.* A few months after the children were brought to Germany, the adoption parents discovered that they were actually stolen from their birth parents.

257 See Chapter VII, section 5.3.

> We travel to the sending countries and accompany them on the ways they usually go. I was in Sri Lanka and accompanied our representative to the child care institutions, the official authorities, introduced myself, talked to them and simply tried to read between the lines and find out if everything was alright…ultimately, you cannot have 100% control. When I come to a child care institution with my representative and hear that there is a child that was relinquished by his/her mother who had signed a form saying that she cannot care for her child and that she wants to give it up for an adoption…ultimately, if it really was the mother or an aunt…there are cases where the father didn't want the child and gave it up while the mother was still recovering from birth…Unfortunately, these cases happen and we try to do everything right. However, I cannot rule out situations that are not in order. Unfortunately, that is the way it is.[258]

Trust plays an important role in the cooperation between the German adoption agencies and the sending countries. Since the geographical distance renders it difficult for the agencies to closely monitor their foreign representatives and partner organizations, confidence in their working methods is key in the transnational collaboration. A staff member of *German adoption agency C* explained:

> A lot is based on trust. We already had inquiries for co-operations, for example, from China…from different countries, even from Bulgaria and so. But if you have the feeling that there is no basis for a collaboration…then you would not start a co-operation. […] We have had co-operation agreements with child care institutions where you need to have trust. We have, for example, co-operated with the orphanage *Kidane Mehret*[259] in Addis Ababa that was led by nuns. We indeed trusted that they were doing a good job.[260]

Trust and confidence in an agency's cooperation partner becomes problematic if it leads the agency to blind out 'red flags', suggesting irregularities in the adoption system. The following section, which zooms in on the child trafficking incidences that emerged in Ethiopia, explains why an adoption agency would be motivated to ignore or downplay the signs of systemic abuse. It will be argued that trust in the foreign cooperation partner creates an important justification for an agency to continue placing children notwithstanding the existence of abusive practices, namely: denial of harm.

258 Interview with the director of German adoption agency A, Germany, 09.06.2015.

259 The orphanage's website is available at http://www.fcj-kmch.org/ (last accessed on 03.08.2018).

260 Interview with a staff member of German adoption agency C, Germany, 10.09.2015.

7 The Ethiopian Child Trafficking Incidents

7.1 Systemic Abuses in the Ethiopian Adoption System

Ethiopia emerged as a significant supply country for a short period of time. It displayed the 'cycle of abuse' that has already been observed in previous 'temporary sending states'.[261] Its development as a sending state can be framed in three phases. In the first phase, only a relatively small number of intercountry adoptions took place in Ethiopia, and they were "welcomed humanitarian venture for the desperately needy few".[262] By 2003, only three licensed adoption agencies, two of them American, were operating in Ethiopia.[263] They sought to place only those children that could not be cared for by their extended family networks – most often AIDS orphans. Intercountry adoption was not considered as the best possible child care option but as a measure of last resort. The government Ministry of Women and Children Affairs (MOWCA) took guardianship of parentless children, assessed whether they were actually orphans, identified the few that were in need of foreign families and approved the adoption. The procedure of identifying orphans and approving adoptions was rather rigorous.[264]

By 2006, however, Ethiopia quickly emerged as a significant supplier in the adoption industry. The number of children sent abroad rose dramatically from 620 in 2000, to 1,527 in 2004, to 4,553 in 2009.[265] Also, the number of licensed adoption agencies increased to more than 70 in 2008.[266] Contributing to that explosive growth was the fact that traditionally significant supply countries limited or entirely banned intercountry adoptions. China and Russia strongly reduced the number of children sent abroad, and Guatemala was about to end adoptions by foreigners after reports of serious abuses.[267] The demand therefore shifted towards African countries, most of which had not ratified the Hague Convention and were thus believed to place fewer barriers between adopters and children.[268] Ethiopia became a

261 Chapter II, section 2.6.

262 E. J. Graff (2014). "They Steal Babies, Don't They?" Pacific Standard, 24.11.2014, available at https://psmag.com/news/they-steal-babies-dont-they-international-adoption-schuster-institute-95027.

263 *Ibid.*

264 *Ibid.*

265 P. Selman (2015). "AFRICA: The 'new frontier' in international adoption." Paper Presented at 2015 SPA Conference, Belfast, available at http://www.adoptionhoksbergen.com/index.php/nl/2-algemeen/87-africa-the-new-frontier-in-international-adoption.

266 E. J. Graff (2014). "They Steal Babies, Don't They?" Pacific Standard, 24.11.2014, available at https://psmag.com/news/they-steal-babies-dont-they-international-adoption-schuster-institute-95027.

267 See Chapter II, section 2.3.1.

268 K. S. Rotabi (2010). "From Guatemala to Ethiopia: Shifts in Intercountry Adoption Leaves Ethiopia Vulnerable for Child Sales and Other Unethical Practices." The Social Work and Society Online News Magazine, available at https://www.uni-vechta.de/fileadmin/user_upload/Soziale_Arbeit/Dokumenten/Kutscher/Socmag_Archiv/June2010/June2010-Rotabi__Kara_Smith-_From_Guatemala_to_Ethiopia__Shifts_in_intercountry_adoption_leaves_ethopia_vunerable_for_child_sales_and_other_unethical_practies.pdf.

particularly attractive source country for adopters, and adoption agencies that sent far more children abroad than all other African states combined.[269] At some point, more people had signed up for adoption than the Ethiopian system could effectively process, and demand began to outstrip supply which resulted in abusive practices. By 2006, the country thus reached the second phase: the 'gold rush'.[270] Graff explains: "there were too many agencies, too many children coming and going, too many people opportunistically looking in the countryside for 'adoptable' children".[271] The large sums of money that Western adopters and agencies brought to Ethiopia turned intercountry adoption into a lucrative business for the locals. In order to keep the supply of children, orphanages began to send out 'child finders' that would solicit children from their poor families in the countryside, sometimes by making false promises to induce abandonment. Media investigations disclosed numerous cases of families who said they were talked into giving up their children by unscrupulous agents who would then sell their children for adoption.[272]

The Dutch adoption agency *Wereldkinderen* was one of the foreign agencies placing children from Ethiopia. Its director, Hut, became suspicious after she heard reports about women who would show up at the entrance of one of the agency's orphanages to search

269 P. Selman (2015). "AFRICA: The 'new frontier' in international adoption." Paper Presented at 2015 SPA Conference, Belfast, available at http://www.adoptionhoksbergen.com/index.php/nl/2-algemeen/87-africa-the-new-frontier-in-international-adoption.

270 E. J. Graff (2014). "They Steal Babies, Don't They?" Pacific Standard, 24.11.2014, available at https://psmag.com/news/they-steal-babies-dont-they-international-adoption-schuster-institute-95027.

271 *Ibid.*

272 In 2006, an illegal adoption was uncovered that involved *Family for you*, the largest private adoption agency in Austria, which had processed some 70 adoptions from Ethiopia. The adoption agency placed a little girl from Addis Ababa whose documents claimed that she was a 4 year-old orphan, placed into a child care institution by her aunt who could not take care of her herself. The girl turned out to be 9 years-old and after she had learned some German, she told her adoptive parents that her mother was still alive. An investigation revealed that the placement office's representative in Ethiopia, a lawyer, had convinced the birth mother to give up her child for adoption in the U.S., promised that she can maintain contact with her daughter and then bribed official authorities to forge the girl's documents (F. Klenk. "Die verlorene Tochter." Zeit Online, 08.01.2008, available at http://www.zeit.de/online/2008/02/adoptionen/komplettansicht). The Austrian authorities and the adoption agency assumed that only this individual case was affected. However, in 2009, two other illegal adoptions from Ethiopia were uncovered. The *modus operandi* employed in these cases were similar to the ones involved in the 2006 scandal: the birth mothers were talked into relinquishing their children and had been promised to keep contract and to see them again, then the children's documents were falsified that declared them as orphans. (A. Rexer (2009). "Adoptionsskandal um äthiopische Kinder: Zwei äthiopische Kinder Mütter klagen an." Profil, 20.01.2009, available at http://www.profil.at/home/adoptionsskandal-kinder-zwei-kinder-muetter-231092.) In 2010, an Australian documentary exposed a child care institution in Addis Ababa as recruiting and buying children from their intact families and misleading adoptive parents about their health and background. It showed a U.S. couple that had adopted three Ethiopian sisters whose mother allegedly died and whose father had been said unable to take care of the children as he was dying of AIDS. After the adoption was finalized, the couple found out that the girls where actually much older than stated in the documents, that their father was healthy and was taking care of his daughters together with an extended family network (including godmothers, aunts, uncles and friends) to which the girls had expected to return. (ABC documentary (2010). "Fly Away Home." 15.03.2010, available at https://documentaries.io/film/fly-away-home/.)

for their children.[273] In 2009, she therefore contracted the organization *Against Child Trafficking (ACT)* to conduct a study into 25 randomly selected adoption files of children that were adopted from five Ethiopian child care institutions between 2004 and 2009.[274] In 19 of these 25 adoption cases, irregularities were detected and analysed. The report, which was finalised in October 2009, exposed a dysfunctional adoption industry in Ethiopia, where children were systematically 'harvested' from their intact families:

> The researched cases give a bleak picture of the Ethiopian adoption reality. It appears that there is a system of collecting children from villages. Orphanages send their busses. Child recruiters are paid monthly salaries. These recruiters are also active in health centres and other places where families go for help.[275]

According to *ACT's* report, no efforts were made to help families stay together; rather, intercountry adoption was offered to them as the best possible option for their children.[276] As it turned out, the relinquishing parents did not often understand the Western concept of adoption that implied a permanent end to the parent-child relationship. Many were promised to receive updates about their children and expected them to return home once they had finished school. After the children were recruited, their documents were typically forged. The study found that in a number of cases, the information in both the adoption file as well as in the Court order were incorrect. For instance, on the adoptees' paperwork, the birth parents would falsely be declared dead, or the children's birth dates or health statuses would turn out to be wrong.[277]

The numerous media investigations and *ACT's* study suggested that it was not just a few individual cases that were affected by irregularities – thus some 'bad apples' – but rather that the abuses were systemic in nature. Extreme poverty, the large sums of money that could be made from intercountry adoptions and the high number of adoption applicants overwhelming the local authorities of the poor country turned the Ethiopian adoption system into a fertile ground for abusive practices and an "ethical Russian roulette".[278] The structural weaknesses rendered adoptions from Ethiopia extremely risky for those who cared about a legal adoption placement procedure. Arguably, the families could not be

273 Interview with I. Hut, director of the Dutch adoption placement agency *Wereldkinderen* between 2003 and 2009, The Netherlands, 06.07.2017.

274 Wereldkinderen and Against Child Trafficking (2009). "Fruits of Ethiopia. Intercountry Adoption: The Rights of the Child, or the "Harvesting" of Children? A Study on Intercountry Adoption in Ethiopia." available at http://www.againstchildtrafficking.org/wp-content/uploads/Second-Interim-Report-FINAL-redacted-for-distribution+annexures.pdf.

275 *Ibid.*, p. 41.

276 *Ibid.*

277 *Ibid.*

278 K. Joyce (2013). "The Child Catchers: Rescue, Trafficking, and the New Gospel of Adoption." Public Affairs, New York, p. 154.

confident that the children they were 'bringing home' were legitimately available for intercountry adoption, and the foreign agencies could not reasonably claim that all the children they were placing were actual orphans.

This is also what the Ethiopian authorities ultimately came to realize. The problem of 'child finders' actively buying and selling children for intercountry adoption became so apparent that the Ethiopian government felt forced to pull the emergency brake. In 2011, Ethiopia finally reached the third stage: the MOWCA decided to dramatically slow down intercountry adoptions.[279] In 2017, the Ethiopian Prime Minister's Office suspended intercountry adoptions[280] and in March 2018, the parliament passed legislation entirely banning adoptions by foreigners.[281]

One of the Ethiopian child care institutions that *ACT's* study identified as problematic was the orphanage *Gelgela* in Addis Ababa.[282] *Gelgela* was cooperating with numerous foreign adoption placement agencies, including two German agencies. In 2010, media investigations found that some of the children from this orphanage that were placed into adoptive families in Canada, were actually not orphans but had living parents or an extended family network in Ethiopia who had previously taken care of them.[283] In the same year, a German newspaper report drew attention to the irregularities involved in an adoption from *Gelgela*.[284] It covered the case of an Ethiopian boy who had been placed to Germany with the involvement *German adoption agency F*, whose father claimed that he had been persuaded by a 'child finder' to give up his son for adoption.[285] According to the child's documents, his mother had already died, but later it turned out that she was alive and had actually never agreed to relinquish her parental rights.[286]

Evidence of abusive practices and flawed documentation in adoption files from *Gelgela* was so overwhelming that the United States embassy in Addis Ababa felt compelled to take extra precautionary measures. In March 2010, it issued a statement announcing that:

279 E. J. Graff (2014). "They Steal Babies, Don't They?" Pacific Standard, 24.11.2014, available at https://psmag.com/news/they-steal-babies-dont-they-international-adoption-schuster-institute-95027.

280 See https://travel.state.gov/content/adoptionsabroad/en/country-information/alerts-and-notices/AdoptionAlertSuspensionofAdoptionsfromEthiopia.html (last accessed on 03.08.2018).

281 See https://travel.state.gov/content/travel/en/News/Intercountry-Adoption-News/ethiopia-adoption-notice--ethiopia-passes-legislation-banning-in.html (last accessed on 03.08.2018).

282 Wereldkinderen and Against Child Trafficking (2009). "Fruits of Ethiopia. Intercountry Adoption: The Rights of the Child, or the "Harvesting" of Children? A Study on Intercountry Adoption in Ethiopia." available at http://www.againstchildtrafficking.org/wp-content/uploads/Second-Interim-Report-FINAL-redacted-for-distribution+annexures.pdf, pp. 45-46.

283 A summary of the CBC documentary is available at http://www.cbc.ca/news/canada/canadian-parents-raise-concerns-1.819903 (last accessed on 03.08.2018).

284 G. Taubert and B. Reuter (2010). "Der verlorene Sohn." TAZ, 15.05.2010, available at http://www.taz.de/!435381/.

285 *Ibid.*

286 *Ibid.*

> Recently, the U.S. Embassy has implemented several changes to the adoption visa process, including conducting a significant additional review of each case and field investigations. In light of our findings, and recent serious allegations and news reports involving Ethiopian adoptions, we will require additional time to process each case from any agency in which the child was processed through *Gelgela* orphanage. Effective immediately, the Embassy will require 8 weeks' processing time for each adoption visa case in which the child was processed through *Gelgela* orphanage. This means that families will not receive an immigrant visa appointment until 8 weeks after the complete case file is submitted to the Embassy. We will not accept incomplete case files in these cases under any circumstances.[287]

Several European adoption placement agencies responded to the scandals revolving around adoptions from Ethiopia by stopping placements from this sending country altogether. For instance in 2009, *Wereldkinderen* - back then the largest adoption ageny in the Netherlands - announced that it would resume adoptions from Ethiopia due to inconsistencies and unreliable information provided about Ethiopian children.[288] In addition, *German adoption agency F*, that had placed the Ethiopian boy who was suspected of having been secured by a child finder, responded to the serious allegations against its partner organization and terminated its cooperation with the *Gelega* orphanage.[289]

However, the other German adoption placement office which was co-operating with *Gelgela* at that time, *adoption agency C*, renewed its collaboration agreement in 2010 for another year.[290] It started placing children for adoption from this orphanage in May 2009, thus at a time when Ethiopia was already in midst of its "gold rush" phase, and after the first reports about abuses and illegal adoption practices had already emerged. Even though it had become apparent that too many foreign adoption agencies were operating in Ethiopia and that the Western run on Ethiopian children was too great to be properly managed by the local authorities, the German agency began its cooperation with *Gelgela*. And despite credible allegations of abuse that were highlighted in *ACT's* report, the media, and the United States embassy in Addis Ababa, the German adoption agency only stopped placing children from *Gelgela* after the orphanage was shut down by the Ethiopian authorities.[291]

287 See http://pear-now.blogspot.nl/2010/03/ethiopia-gelgela-orphange.html (last accessed on 03.08.2018).

288 See https://web.archive.org/web/20090926140159/ http://www.ethiopianreview.com/news/6790 (last accessed on 03.08.2018).

289 G. Taubert and B. Reuter (2010). "Der verlorene Sohn." TAZ, 15.05.2010, available at http://www.taz.de/!435381/.

290 Statement from the heads of the adoption agency, August 2010 (on file with author).

291 Interview with a staff member of German adoption agency C, Germany, 10.09.2015.

7.2 *The German Agency's Ideological and Financial Motivation to Place Children from Ethiopia*

Why would a German adoption placement agency that routinely claims that its mission is to find parents for children and not children for parents (see section 5.2) start a new cooperation in Ethiopia at a time when it had already become apparent that the demand for children was higher than the number of orphans available for international adoption? Why would an agency that repeatedly emphasized that it aims to protect the rights of children and to serve their best interests continue placing children from Ethiopia, even when abuses and irregularities have become apparent? Why would an adoption agency that openly endorses the standards and principles of the Hague Convention and the UNCRC move children from a country that is quite obviously unable to adhere to them? And why would it not end the cooperation with the child care institution after it was exposed to be involved in abusive adoption practices?

One might argue that the agency personnel were just too naïve to acknowledge the risk involved in adoptions from Ethiopia and to be cognizant of the red flags suggesting structural deficiencies in the Ethiopian adoption system. Yet, this argument is difficult to maintain. German adoption agency personnel hold high professional qualifications and have a plethora of experience working in the field of intercountry adoption (see section 5.1). It can thus be assumed that the personnel were well aware of the Ethiopian adoption system's weaknesses that rendered adoptions perilous. This is especially true considering that *German adoption agency C* placed children from Ethiopia as early as 1991. The personnel thus knew the country and its adoption system very well and must have observed how it transformed into a dangerous 'adoption hot spot' with the authorities being overwhelmed by the great Western run on Ethiopian children and the locals being financially motivated to generate 'adoptees'. Considering the agency personnel's high professional competences and their many years of experience with placing children from Ethiopia, there is much to suggest that they did recognize the risk that the adoptions would be affected by irregularities, but they nevertheless accepted it.

A primary motivational driver behind the agency's decision to carry out adoption placements from Ethiopia might have been the appeal to higher loyalties. Adoption agencies usually portray themselves (and are generally perceived) as humanitarian organizations with the generous motive of saving parentless children from the intermediate circumstances in their native countries and providing them with loving families in another country. The names the agencies hold very often illustrate their philanthropic and altruistic identity. Additionally, the information provided on their websites makes it clear that the agencies' primary mission is to serve the best interests of orphaned children by providing them with nurturing homes. Photographs of an adult's white hand clasping a tiny black hand,[292] and 'before' and 'after pictures' of adoptees with sad faces in an institution and then among their new parents and siblings, riding a bike or playing on the beach[293] certainly contribute to the idea that the agencies are strongly committed to the goal of rescuing neglected and forgotten children through adoption. In order to maintain their identity, which is inextricably tied to this ideological mission of saving children, agencies are motivated to keep children moving through the adoption system. And in order to keep children moving, an adoption agency might be motivated to cut ethical corners by continuing to carry out adoption placements from a country in which abuses and irregularities are systemic or by sustaining their cooperation with a shady child care institution. Paradoxically, therefore, an agency might act unethically in order to pursue a higher ethical cause: it may render immoral and harmful decisions for the sake of saving children.

An adoption agency might not necessarily fully appreciate the unethical nature of its decisions. It might genuinely believe that continuing to move children from a country in which child trafficking incidents were uncovered is the right thing to do, as stopping adoptions only because a few single cases were affected by irregularities would harm even more needy children. This conviction is often undergirded by the false assumption of a 'global orphan crisis',[294] as well as a Western understanding of the 'child's best interests' that is based on a liberal and individualistic childhood and which considers the child's community as inferior or even harmful.[295] The idea that intercountry adoption is only needed for a small number of children or that it could even cause harm to them might be counter-intuitive for an adoption agency.

Arguably, *German adoption agency C* did not only have an ideological but also a financial motivation for moving children from Ethiopia to Germany.[296] As was already explained in section 5.2, German adoption placement offices are not provided with financial support by the government. Thus, they have to finance themselves exclusively with the administration fees that are paid by their adoption applicants. Since these fees are the agencies' only revenue, they must place a particular number of children per year to keep their organization up and running. For several years, German agencies have experienced difficulties in achieving this goal as the number of children available for intercountry adoption has been on a steady decrease.[297] The discrepancy between an adoption agency's financial imperative to achieve a particular number of mandates, on the one hand, and the number of (for adopters attractive) children that are legitimately

292 See, for example, http://www.evangelische-adoption.de/node/69 (last accessed on 03.08.2018).

293 See, for example, http://www.zukunftfuerkinder.de/elternberichte (last accessed on 03.08.2018).

294 See Chapter III, section 5.3.

295 See Chapter III, section 6.4.

296 See also D. M. Smolin (2004). "The Two Faces of Intercountry Adoption: The Significance of the Indian Adoption Scandals." Seton Hall Law Review, 35, 403-493, pp. 475-480.

297 See Chapter II, section 2.3.1.

available for intercountry adoption, on the other hand, creates strain. Adoption agencies may respond to this strain by raising the administration fees that are to be paid by the adopters, or by reducing the number of employees (to an extent that is legally permissible) or by bending the ethical rules.[298] They might accept child proposals that include incomplete or inconsistent information about the child or turn a blind eye to or even knowingly accept signs of irregular practices in the sending countries or abusive practices of their cooperation partners in the sending countries.

The agencies' 'hear no evil see no evil' attitude is generally possible because German adoption placement agencies are only accountable for the activities of their representatives in the sending countries, but not for those of the foreign accredited partner organizations or the state authorities.[299] Thus, the agencies cannot be held responsible if it transpires that the cooperation partners have been obtaining children illegally. This lack of agency responsibility is an incentive for adoption agencies to keep children moving from a particular country notwithstanding signs of abuses in the foreign adoption system.[300]

7.3 Hear No Evil, See No Evil - Techniques of Rationalization

The *German adoption agency C*'s decision to continue moving children from Ethiopia to Germany stands in stark contrast to the high ethical standards and principles of due diligence to which the German adoption agencies usually ascribe. After the child trafficking incidents were uncovered vis-à-vis the *Gelgela* child care institution, the heads of the German agency sent out a statement to its members and adoption applicants in 2010 in which they commented on the media reports and explained their decision to retain its cooperation partner.[301] Also, in an interview conducted in 2016, a social worker, who had been working for the agency for more than 20 years, elucidated upon the agency's decision to continue placing children from this orphanage. In both the written statement and the interview, the adoption agency's staff employed a number of rationalization techniques that served to repel criticism, protect the agency from blame and to maintain an image as a child welfare organization abiding by ethical norms and obligations.

'Techniques of rationalization' is a concept that is borrowed from studies on social disorganization and juvenile delinquency, more specifically from the work of Sykes and

298 See R. K. Merton (1938). "Social Structure and Anomie." American Sociological Review, 3, 672-682; N. Passas (1990). "Anomie and Corporate Deviance." Contemporary Crises, 14, 157-178.

299 C. Grünewald and T. Nunez (2017). "Zentralbehörden nach dem HAÜ und deren Aufgaben." In R. Behrentin (ed), "Handbuch Adoptionsrecht." C.H. Beck, München, 76-87, p. 83.

300 See also D. M. Smolin (2006). "Child Laundering: How the Intercountry Adoption System Legitimizes and Incentivizes the Practices of Buying, Trafficking, Kidnapping, and Stealing Children." The Wayne Law Review, 52, 1, 113-200, pp. 192-195.

301 Statement from the heads of German adoption agency C, August 2010 (on file with author).

Matza.[302] They are linguistic devices that allow an individual to maintain a positive and conventional self-image, despite his or her illegal, deviant or unethical behaviour. Rationalization techniques serve individuals to view their decisions as normal or at least justifiable and "to protect the individual from self-blame and the blame of others after the act".[303] Typically, the narratives that individuals advance to make sense of and justify their questionable decisions have already served them as techniques of neutralization *before* the actions occur. Neutralization techniques provide the actors with temporary relief from moral constraint and allow them to engage in illegal or deviant activities without giving up their positive and conventional self-image.[304] Sykes and Matza identified five techniques of neutralization: denial of responsibility, denial of harm, denial of victims, appeal to higher loyalties and condemnation of condemners.[305]

A technique of rationalization that featured strongly in both the interview and the written statement is the *denial of harm*.[306] The social worker denied the risk that the adoption placements they carried out from the *Gelgela* orphanage might be affected by abuses and irregularities as well:

> Well, it did not affect our cases. Our cases were not affected. We have always checked our cases…as did our representatives…their existence relies on that! I think we were well-positioned. It wasn't our cases that were affected in the *Gelgela* orphanage.[307]

The social worker minimized the extent and seriousness of the abuses in the Ethiopian adoption system and of the irregularities that were present in the adoptions from the *Gelgela* orphanage. She insisted that the abusive practices and flawed documentation in the adoption files only affected those individual cases that were exposed, rather than acknowledging that they suggested structural weaknesses in the system:

> *Interviewer*: So you are saying that your cases were not affected, the children that you placed for adoption, and that is why you decided to renew the contract with this orphanage?
>
> *Adoption agency:* Yes, right. You have to look at each individual case. I think that there was a trip to the child care institution where it was checked if it [the

302 G.M. Sykes and D Matza (1957). "Techniques of Neutralization: A Theory of Delinquency." American Sociological Review, 22, 664-670.
303 *Ibid.*, p. 666.
304 *Ibid.*
305 *Ibid.*
306 *Ibid.*
307 Interview with a staff member of German adoption agency C, Germany, 10.09.2015.

> co-operation] was still acceptable. And if the decision was 'yes' then this was legally okay. One cannot put everybody under general suspicion, I find that very difficult. Also, it is easy for someone to judge if they are not at all familiar with the subject matter. And I find the media coverage difficult because it creates a general suspicion. Also, the German authorities put Ethiopia under a general suspicion – always! And I find that totally unfair because not all cases were affected. I think you need to differentiate a bit and take a very close look. And if [*German adoption agency F*] – or who? – decided to do it differently, fair enough! But we made our own decisions and if our boss made a trip [to Ethiopia] and decided that it was acceptable for us because it didn't affect our cases…we cannot simply put all of them under general suspicion.
>
> *Interviewer*: But if a case is being uncovered involving abusive practices, shouldn't you assume that other cases could have been affected as well?
>
> *Adoption agency*: Right, but we checked these other cases.
>
> *Interviewer*: How can you check them?
>
> *Adoption agency*: Can you check everything from bottom to the top or do you rather work? …that is the question! We decided to work because we consider the best interests of the child as our top priority. And for sure we are not an organization that makes money with that.[308]

The social worker claimed that it would be unreasonable to assume that all adoptions from Ethiopia were affected by illegal practices and stressed that each case had to be examined individually. However, at the same time, she conceded that the agency's primary mission – to serve the best interests of the children – would be hampered if the personnel were too cautious and spent too much time on diligently checking the adoption files. Even though she admitted that checking 'everything from the bottom to the top' would not be possible, she maintained that the agency's adoption cases were not affected by abuse and irregularities. The agency's policy might best be described as embracing the principle of 'innocent until proven guilty' in that the personnel would presume that the Ethiopian children they placed were in the intercountry adoption system legally, unless it could be proven otherwise by somebody outside the agency. Despite the overwhelming evidence of abusive and irregular practices in the Ethiopian adoption system and by its own cooperation partner, the agency was willing to place children from the *Gelgela* child care institution for so long

308 Interview with a staff member of German adoption agency C, Germany, 10.09.2015.

as the Ethiopian and German authorities were prepared to approve the adoptions and for so long as irregularities were not uncovered in their own cases.

In addition, the agency's written statement that was sent out to the agency members centred on the denial of harm. It is well-known that poor sending countries often do not have the sufficient resources that are required to establish an effective monitoring and control system, and that widespread corruption renders regulatory institutions ineffective to safeguard the adoption system against abuses.[309] Yet, the agency heads insisted that the very fact that the *Gelgela* orphanage had been accredited and was monitored by official authorities would *ipso eo* exclude their engaging into illegal and abusive practices. Their confidence in the integrity of the authorities and institutions in Ethiopia – arguably created by the distribution of responsibility which constitutes a basic feature in the intercountry adoption system – lent them a justification for continuing to move children from the *Gelgela* orphanage:

> The *Gelgela* institution meets the formal requirements that Ethiopian institutions which want to co-operate with international adoption placement offices have to comply with, according to the directives from May 2009: it was accredited as a national aid organization by the Ethiopian authorities and maintains co-operation agreements with the region/the zones from which children are taken into the institution. As accredited national aid organizations, these institutions are accountable to and are being controlled by the Ethiopian authorities. Engaging so-called 'child finders' is not permitted and would cause their losing their license.[310]

The *appeal to higher loyalties* was not only a motivational driver behind the agency's decision to continue placing children from Ethiopia, but it also served as a rationalization technique in itself. In the interview, the social worker maintained that resuming international adoption placements from *Gelgela* would have been an unreasonable response to the reports about its abusive practices as this would not be in the best interests of the children: "I would not see any reason…if it does not affect us…to deprive the children of the opportunity to being adopted internationally".[311] Also, by pointing to the fact that all the children the agency had placed are doing great now in their new families and that they were better off than they would be in their native countries, the social worker sought to drown out any critical considerations about the Ethiopian adoption system:

309 See Chapter II, section 2.4.1.

310 Statement from the heads of German adoption agency C, August 2010 (on file with author).

311 Interview with a staff member of German adoption agency C, Germany, 10.09.2015.

> Ethiopia was always a difficult country to work in as an adoption agency. For all those children that we have placed – since 1991 we placed more than 500 children, 180 of which were from Ethiopia – intercountry adoption was the right solution. [...] Because...I supervise the adoptive families and I know the stories of the children. There was, for instance, a case of siblings being picked up from the streets by the police who lived in the gully at the age of 4 and 6 years, unaccompanied![312]

Signs of systemic abuses in the Ethiopian adoption system and credible allegations of illegal practices by the *Gelgela* orphanage were minimalized for the sake of a higher value of keeping children moving through the adoption system:

> The *Gelgela* institution...sure, it may be that it did not work properly...it is now closed anyway. But if we came to the conclusion that it was okay to continue co-operating because our cases were not affected...I think, for us, it was about the children and not about the director that might have profited – I don't know if that was really the case if there was anybody who made money, I really cannot tell you that...also because we didn't have so much money. We didn't have money to bribe! There is a lot of corruption in this field, but we have never bribed, we did not have money for that.[313]

This last statement also involves another technique of rationalization: *the denial of responsibility*.[314] The social worker sought to protect the agency from blame by stressing that its personnel did not actively engage in illegal practices. The denial of responsibility also features strongly in the statement that was sent out by the head of the agency:

> We can assure you that [name of the adoption agency] conducted a correct adoption placement procedure. [...] Unfortunately, irregularities occurred in Ethiopia in the last couple of years. However, when assessing these irregularities, the 'driving force' is decisive. We can guarantee that we did not provide any incentive whatsoever for "misconduct". In our view, this is an essential requirement since many grievances are attributable mainly to misconduct of foreign adoption agencies which want to place as many children as possible

312 *Ibid.*
313 Interview with a staff member of German adoption agency C, Germany, 10.09.2015.
314 D. Matza and G. M. Sykes (1961). "Juvenile Delinquency and Subterranean Values." American Journal of Sociology, 26, 712-719, p. 668.

> and as quickly as possible to their waiting adoption applicants. [name of the adoption agency] can only take responsibility for its own work.[315]

From this statement, it becomes obvious that the adoption agency personnel consider themselves responsible only for their own behaviour in Germany, but not for the activities of their partner organization in the sending country. The denial of responsibility is made easy considering the agency's geographical, and concomitant ethical, distance from the illegal practices that took place abroad. This form of rationalization is supported by a German law that does not consider German agencies accountable for the acts of their cooperation partners in the sending states. In their statement, the agency heads downplay the powerful role their adoption agency plays at the demand side of the adoption market. They literally deny the fact that the agency's adoption placement activities, combined with the transfer of money, is already incentive enough for "misconduct" in the intercountry adoption system.

A final technique of rationalization that was advanced during the interview involves the *condemnation of the condemners*, where the focus of attention is shifted away from the deviant acts to the behaviour of those who disapprove of the violations of moral norms.[316] The social worker claims that the critics would lack the necessary know-how to properly assess the incidents surrounding the *Gelgela* orphanage: "it is easy for someone to judge if he is not at all familiar with the subject matter".[317] Furthermore, she denies the nature and extent of the Ethiopian adoption scandals by blaming the media for misrepresenting and exaggerating the facts of the cases:

> You have to take a look at the media coverage. [...] There was a time where this matter was stirred up immensely. Things had been researched and covered by the media that ignored actual facts. I find that very dramatic, honestly! It had brought the entire adoption field into disrepute. Well, I am committed to the work we had done in Ethiopia.[318]

The narratives that the agency personnel advanced in the interview and in the written statement to rationalize their decision to move children from Ethiopia to Germany despite numerous signs of abuses might have also employed as techniques of neutralization before the decision was taken. They provided the agency personnel with temporary relief from moral constraint and allowed them to render an unethical decision without giving up the

---

315 Statement from the heads of German adoption agency C, August 2010 (on file with author).

316 D. Matza and G. M. Sykes (1961). "Juvenile Delinquency and Subterranean Values." American Journal of Sociology, 26, 712-719, p. 668.

317 Interview with a staff member of German adoption agency C, Germany, 10.09.2015.

318 *Ibid.*

agency's image as a philanthropic and altruistic organization that was exclusively serving the best interests of children. The denial of the extent and seriousness of the irregularities in the Ethiopian adoption system and of their responsibility for them allowed them to justify placing children from Ethiopia; the appeal to higher loyalties casts their actions not only as positive but heroic. These narratives are likely to be also advanced by other Western adoption agencies that render unethical decisions based on a self-serving ideology or the financial motivation to keep their organization functioning.

8 The Role of the German Authorities in the Adoption System

8.1 *Accrediting, Authorizing and Controlling German Adoption Agencies*

Germany, a federal state, has a decentralized system of intercountry adoption regulation. As part of the implementation of the Hague Convention, the legislator did not establish one Central Authority but decided to use the already existing decentralized control structure to designate 13 Central Authorities: the Federal Central Office on federal level and 12 Central Adoption Offices on state level (see section 3.1). Whereas the Federal Central Office only has co-ordinating and representative tasks, the 12 Central Adoption Offices are responsible for accrediting and approving the private bodies that are located in their jurisdiction and for controlling their adoption placement activities.

In the course of implementing the Hague Convention, the German legislator has also tightened the regulation system. Germany has reformed the accreditation and authorization procedure for private bodies according to the treaty's standards and provisions, imposed reporting obligations on the accredited adoption agencies and provided the Central Adoption Offices with extensive supervisory powers.

Private agencies are only admitted as international adoption placement offices if (1) they have been accredited as an adoption placement office[319] and (2) were authorized to place intercountry adoptions from one or several particular sending countries.[320] The Central Authority in whose jurisdiction the private agency is located is responsible for providing the necessary accreditation and authorization.

In the accreditation procedure, the private agencies are required to provide the following information:

319 § 4(1) AdVermiG.

320 § 4(2) *leg. cit.*

- specify the agency *personnel* and provide proof of their professional qualifications as well as personal competencies by submitting their diploma, job references and curricula vitae;[321]
- disclose the agency's business plan[322] and *financial situation*,[323] proof of its non-profit objective[324] and provide evidence that they have sufficient financial resources to cover the personnel's salaries as well as other running costs during a period of six months (€100,000); and
- draw up a *concept* for counselling the adoption applicants and assessing their suitability to adopt and for carrying out the adoption placements, in order to comply with the principles of the Hague Convention;[325]

After a private body has been accredited and authorized to carry out intercountry adoption placements, the competent Central Adoption Office must monitor and control its activities. To this end, the adoption agencies have several reporting obligations which include:
- presenting the *child proposals* as well as all consents necessary for an adoption received from the official authorities or the accredited bodies in the sending country (according to Article 16 of the Hague Convention) to the Central Adoption Office for inspection;[326]
- submitting a detailed *annual report on all their placement activities*[327] which must include information on the completed, discontinued and pending adoption placement procedures, a breakdown of the average adoption costs, the nationality and age of the adopted children as well as an annual statement and the adoption placement office's budget;[328] and
- informing the Central Adoption Office about *any substantial changes*, particularly if the agency has employed a new staff member,[329] established a cooperation agreement with a new partner organization or terminated an existing one,[330] if the adoption placement procedure has changed substantially or if the adoption costs increased.[331]

The Central Adoption Offices may request information, inspect adoption files and other documents (such as cooperation agreements, employment contracts, invoices and tax

321 § 1(1)(8) and (9) AdVermiStAnKoV.
322 § 1(1)(3) *leg. cit.*
323 § 1(1)(4) *leg. cit.*
324 § 1(1)(6) *leg. cit.*
325 § 1(1)(7) *leg. cit.*
326 § 11 AdVermiG.
327 § 4(1) *leg. cit.*
328 *Leg. cit.*
329 § 3(5) AdVermiStAnKoV.
330 § 3(6) *leg. cit.*
331 § 3(9) *leg. cit.*

statements)[332] or it may enter the offices of the international adoption placement agencies at any time.[333] They typically either do this randomly or after allegations or indications of irregularities in the adoptions have emerged (e.g. adoption applicants have complained about shady activities in the adoption procedure).

The competent Central Adoption Office must withdraw an agency's accreditation if it finds that the agency does not or can no longer meet the requirements (see section 5.1).[334] An appeal against this withdrawal does not have suspensory effect.[335] The Central Adoption Office therefore has the power to shut down an agency with immediate effect. This is the most extreme sanctioning tool that the Central Adoption Office has at its disposal, which must be used proportionally and only if other measures did not suffice. It can also file criminal charges against it if it suspects staff members of the agency to be involved in criminal activities (see section 9.1.2 and 9.2)

Arguably, the monitoring and control of the German adoption agencies is considerably tight. The Central Adoption Offices have a good insight into the agencies' financial situation as well as their activities in Germany and have the power to intervene if they suspect irregular practices by withdrawing its accreditation. So far, this has happened once in the case of *ICCO* (see section 1).

8.2 *Reviewing Individual Adoptions (Control on Micro Level)*

In Germany, it is the adoption placement agencies and not the Central Authority that are responsible for approving the match between a proposed child and the adopters, according to Article 17(c) of the Hague Convention.[336] After the agency has received the child proposal from the authority in the sending country, it must examine whether the adoption is in the best interests of the child and if an adoption according to German law is possible, or – in case the adoption will be granted in the sending country – if it can be expected that a foreign adoption decision will be recognized in Germany.[337] The adoption agency is obliged to consult the competent youth welfare office,[338] and to present the child proposal together with the consent that is necessary for an adoption (Article 16 Hague Convention) to the competent Central Adoption Office for inspection.[339] This obligation also exists with regard

332 § 4(4) sentence 2 nr. 1 AdVermiG.
333 § 4(4) sentence 2 nr. 2 *leg. cit.*
334 § 4(3) *leg. cit.*
335 § 4(5) *leg. cit.*
336 § 5(3) AdÜbAG.
337 § 5(1) *leg. cit.*
338 § 2(3) AdVermiG; § 5(4) AdÜbAG.
339 § 11 AdVermiG.

to adoptions from non-Hague countries.[340] If the adopters do not reside in the state in which the adoption agency is located, the child proposal does not only have to be presented to the Central Adoption Office which is responsible for monitoring the adoption agency (thus, the Central Adoption Office in whose jurisdiction the adoption placement agency is located), but also to the Central Adoption Office in whose jurisdiction the adopters have their permanent residence.[341]

The German legislator introduced the obligation to present the child proposals to the Central Authority in the course of ratifying the Hague Convention. The objective was to increase the transparency of and the control over the child proposals. It provides the Central Adoption Offices with the opportunity to check the child proposals and their supporting documents and to voice concerns if they consider the information provided to be incomplete or inconsistent.[342]

Article 16(1) of the Hague Convention provides that the child proposal should include information about the child's identity, adoptability, background, social environment, family history, medical history, including that of the child's family and any special needs of the child. It should furthermore be accompanied by proof that the necessary consent to adoption has been obtained (e.g. a relinquishment or abandonment declaration) as well as the reasons for the child's placement.[343] A number of documents that are necessary for the adoption do not have to be included in the child report, such as the child's birth certificate or the parents' death certificate.[344] This is because in many sending countries the judicial adoption proceeding, in which these documents are produced, can only start *after* the match between the proposed child and the adopters has been approved according to Article 17(c) of the Hague Convention.[345] The German adoption agencies and the Central Adoption Offices therefore often only have a limited possibility to check whether the proposed child is legitimately available for intercountry adoption. These documents are (if at all) only presented to the German embassies in the sending countries that process a passport or visa for the adoptee (see section 3.5).

340 R. Reinhardt (2017). "§ 11 AdVermiG." In J. Reinhardt (ed) "Adoptionsvermittlungsgesetz." 4. edition, Nomos Bundesrecht, Erläuterungen, Rn. 9.

341 Interview with J. Reinhardt, international adoption law scholar and head of the Central Adoption Office Bavaria between 2001 until 2008, Germany, 16.03.2015.

342 Before the Hague Convention was implemented in 2002, the adoption agencies were not obliged to present the child proposals to the Central Adoption Offices. The latter only had the chance to check the adoption documents in the judicial conversion procedure that sometimes only took place long after the child moved to Germany. The scandal revolving around the German adoption agency *pro infante action: kind in not* was partly the result of this lax monitoring and control system.

343 Art. 16(2) Hague Convention.

344 Gezamenlijke vergunninghouders interlandelijke adoptie (2013). "Kwaliteitskader Vergunninghouders Interlandelijke Adoptie." 2. Version (on file with author), p. 25.

345 Interview with J. Kouwenhoven, head of and a policy advisor at the Dutch Central Authority, and M. Kroon, official of the Youth Department at the Dutch Ministry of Justice and Security, The Netherlands, 13.07.2017.

According to the head of the Joint Central Adoption Office in Hamburg, the information provided about the proposed children is often very limited or even inconsistent. The Joint Central Adoption Office in Hamburg is the biggest Central Adoption Office in Germany as it has jurisdiction in four German states: Hamburg, Bremen, Lower-Saxony and Schleswig-Holstein. At the moment, no German adoption agency is located in any of these states, but it is presented with all of those child proposals that were accepted by adopters residing in its jurisdiction. The Office therefore has a fair insight into the quality and content of the child proposals that German agencies receive from the sending countries. The head of the Joint Central Adoption Office explains:

> We get the child proposal and see which information about the child is provided by the sending country which is often very rudimental and deficient and partly also inconsistent which gives rise to questions: how come it is stated that the mother is unknown and later that the mother has said this or that?[346]

Also, Reinhardt, the former head of the Central Adoption Office in Bavaria, has observed that the quality of the child proposals was often very low: important documents (e.g. the medical report or proof that the necessary consent for adoption has been given) were either missing altogether or not translated. Interestingly, this did not only apply to proposals from non-Hague states, but also to those from sending countries which have ratified the Hague Convention (e.g. Peru, Burkina Faso) and would thus be obliged to comply with the high standards of Article 16.[347]

If the child proposal is incomplete or inconsistent, the adoption agency or the Central Adoption Office might require additional information from the authorities or cooperation partners in the sending country.[348] Yet, considering the clear division of responsibility between the sending and the receiving country, they are not obliged (and also not allowed) to conduct investigations in the state of origin themselves. The social worker at the Joint Central Adoption Office in Hamburg explains:

> The Hague Convention clearly obliges the countries of origin to examine the history of the child. If they [the competent authorities or the accredited bodies in the sending countries] tell us that the child was found abandoned...well, it does not fall within our competence to double-check that. That is often a

346 Interview with B. Siebert and K. Meissner, head and, respectively, social worker of the Joint Central Adoption Office for Hamburg, Bremen, Lower-Saxony, and Schleswig-Holstein, 25.03.2015.

347 E-mail from J. Reinhardt, international adoption law scholar and head of the Central Adoption Office Bavaria between 2001 until 2008, 21.02.2017.

348 § 3(1) AdÜbAG; § 5(1) AdÜbAG.

> dilemma, I think. We may only raise queries if there are irregularities. In case of doubt, we say that this is too dubious for us.[349]

The Central Adoption Office that is responsible for monitoring the adoption agency might advise the agency to reject a child proposal, if the information provided is insufficient and if the authorities in the sending countries do not provide the requested information or cannot dispel any irregularities. However, ultimately it is the adoption agency's responsibility to accept or reject a child proposal. The competent Central Adoption Office does not have the power to issue directions to the agency in that respect.[350] Yet, if the agency has repeatedly overridden concerns voiced by either the youth welfare office or the Central Adoption Office, the latter might consider sanctions according to § 4(4) AdVermiG, for instance, by withdrawing the agency's authorization to place adoptions from this particular country or – in extreme cases – even withdrawing the agency's accreditation.[351] These supervisory measures must be used proportionally. In practice the competent Central Adoption Office would consider such measures only if no agreement can be found during the supervisory meetings with the adoption agency.[352]

Also, the German embassies in the visa-required sending countries have to be involved in individual adoption procedures, as they have the power to issue a visa or German passport on the basis of the adoption documents presented to them.[353] Yet, they cannot be considered as gatekeepers of the German adoption system that would effectively prevent children that have been obtained illegally from entering into Germany.[354]

Embassies may become askance if they notice a sudden increase in the number of 'abandoned' babies showing up in a particular child care institution or region. However, there is little they can do to actually prove irregular or abusive practices in another sovereign state as they do not generally conduct any investigations into the children's background

349 Interview with B. Siebert and K. Meissner, head and, respectively, social worker of the Joint Central Adoption Office for Hamburg, Bremen, Lower-Saxony, and Schleswig-Holstein, 25.03.2015.

350 H. Bienentreu (2017). "Einzelne Fragestellungen der internationalen Adoptionsvermittlung." In R. Behrentin (ed) "Handbuch für Adoptionen." C.H. Beck, München, 51-70, Rn. 298.

351 Reinhardt (2012). § 5 AdÜbAG.

352 E-mail from Weitzel, head of the German Federal Central Office for International Adoption at the German Federal Office of Justice between 2002 and 2017, 05.04.2017.

353 Generally, German law does not lay down the documents which must be presented to the embassies in the sending countries in the visa or passport procedure. Rather, the embassies determine which documents must be handed in by the adopters. In any case, the adopters have to submit the child's birth certificate and the foreign adoption decision, if the adoption was granted in the sending country. Also, if a full adoption was granted in a Hague country, a certificate of conformity (Article 23) has to be filed with the embassy. In addition, the embassy might require them to present documents that were necessary for an adoption and that were presented during the court procedure (e.g. relinquishment declaration or the birth parents' death certificate).

354 E-mail from Weitzel, head of the German Federal Central Office for International Adoption at the German Federal Office of Justice between 2002 and 2017, 05.04.2017.

to see whether they are real orphans.[355] The embassies only review the submitted documents and they would decline to process a passport or visa if they are not provided with complete or consistent information about the children's origin or background. However, in those cases where the children were laundered 'properly', meaning where all the adoptees' documents appear to be in order, the embassy cannot prevent them from entering Germany, even if it suspects systemic abuses in the host country.

The head of the Joint Central Adoption Office in Hamburg claims that she would often come across incomplete or inconsistent documents of adoptees that had already entered Germany.[356] Basically, the Central Adoption Offices are not only to be involved in the adoption placement procedures but also in the judicial adoption conversion procedures, if the adoptive parents reside in their jurisdiction. If a foreign adoption judgment does not terminate a pre-existing legal parent-child relationship ('simple adoption'), the adoptive parents may request the German court to convert it into a 'full adoption' within the meaning of German adoption law. In such an adoption conversion procedure, the Central Adoption Office has to take a look at the adoption documents and then submits a written statement on the envisaged conversion of the adoption.[357] The head of the Joint Central Adoption Office in Hamburg complains that important information would often be missing from the adoption files:

> Many questions arise from the adoption files that we get…also from the child proposals, where we think, well, interesting that they haven't been clarified before. I mean, why is it only us who raise these questions at the very end, when it is about converting the adoption, why haven't they been raised before?[358]

In its statements, the Central Adoption Office in Hamburg would stress that the information provided in the adoption documents was insufficient. Yet, ultimately it is up to the court to investigate this matter further, for instance, by ordering that the birth parents be contacted again to verify their consent to adoption. According to the head of the Joint Central Adoption Office in Hamburg, this would rarely happen.[359] The German courts would, in many cases, accept the sloppy documentation in the case file and simply convert it into a full adoption. That way, they take the final step in rubberstamping an incomplete adoption case file and maybe even in laundering a child that was in the intercountry adoption system illegally.

355 E-mail from A. Hartung, official at the German Federal Foreign Office, 19.10.2017.

356 *Ibid.*

357 § 5(3) AdWirkG.

358 Interview with B. Siebert and K. Meissner, head and, respectively, social worker of the Joint Central Adoption Office for Hamburg, Bremen, Lower-Saxony, and Schleswig-Holstein, 25.03.2015.

359 *Ibid.*

Why is the German adoption system so permeable, allowing children to enter whose documents do not include all the necessary information? Why would the German adoption agencies, the competent Central Adoption Offices, the German embassy in the sending country and finally the German family court wave through incomplete or even inconsistent adoption files?

The former head of the Central Adoption Office in Munich explains that the German adoption agencies often do not have much time to approve the match between a proposed child and the adopters.[360] He has observed that the foreign partner or authority would often put a lot of pressure on the German agencies to accept the child proposals as fast as possible. This means that the latter, in many cases, do not have time to have important documents translated or legalized.[361] As was already explained in the previous sections, the German agencies are financially and ideologically motivated to keep children moving to Germany. They might thus accept incomplete or inconsistent documents rather than jeopardizing the proposed child placement.

The Central Adoption Offices that are responsible for monitoring the agencies might accept incomplete adoption files because they trust the authorities in the sending countries. As will be explained in the following section, some Central Adoption Offices have particular confidence in the integrity of systems in sending countries that have ratified the Hague Convention.

The German embassy might have failed to notice the inconsistencies in the documents or it may have been reluctant to question the legality of the adoption at the very end, after the German family has legally adopted a child under a foreign law. In most cases, the adoption is granted in the child's country of origin. Refusing to recognize the foreign adoption decision would not only leave the German adopters disgruntled but, more importantly, the child in 'legal limbo'. Under the applicable foreign law, the German couple has already become the child's legal parents, thus refusing to process a passport and thereby preventing the child from entering Germany would mean that the child would need to stay in his or her country of origin, separated from his new family, which cannot be in the child's best interests. The German court that is asked to convert a simple adoption into full adoption might face the same dilemma. Recognizing or converting a foreign adoption decision might be considered to be the lesser evil.

360 E-mail from J. Reinhardt, international adoption law scholar and head of the Central Adoption Office Bavaria between 2001 until 2008, 21.02.2017.

361 *Ibid.*

8.3 *Authorizing, Monitoring and Suspending Adoptions from Sending Countries (Control on Macro Level)*

In Germany, accredited private agencies are only admitted to carry out international adoption placements if they were authorized to do so by the competent Central Adoption Office. Such authorization is issued specifically for one or several sending countries and not for adoption placements in general. In the authorization procedure, the agencies must provide the following information:

- demonstrate *actual cooperation* with the sending country they want to place adoptions from: specify the Central Authority and/or the partner organization(s) they want to collaborate with by presenting the cooperation agreements and disclose the tasks as well as the remuneration of their representatives; if a sending country requires a foreign adoption placement office to get an accreditation, according to its national laws, the German agencies also need to demonstrate such an accreditation in the sending country;[362]
- describe all steps that are usually involved in an intercountry *adoption placement procedure*,[363] including not only the activities that take place in Germany, but also the procedural steps that have to be taken abroad, such as the 'location' of the child, his/her eligibility for an intercountry adoption, the drawing up of the child proposal and its content, the matching process as well as the preparation of the child for the adoption;[364] and
- specify the approximate *costs* that are commonly incurred in an adoption placement procedure,[365] including travel costs, fees for documents and their translation etc.,[366] and to disclose aid projects that they are running or supporting in the sending countries.[367]

The Central Adoption Office must assess, on the basis of the information provided by the agency, whether or not to issue an authorization. It *might* refuse the authorization for a specific sending country if this country does not appear to guarantee the protection of the children[368] or oblige an adoption placement office to apply the standards of the Hague

362 § 2(1)(1) to (5) AdVermiG.
363 § 2(1)(6) *leg. cit.*
364 R. Reinhardt (2017). "§ 4 AdVermiG." In J. Reinhardt (ed) "Adoptionsvermittlungsgesetz." 4. edition, Nomos Bundesrecht, Erläuterungen, Rn. 15.
365 § 2 (1)(7) AdVermiStAnKoV.
366 R. Reinhardt (2017). "§ 4 AdVermiG." In J. Reinhardt (ed) "Adoptionsvermittlungsgesetz." 4. edition, Nomos Bundesrecht, Erläuterungen, Rn. 16.
367 § 4 (1)(2) AdVermiG, § 2(1)(6) AdVermiStAnKoV.
368 R. Reinhardt (2017). "§ 4 AdVermiG." In J. Reinhardt (ed) "Adoptionsvermittlungsgesetz." 4. edition, Nomos Bundesrecht, Erläuterungen, Rn. 11.

Convention to the adoption placement of children from non-Hague countries.[369] The Central Adoption Office *must* refuse the authorization for a specific sending country, if it was contrary to the predominant interests in the cooperation with the corresponding sending country.[370] This is, for instance, the case if competition between several foreign adoption agencies in the sending country is expected to hinder efficient cooperation or where it may decrease the quality of the placement activities.[371]

The competent Central Adoption Office must withdraw an agency's authorization to place adoptions from a particular sending country if it finds that the agency does not or can no longer meet the requirements listed in section 5.1.[372] For instance, it must withdraw the authorization if irregular or abusive practices are uncovered abroad that suggest that the sending country cannot properly protect the best interests of the child. An appeal against this withdrawal does not have suspensory effect.[373] The Central Adoption Office can therefore suspend adoptions from a particular sending country with immediate effect. Yet, this powerful supervisory measure can only be effectively employed if the authorities have a good insight into the conditions and developments in the sending countries. Arguably, this is not the case in Germany, since both the gathering and exchange of information by the Central Adoption Offices are limited.

Unlike the Central Authority in the Netherlands, the German Central Adoption Offices do not have the financial resources to travel to the sending countries tht the German agencies are co-operating with in order to get a better picture of their adoption system and the work of the agencies' foreign representatives and partner organizations. Reinhardt, the former head of the Central Adoption Office in Bavaria, explains:

> If I would have said that I wanted to go on a business trip to Ethiopia to see how *Eltern für Kinder* is operating there...I would not have gotten the permission to do so because there was no money provided for that. [...] There does not exist anything such as a German adoption policy. This is quite different in Italy, Norway, Sweden, and Austria where they have very strong representatives who travel the world and look for good co-operations...supported and agreed by politics. Germany never did that.[374]

369 *Verwaltungsgericht Hamburg, 12.7.2006, 13 E 2153/06.*

370 § 4(2) AdVermiG.

371 R. Reinhardt (2017). "§ 4 AdVermiG." In J. Reinhardt (ed) "Adoptionsvermittlungsgesetz." 4. edition, Nomos Bundesrecht, Erläuterungen, Rn. 17.

372 § 4(3) AdVermiG.

373 § 4(5) *leg. cit.*

374 Interview with J. Reinhardt, international adoption law scholar and head of the Central Adoption Office Bavaria between 2001 until 2008, Germany, 16.03.2015.

The Central Adoption Offices must assess, on the basis of the information provided in the authorization procedure and of the child proposals presented to them by the German agencies, whether or not the authorities and organizations in the sending countries comply with the standards and principles of the Hague Convention and the UNCRC.[375] They may start to question the integrity of the foreign adoption system and/or of the agencies' cooperation partners if the children's documents are inconsistent or incomplete or show patterns of irregular practices. Yet, if the children's documents appear to be in order, the Central Adoption Offices will have little reason to doubt the legitimacy of the adoption procedures in the sending country, unless German adopters report irregular or abusive practices to them:

> The Central Adoption Offices only have a chance if there are dissatisfied adoption applicants. So, if somebody went to the sending country and was asked to pay some extra money or did not get the child or if the adoption procedure was being delayed. That is the only chance that the Central Adoption Office might notice an adoption placement office is not working regularly in the sending country.[376]

The Central Adoption Offices may also become askance if the German embassies report suspicion of irregularities in the sending country. Generally, the embassies have a good insight into the foreign adoption system since all adoptions from their host country have to be channeled through them (unless, of course, the country is a visa-country). In addition, it is common in several sending countries for the embassies to meet up regularly and to talk about their experiences with international adoption. If a German embassy develops doubts as to the integrity of the foreign adoption system or an agency's partner organization, it can report this to the competent Central Adoption Office which might withdraw the agency's authorization to place adoptions from this country.

Generally, the level of suspicion differs between Hague and non-Hague sending countries. Some Central Adoption Offices seem to have more faith in those sending countries that have ratified the Convention than in those that have not. If the child's native country is a Contracting State to the Hague Convention, some Central Adoption Offices in Germany trust that the control structures in the sending country are sufficient to prevent or detect unethical or illegal practices and that the international adoption complies with the general standards and principles. With regards to states of origin that have not ratified

375 § 11(2) AdVermiG.

376 Interview with J. Reinhardt, international adoption law scholar and head of the Central Adoption Office Bavaria between 2001 until 2008, Germany, 16.03.2015.

the Hague Convention, Central Adoption Offices are more careful. Flynn, the current head of the Central Adoption in Bavaria, explains:

> We are usually a bit more suspicious of non-Hague countries because we assume that they probably take liberties with the adoption procedure, the subsidiarity principle, the very important ban on child trafficking or the prohibition to get in touch with the orphanage. There we take a bit of a closer look because we are a bit more suspicious. [With regard to Hague countries] we know that the authorities or the government had dealt with these issues, had enacted laws and procedures and designated Central Authorities. They had given more attention to the issue of child trafficking and how to prevent it.[377]

Another limitation is the fragmented German control structure that impedes the exchange of information about irregularities and unfavourable developments in the sending countries. Germany has designated 12 Central Adoption Offices as Central Authorities on the state level which are responsible for accrediting, authorizing and supervising the adoption agencies located in their jurisdiction. At the time of writing, eight German agencies are authorized to carry out international adoptions,[378] which are monitored by five different Central Adoption Offices. As was illustrated above, the German law provides for a stringent monitoring system. Yet, the Central Adoption Offices must individually decide for themselves as to how they control their adoption agencies and how they respond to indications of irregularities and abuses abroad.

Sometimes, they engage in a concerted response to undesirable developments in the sending countries. For example, in 2015, the Central Adoption Offices in Baden-Württemberg, Rhineland and Rhineland-Pfalz/Hessen withdrew their adoption agencies' authorizations for Ukraine.[379] Shortly before, the regulations of this non-Hague country were changed which provided that child proposals drawn up by the Ministry of Social Policy had to be sent directly to the adoption applicants and not to the competent authority in the receiving countries. The Central Adoption Offices found that this procedure violated the standards and principles of the Hague Convention and jointly suspended intercountry adoptions from Ukraine.

In other incidents of irregular developments in the sending countries, the Central Adoption Offices did not harmonize their reactions. For instance, the former head of the Central Adoption Office in Bavaria explained that the child proposals from Bulgaria were of such low quality that his authority decided at some point to stop the cooperation with

377 Interview with C. Flynn, head of the Central Adoption Office Bavaria, Germany, 24.06.2016.
378 See https://assets.hcch.net/docs/2d171271-b623-4120-9eeb-45c6b64bd84d.pdf (last accessed on 03.08.2018).
379 See https://www.bundesjustizamt.de/DE/Themen/Buergerdienste/BZAA/Aktuelles/2015/2015_node.html (last accessed on 03.08.2018).

this sending state.[380] Bulgaria is a Contracting State of the Hague Convention whose Central Authority, the Ministry of Justice, is responsible for drawing up the child proposals and for doing the matching with the adoption applicants. However, the Central Adoption Offices in Baden-Württemberg and in Rhineland, whose agencies were authorized to place children from Bulgaria, obviously saw it differently. The agencies are still continuing to place children from this country.

The competent Central Adoption Offices also responded differently to the adoption scandals vis-à-vis the Ethiopian child care institution *Gelgela* (see section 7). Whereas the Central Adoption Office in Bavaria advised its agency to discontinue its cooperation with this orphanage,[381] the Central Adoption Office in Rhineland, which is responsible for monitoring the other German adoption agency placing children from the *Gelgela* orphanage, claimed that it did not have any knowledge of *Gelgela* having employed 'child finders' and did not recommend suspending adoptions from Ethiopia.[382] The German agency trusted the judgement of its competent Central Adoption Office and retained its collaboration with this orphanage.

The diffusion of responsibility for monitoring the adoption agencies might cause a diffusion of knowledge about irregularities and unfavourable developments in the sending countries. The personnel of the Central Adoption Office in Rhineland were probably not even aware that their colleagues in Bavaria discovered irregularities in the Ethiopian adoption files and assigned its agency to stop placements from *Gelgela*. This lack of knowledge might even have extended to the Central Adoption Office's agencies. As the agency's social worker was asked why the agency continued collaborating with *Gelgela*, whereas the other agency had terminated the cooperation with this child care institution due to abuses, she responded: "I think you need to differentiate a bit and take a very close look. And if [name of the other German adoption agency that had terminated the collaboration with *Gelgela*] – or who? – decided to do it differently, fair enough!".[383]

The Federal Central Office was established to promote cooperation among the German international placement offices.[384] Its main task is to gain, bundle and then distribute the necessary knowledge about the adoption procedures in the sending countries. It might request, from the Central Authorities in the states of origin, information about their adoption laws, statistics and standard forms or information about the operation of the

380 E-mail from J. Reinhardt, international adoption law scholar and head of the Central Adoption Office Bavaria between 2001 until 2008, 21.02.2017.

381 G. Taubert and B. Reuter (2010). "Der verlorene Sohn." TAZ, 15.05.2010, available at http://www.taz.de/!435381/.

382 Statement from the heads of German adoption agency C, August 2010 (on file with author).

383 Interview with a staff member of German adoption agency C, Germany, 10.09.2015.

384 § 2(2) AdÜbAG; Art. 7 Hague Convention.

Hague Convention[385] and then forward this information to the Central Adoption Offices.[386] However, according to Weitzel, the former head of the Federal Central Office, the exchange as well as distribution of information is often cumbersome in practice. He claims that the Central Authorities in the sending countries would often not respond to inquiries at all, or they would only provide insufficient answers. Another problem is that the Central Adoption Offices would often not request information *via* the Federal Central Office, but rather contact the competent authorities in the sending countries themselves without sharing the information with the other Central Adoption Offices.

Even if the Federal Central Office requests information on behalf of or together with a Central Adoption Office, the distribution of information to the other Central Adoption Offices does not always run smooth in Germany:

> We have thought about ways of changing the system so that the exchange of information could be improved...however, everything is incredibly cumbersome...when I, for instance, want to get in touch with India together with [the Central Adoption Office in] Hamburg in order to discuss the steps of the adoption procedure, then each time a piece of information is delivered I would have to forward it to the other Central Adoption Offices. I would have to establish a huge pot of co-operations, that is difficult![387]

Weitzel believes that a centralized German adoption system with the Federal Central Office as the only Central Authority would allow for better information management and would therefore increase the level of professionalism:

> I think it would have been wiser if Germany had taken the opportunity when ratifying the Hague Convention and created one Central Authority on federal level. [...] In Germany we have had 200 adoptions [in the last year] that took place with the involvement of an adoption placement office. For that, we have 12 Central Adoption Offices and 12 adoption agencies...that is economic nonsense because they need to gather information, store and process them – each office by themselves. I think one office would be much more professional and would have a much better information management than 12 or 24 offices.[388]

385 Art. 7 Hague Convention.

386 Art. 6(2) *leg. cit.*

387 Interview with W. Weitzel, head of the German Federal Central Office for International Adoption at the German Federal Office of Justice between 2002 and 2017, Germany, 21.04.2015.

388 *Ibid.*

Another problem is that the Federal Central Office does not have the authority to issue directions to the German adoption placement offices. If it discovers irregularities or abuses in a particular sending country, it cannot adopt a general ban on adoptions from this state. The Federal Central Office can only advise the Central Adoption Offices to suspend adoptions from a particular country of origin by withdrawing their agencies' authorizations. Yet, ultimately it is up to the Central Adoption Offices to heed this advice. Weitzel, therefore, describes his office as a 'placebo' and explains:

> We do not have any power. Due to the federal structure in Germany, we do not have any power to intervene on state level. If I find that a country is difficult to work with because things are happening that we don't want, I cannot say from here, from the federal level, that the co-operation with this country must be discontinued, period…there won't be any more adoption applicants send to this country! […] We had this problem with Nepal, Haiti and recently Kenya. So there were some countries where the need for action was required. However, I only have co-ordinating functions, I am thus only the holding of the Central Adoption Offices. Three Central Adoption Offices had adoption agencies authorized for Kenya in their portfolios…I can call them together to inform them about what has happened, that we are concerned that not everything is in order and that we aspire to terminate the co-operation or take other measures to respond to development that we considered critically. However, it is up to them to be convinced.[389]

In 2010, the Federal Central Office was able to convince the Central Adoption Offices to ban adoptions from Nepal. Two years prior to that, UNICEF and *terre des hommes* published a report that uncovered illegal and abusive practices within the Nepalese adoption system.[390] On the basis of this report, the Federal Central Office convened the Central Adoption Offices whose agencies were authorized to place adoptions from Nepal who then collectively decided to suspend adoptions from this country.[391]

To counterbalance the lack of power, the Federal Central Office tries to play a strong role in the adoption recognition procedures, according to the AdWirkG, in which it has to be heard (see section 3.4). Weitzel explains:

389 *Ibid.*

390 UNICEF and Terre des Hommes (2008). "Adopting the Rights of the Child, A Study on Intercountry Adoption and Its Influence on Child Protection in Nepal." Available at http://www.bettercarenetwork.org/sites/default/files/attachments/Adopting%20the%20Rights%20of%20the%20Child.pdf (last accessed on 23.07.2018).

391 See https://www.bundesjustizamt.de/DE/Themen/Buergerdienste/BZAA/Aktuelles/2010/Meldungen.html (last accessed on 03.08.2018).

> We realized that we only have little chance to influence intercountry adoption placements. So we said: ok, if we critically assess the end product, then this is the only way to actively exert influence on intercountry adoptions. That is why we perform our task of participating [in the recognition procedure] by drawing up statements that are between 3 and 15 pages long. We present the facts of the case, explain the law of the country in which the adoption took place – so, the requirements of an adoption and its legal effect – and then assess whether the adoption complies with the German ordre public. In the conclusion, we either approve the recognition or say that we have doubts and that there is still need for clarification or we say that it would not be acceptable.[392]

However, obviously, it is up to the German family court to decide whether or not to follow the Federal Central Office's recommendation. And, as was already explained in section 4.3, the latter does not have the possibility to appeal against the court's decision, not even if clear indications of commercial or criminal practices can be found in the adoption documents. The Federal Central Office's actual influence on the outcome of the judicial recognition procedure is therefore very limited.

A possibility to influence intercountry adoption placements to Germany more significantly is provided by Article 44(3) of the Hague Convention. According to this provision, a Contracting State may raise an objection to another country's accession to the treaty. The German Federal Foreign Office is responsible for raising such an objection, and in the past it has done so quite frequently. Usually, the Federal Foreign Office follows the recommendation of the Federal Central Office. The latter assesses the situation of the acceding state and proposes to raise an objection if it finds that it did not establish a functioning Central Authority or if it lacks proper structures which would ensure compliance with the Hague Convention's standards and principles. In the past, Germany has objected to the accession of Cambodia, the Dominican Republic, Mali, Armenia, Rwanda and Lesotho.[393] According to Article 44(3) of the Convention, the objection to a state's accession basically means that the treaty will not apply between the objecting and the acceding country. In Germany, such an objection has the effect of an adoption ban for this country, meaning that the German adoption placement offices are generally not allowed to place children from this state.[394] However, the possibility to ban intercountry adoptions is only available with regard to states which were neither Member States of the Hague

392 Interview with W. Weitzel, head of the German Federal Central Office for International Adoption at the German Federal Office of Justice between 2002 and 2017, Germany, 21.04.2015.

393 See https://www.bundesjustizamt.de/DE/Themen/Buergerdienste/BZAA/Aktuelles/Aktuelles_node.html (last accessed on 03.08.2018).

394 Interview with W. Weitzel, head of the German Federal Central Office for International Adoption at the German Federal Office of Justice between 2002 and 2017, Germany, 12.01.2017.

Conference at the time the 1993 Hague Convention was adopted nor had participated in the drafting procedure and only at the time of the accession (and not afterwards).[395]

8.4 *Central Adoption Offices as Adoption Placement Offices*

In Germany, not only the accredited private agencies are permitted to carry out intercountry adoption placement activities, but so too are the 12 Central Adoption Offices (see section 3.2). In cases where adoption applicants want to adopt a child from a Hague country for which no private adoption agency is authorized, the Central Adoption Office is obliged to process the application,[396] whereas it is at its discretion whether to deal with an application for an international adoption from a non-Hague country.[397] Some Central Adoption Offices recommend adoption applicants to turn to the private adoption agencies and to only handle adoptions from Hague countries for which no agency is authorized (e.g. from India or China). Other Central Adoption Offices do not usually refer adoption applicants to an accredited agency, but rather they carry out the adoption placements themselves (see section 5.3).

The fact that Central Adoption Offices are allowed to carry out intercountry adoption placements is problematic for two reasons. First, as was already mentioned previously (see section 5.3), they might become serious or even existence-threatening competitors for the private adoption agencies, if they are placing children from countries for which one or more agencies have already been authorized. This situation is aggravated by the fact that the Central Adoption Offices also monitor the activities of the private adoption agencies. Some agencies claim that their competent Central Adoption Office 'pull the rug under their feet', as they would use the information that the agency is required to disclose to them in the authorization procedure and carry out the adoption placement for a lower fee. The director of the *German adoption agency B* explains how their competent Central Adoption Office in Baden-Württemberg is systematically adopting their know-how to carry out adoption placements itself:

> They obtain their experiences and knowledge from us because in the authorization procedure we need to disclose our contracts as well as all the procedural steps that need to be taken in the sending country [...] The Central Adoption Office can then work with our experience and expertise that we have gained at our own expenses. [...] We already had a couple of cases where couples adopted

395 Art. 44(3) Hague Convention.
396 § 2(2) sentence 3 AdÜbAG.
397 R. Reinhardt (2017). "§ 2 AdVermiG." In J. Reinhardt (ed) "Adoptionsvermittlungsgesetz." 4. edition, Nomos Bundesrecht, Erläuterungen, Rn. 11.

> the first child with us and their second child via the Central Adoption Office. […] That is bitter for us![398]

Second, unlike the accredited adoption agencies, the Central Adoption Offices are not required to establish actual cooperation with the sending countries (see section 5.1.). Thus, they do not have foreign partner organizations or representatives that would facilitate and oversee the adoption process and help the adoption applicants with bureaucratic matters (see section 6.1). The Central Adoption Offices arrange the adoption placement with the official authorities in the sending countries *via* e-mail or telephone only.[399] The adoption applicants who adopt with the involvement of a Central Adoption Office are therefore completely on their own in the sending country. This is particularly problematic if they do not have knowledge of the official language and are unfamiliar with the local adoption process.[400] They often hire an interpreter and/or a local lawyer to help them handle the adoption. From Germany, however, the Central Adoption Offices cannot monitor the actions of the adoption applicants or their 'facilitators' in the sending country, and particularly, they cannot establish whether the no contact rule in Article 29 of the Hague Convention is being respected. Reinhardt, the former head of the Central Adoption Office in Bavaria, explains the Office' total loss of control with regard to the activities in the sending countries as follows:

> We, the Central Adoption Office, have carried out international adoptions, meaning we have selected adoption applicants that were considered suited to adopt. However, we were not able to control what these people were doing in the sending countries. […] Particularly, if they gave any donations there. The Central Adoption Office is only responsible for checking the adoption applicants. After it has sent the social report to the competent authority in the sending country, our job is done until they send us a child proposal. Yet, we cannot control what people are doing in the meantime. We would not know if the people went to the competent authority in the sending country with an

398 Interview with the director of German adoption agency B, Germany, 23.07.2015.

399 H. Paulitz, et al. (2006). "Adoption: Positionen, Impulse, Perspektiven." C. H. Beck, München, p. 341. This is the reason why they are only obliged to place children from countries that have ratified the Hague Convention, which clearly divides the tasks and responsibilities of the central authorities in Articles 4, 5 and 14 thereof.

400 Most adoptions handled by German Central Adoption Offices are kinship or step-parent adoptions, whereby the adopters have close links to the sending country and thus know the language and might even be familiar with the procedures.

> €10,000 check to get preferential treatment or to get a child that they have already seen in an orphanage.[401]

In contrast to agency adoptions, where the adoption fees have to be channelled through the adoption agencies (this regulation was established to better control cash flow), couples adopting through a Central Adoption Office must pay the adoption costs directly in the sending country. The Central Adoption Office cannot control whether the fees required are reasonably high and where they actually go.

An intercountry adoption that is pursued with the involvement of a Central Adoption Office there lacks two important safeguards: a foreign representative or a partner organization controlling the adoption process in the sending country and the channelling of the adoption costs through the adoption placement office. Ultimately, the difference between an intercountry adoption carried out with the involvement of a German Central Adoption Office and an independent adoption that is pursued without an international adoption placement office whatsoever can, thus, be considered as marginal.

9 Criminal Liability of German Actors

A number of criminal legal provisions are relevant with regard to intercountry adoptions. Some specifically address the circumvention of the adoption laws and the trafficking in children. In the following paragraphs, the most important provisions will be explained.

9.1 *Child Trafficking (§ 236 StGB)*

§ 236 of the German Criminal Code[402] (hereinafter StGB) seeks to protect the dignity and the best interests of children by criminalizing their commodification.[403] § 236(1) StGB criminalizes the sale as well as the purchase of a child (*Kinderhandel*). Birth, adoptive or foster parents or legal guardians[404] who leave their child with another person for an indefinite period of time in return for consideration (money or material goods)[405] or with the intent of enriching themselves or others, are criminally liable if they grossly neglect

401 Interview with J. Reinhardt, international adoption law scholar and head of the Central Adoption Office Bavaria between 2001 until 2008, Germany, 16.03.2015.

402 *Strafgesetzbuch in der Fassung der Bekanntmachung vom 13. November 1998 (BGBl. I S. 3322), das zuletzt durch Artikel 1 des Gesetzes vom 30. Oktober 2017 (BGBl. I S. 3618) geändert worden ist.*

403 B. R. Sonnen (2017). "§ 236 Kinderhandel." In U. Kindhäuser et al. (eds) "Nomoskommentar zum Strafgesetzbuch." 5. edition, Nomos, Baden-Baden, Rn. 9.

404 *Ibid.*, Rn. 13.

405 Wieck-Noodt (2012). "§ 236 Kinderhandel." In W. Joecks et al. (eds) "Münchener Kommentar zum StGB." 2. edition, C.H. Beck, München, Rn 26.

their duties of care and education *(Fürsorge- und Erziehungspflicht)*. The latter element should exclude the criminalization of actions that are socially acceptable and considered to be legitimate, such as the placement of a child with relatives due to long periods of absence of the parents or other long-term foster care arrangements.[406]

Correspondingly, the 'purchasers', the persons taking another person's child into their home and granting (or promising) consideration therefor, are also criminally liable if they know or should have known (*dolus eventualis*) that the child's parent or legal guardian grossly neglects his or her duties of care and education.[407] Selling and purchasing a child is punishable by a fine or imprisonment of up to five years.[408]

§ 236(2) StGB covers the actors that mediate between the 'seller' and the 'purchaser' of a child. § 236(2) sentence 1 nr. 1 StGB criminalizes carrying out illegal adoption placements for consideration or with the intent of enrichment. An adoption placement is illegal if it is undertaken by someone who is not permitted to do so according to § 2a AdVermiG (§ 5(1) AdVermiG).[409] § 236(2) sentence 1 nr. 2 StGB criminalizes mediating between the 'seller' and 'purchaser' of a child with the objective of bypassing the adoption system (§ 5(4) AdVermiG). It covers individuals who mediate between pregnant women and women that are intending to pass off the child as their biological child or men that are willing to wrongfully acknowledge paternity of the child[410] (in Germany, this illegal method is referred to as '*Vaterschaftstrick*').[411]

The illegal adoption placement and mediating activities that are described in § 236(2) sentence 1 StGB are only criminal in nature if they are pursued for consideration or with the intent of enrichment.[412] If they are carried out without consideration or the intent of enrichment, they only constitute a misdemeanour (*Ordnungswidrigkeit*) pursuant to § 14 AdVermiG. The criminal offences found in § 236(2) sentence 1 StGB are punishable by a fine or imprisonment of up to three years. They are punishable by a fine or imprisonment

406 *Beschlußempfehlung und Bericht des Rechtsausschusses (6. Ausschuß) vom 12.09.1997, Deutscher Bundestag, 13. Wahleriode, Bundesdrucksache 13/8511*, p. 40.

407 B. R. Sonnen (2017). "§ 236 Kinderhandel." In U. Kindhäuser et al. (eds) "Nomoskommentar zum Strafgesetzbuch." 5. edition, Nomos, Baden-Baden, Rn. 23.

408 § 236(1) StGB.

409 The placement ban in § 5(1) AdVermiG is not absolute but has exceptions provided in § 5(2) AdVermiG: it does not extend to kinship adoptions and adoptions that are arranged with close friends of parents who, for instance, died unexpectedly in an accident, as long as an adoption placement office or youth welfare office is informed thereof immediately.

410 Wieck-Noodt (2012). "§ 236 Kinderhandel." In W. Joecks et al. (eds) "Münchener Kommentar zum StGB." 2. edition, C.H. Beck, München, Rn 37.

411 See Chapter II, section 2.4.1.

412 Wieck-Noodt (2012). "§ 236 Kinderhandel." In W. Joecks et al. (eds) "Münchener Kommentar zum StGB." 2. edition, C.H. Beck, München, Rn 38.

of up to five years if the actor arranges for the child to be brought to Germany or to be taken abroad[413] (e.g. by providing transportation).[414]

§ 236(2) sentence 2 StGB criminalizes granting consideration to the birth, adoptive or foster parents or legal guardians in exchange for the required consent to the adoption of their child. The German legislator criminalized this particular action in 2008 in the course of ratifying the 2000 Optional Protocol to the UNCRC on the Sale of Children, Child Prostitution and Child Pornography.[415] This offence, too, is punishable by a fine or imprisonment of up to three years. § 236(2) sentence 2 StGB is only applicable in a limited number of cases where consideration for the required consent to the adoption is granted to individuals other than those addressed by § 236(1) StGB (e.g. the child). In all other cases, the actors granting consideration will be liable for instigating the sale of a child according to §§ 26, 236(1) StGB.[416]

The offences listed in § 236(1) and (2) StGB are considered to be aggravated if the perpetrator acts with the intention to make a profit (*Gewinnsucht*) or on a commercial basis.[417] Intention to make a profit must clearly exceed the mere intention of enrichment and it must possess an extraordinary, uninhibited and immoral dimension.[418] This is the case when the offender clearly prioritizes profit prospects over the best interests of the child. The offender acts on a commercial basis if he or she intends to derive a regular income for a certain period of time.[419] Furthermore, the offences listed in § 236(1) and (2) StGB are aggravated if the offender acts as a member of a network (*Bande*), whose purpose is to engage in child trafficking for a certain period of time.[420] The offender is a member of a network if he or she bands together with other persons in Germany or abroad for a certain period of time.[421] As such, the offender is criminally liable for all of the network's actions that he or she agreed upon.[422] Finally, the offences are to be considered aggravated if the offender places the child in danger of a substantial impairment of his or her physical or mental development.[423] These aggravated offences are punishable by imprisonment of between six months and ten years.

---

413 § 236(2) sentence 3 StGB.

414 Wieck-Noodt (2012). "§ 236 Kinderhandel." In W. Joecks et al. (eds) "Münchener Kommentar zum StGB." 2. edition, C.H. Beck, München, Rn 48.

415 See Chapter II, section 3.

416 A. Eser und J. Eisele (2014). "§ 236 Kinderhandel." In Eser et al. (eds), "Strafgesetzbuch Kommentar." 29. Edition, C.H. Beck, München, Rn. 8a.

417 § 236(4)(1) StGB.

418 Wieck-Noodt (2012). "§ 236 Kinderhandel." In W. Joecks et al. (eds) "Münchener Kommentar zum StGB." 2. edition, C.H. Beck, München, Rn 52.

419 *Ibid.*, Rn. 53.

420 § 236(4)(1) StGB.

421 Wieck-Noodt (2012). "§ 236 Kinderhandel." In W. Joecks et al. (eds) "Münchener Kommentar zum StGB." 2. edition, C.H. Beck, München, Rn 54.

422 *Ibid.*, Rn. 55.

423 § 236(4)(2) StGB.

According to § 236(5) StGB, the criminal court may mitigate the sentence of the offenders and their accomplices in case of an (attempted) offence according § 236(1) and the sentences of the accomplices only with regard to an (attempted) offence of § 236(2), if their guilt is only minor, taking into consideration the child's physical and mental well-being.[424] In the case of an (attempted) offence as per § 236(1) StGB, the criminal court may even refrain from imposing a sentence if the offender's guilt is only minor.[425]

The provision of § 236 StGB was created in 1998 as a response to the increasing number of cases where parents – predominantly Romanian asylum seekers in Germany – offered to sell or actually sold their children for remuneration in cash or kind.[426] However, the criminal legal provision is not only applicable to child trafficking activities taking place in Germany, but it also covers cases where the child has been sold or purchased abroad and is then being brought to Germany. It therefore technically also covers cases where children are obtained illegally abroad and then brought to Germany for adoption. In the following section, the question will be addressed as to when German adopters and adoption agencies paying money to the child care institution or the child's birth parents are criminally liable for 'child trafficking' according to § 236 StGB.

9.1.1 Adopters

It is quite common for adopters to provide money or material goods (e.g. clothes, pampers, food) to the orphanage they are adopting a child from. If they pursue a private adoption and get in touch with the child's birth parents, they may even provide money or material goods to them. As was already explained in Chapter II, these contributions are often not granted as explicit considerations for the child but rather as 'donations' or 'gifts'. Nonetheless, they are usually not given out of pure compassion or kindness, but they are implicitly conditioned on the placement or relinquishment of the child. As such, they may incite the director of the orphanage to place the child up for adoption or the birth parents to give up their child. Even considerations that are provided after the adoption of the child could be seen as the fulfilment of an expectation that in itself has induced the placement or relinquishment.[427] Thus, the adopters take another person's child into their home for an indefinite period of time and therefor reward consideration, according to § 236(1) StGB.

424 § 236(5) *leg. cit.*

425 *Ibid.*

426 In 1993 and 1994, a number of cases became public in which parents exchanged their children for money (between €5,000 and €10,000) or goods, such as TVs, cars or apartments. Investigation procedures were started but had to be discontinued as the cases were not considered criminal offences in Germany at that time. In 1989, an accessory criminal legal provision (*'nebenstrafrechtliche Bestimmung'*) was introduced into the AdVermiG (§ 14a) that covered the actions of intermediaries acting on a commercial basis, not, however, the actions of the birth parents or the prospective parents. The comprehensive criminal legal provision of § 236 StGB was implemented in order to close this criminal liability loophole.

427 See Chapter II, section 4.2.2. In several sending countries, the Central Authority or another competent authority decides on the adoption placement of the child, whereas the director of the orphanage (usually

However, international adopters providing money or goods to the orphanage or parents will in most cases not possess the *mens rea* that is required by § 236(1) StGB. Persons purchasing a child according to § 236(1) StGB are only criminally liable if they know or should have known (*dolus eventualis* suffices) that the child's parents or legal guardian grossly neglected their duties of care and education. If the actors believe that they and the child's parents or legal guardians act in the best interests of the child, then the *mens rea* is absent.[428] This is the case if the child's birth parents, respectively the orphanage that is caring for the child, face extreme financial hardship and the adopters purchase the child in order to give him or her a better life.[429] Hence, the element of 'grossly neglecting duties of care and education' in § 236(1) StGB essentially legalizes selling and purchasing children, if their legal guardians or birth parents face extreme poverty and are unable to properly care for the child. Adopters who purchase a child from a so-called 'Third World' country cannot be held criminally liable for child trafficking according to § 236(1) StGB.[430]

Adopters may be liable for participating in one of the offences in § 236(2) StGB if they involve an intermediary who carries out an illegal adoption placement or mediating activities for consideration or financially induces the child's parents' consent to adoption or attempts to do so. However, the court may mitigate the sentence of persons participating in the offence of § 236(2) StGB if their guilt is to be considered as minor.[431] According to the German legislator, this is the case if they acted out of distress or from an unfulfilled desire for a child.[432] Hence, the possibility of mitigating the sentence *de facto* primarily benefits adopters. So far no adopter has ever been convicted of participating in child trafficking according to § 236(2) StGB.[433]

9.1.2 Staff members of an adoption agency

An adoption agency's staff members cannot be held criminally responsible according to § 236(2) sentence 1 StGB. This provision criminalizes actors who carry out illegal adoption placements. It, therefor, covers individuals who act independently or as a member of an

acting as the child's legal guardian) has no say in that regard whatsoever. If money or goods are provided to an orphanage director who cannot decide on the adoption placement of the child, a 'purchase' according to § 236 StGB is excluded.

428 *Ibid.*

429 Wieck-Noodt (2012). "§ 236 Kinderhandel." In W. Joecks et al. (eds) "Münchener Kommentar zum StGB." 2. edition, C.H. Beck, München, Rn. 44; B. R. Sonnen (2017). "§ 236 Kinderhandel." In U. Kindhäuser et al. (eds) "Nomoskommentar zum Strafgesetzbuch." 5. edition, Nomos, Baden-Baden, Rn. 23.

430 See also J. Peters (2014). "Kindheit im Strafrecht: Eine Untersuchung des materiellen Strafrechts mit besonderem Schwerpunkt auf dem Kind als Opfer und Täter." Herbert Utz Verlag, München, p. 235.

431 § 236(5) StGB.

432 *Entwurf eines Sechsten Gesetzes zur Reform des Strafrechts (6.StRG), Deutscher Bundestag, 13. Wahleriode, Drucksache 13/8587*, p. 41.

433 Interview with W. Weitzel, head of the German Federal Central Office for International Adoption at the German Federal Office of Justice between 2002 and 2017, Germany, 21.04.2015.

organization which has not been accredited as an adoption placement office and therefore authorized to carry out intercountry adoptions (see section 5.1). For instance, a lawyer, doctor or nurse who carries out an adoption placement for consideration with the intent of enrichment is criminally liable according to § 236(2) sentence 1 StGB. The objective of this criminal provision is to tackle adoption placements by for-profit individuals and organizations that are not accredited or authorized thereto. It does not cover individuals working for an accredited adoption placement office that is listed in § 2a AdVermiG. If they carry out adoption placement activities for consideration or with the intention of enrichment, their agency's accreditation or authorization may be withdrawn; yet, the individuals cannot be held criminally liable according to § 236(2) sentence 1 StGB.

The staff members of an adoption agency may be held criminally responsible for instigating the sale of a child according to §§ 26, 236(1) StGB, if they grant consideration to the birth, adoptive or foster parents or legal guardians in exchange for the required consent to the adoption of their child. It is quite common for adoption agencies to provide money or material goods to the orphanage they adopt a child from. In some sending countries, this is even explicitly required from foreign agencies. As was explained above, such contributions may incite the director of the orphanage to place children up for adoption as a *quid pro quo*. Yet, in practice, the personnel of a German adoption agency will claim that money or goods were given with a view to improving the living conditions of the children living in the orphanage rather than in exchange for the required consent to the adoption placement of a particular child. But even if money or goods were provided with the intention to obtain the required consent to adoption, criminal liability according to §§ 26, 236(1) StGB will be excluded due to a lack of *mens rea*, as it will be argued that the orphanage was unable to properly care for the child (see section 9.1.1).

In 2010, several staff members of the German adoption agency *ICCO* (section 1) were accused of child trafficking as per § 236 StGB. This was the first time that the criminal provision on child trafficking was applied to a case of intercountry adoption. However, up until the time of writing, the criminal investigation is still ongoing which is why the public prosecutor did not allow access to the case file for the purposes of the present research.

9.2 *Other Relevant Criminal Provisions*

Other provisions of the German Criminal Code may also be relevant for cases whereby children have been obtained illegally and then brought to Germany for adoption. Women who have the birth certificate of someone else's child issued with their name as the biological mother, in order to circumvent the adoption act, are criminally liable according to § 169 StGB (*Personenstandsfälschung*). Private adopters who bring a child to Germany illegally can generally not be held criminally liable for smuggling according to §§ 95, 96 AufenthG (*Einschleusen von Ausländern*), as they do not receive a pecuniary advantage or the promise of a pecuniary advantage in return.

German actors may be held responsible for the abduction of minors from the care of their parents according to § 235 StGB (*Kindesentfuehrung*), if the child was removed from his or her parents by force, threat of serious harm or deception. They may also be held criminally liable for the forgery of documents (§ 267 StGB) or for paying bribes to foreign judges or officials (§ 335a StGB).

So far, no staff member of a German adoption agency has ever been accused of any such criminal offence. Agency personnel in the receiving countries are typically not actively involved in illegal adoption practices in the sending countries and criminal liability for accessory to the foreign parents' commission of these offences by omission is often excluded as their *mens rea* is lacking. In many cases, they can plausibly deny having had knowledge of their foreign partner organizations' illegal practices. And if the information on the child proposals and on the documents necessary for an adoption (e.g. the child's birth certificate, the declaration of relinquishment or the parents' death certificate) is complete and consistent – thus, if the children have been properly laundered – and if there were no other 'red flags' suggesting irregularities in the adoption procedure abroad, the adoption agencies can also claim that they could not have known about their partners' irregular practices abroad.

10 Conclusion and Discussion

In 2001, Germany ratified the Hague Convention. In the course of implementing the treaty's standards and procedures, the German legislator has tightened the regulations for intercountry adoptions: the accreditation and authorization requirements for adoption placement agencies were raised, the Central Adoption Offices were provided with more extensive supervisory powers, and strict reporting obligations were imposed on the adoption placement agencies. Certainly, the German adoption system was improved significantly as a result. Nonetheless, adoption scandals have emerged after the ratification of the Hague Convention, suggesting that the adoption system does not effectively prevent the trafficking of children for adoption purposes. This chapter isolated and explained the criminogenic factors of the German adoption system, meaning its structural features that encourage and facilitate the trafficking in children to Germany:

1) Tolerance towards private adoptions

A major limitation of the German adoption system is the high tolerance towards do-it-yourself adoptions. The law neither explicitly prohibits private adoptions nor does it provide for any negative consequences. This has led to generous case law on the recognition of private adoptions: a study from 2007 revealed that 90% of foreign decisions on an adoption that took place in circumvention of the official adoption placement procedure were recognized by German courts. The latter would argue that the lack of involvement of a German adoption placement office in the adoption procedure would not *per se* be manifestly contrary to German public policy. They assess themselves as to whether the adopters are 'actually' suited to adopt the child at the time of the recognition procedure and – after a positive evaluation – determine that the foreign adoption judgment is to be recognized.

A judgment by the German Supreme Court from 2014 could arguably further increase the family courts' readiness to recognize foreign decisions on private adoptions. In its judgment, it dealt with the question as to whether a Californian court decision that declared a German homosexual couple as the legal parents of a surrogate child was contrary to German public policy. Even though surrogacy is illegal in Germany, the Court declared that the foreign decision had to be recognized, stating that the right to family life (Article 8 ECHR) and the principle of the child's best interests would generally preclude the refusal of a foreign decision only because this might prevent (further) circumventions of the ban on surrogacy agreements. Applying this consideration to intercountry adoptions, this implies that general preventive considerations, namely the consideration that the best interests of the children *in abstracto* can be best served by refusing the recognition and thereby preventing further private intercountry adoption, cannot justify a violation of the rights and the best interests of the child *in concreto*.

Considering the lacking prohibition of private adoptions and the generous case law on their recognition, it will come as no surprise that in Germany an estimated 50% of international adoptions are pursued without the involvement of a German adoption placement office. Arguably, both German law and jurisprudence invite prospective adopters to bypass the typically time-consuming and tedious official adoption placement procedure, and to pursue a more rapid, less bureaucratic private adoption, which are arguably more prone to illegal practices as they take place without there being any opportunity for supervision and control whatsoever.

2) Institutional pressure

Even though private adoptions are particularly prone to commercial and illegal practices, agency adoptions are not without their risks either. In the 90s, it became apparent in Germany that adoptions that were pursued with the involvement of an accredited agency were also not *ipso eo* free from abuses and irregularities. German adoption agencies openly ascribe to the high standards and principles set out in the Hague Convention and the UNCRC. They routinely claim that they exist to serve the best interests of the child and to find parents for children, not children for parents. In the interviews with the agency personnel, it became clear that they had a realistic idea of the pitfalls and risks of the intercountry adoption system, they are well aware of the negative influences that Western money might have on adoption practices in poor sending countries in particular. Hence, many refrain from providing donations to their foreign cooperation partners and from paying 'contingency fees' to their representatives. It is probably fair to say that most German agencies do not actively encourage child trafficking.

However, many agencies passively facilitate the trafficking of children into the German adoption system by failing to scrutinize the adoption fees that their partners determine and to strictly monitor their activities in the sending countries. Control, generally impeded by geographical distance, is substituted by trust in the cooperation partner, the authorities in the countries of origin or even in the adoption applicants. As was explained, trust and confidence become problematic if they lead the agency to ignore the 'red flags' suggesting irregularities in the adoption system. Adoption agencies are ideologically and financially motivated to ignore or minimize signs of systemic abuses. In order to maintain their identity that is inextricably tied to this ideological mission of saving children, agencies may be motivated to keep children moving through the adoption system notwithstanding credible allegations of irregular practices.

Arguably, German adoption agencies do not only have an ideological but also a financial motivation to ignore signs of irregularities in the sending countries. In Germany, all adoption placement offices experience financial strain. They are not provided with financial support by the government which means that they have to finance themselves exclusively with the administration fees paid by their adoption applicants. Since these fees constitute the agencies' only source of revenue, they must place a particular number of children per year to keep their organization up and running. But as the number of (for adopters attractive) children available for intercountry adoption has steadily decreased, the pressure on German agencies to achieve the necessary mandate of placements has intensified. This pressure is exacerbated by the (in relation to the total placement figure) large number of German accredited agencies that not only have to compete with each other as well as with other Western adoption agencies, but also with the German Central Adoption Offices that are permitted to carry out adoption placements.

The discrepancy between an adoption agency's financial imperative to achieve a particular number of mandates, on the one hand, and the number of (for adopters attractive) children that are legitimately available for intercountry adoption, on the other hand, creates strain. Adoption agencies respond to this strain by either raising the administration fees that are to be paid by the adopters, reducing the number of employees (to an extent that is legally permissible) or by bending the ethical rules. They may continue to move children from a sending country, even after signs of systemic irregularities have become apparent and retain their foreign cooperation partner that was exposed to have been engaged in illegally securing children for adoption. Different techniques of rationalization would serve the agency personnel to allow them to repel criticism, protect the agency from blame and to maintain an image as a child welfare organization abiding by ethical norms and obligations. They might a) deny the extent and seriousness of the abusive practices abroad by insisting that they were incidental rather than systemic, b) emphasize the higher cause of saving children through adoption, c) deny their responsibility by claiming that they did not actively engage in illegal practices themselves (e.g. by bribing) and by denying their powerful role at the demand end of the adoption market and d) condemn critics for lacking the necessary know-how to properly asses the incidences abroad and the media for misrepresenting and exaggerating the facts of single cases.

3) Unregulated flow of money into the sending countries

German law fails to establish financial limits or guidelines on intercountry adoptions. It does not restrict the amount of money German agencies pay to their foreign cooperation partners, for instance, by providing guidelines on reasonable fees and remuneration. Moreover, the German Central Adoption Offices have not specified as to which adoption costs should be considered as 'reasonable'. They commonly leave it up to the Central Authority of the sending countries to establish standards for fees and remunerations. German law also lacks specific provisions regulating donations and contributions to sending countries. In particular, it does not explicitly prohibit adoption placement offices from donating money or material goods to child care institutions they are cooperating with. The German adoption system thus allows inordinate sums of money to be introduced into the international adoption system, which might facilitate and encourage abusive and illegal practices as a consequence.

4) Fragmented monitoring and control structure

The monitoring and control of the German adoption agencies is considerably tight. The Central Adoption Offices have a fair insight into the agencies' financial situation, as well as their activities in Germany and have the power to intervene if they suspect irregular practices by withdrawing its authorization to place international adoptions or even its accreditation. Yet, the monitoring system established in Germany has its limitations.

First, the German Central Adoption Offices do not have the financial resources to regularly travel to the sending countries, with which the German agencies are cooperating, in order to gain a better understanding of their adoption system and the work of the agencies' foreign representatives and partner organizations. The Central Adoption Offices can only assess on the basis of the information provided during the authorization procedure and of the child proposals that are presented to them by the German adoption placement agencies whether or not the authorities and organizations in the sending countries comply with the standards and principles set out in the Hague Convention and the UNCRC.

Second, Germany's monitoring structure that has been established to control intercountry adoptions is so fragmented and cumbersome that it cannot be considered suited to effectively prevent the laundering of children. A total of 13 Central Authorities were designated that have different tasks and responsibilities. The 12 Central Adoption Offices at state level are in charge of accrediting, approving and supervising the adoption agencies that are located within their jurisdiction. In practice, each Central Adoption Office decides itself as to how to control the agencies and how to respond to allegations or indications of adoption irregularities and abuses. In the past, they have rarely engaged in a concerted response to undesirable developments in the states of origin. The dispersion of responsibility has more than likely led to a situation whereby none of them can see the big picture of the processes and possible pitfalls in the sending country's adoption systems. The Central Adoption Offices' lack of control and of a general overview of the activities in the states of origin appears to have been compensated by the trust that is placed in the competent authorities in the sending countries. This is particularly the case if they are States Parties to the Hague Convention.

The Federal Central Office was established so as to prevent the diffusion of knowledge about irregularities and unfavourable developments in the sending countries. As a 'holding' of the Central Adoption Offices, it is responsible for collecting and distributing the necessary information and promoting cooperation among them. However, it often experiences difficulties in distributing the necessary information about the sending countries. Furthermore, the Federal Central Office does not have the authority to issue directions to the Central Adoption Offices. If it discovers irregularities or abuses in a particular sending country, it can only advise them to stop placing children from this state and to withdraw their agencies' authorizations. The Federal Central Office can significantly influence intercountry adoptions to Germany by proposing to raise an objection to a sending country's accession to the Hague Convention. This basically has the effect that adoptions from this state are blocked. Yet, this possibility to ban intercountry adoptions is only available with regard to states which neither were Member States of the Hague Conference at the time the 1993 Hague Convention was adopted nor had participated in the drafting procedure and only at the time of the accession (and not afterwards).

5) Central Adoption Offices as adoption placement offices

The Central Adoption Offices are not only responsible for licencing and monitoring the German adoption agencies, but they are also permitted to handle intercountry adoption placements themselves. This is problematic for two reasons. First, the financial pressure on the German adoption agencies will be further increased if the Central Adoption Offices are placing children from those countries for which the former has been authorized. Second, intercountry adoptions that are handled by Central Adoption Offices lack two important safeguards: a foreign representative or partner organization controlling the adoption process in the sending country and the channelling of the adoptions costs through the adoption placement office. Thus, ultimately the difference between a private intercountry adoption and an adoption carried out with the involvement of a German Central Adoption Office is only marginal.

6) No criminal liability of German adopters and adoption agencies

In most cases of child laundering, both the adopters and the adoption agencies in Germany can plausibly deny having had knowledge of the illegal practices in the sending country. Yet, even if they engage in illicit practices themselves, they can often not be held criminally responsible. The provision found in § 236 StGB criminalizes the sale, as well as the purchase, of children. However, it does not cover adopters providing money or goods to the orphanage or the child's birth parents who may be facing extreme financial hardship (which is most often the case in international adoption). Furthermore, accredited agencies carrying out adoption placements for consideration or with the intention of enrichment or providing money or goods to the orphanage in the sending countries they place children from can generally not be held criminally liable according to § 236 StGB.

VI The Dutch Intercountry Adoption System

1 Introduction

Irregular and abusive adoption practices in the sending countries often remain invisible to the stakeholders in the receiving countries. Yet, a relatively high number of child laundering cases have been uncovered in the Netherlands. This is particularly due to numerous documentaries that have been shown on Dutch television programmes like *Netwerk,*[1] *Brandpunt*[2] and *Zembla,*[3] which conducted investigations in sending countries and

---

1 For example, in 2007, *Netwerk* broadcast a documentary about the child laundering case involving the Indian boy Rahul who was stolen from his sleeping parents laundered through the adoption system and then adopted by a Dutch couple who did not know about his actual origin (Netwerk (2007). "India eist gestolen adoptiekind uit Nederland terug." 22.05.2007, available at http://www.uitzendinggemist.net/aflevering/86316/Netwerk_eo_Ncrv.html.) Only one year after the Indian child laundering case was reported, *Netwerk* investigated the illegal adoption practices employed in China. The documentary, broadcast on 11 March 2008, showed how family planning officials in Gaoping, a city in the Chinese province Shanxi, confiscated thirteen over-quota or unregistered children and then turned them into the Shaoyang orphanage for intercountry adoption. The parents were told that they could only retrieve their child if they paid an amount of money they obviously did not have. The documentary brought to light irregularities in the Chinese adoption system that the Dutch adoption agency Wereldkinderen sought to clarify with the help of the Ministry of Justice and Security for already several years (I. Pronk (2008). "Weer ophef rond adoptie uit China." Trouw, 11.03.2998, available at https://www.trouw.nl/home/weer-ophef-rond-adoptie-uit-china~af540f5a/).

2 In 2011, *Brandpunt* broadcast a documentary about irregular adoption practices in Ethiopia. Based on the findings of *ACT's* study, the programme conducted an investigation into the Ethiopian adoption system. The documentary describes how child care institutions would deceive parents about the consequences of an adoption, falsify the children's birth certificates or relinquishment deeds and then send the children abroad as 'orphans'. This was also the case with Betty and her sister, two Ethiopian girls adopted by a Dutch couple. The siblings' documents said that both their parents were dead and that there was no family member able to care for them. Also, Betty was actually older than indicated on her birth certificate. *Brandpunt* accompanied the teenager to Ethiopia to trace down her mother. In 2013, an Ethiopian court even revoked Betty's adoption. (Brandpunt (2011). "Kinderen te koop." 11.01.2011, available at https://brandpunt.kro-ncrv.nl/brandpunt/broadcasts/segment/68/.) In 2013, an Ethiopian court even revoked Betty's adoption (Brandpunt (2013). "Kinderen te koop" 24.02.2013, available at https://www.npo.nl/brandpunt/04-08-2017/WO_KRO_795126). In 2015, Brandpunt broadcast a report about illegal practices in the Bulgarian adoption system. It describes how Bulgarian authorities would remove children from their poor families and then send them abroad for adoption with the parents' consent. The parents were not provided with any assistance to keep their children and no efforts were made to find an adoptive family in Bulgaria (Brandpunt (2015). "De Bulgaarse adoptie-industrie" 18.10.2015, available at https://www.npo.nl/brandpunt-reporter/18-10-2015/KN_1673048).

3 In 2017 and 2018, *Zembla* broadcast three documentaries about illegal adoptions practices in Sri Lanka in the 70s and 80s: Zembla (2017). "Adoptiebedrog." 17.05.2017, available at https://www.npo.nl/zembla/17-05-2017/VARA_101382216; Zembla (2017). "Adoptiebedrog (2)." 20.09.2017, available at http://www.uitzendinggemist.net/aflevering/406615/Zembla.html; and Zembla (2018). "Adoptiebedrog (3)." 12.07.2018, availabe at https://tvblik.nl/zembla/adoptiebedrog-iii.

uncovered cases involving illegally obtained children that were adopted by Dutch families. Their reports have triggered many debates about the legitimacy of intercountry adoption, also in the Dutch parliament. It is furthermore due to the commitment of the former director of the Dutch adoption agency *Wereldkinderen*, Ina Hut, why illegal adoption practices have become visible in the Netherlands. She had irregular adoption practices in Ethiopia investigated, demanded the Dutch Ministry of Justice and Security to take an active role in clarifying abusive practices in China and openly talked about the weaknesses in the intercountry adoption system.

Considering the numerous reports about irregular and abusive adoption practices in the sending countries, it does not come as a surprise that the *Raad voor Strafrechtstoepassing en Jeugdbescherming (RSJ)* recommended banning intercountry adoptions to the Netherlands altogether in 2016. After having analysed the numerous weaknesses in the intercountry adoption system and discussed the possible scenarios for dealing with international adoption in the future, the *RSJ* concluded that:

> The RSJ is of the opinion that intercountry adoption is not the best means to protect children and appeals to the Dutch authorities to shift the focus and support these children by helping to build up and improve the child protection system in the country of origin.[4]

However, the Dutch Ministry of Justice and Security announced that it would continue with intercountry adoptions, claiming that it should remain available for children that cannot be cared for in their home countries.[5] And there is much to suggest that reports about illegal and abusive adoption practices in the sending countries will continue to emerge, thereby triggering further political discussions in the Netherlands.

This Chapter seeks to identify and explain the structural features in the Dutch adoption system that work to facilitate the trafficking in children to the Netherlands for adoption purposes. Section 2 gives a brief overview of the history, development and current trends of international adoption in the Netherlands. Section 3 describes the Dutch legal framework of intercountry adoption. It explains the relevant Dutch adoption laws and policies and outlines the steps that are involved in an official intercountry adoption placement procedure.

Section 4 takes a closer look at independent adoptions – adoptions that are arranged by adopters themselves. It explains the risks that are involved in partial-do-it-yourself adoptions (*deelbemiddelingen*) which couples and individuals pursue with the help of a private contact that is approved by the Dutch Ministry of Justice and Security. Furthermore,

4 *Bezinning op Interlandelijke Adoptie, Advies van de Afdeling advisering van de Raad voor Strafrechtstoepassing en Jeugdbescherming (RSJ), 16.11.2016, Kamerstukken II 2015-216, Nr. 60 839,* p. 68.

5 *Brief van de Staatssecretaris van Veiligheid en Justitie, 31.01.2017, Kamerstukken II 2016-2017, 31 265, Nr. 62,* p. 4.

it describes how private adoptions, namely adoptions that take place without any form of state involvement, are responded to in the Netherlands.

The subsequent sections then zoom in on agency adoptions, meaning adoptions that are arranged by Dutch adoption placement offices, and seek to explain why they, too, are not free from abusive or irregular practices. Section 5 takes a closer look at the Dutch agencies' accreditation requirements as well as financial situation and explains why they find themselves caught up in a tension between integrity and money. Section 6 zooms in on the Dutch adoption agencies' cooperation with the sending countries. In particular, it examines how the agencies pay their foreign representatives and partner organizations and how they monitor what occurs abroad.

Section 7 analyses the role of the Dutch authorities in the adoption system. It explains the control loopholes in the adoption review process for full adoptions from Hague countries. Furthermore, using the example of the Chinese child laundering incidents, the section illustrates how trust in the authorities of Hague sending countries, as well as diplomatic and other interests, may hinder an effective response by Dutch authorities to irregularities in the sending countries. Section 8 discusses the criminal liability of Dutch actors that are involved in illegal adoptions. Section 9 concludes by summarizing the weaknesses, or criminogenic factors, of the Dutch adoption system.

2 History, Developments and Current Trends

In the Netherlands, the phenomenon of intercountry adoption began in the 1950s with the adoption of children from Greece (almost 400 children, which ceased in 1979), Austria (about 300 children, which ceased in 1984), Germany (about 150 children, which ceased in 1982) and other European countries.[6] The economic hardship that was felt after World War II forced many families to give up their children and since these countries could not themselves take care of them, they were sent to adoptive parents in the Netherlands, the United States, Scandinavia and other Western countries. Many of the foreign children were placed to the Netherlands with the help of the organization *Nederlandse Vereniging voor Pleeggezinnen* (NVP) that was established in 1950.

In the late 60s, beginning of the 70s, Dutch couples gradually began to adopt children from countries outside Europe. Television broadcasts about military conflicts as well as poverty in Asian and South American countries broadcast the suffering of millions of children, prompting the foundation of Dutch humanitarian organizations with the goal

6 R. A. C. Hoksbergen (1991). "Intercountry Adoption Coming of Age in The Netherlands: Basic Issues, Trends, and Developments." In H. Altstein and R. J. Simon (eds), "Intercountry Adoption: A Multinational Perspective." Praeger, New York, 141-158, p. 142.

of helping these children.[7] *Nederlandse Stichting voor Interlandelijke Adoptie* (SIA), founded in 1969, and *Wereldkinderen*, established in 1971 by adoptive parents, were the first Dutch organizations set up with the aim of placing foreign children from war and poverty-ridden countries to the Netherlands.[8] In 1969, the first 10 adoptees from South Korea arrived in the Netherlands. Between 1971 and 1980, about 9,000 children were adopted by Dutch families, most of them less than two years-old, coming from South Korea (2317), Indonesia (1788), India (865), Lebanon (335), Sri Lanka (158), Peru (112) and Colombia (106).[9]

The generation of adoptive parents of the period 1971-1980 mainly had idealistic motivations in adopting a child from abroad. Often they already had their own biological children and wanted to take care of children suffering from the consequences of war, natural disasters or starvation in other parts of the world.[10] Since about 1984, however, the motives for adopting internationally has gradually changed, as the adopting couples' own interests and needs began to play a more central role.[11]

In the Netherlands, the number of couples wishing to adopt a child has increased dramatically since the 1950s. Whereas 38 domestic adoptions were recorded in 1957, the figure was 416 in 1965 and 1,032 in 1970.[12] However, as in other industrialized countries, the number of Dutch children available for adoption has fallen drastically since the mid-70s. Due to several reasons that were already explained earlier,[13] the domestic adoptions fell from 1,259 in 1974 to 144 in 1984.[14] Yet, the number of Dutch couples (the majority of them involuntarily childless) wishing to adopt continued to increase and for many, intercountry adoption became an attractive solution to having their own child. Between 1981 and 1992, more than 11,000 children were adopted from abroad.[15]

Yet, from 1980 the number of foreign children adopted by Dutch families has steadily decreased. Whereas almost 1,600 intercountry adoptions were recorded in 1980 (the highest number of international adoptions ever recorded in the Netherlands), the figure was only about 600 in 1993.[16] This dramatic drop is due to several reasons both within the

---

7 *Ibid.*

8 *Ibid.*

9 R. A. C. Hoksbergen (2000). "Vijftig Jaar Adoptie in Nederland, Een historisch-statistische beschouwing." Utrecht, available at http://www.vijfeeuwenmigratie.nl/sites/default/files/bronnen/VIJFTIG%20JAAR%20ADOPTIE.pdf, pp. 8-9.

10 *Ibid.*, pp. 7-9.

11 R. A. C. Hoksbergen (1991). "Intercountry Adoption Coming of Age in The Netherlands: Basic Issues, Trends, and Developments." In H. Altstein and R. J. Simon (eds), "Intercountry Adoption: A Multinational Perspective." Praeger, New York, 141-158, p. 150.

12 R. A. C. Hoksbergen (2000). "Vijftig Jaar Adoptie in Nederland, Een historisch-statistische beschouwing." Utrecht, available at http://www.vijfeeuwenmigratie.nl/sites/default/files/bronnen/VIJFTIG%20JAAR%20ADOPTIE.pdf, pp. 8-9.

13 See Chapter II, section 2.2.1.

14 *Ibid.*, pp. 8 and 10.

15 *Ibid.*, p. 12.

16 *Ibid.*

sending countries as well as in the Netherlands. On the one hand, Indonesia shut down its intercountry adoption system due to recurring reports of illegal activities and South Korea sought to minimize the number of children sent abroad. On the other hand, the number of Dutch adoption applicants decreased due to economic difficulties in that time, as well as a result of critical voices about illegal adoptions and studies which illustrated that adoptive parents faced several difficulties in adopting a foreign child.[17]

From 1995, the number of intercountry adoptions increased once again, peaking in 2004 with 1,300 adoptions.[18] The number of adoption applications rose significantly, particularly due to an economic revival as well as due to the fact that in 1998, it became possible for single and same sex parents to adopt a child[19] The growing demand for adoptable children was paralleled by an increase in the supply of children, particularly in China and Colombia but also in countries from the former Soviet Union, like Romania and Poland.[20] Ever since 2004, however, the number of foreign children placed to the Netherlands has dramatically decreased. Whereas more than 1,000 intercountry adoptions were recorded in 2005,[21] the figure was only about 700 in 2010[22] and 210 in 2017.[23] The number of foreign children placed to the Netherlands is currently as low as it was back in the early 70s. The reasons for the dramatic drop in intercountry adoptions worldwide are further discussed in Chapter II.

---

17 *Ibid.*, p. 10.

18 Ministerie van Justitie en Veiligheid (2007). "Statistische gegevens betreffende de opneming in gezinnen in Nederland van buitenlandse adoptiekinderen in de jaren 2002-2006." Available at https://adoptie.nl/wp-content/uploads/2017/03/Statistieken.pdf.

19 R. A. C. Hoksbergen (2000). "Vijftig Jaar Adoptie in Nederland, Een historisch-statistische beschouwing." Utrecht, available at http://www.vijfeeuwenmigratie.nl/sites/default/files/bronnen/VIJFTIG%20JAAR%20ADOPTIE.pdf, p. 13.

20 *Ibid.*, p. 12.

21 Ministerie van Justitie en Veiligheid (2010). "Adoptie, Trends en Analyse, Statistisch overzicht interlandelijke adoptie over de jaren 2005 tot en met 2009." (on file with author).

22 Ministerie van Justitie en Veiligheid (2013). "Adoptie, Trends en Analyse, Statistisch overzicht interlandelijke adoptie over de jaren 2008 tot en met 2012." Available at https://adoptie.nl/wp-content/uploads/2017/03/Adoptie_trends_en_analyse_2013.pdf.

23 Ministerie van Justitie en Veiligheid (2018). "Adoptie, Trends en Analyse, Statistisch overzicht interlandelijke adoptie over de jaren 2013 tot en met 2017." Available https://www.rijksoverheid.nl/documenten/rapporten/2018/03/07/adoptie-trends-en-analyse.

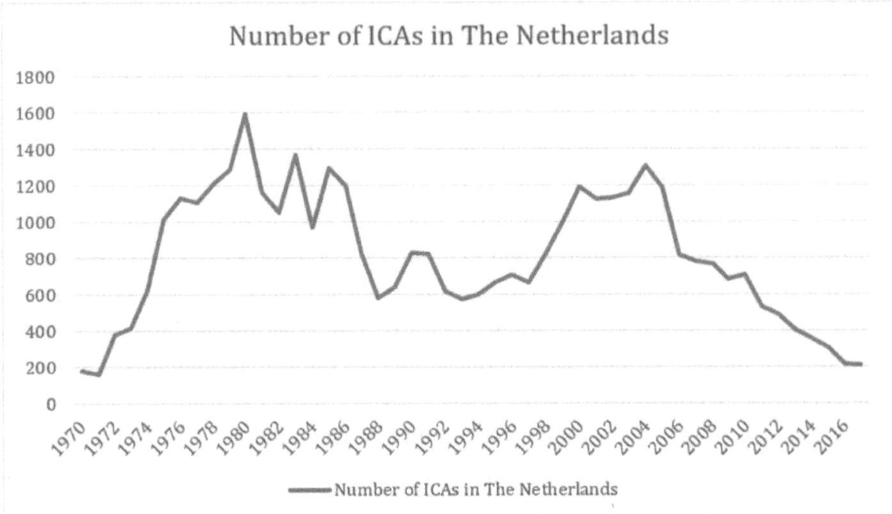

3 The Dutch Legal Framework of Intercountry Adoption

As with all other receiving countries, in the Netherlands, the first intercountry adoptions took place in a rather unregulated manner. There were no legal standards or guidelines to follow and no official qualifications were required in order to organize intercountry adoptions. Thus, anyone could act as an intermediary between the Dutch prospective adoptive parents and a sending country. In this legal vacuum, adoptive parents who wanted to help children orphaned by the wars in Vietnam and Biafra established *Wereldkinderen* in 1971, the largest and oldest Dutch international adoption agency of its kind.[24]

By the end of the 1970s, however, experts began to claim that the operation of adoption organizations needed to be regulated and controlled.[25] In 1988, the first law on intercountry adoptions, the Act on the Placement of Foreign Foster Children[26] (hereinafter WOBP), was enacted and came into force in 1990. It provides that only accredited Dutch organizations are permitted to carry out international adoptions and it stipulates specific requirements that they must meet (e.g. non-profit objectives, actual cooperation with organizations and institutions in the sending countries, placements must be carried out by qualified

24 R. A. C. Hoksbergen (1991). "Intercountry Adoption Coming of Age in The Netherlands: Basic Issues, Trends, and Developments." In H. Altstein and R. J. Simon (eds), "Intercountry Adoption: A Multinational Perspective." Praeger, New York, 141-158, p. 145.

25 See, for example, R. A. C. Hoksbergen, et al. (1979). "Adoptie van Kinderen Uit Verre Landen." Van Loghum Slaterus, Deventer.

26 *Wet van 8 december 1988, houdende regelen inzake de opneming in Nederland van buitenlandse pleegkinderen met het oog op adoptie.*

psychologists and social workers).[27] Furthermore, the Act regulates the procedural steps that the prospective adoptive parents must undergo.

The Netherlands ratified the treaty in 1998 by enforcing the Act of 14 May 1998 on the Implementation of the Hague Convention on Intercountry Adoptions of 29 May 1993[28] (hereinafter *Uitvoeringswet*). In the course of implementing the Hague Convention, the Netherlands adapted the national adoption law that was promulgated in 1988. The legislator modified the WOBP and renamed it the Act on the Placement of Foreign Children with a View to Adoption[29] (hereinafter WOBKA) which came into force in 1989. The WOBKA *inter alia* provides the requirements for prospective adoptive parents' principle approval to adopt internationally, lays down the prerequisites for the placement of a foreign child and regulates the accreditation and the activities of Dutch adoption agencies as well as the monitoring and control thereof. It has been modified several times and is further elaborated upon in a number of decrees and guidelines which are set out below:

- Decree on the Placement of Foreign Children with a View to Adoption[30] (hereinafter BOBKA) which regulates the requirements, activities, and financing of the Foundation Adoption Services as well as the organization and tasks of the accredited Dutch adoption agencies;
- Guidelines on the Placement of Foreign Children with a View to Adoption 2000[31] (hereinafter ROBKA) stipulating when and under what circumstances the Minister of Justice might deviate from the age requirements for granting principle approval to prospective adoptive parents;
- Decree on Complaints Commission Accredited International Adoption Placement Agencies,[32] determining the procedure concerning complaints by prospective adoptive parents against the actions and decisions of Dutch accredited adoption agencies;

27 R. A. C. Hoksbergen (1991). "Intercountry Adoption Coming of Age in The Netherlands: Basic Issues, Trends, and Developments." In H. Altstein and R. J. Simon (eds), "Intercountry Adoption: A Multinational Perspective." Praeger, New York, 141-158, p. 145.

28 *Wet van 14 mei 1998 inzake de uitvoering van het op 29 mei 1993 tot stand gekomen verdrag inzake de bescherming van kinderen en samenwerking op het gebied van interlandelijke adoptie en, in verband daarmee, wijziging van de Wet opneming buitenlandse pleegkinderen en enige andere wetten (Uitvoeringswet Verdrag inzake de bescherming van kinderen en de samenwerking op het gebied van de interlandelijke adoptie), Stb. 1998, 302, zoals laatstelijk gewijzigd op 13 juli 2016, Stb. 2016, 290.*

29 *Wet van 8 december 1988, houdende regelen inzake de opneming in Nederland van buitenlandse pleegkinderen met het oog op adoptie (Wet opneming buitenlandse kinderen ter adoptie), Stb. 1988, 566, zoals laatstelijk gewijzigd op 15 november 2014, Stb. 2014, 442.*

30 *Besluit van 4 juli 1989, houdende vaststelling van het Besluit opneming buitenlandse pleegkinderen en wijziging van het Uitvoeringsbesluit Kinderbescherming (Besluit opneming buitenlandse kinderen ter adoptie), Stb. 1989, 262, zoals laatstelijk gewijzigd op 25 october 2011, Stb. 2011, 480.*

31 *Richtlijnen van 10 november 2000 (Richtlijnen opneming buitenlandse kinderen ter adoptie), Stcrt. 2000, 234, zoals laatstelijk gewijzigd op 29 september 2010, Stb. 2010, 15596.*

32 *Besluit van 13 maart 2000, houdende regels ter uitvoering van artikel 24a van de Wet opneming buitenlandse kinderen ter adoptie alsmede inwerkingtreding van dat artikel (Besluit klachtencommissie vergunninghouders interlandelijke adoptie), Stb. 2000,120, zoals laatstelijk gewijzigd op 5 juli 2005, Stb. 2005, 435.*

- Decree on Research into Foreign Contacts of Prospective Adoptive Parents[33] and the Protocol on Research into Foreign Contacts and Partial Agency Intercountry Adoption Placement[34] which regulate the application for and the approval of a partial do-it-yourself adoption;
- Regulations on Foreign Cooperations of Intercountry Adoption Agencies,[35] laying down the information that Dutch agencies are required to provide in the accreditation procedure; and
- Regulation on an Agency's Application for an Intercountry Adoption Placement Approval,[36] which contains rules concerning the information that accredited adoption bodies are required to provide regarding their cooperation with institutions and organizations in the sending countries.

Unlike the regulations of the *Uitvoeringswet*, the provisions of the WOBKA and of the listed decrees and guidelines are applicable to both adoptions from Hague countries and non-Hague countries.

In 2008, representatives of the Dutch adoption agencies and the Dutch Minister of Justice agreed upon the Quality Framework (*Kwaliteitskader vergunningouders interlandelijke adoptie)* which was modified in 2013. The Framework lays down standards and guidelines concerning the agencies' personnel, the adoption placement procedure and the cooperation with the sending countries that the Dutch adoption agencies agree to comply with. It is not part of the Dutch legal framework, but it nevertheless serves as a guideline in monitoring and controlling the adoption agencies (see section 7.1).

3.1 *Stakeholders in the Dutch Adoption System*

The Netherlands has designated the Ministry of Justice and Security (*Ministerie van Justitie en Veiligheid*) as the Central Authority within the meaning of Article 6 of the Hague Convention.[37] Public authorities and accredited bodies within the meaning of Article 9 and 22(1) of the Hague Convention are:

33 *Besluit van 18 mei 1995, houdende vaststelling van maatstaven die bij het in artikel 7a, eerste lid, van de Wet opneming buitenlandse pleegkinderen bedoelde onderzoek dienen te worden gehanteerd (Besluit inzake het onderzoek naar buitenlandse contacten van aspirant-adoptiefouders), Stb. 1995, 275, zoals laatstelijk gewijzigd op 30 juni 1998, Stb. 1998, 388.*

34 *Protocol van 25 september 1995 inzake onderzoek naar buitenlandse contacten en deelbemiddeling bij interlandelijke adoptie, 25 september 1995/Nr. 516934/95/PJR.*

35 *Regeling van 17 augustus 1998 (Regeling gegevens buitenlandse betrekkingen vergunninghouder interlandelijke adoptie), Stcrt. 1998, 171.*

36 *Regeling van 17 augustus 1998 (Regeling aanvraag vergunning bemiddeling interlandelijke adoptie), Stcrt. 1998, 171.*

37 Art. 2(1) *Uitvoeringswet.*

- the Youth Care Inspectorate (*Inspectie Jeugdzorg*);[38]
- the Foundation Adoption Services (*Stichting Adoptievoorzieningen*);
- the Child Protection Council (*Raad voor de Kinderbescherming*); and
- accredited intercountry adoption agencies (*vergunninghouders*)

The Minister of Justice is responsible for approving Dutch adoption agencies to place international adoptions and for deciding on couples' or individuals' applications for principle approval to adopt a child from abroad. Furthermore, together with the Youth Care Inspectorate, it is in charge of controlling the adoption agency's activities. In the following paragraphs, the terms 'Dutch Central Authority' and 'Dutch Ministry of Justice and Security' will be used interchangeably.

The Foundation Adoption Services is responsible for counselling prospective adoptive parents on the placement and adoption of a foreign child, as it is envisaged according to Article 5 of the Hague Convention. It ensures that the prospective adoptive parents have been counselled and determines that the child is or will be authorized to enter and reside permanently in that state. In addition, the Foundation Adoption Services provides post-adoption services according to Article 9 of the treaty.

The Child Protection Council is an executive body of the Ministry of Justice and Security and is in charge of examining the adoption applicants' suitability and eligibility to adopt and for drawing up a home study report.

The accredited adoption agencies act as mediators between the adoption applicants and the competent authorities and organizations in the sending countries. Only they are admitted as international adoption placement offices in the Netherlands. Private bodies that have not been accredited and independent agents are prohibited from operating in the Dutch adoption system. The Netherlands does therefore not use the limited possibility of independent adoptions that is provided for in Article 22(2) of the Hague Convention.

3.2 *International Adoption Placement Procedure*

Couples and individuals that are permanently residing in the Netherlands and who wish to adopt a child from abroad have to request principle approval (*beginseltoestemming*) from the Minister of Justice.[39] They need to contact the Foundation Adoption Services, which then registers their official request on behalf of the Minister of Justice.[40] The Foundation is an institution that is appointed by the Minister of Justice, which is in charge of

38 In 2017, the *Inspectie Jeugdzorg (IJZ)* was merged with the *Inspectie voor de Gezondheidszorg (IGZ)* and is now called the *Inspectie Gezondheidszorg en Jeugd (IGJ)*.

39 Art 5 *Uitvoeringswet*; Art. 4 WOBKA.

40 Art. 5(2) WOBKA.

providing counselling (*algemene voorlichting*) to prospective adoptive parents who want to adopt a foreign child for the first time.[41] After the prospective adoptive parents have completed a number of obligatory information sessions, the Foundation Adoption Services forwards the applicant's data to the Child Protection Council.

The Child Protection Council is part of the Ministry of Justice and Security and has seven offices in the Netherlands which conduct assessments of the adoption applicants' eligibility and suitability to adopt (*gezinsonderzoek*).[42] For the purposes of this assessment, the prospective adoptive parents have to undergo psychological and medical examinations as well as criminal background checks, document their financial situation and complete home visits as well as a number of interviews with a social worker.[43] The Child Protection Council will suspend the assessment procedure if the family situation has changed, for instance, if the adopters become pregnant or undergo fertility treatments, or if they are getting divorced or one of them has died.

The Child Protection Council draws up a home study report that evaluates the applicants' suitability to adopt internationally, clarifies the characteristics of the children for which they would be qualified to care for and finally gives advice for granting the principle approval.[44] This report is then discussed with the adopters and then forwarded to the Minister of Justice.[45] Previously, a copy of the home study report was also sent out to the adoption applicants. This practice, however, is now prohibited as it has happened in the past that adopters pursued a private adoption, submitting a copy of this report as proof of their suitability to adopt (which was commonly accepted by the foreign authorities in the sending countries).[46]

On the basis of the report drawn up by the Child Protection Council, the Minister of Justice decides on granting the principle approval.[47] It will deny the principle approval: 1) if he or she thinks that a prospective adoptive parent is not eligible and suited to care for and raise a child from another country, 2) if one prospective adoptive parent has already reached the age of forty-two at the moment the request for the principle approval was submitted or 3) if it is to be expected that at the moment a foreign child could be placed, the difference in age between one of the parents and the child will be more than forty years.[48] In case one of the two parents does not comply with the age requirements, the

41 Art. 4 BOBKA.

42 Art. 5(1) WOBKA.

43 J. van den Braak et al. (2004). "Evaluatieonderzoek Wobka, Een evaluatieonderzoek naar de Wet opneming buitenlandse kinderen ter adoptie." WODC, Adviesbureau Van Montfoort, Woerden, p. 46.

44 Art. 5 (1) WOBKA.

45 Art. 5 (4) *leg. cit.*

46 J. de Heer (2016). "Wet opneming buitenlandse pleegkinderen ter adoptie. "In M. J. C. Koens and A. P. M. J. Vonken (eds) "Personen- en familierecht, Tekst & Commentaar." Wolters Kluwer, Deventer, 2697-2741, pp. 2708-2709.

47 Art. 5(1) WOBKA.

48 Art. 5(5) and (6) *leg. cit.*

Minister may find that special circumstances make it desirable to grant the principle approval anyway.[49] This may be the case if the prospective adoptive child is older than two years-old or has special needs or if the parents have already adopted from abroad and now consider adopting another (older) child or the adoptee's sibling.[50]

If none of the reasons for denial applies, the Minister of Justice issues its principle approval (he usually follows the advice of the Child Protection Council) for the placement of one child or of two or more foreign children if they are siblings or if they are in another way so attached to each other that it would be undesirable to separate them.[51] The principle approval is valid for four years and can be prolonged for another four years after the Child Protection Council has once again assessed the adoption applicants' eligibility and suitability to adopt a foreign child. Its validity expires when one of the prospective adoptive parents has reached the age of forty-six years, unless the Minister of Justice finds that special circumstances indicate otherwise.[52]

If the Minister of Justice decides to grant principle approval to the prospective adoptive parents, he places them on the central waiting list and then sends the home study report to a Dutch accredited adoption agency that is selected by the prospective adoptive parents.[53] The agency either carries out the adoption placement in cooperation with its partner organizations in the sending country (*volledige bemiddeling*), or – in case the adoption applicants want to pursue a do-it-yourself adoption (*deelbemiddeling)* according to Article 7a WOBKA – assesses the integrity and diligence of the private contact abroad (see section 4.1). An accredited agency is permitted to handle intercountry adoption placements only for prospective adoptive parents with principle approval.[54]

If the Dutch adoption agency carries out the adoption placement itself, it sends the home study report, together with other required application documents, to the Central Authority or another competent authority in the sending country which usually does the 'matching'. After the latter have accepted the adopters' application and found an adoptable child whose profile fits the profile of the adopters, it sets up a child proposal which is sent to the Dutch adoption agency.[55] The child proposal then has to be presented to the Dutch Ministry of Justice and Security together with substantiated written advice as to whether there are any objections against the envisaged placement. The Dutch Ministry then decides on whether to approve the adoption or whether to attach certain conditions thereto.[56]

49 Art. 5(6) WOBKA.
50 Art. 2 and 3 ROBKA.
51 Art. 3(2) WOBKA.
52 Art. 3(1) *leg. cit.*
53 Art. 5(4) *leg. cit.*
54 Art. 20(1) *leg. cit.*
55 Art. 16(2) Hague Convention; Art. 7(1) *Uitvoeringswet.*
56 Art. 7(2) and (3) *Uitvoeringswet.*

If the child proposal is approved by the Ministry of Justice and Security and accepted by the prospective adoptive parents, the Dutch agency has to notify the Central Authority, another competent authority or the approved contact in the sending country to intimate to them that the adoption may proceed.[57] The child may then be brought to the Netherlands – either with a Dutch passport or a visa (see section 3.5) – if the requirements laid down in Article 8 WOBKA are met, namely:

- the *child is not older than* 6 years at the time of arrival, unless the Minister of Justice has made an exemption due to special circumstances;[58] the Minister might make an exemption, for instance, if the prospective adoptive parents want to adopt two foreign children or an older sibling of the child they already adopted;[59]
- the prospective adoptive parents are required to produce a *medical report* about the child[60] that must be drawn up by an admitted physician in the sending country;[61]
- they have to clarify as to how they made use of an *accredited Dutch adoption* agency;[62] and
- they must produce documents satisfactorily showing that the *relinquishment* of the child by his or her biological parents has been *regulated properly*[63] and that the authorities in the sending countries agree with the envisaged placement of the child.[64]

3.3 *Judicial Adoption Procedure*

After the child has been matched with a Dutch couple or individual suited to adopt, a judgment on the intercountry adoption must be rendered by a competent court either in the child's country of origin or in the Netherlands.[65] If the judgment is rendered in the Netherlands, then Articles 1:227 to 1:232 of the Dutch Civil Code[66] (*Burgerlijk Wetboek*, hereinafter BW) are applicable (Article 10:105 BW[67]). According to these provisions, the following requirements need to be fulfilled:

57 Art. 8 *leg. cit.*

58 Art. 8(a). WOBKA.

59 Art. 4 ROBKA.

60 Art. 8(b) WOBKA.

61 J. de Heer (2016). "Wet opneming buitenlandse pleegkinderen ter adoptie. "In M. J. C. Koens and A. P. M. J. Vonken (eds) "Personen- en familierecht, Tekst & Commentaar." Wolters Kluwer, Deventer, 2697-2741, p. 2716.

62 Art. 8(c) WOBKA.

63 Art. 8(d) *leg. cit.*

64 Art. 8(e) WOBKA.

65 In fact, several sending countries allow the child's departure to the receiving country only after the child has been adopted according to their laws.

66 *Burgerlijk Wetboek Boek 1, inwerkingtreding 1 januari 1970, zoals laatstelijk gewijzigd met Stb. 2017, 245.*

67 *Burgerlijk Wetboek Boek 10, inwerkingtreding 1 januari 2012, Stb. 2011, 272, zoals laatstelijk gewijzigd met Stb. 2016, 290.*

- a joint request by one person[68] or by two persons that have lived together for at least three consecutive years immediately preceding the filing of the request;[69]
- the adoption is manifestly in the best interests of the child;[70]
- it has been ascertained that the child to be adopted, at the moment on which the request was filed and in the reasonably foreseeable future, may expect nothing of his parent or parents to the point of parenthood;[71]
- the adopter(s) is/are at least eighteen years older than the child;[72]
- neither of the biological parents raises objections to the request;[73]
- the adopter(s) of the child has/have cared for and raised that child for at least one year;[74] and
- the biological parents do not or no longer have legal responsibility for the child.[75]

The law of the state whose nationality the child has shall apply to the consent and counselling of the child's biological parents or other persons, institutions and authorities whose consent is necessary for the adoption.[76] However, if the law of the child's country of origin does not provide rules for an adoption, then only Dutch law is applicable.[77]

3.4 *Adoption Recognition and Conversion Procedure*

If the judicial decision about an intercountry adoption was rendered in the child's country of origin, then it needs to be recognized in the Netherlands. An adoption granted in a sending country that *is* a State Party to the Hague Convention is to be recognized *ex lege*, according to Articles 23 and 24 of the Hague Convention. Thus, if the adoption is certified by the foreign competent authority as having been made in accordance with the Convention, it has to be recognized automatically, without a Dutch judicial or administrative decision being required. Dutch courts and authorities must recognize "[a]n adoption certified by the competent authority of the State of the adoption as having been made in accordance with the Convention" (Article 23), unless "the adoption is manifestly contrary to its public policy, taking into account the best interests of the child" (Article 24).

68 Art. 1:227(1) BW.
69 Art. 1:227(2) *leg. cit.*
70 Art. 1:227(3) *leg. cit.*
71 *Leg. cit.*
72 Art. 1:228(c) *leg. cit.*
73 Art. 1:228(d) *leg. cit.*
74 Art. 1:228(1)(f) *leg. cit.*
75 Art. 1:228(g) *leg. cit.*
76 Art. 10:105(2) *leg. cit.*
77 Art. 10:105(3) *leg. cit.*

If an adoption decision was rendered in a sending country that is *not* a State Party to the Hague Convention, Section 10.6.3. of the Dutch Civil Code is applicable,[78] which regulates the recognition of foreign adoption judgments. According to Article 10:109 BW, a foreign adoption decision is to be recognized *ex lege* if a) the provisions of the WOBKA were complied with, b) the recognition obviously is in the best interests of the child and c) no ground of exclusion is applicable.[79] Whether the provisions of the WOBKA were complied with can be derived from the principle approval and the visa.[80] Whether or not the recognition is in the best interests of the child has to be assessed at the time of the Dutch recognition procedure and not at the time when the foreign adoption decision was rendered.[81] The grounds of exclusion are listed in Article 10:109(1)(c) and Article 10:108(2) and (3) BW as follows:

- it was obviously not preceded by a proper investigation or a proper administration of justice[82] (e.g. the consent by the biological parent(s) was not obtained properly);[83]
- it is not recognized in the State in which the child resided at the time on which an application for this adoption was lodged, as well as at the time of the adoption order;[84]
- recognition is manifestly contrary to Dutch public order;[85] (if the adoption took place with the involvement of a Dutch adoption agency and in accordance with the regulations of the WOBKA, a Dutch court generally assumes that recognition is not contrary to Dutch public order);[86]
- if the adoption obviously was a sham action,[87] for instance, because the legal institute of adoption was manifestly misused in order to gain a permanent Dutch visa or the Dutch nationality.[88]

The recognition of a foreign adoption decision includes the recognition of a) the parent-child relationship between the child and his or her adoptive parents, b) parental responsibility of the adoptive parents for the child and c) the termination of the pre-existing legal

78 Art. 10:107 *leg. cit.*
79 Art. 10:109(1) *leg. cit.*
80 L. Hertsig (2005). "Adoptie van buitenlandse kinderen door Nederlandse adoptiefouders." Familie- en Jeugdrecht, 9, p. 2.
81 *Gerechtshof Leeuwarden*, 02.12.2010, 200.069.042, ECLI:NL:GHLEE:2010:BP0604.
82 Art. 10:108(2)(a) BW.
83 M. J. C. Koens and A. P. M. J. Vonken (eds) (2016). "Personen- en familierecht, Tekst & Commentaar." Wolters Kluwer, Deventer, p. 2650.
84 Art. 10:108(2)(b) BW.
85 Art. 10:108(2)(c) *leg. cit.*
86 L. Hertsig (2005). "Adoptie van buitenlandse kinderen door Nederlandse adoptiefouders." Familie- en Jeugdrecht, 9, p. 6.
87 Art. 10:108(3) BW.
88 M. J. C. Koens and A. P. M. J. Vonken (eds) (2016). "Personen- en familierecht, Tekst & Commentaar." Wolters Kluwer, Deventer, p. 2650.

familial relationship between the child and his or her biological family, if the adoption has the effect in the state in which it took place (full adoption).[89]

However, if a foreign adoption does not have the effect of terminating the pre-existing legal parent-child relationship (simple adoption) in the State in which it took place (e.g. an adoption from Haiti), then it does not have this effect in the Netherlands either.[90] In this case, the adoptive parents might apply for a conversion to a full adoption according to Dutch law.[91] In case of an adoption from a country that is party to the Hague Convention, the accredited bodies must ensure that a request for an adoption conversion will be submitted to the courts in the Netherlands.[92]

Upon request, the Dutch court will convert a simple adoption into a full adoption a) if the law of the receiving State so permits, b) if this is manifestly in the child's best interests and c) if the biological parents have given the required consent for an adoption of this nature, after having been informed of the consequences of their consent.[93] Where this consent has not been obtained, or the biological parents are not willing to give this consent, a conversion of a simple adoption into a full adoption is not possible.

3.5 *The Child's Entry into the Netherlands*

If a full adoption was granted in the child's country of origin which was certified as having been made in accordance with the Hague Convention (Article 23(1)) or which has to be recognized according to Dutch law (see section 3.4), and at least one of the adoptive parents is a Dutch national, then the child will acquire the Dutch nationality *ex lege*.[94] He or she needs a Dutch passport,[95] which is applied for at the Dutch embassy in the sending country and then processed by the Dutch Ministry of Foreign Affairs in The Hague, in order to be permitted to enter the Netherlands (see section 7.2).

If an adoption decision is still to be rendered by a court in the Netherlands (for instance, after a particular period of foster care has expired) or if the adoption granted in the sending country was merely a simple adoption, the child might require a visa, namely a regular provisional residence permit (*afgifte machtiging tot voorlopig verblijf*), in order to be able

89 Art. 26(1) of the Hague Convention, Art. 10:110(1) BW.

90 Art. 10:110(2) BW.

91 Art. 1:229 BW, Art. 11(1) *Uitvoeringswet*, Art. 10:111 BW.

92 Art. 11(1) *Uitvoeringswet.*

93 Art. 10:111 BW in conjunction with Art. 11 of the *Uitvoeringswet* and Artt. 1:227(3) and 1:228(1)(d) BW.

94 Art. 5a *Rijkswet van 19 december 1984, houdende vaststelling van nieuwe, algemene bepalingen omtrent het Nederlanderschap ter vervanging van de Wet van 12 december 1892, Stb. 268 op het Nederlanderschap en het ingezetenschap, zoals laatstelijk gewijzigd op1 maart 2017, Stb. 2017, 52, 53.*

95 § 1 Artikel 9 *Rijkswet van 26 september 1991, houdende het stellen van regelen betreffende de verstrekking van reisdocumenten, Stb. 1991, 498, zoals laatstelijk gewijzigd op 17 mei 2017, Stb. 2017, 217.*

to enter the Netherlands.[96] A visa is not required if the child comes from a visa-free state, such as, for instance, an EU or EEA country, Brazil, Colombia, Argentina, Guatemala, South Korea or the United States.[97] The required visa will be processed by the Dutch Immigration and Naturalisation Service in The Hague (*Immigratie- en Naturalisatiedienst*, hereinafter IND) if the adopters were granted a valid principle approval by the Dutch Ministry of Justice and Security[98] and if the requirements laid down in the WOBKA are fulfilled[99] (see section 7.2).

4 Independent Adoptions

4.1 *Partial Do-It-Yourself Adoptions (deelbemiddelingen)*

In the Netherlands, couples and individuals are prohibited from pursuing a private adoption, meaning an adoption that takes place without the involvement of the Dutch authorities (see section 4.3). However, Dutch adoption law provides the possibility of partial do-it-yourself adoptions (*deelbemiddeling*). According to Article 7a WOBKA, couples and individuals who have been granted principle approval according to Article 2 WOBKA are allowed to adopt *via* a foreign private contact (an authority, institution or individual in the sending country which is not the cooperation partner of a Dutch adoption agency), if this has been approved by the Dutch Ministry of Justice and Security.

In the past, only a small fraction of all registered intercountry adoptions to the Netherlands were *deelbemiddelingen* (in 2004, there were 29 partial do-it-yourself adoptions and 1,276 agency adoptions ; in 2005 the ratio was 38:1,147; in 2006 it was 44:772 and in 2007 it was 48:735).[100] The majority of partial do-it-yourself adoptions involved a child from the United States (2004: 18; 2005: 32; 2006: 38, 2007: 39) and were mainly pursued by same-sex Dutch couples.[101] Since do-it-yourself adoptions are not compatible with the standards and principles of the Hague Convention, (see section 4.2), they are only allowed

96 Art. 3.6. *Besluit van 23 november 2000 tot uitvoering van de Vreemdelingenwet 2000 (Vreemdelingenbesluit 2000), Stb. 2000, 497, zoals laatstelijk gewijzigd op 9 April 2018, Stb. 2018, 107.*

97 See https://www.netherlandsandyou.nl/travel-and-residence/visas-for-the-netherlands/short-stay-schengen-visa (last accessed on 03.08.2018).

98 Paragraaf B7/3.6.2 *Besluit van de Staatsecretaris van Justitie en Veiligheid van 21 juni 2018, nummer WBV 2018/4, houdende wijziging van de Vreemdelingencirculaire 2000, Stcrt. 2018, 36067; Art. 2 WOBKA.*

99 Paragraaf B7/3.6.2 *Vreemdelingencirculaire 2000.*

100 Ministerie van Justitie en Veiligheid (2007). "Statistische gegevens betreffende de opneming in gezinnen in Nederland van buitenlandse adoptiekinderen in de jaren 2002-2006." Available at https://adoptie.nl/wp-content/uploads/2017/03/Statistieken.pdf.

101 *Ibid.*

from states that have not ratified the treaty.[102] Thus, since the United States became a party to the Hague Adoption Convention in 2008, *deelbemiddeling* from this country are no longer permitted.[103] As the number of sending countries ratifying the Hague Convention is increasing, the number of partial do-it-yourself adoptions is decreasing as a result. Whereas in 2008, a total of 61 cases of *deelbemiddeling* were recorded, there were only 25 in 2010 and 8 in 2012.[104] In 2013, 2014 and 2016 no partial do-it-yourself adoptions took place and in 2015, there was only one adoption of a child from Nigeria.[105]

Prospective adoptive parents choose to pursue a partial do-it-yourself adoption for a number of reasons. First, they can play a more active role in the matching process than in an agency adoption,[106] as they are better able to select a child that meets their interests and expectations. They have already established contact with an institution or individual abroad (e.g. during a vacation or on the internet)[107] and might even also have a specific child in mind that they wish to adopt. Second, adopters decide to pursue a *deelbemiddeling* if they want to adopt a child from a sending country in which no Dutch accredited agency has a cooperation partner (e.g. Bangladesh, India and Ethiopia).[108]

If prospective adoptive parents want to pursue a do-it-yourself adoption, the accredited Dutch agency, to which the adopters' home study report is sent, examines the integrity and diligence of their private contact.[109] In case the prospective parents already have a particular child in mind that they wish to adopt, the agency also evaluates whether the

102 J. de Heer (2016). "Wet opneming buitenlandse pleegkinderen ter adoptie. "In M. J. C. Koens and A. P. M. J. Vonken (eds) "Personen- en familierecht, Tekst & Commentaar." Wolters Kluwer, Deventer, 2697-2741, p. 2712; see also Verslag van een Algemeen Overleg, 11 juni 2009, Tweede Kamer 2008-2009, 31 265, Nr. 26.

103 However, A. Mens (2009). "Interlandelijke adoptie, Is deelbemiddeling in verdragslanden mogelijk?" Familie- en Jeugdrecht, 67, p. 5, argues that an international adoption which is pursued by a same-sex couple (which is permitted in The Netherlands since 2009) falls outside the scope of the Hague Convention (which does only acknowledge adoptions by couples of different sex) and can thus still be done according to Article 7a WOBKA, even if the sending country (e.g. the United States) is a State Party to the Hague Convention (pp. 6-7).

104 Ministerie van Justitie en Veiligheid (2013). "Adoptie, Trends en Analyse, Statistisch overzicht interlandelijke adoptie over de jaren 2008 tot en met 2012." Available at https://adoptie.nl/wp-content/uploads/2017/03/Adoptie_trends_en_analyse_2013.pdf.

105 Ministerie van Justitie en Veiligheid (2017). "Adoptie, Trends en Analyse, Statistisch overzicht interlandelijke adoptie over de jaren 2012 tot en met 2016." Available https://adoptie.nl/wp-content/uploads/2017/03/2012-2016-Trends-en-analyse-interlandelijke-adoptie.pdf.

106 J. van den Braak et al. (2004). "Evaluatieonderzoek Wobka, Een evaluatieonderzoek naar de Wet opneming buitenlandse kinderen ter adoptie." WODC, Adviesbureau Van Montfoort, Woerden, p. 92.

107 *Ibid.*, p. 110.

108 N. A. Kalsbeek et al. (2008). "Report on Intercountry Adoption - "All things of value are defenceless"." Committee on Lesbian Parenthood and Intercountry Adoption, available at http://poundpuplegacy.org/files/10866_Interlandelijke-Adoptie_tcm34-137684.pdf, p. 40.

109 Art 7a WOBKA.

envisioned placement complies with the requirements that are laid down in Dutch adoption law.[110] The agency assesses the following aspects:

- the *capacity* in which the foreign intermediary acts, its competencies, expertise as well as the manner in which it carries out its activities;[111]
- the *costs* that the institution or individual charges for its services, in order to determine whether they are reasonably high;[112]
- the *information about the child's* identity, origin and health status, the foreign state's regulations on the relinquishment or abandonment of a child and the manner in which he or she was considered for an intercountry adoption;[113]
- the measures which were taken to find an alternative care solution in the child's country of origin (*subsidiarity principle*) and whether the competent authorities in the country of origin have approved the adoption by the prospective adoptive parents;[114] and
- whether the *foreign intermediary* has complied with the sending state's legal provisions on the international adoption placement (e.g. the regulations in do-it-yourself-adoptions).[115]

The prospective adoptive parents are obliged to assist the adoption agency in assessing the foreign institution or individual that should carry out the adoption placement. To this end, they have to submit all documents which provide information about their intermediary's identity, contact details and capacity, as well as its placement activities and remuneration.[116] In addition, the prospective adoptive parents have to submit all correspondence that they have had with the private contact.[117] In case they already have a particular child in mind that they wish to adopt, they have to hand in the abandonment or relinquishment documents as well as the child's medical reports.[118] To verify the accuracy of the information provided by the parents, the accredited agency is required to conduct additional investigations insofar as this is necessary and possible.[119]

---

110 J. de Heer (2016). "Besluit in zake het onderzoek naar buitenlandse contacten van aspirant-adoptiefouders. "In M. J. C. Koens and A. P. M. J. Vonken (eds) "Personen- en familierecht, Tekst & Commentaar." Wolters Kluwer, Deventer, 2753-2756, p. 2754.

111 Art. 1(1)(a) and (b) Decree on Research into Foreign Contacts of Prospective Adoptive Parents.

112 Art. 1(1)(c) *leg. cit.*

113 Art. 1(1)(d) and (f) *leg. cit.*

114 Art. 1(1)(c) *leg. cit.*

115 Art. 1(1)(g) *leg. cit.*

116 *Protocol inzake onderzoek naar buitenlandse contacten en deelbemiddeling bij interlandelijke adoptie van 23 januari 2013.*

117 J. de Heer (2016). "Wet opneming buitenlandse pleegkinderen ter adoptie. "In M. J. C. Koens and A. P. M. J. Vonken (eds) "Personen- en familierecht, Tekst & Commentaar." Wolters Kluwer, Deventer, 2697-2741, p. 2713.

118 *Ibid.*

119 *Ibid.*

Following its assessment, the adoption agency will write an advice to the Minister of Justice,[120] which then has to decide whether or not to approve the partial do-it-yourself adoption. Where necessary, the Minister of Justice will request further information from the prospective adoptive parents, the Ministry of Foreign Affairs[121] or from an international organization with experience in the field of intercountry adoption (e.g. ISS, EurAdopt).[122] The Minister of Justice will refuse to approve the *deelbemiddeling* 1) if it is likely that the prospective adoptive parents will not comply with Article 8(d) and (e) WOBKA, 2) if it is likely that the parents' actions will cause harm to the relation between the accredited body and the institutions, authorities or individuals abroad or 3) when there are reasonable grounds to doubt the integrity and diligence of these foreign intermediaries.[123] Such a reasonable ground exists in any case when the prospective adoptive parents are required to pay costs that are unreasonably high in relation to the services rendered by their foreign intermediary.[124]

If the Minister of Justices approves the *deelbemiddeling*, he might impose specific conditions on the prospective adoptive parents or the adoption agencies, for instance, by requiring additional documents or further investigations.[125] In case the partial do-it-yourself adoption is approved, the adoption agency must make sure that the home study report, as well as the documents submitted by the prospective adoptive parents, are translated, legalized and sent to the approved intermediary abroad.[126] The adoption file thus has to be channelled through the accredited body and is not handed out to the prospective adoptive parents due to reasons that were already elaborated upon above.

4.2 *Risks and Limitations of Partial Do-It-Yourself Adoptions*

Partial do-it-yourself adoptions are not without risks and limitations. First, a thorough evaluation of a foreign contact is difficult. The Dutch adoption agencies are required to finish the assessment and draw up written advice for the Minister of Justice within 8 weeks after the prospective adoptive parents have reported their foreign contact to them.[127] The

120 Art. 7a(4) WOBKA.

121 J. van den Braak et al. (2004). "Evaluatieonderzoek Wobka, Een evaluatieonderzoek naar de Wet opneming buitenlandse kinderen ter adoptie." WODC, Adviesbureau Van Montfoort, Woerden, p. 86.

122 J. de Heer (2016). "Besluit in zake het onderzoek naar buitenlandse contacten van aspirant-adoptiefouders. "In M. J. C. Koens and A. P. M. J. Vonken (eds) "Personen- en familierecht, Tekst & Commentaar." Wolters Kluwer, Deventer, 2753-2756, p. 2755.

123 Art. 7a(3) WOBKA.

124 *Leg cit.*

125 J. de Heer (2016). "Wet opneming buitenlandse pleegkinderen ter adoptie. "In M. J. C. Koens and A. P. M. J. Vonken (eds) "Personen- en familierecht, Tekst & Commentaar." Wolters Kluwer, Deventer, 2697-2741, p. 2714.

126 *Ibid.*

127 Art. 7a(4) WOBKA.

limited amount of time available, as well as the lack of financial resources, make it difficult for the agencies to thoroughly examine the intercountry adoption laws and practices in the sending country as well as the integrity of the private contact. They must determine the intermediaries' integrity and diligence on the basis of the documents that have been submitted to them by the prospective adoptive parents. It would, however, be too expensive to send somebody to the sending country to evaluate the work of the intermediaries. They do also not establish a direct contact with them.[128] Since a lot of effort needs to be put into assessing the structure of the intercountry adoption system in the sending country and the private contact with only limited financial resources, many Dutch adoption agencies refuse to assess partial do-it-yourself adoptions in general or from countries whose adoption systems they are not familiar with[129] (e.g. *Stichting Meiling* and *Wereldkinderen*). Others evaluate private contacts only in exceptional cases (*Kind en Toekomst*).

Second, it cannot be ruled out that the prospective adoptive parents will contact the parents or another person who has the actual care of the child (e.g. the director of an orphanage or a child care institution) *before* the matching takes place. In fact, Dutch law even takes into consideration a situation whereby prospective adoptive parents have already selected a particular child before their foreign contract is assessed by a Dutch accredited agency and subsequently approved by the Minister of Justice. According to Article 1(1)(d) of the Decree on Research into Foreign Contacts of Prospective Adoptive Parents, the Dutch adoption agency must also review the information about the identity and origin of an already selected child and the manner in which he or she was considered for an intercountry adoption in the sending country in its assessment.

Third, Dutch authorities do not monitor the adoption placement process *after* the Minister of Justice has approved the *deelbemiddeling*. In particular, it is not controlled if the prospective adoptive parents pay additional costs (to the birth parents, the child care institution or an official authority) or engage in other irregular practices to facilitate the adoption process.[130] Moreover, in cases where the Minister has attached particular conditions to his approval, it is not assessed as to whether the adoptive parents have actually complied with these conditions. Unlike with agency adoptions from Hague countries, the Dutch authorities do not review and approve the proposed match between the adoptive parents and the child in a partial do-it-yourself adoption. Basically, adoptive parents who pursue a do-it-yourself adoption are obliged to submit all of the relevant adoption docu-

128 J. van den Braak et al. (2004). "Evaluatieonderzoek Wobka, Een evaluatieonderzoek naar de Wet opneming buitenlandse kinderen ter adoptie." WODC, Adviesbureau Van Montfoort, Woerden, pp. 93, 99.

129 Interview with J. Kouwenhoven, head of and a policy advisor at the Dutch Central Authority, and M. Kroon, official of the Youth Department at the Dutch Ministry of Justice and Security, The Netherlands, 13.07.2017.

130 J. van den Braak et al. (2004). "Evaluatieonderzoek Wobka, Een evaluatieonderzoek naar de Wet opneming buitenlandse kinderen ter adoptie." WODC, Adviesbureau Van Montfoort, Woerden, p. 95.

ments to the Dutch agency after they have come back to the Netherlands.[131] However, the agencies do not have the possibility to impose sanctions on the adoptive parents in case they fail to do so.[132]

As a result of these limitations, partial do-it-yourself adoptions are not compatible with the standards set out in the Hague Convention,[133] particularly the no contact rule that is found in Article 29,[134] Article 17(b) which requires the Central Authority of the receiving state to approve the matching proposal that is set up by the authorities in the sending country and Article 19(2) which obliges the Central Authorities of both countries to ensure that the transfer of the child from the sending to the receiving state takes place under secure and appropriate circumstances.[135] A partial do-it-yourself adoption is thus generally not allowed from a sending country which is a party to the Hague Convention.

In the Netherlands, therefore, different standards apply to do-it-yourself adoptions from non-Hague countries and adoptions from Hague countries. However, this weakness is more or less only a theoretical one. Since the number of non-Hague countries from which *deelbemiddelingen* are permitted is decreasing and given that most Dutch adoption agencies refuse to assess private contacts in sending countries that they are not familiar with, adopters no longer pursue do-it-yourself adoptions (or only in exceptional cases), as can be seen from the statistics.

---

131 *Protocol van 25 september 1995 inzake onderzoek naar buitenlandse contacten en deelbemiddeling bij interlandelijke adoptie.*

132 J. van den Braak et al. (2004). "Evaluatieonderzoek Wobka, Een evaluatieonderzoek naar de Wet opneming buitenlandse kinderen ter adoptie." WODC, Adviesbureau Van Montfoort, Woerden, p. 98.

133 A. Mens (2009). "Interlandelijke adoptie, Is deelbemiddeling in verdragslanden mogelijk?" Familie- en Jeugdrecht, 67, p. 5; Different view: I. Curry-Sumner and M. Vonk (2008). "Ontwikkelingen op het gebied van internationale adoptie." Familie- en Jeugdrecht, 108, pp. 2-5 who argue that Art. 22(2) of the Hague Convention allows its Contracting States to permit independent non-accredited agents or agencies to handle intercountry adoption placement if they have been approved (e.g. Colombia and the United States have used this limited possibility of independent adoptions).

134 It is worth noting that Art. 29 of the Hague Convention generally permits the Contracting States to allow contact between the prospective adoptive parents and the birth parents or the person actually caring for the child and some, e.g. United States, have done so. However, under the treaty, the prospective adoptive parents are not allowed to directly arrange the adoption with the birth parents, thus, to be involved in the matching process (see Chapter IV, section 5.1.3).

135 A. Mens (2009). "Interlandelijke adoptie, Is deelbemiddeling in verdragslanden mogelijk?" Familie- en Jeugdrecht, 67, p. 5, arguing that an international adoption which is pursued by a same-sex couple (which is permitted in The Netherlands since 2009) falls outside the scope of the Hague Convention (which does only acknowledge adoptions by couples of different sex) and can thus be done according to Article 7a WOBKA, even if the sending country (e.g. the United States) is a State Party to the Hague Convention (pp. 6-7).

4.3 *Private (Illegal) Adoptions – Prohibited but Not Properly Sanctioned*

In the Netherlands, couples and individuals are only permitted to adopt internationally if they have been granted principle approval by the Dutch Minister of Justice and Security (Article 2 WOBKA) and if an accredited Dutch adoption agency is involved in the adoption procedure. The latter either carries out the adoption placement in cooperation with one of its cooperation partners in the sending countries (*volledige bemiddeling*) or assesses the integrity of the foreign private contact in a do-it-yourself-adoption (*deelbemiddeling*). A principle approval from the Dutch Ministry of Justice and Security is also required if the child has been adopted in the sending country and is subsequently being brought to the Netherlands by the adopters.[136]

As was explained in the previous Chapter, private adoptions are arguably more susceptible to illegal and irregular practices than agency adoptions.[137] The adoption placement procedure is not supervised and controlled by the adoption placement office and the authorities in the receiving countries and the adopters are often not sensitized to the risks that are involved in an intercountry adoption procedure.[138] In the following sections, the term 'private' or 'illegal adoption' does not only refer to an official adoption that is granted by a court in the sending country and that was pursued without the adopters having received the necessary principle approval. It also refers to a *de facto* adoption where a couple or individual bring someone else's child to the Netherlands for an indefinite period of time for the purpose of care, without having pursued a legal adoption procedure in the child's country of origin.[139]

Intercountry adoptions are pursued privately for a variety of reasons. Some people are unaware of the fact that if they adopt internationally the WOBKA regulations need to be complied with. This is particularly the case in intercountry step-parent or kinship adoptions or in cases where couples or individuals adopt from their own country of origin. However, others maliciously circumvent the adoption placement procedure as they find it too lengthy and cumbersome or because they do not actually fulfil the requirements laid down in the WOBKA (e.g. the age limits).[140]

There is no way to accurately estimate the number of private adoptions that have taken place in the Netherlands.[141] Published case law shows that Dutch courts have to regularly deal with intercountry adoptions that were pursued in circumvention of the official procedure, and there is much to suggest that these cases are only the tip of the iceberg. Some

136 See, for instance, *Rechtbank Rotterdam, 20.03.2012, 10/700429-11, ECLI:NL:RBROT:2012:BV9978.*
137 See Chapter V, section 4.1.
138 *Ibid.*
139 See Chapter I, section 4.
140 See Chapter V, section 4.2.
141 K. Boele-Woelki, et al. (2011). "Draagmoederschap en illegale opneming van kinderen." WODC, Ministerie van Veiligheid & Justitie, p. 88.

private adopters bring the child to the Netherlands as their biological child after having the child's birth certificate falsified or fabricated. For obvious reasons, these cases would not appear in the official adoption statistics and may only be detected if there is reasonable suspicion to start an investigation into the child's actual origin.[142]

In the Netherlands, private adoptions are explicitly prohibited by law and constitute a misdemeanour (*overtreding*). According to Article 28 WOBKA, adopters who pursue an intercountry adoption without valid principle approval from the Dutch Ministry of Justice and Security according to Article 2 WOBKA, and hence without the involvement of an accredited Dutch adoption agency, are punishable by a fine of up to €8,200. In addition, the court might oblige the prospective adoptive parents to pay those financial benefits that they derived from having circumvented the official adoption placement procedure as per the WOBKA.[143]

Pursuant to Article 10 WOBKA, the family court may entrust the Dutch Youth Welfare Office with interim guardianship (*voorlopige voogdij*) of the child. The interim guardianship of the Dutch Welfare Office ends when the child is placed with an adoptive family that has been granted principle approval (this can be the original or new parents) or after he or she has been sent back to the country of origin.[144] However, this measure may only be ordered if it is commensurate with the child's best interests. It is therefore not *ipso eo* excluded that the child remains with the family that adopted illegally. In 2000, the Dutch Supreme Court ruled that a child may stay with adopters, even though they had maliciously violated the regulations contained in the WOBKA.[145] In this particular case, a Dutch couple travelled to the Philippines where they sourced a child (Fréderique) with the help of a private contact. After they had the child's birth certificate issued with their names as the biological parents, they brought the child to the Netherlands. The illegal activities were uncovered after someone made an anonymous disclosure to the Dutch police. The court in Eindhoven left the child with the adopters, stipulating that it would not be in her best interests to be placed with another family. The decision was confirmed by the court in the second instance and finally also by the Dutch Supreme Court. The latter ruled that it is at the discretion of the court to decide on a particular measure laid down in Article 10 WOBKA and that, when so doing, it must take the child's best interests into consideration.[146] This means that the court cannot place the child into another family (which has principle approval) if there is a real risk that he or she will be exposed to physical or psychological harm.

142 See Chapter II, section 4.2.2.

143 J. de Heer (2016). "Wet opneming buitenlandse pleegkinderen ter adoptie. "In M. J. C. Koens and A. P. M. J. Vonken (eds) "Personen- en familierecht, Tekst & Commentaar." Wolters Kluwer, Deventer, 2697-2741, p. 2740.

144 Art. 10(2) WOBKA.

145 *Hoge Raad, 01.12.2000, HR2000AA8715, ECLI:NL:PHR:2000:AA8715.*

146 *Ibid.*, para. 2.1.4.

In most private adoption cases, the Dutch court will leave the child with the couple that illegally brought the child to the Netherlands and will either grant them guardianship (Articles 1:241(1) and 1:295 BW) or adoption (Articles 1:227 and 228 BW). In their considerations, the best interests of the child, as well as the right to family life according to Article 8 ECHR, play an important role. As was explained in Chapter V, the child's and the adopters' right to family life laid down in Article 8 ECHR may be violated if a request for adoption or guardianship is rejected by the court.[147] A child may be removed from the caretakers with whom he or she already has close *de facto* ties, only if this is necessary to protect the child's best interests.[148]

In a spectacular case involving a surrogate baby (Donna) from Belgium, the *Rechtbank Utrecht* decided to leave the child with the Dutch couple that illegally brought her to the Netherlands, arguing that a *de facto* bond existed, which amounted to family life according to Article 8 ECHR.[149] The Dutch couple bought the child online and then brought her to the Netherlands for the purpose of care, without receiving the necessary principle approval according to Article 2 WOBKA. The child's biological mother acted as a surrogate for a Belgian couple and offered the child on the internet after she had an argument with the intended parents. The court in Utrecht ruled that the child should stay with the Dutch couple, ruling that a family life bond had emerged between them and the baby, for whom they had continuously cared since her birth.[150] Several months later, the court in Utrecht finally granted the Dutch couple guardianship of the child.[151]

In 2008, the *Rechtbank Zwolle-Lelystad* decided on another case concerning an illegal adoption from Belgium.[152] A Dutch couple brought a child (Jayden), who was offered on the internet by her mother, to the Netherlands illegally. Contrary to the case of baby Donna, baby Jayden's documents were forged so as to hide her actual origin. After she was born, her mother filled out the child's birth certificate with the name of the Dutch woman. The latter then registered the child as her own child at the local municipality in the Netherlands. The Dutch couple requested interim guardianship of the child after their illegal practices were uncovered. Stressing the decision of the Dutch Supreme Court from 2000, they argued that placing the child within another family would be contrary to her best interests. However, the *Rechtbank Zwolle-Lelystad* rejected the Dutch couple's request. It argued that the manner in which the couple had adopted the child would threaten her development and that it would not be contrary to the child's best interests for her to be placed into another family as she was only 5 months old (thus younger than the Filipino child in the Supreme

147 See, for instance, *Gerechtshof Amsterdam, 16.03.2000, 439/99, ECLI:NL:GHAMS:2000:AA5155, which referred to the European Commission of Human Rights in Akin vs. The Netherlands, 01.07.1998, No. 34986/97.*

148 Chapter V, section 4.3.

149 *Rechtbank Utecht, 26.10.2005, 197521/FA RK 05-3560, ECLI:NL:RBUTR:2005:AU4934.*

150 *Ibid.*

151 P. Dorhout (2008). „Baby Donna, waar ging het mis?" Tijdschrift voor Familie- een Jeugdrecht, 70.

152 *Rechtbank Zwolle-Lelystad, 27.11.2008, 151779 / JZ RK 08-908, ECLI:NL:RBZLY:2008:BG5827.*

Court ruling) and because she had not yet bonded with the Dutch couple. Finally, baby Jayden was sent back to Belgium where she was placed in an approved foster family.

Dutch family courts may even grant adoption – and not only interim guardianship – to couples who have adopted illegally. For instance, in 2005, the *Gerechtshof Amsterdam* had to decide on a case whereby a Dutch couple adopted a child in Russia and then brought him to the Netherlands without having received principle approval and a valid visa.[153] The boy was not granted a visa, as the requirements of the WOBKA were not met (see section 7.2). The couple, therefore, requested an adoption which was granted in the second instance. The *Gerechtshof Amsterdam* held that neither the principle approval according to Article 2 WOBKA nor a visa is a requirement for an adoption according to Articles 1:227 and 1:228 BW (see section 3.3). It furthermore stated that it was in the best interests of the child to remain within a setting that was already familiar to him, whereas sending him back to Russia would pose a severe threat to his development.

One year later, the *Rechtbank Zwolle-Lelystad* advanced a different rationale, but nevertheless came to the same conclusion.[154] In this case, a Dutch couple brought a child that they had adopted in Russia to the Netherlands without having received principle approval and a valid visa. Since the Dutch immigration court refused to grant a visa to the boy, the couple decided to adopt him. Contrary to the *Gerechtshof Amsterdam* in the previous year, the *Rechtbank Zwolle-Lelystad* argued that in order for an adoption to be validly concluded, not only do the requirements laid down in Articles 1:227 and 1:228 BW have to be fulfilled, but the provisions of the WOBKA must also be complied with. However, it nevertheless granted the adoption, arguing that the child had already bonded with the Dutch couple and that – considering his health status and emotional development – it would not be in his best interests to be separated from his new caretakers and sent back to Russia.

Both the decision of the *Gerechtshof Amsterdam* and the *Rechtbank Zwolle-Lelystad* illustrate how civil law and immigration law can clash in cases of illegal intercountry adoptions.[155] Such a clash is also apparent in the decision from the *Rechtbank Utrecht* in 2002, whereby the court granted an adoption to a woman that had illegally brought a 12 year-old child from Suriname to the Netherlands for the purpose of care.[156] The court in Paramaribo ended the parental rights of the child's biological mother and granted guardianship to the Dutch woman, who then brought the child to the Netherlands without principle approval and without a visa. The Dutch immigration court refused to legalize the child's residency in the Netherlands, arguing that the requirements of the WOBKA were not met. The woman, therefore, requested an adoption to be granted. The *Rechtbank*

153 *Gerechtshof Amsterdam, 05.04.2004, 1288/2003, ECLI:NL:GHAMS:2004:AP0522.*

154 *Rechtbank Zwolle-Lelystad, 12.01.2006, 107814/FARK05-1186, ECLI:NL:RBZLY:2006:AV4706.*

155 T.E.G. Seedorf (2006). "Interlandelijke adoptie; jurisprudentie houvast voor aspirant-adoptiefouders zonder beginseltoestemming?" Tijdschrift voor Familie- en Jeugdrecht, 17.

156 *Rechtbank Utrecht, 24.07.2002, 137028/FARK01-5441, ECLI:NL:RBUTR:2002:AN9168.*

Utrecht stressed that due regard had to be paid to the desirability of continuity in a child's upbringing, especially if he or she cannot grow up within their own families (Article 20 UNCRC). It then relied on Article 12 of the 1980 Convention on the Civil Aspects of International Child Abduction to answer the question as to whether sending the child would be possible in the context of continuity. According to this provision, the authority shall only order the return of a child that has been illegally removed from his or her parents, if less than one year has elapsed from the date of the removal. The *Rechtbank Utrecht* argued that the child had stayed with the Dutch woman for more than 2.5 years and that she was therefore already rooted in the Netherlands. Sending the child back to Suriname would thus be contrary to the child's best interests. Hence, it granted the adoption by arguing that the child's best interests had priority over Dutch immigration law.

An adoption is usually not granted if the adopters have maliciously bypassed the official adoption procedure, for instance, by means of deception. In 2001, the *Rechtbank Rotterdam* had to decide on an illegal domestic adoption from Brazil.[157] A Dutch woman adopted a child in Brazil without having received principle approval. She applied for such approval, but then stopped the procedure after she learned that no Dutch agency was cooperating with Brazil and that a partial do-it-yourself adoption was not possible since Brazil was a Hague country. The Brazilian judge granted a domestic adoption based on the assumption that the woman had her permanent residence in Brazil and that the boy would remain with her in his country of origin. She then brought the child to the Netherlands, where she sought to register him by presenting his birth certificate that showed her as the biological mother. After the Dutch civil registrar became suspicious, she laid open the fact that she had actually adopted the child. She requested the *Rechtbank Rotterdam* to recognize the Brazilian adoption decision or, alternatively, to grant the adoption in accordance with Dutch law. However, the court rejected both her requests. It argued that the Brazilian adoption decision was obviously not preceded by a proper investigation and administration of justice, given the fact that the court in Brazil was deceived about the actual nature of the adoption and that recognition would be contrary to public order. Furthermore, it held that the recognition of the foreign decision could not take place as the requirements of the WOBKA were not complied with, because the woman did not have the necessary principle approval. The *Rechtbank Rotterdam* also refused to grant the adoption in accordance with Dutch law due to the woman's lack of good faith. Yet, it granted the woman guardianship, reasoning that it would not be in the child's best interests to be separated from the woman and her husband who, the court held, had the required pedagogic insight and empathy to care for the child.[158]

---

157 *Rechtbank Rotterdam, 26.09.2011, 371367/F2RK11-133 en 370919/F2RK11-104, ECLI:NL:RBROT:2011: BT8220.*

158 *Ibid.*

In another illegal adoption case, the court decided to split guardianship between the adopters and a certified Dutch institution (*gecertificeerde instelling*).[159] In this case, a German couple adopted a 6-year old boy in Ghana and then brought him to the Netherlands without principle approval and without a visa. The *Rechtbank 's-Gravenhage* held that the adoption in Ghana (a non-Hague country) was not valid, according to Dutch law, and that the couple was therefore not to be considered as the legal guardians of the boy in the Netherlands. The Dutch court then, however, granted the German couple guardianship of the boy. It held that family life had emerged between them and that it was in the child's best interests to stay with his new caregivers.[160] This decision was overturned by the court in the second instance, and whereby the court split the guardianship between the couple and the Youth Welfare Office, reasoning that there were not only many ambiguities concerning the actual origin of the child but that the couple had also lost sight over the problems the child might face in the future.[161] This decision was confirmed by the Dutch Supreme Court.[162] The latter argued that the couple was not willing or able to reflect upon their actions regarding the illegal adoption of the child. They were not open about the boy's actual origin (it was unclear whether his parents were still alive) and the circumstances under which they had brought him to the Netherlands. Thus, the court had severe doubts as to whether they would explain, at some point in the future, the boy's future to him in a desired manner and therefore it considered that it would be in the best interests of the child to involve a certified institution in raising him.

In another illegal adoption case, the court found that leaving the child within the family was not in the child's best interests and therefore the court refused to grant guardianship to the adopters.[163] In this case, a Dutch couple had brought two Polish girls (from two different biological mothers) to the Netherlands without principle approval. The man claimed to be the children's biological father (which was confirmed by both biological mothers). He acknowledged paternity of one girl, whereas his wife adopted the other girl in Poland. In the Netherlands, the children were placed with a foster family and the couple's request for guardianship was rejected. The *Rechtbank 's-Gravenhage*[164] held that the paternity acknowledgement was not valid according to Dutch law, as the man was married to a woman other than the biological mother at the time of the acknowledgement (Article 1:204(1)(e) BW).[165] It furthermore refused to recognize the Polish adoption decision,

---

159 *Rechtbank 's-Gravenhage, 08.06.2011, 376129-FARK10-7586, ECLI:NL:RBSGR:2011:BQ8583.*

160 *Ibid.*

161 *Gerechtshof 's-Gravenhage, 21.03.2012, 200.093.249-01, ECLI:NL:GHSGR:2012:BX0126.*

162 *Hoge Raad, 19.04.2013, 12/02994, ECLI:NL:HR:2013:BZ7948.*

163 *Rechtbank 's-Gravenhage, 11.03.2010, 334600 / 09-2668, ECLI:NL:RBSGR:2010:BM2880; Gerechtshof 's-Gravenhage, 13.04.2011, 200.068.764-01, ECLI:NL:GHSGR:2011:BQ2937.*

164 *Rechtbank 's-Gravenhage, 11.03.2010, 334600/09-2668, -ECLI:NL:RBSGR:2010:BM2880.*

165 Pursuant to Art. 10(2)(a) Conflictenrecht Afstamming (Wca), the recognition of the paternity acknowledgement was to be refused as it was not valid according to Dutch law (Art. 1:204(1)(e) BW). The objective of

claiming that the requirements laid down in the WOBKA were not fulfilled. The court nevertheless established that family life had emerged between the children and the couple, whom together cared for the children as if they were their biological parents, reasoning that it was not only the legal, but rather the factual situation, that was decisive for the question as to whether or not family life had emerged. However, it held that an interference with their right to family life was necessary in the best interests of the child. The court argued that the couple had maliciously bypassed the official adoption procedure and they were not willing to help clarify the actual origin of the children (the father refused to take a DNA test which ought to have verified whether he really was the girls' biological father). Furthermore, the children had already bonded with the new foster family that they were placed into, and removing them would be traumatizing for them and hence not in their best interests. This decision was confirmed by the court in the second instance, which ruled that the best interests of the two children outweighed the couples' right to family life as laid down in Article 8 ECHR.[166]

In the Netherlands, pursuing a private adoption is explicitly prohibited by law. Article 10 WOBKA basically leaves it to the discretion of the judge to place an illegally adopted child under the interim guardianship of a certified Dutch institution or with adoptive parents that have been granted principle approval. However, in most cases, the courts decide to leave the child with the private adopters, even if they have maliciously bypassed the legal adoption procedure as per the WOBKA, for instance, by forging birth certificates or deceiving the court in the sending country about the international nature of the adoption. The best interests of the individual child, as well as the right to family life in Article 8 ECHR, often make it impossible to remove the child from the couple or individual that has adopted privately but generally seem to be suited to care for the child. Depending on the nature of the adopters' illegal actions and their willingness to clarify them, the court either grants them adoption according to Dutch law, full guardianship or guardianship that is split with a Dutch child welfare institution. A valid principle approval is not a requirement for either of them.[167] Only the recognition of a foreign adoption decision is excluded, as this would require compliance with the provisions of the WOBKA.

In only two published cases has the Dutch court decided to remove the child from the couple that has illegally adopted. In one case (involving baby Jayden), the court held that the manner in which the couple had adopted the child would threaten her development and that it would not be contrary to the child's best interests for it to be placed into another family as she was only 5 months old at the time of the decision. In another case (involving

Art.10 Wca is to prevent the circumvention of the official adoption procedure by acknowledging paternity of a child.

166 *Gerechtshof 's-Gravenhage, 13.04.2011, 200.068.764/01, ECLI:NL:GHSGR:2011:BQ2937.*

167 S. W. E Rutten, and K. J. Saarloos (2007). "De erkenning van de kafala in het IPR en het vreemdelingenrecht." Tijdschrift voor Familie- en Jeugdrecht, 125, p. 4.

two babies from Poland), the court found that family life already existed, but it held that removing the children was justified as being in their best interests as the adopters were unwilling to clarify their illegal actions and the children's true origin.

For the court, the individual interests of the child involved in an illegal adoption are decisive factors when deciding on a measure laid down in Article 10 WOBKA. The decision to leave a privately adopted child within the family may be in the best interests of the particular child and thus the right decision on a micro level. However, such a decision is harmful to the best interests of the child on a macro level. The tendency of the Dutch courts to allow adopters to keep a child that they illegally brought to the Netherlands by referring to the best interests of the individual child undermines the strict international adoption procedure that is laid down in the WOBKA, which seeks to protect not only the best interests of individual children but also the best interests of children in general. It invites adopters to circumvent the official legal procedure and to pursue (if necessary with the means of deception) a more rapid and less bureaucratic independent adoption. In a sense then, the courts' focus on the individual interests of a particular child that has been involved in an illegal adoption lowers the protection of the best interests of the children in general. As Rutten and Saarloos note:

> It seems that judges in the Netherlands [...] give priority to the interests of the child *in concreto* over the abstract but not less fundamental interests of the child that the international adoption process aims to protect.[168]

Illegally adopting a child is a misdemeanour and punishable by a fine of up to €8,200, according to Article 28 WOBKA. However, the statute of limitation for prosecuting this misdemeanour is only three years, which may be the reason why there is only a small number of published cases were adopters were successfully prosecuted and convicted of having violated the regulations contained in the Dutch adoption law.[169] Yet, even if they are convicted, the fines are usually considerably low. For instance, in the case involving baby Jayden from Belgium, the adopters were fined €1,000 for having bypassed the official adoption procedure.[170] The Dutch woman who brought the boy from Brazil to the Netherlands without principle approval received a fine of only €2,400.[171]

168 S. W. E. Rutten and K. J. Saarloos (2007). "De erkenning van de kafala in het IPR en het vreemdelingenrecht." Tijdschrift voor Familie- en Jeugdrecht, 125, p. 4.

169 L. Bosch (2016). "Promising Practice: Legal Paths to Justice in the Netherlands." In International Social Service (2016). "Responding to Illegal Adoptions: A Professional Handbook." Available at https://fiom.nl/sites/default/files/responding-to-illegal-adoptions-a-professional-handbook-iss-april-2016.pdf, 40-44, p. 42.

170 *Gerechtshof Zwolle-Lelystad, 07.400176-09, ECLI:NL:RBZLY:2011:BR1615.*

171 *Rechtbank Rotterdam, 20.03 2012, 10/700428-11, ECLI:NL:RBROT:2012:BV9975.*

As will be explained in section 8.1, illegal adopters may be held liable for criminal offences such as forgery of documents or even smuggling of human beings. However, if adopters are convicted at all, they are usually sentenced to community work or imprisonment on probation. Only in one published case were the illegal adopters sentenced to 90 days in prison. Whether such mild sentences have any deterrent effect is questionable. As we will see in Chapter VII, the adopters' desire for a child of their own is too strong and they are probably willing to accept such mild sentences. As long as they get to keep the child, they may not be discouraged by a sentence on probation and even less so by fines. Given the large sum of money that adopters are willing to pay for a child to love, a fine of €1,000, €2,400 or even €8,200 is but another expense that they are ready to accept.

What may be deterring for couples and individuals considering a private adoption, however, are possible future legal actions by their illegally adopted children. For instance, in a recent case, a 37 year-old adoptee from Brazil sued his adoptive parents for damages.[172] They had adopted him with the help of a private contact in Brazil when he was only a couple of days old. They provided money to the birth mother (approximately €72 which back then amounted to an employee's monthly salary) as well as a 'donation' (about €290) to the child care institution that had cared for him after his birth. After they had his birth certificate issued with their names as his biological parents, they illegally brought him to the Netherlands. The adoptee grew up knowing that he was adopted. When he was 21 years-old, he started searching for his biological parents. It was only then that his adoptive parents told him that they had passed him off as their biological son in order to circumvent the official adoption procedure. Sixteen years later, he sued his adoptive parents for having adopted him without principle approval and for having indicated to be his biological parents. The *Rechtbank Den Haag* rejected the claim as it was already time-barred. However, in its assessment it basically acknowledged the harm suffered by somebody that has been adopted illegally:

> It is of great importance that a child is correctly informed about his origin from an early age on. Adopting illegally and knowingly providing [the plaintiff] until adulthood misrepresenting facts about it by the legal parents is to be considered as an unlawful act against [the plaintiff] which has caused him harm. Due to the behaviour of the legal parents, there are, other than this would (most likely) have been the case in a legal adoption, no correct birth dates available for [the plaintiff]. That such a situation of lacking knowledge can have a major impact, also in adulthood, is now well known. The fact that the legal parents told [the plaintiff] already at an early stage that he was not their biological child and the

172 *Rechtbank Den Haag, 05.07.2017, C/09/515621 / HA ZA 16-893, ECLI:NL:RBDHA:2017:6711.*

> circumstances that the legal parents strove to provide [the plaintiff] a carefree youth does not matter.[173]

The court's argumentation is interesting, as it acknowledges the harmful consequences that an illegal adoption might have on the adoptee. In particular, the court does not accept the fact that the adopters had put a lot of effort into providing the adoptee with a carefree childhood, or generally a better life, as an excuse. Perhaps the court would have granted the adoptee damages, had he filed his complaint in good time.

5 Dutch Adoption Agencies

5.1 Accreditation and Authorization Requirements

In the Netherlands, private agencies are only permitted to place international adoptions if they have been accredited by the Ministry of Justice and Security.[174] Conducting placement activities without being accredited is punishable pursuant to Articles 27 and 28 WOBKA. An accreditation is granted upon the request of a legal person located in the Netherlands[175] who meets the requirements contained in Article 16 WOBKA.

First, it must have the objective to carry out international adoption placements only in those situations where this is in the *best interests of the involved children.*[176] This means that an intercountry adoption must only be considered if no alternative care solution can be found in the child's country of origin. The same basically applies to partial do-it-yourself adoptions.[177]

Second, the agency must *not pursue profit objectives*. It must not have the intention to profit from the placement activities.[178] This does not mean that cost-covering incomes or proportionate financial contributions from prospective adoptive parents are excluded. However, deriving improper financial or other gain or charging fees that are unreasonably high is prohibited.

Third, the *adoption agency' board*, which is responsible for monitoring the activities of the agency personnel and its foreign contacts, must consist of at least three members and it must be composed in such a way that both the best interests of the children, as well

173 *Ibid.*, para. 4.5.

174 Art. 15 WOBKA.

175 Art. 16(1) *leg. cit.*

176 Art. 16(2) *leg. cit.*

177 J. de Heer (2016). "Wet opneming buitenlandse pleegkinderen ter adoptie. "In M. J. C. Koens and A. P. M. J. Vonken (eds) "Personen- en familierecht, Tekst & Commentaar." Wolters Kluwer, Deventer, 2697-2741, p. 2725.

178 Art. 16(3) WOBKA.

as the needs and wishes of the adopters, can be taken into professional consideration.[179] Hence, the board should be composed of personnel from different backgrounds in, for instance, law, social sciences and accounting.[180] The agency personnel do not have to meet specific requirements. If volunteers are working for the agency, the agency is responsible for their activities,[181] meaning that the monitoring by the Minister of Justice as well as the Youth Inspectorate also covers their activities.[182]

Fourth, the adoption agency must be equipped in such a way that a *careful and effective fulfilment of its tasks and responsibilities* (as is laid down in Articles 17a to 17g WOBKA) can be guaranteed.[183] It needs to have adequate office premises which can ensure confidential conversations about intercountry adoptions, as well as safe archival storage for all adoption case files.[184]

Fifth, it must be prepared to *cooperate with other accredited bodies*, in particular with regard to informing the prospective adoptive parents,[185] but also with regard to post-adoption services.[186]

In addition to the requirements laid down in the WOBKA, the adoption agencies also have to fulfil the standards provided in the Quality Framework. Until 2008, agency personnel were not required to meet any *professional competencies.*[187] This was amended by the Quality Framework that the Dutch adoption agencies agreed upon in 2008 and which was modified in 2013. The Quality Framework raised the level of professionalism by requiring agency personnel to have knowledge in the field of finance and administration (in order to be able to read and understand the information about their foreign partners), social-pedagogy, psychology and medicine, as well as social expertise to be able to work with prospective adoptive parents.[188] Furthermore, it requires the agency personnel to be familiar with the relevant international regulations and adoption laws (of both the

179 Art. 16(4) *leg. cit.*

180 *Kamerstukken II, 20 046, nr. 3*, p. 20; J. de Heer (2016). "Wet opneming buitenlandse pleegkinderen ter adoptie. "In M. J. C. Koens and A. P. M. J. Vonken (eds) "Personen- en familierecht, Tekst & Commentaar." Wolters Kluwer, Deventer, 2697-2741, p. 2725.

181 Art. 14 BOBKA.

182 J. de Heer (2016). "Besluit opneming buitenlandse kinderen ter adoptie. "In M. J. C. Koens and A. P. M. J. Vonken (eds) "Personen- en familierecht, Tekst & Commentaar." Wolters Kluwer, Deventer, 2743-2752, p. 2751.

183 Art. 16(5) BOBKA.

184 J. de Heer (2016). "Besluit opneming buitenlandse kinderen ter adoptie. "In M. J. C. Koens and A. P. M. J. Vonken (eds) "Personen- en familierecht, Tekst & Commentaar." Wolters Kluwer, Deventer, 2743-2752, p. 2751.

185 Art. 16(6) BOBKA.

186 J. de Heer (2016). "Wet opneming buitenlandse pleegkinderen ter adoptie. "In M. J. C. Koens and A. P. M. J. Vonken (eds) "Personen- en familierecht, Tekst & Commentaar." Wolters Kluwer, Deventer, 2697-2741, p. 2725.

187 J. van den Braak et al. (2004). "Evaluatieonderzoek Wobka, Een evaluatieonderzoek naar de Wet opneming buitenlandse kinderen ter adoptie." WODC, Adviesbureau Van Montfoort, Woerden, p. 63.

188 *Ibid.*

Netherlands and the states with which they co-operate), the cultural, social and political developments in the sending countries and their official or working language.[189]

The Quality Framework also lists a number of *personal competencies* that agency personnel with core functions need to have in addition to the aforementioned qualifications. They must show professional integrity, be accurate and critical, client-oriented, co-operative as well as social and communicative.[190]

If an accredited Dutch adoption agency wishes to carry out adoption placements from a country that is State Party to the Hague Convention, it is required to have authorization from the Dutch Minister of Justice.[191] Such an authorization will be granted only if the adoption agency has obtained an identical authorization from the competent authority in the sending country.[192] The Ministry may deny an authorization if one or more other agencies are already approved to operate in the country of origin from which the Dutch agency wishes to place children. Authorization from the Ministry of Justice and Security is not required if an agency wants to carry out placements from a non-Hague country (see section 7.3).

5.2 *Financial Strain*

In the Netherlands, there are currently five adoption agencies that are accredited: *Vereniging Wereldkinderen, Nederlandse Adoptie Stichting (NAS), Stichting Meiling, Stichting Kind en Toekomst* and *Adoptiestichting A New Way*. *Wereldkinderen* is the most significant Dutch adoption agency with 64 international adoption placements in 2016 (36%).[193] In the same year, *Kind en Toekomst* completed 50 adoption placements, *Meiling* 47 and *NAS* 33. *A New Way*, a young agency founded in 2011 which only places children from the United States, carried out a total of 20 adoptions.[194]

Similar to the German adoption agencies, the Dutch adoption agencies openly endorse the standards and principles of the Hague Convention as well as the UNCRC.[195] They

189 Gezamenlijke vergunninghouders interlandelijke adoptie (2013). "Kwaliteitskader Vergunninghouders Interlandelijke Adoptie." 2. Version (on file with author), pp. 13-14.

190 *Ibid.*

191 Art 12 Hague Convention; Art. 4(1) *Uitvoeringswet.*

192 Art. 4(1) *Uitvoeringswet.*

193 Ministerie van Justitie en Veiligheid (2017). "Adoptie, Trends en Analyse, Statistisch overzicht interlandelijke adoptie over de jaren 2012 tot en met 2016." Available https://adoptie.nl/wp-content/uploads/2017/03/2012-2016-Trends-en-analyse-interlandelijke-adoptie.pdf.

194 *Ibid.*

195 See, for example, Wereldkinderen: "The agency's objective is to help children in need. [...] We provide this help in accordance with the 'Convention on the right of the child'." (Art. 2(1) and (2) of the Statute from Sep. 26th, 2014); "Our vision corresponds to the United Nations Convention on the Rights of the Child (art. 21) and the international Hague Adoption Convention." (Wereldkinderen (2016). "Annual report

claim that their mission is to serve the best interests of children and to find parents for children, not children for parents.[196] Many maintain that they would promote the subsidiarity principle by supporting aid projects in the sending states, which aim to help children to grow up in their own countries of origin, and they emphasize that intercountry adoptions should be a child care measure of last resort.[197] Some clarify that it is therefore not healthy infants that they are placing for adoption, but primarily older children with special needs (e.g. with mental or physical diseases, or a social stigma) for whom no proper childcare solution can be found in their native country.[198]

However, in practice, the high standards and principles that the agencies claim to abide by are susceptible to being undermined, because in the Netherlands, like in Germany, the adoption placement agencies experience financial strain.[199] Dutch adoption agencies do not receive financial support to handle intercountry adoption placements. If at all, government subsidies are only provided for financing aid projects in the sending countries. The agencies have to finance themselves exclusively with the 'administration fees' (*Bureaukosten* or *Nederland kosten*) that are paid by their adoption applicants. This fee is calculated on the basis of the running costs that the agency incurs annually and the figure currently varies somewhere between €8,400 and €11,000.[200]

2015 Wereldkinderen." Available at https://www.wereldkinderen.nl/websites/implementatie/mediadepot/1443483d20c4.pdf, p. 4).

196 See, for example, *Stichting Meiling*: "The main point of departure always is and remains the perceived interests of the child. The child qualifying for adoption is the starting point, for whom suitable parents have to be found." (Stichting Meiling (2015). "Annual Report 2014." (on file with author), p. 7); „The interests of children are our priority. [...] Our objective is to find the best suitable parents for a child, not vice versa." (Website Stichting Meiling, avilable at https://www.meiling.nl/index.php?option=com_content&view=article&id=136&Itemid=666&lang=en.)

197 See, for example, *Wereldkinderen:* "We work together with local organizations that prevent children from ending up in the streets or in children's homes. If it is not possible for a child to grow up in his or her own family, we feel that a local foster family is a good alternative. If this is not possible, we act as a mediator for intercountry adoption." (Wereldkinderen (2016). "Annual report 2015 Wereldkinderen." Available at https://www.wereldkinderen.nl/websites/implementatie/mediadepot/1443483d20c4.pdf, p. 4); *Stichting Kind en Toekomst*: "With Stichting Kind en Toekomst, project aid and sponsoring are always aimed at the welfare of the most vulnerable group in society: children. [...] In some cases, international adoption can be prevented because due to project help and sponsoring, children can be helped in their own countries." (Stichting Kind en Toekomst (2016). "Jaarverslag 2015." (on file with author), p. 7); *Nederlandse Adoptie Stichting*: "Starting point of a[n adoption] placement is that it takes place in the best interests of the child and that there are no alternative child care solutions in the child's native country according to the subsidiarity principle." (Nederlandse Adoptie Stichting (2015). "Jaarverslag 2014." Available at http://www.nederlandseadoptiestichting.nl/documents/NAS_Jaarverslag2014.pdf, p. 3).

198 See, for example, *Wereldkinderen:* "We increasingly receive files of children from China with complex health issues. Many children have one or more serious disorders, a considerable lag in development or a combination of both." (Wereldkinderen (2016). "Annual report 2015 Wereldkinderen." Available at https://www.wereldkinderen.nl/websites/implementatie/mediadepot/1443483d20c4.pdf, p. 15).

199 Vergunninghouders Adoptie (2014). "De Adoptieketen in 2020, Advies van de Samenwerkende Vergunninghouders Adoptie", p. 8.

200 For example, the adoption placement office *Stichting Kind en Toekomst* charges an administration fee of €7,950 plus €400 fixed costs. Adoption applicants who adopt a child from Nicaragua with the involvement

Since the administration fee is the adoption agencies' only revenue stream, their existence is thus reliant on a particular number of adoption placements. As was already explained in Chapter V, this dependency is problematic for a variety of reasons. For one, agencies might be inclined to accept more adoption applicants than they can find children for, and thereby create expectant prospective adoptive parents who put pressure on the agency personnel and on the sending countries as a result.[201]

Second, they cannot easily afford to discontinue cooperation with a foreign partner organization, especially if they only have one or two partners, since doing so might spell the end of their existence. For several years, Dutch agencies have faced difficulties in carrying out enough placements to keep their organization up and running. Just like in all other receiving countries, intercountry adoptions are on a dramatic decrease in the Netherlands: whereas in 2004, 1,304 children were placed, the figure was only 528 in 2011 and 214 in 2016 (see section 2). The decreasing number of adoption placements, combined with the continued high competition between Dutch and foreign adoption agencies, places financial strain on the agencies.[202] All of them have responded to this pressure by increasing the administration fees as well as by restructuring their organization. For instance, *Wereldkinderen* which was working with 60 staff members (48 fte) in 2003,[203] reduced the number of employees to six (4.5 fte) in 2017. Some Dutch adoption agencies dropped out entirely (*Stichting HOGAR, Stichting Flash* and *Stichting Afrika*), one of the reasons being the financial difficulties that have been caused by the decreasing numbers of intercountry adoption.

As was explained in the previous Chapter, the financial strain is a highly criminogenic condition in the adoption system of a receiving country. It might motivate the adoption agencies to turn a blind eye on or even knowingly accept signs of irregular practices in the sending countries or of abusive practices of their foreign partner organisations or representatives in order to survive.[204] Even the most benevolent agency personnel might be inclined to cut ethical corners if this is necessary to secure the organization's continued existence and their own jobs.

---

of the agency *Nederlandse Adoptie Stichting* have to pay €11,000 which is composed of procedural costs (for shipping, courier service, money transaction, MVV, dossier storage), personnel costs as well as overhead costs (for visits to the sending countries, accounting, quality assurance, rent, and counselling). This fee is similarly high for adoption placements from the United States that are handled by the *Stichting A New Way*. Usually, the adoption applicants pay this administration fee in instalments vis-à-vis the accomplished steps of the placement procedure.

201 Chapter V, section 5.2.

202 See also Smits et al. (2016). "De Toekomst van de keten voor interlandelijke adoptie." 17.05.2016, GV349/conceptrapport, Andersson Elffers Felix, available at https://www.rijksoverheid.nl/documenten/rapporten/2016/05/17/de-toekomst-van-de-keten-voor-interlandelijke-adoptie, p. 4.

203 Interview with I. Hut, director of the Dutch adoption placement agency *Wereldkinderen* between 2003 and 2009, The Netherlands, 06.07.2017.

204 See Chapter V, section 7.2.

6 Cooperation with the Sending Countries

6.1 *Dutch Adoption Agencies' Partners and Their Tasks in the Sending Countries*

Dutch adoption agencies place children from a total of 25 countries, many of which have ratified the Hague Convention: Taiwan, China, Suriname, Thailand, Philippines, India, Sri Lanka, Kyrgyzstan, South Africa, Lesotho, Nigeria, Namibia, Burkina Faso, Bolivia, Dominican Republic, Haiti, Panama, Hungary, Poland, Bulgaria, Slovakia, Czech Republic, Turkey, Portugal and the United States. Adoption agencies are responsible for maintaining contacts and cooperating with the authorities, organizations and individuals in the countries from which they place children.[205]

Dutch adoption law seeks to manage the cooperation with the sending countries. Dutch adoption agencies are not allowed to cooperate with a foreign institution or organization that already has a collaboration agreement with another Dutch adoption agency.[206] This could mean that only one Dutch agency is permitted to place children from a country in which solely one institution or partner organization is available for a cooperation (like, for instance, in China). However, it is possible to split the country up into several regions and then assign these regions to the agencies.[207] This regulation ought to avoid competition between Dutch adoption agencies, as well as to reduce the pressure on the institutions and organizations in the sending countries.

Dutch adoption agencies must fulfil certain tasks and responsibilities with regard to the adoption steps that are taken in the sending countries. They must support the prospective adoptive parents in the adoption procedure abroad and assist them in obtaining the documents that are necessary for the child's admission to the Netherlands (Article 8 WOBKA).[208] Furthermore, they are required to make sure that no contact is established between the adopters and the biological parents of the child or another person or institution that is actually caring for the child until it has been determined 1) that the child is adoptable, 2) that the authorities of the state of origin accepted the placement of the child with the prospective adoptive parent and 3) that the required consent to adoption of the persons and institutions in the states of origin has been obtained.[209]

---

205 Art. 17a(1)(a) WOBKA.

206 Art. 20(4) *leg. cit.*

207 J. de Heer (2016). "Wet opneming buitenlandse pleegkinderen ter adoptie." In M. J. C. Koens and A. P. M. J. Vonken (eds) "Personen- en familierecht, Tekst & Commentaar." Wolters Kluwer, Deventer, 2697-2741, p. 2733.

208 Art. 17a(1)(c) WOBKA.

209 Art. 17(1)(d) *leg. cit.*

6.2 *Adoption Costs, Donations and 'Facilitation Payments'*

In addition to the 'administrative fee', the Dutch adoption agency charges for the services rendered in the Netherlands (see section 5.2), the adoption applicants also need to pay a fee for the services rendered by the agency's cooperation partner and representative abroad, which is referred to as the 'country fee' (*buitenlandkosten*). This fee does not cover the procedural adoption steps that have to be followed in the sending countries. Thus, fees for legalisation, court hearings, lawyers or the issuance of a visa or passport (often called 'procedural fees') need to be incurred by the adopters.

In order to avoid financial inducements for actors in the sending countries, which may lead them to engage in abusive or illegal practices, Article 20(3) WOBKA prohibits Dutch adoption agencies from paying unreasonably high fees to their foreign cooperation partners and representatives. Fees are considered to be unreasonably high if they are disproportionate compared to the average income in the sending country.[210] Dutch adoption agencies that violate this provision commit a misdemeanour that is punishable by a fine (Article 28 WOBKA) or – in case they act with the objective to profit – face criminal sanctions (Article 27 WOBKA) (see section 8.2). Furthermore, the Dutch Ministry might withdraw the adoption agencies' accreditation (see section 7.1).

Generally, the country fees vary greatly between cooperation partners and sending countries and they are dependent on the form of cooperation, the services provided by the foreign partners, the laws and regulations in the sending country as well as the number of adoption placements carried out per year. Usually, they are determined individually by the Dutch adoption agencies together with their foreign representatives or partner organizations. The latter estimate the costs that they incur annually by assisting the adopters (travel, accommodation and translation costs) and by running a representative office, which is obligatory in some sending countries (e.g. Kazakhstan). These costs are added to the fixed monthly salaries that the Dutch agencies pay their foreign representatives and the figure is then divided by the number of adoption placements carried out the previous year. The resulting country fee will, therefore, be higher for adoptions from countries in which the agencies have to establish a representative office and/or where the volume of placements is low. And it will comparably be lower for adoptions from countries from which many children are placed and/or in which the agency co-operates with an orphanage or accredited adoption agency that is also collaborating with other foreign adoption agencies

Due to the numerous factors that influence the amount of the country fees, it is often difficult for somebody outside the agency to determine whether they are reasonably high. However, in some instances the country fees that the Dutch agencies charge can hardly

210 Kamerstukken II, 20 046, Nr. 6, p. 38.

be considered reasonable. For instance, *Dutch adoption agency Y* charges a country fee of €7,225 and an additional 'procedure fee' of €1,172 for an adoption placement from Nigeria - a non-Hague country. Both fees exclude the costs that the adopters have to pay to travel to the sending country as well as for their accommodation. The Dutch agency collaborates with an accredited Nigerian organization that has strong links to local orphanages all over the country from which it also places children up for adoption. In an interview, the director of the agency was asked to break down the fees that are transferred to the Nigerian partner organization and to explain what they are being used for. She disclosed that some €2,000 of the country fee is used to pay the salaries of the organization's staff members. Yet, when asked how the rest of the money is spent abroad, the agency's head appeared to have difficulties justifying them:

> Yes, for a lot, for the parents who have to fly [within Nigeria], they have to...the child has to be prepared for the procedure, so that you have all the data, they have to get back to the [partner organization], if we miss something, to have that being done again. If, for example, there is a blood test showing high values, the Ministry of Justice and Security says: yes, that value is high, if the doctor has said so, can you let that be checked again? Well, fine, but then somebody has to travel with the child from the child care institution and then you often have to take the plane, of course, because the distances there are huge! And, of course you have the passport requests, which need to be paid, the birth certificates, if necessary, the death records. If there is no gas supply and the judge says: well, I will not come to trial because I cannot use my car then taxis have to be rented to get that judge there. So yes, that's how it works.[211]

She furthermore claimed that the remaining fees are also used to pay medical costs that might arise if a child falls ill:

> If a child gets malaria or an epileptic seizure or whatever, [nannies in the orphanage] go to the hospital. That must be paid. We also do not say to parents: well, you are really very unfortunate, you have to pay extra, your child has gotten sick. We now have [...] a couple [in Nigeria], they got a proposal for a child that had quite a special need. [...] So we paid for that operation, but then you lost 3,500 euro for the operation and 2,000 for the physio. You lose 5,000 euro in one fell swoop. This was a huge situation, and fortunately you do not

211 Interview with the director of Dutch adoption agency Y, The Netherlands, 13.11.2017.

> have that so often, thus we just paid extra for that child. We did not charge the parents. [...] That's what you have reserves for.[212]

Even if the total costs for medical treatments are split up among all adoption applicants, a country fee of more than €7,000 is difficult to comprehend. The case that the agency's head described was an exception and as she explained herself, high medical costs rarely have to be incurred. When she was asked if she did not think that the country fee was unreasonably high for the services she itemized, considering the average costs in Nigeria, she replied:

> We work with this country since 1993 and [back than the costs] were lower. If you see, for example, how the travel costs were considering gas...then and now...yes, then you have to go up [with the fees] to get things done. When I go there and travel myself, I am very surprised to see that the gas is as much as I would pay here [...]. That is not like that in every country, and then you can also buy gasoline in a jerry can at the side of the road, but then you never know how far you will come. Well, you know, such things, yes. Yes, if you look at it like that, what you said, then I think, yes...I can imagine that you look at it that way. But it is absolutely not an organization that, no...[213]

During the interview, the head of the Dutch adoption agency could not explain in a comprehensive manner as to how the country fees that the adopters have to pay are being used in Nigeria. Neither did she want to disclose the costs nor did she know exactly how the cooperation partner uses them. As a policy advisor of the Central Authority explained in an interview, some sending countries are rather unwilling to properly disclose and explain the costs that adopters are required to pay (see section 7.3). As was argued in the previous Chapter, the motivation of the adoption agencies to carefully examine the country fees and how they are actually being used abroad might be limited.[214]

It is not only unreasonably high country fees, but also donations that may engender inducements for the partner organizations in the sending countries. Three of the five Dutch adoption agencies have established or support aid projects in the countries from which they place children. One Dutch adoption agency, that places children from Taiwan, transfers donations to all three of the orphanages it is cooperating with. In addition to the country fee of €7,100, its adopters are required to pay a 'fixed contribution' of between

212 *Ibid.*
213 *Ibid.*
214 Chapter V, section 6.2.

€7,000 and €12,000 to the orphanage they adopt from.[215] Such contributions are usually provided with good intentions, namely to help improve the living conditions for the children, especially those that cannot be placed for adoption. Yet, they may actually do more harm than good as they could influence the decision of the orphanage personnel concerning the placement of their children. Donations might induce them to supply the Dutch cooperation partner with 'adoptable children', either due to the necessity to cover the institution's expenses or with the intention to profit financially.[216]

Two of the Dutch adoption agencies seek to separate developmental aid from the adoption placement activities by supporting aid projects that are not directly linked to intercountry adoptions (e.g. a milk project for school children in Thailand, foster parents programme). Some sending countries (e.g. Ethiopia, Haiti and China) would only allow foreign adoption agencies to place children if they support local aid projects or to donate money to the government to help finance the local child welfare system and to thereby implement the subsidiarity principle. But even if there is no obvious or direct link between the local aid projects and intercountry adoptions, donations could nevertheless have the effect of perpetuating the intercountry adoption system. If the welfare systems in the sending countries are primarily financed by foreign money, contributions might induce the governments to provide children for intercountry adoption.[217]

Dutch law only stipulates that the fees that Dutch adoption agencies pay to their foreign representatives and partner organizations be reasonable. However, it lacks specific provisions regulating donations and contributions to sending countries. Particularly, it fails to prohibit Dutch adoption agencies from contributing money or material goods to the child care institutions they are cooperating with and it does not limit the amount of money they are allowed to donate to the government. Also, the Quality Framework lacks standards and guidelines for donations.

In some sending countries, it is common for the authorities involved in intercountry adoption to ask foreign adoption agencies to pay bribes. According to Hut, the former director of the agency *Wereldkinderen*, the authorities in Haiti, for instance, required €1,000 per adoption in addition to the fees the adopters had to pay for the bureaucratic steps. She explains: "They did not label it [as a bribe] but they could not show us where the money goes to [...] and we knew already from our own experience that it was divided between about twenty officials from the government; each of them got fifty dollars or euros, but it was not transparent".[218] The authorities in the Netherlands tolerate such

215 See https://www.meiling.nl/index.php?option=com_content&view=category&layout=blog&id=88&Itemid=484&lang=nl (last accessed on 07.08.2018).

216 See Chapter II, section 2.5 and 4.2.2.

217 See Chapter V, section 6.4. and Chapter VI, section 7.4.1.

218 Interview with I. Hut, director of the Dutch adoption placement agency *Wereldkinderen* between 2003 and 2009, The Netherlands, 06.07.2017.

'facilitation payments'. Hut claims: "I told our Ministry of Justice and Security that we had to pay bribes to the government in Haiti, but they said: 'oh, that's no problem, if you are transparent in your administration, that's okay with us'".[219] Also, the Dutch Committee on Lesbian Parenthood and Intercountry Adoption, which the Dutch Ministry of Justice and Security asked to advise on the future of intercountry adoption in the Netherlands, condones the practice of bribing authorities in the sending countries where this is customary. Its report, which discusses a number of weaknesses in the Dutch adoption laws and procedures, says:

> the Committee [...] observes that it may be customary in certain countries of origin to make a small payment to the individuals or authorities involved in an adoption. The Committee points out that, in principle, the payment of bribes to foreign officials is liable to punishment in the Netherlands [...]. The engagement of local agents or representatives for the actual payment of bribes may result in liability for punishment in the Netherlands. This also applies to accredited bodies. Nevertheless, the Public Prosecution Service will not decide to prosecute where so-called 'facilitation payments' are concerned, namely small payments that serve to urge government officials to perform their tasks. The Committee is of the opinion that accredited bodies must have the scope to make 'facilitation payments' of this nature where this is customary in certain countries. However, in these situations, the payments must be small and it must be possible to consider them acceptable.[220]

In many sending countries, extra payments for services or approvals are commonplace. The Committee arguably supposes that bribes or 'facilitation payments' that are made to secure necessary services or approvals for an adoption within a society where such payments are common would not necessarily distort the intercountry adoption system. After all, in some sending countries, government officials or orphanage directors may demand extra payments for providing a service or approval that is entirely legitimate. In that sense, it might be argued, bribes simply accelerate the legal adoption procedure. Considering the negative effects that delays in the adoption procedure have on the institutionalized child, facilitation payments may be considered as a necessary evil to bring about a greater good:

219 *Ibid.*

220 N. A. Kalsbeek et al. (2008). "Report on Intercountry Adoption - "All things of value are defenceless"." Committee on Lesbian Parenthood and Intercountry Adoption, available at http://poundpuplegacy.org/files/10866_Interlandelijke-Adoptie_tcm34-137684.pdf, p. 52.

saving the child from the immediate circumstances in an orphanage and providing him or her with a loving family and a stable life as quickly as possible.[221]

However, in a corrupt adoption system, money does not only speed up legal adoption procedures but also procures approvals and false paperwork in cases where children are illegally obtained for intercountry adoption. In poor sending countries, Western money creates an incentive to illicitly source children and then launder them through the adoption system.[222] In the end then, it is not possible to distinguish the legal from the illegal adoptions. Smolin explains:

> The combination of a system where permissions/approvals are commonly based on money or personal connections, with a large monetary incentive toward foreign adoptions, can lead to a systematically corrupt adoption system. [...] Within such a system, it can become virtually impossible to tell which adoptions were legitimate, and which were not, as the system may operate in largely the same way for both. Both involve the use of personal connections or bribery for approvals, and both involve disproportionately large monetary incentives toward intercountry adoption. The question of whether children really were orphans needing a home, or could have been placed in-country, can be obscured in a system already corrupted by the power of money and personal connections.[223]

The Committee suggests limiting 'facilitation payments', claiming that they should be 'small' and 'acceptable'. However, what can be considered small and acceptable, especially in countries where a large proportion of the population lives in poverty? Given the economic asymmetries between the Netherlands and the sending states, even (by Western standards) modest payments could have a corrupting effect and facilitate the laundering of illegally obtained children.

6.3 *Supervision of Foreign Representatives and Cooperation Partners*

Dutch adoption laws do not specify as to how adoption agencies should monitor and control their partner organizations and representatives in the sending countries. However, the Quality Framework provides standards and guidelines to this effect. The Framework

221 D. M. Smolin (2006). "Child Laundering: How the Intercountry Adoption System Legitimizes and Incentivizes the Practices of Buying, Trafficking, Kidnapping, and Stealing Children." The Wayne Law Review, 52, 1, 113-200, p. 115.

222 See Chapter II, section 2.5.

223 D. M. Smolin (2004). "The Two Faces of Intercountry Adoption: The Significance of the Indian Adoption Scandals." Seton Hall Law Review, 35, 403-493, p. 448.

was drafted in 2008 following the disclosure of a child laundering case involving an illegally obtained Indian child that was adopted by a Dutch couple.[224] The child, a 1½-year old boy (Rahul), was kidnapped from his sleeping parents in 1999, and who were desperately searching for his whereabouts for six years. In 2005, a child kidnapping network was uncovered in Chennai, whose members allegedly stole children and then sold them to *Malaysian Social Service (MSS)*, an Indian orphanage that was accredited and controlled by the Central Authority *CARA*. The orphanage personnel were later found guilty of having kidnapped children from the streets, slums, hospitals and busy markets.[225] According to the Indian authorities, at least 350 adoptions that were arranged by this orphanage involved illegally obtained children.

MSS was the cooperation partner of the Dutch adoption agency *Meiling*. Between 1995 and 2002, *Meiling* had placed 35 children from this orphanage, including, as it later turned out, Rahul. The Indian kidnappers brought the boy to the orphanage *MSS*, whose director fabricated the surrender deed, signed it as the child's mother and then sent the child to the Netherlands where he was later adopted. The case only came to light in 2008, after the Dutch TV programme *Network* broadcast a documentary thereon.

Upon the request of the Dutch Minister of Justice, the Youth Inspectorate examined whether the adoption agency *Meiling* had properly monitored and controlled the reliability of its Indian cooperation partner and whether it had adequately responded to signs of possible irregularities in India.[226] The report concluded that *Meiling* failed to screen *MSS* in a "professional and structured" manner.[227] Instead, it simply relied on the information that was provided by the Indian authority *CARA*, rather than conducting an independent assessment of its cooperation partner's integrity.[228] *Meiling* did not only trust the information *CARA* provided about *MSS*, but it also blindly trusted the reliability of the child reports without making its own assessment regarding the child's adoptability:

> For *Meiling*, the child is in principle adoptable when the Indian authorities have completed their procedures and have put all their stamps. *Meiling* does not itself determine on the basis of set standards whether or not all conditions for an adoption were met. Nor does it have a guideline for the manner in which

---

224 Netwerk (2007). "India eist gestolen adoptiekind uit Nederland terug." 22.05.2007, available at http://www.uitzendinggemist.net/aflevering/86316/Netwerk_eo_Ncrv.html.

225 Aravamudan, G. (2017) "Child trafficking, 'manufactured orphans': The dark underbelly of inter-country adoption in India." Firstpost, 03.09.2017, available at http://www.firstpost.com/india/child-trafficking-manufactured-orphans-the-dark-underbelly-of-inter-country-adoption-in-india-4000837.html.

226 *Meiling en adoptie uit India; Onderzoek naar het handelen van vergunninghouder interlandelijke adoptie Meiling in de periode 1995 t/m 2002 naar aanleiding van signalen over mogelijke misstanden in India, 09.11.2007, Kamerstukken II 2007-2008, 31 265, Nr. 1*

227 *Ibid.*, p. 14.

228 *Ibid.*

it makes sure that the adoption of the child in the Netherlands can be considered in the interests of the child.[229]

In its conclusions, the Youth Inspectorate suggested that the Dutch Ministry promulgate standards and guidelines together with the other Dutch agencies. The Quality Framework that was agreed upon by the Dutch agencies in 2008 and further modified in 2013 determine, *inter alia*, the standards for controlling the agency's representatives and partner organizations in the sending countries. It provides that the agencies are responsible for the work of their foreign representatives. With regard to their foreign partner organizations, the Framework obliges the agencies to assess and monitor them to the best of their abilities, both before and after having begun their cooperation.[230] Particularly, they must check whether the following criteria are met:

- the adoption laws and policies in the sending country (particularly the relinquishment procedure and the legal adoptability) are compliant with the Hague Convention and the UNCRC;[231]
- the partner organization has an accreditation or permission with regard to intercountry adoption and its objectives are consistent with the standards and principles set out in the Hague Convention and the UNCRC;[232]
- the partner organization must be willing to make its structure, organization, tasks and responsibilities, activities and procedures (particularly with regard to foundlings), financial situation as well as the adoption costs (including the costs that are spent on aid projects) transparent and they must provide general information (for example, on the number of adoptions as well as the percentage of foundlings and of relinquishment declarations);[233] and
- the partner organization or another competent authority in the sending country must examine whether a suitable domestic child care option is available for the child before considering intercountry adoption (subsidiarity principle).[234]

These standards make it clear that the Dutch agencies must assume an active role in controlling their partner organizations abroad. They must not blindly trust the information that has been provided by the authorities and its cooperation partners in the sending country; they are also required to make their own assessments regarding the integrity of

229 *Ibid.*

230 Gezamenlijke vergunninghouders interlandelijke adoptie (2013). "Kwaliteitskader Vergunninghouders Interlandelijke Adoptie." 2. Version (on file with author), p. 28.

231 *Ibid.*, p. 31.

232 *Ibid.*

233 *Ibid.*, pp. 32-33.

234 *Ibid.*, p. 33.

the foreign adoption system and their partner organization, as well as the reliability of the information that has been provided regarding the children.

The two Dutch adoption agencies that were interviewed use the same measures to monitor and control their foreign representatives and partner organizations as the German agencies.[235] First, their personnel travel to the sending countries roughly once a year in order to inspect the conditions and their partners' working methods. Second, they ask their adoption applicants to report any irregularities they notice during the adoption procedure. Finally, they assess the integrity of the foreign adoption system on the basis of the information contained in the child proposals. As was explained in Chapter V, all of these monitoring measures have their limitations and they cannot guarantee strict supervision of the activities abroad. Since a strict control of the activities in the sending countries is difficult in the Netherlands, trust plays an important role in the cooperation between the Dutch agencies and their partner organizations.

The Quality Framework emphasizes the adoption agencies' co-responsibility for the adoption steps that are taken in the sending countries, also with regard to the question as to whether the envisaged intercountry adoption is indeed in the child's best interests.[236] However, it explicitly excludes the Dutch adoption agencies' *legal* responsibility for the activities of their cooperation partners in the sending countries.[237] Thus, they cannot be held responsible if it transpires that the organization they work with has been illegally obtaining children. The adoption agency *Meiling* did not face any regulatory consequences for the aforementioned incident, even though its partner organization was found guilty of child trafficking. This lack of agency responsibility, combined with the financial and ideological motive to carry out international adoptions, arguably lowers the agencies' motivation to properly control their foreign partners and even proclives them to turn a blind eye on or wilfully accept any signs of irregularities in the sending countries.

The Quality Framework requires the Dutch adoption agencies to request advice from an individual or institution in the sending country (Central Authority or Dutch embassies) or in the Netherlands (Central Authority) or to demand further investigations in the State of origin, if they have doubts as to the reliability of the information that has been provided by their foreign partner organization (e.g. if the information in the child proposal is incomplete or inconsistent).[238] If these doubts cannot be dispelled or if the Central Authority in the sending country refuses to communicate with the adoption agencies,[239] the latter must notify the Dutch Central Authority. The Dutch Central Authority then

---

235 See Chapter V, section 6.4.

236 See principle of co-responsibility explained in Chapter IV, section 4.6.

237 Gezamenlijke vergunninghouders interlandelijke adoptie (2013). "Kwaliteitskader Vergunninghouders Interlandelijke Adoptie." 2. Version (on file with author), p. 28.

238 *Ibid.*, p. 30.

239 Sometimes foreign Central Authorities are only willing to communicate with their formal counter parts in the receiving countries and not with the adoption agencies (see section 7.4.1).

needs to seek further information from the Central Authority in the sending country. In case the issue cannot be resolved that way, it shall take further actions *via* the Dutch Ministry of Foreign Affairs and/or the Permanent Bureau of the Hague Conference. On the basis of a thorough investigation, the Central Authority may finally decide to (either permanently or temporarily) suspend adoptions from that sending country (see section 7.3). Of course, the adoption agencies also have recourse to this possibility.[240] The Quality Framework thus involves the Dutch authorities monitoring and controlling the activities taken in the sending countries. Yet, as we shall see below (see section 7.4), as a result of diplomatic sensibilities, the Dutch Ministry of Justice and Security may be reluctant to put pressure on the authorities in the sending countries in order to get further information or suspend intercountry adoption altogether, especially where there are continuing reports of irregularities and abuses in the foreign adoption system.

7 The Role of the Dutch Authorities in the Adoption System

7.1 *Accrediting and Controlling Dutch Adoption Agencies*

Dutch private agencies are admitted to carry out intercountry adoption placements, however, only if they have been accredited.[241] The Dutch Ministry of Justice and Security is responsible for granting, extending and withdrawing the accreditations of the Dutch adoption agencies. In the accreditation procedure, the agencies are required to provide the following information:

- a copy of their *statute*;[242]
- a precise description as to the manner in which they make sure that the placement of a foreign child to the Netherlands can be considered in his or her *best interests*;[243]
- information about the *composition of their board* and an explanation of how this composition ensures that both the interests of foreign children, as well as the needs and wishes of prospective adoptive parents, can be taken into consideration;[244]
- an explanation as to the nature of their placement activities and of the *international adoption procedure* that prospective adoptive parents have to undergo in the different sending countries;[245]

---

240 Gezamenlijke vergunninghouders interlandelijke adoptie (2013). "Kwaliteitskader Vergunninghouders Interlandelijke Adoptie." 2. Version (on file with author), p. 30.

241 Art. 15 WOBKA.

242 Art. 1(a) Regeling gegevens buitenlandse betrekkingen vergunninghouder interlandelijke adoptie.

243 Art. 1(b) *leg. cit.*

244 Art. 1(c) *leg. cit.*

245 Art. 1(d) *leg. cit.*

- in case the agencies have already carried out *placement activities* before, and where they are applying for a renewal of its accreditation for another four-year period: a report about their activities, as well as a balance sheets and a statement of income and expenses with explanations about the previous year and the year in which the accreditation has been requested;[246]
- information about the *individuals and authorities in the sending countries* with which the agencies cooperate, including: judicial and other competent authorities, orphanages, lawyers and other individuals and/or organizations which are involved in the adoption placement procedure; in case individuals and/or organizations work with each other this must be reported as well;[247] and
- a description of *post-adoption services* that the agencies plan to provide.[248]

The accreditation is provided for a period of three years and must be renewed every five years.[249] The temporary granting of the accreditation was one of the changes brought about by the WOBKA. The objective was to tighten control over the adoption agencies by giving the Ministry of Justice and Security the opportunity to evaluate their organization and activities on a regular basis. In the accreditation renewal procedure, the Youth Inspectorate and the financial audit unit of the Ministry of Financial Affairs are responsible for inspecting the adoption agencies.[250]

During the accreditation renewal procedure, the Youth Inspectorate checks whether the agencies continue to meet the accreditation requirements according to Article 16 WOBKA (see section 5.1) and whether they fulfil the tasks and obligations that are laid down in Articles 20 to 23 WOBKA,[251] as well as in the Quality Framework. The Inspectorate, in particular, checks how the agencies assist the adopters in the procedures that are to be followed abroad,[252] looks at the quality of the matching proposals, the manner in which they cooperate with the authorities and their partner organizations in the sending countries,[253] and how they deal with complaints by adoptive parents.[254] After having conducted the inspection, the Inspectorate draws up a report detailing its findings and, if necessary, recommendations on how the agencies should improve. The financial audit unit of the Ministry of Financial Affairs inspects the administrative aspects of the agencies' organiza-

246 Art. 1(e) *leg. cit.*
247 Art. 1(f) *leg. cit.*
248 Art. 1(g) *leg. cit.*
249 Art. 16a WOBKA.
250 Interview with A. van Leur, policy advisor at the Dutch Central Authority, The Netherlands, 28.07.2017.
251 Art. 25(1) WOBKA.
252 Art. 20(1) WOBKA.
253 Art. 17a(1)(a) *leg. cit.*
254 Interview with A. van Leur, policy advisor at the Dutch Central Authority, The Netherlands, 28.07.2017.

tion. Particularly, they check whether agencies keep adequate records of their financial situation.[255]

On the basis of the inspection findings, the Ministry of Justice and Security then decides as to whether or not to renew an agency's accreditation. It will deny (the renewal of) an accreditation where it has reasonable grounds to believe that the agency will not comply with the accreditation requirements or if it expects that the adoption agency has too few possibilities in the future to handle intercountry adoption placements.[256] However, if an agency meets all the legal requirements, the Ministry will grant an accreditation, if necessary with specific conditions attached thereto. So far the Ministry has never rejected an agency's request for an accreditation (renewal).[257]

The Ministry of Justice and Security meets up with the staff members of the agencies at least twice a year at their offices to talk about the cooperation with their sending countries and their foreign cooperation partners. In addition, the adoption agencies have reporting obligations towards the Ministry, which include the following:

- notifications about *any change* of its statute or of the composition of its board;[258]
- information about *any intercountry adoption placement* carried out for prospective adoptive parents who are registered with them;[259]
- notification of prospective adoptive parents who have cancelled their *registration* with them in order to be registered with another adoption agency;[260] and
- a detailed *annual report* on all the agencies' activities performed within and outside the Netherlands, as well as their balance sheets and an annual financial statement[261] which is assessed by the *Directie Control Bedrijfsvoering en Juridische Zaken* of the Minister of Justice.[262]

Moreover, the Youth Inspectorate inspects the adoption agencies between the accreditation renewals, usually after calamities have occurred and it will do so either on its own initiative or upon request of the Ministry of Justice and Security or the adopters.[263] According to Article 24a WOBKA, (prospective) adoptive parents can file a complaint about the conduct of an adoption agency to the Complaints Commission (*Klachtencommissie Vergunninghouders Interlandelijke Adoptie,* hereinafter KVIA).[264] Previously, such complaints had to be

255 Art. 23 WOBKA.
256 Art. 17 *leg. cit.*
257 Interview with A. van Leur, policy advisor at the Dutch Central Authority, The Netherlands, 28.07.2017.
258 Art. 13 BOBKA.
259 Art. 23(1) WOBKA.
260 Art. 21(6) *leg. cit.*
261 Art. 23(1) *leg. cit.*
262 Interview with A. van Leur, policy advisor at the Dutch Central Authority, The Netherlands, 28.07.2017.
263 *Ibid.*
264 Art. 24a WOBKA.

channelled through the adoption agencies and could not be directly submitted to the KVIA. This was problematic as adopters, who are more or less reliant on their agencies, might have feared that a complaint about their conduct could result in a suspension of the placement procedure or decrease their chances of getting a child proposal. As a result of this, the procedure was amended in 2008. It is the now the case that complaints against the agencies can be submitted directly to the KVIA.[265] The latter publishes an annual report which provides an overview of the number and the nature of the complaints. This report is sent to the Ministry of Justice and Security and to the Youth Inspectorate, which may then decide to inspect the adoption agency if necessary.

The Minister *might* withdraw the accreditation of an adoption agency that has not complied with the provisions contained in Articles 8 and 20 to 23 WOBKA[266] (in case the agency has violated the requirements of Article 8, it might also be liable towards the prospective adoptive parents),[267] or if it has not completed any intercountry adoption placement for at least two years.[268] The Ministry of Justice and Security *must* withdraw the accreditation if it finds: 1) that the agency no longer meets the accreditation requirements laid down in Article 16 WOBKA,[269] or 2) where the data, that is presented to obtain the accreditation, appear to be so incorrect or incomplete that the accreditation would not have been granted if the Ministry had known at the time of its decision that the information was incomplete or incorrect.[270] In addition to that, it might report an accredited body to the police if it violates the provisions of Articles 2, 8, 15, or 20 WOBKA, which is punishable according to Articles 27 or 28 WOBKA.[271] Withdrawing an agency's accreditation is the Dutch Ministry's most serious supervisory measure and has so far never been used.

The monitoring and control of the adoption agencies in the Netherlands is considerably tight. Numerous stakeholders are involved in supervising the agencies, which all have to report their findings and observations to the Ministry of Justice and Security. The latter has a good insight into the agencies' financial situation and their activities in the Netherlands, and it has the power to intervene by withdrawing or refusing to extent the agency's accreditation, if it suspects any irregular or illegal practices.

265 Beleidsdoorlichting Interlandelijke Adoptie, 15.03.2012, Bijlage bij Kamerstukken II, 2011-2012 33 199, Nr. 1, p. 26.
266 Art. 18(2)(a) WOBKA.
267 J. de Heer (2016). "Wet opneming buitenlandse pleegkinderen ter adoptie. "In M. J. C. Koens and A. P. M. J. Vonken (eds) "Personen- en familierecht, Tekst & Commentaar." Wolters Kluwer, Deventer, 2697-2741, p. 2731.
268 Art. 18(2)(b) WOBKA.
269 Art. 18(1)(a) *leg. cit.*
270 Art. 18(1)(b) *leg. cit.*
271 Art. 28 *leg. cit.*

7.2 *Reviewing and Approving Individual Adoptions (Control on Micro Level)*

Pursuant to Article 17(c) of the Hague Convention, the Central Authorities of both the sending and the receiving country must approve the match between a proposed child and the adopters. Hence, the Dutch adoption agencies must present to the Dutch Central Authority all child proposals they have received from the countries of origin[272] together with substantiated written advice on whether the envisioned placement should take place.[273] As was already mentioned in Chapter V, the content and quality of the child proposals differ substantially between the sending countries. The Quality Framework provides which information the social, medical and the development report about the child need to include in any case.[274] If this information is missing or insufficient, the adoption agency must request additional information (either itself or *via* the Dutch Central Authority) or otherwise it will have to reject the child proposal.[275] The Ministry reviews the information that is provided in the child proposal and then decides whether or not to approve the proposed match, and if so, whether to attach certain conditions to the adoption.[276]

According to Dutch law, the adoption agencies only have to present to the Ministry the child proposals from sending countries that are States Parties to the Hague Convention. However, the Ministry requires the agencies to present all child proposals, including those from non-Hague sending countries.[277] Since the Dutch Ministry of Justice and Security must approve the proposed match according to Article 17(c) of the Hague Convention, it has the final word in deciding on whether or not a child proposal will be accepted. This is different in Germany, where it is the adoption placement agencies that are ultimately responsible for approving a child proposal.[278]

The child report must be accompanied by proof that the necessary consent for the adoption has been obtained.[279] Yet, several documents that are necessary for the adoption, like the child's birth certificate, the declaration of relinquishment or the parents' death certificate, are often not included within the child report. The Dutch adoption agency and the Ministry therefore only have limited possibility to check whether the proposed child is legitimately available for intercountry adoption. These documents are only presented

---

272 Art. 7(1) *Uitvoeringswet*; Art. 16 Hague Convention.

273 Art. 7(2) *Uitvoeringswet.*

274 Gezamenlijke vergunninghouders interlandelijke adoptie (2013). "Kwaliteitskader Vergunninghouders Interlandelijke Adoptie." 2. Version (on file with author), pp. 23-25.

275 *Ibid.*, p. 23.

276 Art. 7(3) *Uitvoeringswet*

277 Interview with J. Kouwenhoven, head of and a policy advisor at the Dutch Central Authority, and M. Kroon, official of the Youth Department at the Dutch Ministry of Justice and Security, The Netherlands, 13.07.2017.

278 See Chapter V, section 8.2.

279 Art 16(2) Hague Convention.

to the IND or the Ministry of Foreign Affairs that process a visa or, respectively, a Dutch passport for the adoptee (see section 3.5).

The IND will process a visa for the child, only if the requirements laid down in the WOBKA are met:[280]

- the Dutch Ministry of Justice and Security has granted principle approval,[281] and has approved the match between the proposed child and the adopters;[282]
- there is a medical report about the child;[283]
- the relinquishment of the child by his or her parents is regulated properly;[284] and
- the authorities in the sending countries agree with the envisaged adoption of the child.[285]

The IND conducts an accelerated application review procedure, which only takes two weeks if the accredited Dutch adoption agency handling the placement procedure applies for a visa on behalf of the adopters.[286] The IND then checks whether the Dutch Ministry of Justice and Security has granted principle approval and has approved the match between the proposed child and the adopters. If these conditions are met, the IND will give the Dutch embassy its consent to process a visa, only if the adopters file the documents substantiating the remaining requirements of Article 8 WOBKA with the Dutch embassy, which are: the child's medical report, a relinquishment declaration signed by the child's biological parents and a declaration of the competent authorities in the sending country approving the envisaged adoption (the judicial adoption decision).[287] If there is no relinquishment declaration because the child is a foundling, other documents need to be presented showing that the requirements were complied with. The declarations need to be legalized and must prove, in a satisfactory manner, that the child was given up for adoption in accordance with the norms and standards of both the sending country and the Netherlands.[288]

The Dutch embassy reviews these documents and then decides on whether to process a visa. The application for a visa is rejected if a document required for traveling to the Netherlands is missing and the child's identity cannot be proven in another manner.[289] If it has doubts about the reliability of the submitted documents, it must present the case

280 Paragraaf B7/3.6.2 *Vreemdelingencirculaire 2000.*
281 Art. 2 WOBKA.
282 Art. 7(1) *Uitvoeringswet*; Art. 16 Hague Convention.
283 Art. 8(b) WOBKA.
284 Art. 8(d). *leg. cit.*
285 Art. 8(e). *leg. cit.*
286 Paragraaf B7/3.6.2 *Vreemdelingencirculaire 2000.*
287 *Leg. cit.*
288 J. de Heer (2016). "Wet opneming buitenlandse pleegkinderen ter adoptie. "In M. J. C. Koens and A. P. M. J. Vonken (eds) "Personen- en familierecht, Tekst & Commentaar." Wolters Kluwer, Deventer, 2697-2741, p. 2716.
289 *Ibid.*

and all its supporting documents to the IND[290] and inform the Dutch Central Authority thereon.[291] The latter might then send a delegation to the sending country so as to investigate individual adoption cases. This has happened once, after the Dutch embassy voiced suspicions about adoptions from Uganda (see section 7.3). The Dutch embassies themselves, however, do not conduct any investigations in the sending states.[292]

In case the child has been adopted in a Hague sending country and the adoption is a full adoption that is certified by the foreign competent authority as having been made in accordance with the Hague Convention, the adoption must be recognized *ex lege* by the Dutch authorities, unless the adoption is manifestly contrary to Dutch public policy (see section 3.4). In case of an *ex lege* recognition, the child instantly acquires the Dutch nationality if at least one of the adoptive parents is a Dutch national. The child does not need a visa from the IND, but rather a Dutch passport, in order to be able to enter the Netherlands (see section 3.5). The Dutch passport is applied for at the embassy in the receiving country which sends the application and the necessary documents – the child's birth certificate, the foreign adoption decision (including documents that are necessary for an adoption, like, for instance, an abandonment declaration), and the conformity certificate (Article 23 Hague Convention) – to the Dutch Ministry of Foreign Affairs in The Hague. The latter then processes a Dutch passport after having checked whether the application is complete and if the submitted documents are authentic. Yet, it will not conduct investigations in the sending countries to verify the accuracy of the content of the submitted documents:

> If there is a document saying that the child has been abandoned and it is part of the court decision, we are not going to check whether the child was really abandoned but we check whether these documents were available and which judge made a decision.[293]

The Dutch Ministry of Foreign Affairs will also not examine whether the authorities in the sending countries have fulfilled their duties allocated to them by the Hague Convention, and whether the adoption actually complies with the treaty's standards and principles:

> We do not check whether the country fulfilled all the requirements under the [Hague] Convention, that is why we have the Convention. […] We cannot check with every adoption under the Convention whether all steps have been

290 Paragraaf B7/3.6.2 *Vreemdelingencirculaire 2000.*

291 Interview with two advisors of the Dutch Immigration and Naturalisation Service, The Netherlands, 15.11.2017.

292 Interview with two policy officers at the Dutch Ministry of Foreign Affairs, The Netherlands, 16.03.2018.

293 *Ibid.*

> done properly. That's up to the judge or the authority in that country to determine. If we do not trust that authority to do its work properly, then there is something wrong with the Convention.[294]

The adoptee is thus granted entry to the Netherlands on the basis of trust, namely that he or she is in the intercountry adoption system legally.

7.3 *Authorizing, Monitoring and Suspending Adoptions from Sending Countries (Control on Macro Level)*

If an accredited Dutch adoption agency wishes to carry out adoption placements from a country that is State Party to the Hague Convention, it is required to have authorization from the Dutch Minister of Justice. Such an authorization is not required for adoption placements from non-Hague sending countries (see section 5.1).

According to the head of the Central Authority, the Ministry of Justice and Security has so far granted authorizations without having done any inquiries in the sending country that the agency would like to cooperate with. Hence, it only gets an idea of the adoption system in the country of origin once it has received the first child proposals:

> If an adoption agency wants [an authorization] for working in [sending country] we initially do not know anything about the procedure in [the sending country]. We only know about the specific situation in [the sending country] when we get the first child proposal. That is a thing that we want to do in a more proper way in the future, for example, by going to [the sending country] together with the adoption agency to do the conversations, to make the arrangements and to see if all requirements are met.[295]

In addition, the policy advisor working at the Central Authority criticizes the Dutch Ministry's lack of involvement when Dutch adoption agencies wish to arrange a new cooperation with a sending country: "We used to say: okay, on paper it seems like a good plan, just start and we will see, but now we will change that, [we want] more check[s] before they start and if necessary we as a Central Authority travel to that specific country to see whether everything is all right to start".[296]

---

294 *Ibid.*

295 Interview with J. Kouwenhoven, head of and a policy advisor at the Dutch Central Authority, and M. Kroon, official of the Youth Department at the Dutch Ministry of Justice and Security, The Netherlands, 13.07.2017.

296 Interview with A. van Leur, policy advisor at the Dutch Central Authority, The Netherlands, 28.07.2017.

Unlike the authorities in Germany, the Dutch Central Authority travels to the sending countries that the Dutch adoption agencies cooperate with in order to take a look at the adoption system. It does so two or three times a year, particularly after irregular practices have been uncovered or are being suspected by a Dutch adoption agency or embassy. In the sending country, the Dutch Central Authority meets with the competent authorities, talk to NGOs and other embassies, visit the Dutch adoption agencies' cooperation partners (orphanages) and maybe look into adoption files in order to get an idea of the adoption system's integrity. The aim is to ascertain an understanding of the adoption procedure, particularly the subsidiarity principle and the manner in which biological parents are informed about the consequences of an adoption. However, according to the policy adviser of the Central Authority, in some countries it is impossible to look into an adoption's financial aspects:

> It's difficult to talk about finances, particularly in African countries. [...] I think, on the one hand, it is: why do you interfere with that? We do regulate this properly. And, on the other hand, I think there's always something accusatory in it or something like that. It is always really difficult to ask questions about it. [...] You have to be careful with that. It is difficult to go there and say: okay, tell me what do you use this for, that for, that for, that for? So, you have to be careful with that.[297]

In case any irregularities are suspected, the Ministry may also ask the Dutch embassy in the sending country to conduct investigations. If the Dutch Central Authority or embassy finds that the adoption procedures are not properly carried out, the Ministry may decide to suspend intercountry adoptions from this particular sending country. This measure is not provided for in the WOBKA.[298] However, the Ministry has nevertheless suspended adoptions from a number of sending countries which has always been accepted by the Dutch agencies. The head of the Central Authority explains why this is the case: "We invest a lot in the contact with the accredited adoption agencies so that they know what is going on. We do not have a legal basis [for a suspension], however, they still agree with it".[299]

In 2001, the Ministry of Justice and Security decided to suspend intercountry adoptions from Guatemala as a 'political signal' after extensive child laundering practices were

297 Interview with A. van Leur, policy advisor at the Dutch Central Authority, The Netherlands, 28.07.2017.

298 J. van den Braak et al. (2004). "Evaluatieonderzoek Wobka, Een evaluatieonderzoek naar de Wet opneming buitenlandse kinderen ter adoptie." WODC, Adviesbureau Van Montfoort, Woerden, p. 155.

299 Interview with J. Kouwenhoven, head of and a policy advisor at the Dutch Central Authority, and M. Kroon, official of the Youth Department at the Dutch Ministry of Justice and Security, The Netherlands, 13.07.2017.

uncovered.[300] It based its decision on the report of the Commission on Human Rights,[301] according to which the vast majority of intercountry adoptions (99%) were privately organized by lawyers who made large profits by offering their adoption services and who resorted to a number of illegal practices to sustain the supply of adoptees. They would obtain children through purchase, abduction, force or deception and then falsify their paperwork so as to hide their true origin.[302] The findings of this report were backed-up by a study conducted by ILPEC,[303] as well as by observations of the International Social Service (ISS).[304] After the report of the Commission on Human Rights was published, a Special Commission on the Practical Operation of the Hague Convention took place whereby a number of organizations and delegations met in order to discuss the situation in Guatemala after which some countries, including the Netherlands, decided to suspend intercountry adoptions from this country.[305] Interestingly, many members of the Second Chamber criticized the Ministry's decision, arguing that there was no need to stop with adoptions to the Netherlands as they all took place *via* the agency *Kind en Toekomst* and were thus controlled by the state.[306] However, the Ministry stressed that it did not want to take the risk of placing children that were kidnapped or stolen and therefore it decided to uphold the suspension.[307]

Two years later, in 2003, the Minister of Justice decided to suspend adoptions from Cambodia.[308] After the Ministry received a number of requests for *deelbemiddelingen*, from which it appeared that the adoption procedure in Cambodia was rather poor, it asked the Dutch embassy in Thailand to conduct investigations into the Cambodian intercountry adoption system.

The latter found that the procedure did not comply with the important requirements. Intermediaries would buy children from their biological parents, many of whom did not understand the consequences of an adoption and were thus not aware of the fact that their child was going abroad forever. Furthermore, it was almost impossible to verify the status of the child. Since the country was suffering from high levels of corruption, it was easy to

300 *Brief van de Minister van Justitie, 18.04.2001, Kamerstukken II 2001-2002, just000339.*

301 UN Commission on Human Rights (2000). "Report of the Special Rapporteur on the Sale of Children, Child Prostitution and Child Pornography." 27.01.2000, E/CN.4/2000/73/Add.2.

302 *Ibid.*, para. 13.

303 Latin American Institute for Education and Communication (ILPEC) (2000). "Adoption and the Rights of the Child in Guatemala." Available at http://poundpuplegacy.org/files/Guatemala-UNICEFILPECENG.pdf.

304 *Brief van de Minister van Justitie, 18.04.2001, Kamerstukken II 2001-2002, just000339.*

305 The Permanent Bureau of the Hague Conference on Private International Law (2000). "Report and Conclusions of the Special Commission on the practical operation of the Hague Intercountry Adoption Convention of 29 May 1993 on Protection of Children and Co-operation in Respect of Intercountry Adoption 28 November-1 December 2000." The Hague.

306 *Verslag van een Algemeen Overleg, 30.05.2001, Kamerstukken II 2000-2001, 27 256, Nr. 8.*

307 *Ibid.*, p. 4.

308 *Verslag van een Algemeen Overleg, 17.09.2003, Kamerstukken II 2003-2004, 28 457, Nr. 7*, p. 6.

get a birth certificate or a relinquishment document for small amounts of money in order to hide the actual origin of the illegally obtained child. In addition, the investigation revealed that the authorities in Cambodia has not taken any efforts whatsoever to comply with the subsidiarity principle. Based on these findings, the Minister of Justice decided to suspend intercountry adoptions from Cambodia, arguing that they would not be compliant with the Hague Convention and the UNCRC.

In 2010, the Minister suspended adoptions from Haiti. In the immediate aftermath of the earthquake which rocked the country in December 2010, the Minister installed an accelerated adoption placement procedure to quickly bring 105 children from Haiti to the Netherlands, most of which were already adopted or at least matched with Dutch couples.[309] A couple of months later, he then formally suspended adoptions from Haiti altogether, arguing that proper adoption placement procedures could not be guaranteed any longer as the state structures had collapsed and the risk of corruption and illegal adoption practices had therefore increased.[310] The Netherlands resumed adoptions from Haiti in 2013, after the country decided to ratify the Hague Convention.[311]

In 2012, the Ministry also decided to stop with adoptions from Uganda. It sent a delegation to Uganda after the Dutch embassy in Kampala voiced suspicions about the Ugandan intercountry adoption system's integrity.[312] The Dutch delegation found that the children's origin and background were not properly investigated and that the stakeholders involved in intercountry adoptions demanded money for setting up their reports. The risk was therefore high, it claimed, that the biological parents were falsely informed about the consequences of an intercountry adoption and it was questionable whether the subsidiarity principle was complied with. Based on the delegation's report, the Ministry of Justice and Security banned intercountry adoptions from Uganda and announced 'additional individual investigations' into the adoption files of the 22 Ugandan children that were already proposed to Dutch couples.[313]

A couple of weeks later, it sent a Dutch delegation to Uganda that investigated the manner in which these children were given up for adoption.[314] Particularly, it interviewed the children's biological parents to verify whether or not they were actually aware of an

309 *Brief van de Minister van Justitie, 20.01.2010, Kamerstukken II 2009-2010, 31 265, Nr. 30; Brief van de Minister van Justitie, 18.02.2010, Kamerstukken II 2009-2010, 31 265, Nr. 33.*

310 *Brief van de Staatssecretaris van Veiligheid en Justitie, 10.12.2010, Kamerstukken II 2010-2011, 31 265, Nr. 36.*

311 Ministerie van Justitie en Veiligheid (2016). "Adoptie, Trends en Analyse, Statistisch overzicht interlandelijke adoptie over de jaren 2011 tot en met 2015." Available at https://adoptie.nl/wp-content/uploads/2017/03/2011_tm_2015_Trends_en_analyse_interlandelijke_adoptie.pdf.

312 *Brief van de Staatssecretaris van Veiligheid en Justitie, 11.06.2012, Kamerstukken II 2011-2012, 31 265, Nr. 43.*

313 *Ibid.*

314 *Brief van de Staatssecretaris van Veiligheid en Justitie, 04.10.2012, Kamerstukken II 2012-2013, 31265, Nr. 44.*

adoption's consequences and it conducted DNA examinations to check whether they were the real parents of the children. Ultimately, the Ministry approved 18 of the 22 child proposals. In eight cases, the children's parents did not know about the intercountry adoption's implications. Four families decided to give up their children for intercountry adoption after they had been counselled and informed about the domestic child care options. Three families withdrew their consent to adoption after its implications were explained to them, and one biological father asked for more time to make a final decision.[315] The Ministry explained that it would not conduct an investigation into the background and origin of the Ugandan adoptees that were already placed into Dutch adoptive families (according to the statistics it was 21)[316] as this would not be in the children's best interests[317] and since an already granted adoption cannot be repealed in any case.[318]

The fact that the Minister did not investigate the origin and background of the children that were already placed for adoption in the Netherlands is objectionable. Both the adopters and adoptees, who will perhaps eventually seek their true origin, deserved clarity about the legitimacy of their adoptions. This was also criticized by some members of the Second Chamber.[319] However, apart from that, The Ministry's response to the irregularities in the Ugandan adoption system certainly is remarkable. It took the Dutch embassy's allegations of abusive practices very seriously, sent a Dutch delegation to Uganda to conduct inquiries and then decided to suspend adoptions altogether. With regard to the 22 children that were already proposed to Dutch couples, the Ministry did not want to take any risks but demanded in depth investigations into each individual case and finally let only those children pass the adoption system, after the child's biological parents were properly informed about the consequences of an intercountry adoption.

With regard to adoptions from Guatemala, Cambodia, Haiti and Uganda, all non-Hague sending countries at that time, the Dutch Minister of Justice did not want to take any risks. Based on the reports about illegal practices, he suspended adoptions from these countries. In 2005/2006, however, after serious allegations of abusive practices in the Chinese adoption system became public, the Minister adopted a more reticent attitude. The following section outlines the child laundering incidents that were uncovered in China and describes the manner in which the Chinese authorities and the Dutch Ministry

315 *Ibid.*

316 Ministerie van Justitie en Veiligheid (2013). "Adoptie, Trends en Analyse, Statistisch overzicht interlandelijke adoptie over de jaren 2008 tot en met 2012." Available at https://adoptie.nl/wp-content/uploads/2017/03/Adoptie_trends_en_analyse_2013.pdf; Ministerie van Justitie en Veiligheid (2016). "Adoptie, Trends en Analyse, Statistisch overzicht interlandelijke adoptie over de jaren 2011 tot en met 2015." Available at https://adoptie.nl/wp-content/uploads/2017/03/2011_tm_2015_Trends_en_analyse_interlandelijke_adoptie.pdf.

317 *Brief van de Staatssecretaris van Veiligheid en Justitie, 04.10.2012, Kamerstukken II 2012-2013, 31265, Nr. 44.*

318 *Verslag van een Algemeen Overleg, 13.12.2012, Kamerstukken II 2012-2013, 31 265, Nr. 45,* pp. 13-14.

319 *Ibid.*

responded to them. It then seeks to explain why the Dutch Ministry was reluctant to put pressure on the Chinese authorities or to suspend intercountry adoptions altogether, despite regular reports about irregular and abusive adoption practices in China.

7.4 *The Dutch Ministry's Deference to China*

7.4.1 The Chinese child trafficking incidents

China began sending children abroad for the purposes of intercountry adoption in the 1990s. Western commentators believe that China's one-child policy, that was introduced in the 1980s, combined with the cultural preference for sons has led to a dramatic increase in abandoned female children.[320] In order to relieve the financial burden on the state welfare system, China set up an intercountry adoption programme in 1992.[321] Intercountry adoptions not only aimed to reduce the number of institutionalized children. It also provided a way to generate large sums of money – paid by foreign adopters in the form of fees and mandatory donations – to finance child care institutions and to care for the children that could not be placed for adoption.[322] In 1997, the Chinese Ministry of Civil Affairs established the China Centre for Adoption Affairs (CCAA), which is responsible for approving Chinese orphanages to participate in the intercountry adoption programme, handling foreign adoption applications including the home study reports and doing the matching.[323]

China became one of the most significant suppliers of adoptable children. After it had opened its doors for foreign adopters in the 1990s, the number of intercountry adoptions increased each year, peaking in 2005 with 14,500 children sent abroad,[324] the majority of them immigrating to the United States. Also for the Netherlands, China gradually evolved as an important sending country. Whereas in 1993 only 29 Chinese children were adopted by Dutch parents, the numbers rapidly increased to 457 in 2000, peaking in 2004 with 800 adoptions, comprising about 60% of all intercountry adoptions in the Netherlands.[325]

---

320 K. A. Johnson (2004). "Wanting a Daugther, Needing a Son." Yeong & Yeong, Minneapolis.

321 N. Luo and D. M. Smolin (2004). "Intercountry Adoption and China: Emerging Questions and Developing Chinese Perspectives." Cumberland Law Review, 35, 3, 597-618, pp. 599-607.

322 *Ibid.*

323 P. J. Meier and Z. Xiaole (2008). "Sold into Adoption: The Hunan Baby Trafficking Scandal Exposes Vulnerabilities in the Chinese Adoptions to the United States." Cumberland Law Review, 39, 1, 87-130, p. 96.

324 P. Selman (2012). "The Global Decline of Intercountry Adoption: What Lies Ahead?" Social Policy and Society, 11, 03, 381-397, p. 384.

325 R. A. C. Hoksbergen (2000). "Vijftig Jaar Adoptie in Nederland, Een historisch-statistische beschouwing." Utrecht, available at http://www.vijfeeuwenmigratie.nl/sites/default/files/bronnen/VIJFTIG%20JAAR%20 ADOPTIE.pdf, p. 256.

It was long assumed that China's intercountry adoption system was free from abuses and irregularities.[326] There was little reason to believe that Chinese children adopted by Western couples and individuals were not eligible for intercountry adoption. The adoption system appeared to be well organized and strictly controlled by the Chinese government and it was perceived that China's one-child policy produced countless abandoned and unwanted baby girls who were in need of intercountry adoption.[327] However, this widely held assumption was challenged in 2005, when a child trafficking network was uncovered in Hunan province, involving six (identified) orphanages which had been buying and reselling children for the purposes of intercountry adoption since 2002.[328]

After the Hunan scandal became public – not only nationally but also internationally – the Chinese government sought to maintain the reputation of their intercountry adoption programme. Chinese officials arrested 27 suspects and, only three months later, ten people involved in the child buying scheme were convicted. The director of the key orphanage (the Hengyang Social Welfare Institute) was sentenced to one year in prison, three traffickers received a sentence of 15-years imprisonment and a fine of 50,000 yuan each (about €6,500) and six other traffickers were sentenced to imprisonment between three and thirteen years. Moreover, the government fired 23 county officials in Hengyang and prohibited intercountry adoptions from Hunan Province for several months. Shortly after the trial, the Chinese government censored media coverage on this subject.[329] The convictions and imposed sentences certainly appeared impressive considering the low changes that people involved in child trafficking for adoption purposes receive a serious official response.[330]

After the adoption scandal in Hunan was uncovered in 2005, Ina Hut, director of *Wereldkinderen*, the largest Dutch adoption agency placing the majority of Chinese adoptees, sought clarity of the matter. She wanted to find out whether the adoptions to the Netherlands, particularly those that were carried out by her agency, were also affected. She traveled to China in order to ask the Chinese Central Authority, the CCAA, whether the adoptees that *Wereldkinderen* placed were also illegally obtained by the orphanages. However, the CCAA refused to disclose information on the identity of the children involved in the child buying scandal, claiming that the Dutch adoption agency was not its formal counterpart and that all communication had to take place via the Dutch Central Authority.

---

326 B. H. Stuy (2014). "Open Secret: Cash and Coercion in China's International Adoption Programm." Cumberland Law Review, 44, 3, 355-422, p. 371; D. M. Smolin (2011). "The Missing Girls of China: Population, Policy, Culture, Gender, Abortion, Abandonment, and Adoption in East-Asian Perspective." available at https://works.bepress.com/david_smolin/9/, p. 59.

327 *Ibid.*

328 P. J. Meier and Z. Xiaole (2008). "Sold into Adoption: The Hunan Baby Trafficking Scandal Exposes Vulnerabilities in the Chinese Adoptions to the United States." Cumberland Law Review, 39, 1, 87-130.

329 B. H. Stuy (2014). "Open Secret: Cash and Coercion in China's International Adoption Programm." Cumberland Law Review, 44, 3, 355-422, pp. 89-90.

330 See Chapter II, section 4.2.5.

Hence, Hut urged the Dutch Ministry of Justice and Security to intervene and press for clarification as regards the adoptees' identities. Upon Hut's request, the Minister sent an official delegation to Beijing which met with the CCAA in 2006. The latter reassured that it "had the scandal well under control", "that none of the children [involved in the Hunan scandal] went to the Netherlands and that in all cases where children have gone for adoption abroad, the embassies of the countries concerned were informed".[331]

However, Hut was not reassured by the CCAA's answer. To her, it became apparent that the CCAA told all receiving countries that the children sent to them were not involved in the Hunan child buying scandal. Moreover, new reports emerged indicating that more children were illegally obtained by the child buying network than the CCAA had earlier admitted. Thus, Hut urged the Dutch Ministry of Justice and Security to demand clarification on this matter. The latter sent a letter to the CCAA, asking if new circumstances had emerged since its visit to China which would indicate that the adoptions to the Netherlands had also been affected by abusive practices. It furthermore asked which measures the CCAA intended to take in order to prevent children being illegally placed for intercountry adoptions, meaning in violation of the principles Hague Convention and the UNCRC. Only after the Ministry of Justice and Security (upon *Wereldkinderen's* request) urged the CCAA to respond, did the director of the CCAA send an answer, claiming that the Hunan scandal was an aberration unrelated to intercountry adoption:

> all children involved for inter-country adoption are all [sic] abandoned children, who were placed for adoption in accordance with the principle of 'children's interests as the priority' and the whole procedure was legal and in light of the spirits [sic] of [the] Hague Convention. The adoptions are protected by law and will not cause any problems for the adoptive families. It is known that these children are well cared for in the adoptive families and are doing fine. It is better not to pursue, expand or elaborate on this issue further and to keep secret for related families in order not to interrupt the bond established between the adoptive parents and the children and impose any unnecessary pressure on them.[332]

While the Chinese government took great efforts to characterize the Hunan scandal as an incident that was properly dealt with, the evidence that was accumulated suggests that the

331 I. Hut (2009). "Bevindingen met betrekking tot Interlandelijke Adoptie t.b.v. het Algemeen Overleg Adoptie op 6 oktober 2009." 01.10.2009, available at http://poundpuplegacy.org/files/Reactie%20Ina%20HR%20Hut%20ivm%20AO%206%20okt%202009.pdf, p. 2.

332 Letter from Lu Ying, Dir.-Gen. of the China Center of Adoption Affairs (CCAA) to N.P. Levenkamp, Dir., Ministry of Justice, 20.02.2008, cited in B. H. Stuy (2014). "Open Secret: Cash and Coercion in China's International Adoption Programm." Cumberland Law Review, 44, 3, 355-422, p. 412.

problem was systemic. Numerous reports about irregular adoption practices laid bare the severe weaknesses of the Chinese intercountry adoption system and challenged the widely held Western assumption that there was an endless supply of adoptable healthy female babies from China.[333]

Whereas China had to deal with a plight of abandoned children in the 80s and 90s, the situation apparently changed in the early 2000s. Sex-selective abortions replaced sex-selective abandonment, restrictions on domestic adoption were lifted and incomes were rising, which in turn led to a decrease in the number of institutionalized children.[334] However, financial inducements for sending children abroad for adoption purposes were still there. For the Chinese child care institutions, participating in the intercountry adoption programme was attractive as considerable revenues could be generated by placing children abroad. Foreign adopters had to pay mandatory donations of $3,000-4,000 (sometimes called a 'child-rearing fee') to provincial officials – a sum nearly twice the average annual Chinese income.[335] In addition, many contributed voluntary monetary or material support to the orphanage after the adoption in order to improve the living conditions for the 'remaining children'.[336] These large sums of foreign money formed a strong incentive for Chinese orphanages to obtain as many children as possible and then place them up for intercountry adoption.

In order to keep a steady supply of adoptable young and healthy children, Chinese orphanages used various means to obtain them. Since at least 2001, it appeared, orphanages were purchasing and reselling children for international adoption. They actively used 'child finders' who recruited and sought children from neighbouring provinces, sometimes by

333 P. S. Goodman (2006). "Stealing Babies for adoption." Washington Post, 12.03.2006, available at http://www.washingtonpost.com/wp-dyn/content/article/2006/03/11/AR2006031100942.html; P. J. Meier and Z. Xiaole (2008). "Sold into Adoption: The Hunan Baby Trafficking Scandal exposes Vulnerabilities in the Chinese Adoptions to the United States." Cumberland Law Review, 39, 1, 87-130; B. Demick (2009). "A young Chinese girl pines for her twin." LA Times, 20.09.2009, available at http://articles.latimes.com/2009/sep/20/world/fg-china-twins20; B. Demick (2009). "Some Chinese parents say their babies were stolen for adoption" LA Times, 20.09.2009, available at http://articles.latimes.com/2009/sep/20/world/fg-china-adopt20; B. Demick (2010). "A family in China made babies their business." LA Times, 24.01.2010, available at http://articles.latimes.com/2010/jan/24/world/la-fg-china-adopt24-2010jan24; B. Loyd (2008). "China's lost children." ABC News, 12.05.2008, available at http://abcnews.go.com/International/story?id=4774224; The Schuster Institute for Investigative Journalism, News reports of Adoption Irregularities in China (2006-2011), available at https://www.brandeis.edu/investigate/adoption/china-news.html.

334 D. M. Smolin (2011). "The Missing Girls of China: Population, Policy, Culture, Gender, Abortion, Abandonment, and Adoption in East-Asian Perspective." available at https://works.bepress.com/david_smolin/9/, pp. 55-59.

335 B. H. Stuy (2014). "Open Secret: Cash and Coercion in China's International Adoption Programm." Cumberland Law Review, 44, 3, 355-422, p. 364.

336 *Ibid.*, p. 365.

making false promises to the parents so as to induce abandonment.[337] Furthermore, they bought children from child care institutions that were not approved to participate in the intercountry adoption programme.[338] In addition, population control officials sometimes obtained children from their families by force with the motivation to sell them to orphanages participating in the intercountry adoption programme.[339] In order to hide the illegal procurement of the children, finding certificates were fabricated providing fake information about the time and location the 'abandoned' child was found.[340] Smolin claims: "the increase in intercountry adoptions from 2000 to 2005 was driven by orphanages entering the illicit market for healthy baby girls" and "[t]hese child trafficking practices also clearly explain the drop in intercountry adoptions since 2005".[341]

At the beginning of 2008, the Dutch TV Programme *Netwerk* (EO) investigated the illegal adoption practices that were employed in China. The documentary, broadcast on March 11, showed how family planning officials in Gaoping, in the province Shanxi, confiscated thirteen over-quota or unregistered children and then turned them into the *Shaoyang* orphanage for intercountry adoption.[342] The parents were told that they could only retrieve their child if they paid an amount of money they did not have.[343] The *Netwerk* documentary increased the pressure on the Dutch Ministry. After a member of the Second Chamber urged the Minister to respond to these allegations, the latter reassured that he was planning to send a diplomatic delegation to China to ask the CCAA for clarifications.[344] However, he stressed that the Dutch Ministry as the Central Authority must have faith that the other Central Authorities fulfil their responsibilities and that "in contacts with the CCAA in 2006 and 2007 the image emerged of an organization with the intent to put things

337 P. J. Meier and Z. Xiaole (2008). "Sold into Adoption: The Hunan Baby Trafficking Scandal exposes Vulnerabilities in the Chinese Adoptions to the United States." Cumberland Law Review, 39, 1, 87-130, pp. 102; B. Demick (2010). "A family in China made babies their business." LA Times, 24.01.2010, available at http://articles.latimes.com/2010/jan/24/world/la-fg-china-adopt24-2010jan24; B. Demick (2009). "Some Chinese parents say their babies were stolen for adoption" LA Times, 20.09.2009, available at http://articles.latimes.com/2009/sep/20/world/fg-china-adopt20; The Schuster Institute for Investigative Journalism, News reports of Adoption Irregularities in China (2006-2011), available at https://www.brandeis.edu/investigate/adoption/china-news.html.; P. S. Goodman (2006). "Stealing Babies for adoption." Washington Post, 12.03.2006, available at http://www.washingtonpost.com/wp-dyn/content/article/2006/03/11/AR200603 1100942.html.

338 *Ibid.*

339 *Ibid.*

340 B. H. Stuy (2014). "Open Secret: Cash and Coercion in China's International Adoption Programm." Cumberland Law Review, 44, 3, 355-422, p. 384.

341 D. M. Smolin (2011). "The Missing Girls of China: Population, Policy, Culture, Gender, Abortion, Abandonment, and Adoption in East-Asian Perspective." available at https://works.bepress.com/david_smolin/9/, pp. 62-63.

342 I. Pronk (2008). "Weer ophef rond adoptie uit China." Trouw, 11.03.2998, available at https://www.trouw.nl/home/weer-ophef-rond-adoptie-uit-china~af540f5a/).

343 *Ibid.*

344 *Brief van de Minister van Justitie, 14.03.2008, Kamerstukken II 2007-2008, 31 265, Nr. 3.*

in order".[345] He furthermore stressed, "as in 2005 the irregularities in Hunan were uncovered, it was the CCAA that intervened and made sure that all those involved in child trafficking were convicted".[346]

In May 2008, the Dutch Ministry sent a diplomatic delegation to China where it met with the CCAA, the National Population and Family Planning Commission, the French and Spanish embassies in Beijing, Save the Children UK, UNICEF as well as "several individual persons working in the field of intercountry adoption" and it also visited a child care institution.[347] Upon returning to the Netherlands, the Minister reported to the Dutch adoption agencies placing children from China that the Chinese authorities had everything under control and that he saw no reason to stop adoptions from China.

For *Wereldkinderen*, the Ministry's inquiries in China did not go far enough. They criticized the Dutch delegation for not having conducted investigations themselves, particularly in the provinces, and for being content with the statements of the Chinese authorities. Before the Minister sent his letter to the second Chamber, *Wereldkinderen* went to China – both to Beijing and some provinces – to seek more clarity. They spoke to the CCAA, local authorities, directors and staff members of child care institutions, staff members of other foreign adoption agencies, an investigative journalist, an expert from UNICEF, ILO, a Chinese Dutch scholar, the Dutch ambassador as well as to their own Chinese representatives.[348] *Wereldkinderen* thereby got the impression that paying for children that were brought to child care institutions would not just happen incidentally but rather on a large scale, that the subsidiarity principle is not actually implemented, that the Chinese local authorities and child care institutions have more information about the child than is being presented to the foreign adoption agencies and that there are enough couples in China willing to adopt.[349] Hut shared her impressions with the Dutch Minister who, however, was not convinced. In his letter to the Second Chamber he reported the following findings of the Dutch delegation's visit in China:

- according to the Chinese authorities, all children placed for adoption from China have been abandoned by their parents (most of them are girls or special-needs children);[350]
- in order to make sure that the children have been abandoned voluntarily, the origin of the children was being investigated by the authorities;[351]

345 *Ibid.*

346 *Ibid.*

347 *Brief van de Minister van Justitie, 03.06.2008, Kamerstukken II 2007-2008, 31 265, Nr. 7.*

348 I. Hut (2009). "Bevindingen met betrekking tot Interlandelijke Adoptie t.b.v. het Algemeen Overleg Adoptie op 6 oktober 2009." 01.10.2009, available at http://poundpuplegacy.org/files/Reactie%20Ina%20HR%20Hut%20ivm%20AO%206%20okt%202009.pdf, p. 9.

349 *Ibid.*, p. 10.

350 *Brief van de Minister van Justitie, 10.09.2008, Kamerstukken II 2007-2008, 31 265, Nr. 9,* p. 2.

351 *Ibid.*, p. 3.

- paying money for children is prohibited in China; however, donations to the child care institutions are permitted; they are regulated and controlled by the Chinese authorities;[352]
- the Chinese Central Authority explained that it is quite common for child finders to be given money (usually only 'symbolic' amounts) as a sign of gratitude that they brought the children to the orphanage; it stressed that it opposed this practice and that it had started a campaign to raise awareness that foundlings should be brought to the police rather than to an orphanage;[353]
- the numbers of Chinese couples willing to adopt are increasing and the authorities prioritize the placement of children within Chinese adoptive or foster families; China is thus primarily placing special-needs children for intercountry adoption;[354]
- the one-child policy is exerting pressure on the Chinese people; however, according to the Chinese Central Authority, no pressure is being exerted on the parents to relinquish their over-quota children who are subsequently being placed for intercountry adoption;[355] and
- the child dossiers that were presented to the Dutch delegation for inspection made a professional impression.[356]

Based on these findings, the Minister concluded that "the regulations in China are in accordance with the principles of the Hague Convention and [that] the authorities in Beijing made a lot of effort to make sure adoptions are in accordance with the Hague Convention".[357] The Chinese authorities were aware that irregularities could occur and they promised to take actions if they were uncovered. According to the Minister, "the manner in which the authorities responded to the irregularities in Hunan confirms that".[358] He emphasized that it falls within the responsibility of the competent authorities in the sending countries to control whether the requirements of the Hague Convention are being met and that he must have faith that they are doing so.[359] Finally, he concluded that "there is no reason to reconsider the existing adoption relationship between the Netherlands and China".[360] He promised to increase the collaboration with China as well as to establish a

352 *Ibid.*
353 *Ibid.*, p. 4.
354 *Ibid.*, pp. 3-4.
355 *Ibid.*, p. 4.
356 *Ibid.*, p. 5.
357 *Ibid.*, p. 6.
358 *Ibid.*
359 *Ibid.*
360 *Ibid.*, p. 7.

special advisor (*special adviseur*) at the Dutch Central Authority that would be responsible for the communication.[361]

In 2009, the Dutch newspaper *Trouw* covered another adoption scandal, reported by the Chinese media, which occurred in Zhenyuan in the province Guizhou.[362] Since 2001, about 80 over-quota children were removed from their families by the Chinese authorities and then placed in an orphanage. After the children's documents were falsified by the orphanage, together with the Chinese authorities, to make them look like foundlings, they were sent abroad for adoption, some of them to the Netherlands. It transpired that seven Chinese children adopted by Dutch families came from this orphanage in Zhenyuan.[363]

A member of the Second Chamber asked the Minister whether he intended to investigate these allegations and to clarify whether Chinese adoptions to the Netherlands were affected.[364] The Minister responded that he asked the Chinese authorities to clarify whether the seven children adopted by families in the Netherlands were affected by the irregular practices in Zhenyuan. Furthermore, he requested the Youth Inspectorate to look into the seven adoption placements and to find out whether the Dutch adoption agencies had acted diligently.[365] With regard to the question of whether he intended to stop adoptions from China, the Minister replied that he wanted to wait for the results of the investigation of the Chinese authorities. Furthermore, he said: "[f]rom the reports so far, I cannot say that there are structural irregularities. […] On the basis of the information available now, the case seems to be an isolated one. I do thus not see a reason to stop with adoptions of children from China altogether".[366]

Two weeks after the Minister sent his response, Hut stepped down as the director of *Wereldkinderen*. On TV, Hut explained that the inquiries by the Dutch authorities in China did not go far enough, that *Wereldkinderen* wanted to conduct more thorough investigations itself, but that two officials of the Dutch Ministry of Justice and Security threatened to withdraw the agency's accreditation if such investigations took place.[367] This, she clarified, was one of the main reasons why she decided to quit.[368] Later she explained that:

> In my endeavour for transparency and open procedures and in my endeavour to establish the truth with regard to the background of the adoptees, I am not

361 *Ibid.*

362 M. Roessingh (2009). "Weer adoptieschandaal China." Trouw, 03.07.2009, available at https://www.trouw.nl/home/weer-adoptieschandaal-china~a0620ea0/.

363 *Brief van de Minister van Justitie, 15.02.2010, Kamerstukken II 2009-2010, 31 265, Nr. 31.*

364 *Ministerie van Justitie, Antwoorden kamervragen over gestolen Chinese adoptiekinderen, 04.08.2009, Kamerstukken II 2009-2010, 5610670/09/DJJ.*

365 *Ibid.*

366 *Ibid.*

367 Netwerk (2009). "Directeur adoptieorganisatie stapt op na intimidatie Netwerk." 18.08.2009, available at https://www.youtube.com/watch?v=rKzle3UQFoI.

368 *Ibid.*

> sufficiently supported but restrained by the Minister of Justice. [...] The Ministry of Justice and Security needs to give primacy to the best interests of adoptees and children. My experience is that [...] the [Minister] prioritizes economic, diplomatic and also political interests over the interests of children and adoptees.[369]

Hut's resignation further increased pressure on the Dutch Minister of Justice. In October 2009, a general consultation of the Second Chamber over intercountry adoptions from China took place.[370] In this session, the Dutch Minister was exposed to vehement criticism regarding the manner in which the Ministry responded to the adoption scandal in China. Members of the Second Chamber wanted to know why the Ministry impeded investigations by *Wereldkinderen*,[371] why it still trusted the CCAA's explanations despite recurring reports about irregularities[372] and why the Dutch delegation did not conduct proper inquiries in China. The Minister sought to conciliate by explaining that he was still waiting for the findings of the investigation into the adoption scandal in Zhenyuan, that were conducted by the Chinese authorities as well as the Youth Inspectorate. He furthermore stressed that:

> [It is] worth noting that we are not dealing with a Chinese agency but with a state: The Republic of China. That also was decisive for the way we have approached the idea of an own-initiative inquiry. The Republic of China is our contract partner. It would be very wrong to negate that. We would create the impression that we are investigating on our own initiative into something that falls within the responsibility that we states must address.[373]

At the beginning of 2010, the Minister shared the findings of the Youth Inspectorate's investigation with the Second Chamber.[374] In its report, the Inspectorate concluded that the two adoption agencies placing children from the orphanage in Zhenyuan acted within the available possibilities and that the information provided about the adoptees were not always reliable.[375] It described a tension between the principle of trust as laid down in the

369 I. Hut (2009). "Bevindingen met betrekking tot Interlandelijke Adoptie t.b.v. het Algemeen Overleg Adoptie op 6 oktober 2009." 01.10.2009, available at http://poundpuplegacy.org/files/Reactie%20Ina%20HR%20Hut%20ivm%20AO%206%20okt%202009.pdf, p. 18.

370 *Verslag van een Algemeen Overleg, 06.10.2009, Kamerstukken II 2009-2010, 31 265 Nr. 28.*

371 *Ibid.*, p. 3.

372 Langkamp (SP) said: "Why does the Minister still have trust in the CCAA's investigation? It became already obvious that they [the Chinese authorities] were not right when they said that there is nothing wrong." *Ibid.*, p. 19.

373 *Ibid.*, p. 19.

374 *Brief van de Minister van Justitie, 23.07.2010, Kamerstukken II 2009-2010, 31 265 Nr. 35.*

375 *Achtergrond Onbekend? Onderzoek naar het Handelen van Twee Vergunninghouders bij de Interlandelijke Adoptie van Zeven Chinese Kinderen, 13.01.2010, Kamerstukken II, 2009-2010, 31265, Nr. 29.*

Hague Convention, on the one hand, and the responsibility of the adoption agencies' to control the reliability of the adoptees' information, on the other. The Inspectorate also stressed that the Dutch Central Authority must take on a more active role and stop intercountry adoptions if the risks of irregularities are too high.[376]

One month later, the Minister reported to the Second Chamber that he had also received a response from the CCAA.[377] According to the latter, investigations revealed that the report on illegal adoption practices in Zhenyuan was incorrect. The CCAA explained that the adoption placements from the orphanage were carried out in accordance with Chinese laws and procedures and reassured all stakeholders that the adoptions of the seven Chinese children placed with families in the Netherlands were legal.[378] In his letter, the Dutch Minister reiterated the sending countries' responsibility to control whether the Hague Convention's requirements are met as well as the principle of trust and concluded: "On the basis of the aforesaid I do therefore not see a reason to take further steps".[379]

A couple of months later, the Minister sent another letter informing the Second Chamber that a Dutch delegation went to China where it met with the CCAA, the Chinese Ministry of Public Security, representatives of an U.S. adoption agency and volunteers of 'Baby Come Home', an organization established by parents whose children have been stolen. The Chinese authorities, the letter stated, would admit that child trafficking for the purposes of domestic adoption is a problem in China (since the demand for children is increasing), but that there was no link between child trafficking and intercountry adoption. According to the Chinese authorities, the risk that children are obtained from their families and then illegally placed for intercountry adoption is very rare.[380]

7.4.2 Trust in the authorities of Hague sending countries

China's intercountry adoption system is unique insofar as it is entirely state-run. Foreign adoption placement agencies do not cooperate with Chinese partner organizations, like adoption agencies or child care institutions. Rather, they must collaborate with the Chinese Central Authority, the CCAA, which is responsible for matching foreign adoption applicants with children from child care institutions that are permitted to participate in the intercountry adoption programme.[381] Many foreign adoption agencies have representatives in China which mediate between them and the CCAA. Particularly, they accompany the adopters in China and assist them in carrying out the bureaucratic procedures. However, they are prohibited from directly contacting the Chinese child care institutions from which the

376 *Ibid.*
377 *Brief van de Minister van Justitie, 15.02.2010, Kamerstukken II 2009-2010, 31 265, Nr. 31.*
378 *Ibid.*
379 *Ibid.*
380 *Ibid.*
381 P. J. Meier and Z. Xiaole (2008). "Sold into Adoption: The Hunan Baby Trafficking Scandal exposes Vulnerabilities in the Chinese Adoptions to the United States." Cumberland Law Review, 39, 1, 87-130, p. 96.

adoptees are placed. Hence, given the closed nature of the adoption system in China, foreign adoption agencies only have limited possibilities to control the legitimacy of the adoption placements they carry out. They can only assess whether the envisaged adoptions are legitimate on the basis of the documents they receive from the CCAA. This was also the conclusion of the Youth Inspectorate's investigation into the two Dutch adoption agencies placing children from China at the time the scandals were exposed (*Wereldkinderen* and *Meiling*).[382]

Also, the authorities in the receiving countries only have limited possibilities to control the legitimacy of the adoption placements. They may travel to the states of origin, meet with the authorities and request (additional) information on the background of the adoptees or demand access to the child care institutions. In addition, they may seek background information from NGOs (such as UNICEF and/or Save the Children). However, their assessment regarding the trustworthiness of the foreign adoption stakeholders is ultimately confined to the information that is provided by foreign authorities or NGOs. It could not have been expected from the Dutch delegation that traveled to China after the adoption scandals were uncovered to conduct investigations into the adoption system itself without the knowledge and approval of the Chinese authorities. It is therefore understandable that the Dutch Minister was opposed to own-initiative investigations by the Dutch delegation.

Yet, what is not understandable is that the Minister accepted quite uncritically, as it seems, the explanations and reassurances given by the Chinese authorities, notwithstanding the existence of recurring reports on irregular adoption practices and *Wereldkinderen*'s own investigation which signalled systemic abuses in the Chinese adoption system. In his statements to the Second Chamber – many of whose members strongly criticized the Minister for his reticent attitude – he repeatedly stressed the principle of mutual trust between Hague countries.[383] He explained that the responsibility to control whether an adoption complies with the Convention's requirements rests with the country of origin and that the Netherlands needs to have confidence in the foreign authorities' integrity and in the reliability of the information provided on the children. If doubts arise, he asserted, the Dutch Central Authority or the Ministry of Foreign Affairs must ask the foreign authorities in the sending countries for more information and may urge them to take measures.[384]

The Minister had already previously emphasized the responsibilities of the authorities in the states of origin and mutual trust. In 2005, an Indian adoption agency - Malaysia

382 *Achtergrond Onbekend? Onderzoek naar het Handelen van Twee Vergunninghouders bij de Interlandelijke Adoptie van Zeven Chinese Kinderen, 13.01.2010, Kamerstukken II, 2009-2010, 31265, Nr. 29.*

383 *Brief van de Minister van Justitie, 10.09.2008, Kamerstukken II 2007-2008, 31 265, Nr. 9, p. 6.; Vragen gesteld door de leden der kamer, met de daarop door de regering gegeven antwoorden, 02.09.2009, Kamerstukken II 2008-2009, 2009Z14923, p. 7804; Verslag van een Algemeen Overleg, 06.10.2009, Kamerstukken II 2009-2010, 31 265 Nr. 28,* p. 20.

384 *Brief van de Minister van Justitie, 10.09.2008, Kamerstukken II 2007-2008, 31 265, Nr. 9,* p. 6.

Social Service Centre (MSSC) - was accused and found guilty of having kidnapped children from the streets, slums, hospitals and busy markets and then placing them up for intercountry adoption.[385] The Dutch adoption agency *Meiling* cooperated with MSSC between 1995 and 2002[386] and, as it later turned out, had placed a kidnapped child (named Rahul) into an adoptive family in the Netherlands (see section 6.3). In his letter to the Second Chamber, the Dutch Minister explained why the Ministry did not know and also could not have known about the uncovered illegal practices in India:

> In the treaty [the Hague Convention], duties and responsibilities are being allocated to the Central Authorities of the sending as well as the receiving countries, assuming mutual trust that each of the contracting states accepts and fulfils the allocated tasks and responsibilities. [...] Regarding the performance of the contractual duties, the Netherlands, just like other countries, must (can) thus to a great extent rely on the integrity of the institutions and authorities in the 'sending' countries.[387]

Indeed, the Hague Convention distributes the responsibility for fulfilling the requirements of an international adoption between the sending and the receiving countries. Whereas the authorities in the receiving countries have to examine the adopters' eligibility and suitability to adopt, the authorities in the sending countries have to verify the child's adoptability, ensuring that the necessary consent for an adoption have been freely given, fully informed, counselled, without any financial inducement and in the required form and determining that the subsidiarity principle is complied with.[388] The Convention allocates the lion's share of responsibility to the states of origin.[389] This makes sense as the competent authorities in the child's native country are better positioned than foreign authorities to determine whether the child is actually available for an intercountry adoption.

However, despite the Hague Convention's allocation of the most important duties to the sending countries, the receiving nations are still required to make assessments themselves regarding the integrity of the sending countries' intercountry adoption system and

385 Aravamudan, G. (2017) "Child trafficking, 'manufactured orphans': The dark underbelly of inter-country adoption in India." Firstpost, 03.09.2017, available at http://www.firstpost.com/india/child-trafficking-manufactured-orphans-the-dark-underbelly-of-inter-country-adoption-in-india-4000837.html.

386 *Meiling en adoptie uit India; Onderzoek naar het handelen van vergunninghouder interlandelijke adoptie Meiling in de periode 1995 t/m 2002 naar aanleiding van signalen over mogelijke misstanden in India, 09.11.2007, Kamerstukken II 2007-2008, 31 265, Nr. 1.*

387 *Brief van de Minister van Justitie, 07.11.2007, Kamerstukken II 2007-2008, 31 265, Nr. 1,* p. 6.

388 Art 4. Hague Convention.

389 R. Rios-Kohn (1998). "Intercountry adoption: An international perspective on the practice and standards." Adoption Quarterly, 1, 4, 3-32, p. 27.

on the reliability of the information provided about the children.[390] As was already explained, many sending countries, including those which have ratified the Hague Convention, suffer from high levels of corruption. Authorities in the receiving states can therefore *not* necessarily trust that their foreign counterparts properly fulfil the tasks and responsibilities assigned to them by the treaty and that the proposed children are legitimately available for intercountry adoption.[391] Thus, the Convention's Guide to Good Practice No. 2 emphasizes a mandate of 'shared' or 'joint responsibility':

> The Contracting States must not only assume their own specific responsibilities, but also share certain others. In essence, receiving States and States of origin have a collective responsibility to make the Convention work as it was intended, and they must work together to ensure the effective regulation of intercountry adoptions.[392]

This also means, the Guide further explains, that receiving countries need to take proactive steps when systemic abuses occur, by trying to eliminate them, by discontinuing or refusing adoptions from an underperforming sending state, if this is necessary.[393] However, the Dutch Ministry interpreted the treaty's allocation of duties as relieving the receiving countries from the responsibility for the adoption steps taken in the countries of origin. It claims that the Netherlands should not only, but actually must, have confidence in the integrity of the foreign authorities in the Hague sending countries and trust that they will fulfil the tasks assigned to them by the Convention.

With regard to adoptions from China, trust on part of the Netherlands arguably was misplaced. The letter sent by the CCAA's director to the Dutch Central Authority, which demanded clarifications after the Hunan scandal, signalled that the Chinese authorities were unwilling to properly investigate the origin and background of the children from Hunan that were placed for intercountry adoption ("It is better not to pursue, expand or elaborate on this issue further and to keep secret for related families in order not to interrupt the bond established between the adoptive parents and the children and impose any unnecessary pressure on them"). Furthermore, recurring media reports about irregular adoption practices in China, including the findings of *Wereldkinderen's* own investigation, contradicted the Chinese authorities' assurances, namely that the uncovered scandals in Hunan and Zhenyuan were only a few bad apples in an overwhelmingly Hague compliant

390 B. H. Stuy (2014). "Open Secret: Cash and Coercion in China's International Adoption Programm." Cumberland Law Review, 44, 3, 355-422, p. 358.

391 See Chapter IV, sections 5.3. and 5.4.

392 The Permanent Bureau of the Hague Conference on International Private Law (2012). "Accreditation and Adoption Accredited Bodies: Guide to Good Practice No. 2." The Hague, para. 551.

393 *Ibid.*, para. 553.

adoption system. Finally, CCAA's downplaying of the role that money and the one-child policy played in the Chinese intercountry adoption system showed that the authorities in China were not prepared, as they assured, to properly tackle irregular practices.

However, the Dutch Minister seemed to have been unimpressed by the numerous red flags. He brushed aside signs of systemic irregularities in the Chinese adoption system, readily accepted the flimsy explanations that he and his delegation were presented with by the Chinese authorities and was dazzled by adoption paperwork that, he praised, "made a professional impression". Rather than urging the Chinese authorities to investigate the adoption scandals thoroughly, the Minister asked the Youth Inspectorate to examine whether the two Dutch adoption agencies that were placing children from the orphanage in Zhenyuan at that time (*Wereldkinderen* and *Meiling*) had properly examined the Chinese adoption files. Instead of putting pressure on the CCAA to disclose more information on the children sent to the Netherlands that came from the orphanages involved in the scandals – if necessary by threatening to discontinue adoptions from China altogether – the Ministry hid behind the mantra of shared responsibility and mutual trust.

7.4.3 Diplomatic and other interests in intercountry adoptions

It is not only the interpretation regarding the Hague Convention's allocation of responsibilities as a mandate of deference and mutual trust which explains the Minister's reluctance to exert pressure on the Chinese authorities. Also, diplomatic, as well as other interests that were at stake at that time might have influenced his reticent attitude towards the Chinese authorities. Generally speaking, a receiving country's decision regarding the manner in which to respond to signs of irregular adoption practices in a sending country is not only based on the best interests of children but also takes into account diplomatic interests as well as the interests of adoption agencies and (prospective) adopters.

The important relationship between China and the Netherlands might have been one of the reasons why the Dutch Ministry was reluctant to exert pressure on the Chinese authorities or to discontinue intercountry adoptions altogether. China was - and still is - one of the biggest trading partners of the Netherlands. Dutch exports have increased tenfold in the last ten years to €7.8 billion in 2013 and China's investments in the Netherlands have increased tenfold since 2006 to over €700 million.[394] Numerous Dutch companies have expanded their business to China. This has been partly due to the port in Rotterdam, whereby the Netherlands has become China's entrance to Europe and other European trade partners.[395] In 2007 - at that time the Netherlands still was China's second economic partner in the EU - the state secretary of the Dutch Ministry of Economic Affairs and the

394 F. Harm (2014). "Wat doet China in Nederland?" NOS, 22.03.2014, available at https://nos.nl/artikel/626521-wat-doet-china-in-nederland.html.

395 *Ibid.*

Chinese Vice-President agreed to further intensify the economic relationship at the Joint Economic Committee in The Hague.[396] As the irregular adoption practices were uncovered in Hunan one year later, the Ministry probably sought to deal with the scandal in a manner that would not impede the flourishing economic relationship with China. Hence, it not only refused to increase the pressure on the Chinese authorities, it also explicitly prohibited *Wereldkinderen* from conducting its own investigations. After Hut resigned as a director of *Wereldkinderen*, the Minister clarified in his response to a number of critical parliamentary questions as to why the agency was prohibited from carrying out its own investigations:

> I find it important to stress that it is customary that the Netherlands approaches states with whom it sustains a contractual relationship in international legal relations. An undercover investigation is not consistent with that. Such an investigation could have unintended and undesirable consequences for the cooperation between the Netherlands and China, first and foremost in the field of adoption, but also with regard to other relations.[397]

The Quality Framework basically obliges the Dutch adoption agencies to check their foreign partner organizations' integrity and to monitor and control their activities. Yet, as the Dutch Minister emphasized, the agencies' mandate to supervise their partners in the sending countries is limited by diplomatic customs:

> I expect from the agencies that an investigation into the integrity of their foreign partner organization does not go further than what is condign in international legal relations and what is laid down in the Quality Framework. In case only insufficient information can be obtained, the agencies do have the possibility to call in the Dutch Central Authority to try to get the needed information.[398]

Interestingly, the Ministry did not have a problem with the investigation that *Wereldkinderen* had carried out in relation to Ethiopia in 2009. The agency's director, Ina Hut, had become suspicious about the legitimacy of adoptions from Ethiopia after having received several reports that women would show up at the entrance of its orphanage and ask for information about their children. Thus, Hut contracted the organization *Against Child Trafficking (ACT)* to conduct a study into 25 randomly selected adoption files of children placed from five child care institutions throughout Ethiopia between 2004 and

396 "Nederland en China versterken economische relatie." Trouw (10.09.2007), available https://www.trouw.nl/home/nederland-en-china-versterken-economische-relatie~a3883370/.

397 *Vragen gesteld door de leden der kamer, met de daarop door de regering gegeven antwoorden, 02.09.2009, Kamerstukken II 2008-2009, 2009Z14923.*

398 *Ibid.*

2009.[399] These files were cross-checked during field visits in Ethiopia, where the children's birth families were traced and interviewed. In 19 of the 25 adoption cases, irregularities were detected and analysed which were described in the report entitled "Fruits in Ethiopia". The study exposed a dysfunctional adoption industry in Ethiopia whereby children were systematically being "harvested" from their intact families. According to the report, no efforts were made to help the families stay together; rather, intercountry adoption was offered to them as the best possible option for their children. It is the case that the relinquishing birth parents typically do not understand the Western concept of adoption. Many are promised to receive updates about their children and expect them to return home once they finish school abroad. After the children have been recruited, their documents are often forged. The study found that in a number of cases the information in both the adoption file as well as the Court order was incorrect. For example, the parents were falsely declared dead and the children's birth dates or health status turned out to be wrong.[400] Based on these findings, the Dutch adoption agency *Wereldkinderen* decided to suspend adoptions from Ethiopia.[401] In a general consultation of the Second Chamber over intercountry adoptions from China which took place in October 2009, the Minister applauded *Wereldkinderen's* initiative with regard to Ethiopia:

> I find the decision of Stichting Wereldkinderen to temporarily suspend [adoptions from Ethiopia] and to conduct investigations courageous. Also, I appreciate that one takes such a step if he finds that there is the reason for that. This critical attitude is very much appreciated. I follow this investigation with great interest.[402]

Not only diplomatic interests, but also the interests of Dutch adopters and adoption agencies might have somewhat influenced the Dutch Minister's decision to continue intercountry adoptions from China or to refrain from increasing the pressure on the CCAA, despite reports of systemic abuses. For several years, China has been the most dominant sending country for the Netherlands in terms of the number of children placed. In 2007, China sent 365 children to the Netherlands for intercountry adoption, comprising almost

399 Wereldkinderen and Against Child Trafficking (2009). "Fruits of Ethiopia. Intercountry Adoption: The Rights of the Child, or the "Harvesting" of Children? A Study on Intercountry Adoption in Ethiopia." available at http://www.againstchildtrafficking.org/wp-content/uploads/Second-Interim-Report-FINAL-redacted-for-distribution+annexures.pdf.

400 *Ibid.*

401 See https://web.archive.org/web/20090926140159/ http://www.ethiopianreview.com/news/6790 (last visited on Sep. 29th 2016).

402 *Verslag van een Algemeen Overleg, 06.10.2009, Kamerstukken II 2009-2010, 31 265 Nr. 28*, p. 24.

50% of all international adoptees coming to the Netherlands.[403] For many Dutch adopters, China was an attractive sending country. The placement procedures were relatively fast and it sent the kind of adoptees that most applicants were looking for: young and healthy girls. *Wereldkinderen* placed most of the children (163 in 2007), followed by *Kind en Toekomst* (149) and *Meiling* (53).[404] For all these agencies, adoptions from China had made up the lion's share of all their placements: for 51% for *Wereldkinderen*, 58% for *Meiling* and even 66% for *Kind en Toekomst*.[405] At this point in time, it would therefore have been a major shock if the Dutch Minister decided to suspend adoptions from China. The Netherlands would have lost its most important supply country overnight, thereby probably forcing *Kind en Toekomst* and *Meiling* to shut down their adoption business and leaving many Dutch prospective adopters disgruntled, especially those who had been on the waiting list for several months. In 2007, more than 1,500 principle approvals were provided and 2008 the figure was some 1,000.[406] Adding to these newly approved adoption applicants were adopters who had received their approval in previous years, but were still waiting for a child proposal. Hence, the pressure to adopt internationally was intense in the Netherlands at that time, and the Minister probably would have had to deal with strong opposition from Dutch adopters and agencies if he decided to ban adoptions from China.

In the Netherlands, adoption agencies and (prospective) adoptive parents have a powerful voice in the debates on intercountry adoption. International adopters are organized into interest groups (*Adoptie Ouders Overleg AdoptieVereniging Gereformeerde Gezindte, De Adoptievereniging de Rode Draad* and *Belangenvereniging Zelfdoeners in Adoptie*) which also seek to influence policies and decisions on intercountry adoption. Two days after intercountry adoptions from China were discussed in the Second Chamber, a round-table discussion about this issue took place whereby scholars, adoptees, adoptive parents, adoptions agencies and other organizations were in attendance. The two adoption agencies placing children from China at that moment in time were content with the Dutch Ministry's investigation. For instance, in its position paper, *Meiling* wrote:

> The outcome of the investigation as sent to you by the Minister appears to the agency as a sound investigation. This letter shows that there is no reason to assume that there are irregularities on a structural level. This has been confirmed by UNICEF and Save the Children. *Meiling*, therefore, endorses the conclusion of the Minister of Justice that there is no direct reason to mistrust the integrity of the Central Chinese adoption authority (CCAA) or to stop with adoptions

403 Ministerie van Justitie en Veiligheid (2010). "Adoptie, Trends en Analyse, Statistisch overzicht interlandelijke adoptie over de jaren 2005 tot en met 2009." (on file with author).

404 *Ibid.*

405 *Ibid.*

406 *Ibid.*

from China. *Meiling* does thus also not consider stopping with the placement of children from China.

Also, the *De Adoptievereniging de Rode Draad* (*ARD*) was convinced by the Ministerial letter. In its position paper, it wrote: "The ARD appreciates the fact that the government has straightforwardly addressed the reported irregularities with the Chinese authorities". The statements of both the adoptive parents and the adoption agencies supported the Ministry's approach towards the scandals in China.

8 Criminal Liability of Dutch Actors

8.1 *Adopters*

Article 278 of the Dutch Criminal Code[407] (*Wetboek Strafrecht*, hereinafter Sr.) criminalizes human kidnapping (*mensenroof*) and can be applicable to cases whereby children are trafficked to the Netherlands for the purposes of adoption.[408] This provision was meant to protect vulnerable individuals from being transferred out of Europe: "Any person who takes another person across the borders of the Kingdom in Europe, with the intention of unlawfully placing him under the control of another person or placing him in a powerless situation, shall be guilty of kidnapping". Human kidnapping is punishable by a fine or imprisonment of up to 12 years and has a prosecution deadline of 20 years.

In 1999, Article 278 Sr. was applied to a case of an illegal intercountry adoption for the first time.[409] Two individuals falsified the documents of a one year-old baby (Lisa) and then brought her from Brazil to the Netherlands with the aim of handing her over to a Dutch couple, whom intended to pass the child off as their biological child. Both individuals were charged with falsifying documents and for human kidnapping as they had trafficked the baby across European borders with the intention of unlawfully placing her under the control of the Dutch couple (namely outside the official intercountry adoption procedure) and in a powerless situation, considering the child's age and the fact that she was lacking official status because her documents were falsified.

The Court of the Second Instance acquitted the accused of the human kidnapping charge because they had brought the child into and not out of Europe. However, the Dutch Supreme Court overturned this decision, arguing that Article 278 Sr. is to be broadly interpreted so as to also cover the transfer of persons to the Netherlands from abroad since

407 *Wetboek van Strafrecht van 30 januari 1886, zoals laatstelijk gewijzigd met Stb. 2017, 317.*

408 P. P. J. Van der Meij (2016). "Commentaar op art. 278 Sr." In C.P.M. Cleiren et al. (eds), "Strafrecht, Tekst en Commentaar Strafrecht." Wolters Kluwer, Deventer.

409 *Hoge Raad, 20.11. 2001, 00460/00, ECLI:NL:HR:2001:AB2809.*

they, too, require protection.[410] The accused was finally convicted of human kidnapping and sentenced to 11 months' imprisonment, of which he had to spend 3 months in jail.[411] In the decision, the court motivated the sentence as follows: "by these actions, the rule of law has been seriously undermined, because a little girl has been brought to the Netherlands as if she was a piece of commodity, with large sums of money being involved. Furthermore, it cannot be excluded that the child will later suffer psychically from these actions. [The accused] made sure that the child has been taken her real identity, she no longer has her own name and only false documents, including a passport, are available about her".[412]

The Dutch Supreme Court's broad interpretation of Article 278 Sr. has opened the possibility of applying the criminal provisions on human kidnapping to cases of child trafficking for adoption purposes. However, in practice, it is only the adopters' intermediaries that are being held liable for human kidnapping and not the adopters themselves. If couples or individuals traffic a child with the intention of taking care or adopting him or her, they can only be criminally liable for placing another person 'into a powerless situation' (not, however, for placing the child 'under the control of *another* person'). Yet, this element is very difficult to prove. For instance, in 2005, a couple that trafficked a baby from Turkey to the Netherlands as their own biological child was charged *inter alia* with human kidnapping. The court held that a person is placed in a powerless situation according to Article 278 Sr. only if his or her health or life is endangered.[413] It argued that the fact that the child was only one year-old and could not care for herself did not *ipso eo* mean that she was placed in a powerless situation. Since the couple wanted to take care of the child instead of endangering her health or life, they were acquitted of the human trafficking charge.[414] This line of argumentation was also advanced in other published decisions on similar cases.[415]

Adopters may be held criminally liable for child abduction according to Article 279 Sr. (*onttrekken aan gezag*), if they take a child from the parents or legal guardian without the required consent. If they use deception, violence or threats of violence to remove a child under the age of 12 years-old, then they commit an aggravated offence according to Article 279(2) Sr. However, in practice this criminal provision is difficult to prove in cases of intercountry adoption. For instance, in 2009 a Dutch couple that illegally transferred a child from the Philippines to the Netherlands (without the principle approval) for the purposes of care were accused of *inter alia* child abduction according to Article 279(2) Sr.

410 *Ibid.*

411 *Gerechtshof Arnhem, 12.11.2002, 21-21000804-02, ECLI:NL:GHARN:2002:AF4646; Gerechtshof Arnhem, 18.11.2002, 21-000799-02, ECLI:NL:GHARN:2002:AF4646.*

412 *Ibid.*

413 *Rechtbank Almelo, 21.06.2005, 08/005134-04, ECLI:NL:RBALM:2005:AT7809.*

414 *Ibid.*

415 *Rechtbank Almelo, 21.06.2005, 08/005134-04, ECLI:NL:RBALM:2005:AT7809; Rechtbank Leeuwarden, 29.09.2009, 17/885167-09 VEV, ECLI:NL:RBLEE:2009:BJ8794.*

They had the child's birth certificate issued with their names as the biological parents and claimed that the actual mother, an 18 year-old woman, handed her over to them shortly before she passed away because she could not care for the child. The child's biological father, they alleged, was unknown to them.

The court in Leeuwarden acquitted the couple of the child abduction charge. It held that it could not establish as to who had custody over the child on the day she was brought to the Netherlands and that it could therefore not be proven that the couple had taken the child from her mother without consent.[416] The acquittal was confirmed by the Court in the Second Instance[417] The prosecution brought the case to the Dutch Supreme Court.[418] It argued that the intercountry adoption took place unlawfully, which is why custody was never been transferred to the Dutch couple. Thus, if the latter did not have custody over the child, somebody else therefore did – either the biological mother when she was still alive, the biological father, other family members or the Philippine state. This, it was argued, is why the couple must be held criminally liable for taking away somebody else's child according to Article 279 Sr.[419] The Dutch Supreme Court did not follow the prosecution's argumentation, however. It held that the fact that the couple had brought the child to the Netherlands in circumvention of the official international adoption procedure would not *per se* make them criminally liable for child abduction according to Article 279 Sr.[420] Furthermore, the Court argued, neither the Hague Convention nor the UNCRC (notably Article 21 thereof) is compatible with the requirement to prove from whose custody the child was removed illegally.[421]

Adopters can be held criminally liable for forgery of documents according to Articles 225, 227 and 231 Sr. (*valsheid in geschrifte*), if they falsify a document and/or intentionally use a false document, such as a birth document, passport or visa. This offence is relatively easy to prove and there are several published criminal decisions whereby international adopters were found guilty of this offence.[422] For instance, in 2012, a Dutch couple was found guilty according to Articles 225(1) and (2) and 231 Sr.[423] They went to Turkey where they got in contact with a Turkish couple who agreed to give up their newborn baby for adoption. The Dutch couple had the child's birth certificate issued with the Dutch woman's

416 *Rechtbank Leeuwarden, 29.09.2009, 17/885166-09 VEV, ECLI:NL:RBLEE:2009:BJ8794.*

417 *Gerechtshof Leeuwarden, 08.04.2010, 24-002474-09, ECLI:NL:GHLEE:2010:BM0459.*

418 *Hoge Raad, 31.01.2012, S 10/01756, ECLI:NL:HR:2012:BU6921.*

419 *Ibid.*, para. 4.3.

420 *Ibid.*, para. 3.4.1.

421 *Ibid.*, para. 3.4.2.

422 *Rechtbank Almelo, 21.06.2005, 08/005134-04, ECLI:NL:RBALM:2005:AT7809; Gerechtshof Leeuwarden, 08.04.2010, 24-002474-09, ECLI:NL:GHLEE:2010:BM0459; Rechtbank Zwolle-Lelystad, 12.02.2010, 07.400121-08, ECLI:NL:RBZLY:2010:BL4061; Rechtbank Zwolle-Lelystad, 14.07.2011, 07.400176-09, ECLI:NL:RBZLY:2011:BR1615; Rechtbank Middelburg, 08.11.2012, 12/708507-08[P], ECLI:NL:RBMID:2012:BY2679; Rechtbank Oost-Brabant, 12.02.2013, 01-810049-07 en 01-810050-07, ECLI:NL:RBOBR:2013:BZ1186.*

423 *Rechtbank Middelburg, 08.11.2012, 12/708507-08[P], ECLI:NL:RBMID:2012:BY2679.*

name as the biological mother and with a false birth date, and then used this false document to get a false passport for the child. In the Netherlands, the Dutch couple registered the child within their municipality by using both the false birth document and passport. In addition, the Dutch couple was convicted of human smuggling according to Article 197a(1) Sr. (*mensensmokkel*) as they had illegally brought the child to the Netherlands, without valid travel documents.

Finally, adopters may be liable pursuant to Article 28 WOBKA if they have pursued an intercountry adoption without principle approval from the Ministry of Justice and Security according to Article 2 WOBKA. In addition, this misdemeanour is relatively easy to prove.[424] Article 8 WOBKA establishes five other requirements which need to be fulfilled, regarding limitations on the age of the child, medical reports, mediation by recognized adoption organizations, the document of relinquishment by the biological parents and the agreement of the foreign authorities. If these requirements are not met, a maximum fine of €8,200 may be imposed (Article 28 WOBKA). However, prosecution based on this article is challenging. For example, the verification of the document of relinquishment by the biological parents demands extensive international investigations, which rarely take place in practice. The deadline for prosecuting a misdemeanour according to Article 28 WOBKA is only three years, which is why there are only a few published cases whereby adopters were successfully prosecuted and convicted of having violated the adoption law regulations.[425]

If adopters are convicted of their illegal actions, they commonly receive only relatively mild sentences. Since they do not have a criminal record, they are usually sentenced to community work or to imprisonment on probation. Only in one published case were illegal adopters convicted to community work and imprisonment of 189 days, respectively 240 days, of which they had to spend 90 days in prison.[426] In this case, a Dutch couple fabricated principle approval from the Minister of Justice which it had then used to adopt a child (Milan) from Sri Lanka. In addition to probation, the adopters may be given a fine for having circumvented the official adoption procedure (Article 28 WOBKA). However, as was already explained above, these fines – if passed down at all – are often very low. If such mild sentences have any preventative effect at all, remains questionable.

424 *Rechtbank Rotterdam, 20.03.2012, 10/700428-11, ECLI:NL:RBROT:2012:BV9975; Rechtbank Zwolle-Lelystad, 14.07.2011, 07.400176-09, ECLI:NL:RBZLY:2011:BR1615.*

425 L. Bosch (2016). "Promising Practice: Legal Paths to Justice in the Netherlands." In International Social Service (2016). "Responding to Illegal Adoptions: A Professional Handbook." Available at https://fiom.nl/sites/default/files/responding-to-illegal-adoptions-a-professional-handbook-iss-april-2016.pdf, 40-44, p. 42.

426 *Rechtbank Zwolle-Lelystad, 16.02.2010, 07.400121-08 and 07.400120-08, ECLI:NL:RBZLY:2010:BL4062.*

8.2 *Staff Members of an Adoption Agency*

Adoption agencies in the receiving countries are typically not actively involved in illegally obtaining and laundering children for intercountry adoption purposes. In case illegal adoption practices of their foreign partner organizations are uncovered, they can usually plausibly deny having been aware of what occurred in the sending country. If the information in the child proposals and on the documents necessary for an adoption (e.g. the child's birth certificate, the declaration of relinquishment or the parents' death certificate) is complete and consistent, they can also claim that they could not have known about their partners" irregular practices abroad. Hence, criminal liability of the agency personnel as accessories to the foreign parents' commission of offences, like the forgery of documents (Articles 225, 227 and 231 Sr.) or child abduction (Article 279 Sr.) by omission, is usually excluded since the necessary *mens rea* is lacking.

If Dutch adoption agencies make 'facilitation payments' to authorities in the sending countries, their personnel are theoretically liable for bribery (*Misdrijven tegen het openbaar gezag*), according to Articles 177, 177a and 178a Sr. However, the Dutch Public Prosecutor's Office generally refrains from prosecution, if such payments are made to get an authority's approval or service.[427] Thus, if the staff members of an adoption agency pay bribes in a country were such payments are common, 'only' to accelerate the adoption placement procedure, then they are not held liable therefor (see section 6.2).

Yet, adoption agency personnel can be held liable for violating the provisions of the WOBKA. Carrying out adoption placement activities without the required accreditation,[428] placing a child with a couple or individual which does not have principle approval,[429] or paying unreasonably high fees to foreign cooperation partners and representatives[430] is a misdemeanour according to Article 28 WOBKA and punishable with a fine of up to €8,200. If these actions were committed in order to make a profit, then they constitute a criminal offence according to Article 27 WOBKA and are punishable with a fine of up to €8,200 or with imprisonment for a maximum period of six months.[431]

In addition, criminal liability pursuant to Article 151 Sr. may be possible. According to this provision, any person who, for reasons of financial gain, intentionally facilitates the placement of an infant younger than six months, who is not under the guardianship of a legal person, in a foster family without the prior written consent of the Child Protection Council, shall be liable to a term of imprisonment not exceeding six months or a fine of

427 N. A. Kalsbeek et al. (2008). "Report on Intercountry Adoption - "All things of value are defenceless"." Committee on Lesbian Parenthood and Intercountry Adoption, available at http://poundpuplegacy.org/files/10866_Interlandelijke-Adoptie_tcm34-137684.pdf, p. 52.

428 Art. 15 WOBKA.

429 Art. 2 and 20(1) *leg. cit.*

430 Art. 20(3) *leg. cit.*

431 Art. 27 *leg. cit.*

up to €8,200. However, so far, no staff member of an accredited Dutch adoption agency has ever been convicted of any such offence or misdemeanour.

9 Discussion and Conclusion

Compared to Germany, a relatively high number of child trafficking cases have been uncovered in the Netherlands which have triggered numerous debates about the legitimacy of intercountry adoption, especially in the Dutch parliament and the media. The Dutch authorities not only had to deal with a number of privately arranged adoptions, but also with (signs of) irregularities and abuses in regular agency adoptions. Particularly, the case involving the stolen Indian boy Rahul and the child trafficking incidences in China, as well as the role of Dutch stakeholders, were the subject of heated discussions in the Netherlands. This chapter isolated and explained the factors of the Dutch adoption system that might work to encourage and facilitate the trafficking of children to the Netherlands that are not otherwise legitimately available for intercountry adoption.

1) Deelbemiddelingen

Dutch adoption law provides for the possibility of partial do-it-yourself adoptions (*deelbemiddeling*). Couples and individuals who have been granted principle approval are allowed to adopt *via* a foreign private contact (an authority, institution or individual in the sending country which is not the cooperation partner of a Dutch adoption agency) if this contact was assessed by a Dutch adoption agency and ultimately approved by the Dutch Ministry of Justice and Security. *Deelbemiddelingen* are riskier than agency adoptions. First, the limited amount of time available and the lack of financial resources make it difficult for the agencies to thoroughly examine the intercountry adoption laws and practices in the sending country, as well as the integrity of the private contact. Second, it cannot be ruled out that adopters establish contact with the birth parents or the orphanage caring for the child *before* the matching has taken place. In fact, Dutch law even takes into consideration situations whereby adopters have already have selected a particular child before their foreign contract is approved by the Ministry. As was already explained, allowing the adopters to get in touch with the child's birth parents' or legal guardians is problematic as it becomes impossible to prevent adopters from influencing their decision to place the child for adoption. Adopters may provide assistance in the form of money or goods or exert (probably even unintentionally) psychological pressure on them and thereby induce their consent to adoption.[432] However, the possibility to pursue a *deelbemiddeling* is only a theoretical weakness in the Dutch adoption system. Since the number of non-Hague

432 See Chapter IV, section 5.1.3.

countries, from which *deelbemiddelingen* are still permitted, is decreasing and most Dutch adoption agencies refuse to assess private contacts in countries they do not know, the numbers have decreased dramatically.

2) Tolerance towards private adoptions

Unlike in Germany, private adoptions are explicitly prohibited by law and constitute a misdemeanour pursuant to Dutch law. Adopters who pursue a private adoption are punishable with a fine of up to €8,200 (Article 28 WOBKA). In addition, the Dutch family court may place the privately adopted child in an approved Dutch foster family or send the child back to the country of origin. However, in practice, private adoptions must often be tolerated. In many cases, the best interests of the individual child as well as the right to family life according to Article 8 ECHR may make it impossible for the Dutch family courts to remove the child from the illegal adopters. Furthermore, adopters are rarely held liable for violations of Article 28 WOBKA as the deadline for prosecuting this misdemeanour is only three years. And even if they are convicted, the fines are considerably low. Illegal adopters may be held liable for criminal offences, such as forgery of documents or even human smuggling. However, if adopters are convicted at all, they are usually only sentenced to community work and imprisonment on probation. Whether such mild sentences act as a deterrent for future couples and individuals, considering a private adoption, is questionable. As we will see in the following Chapter, the adopters' desire for a child is often so strong that they are probably willing to accept such mild sentences. As long as they get to keep the illegally adopted child, they may not be discouraged by a sentence on probation and even less so by fines. Given the large sums of moneys adopters are willing to pay for a child to love, a fine might be but another expense that they are ready to accept.

3) Institutional pressure

In the Netherlands, like in Germany, adoption agencies experience financial strain. They do not receive any public funding but rather they have to finance themselves primarily by the 'administration fees' that are paid by their adoption applicants. Hence, to keep their business up and running they have to handle a particular number of intercountry adoptions per year. This financial dependency on placements is problematic as agencies cannot easily afford to discontinue the cooperation with a foreign partner organization, especially if they only have one or two partners, as doing so might spell the end of their existence. For several years, Dutch agencies have had difficulties placing enough children in order to keep their organization up and running. Just like in all other receiving countries, intercountry adoptions are on a dramatic decrease in the Netherlands. The decreasing numbers of adoption placements, combined with the continued high competition between Dutch and foreign adoption agencies, create financial strain for the agencies. All of them responded to this pressure by increasing the administration fees as well as by restructuring their organization. Some Dutch adoption agencies dropped out entirely as they could not manage to keep their organization up and running. The financial strain is a criminogenic condition in the Dutch adoption system: agency personnel might be motivated to turn a blind eye on or even knowingly accept signs of irregular practices in the sending countries, or they may be reluctant to assess whether the country fees that their cooperation partners require adopters to pay are reasonably high and what they are being used for. Even the most benevolent agency personnel are inclined to keep their eyes wide shut, if this is necessary to secure the organization's continued existence and their own jobs.

4) Inconsistent restriction of the money flow to the sending countries

Dutch law seeks to restrict the transfer of money to the sending countries by prohibiting Dutch adoption agencies from paying unreasonably high fees to their foreign partner organizations and representatives. The country fees that the adoption agencies transfer for the services rendered abroad must be disproportionate compared to the average income in the sending country.[433] Dutch adoption agencies that violate this provision commit a misdemeanour that is punishable by a fine (Article 28 WOBKA) or – in case they act with the objective to profit – even a criminal offence (Article 27 WOBKA) and might have their accreditation withdrawn. In practice, some country fees that the Dutch agencies charge their adopters seem rather unreasonable, considering the average costs in the sending state. In some sending countries, the actors are reluctant to properly itemize the fees that foreign adopters are required to pay, making it difficult for the foreign adoption agencies to assess whether or not they are actually reasonable. Considering the agencies' financial and ideological motivation to keep children moving through the adoption system, they might be reluctant to ask too many questions about the country fees that their established cooperation partners seek.

Unfortunately, the objective of the Dutch adoption system to prevent financial inducements by restricting the transfer of money to the sending countries is not consistent. First, Dutch law only prohibits adoption agencies from paying unreasonably high fees to their partner organizations and representatives, but it does not provide any provisions regulating donations or contributions. Money or goods that foreign adoption agencies donate to child care institutions create inducements for the personnel to keep children moving for intercountry adoption and could thus encourage them to engage in abusive practices. Also, contributions that are made to help finance the child welfare system of the sending country might have such a harmful effect. Second, the Dutch Central Authority tolerates 'facilitation payments' to authorities in sending countries where bribes are customary. How useful is it to prohibit adoption agencies from paying unreasonably high fees

433 *Kamerstukken II, 20 046, nr. 6*, p. 38.

for services abroad when there are no regulations whatsoever with regard to donations and when 'facilitation' payments are generally tolerated?

5) Trust and Diplomatic Deference

The issue of trust in the authorities in Hague sending countries also becomes apparent when looking at how the Dutch Ministry of Justice and Security responded to irregular adoption practices in countries which have ratified the treaty. Generally, the Dutch Ministry has the possibility to send a delegation to the sending countries, if an adoption agency or embassy suspects or uncovers irregular practices therein. The Dutch delegation typically meets with the competent authorities, talks to NGOs and other embassies, visits the Dutch adoption agencies cooperation partners (orphanages) and potentially looks into adoption files. The possibility of the Dutch authorities actually travelling to the sending countries is important as the integrity of a foreign adoption system can be better assessed on-site than from the Netherlands – the Central Authorities in Germany do not have this option! Alternatively, the Ministry may ask a Dutch embassy in the sending country to conduct the necessary investigations. If the Dutch delegation or embassy finds that the adoptions procedures are not properly carried out, the Ministry may decide to suspend intercountry adoptions from this particular sending country. It has already done so with regard to Guatemala, Cambodia, Haiti and Uganda, all of which are non-Hague sending countries. However, in 2005/2006, after serious allegations of abusive practices in the Chinese adoption system became public, the Minister adopted a more reticent attitude. He accepted - quite uncritically - the explanations and reassurances of the Chinese authorities, notwithstanding recurring reports about irregular adoption practices and *Wereldkinderen*'s own investigation which signalled systemic abuses in the Chinese adoption system, by stressing the principle of trust. In several statements, he explained that the responsibility to control whether an adoption complies with the Convention's requirements rests with the country of origin and that the Netherlands needs to have trust in the foreign authorities' integrity and the reliability of the information provided on the children.

Yet, it was not only the interpretation of the Hague Convention's allocation of responsibilities as a mandate of deference and mutual trust which explains the Minister's reluctance to exert pressure on the Chinese authorities. Also, diplomatic as well as other interests that were at stake at that time might have influenced his reticent attitude towards the Chinese authorities. China was - and still is - an important trade partner for the Netherlands. As the irregular adoption practices were uncovered in China, the Ministry had probably sought to deal with the scandal in a manner that would not impede this flourishing economic relationship between the two countries. It not only refused to increase the pressure on the Chinese authorities, it also explicitly prohibited *Wereldkinderen* from conducting its own investigations. Finally, the interests of Dutch adopters and adoption agencies might also have played a crucial role in this regard. At that time, China was by far the most significant sending country for the Netherlands in terms of adoption placements. At this point in time, it would therefore have been a major shock for the Dutch agencies and adopters on the waiting list for a child proposal from China, if the Dutch Minister decided to suspend adoptions from this country altogether.

VII Parenthood, Consumption and Narratives of Rescue and Love in Intercountry Adoption

1 Introduction

In contemporary Western societies, children are considered to be priceless who cannot and should not be paid for. Moreover, the relationship between children and their parents is understood as defying commodification, as it is understood to be so sacrosanct that no price can be attached to it whatsoever. Parenthood is traditionally relegated to the intimate, private realm and it is understood as non-economic in scope. Contrasted with this ideology, which separates children and intimate relationships from the market sphere, is the social practice of intercountry adoption where privileged wealthy adopters, most often involuntarily childless, pay large sums of money for a child to love. This chapter seeks to explore how parents who have internationally adopted their child manage the mingling of what is culturally considered to be incompatible: parenthood and consumption, love and money.

A narrative analysis of autobiographical stories written by German and Dutch adopters, in which they explain how they came to adopt from a foreign country and describe their transition to adoptive parenthood, will be conducted. The aim is to identify recurring tropes and commonplaces that the authors mobilize, on their route to adoptive parenthood, in order to resolve the moral tension between the cultural conception of children as being priceless and them exercising key market components: choice concerning the child's characteristics and payments. It will be explained that the adopters' narratives are the visible manifestation of tacit, invisible values and beliefs, shaped by the authors' culture, that they unwittingly take for granted and which might probably also be observed in other international adopters. These values and beliefs, it will be explained, are but another factor in the intercountry adoption system which is conducive to the laundering of children.

The chapter is organized into six sections. Section 2 describes in more detail the ideological separation between the intimate and the economic sphere and explains when and why children nevertheless came to be treated as commodities in Western societies. Section 3 lays out the methodology and the theoretical background of this chapter. Sections 4 and 5 form the core of this chapter, depicting the route to adoptive parenthood. Section 4 focuses on the pre-assignment phase, the phase which begins with the prospective adoptive parents' desire to have children, ending with the assignment of a particular adoptee. Section 5 examines the post-assignment stage which starts with the matching of the adopting couple with a child. Section 6 then concludes this chapter.

2 The Tension between Consumption and Parenthood in Intercountry Adoption

Parenting a child, we like to believe, cannot be paid for nor consumed. A child is not a piece of private property that can be transferred from one owner to another in exchange for money. Treating a child as a commodity degrades the child and fails to value him or her as a human being that is worthy of dignity and respect. This cultural conception of children, or human beings in general, is mirrored in the German Constitution whose Article 1(1) provides one of the most fundamental constitutional principles: "human dignity shall be inviolable". It is furthermore reflected in several international human rights instruments which lay down that all human beings are born with dignity. Attaching a price to a person, and even more so to a child, would violate his or her dignity and this would therefore be perceived as morally objectionable and in most countries it is considered to be a crime. Kopytoff notes that in most Western liberal societies, a cultural separation exists between things that are understood to be saleable and persons, who are considered to be precluded from being commoditized:

> In contemporary Western thought, we take it more or less for granted that things – physical objects and rights to them – represent the natural universe of commodities. At the opposite pole we place people, who represent the natural universe of individuation and singularization.[1]

In addition, intimate relationships between two human beings are culturally understood as defying their commodification. Especially the intimacy between a parent and his or her child is considered to be so sacrosanct that no price can be attached to it whatsoever. As Wilson argues, the intimate and the economic realms are generally considered to be distinct and independent:

> Common sense understands the intimate realm to be *non-economic*, or at least nonproductive: part of what defines the values of family, romance, and friendship is their stark difference from market values (a distinction that attributes masculinity to the market sphere and femininity to the domestic sphere).[2]

1 I. Kopytoff (1986). "The Cultural Biography of Things: Commoditization as Process." In A. Appadurai (ed), "The Social Life of Things: Commodities in Cultural Perspective." Cambridge University Press, New York, 64-91, p. 64.

2 A. Wilson (2012). "Intimacy: A Useful Category of Transnational Analysis." In G. Pratt (ed), "The Global and the Intimate: Feminism in Our Time." Columbia University Press, New York, 31-56, p. 41.

Our ideological understanding of human beings and their intimacies as being separate from the economic sphere, however, is in stark contrast with the social reality. In this day and age, almost everything can be bought and sold. According to consumer-capitalism, markets have expanded to cover all thinkable aspects of societal life. Today, not only are things being commodified, but it also follows that human beings, their life, organs, sexuality, fertility, and labour as well as their intimate relationships are slowly being turned into objects of economic value and bought and sold either openly or on black markets.[3]

Moreover, parenting a child, which is culturally relegated to the intimate, private realm and therefore understood as non-economic in scope, is complexly intertwined with consumption and commodification.[4] Whether shopping for children's clothes, childbirth or child care services or paying for family formation techniques including surrogacy or fertility treatments: becoming a parent and parenting, in general, is deeply influenced by money and consumption.[5] Katz Rothman notes: "[T]here seems no way to think beyond consumerism. One can consume differently, but almost whatever one does as a mother becomes just one more cog in the consumer wheel".[6]

The interrelation between the economic and the intimate sphere, between parenthood and consumption and between money and love is particularly visible in intercountry adoptions.[7] Couples and individuals that are willing to adopt a child internationally have to pay high adoption costs, depending on the adoption agency as well as the sending country they choose to adopt from. Financial transactions, including fees paid to the adoption agencies, family courts, government officials, orphanages, visa bureaus etc. make international adoption a lucrative business. Such financial exchanges, although characterized as 'service costs' or 'administrative fees', resemble payments as they are understood in most other economic spheres.[8] Spar notes:

3 M. J. Sandel (2012). "What money can't buy, The Moral Limits of Markets." Farrar, Straus and Giroux, New York.

4 See, for example, I. Kopytoff (2004). "Commoditizing Kinship in America." In J. S. Taylor et al. (ed), "Consuming Motherhood." Rutgers University Press, London, 271-279.

5 J. S. Taylor, et al. (2004). "Consuming Motherhood." Rutgers University Press, New Brunswick.

6 B. Katz Rothman (2004). "Caught in the Current." In J. S. Taylor et al. (eds), "Consuming Motherhood." Rutgers University Press, London, 279-288, pp. 286-287.

7 M. Homans (2013). "The Imprint of Another Life: Adoption Narratives and Human Possibility." University of Michigan Press, Ann Arbor, p. 26; See also S. K. Dorow (2002). ""China 'R' Us?": Care, Consumption, and Transnationally Adopted Children." In D. T. Cook (ed), "Symbolic Childhood." Peter Lang, New York, 149-168.

8 M. Goodwin (2010). "Baby Markets: Money and the New Politics of Creating Families." Cambridge University Press, pp. 4-5.

> When parents choose a child to adopt [...] they are doing business. Firms are making money, customers are making choices, and children – for better or worse – are being sold.[9]

The lucrative business with adoptable children is not an old phenomenon. According to Zelizer, it only developed in the 20th century as a consequence of the profound cultural transformation in children's economic and sentimental value.[10] Back in the 19th century, children were considered as an economic benefit to their birth or foster families because they were expected to help out with farm chores and household tasks. As a result, their capacity for labour determined their worth. Thus, strong, older children - preferably male - were favoured.[11] However, between the 1870s and the 1930s, the economically useful child was gradually displaced by the economically useless, but emotionally priceless, child.[12] The market for child labour disappeared and children came to be valued for non-economic reasons. Sentimental adoption, still rare in the 19th century, rapidly displaced earlier instrumental fostering arrangements in the 1920s and 1930s[13] and created an unprecedented demand for children under the age of three, especially female infants.[14] A growing number of enthusiastic prospective adoptive parents queued up, willing to pay inordinate sums of money for a child to love.[15] Zelizer explains,

> The sentimentalization of adoption, thus, led paradoxically to a greater commercialization and monetization of child life. [...] An apparently profound contradiction was thereby created, between a cultural system that declared children priceless emotional assets, and a social arrangement that treated them as 'cash commodities'.[16]

The paradox between the cultural conception of children as being priceless, on the one hand, and the social reality in which they are commodified, on the other hand, creates strong moral tensions for the people involved in the intercountry adoption system. Adoption agencies do not want to be confronted with accusations of doing business with adoptable children or to profit from intercountry adoptions. They commonly portray

9 D. L. Spar (2006). "The baby business: How money, science, and politics drive the commerce of conception." Harvard Business School Press, Boston, p. xi.

10 V. A. Zelizer (1994). "Pricing the Priceless Child, The Changing Social Value of Children." Princeton University Press, Princeton, New Jersey, p. 195.

11 *Ibid.*, pp. 171-175.

12 *Ibid.*, p. 209.

13 *Ibid.*, p. 189.

14 *Ibid.*, p. 192.

15 *Ibid.*, p. 195.

16 *Ibid.*, p. 201.

themselves as humanitarian, charitable organizations with names like *Child and Future, Help a Child, Parents-Child-Bridge* or *Parents for Children*. Most of them support aid programmes in the sending states and claim that they only place those children who cannot be cared for in their native countries. Furthermore, they routinely stress that they exist to serve the best interests of the child and stress that their mission is to find parents for children and not the other way around.

In addition, adoptive parents do not want to be reproached for having bought their adopted child as they do not consider themselves as 'shopping for their offspring'. Yet, they are involved in a market operation by paying large sums of money for a child. This Chapter explores the relationship between parenthood and consumption as is conceived by German and Dutch parents who seek to adopt a child internationally. It is particularly concerned with the question as to how these prospective adoptive parents manage the mingling of what is culturally considered to be incompatible: parenthood and consumption, and love and money.

3 Methodology and Theoretical Background

This Chapter conducts a narrative analysis of autobiographical stories that have been written by German and Dutch adopters, explaining how they came to adopt internationally and describing their transition to adoptive parenthood. It zooms in on the role that money and consumption plays in the adopters' stories and it aims to uncover the linguistic choices they use to resolve the moral tension between, on the one hand, the cultural belief that children are priceless and that parenthood is separated from the economic sphere and, on the other hand, the fact that they have to pay considerable sums of money in the adoption procedure to accomplish the goal of having their own child.

Fifteen autobiographical stories have been selected for narrative analysis, eight of them were written by German adoptive parents and seven were authored by Dutch adopters.[17]

17 German book: M. Gaedicke (2009). "Wunschkind, Geschichte einer Adoption." Hoffmann und Campe, Hamburg; A. Michaela (2014). "Neun Monate Sommer, Tagebuch einer Adoptionsschwangerschaft in Kenia." Tausendschlau Olga Bien, Munich; A. Palm-Hensel (2008). "Stella, Unser Stern aus Indien, Die Geschichte einer glücklichen Adoption." Kleine Schritte, Trier; B. Schulz (2005). "Tochter Indira, Die Geschichte einer Adoption aus Indien." Ullstein, Berlin; T. Schumann (2012). "Faith - Adoption in Kenia, Ein Vater erzählt." Norderstedt, Books on Demand; T. Schumann (2014). "Hope - Adoption in Haiti, Ein Vater erzählt." Books on Demand, Norderstedt; A. Wenzek-Grüneberg (2005). "Das Regenbogenkind, Die Geschichte einer Auslandsadoption." Books on Demand, Norderstedt; R. Vollmer (2004). "Mein Kind aus der Fremde." Rowohlt, Reinbek bei Hamburg. Dutch books: M. & K. Van der Staaij (2004). "Liefs uit Bogotá, Ons verhaal over adoptie." Uitgeverij Boekencentrum, Zoetermeer; G. Bakker (2008). "Het Adoptieboek, Stap voor Stap, Stress Tijdens de Adoptie Periode." Uitgeverij Aspekt, Soesterberg; D. Michielsen (2005). "Dochters van ver, belevenissen van een adoptiemoeder." Archipel, Amsterdam; I. Holla (2005). "Mijn droom van een kind, Waargebeurd verhaal van een vrouw die haar wens om moeder te worden niet opgeeft." Uitgeverij Sirene, Amsterdam; M. & I. Koolen (2009). "Moeders mooiste, vaders trots, Een bijzonder verslag

The stories were recommended on websites, online forums, and blogs where involuntarily childless and (prospective) adopters would relay all kinds of information, share experiences and provide advice.[18] One adoption story, *Wunschkind, Geschichte einer Adoption* even served as the basis for a movie that was broadcast on German television in 2017. Two stories were authored by adoptive couples, two stories by one adoptive father and the remaining ones were by adoptive mothers, all of whom were married. The narratives describe the international adoption of a total of 19 children from Kenya (5 children), China (4), India (2), Russia (2), Colombia (2), Argentina (1), Haiti (1), Ukraine (1) and Sri Lanka (1). Nine of the children were less than one year-old at the time of the assignment (one was only two weeks-old), three children were younger than two and one girl was four when the adopters met her for the first time. Most parents pursued the adoption with the involvement of an adoption agency, four authors adopted their child independently. Five of the international adoption procedures took place in the adopters' home country, which had ratified the Hague Convention (the Netherlands in 1998 and Germany in 2001).

For the purposes of this chapter, the adopters' autobiographical stories are considered the best source of information. They allow the researcher to observe how adopters deal with the issue of consumption and money in an intercountry adoption without the potential of researcher contamination that could otherwise arise in interviews, especially given the delicate nature of the present study's topic. The adopters do not perform for the researcher by giving answers to specific questions, but rather they write freely. Whereas an interview is about the interviewer, a narrative is about the writer. Narratives thus provide the researcher with the unique opportunity to explore the adoptive parents' unmasked views, opinions and attitudes.

A narrative approach to data collection has been chosen due to the social and psychological functions that storytelling fulfils. Narrative is an important means by which individuals integrate and give meaning to past episodes in their lives and, subsequently construct their identity.[19] Carr notes: "Narrative is not a dress which covers something else but the structure inherent in human experience and action".[20] The narrative structure is used to craft private and personal stories by weaving together diverse actions and events into an understandable unity. By being incorporated into a plot, the individuals' experiences shape

van de lange weg naar adoptie." The house of books, Antwerpen; I. Andersson (2006). "Bloem van China, Dochter in Nederland." Free Musketeers, Woerden; I. Andersson (2009). "Dochters van China, Zusjes in Nederland." Free Musketeers, Zoetermeer.

18 https://www.kinderlosenberatung.de/literatur/, http://ungewolltkinderlos.de/index.php?article_id=131, http://www.adoption-indien.de/10.html, http://das-elternhandbuch.de/, https://charlottesadoptionsblog.com/tag/wunschkind/, http://hopeadoptionhaiti.blogspot.nl/, http://faithkenia.blogspot.nl/, http://www.adoptionsforum-stuttgart.de/Index.html, http://www.adoption.de/aktuell.htm, http://adoption-forum.phpbb8.de/, http://dedochtersuitchina.blogspot.nl/, https://adoptieoudersonline.nl/, https://www.zappy.be/nl/, https://www.dela.nl/blog/voorelkaar, https://babyblog.nl/, https://www.freya.nl/ (last accessed on 07.08.2018).

19 A. D. Brown et al. (2008). "Making Sense of Sensemaking Narratives." Human Relations, 61, 8, 1035-1062.

20 D. Carr (1986). "Time, narrative, and history." Indiana University Press, Bloomington, p. 65.

their stories and give them a certain direction or intent of meaning.[21] The stories are the basis of individuals' identity and self-understanding. As Polkinghorne explains: "It is only by use of narrative conceptualization that we can produce out of our separate life events the meaningful whole that we are".[22] In other words, narrative helps individuals to make sense of their lives and of their selves. Thus, as Shankar et al. point out, constructing stories has an "ontological status", in the sense "that the process of telling stories is an act of creation and construction and not simply an act of remembering or retelling".[23]

Narrative plays a particularly crucial role for adopters in the process of constructing their identity as parents.[24] Since blood ties are absent, adopters invest considerable work in crafting compelling life stories which help them to reinvent themselves as parents and to forge a family link between them and the biologically unrelated adoptive child.[25] Life stories also serve adopters to justify and legitimize intercountry adoption, a non-normative means of having children which has been criticized by many for its self-serving, imperialistic and exploitative nature. These are the reasons, González and Wesseling argue, why adoptive parents engage quite extensively in various forms of life writing.[26] They craft autobiographies, entries on online forums, blogs and websites whereby they talk about the adoption of their child as well as their lives after the arrival of the adoptee.[27] The narrative structure that is employed to craft their stories allows the adopters to give meaning to the events they have experienced and the actions they have taken on their route to parenthood – including the failure to reproduce a biological child and the decision to pursue an international adoption.

Sometimes specific life events may seem difficult to integrate into the plots that individuals employ to identify themselves and to give meaning to their experiences.[28] In their narratives, parents typically use plot lines based on the idea that their children are priceless and that parenthood is so sacrosanct that it cannot be consumed nor paid for. In case of an international adoption, such a plot cannot easily absorb and make sense of the fact that the parents made rational choices concerning their prospective child's characteristics and origin and had to pay considerable amounts of money to achieve the desired goal of par-

21 P. Brooks (1992). "Reading for the Plot: Design and Intention in Narrative." Harvard University Press, London, p. xi.

22 D. E. Polkinghorne (1991). "Narrative and Self-Concept." Journal of Narrative and Life History, 1, 2 & 3, 135-153, p. 137.

23 A. Shankar et al. (2009). "Identity, Consumption and Narratives of Socialization." Marketing Theory, 9, 1, 75-94, p. 79.

24 M. G. González and E. Wesseling (2013). "The Stories We Adopt By: Tracing" The Red Thread" in Contemporary Adoption Narratives." The Lion and the Unicorn, 37, 3, 257-276, p. 258.

25 *Ibid.*

26 *Ibid.*

27 *Ibid.*

28 D. E. Polkinghorne (1991). "Narrative and Self-Concept." Journal of Narrative and Life History, 1, 2 & 3, 135-153, p. 149.

enthood. This Chapter seeks to uncover and explain the linguistic tools, tropes and commonplaces that adoptive parents appropriate in order to weave the aspects of money and consumption into a plot which is based on the cultural belief that human beings and their intimate relationships are separate from the economic sphere.

Tropes or metaphors are rhetorical devices that project a "system of associated commonplaces" which make up the meaning of one term onto another term, and vice versa.[29] Through a trope, the characteristic features of both terms merge, the features of one term functioning as a focus on the other, and vice versa. That way some features are shaped whereas others are minimized.[30] Commonplaces, or '*topoi*', are statements reinforcing values and beliefs that are commonly shared by members of an audience or a community. Such commonplaces need not actually be true – in fact, they might even include "downright mistakes" – rather, they must only be "readily and freely evoked" by a given community.[31]

Life stories, or more specifically the plot or storylines used in the construction of self-narratives, are usually not construed from scratch. Rather, they are influenced and shaped by an individual's culture.[32] Geertz defines culture as "a system of inherited conceptions expressed in symbolic forms by means of which men communicate, perpetuate, and develop their knowledge about and attitudes toward life".[33] These inherited conceptions are often embedded within exemplary narrative plots which can be found in literary and oral stories that are produced by one's culture.[34] May gives examples of four sources that supply an individuals' "cultural stock of narrative plot": (a) myths, (b) classical drama, (c) masterworks of European culture and (d) contemporary drama, films and novels.[35] These sources provide repertoires of stereotypical narratives, tropes and commonplaces upon which people draw in order to give meaning to the actions and events in their own life.[36] They are often not deliberately sought after by individuals but rather work unconsciously, carrying the character of the culture.[37] The narrative plots in the individual's life stories, which are adaptations from the cultural repertoire, then influence the individual's culture in a feedback

29 M. Black (1955). "XII.—Metaphor." Proceedings of the Aristotelian Society, 55, 1, 273-294.

30 E. Wesseling (ed.) (2016). "The Child Savage, 1890–2010: From Comics to Games." Routledge, New York, p. 12.

31 M. Black (1955). "XII.—Metaphor." Proceedings of the Aristotelian Society, 55, 1, 273-294, p. 287.

32 D. E. Polkinghorne (1991). "Narrative and Self-Concept." Journal of Narrative and Life History, 1, 2 & 3, 135-153, p. 147.

33 C. Geertz (1973). "The Interpretation of Cultures." Basic Books, New York, p. 89.

34 D. E. Polkinghorne (1991). "Narrative and Self-Concept." Journal of Narrative and Life History, 1, 2 & 3, 135-153, p. 147.

35 R. May (1975). "Values, myths, and symbols." The American journal of psychiatry, 132, 703-706.

36 *Ibid.*

37 D. E. Polkinghorne (1991). "Narrative and Self-Concept." Journal of Narrative and Life History, 1, 2 & 3, 135-153, p. 148.

loop. Polkinghorne explains: "The individual and culture are melded [...] – the person shaped by the cultural stock, and the stock reshaped by the person's adaptation".[38]

Life stories, thus, are the visible manifestation of the authors' invisible values, beliefs, assumptions and commonplaces which are unconsciously shaped by their culture, and vice versa. This finds expression in the metaphor of an iceberg – with a small visible part (on the surface) and a relatively large invisible part (below the surface) – which is often advanced to explain culture.[39] Elements of culture which can be plainly observed and which may or may not be obvious to people, such as language, behaviours, customs, traditions and even laws, are represented by the upper portion: the tip of the iceberg. Those elements which are not observable and which people might not necessarily be aware of are represented by the much larger portion of the iceberg, which is underwater and include cultural beliefs, norms, values, perceptions and expectations etc.

A narrative analysis of the autobiographic stories written by adopters does thus not only provide the opportunity to detect and understand the recurring linguistic choices that adopters use to manage the tension between consumption and parenthood. It also helps to unearth tacit, invisible values and beliefs, shaped by the authors' culture which they unwittingly take for granted and which might probably also be observed in other international adopters. That being said, however, it must be stressed that the findings which will be presented in the following paragraphs are not representative in a social scientific sense. Each adoption story is different and the individual experiences of the authors must be seen in a particular context. Also, not all adopters write stories about their experiences. Arguably, the very fact that some adopters do craft autobiographies already distinguishes them from those adoptive parents who do not. Thus, the collected results may have only limited application to other adopters and cannot be generalized to the population of adoptive parents as a whole.

38 *Ibid.*
39 E. T. Hall (1989). "Beyond Culture." Anchor Books, New York.

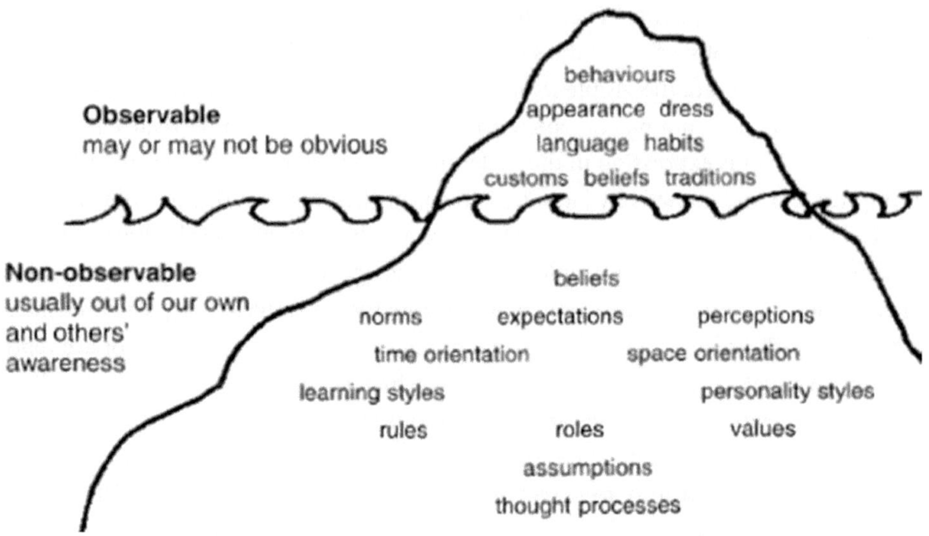

Source: http://myiepclass.weebly.com/cultural-aspects.html (last accessed on 07.08.2018).

What all German and Dutch adoptive parents, in fact almost all international adopters, have in common is that they are socially advantaged members of a capitalist Western society which shapes and is being shaped by the culture of 'individualization'. This culture, this chapter will show, strongly manifests itself in the adopters' autobiographic stories. According to Beck, individualisation "means, first, the disembedding and, second, the re-embedding of industrial society ways of life by new ones, in which the individual must produce, stage and cobble together their biographies themselves".[40] In late modernity, Beck, as well as numerous other sociologists explain,[41] most Western societies underwent a process of 'de-traditionalisation' which involved the 'liberation' (*Freisetzung*) of individuals from traditional bonds and affiliations.[42] People's lives and identities, which were once structured by their social class, gender, religious beliefs etc., are now increasingly shaped by the individuals themselves. People are left to their own devices in terms of making life decisions, choosing their social bonds and constructing their identities without the shackles of traditional norms and religious ideologies, which once limited the options for individual self-development.[43] This is not to say that tradition and religion no longer play

40 U. Beck, et al. (1994). "Reflexive Modernization: Politics, Tradition and Aesthetics in the Modern Social Order." Stanford University Press.

41 A. Giddens (1991). "Modernity and Self-Identity, Self and Society in the Late Modern Age." Stanford University Press; Z. Bauman (2001). "The Individualized Society." Polity Press, Cambridge.

42 *Ibid.*

43 *Ibid.*

a role, but that they only "have force" for individuals who choose them to have force.[44] People now have the freedom to 'individualize' their life courses and identities, by determining the directions their lives shall take and their social networks and by exercising a myriad of choices along the way. Where once there was a 'standard biography', there is now an 'elective biography' a 'do-it-yourself biography'.[45] Beck explains: "Individualization is a compulsion, [...] to stage manage, not only one's own biography but the bonds and networks surrounding it".[46]

In late modern Western societies, Giddens argues, fate and destiny have lost significance: "Fate and destiny have no formal part to play in [...] a system, which operates (as a matter of principle) via what I shall call open human control of the natural and social world".[47] He continues by saying that: "Fate is taken to mean a form of preordained determinism, to which the modern outlook stands opposed".[48] Whereas previously, the concept of fate or *fortuna* played an important role, reflecting the idea of a predestined life path, often charted by religious cosmologies or the behaviour of older generations, in the era of individualization, fate and destiny have lost their hold on individual human control.[49] Now there is a general perception that individuals are able to control their fates and shape their own destinies by overcoming any natural and social obstacles. The culture of individualization, it will be explained in this Chapter, is the driving force behind the international adoption of foreign children to Western countries.

4 The Desire to Achieve Parenthood

4.1 *Involuntary Childlessness and the Powerful Wish to Have a Child*

Notwithstanding the numerous role options that are afforded to men and women in individualized Western societies, achieving parenthood is still a highly-valued life goal for many couples and individuals.[50] The reasons for having children, however, have changed over the last couple of years. As was already explained earlier in this study, whereas having children primarily served economic purposes until the 19th century (and still does in other

44 U. Beck (2002). "Individualization: Institutionalized Individualism and Its Social and Political Consequences." Sage, London, pp. 27-28.
45 *Ibid.*, p. 24.
46 *Ibid.*, p. 4.
47 A. Giddens (1991). "Modernity and Self-Identity, Self and Society in the Late Modern Age." Stanford University Press, p. 109.
48 *Ibid.*, p. 110.
49 A. Giddens (1999). "Risk and Responsibility." The Modern Law Review, 62, 1, 1-10.
50 J. McQuillan et al. (2003). "Frustrated Fertility: Infertility and Psychological Distress Among Women." Journal of Marriage and Family, 65, 1007-1018.

societies), children are now valued mainly for sentimental reasons. In an individualized society in which divorce rates are increasing and traditional family agreements are breaking down, children fulfill important affective functions. They serve their parents to countervail the eroding chances of having a partner relationship that lasts as well as to avoid loneliness, particularly in old age. Beck et al. explain: "The child becomes the last remaining, irrevocable, unique primary love object. Partners come and go, but the child stays. Everything one vainly hoped to find in the relationship with one's partner is sought in or directed at the child".[51] Paradoxically, thus, in times where birth rates are on a constant decline, Beck et al argue, "children have never been more important".[52]

Children also serve Western couples and individuals in building their social and cultural capital. Anagnost claims that (in the context of the United States) parenting has been "increasingly marked as a measure of value, self-worth, and citizenship".[53] Achieving parenthood is necessary in order to be a "fully realized" citizen.[54] This is not only true for heterosexual couples but, increasingly, also for homosexual couples as well as singles who seek recognition within their community.[55] Nelson argues that there is "the enormous cultural pressure to complete one's life with family (which includes children)".[56] Just like having an education, pursuing a career, getting married or purchasing an apartment, starting a family is an important life course milestone which ought to further the process of self-optimization and identity formation. Having a child is also a means of expressing one's wealth and status in society. For example, Koolen, a Dutch woman, writes:

> Of course, we were well off financially, with a nice house and two cars in front of the door. But still something was missing and that was a child. Only with such a little one would our lives really be complete.[57]

Having children is central to many people's identities and, for parents, is usually the most salient identity.[58] According to feminists, having children is particularly salient for women

51 U. Beck and E. Beck-Gernsheim (1995). "The Normal Chaos of Love." Polity Press, Cambridge, p. 37.

52 *Ibid.*

53 A. Anagnost (2000). "Scenes of Misrecognition: Maternal Citizenship in the Age of Transnational Adoption." Positions: east asia cultures critique, 8, 2, 389-421, p. 391.

54 *Ibid.*, p. 392.

55 D. L. Eng (2006). "Political Economics of Passion: Transnational Adoption and Global Woman: Roundtable on Global Woman." Studies in Gender and Sexuality, 7, 1, 49–59, p. 57.

56 K. P. Nelson (2006). "Shopping for children in the international marketplace." In J. J. Trenka et al. (eds), "Outsiders Within: Writing on transracial adoption." South End Press, Cambridge, 89-104, p. 89.

57 M. and I. Koolen (2009). "Moeders mooiste, vaders trots, Een bijzonder verslag van de lange weg naar adoptie." The house of books, Antwerpen, p. 21.

58 P. A. Thoits (1992). "Identity structures and psychological well-being: Gender and marital status comparisons." Social Psychology Quarterly, 55, 236-256

as a consequence of the pronatalist ideology that many Western societies still embrace.[59] This ideology embodies the belief that a woman's social value is, first and foremost, linked to bearing children and that motherhood is an integral part of a woman's identity. As Fisher explains, "most women experience considerable pressure to bear and/or raise children. This pressure may become nearly intolerable at times, as parents and relatives [and society] convey the notion that women 'owe' their family children".[60]

However, some couples and individuals fail to achieve the identity as a parent: they are involuntarily childless, meaning that they want to have a child but are not able to conceive. According to a study published in 2007, 1.4 million German men and women between the age of 25 and 59 are involuntarily childless due to medical reasons.[61] In the Netherlands, 10% of couples cannot have a child of their own.[62] Some of them resign themselves to their faiths; others are willing to do whatever it takes and whatever the cost, to achieve the life goal of having a child. For some involuntarily childless persons, intercountry adoption offers a last resort means to embrace the identity of a parent in order to become a fully realized citizen in their community. The benevolent and ostensible altruistic character of an adoption thereby makes up for the fact that the child is not a biological one.

As was already mentioned, infertility is now the primary motivation to pursue an international adoption. Both in Germany as well as in the Netherlands, the majority of adopters (some 90%) are involuntarily childless and many of them consider intercountry adoption as their last chance to have children. The remaining 10% adopt a child internationally primarily due to idealistic reasons. This is reflected by the authors of the adoption narratives that were analysed in this study. Almost all of them claim that they were not able to produce their own children. Only one adoptive father did not report any infertility issues and would not rule out biological parenthood at the time he and his wife applied for their first adoption in Kenya.[63] As will be explained in the following, this couple's motivation to adopt internationally revolved mainly around an altruistic, religious core.

The involuntarily childless couples' desire to have 'a child of their own'[64] has stretched over a period of several years, characterized by numerous unsuccessful pregnancies, feelings of extreme frustration, desperation and loss of control. All of them have embarked on

59 M. Ulrich and A. Weatherall (2000). "Motherhood and Infertility: Viewing Motherhood through the Lens of Infertility." Feminism & Psychology, 10, 3, 323-336.

60 B. Fisher (1992). "Against the grain: Lives of women without children." IRIS: A Journal About Women, 2, 46-51.

61 Institut für Demoskopie Allensbach (2007). "Unfreiwillige Kinderlosigkeit." Nr. 11, available at https://www.ifd-allensbach.de/uploads/tx_reportsndocs/prd_0711.pdf.

62 K. Bos (2016). "Baby? Dat gaat niet meer gebeuren.", NRC, 14.05.2016, available at https://www.nrc.nl/nieuws/2016/05/14/baby-dat-gaat-niet-meer-gebeuren-1620805-a325064.

63 T. Schumann (2012). "Faith - Adoption in Kenia, Ein Vater erzählt." Norderstedt, Books on Demand.

64 B. Katz Rothman (2004). "Motherhood under Capitalism." In J. S. Taylor et al. (eds), "Consuming Motherhood." Rutgers University Press, London, 19-30, p. 25.

expensive medical treatments to overcome their infertility. Advances in procedures and new technologies gave the couples hope of having their own child and temporarily reinstalled a sense of control over their life plans. Satisfying the desire to achieve parenthood has become a mission that a great deal of time, money and physical as well as mental energy is devoted to. Bakker describes the number of fertility treatments she has undergone:

> [I have had] four laparoscopies, my cysts removed, a number of hormonal treatments which resulted in a chemical menopause, all these treatments multiplied by two because as I got married a second time my gynaecologist wanted the latest data, four IUIs and four IVFs over the course of 10 years.[65]

As the number of unsuccessful attempts to get pregnant or maintain a pregnancy increases, the loss of control over their sexuality and over achieving the desired identity as parents intensifies for the authors. Palm-Hensel, a woman who had nine in-vitro fertilizations over a 1 ½-year-period, describes her ordeal to conceive and how she finally realized that she would never be able to accomplish a pregnancy:

> I have gained a lot of weight due to the massive dosage of hormones I took during the treatments. Moreover, the many disappointments have devastated me physically and mentally. I had to cope with the idea that I would not be granted to feel something growing in me and to hold our baby in my arms.[66]

All authors are socially and economically advantaged. They are well-educated, pursue a career and are financially well off. This mirrors the demographics of international adopters who are typically from the middle or upper social class. Studies suggest that birth rates are generally declining in Western countries, but that fertility rates are lowest among the better educated and financially secure couples and individuals.[67] This has to do with the fact that middle-class women tend to postpone parenthood to a later stage in life – often into their 30s or even 40s – when they have completed their education and after they have commenced their career.[68] In the wake of individualization, women have emancipated themselves from their traditional roles as mothers and wives 'living for others' and have demanded 'a life

65 G. Bakker (2008). "Het Adoptieboek, Stap voor Stap, Stress Tijdens de Adoptie Periode." Uitgeverij Aspekt, Soesterberg, p. 158.

66 A. Palm-Hensel (2008). "Stella, Unser Stern aus Indien, Die Geschichte einer glücklichen Adoption." Kleine Schritte, Trier, p. 11.

67 S. A. Scritchfield (1995). "The social construction of infertility: From private matter to social concern." In J. Best (ed), "Images of issues: Typifying contemporary social problems." (2nd edition) Aldine de Gruyter, Hawthorne, 131-146, p. 136.

68 *Ibid.*

of their own'.[69] They are no longer dependent on their husbands or families but have the freedom to shape their lives and identities themselves. Today, many women pursue an education and get a job, and when they finally decide that it is time to have children, some realize that "mother nature" no longer cooperates.

The authors' failure to achieve the life goal of having a child causes extreme pain and stress. Schulz, a woman in her 40s, who tried numerous reproductive treatments without success, describes her increasing frustration with the inability to conceive a child:

> I was obsessed with the idea that a pregnancy must be accomplished. In my life, I have not had any setbacks so far, neither in school, during my studies, in my career, nor in my marriage. I could not and did not want to realize that my body was not functioning. I became impatient. I have worked hard and so far I have always been rewarded for my performances. I perceived it as unfair that I was not able to have a child. I thought of being entitled to have my offspring and was annoyed by all pregnant women I saw.[70]

Experts suggest that people with more resources are commonly better able to cope with a given stressor and that stress is least evident among those with more advantaged social statuses. However, in the specific case of infertility, the failure to conceive is said to be particularly painful for socio-economically advantaged women.[71] Their privileged position in society gives them a strong sense of personal control in all aspects of their life, including their family planning.[72] They are comforted with the idea that success is the result of one's own actions and therefore perceive their infertility as an obstacle that can and that must be overcome with hard work, persistence and money. Just like Schulz, many authors believe that they deserve to become parents and that they are entitled to have children. They have spent a great deal of time, money and effort on getting pregnant, and they therefore feel that they have to be 'rewarded' for their 'performances'. Some authors describe how they perceive it to be 'unfair' that their hard work did not pay off, whereas many women in their surroundings got pregnant quite effortlessly.

These narratives illustrate the culture of individualization which has shaped modern Western societies. The authors of the adoption narratives demand an active role in managing their family planning and in forming their identities as biological parents. They have decided to produce a child and believe that – just like in other aspects of their life – they

69 *Ibid.*

70 B. Schulz (2005). "Tochter Indira, Die Geschichte einer Adoption aus Indien." Ullstein, Berlin, p. 111.

71 S. A. Scritchfield (1995). "The social construction of infertility: From private matter to social concern." In J. Best (ed), "Images of issues: Typifying contemporary social problems." (2nd edition) Aldine de Gruyter, Hawthorne, 131-146.

72 *Ibid.*, p. 136.

can have full measure of control over accomplishing this goal. The couples and individuals are not willing to resign themselves to their infertility and they refuse to accept the fact that reproduction is often not a matter of choice, regardless of the new advances in reproductive medical technologies. Rather, they want to believe they can take active measures to change their status as childless. Palm-Hensel explains: "I wanted a child badly and I wanted to defeat my fate".[73] Yet, as will be shown below, the narrative of fate and destiny plays an important role in a later stage on the route to adoptive parenthood.

Realizing that a pregnancy cannot be accomplished by their own actions and that their behaviour does not have any effect on their situation at all, causes severe frustration for many authors. Having children is so central to their identity that they experience a real and stressful "transition to nonparenthood" despite the fact that no objective change has occurred in their status.[74] As one female author describes it: "You lose something that you have never had (a child)".[75] Their infertility is an example of what Goffman refers to as 'spoiled identity' or stigma. Childlessness becomes the authors' master status that dominates their lives and is the main lens through which they define themselves.[76] This is illustrated by Vollmer, a woman who had four miscarriages and was finally diagnosed with infertility. In her book, she describes how her desire for a child perverted into an obsession that dominated her life:

> I was suffering from some sort of child mania. I was running after strange women on the streets who were pushing their buggies, only to sneak a peek on their children. I was buying children's clothes and watched children's movies. [...] It was an obsession. [...] It [the realization that she was infertile] was a horrible realization that made me become shallow and egotistical. I only saw me and the child that would never exist.[77]

Vollmer created a particular image of the child that she wanted to have and that would finally transform her into a mother. To make this image more tangible, she started purchasing and acquiring material goods:

> My child, in case I got a girl – and I was pretty sure about that – should be named Scarlett. Later I liked the combination of Scarlett and Vivien even better.

73 A. Palm-Hensel (2008). "Stella, Unser Stern aus Indien, Die Geschichte einer glücklichen Adoption." Kleine Schritte, Trier, p. 11.

74 R. Matthews and A. M. Matthews (1986). "Infertility and involuntary childlessness: The transition to nonparenthood." Journal of Marriage and the Family, 48, 641-649.

75 G. Bakker (2008). "Het Adoptieboek, Stap voor Stap, Stress Tijdens de Adoptie Periode." Uitgeverij Aspekt, Soesterberg, p. 161.

76 E. Goffman (2009). "Stigma: Notes on the Management of Spoiled Identity." Simon and Schuster, London.

77 R. Vollmer (2004). "Mein Kind aus der Fremde." Rowohlt, Reinbek bei Hamburg, pp. 95-96.

> Since then, nobody could dissuade me from that. I have even purchased a bracelet with her name engraved on it.[78]

For several thousand Euros, Vollmer also bought baby toys and clothing, a pink baby dresser as well as a crib that she "fell in love with" and started decorating a nursery in her house, even though she knew that she would never be able to conceive a child.[79] The acts of consumption served Vollmer with the means to regain a sense of power and control in her life. The purchases and acquisitions helped her to construct the identity of the desired baby and to simulate her transformation from a childless woman into a 'mother-to-be'. She explains, "it was like an inner compulsion. [...] Afterwards, I felt better. I saw it as a sign, as a good sign that sooner or later will bring me luck".[80] Later Vollmer wondered if her extremely strong desire for a child was already of pathological nature:

> I asked myself if I really wanted a child or if I already became the victim of a sick obsession. How many people cannot accept the facts? And how many of them are pathological cases?[81]

Only after a period of unsuccessful attempts to achieve pregnancy with technological intervention, do the authors consider adopting internationally as a backup or a last resort measure to have their own child. Three authors recall being interested in adopting even before they and their husbands discovered that they could not have biological children.[82] One woman writes that she perceived an adoption as "too risky" at the beginning. She was concerned about the fact that she did not know anything about possible genetic diseases, complications during pregnancy, the birth mother, the birth nor about the child's life in the institution.[83] Also, she had feared that she would not be able to accept an adopted child the way she would accept a biological one.[84] Another woman describes how she had initially rejected the idea of adopting internationally because she was worried that a child from another country might be subjected to racism in Germany.[85] However, the more cumbersome and futile the attempts to achieve pregnancy became, the more the women would embrace the idea of adopting a child. Many contemplated a domestic adoption but did

78 *Ibid.*, p. 137.
79 *Ibid.*, pp. 28-31.
80 *Ibid.*, pp. 30-31.
81 *Ibid.*, p. 152.
82 A. Michaela (2014). "Neun Monate Sommer, Tagebuch einer Adoptionsschwangerschaft in Kenia." Tausendschlau Olga Bien, Munich, p. 25.
83 B. Schulz (2005). "Tochter Indira, Die Geschichte einer Adoption aus Indien." Ullstein, Berlin, p. 101.
84 *Ibid.*, p. 99.
85 Wenzek-Grüneberg (2005). "Das Regenbogenkind, Die Geschichte einer Auslandsadoption." Books on Demand, Norderstedt, p. 5.

not meet the stringent requirements (age limit) or were deterred by the long waiting times and the slim chances of being matched with a young child. For all authors, intercountry adoption was, thus, the very last chance to have a child and to accomplish the goal of parenthood. One author explains: "Pregnancy was a dream, adoption is reality and thus the new dream".[86] Another woman writes:

> It [adoption] is nothing I have ever dreamed of, however, I could love every child. I came to realize that I demand a child, no matter if he/she is from us or not.[87]

Many authors describe how deciding to pursue an international adoption meant taking matters into their own hands again. After years of fertility treatments, whose success was beyond their power, the decision to adopt restored the feeling of having control over their family planning in many authors. Schulz explains how the idea of adopting internationally gave her new perspectives, "I was immersing myself in adoption books and that helped me. I suddenly became calm. An adoption was a huge challenge. But it was a goal. An alternative".[88] Van der Staaij explains: "It was almost strange to notice how well that thought [to adopt] felt. It also felt like being relieved of all the pain and efforts we had endured".[89] Going through the bureaucratic adoption process made the authors feel that they could achieve parenthood through their own actions. The many bureaucratic steps in the adoption procedure kept them busy and gave them the feeling of being in charge of their own life path. However, as soon as they finished the lengthy assessment procedure and submitted all necessary adoption documents, the waiting period began, which was perceived by most adoptive parents as a time in which they felt being at the mercy of other people.

4.2 *Saving a Child*

For many authors, the humanitarian aspect of intercountry adoption became an important argument in the process of rationalizing their decision to adopt a child from another country. Schulz who underwent a laparoscopy, numerous hormonal therapies as well as artificial inseminations over several years and finally decided to try in-vitro fertilization, explains why she finally decided to pursue an international adoption:

---

86 G. Bakker (2008). "Het Adoptieboek, Stap voor Stap, Stress Tijdens de Adoptie Periode." Uitgeverij Aspekt, Soesterberg, p. 137.

87 I. Holla (2005). "Mijn droom van een kind, Waargebeurd verhaal van een vrouw die haar wens om moeder te worden niet opgeeft." Uitgeverij Sirene, Amsterdam, p. 29.

88 B. Schulz (2005). "Tochter Indira, Die Geschichte einer Adoption aus Indien." Ullstein, Berlin, p. 117.

89 M. K. Van der Staaij (2004). "Liefs uit Bogotá, Ons verhaal over adoptie." Uitgeverij Boekencentrum, Zoetermeer, p. 14.

> [...] during the preparations for the in-vitro surgery our doubts were increasing. Why should we force a pregnancy and have a child when there are thousands of children in institutions without parents? We have never found a convincing answer and it became our strongest argument for considering an adoption. Despite all the fear of an adoption, we came to perceive reproductive treatments as a betrayal of an institutionalized child. Somewhere in this world, there is a child that does not have parents and that has to wait longer to have parents, only because I was shying away from the risks and could not make a decision. I ran away from myself and the techniques in gynecology helped me with that.[90]

The logic of 'global motherhood', as described by Shome, serves these authors with a means to come to terms with their decision to adopt a child from another country. Shome argues: "It is now commonplace and even fashionable to see white Western women saving, rescuing, or adopting international children from underprivileged parts of the world. [...] Global motherhood has surfaced as a logic through which white women's bodies are spilling into the global community and offering visions and hopes of a multicultural family".[91] Briggs has shown how media images of the poor have provided a basis for middle-class white people in the West to imagine the needs of adoptable children and to position themselves as their rescuers.[92]

Two female authors make clear that they did not consider themselves as "saving a child". Schulz, who travelled to India to adopt, remarks: "I am not a holy Samaritan. No, there is also a large portion of egoism that I am searching for a child here".[93] Also, Michielsen points out that she did not have an altruistic motivation to adopt: "I did not want to adopt to make the world a better place, but just to start a family".[94] However, in most other adoption stories, the "save a child" narrative, in which children from "Third World Countries" are portrayed as children in desperate need of being saved from their immediate circumstances through adoption, finds strong expression. Palm-Hensel, for instance, explains: "We just want to provide a poor, parentless child with a new home and a future that he/she would never have in his/her native country".[95] Another female author writes that she already developed an idealistic idea of 'saving the world' when she was a

90 B. Schulz (2005). "Tochter Indira, Die Geschichte einer Adoption aus Indien." Ullstein, Berlin, p. 116.

91 R. Shome (2011). ""Global Motherhood": The Transnational Intimacies of White Femininity." Critical Studies in Media Communication, 28, 5, 388-406, p. 389.

92 L. Briggs (2003). "Mother, Child, Race, Nation: The Visual Iconography of Rescue and the Politics of Transnational and Transracial Adoption." Gender & History, 15, 2, 179-200.

93 B. Schulz (2005). "Tochter Indira, Die Geschichte einer Adoption aus Indien." Ullstein, Berlin, p. 34.

94 D. Michielsen (2005). "Dochters van ver, belevenissen van een adoptiemoeder." Archipel, Amsterdam, p. 15.

95 A. Palm-Hensel (2008). "Stella, Unser Stern aus Indien, Die Geschichte einer glücklichen Adoption." Kleine Schritte, Trier, p. 13.

young girl. At the age of 10, she already knew that she would once adopt "children from a distant, hot and primarily poor country".[96] As the woman later realized that she would not be able to produce her own children, the idea of intercountry adoption came up again:

> Only when we began loving to travel to distant countries and there came into contact with countless children who did not really live a carefree life, the adoption ideal resurged for both of us. Why placing a child into a world when there are an awful lot of them wandering around, who would be thriving better if they got loving parents who were also to take care of them in material terms?[97]

The 'orphan crisis' in the 'Third World' is a dominant commonplace throughout the adoption narratives. The countries that the authors wish to adopt from are usually conceptualized as a perpetual source of orphaned children that need to be provided with a family and that would otherwise endure a miserable life in an impoverished child care institution and then on the streets. Michaela, for example, referrs to orphan statistics to stress the urgency of adopting a child from Kenya:

> In Kenya, 20 percent of the children are orphans. Their parents either abandoned them or died of AIDS. According to the information of the AS, it is difficult to establish accurate figures, however, it is estimated that more than 2,7 million orphans are living in Kenya. The majority of these small human beings are being abandoned or relinquished by their mothers after birth. Some children first live with their relatives or neighbours and then end up on the streets of Nairobi or Kisumu where they somehow fight for their survival. Many of them are addicted to drugs. Sniffing glue is the cheapest way to numb their pain.[98]

As was already explained in Chapter III, estimates on orphaned children published by UNICEF and other international organizations are partly responsible for this erroneous assumption of an 'orphan crisis'. These organizations adopted a broad definition of 'orphanhood' in the mid-1990s in order to draw developmental aid's attention to the growing AIDS crisis. Their estimates on orphans are inflated, including all children under 18 years who have lost one or two parents. Most of those children that have actually lost both parents live within their extended family network and are therefore not in need of

96 I. Andersson (2006). "Bloem van China, Dochter in Nederland." Free Musketeers, Woerden, p. 7.

97 *Ibid.*

98 A. Michaela (2014). "Neun Monate Sommer, Tagebuch einer Adoptionsschwangerschaft in Kenia." Tausendschlau Olga Bien, Munich, p. 31-32.

new parents. Yet, as Joyce explains: "In the popular imagination these hundreds of millions of orphans have become a mass of potential adoptees".[99]

The narratives of 'saving poor children' by way of adoption strongly feature in the adoption stories, whereas alternative forms of intervention (supporting local child protection and family welfare programmes), which would be more cost efficient and would not only benefit a few individual children that meet the adopters' desires, are not mentioned nor contemplated at all by the authors. Obviously, it is only by saving a child from a poor country that the authors are able to accomplish their life goal of becoming a parent. The adoptees aid the adopters in embracing the identity as parents and thereby help them to achieve the status of, what Anagnost calls, a "fully realized citizen"[100] in their community. They furthermore serve the Western adopters as a "primary love object" which compensates for the eroding family ties and love relationships.[101] Scholars in postcolonial and transnational feminism have illustrated how "global women" – as nannies, sex workers, nurses or mail-order brides – have contributed to the lifestyle of people in the Western countries by performing not only physical, but also affective labour that is traditionally associated with a wife's role.[102] Ehrenreich et al. explain: "It is as if the wealthy parts of the world are running short in precious emotional and sexual resources and have had to turn to poorer regions for fresh supply".[103]

Eng points out that in the context of international adoption, the child performs a kind of emotional work, similar to that of the 'global woman'. He argues that the transnational adoptee functions as an unconsenting affective laborer for his or her parents' access to full recognition by the community.[104] Hübinette even goes so far as to describe adoptees as slaves "brought over only to satisfy the needs and desires of their well-to-do acquirers".[105] Cheney perceives this as a paradox: "While adoption is ostensibly initiated to 'save' them, adopted children may actually serve as vital forms of social capital that end up 'saving' the

99 K. Joyce (2013). "The Child Catchers: Rescue, Trafficking, and the New Gospel of Adoption." Public Affairs, New York, p. 63.

100 A. Anagnost (2000). "Scenes of Misrecognition: Maternal Citizenship in the Age of Transnational Adoption." Positions: east asia cultures critique, 8, 2, 389-421, p. 392.

101 U. Beck and E. Beck-Gernsheim (1995). "The Normal Chaos of Love." Polity Press, Cambridge, p. 37.

102 B. Ehrenreich and A. R. Hochschild (2002). "Global Woman: Nannies, Maids, and Sex Workers in the New Economy." Henry Holt, New York.

103 *Ibid.*, pp. 4-5.

104 D. L. Eng (2006). "Political Economics of Passion: Transnational Adoption and Global Woman: Roundtable on Global Woman." Studies in Gender and Sexuality, 7, 1, 49–59, p. 57.

105 T. Hübinette (2006). "From Orphan Trains to Babylifts: Colonial Trafficking, Empire Building, and Social Engineering." In J. J. Trenka et al. (eds), "Outsiders Within: Writing on Transracial Adoption." South End Press, Cambridge, 139-149, p. 143.

adoptive family by performing the emotional labor necessary for social reproduction. This begs the question of who is really giving what to whom in adoption".[106]

The logic of 'saving' children from underprivileged parts of the world is not only advanced by infertile couples as a means to rationalize their decision to pursue an international adoption. For Schuman and his wife, a couple that were not involuntary childless, the motivation to adopt a child from another country revolves mainly around a religious core. When their caseworker from the adoption agency asked why they wanted to adopt a child from Kenya, the man, an evangelic pastor, replied:

> Before bringing a biological child into this world, we would like to provide a child with a family, that is already in this world and that does not have any parents. [...] We have good reasons to adopt a child. These include our knowledge and belief in Jesus' words that it is good to accept and take care of a child. Also, we are touched by the suffering of AIDS orphans, so we decided to adopt from Africa.[107]

The adoptive father bought into the discourse of saving children, claiming that the Bible commands him (as a Christian) to help orphans. Schumann argues that contributing money to a child care institution so as to help these children in their native countries would not go far enough, since money can never replace what they really need: loving parents. The author explains, "we would like to adopt a child and provide him with what you cannot buy with money: a family".[108] In his opinion, therefore, intercountry adoption appears to be the only entirely altruistic and humanitarian solution for children in need.

Adoptive parents like the Schumans who want to adopt primarily due to religious motivations are not an exception. Joyce points out that in the United States, a powerful Christian adoption movement emerged in the early 2000s which seeks to mitigate the global 'orphan crisis' through intercountry adoption. These conservative evangelic Christians' main intention is not to start a family in the wake of infertility, but instead to answer a biblical mandate to care for orphaned children.[109] For them, intercountry adoption does not so much serve as a means to embrace the identity as a family (most often they already have biological children) but the identity as a good Samaritan living according to the spirit

---

106 K. E. Cheney (2014). "'Giving Children a Better Life?' Reconsidering Social Reproduction, Humanitarianism and Development in Intercountry Adoption." The European Journal of Development Research, 26, 2, 247-263, p. 258.

107 T. Schumann (2012). "Faith - Adoption in Kenia, Ein Vater erzählt." Norderstedt, Books on Demand, p. 17.

108 *Ibid.*, pp. 8, 16.

109 K. Joyce (2013). "The Child Catchers: Rescue, Trafficking, and the New Gospel of Adoption." Public Affairs, New York.

of the Bible. The international adoptee functions as an emotional laborer for his or her parents' access to full recognition by the Christian community.

Arguably, all children – biological as well as adopted – fulfil affective and social functions for their parents. Homans stresses: "Against the charge that adopted children are singled out to perform uncompensated labour for their parents, I suggest that children in all kinds of families are instrumentalized every day [...]".[110] As was explained, in an individualized society where divorce rates are increasing, children become "the last remaining, irrevocable, unique primary love object[s]" which serve their parents with some sort of 'emotional provisions'. However, the financial transactions involved in intercountry adoption, as well as the fact that the child is not biologically related to his or her adoptive parents (which is in many cases apparent), make the instrumentalization of children particularly visible in adoptive parenthood. The narrative of adoption as rescuing a child serves the adopters with a powerful tool to obscure the economics of intercountry adoption and the commodification of the adoptee.

4.3 *Choosing the 'Right' Child*

Many authors repeatedly stress their intention to rescue a child without, however, concealing their own desires and needs in an intercountry adoption. For almost all of them, international adoption is their last chance to have a child. When an adopting couple was asked by a colleague if true, altruistic love would not actually meant financially supporting the birth family instead of adopting the child, the man replied:

> Of course, we are not selfless. We never claimed to be. Loving a child also means being loved, getting something back from this little creature. We want to be parents but that does not make us cold-hearted, mean capitalists![111]

Adopting parents often note the mutually beneficial nature of an intercountry adoption. They perceive this childcare option as a win-win-situation, as a logical solution to two problems: the child's need for parents and the couple's desire for a child. Due to the myth of an 'orphan crisis', many authors imagine a plight of orphans in developing countries from which they can literally pick 'a suitable child' or 'the right child'. They often picture overcrowded child care institutions, where they simply need to choose a child that meets their wishes and expectations. For instance, a woman who travelled to Argentina after her husband's business partner promised to find a child for her to adopt, describes the

110 M. Homans (2013). "The Imprint of Another Life: Adoption Narratives and Human Possibility." University of Michigan Press, Ann Arbor, p. 21.

111 M. Gaedicke (2009). "Wunschkind, Geschichte einer Adoption." Hoffmann und Campe, Hamburg, p. 228.

romanticized image of herself in an orphanage choosing a suitable child from a wide selection of orphans:

> I pictured a large dormitory with white walls and a highly vaulted ceiling. A large wooden cross was hanging on the front side of the room. The floor was paved with bricks and in the middle, there was a wide corridor. On the right and on the left side of the room were white wooden cribs lined up. Small plates were attached to the ends of the cribs containing the name and the birth date of the particular child. I imagine myself slowly walking along the corridor. The idea that I could choose any of these babies, that I simply had to settle for one of them and that all my sorrow would be gone instantly put me in a peculiar sense of delight, in a mixture of euphoria and astonishment.[112]

Also, another woman, Wenzek-Grüneberg, describes the expectations that she and her husband had when – after numerous unsuccessful attempts to conceive – they finally decided to pursue an adoption in Ukraine:

> Of course, we do not have any guarantee that we will find a child that we like and that suits us. However, in those institutions [in Ukraine] there are more than 100.000 children without parents. There must also be a child for us, right?[113]

For most adopters, a 'suitable child' is a healthy baby. Couples pursuing an agency adoption are commonly asked to fill out a form in which they have to articulate preferences concerning the age of the child (usually adopters can choose between several age ranges) and whether or not they would be willing to accept an adoptee with a 'special need', meaning a mental or physical disability. In Germany, adopters are asked by their agency to tick off those special needs they think they could accept. Caseworkers (often those in the sending country) then use the chosen criteria to 'match' a child with the couple. One author decided to accept a young child with an operable special need. Another woman did not have any preferences concerning the child's age or health status, explaining: "[w]hen you become pregnant naturally you also do not get to choose gender, appearance, and health".[114] All of the other authors, however, did not want to leave their future child's characteristics to chance, but explicitly stated that they wished to adopt a child that was healthy and as young

---

112 R. Vollmer (2004). "Mein Kind aus der Fremde." Rowohlt, Reinbek bei Hamburg, p. 43.

113 A. Wenzek-Grüneberg (2005). "Das Regenbogenkind, Die Geschichte einer Auslandsadoption." Books on Demand, Norderstedt, p. 12.

114 A. Palm-Hensel (2008). "Stella, Unser Stern aus Indien, Die Geschichte einer glücklichen Adoption." Kleine Schritte, Trier, p. 18.

as possible. In order to fulfil this desire, most were even ready to accept longer waiting periods:

> We had the feeling that, after years of waiting and of intense emotions, and also taking into consideration my heavy migraine which put a strain on both of us, we should not deliberately choose a 'special need' child but think of ourselves, even though this choice would extend the waiting period.[115]

Adoption applicants also typically choose the country they wish to adopt from, which is often done according to practical criteria. Most would settle for a sending state where the prospects of adopting a young child are high and adoption procedures are known to be unbureaucratic and speedy. Two authors particularly preferred adopting a young girl: China with its apparent surplus of abandoned female babies, as well as its relatively short waiting lists, was thus an attractive sending country for them. Koolen explains why she and her husband deliberately chose China as an adoption country:

> We decided to adopt a child from China. In this far, for us so mysterious, country there were still opportunities to adopt a healthy baby. We wanted a child as young as possible as we wished to experience the child's first words and steps. In addition, this choice was a pragmatic one: we have already been busy for five years with having children, thus, the factor time and the length of the waiting list played an important role for us. We heard an adoption of a child from China went reasonably fast if you had a valid principle approval. Moreover, in other adoption countries the adoption criteria were tightened, the waiting periods lengthening or adoption was even banned.[116]

For some authors, the range of choices and the scope of autonomy afforded to them in an agency adoption procedure were too limited. An adoption can only be pursued in a country with which the agency has established cooperation. Furthermore, the adopters are reliant on other people's actions and they hardly have any say in the adoption process. They are expected to follow the steps in the adoption procedure, which many consider as inefficient and needlessly bureaucratic, with little scope for decision-making as they are moved through the adoption system. Even after the applicants have undergone a lengthy assessment procedure (which many perceive as too intrusive or even humiliating) and have submitted all of the necessary adoption documents, they still have to wait – sometimes

115 M. & I. Koolen (2009). "Moeders mooiste, vaders trots, Een bijzonder verslag van de lange weg naar adoptie." The house of books, Antwerpen, p. 30.

116 *Ibid.*, pp. 35-36.

even years if they choose to adopt a healthy baby – without being able to move the process forward.

This lack of autonomy in an agency adoption is not an option for some. They have already experienced a complete lack of control over their family planning for several years and they are not ready to hand over the steering wheel to another person. Thus, in order to maintain a degree of individual initiative in the adoption procedure, as well as to be able to exercise a greater choice over the matching, some authors decide to pursue a do-it-yourself adoption. For instance, Schulz was not willing to accept the long waiting times that her caseworker predicted. The previous months of waiting for a child proposal created a feeling of powerlessness in her, so that she decided to finally "take matters into her own hands" by travelling to India and visiting numerous orphanages to choose a suitable child.[117] Also, Holla and her husband decided to adopt independently:

> Of course, we could save ourselves a lot of effort by having our names placed on the waiting list of an adoption agency. However, we did not like this idea. We already had to wait too often and we preferred taking action and create opportunities.[118]

The demand to take an active role in the adoption procedure and to influence its outcome illustrates, once again, the Western culture of individualization that was described earlier. Do-it-yourself adopters are not willing to be dependent on anybody else's actions, but rather they want to be in full control of accomplishing their goals. In order to get an adoptive child as quickly as possible, one author, Michielsen, even considered a number of illegal means. As they learned from a French acquaintance about a Filipino woman who was willing to give her child up for adoption, the couple thought about different opportunities to smuggle the child to the Netherlands. As their plan did not work, they considered searching for an adoptable child with the help of a befriended couple working at the UNHCR in Vietnam. The woman explains why they considered illegal actions:

> [Y]ou feel easily inclined to do something unethical if you want to chase an adoption – [...] we wanted to organize an adoption ourselves. We couldn't stand waiting until it was our turn. I felt obliged to take actions myself.[119]

117 *Ibid*, p. 14.

118 I. Holla (2005). "Mijn droom van een kind, Waargebeurd verhaal van een vrouw die haar wens om moeder te worden niet opgeeft." Uitgeverij Sirene, Amsterdam, pp. 90-91.

119 D. Michielsen (2005). "Dochters van ver, belevenissen van een adoptiemoeder." Archipel, Amsterdam, p. 36.

Do-it-yourself adopters play a very active role in choosing their future child. Some use their private contacts to child care institutions or hire an independent agent in the sending country to secure an adoptable child. For instance, one woman adopted a child from an institution in Kenya which she helped establish years before. Two other authors travelled to the sending country and visited a number of orphanages in order to find a child to adopt. After having spent some time in the sending country, many adopters realize that the majority of children available for intercountry adoption do not live up to their expectations as they are already older or have disabilities. Wenzek-Grüneberg describes how frustrating the search for a suitable child in Ukraine was for her and her husband:

> At first, we were in an institution where there were only handicapped children. One was mentally disabled, another one had a heart defect and the third child was epileptic. That was very depressing and we feared that we would not find a healthy child for us.[120]

Later, in a Ukrainian adoption center, Wenzek-Grüneberg and her husband went through numerous pictures of orphans that were available for intercountry adoption, whereby they had to reject most of the children they did not find suitable:

> They saw a beautiful girl with dark hair that, however, was already six years old. They liked her but then they heard that she was mentally ill. Änne und Peter looked at each other. No, their eyes said, we want a healthy child, somehow feeling a bit bad. […] Two hours passed and they were sitting in a pile of pictures and could still not make up their mind.[121]

As becomes apparent from the stories, adopters exercise a key market component: choice.[122] First of all, they must choose international adoption as a means of having a child. After they have decided to pursue an adoption, they get to indicate age preferences and choose between a healthy child and an adoptee with a special need. If they are ready to receive a special need child, they have to decide which kind of disability they are willing to accept. By determining the sending country, adopters might also choose the child's sex or even skin colour. Couples and individuals wishing to adopt a child with a fair skin tone, might, for instance, choose to adopt from Russia or an Eastern European state. Those who wish to have a young girl might want to consider an adoption from China.

---

120 *Ibid.*, p. 30.
121 *Ibid.*, p. 81.
122 M. Goodwin (2010). "Baby Markets: Money and the New Politics of Creating Families." Cambridge University Press, p. 10; S. Marijnen and J. Doomernik (2015). "Baby Migration." AEMI Journal, 13, 133-149, p. 140.

It is not only preferences concerning the child's characteristics that might influence the country choice, but also practical considerations, such as waiting lists and the level of bureaucracy with the authorities. Most adopters wish to achieve their goal of parenthood as soon as possible and thus seek to adopt from a sending country which seems to promise fast adoption procedures. Those who want to exercise greater choice and autonomy over selecting the 'right child' might want to pursue a do-it-yourself adoption, which allows them to maintain a higher degree of individual initiative during the selection process.

Some adopters feel uncomfortable with exercising choice in the adoption procedure, as for them it feels like shopping for their child. One woman, for instance, who had already adopted a baby girl from China and decided to adopt her second child - this time a baby boy - describes the feeling of unease she had when she and her husband deliberately chose Thailand as a sending country for their second adoption:

> Suddenly we realized how bizarre the situation was: the country of birth is decisive for the child's sex. As if you are checking out a holiday brochure and the type of beach – sand or stones – determines your destination. It felt differently years before when we choose for China. That was because we were busy for such a terribly long time with having a child and because an adoption from China seemed to go fast. Furthermore, it had to do with the fact that I wanted to go to Asia due to my Indian roots. The choices you sometimes have to make are too absurd as to think about them 'rationally'. To China for a girl and to Thailand for a boy: suddenly it began to look a lot like shopping.[123]

In order to downplay the commercial component of the selection process in an international adoption, Bakker, an adoptive mother of two Kenyan children, explains to aspirant adopters the following:

> You are the ones who make a choice. You choose an adoption, for whatever reason. However, there is also another aspect. Namely the one of being chosen. The choice of the child. [...] Not you alone are busy with choosing a child, also the child chooses you. Many prospective adoptive parents have problems seeing an agency determining which child will finally find a place in your family and your heart. [...] But don't worry so much. The energy in the universe is so strong that there are already vibes between child and parents which are

123 D. Michielsen (2005). "Dochters van ver, belevenissen van een adoptiemoeder." Archipel, Amsterdam, p. 163.

> unmeasurable but which are definitely there. The child that ultimately will be placed in your family has already chosen you.[124]

By suggesting that it is actually the adoptee that chooses his or her parents, Bakker minimalizes the superior role that adopters play in an international adoption by virtue of their class and race privileges.[125] She explains that it is not the rational choices made by adoptive parents (and then by adoption agencies) but the undeliberate choices of the child which, with the help of cosmic forces, will ultimately bring the adoptee and adopter together. Ironically, the same adopters who were refusing to resign themselves to fate – in the form of involuntary childlessness – and did everything they could to regain a full measure of control over accomplishing parenthood, appropriate the concept of destiny to deny their role as consumers and the instrumentalization of a child. As will be shown, such 'rhetorics of disavowal'[126] are recurring throughout all stages of the route to adoptive parenthood.

Adopters might not only feel uncomfortable with deliberately choosing a 'suitable child'. Many authors write that they feel guilty for the children they did *not* choose to adopt as they did not meet their wishes and expectations. They describe feelings of unease about the tension between, on the one hand, the moral imperative to save a child that urgently needs loving parents but that does not have the desired characteristics and, on the other hand, their own desires and preferences: adopting a healthy baby. For instance, Schulz who visited several child care institutions in Bombay describes the emotional stress that she felt after she decided to refuse to adopt from an orphanage where the children were living in deplorable conditions:

> In the cab, I started feeling guilty [...] about the children. Actually, we should adopt a child from here. Here, where the children are hit very hard, where they are neglected and sick from loneliness and sadness, where their souls are atrophy. However, I am not that forceful, not that brave, not that honest. I know that in this institution time has left deep traces in the children's psyches. They will have to struggle with the consequences of this traumatizing experience for a long time, or forever.[127]

Many adopters provide generous contributions, either in the form money or goods, to the orphanage they adopt from. Several authors describe how they went to shopping malls in

---

124 G. Bakker (2008). "Het Adoptieboek, Stap voor Stap, Stress Tijdens de Adoptie Periode." Uitgeverij Aspekt, Soesterberg, p. 190.

125 See, for instance, T. L. Perry (1998). "Transracial and International Adoption: Mothers, Hierarchy, Race, and Feminist Legal Theory." Yale Journal of Law and Feminism, 10, 101-164.

126 *Ibid.*

127 *Ibid.*, p. 45.

the country they adopted from (most often these malls meet Western standards and are not affordable for the majority of locals) to purchase pampers, baby food, bottle-heaters, lotions and other baby products for the child care institution they adopted from. Arguably the contributions and donations help adopters to buy their way out of feelings of guilt and unease that is caused by their rational choice to adopt a suitable child, leaving behind many other children that do not meet their expectations but that would probably need 'to be saved' more urgently.

4.4 *Paying for an Adoption*

Not only choice but also the payment of money is a key component of the adoption market and is an uncomfortable factor for many adopters. As Anagnost observes, "[t]he anxiety that the child might be a commodity is aroused by the incontrovertible fact that as the child moves from one site of nurture to another, money has to change hands; agencies are established; 'baby flights' are chartered; tour packages are assembled".[128] Some authors do not mention the adoption costs in their stories at all and omit any possible thoughts about the economics in a transnational adoption. Yet others do deal with the financial aspects, seeking ways to manage the anxiety that they are exchanging money for a child.

In her book, Schulz describes the conversation she had with an Indian woman who she met in front of a child care institution in Bombay and who told her that her sister also wanted to adopt a child.[129] Soon it became clear that the Indian woman's motivation to adopt was quite different to Schulz's. The woman explained that her sister, who 'only has a daughter', urgently needed a son otherwise her husband's family would cease to exist. Since they found the official adoption procedure too time-consuming and intrusive, they decided to purchase a baby boy from a mother who wanted to drop off her child in the child care institution. She revealed that she and her sister are willing to pay 1,000 to 2,000 Rupees (about €30), depending on the child's condition. Schulz was appalled as the Indian woman asked her how much she herself was willing to pay for a child:

> 'Nothing. I am not paying anything. Otherwise, I would be arrested', I reply. I explain that a child should not be paid for, that this is considered to be child trafficking, no matter if you are in India, Europe, America or anywhere else. "But you want to have a child. A child brings happiness and saves the family. You need to pay for that. You cannot have that for free", she asserts. After all, you need to pay for everything. [...] I talk about human dignity and child

128 A. Anagnost (2004). "Maternal Labor in a Transnational Circuit." In J. S. Taylor et al. (eds), "Consuming Motherhood." Rutgers University Press, New Brunswick, 139-167, p. 147.

129 B. Schulz (2005). "Tochter Indira, Die Geschichte einer Adoption aus Indien." Ullstein, Berlin, pp. 47-50.

> trafficking and international law. But she does not listen to me anymore. I lost all her respect. Rich Western women that come to India and want to have a child for free.[130]

This conversation reveals two fundamentally different cultural conceptions of the child and an adoption. For the Indian woman, a male child fulfills a clear function, namely to protect the family's fortunes and preserve its name. She considers the child to have an economic benefit for the family and was willing to pay the price for him. For Schulz, on the contrary, adoption does not serve an instrumental but rather a sentimental purpose. She is searching for what Zelizer refers to as 'an economically useless child' to love and nurture, preferably a young girl. Contrary to the Indian woman, Schulz considers a child as priceless and stressed that he or she cannot and should not be valued in monetary terms. Even though she is most probably spending a lot of money in the adoption process (more than just €30), she insists that she is not paying anything for the child.

Schulz's answer to the Indian woman's question as to how much she was willing to pay for a child illustrates what Anagnost refers to as 'a refusal and resignification of the meaning of monetary exchanges', a rhetorical device often detected in adopting parents' stories that mask their discomfort with the possible commodification of an adoptive child.[131] Even though adopters spend huge amounts of money in an intercountry adoption process, they repeatedly emphasize that they are not technically paying for a child and thereby they deny the role that their money plays in the adoption system. Again, such 'rhetoric of disavowal'[132] serves them with a tool to distance themselves from a situation that they strongly reject: engaging in a market in children.

Also, Schumann, another adopting mother, disavowed the significance of money in the adoption from Kenya.[133] When asked by her colleague how much she was willing to pay for a child, she reprovingly answered: "[we]e are adopting a child, we are not purchasing a child",[134] thereby stressing that adoption and commerce are two intrinsically contradictory and mutually exclusive domains. Later in the book, the author stresses that "a child is a treasure that is much greater than money."[135] By arguing that children are priceless and *ipso facto* beyond commerce, both Schulz and Schumann do not only tacitly deny their engagement in a market in children, but that a market in children exists in the first place. After all, how can children be bought if their worth cannot be assessed in monetary terms?

---

130 *Ibid.*

131 A. Anagnost (2004). "Maternal Labor in a Transnational Circuit." In J. S. Taylor et al. (eds), "Consuming Motherhood." Rutgers University Press, New Brunswick, 139-167, p. 147.

132 *Ibid.*

133 *Ibid.*

134 T. Schumann (2012). "Faith - Adoption in Kenia, Ein Vater erzählt." Norderstedt, Books on Demand, p. 28.

135 *Ibid.*, p. 72.

One adoptive mother downplays the meaning of monetary exchanges in an intercountry adoption by aligning adoption with reproductive treatments, both – she argues – of which are costly means of having a child.

> We were happy about investing all our savings in our "child project". What could be more precious than seeing a happy child, what could be better and more satisfying than finally being mommy and daddy? A reproductive treatment also costs money and you can never be sure if it will result in a pregnancy after all. Every couple spends money on this very special desire – some more, some less. However, you do not have to be rich.[136]

Also, other authors compare adoption to reproductive treatments or to a pregnancy. For instance, Michaela's book, in which she describes the nine months she and her husband were obliged to stay in Kenya with their adoptive son until the adoption proceedings could be finalized, is titled: "Nine months of summer. A diary about an adoption pregnancy".[137] Similarly, Palm-Hensel compares waiting for the assignment of a particular child with a pregnancy: "It took nine months until one day we got a call from the adoption agency. Nine months of my 'pregnancy' that felt like nine years for us".[138] The pregnancy-metaphor serves the adopters with a means to suppress the role that money and their rational choices play in an adoption and thereby 'renaturalizes' and 'decommodifies' the adoption process.[139]

One couple who underwent several reproductive treatments without success and finally decided to pursue an international adoption argues that it is actually far less selfish to spend money on an adoption than trying to have one's own biological child. The 'save a child' narrative is therefore appropriated to sanctify an intercountry adoption as a nobler means to have a child than recourse to reproductive treatments:

> If we had to choose again between a reproductive treatment and an adoption, we would immediately go for an adoption. Obviously, both cost money and is nerve-racking. But in an adoption, you help a child that does not have parents. And it is not as exhausting as a reproductive treatment. [...] In retrospective, I think that we were quite selfish. We needed our own child to be a family –

136 A. Michaela (2014). "Neun Monate Sommer, Tagebuch einer Adoptionsschwangerschaft in Kenia." Tausendschlau Olga Bien, München, p. 190.

137 A. Michaela (2014). "Neun Monate Sommer, Tagebuch einer Adoptionsschwangerschaft in Kenia." Tausendschlau Olga Bien, Munich.

138 A. Palm-Hensel (2008). "Stella, Unser Stern aus Indien, Die Geschichte einer glücklichen Adoption." Kleine Schritte, Trier, p. 24.

139 M. Sandelowski (1993). "With Child in Mind: Studies of the Personal Encounter With Infertility." University of Pennsylvania Press, p. 193.

> no matter how much it costs. Every unsuccessful reproductive treatment claimed a life. Adopting saved a life.[140]

Another book also provides an example of refusing and resignifying the meaning of monetary exchanges in an adoption, though this is an extreme example. Vollmer, who went to Argentina to find an adoptable child with the help of her husband's shady business partner (without the involvement of any German adoption agency), repeatedly stresses that she did not want to violate any laws and that anything else than a 'regular' adoption would be out of the question.[141] She refused to accept a baby girl that was offered to her by an Argentinian beggar woman she passed by on the streets of Buenos Aires (even though in her words "the temptation was great"), by claiming that this is something that she 'would never be able to do".[142] However, as the business partner acting as an intermediary later demanded 2,000 Dollars as a "down payment" for a doctor who allegedly had a suitable child for her, she unhesitatingly paid the amount without questioning the nature or legitimacy of the payment.[143] When her private agent did not show up with the promised child, Vollmer writes:

> [He] should keep the agreement [...]. If I would have known back then that he had arranged a broker's commission of fifteen thousand dollars with Harry [her husband], I would not have given him a break. I pressured him until he gave me a new appointment.[144]

In order to deal with their anxiety that the child might be a commodity that is bought and sold, adopters deny the significance of payments in the adoption procedure by reframing and resignifying them. Financial transactions made to adoption agencies, family courts, government officials etc. are characterized as 'service costs' or 'administrative fees' and money or goods provided to the institution where the child was adopted from are defined as 'contributions' and 'donations'. However, not only legitimate payments but also clearly illegal payments are reframed to obscure the economics in an international adoption. Money or goods offered to the child's birth mother are labelled as 'gifts' and payments made to private intermediaries sourcing a suitable child to adopt are characterized as 'down payments' or 'broker's commission': anything but the payment for a child.

140 T. Schumann (2012). "Faith - Adoption in Kenia, Ein Vater erzählt." Norderstedt, Books on Demand, p. 192-193.

141 R. Vollmer (2004). "Mein Kind aus der Fremde." Rowohlt, Reinbek bei Hamburg, pp. 36-38, 109, 153-154.

142 *Ibid.*, p. 50.

143 *Ibid.*, p. 139.

144 *Ibid.*, p. 150.

5 Becoming Parents

5.1 *Finding the 'Meant-To-Be'-Child*

The assignment of a particular child is a crucial moment for adopters. It terminates the pre-matching waiting period and transforms the abstract wish for a child into a tangible subject of anticipation. Couples and individuals pursuing an agency adoption usually receive a photograph and/or a brief description of the child that was selected for them.[145] According to Sandelowski who studied women's and couples' narrative accounts of adoption, "these artifacts provid[ed] couples with a new, material reality; like couples learning of a pregnancy, they now knew of the existence of a specific child 'earmarked' for them".[146] Like an ultrasound picture for childbearing couples, the profile of the child serves adopters with a reassurance that they will finally get a child, but it also constitutes as an important source of information to construct a clear image of the child that is supposed to be theirs. Michielsen writes:

> How happy can you be with such a photo? Incredible. […] Our first family portrait! We slept with the photograph in our bed, I carried a smaller size of it in my wallet as well as in my agenda […] Our virtual child finally was of flesh and blood![147]

In the case of do-it-yourself adoptions, adopters who are often in the sending country commonly directly meet the child selected for them without having received a photograph beforehand. Right after the adopters have seen the child for the first time (either on a photograph or in *natura*), they engage in 'parental claiming' so as to demand the status as parents of the biologically unrelated child. This is a deliberative process which Sandelowski describes as "the special kind of emotional and intellectual work that adopting couples [do] […] to make someone else's child, 'somewhere out there', their own child".[148] Parental claiming can also be observed in childbearing couples, it is, however, particularly crucial for adopters as the child selected for them does not naturally belong to them.[149] Howell describes the imaginative and symbolic work that adopters engage in to forge family ties

145 Adopting parents that, however, pursue a private adoption, meet their prospective adoptive child in the child care institution for the first time.

146 M. Sandelowski (1993). "With Child in Mind: Studies of the Personal Encounter With Infertility." University of Pennsylvania Press, p.185.

147 D. Michielsen (2005). "Dochters van ver, belevenissen van een adoptiemoeder." Archipel, Amsterdam, p. 73.

148 *Ibid.*, p. 188.

149 *Ibid.*, pp. 188-189.

between them and the unrelated child as 'kinning', a process which involves 'transubstantiating' the child's identity (as somebody else's child into the adopters' child). She explains: "Through a process of kinning and transubstantiation, adoptive parents not only incorporate their children into their own kin, they also transform themselves into parents, thereby negating the separation between social and biological that is encountered elsewhere in society".[150]

Many adopting parents actively construe a biologically unrelated child as 'their child' by maintaining that the child was supposed to be theirs. They see the hand of God, fate or cosmic forces bringing them together. One author, for instance, concludes that the fact that the proposed Chinese girl was born the day after her father passed away proved that this child was destined for her and her husband.[151] Another author remarkes that the girl selected for her was born the day she set foot in Sri Lanka, "as if we landed on this piece of earth on the same day".[152] Later in her book, she notes that she believed it was her triplets that she had lost a couple of days after birth who brought her together with her adoptive child.[153] One woman who adopted two children from Kenya writes:

> What I feel very strongly is that these children are destined for us. [They] came on our path to embark on their life journey together with us. I believe in the steering of God, of almightiness.[154]

Wenzek-Grüneberg concludes that the Ukrainian boy offered to her and her husband was meant for them as the German translation of the boy's last name is "everything is white" *("alles ist weiß")*, which strongly resembles the couple's last name: "Coincidence? Fate? Hand of God? It was as if everything fell into place".[155] She also recognizes physical similarities between the boy and her husband (both blond, a bit chubby and with blue eyes), supporting her assumption that the child was destined to be their child.[156] Another female author who adopted two girls from China writes of how she endorsed the idea of an invisible 'red thread' connecting her with her adoptive daughters who, she believes, she

150 S. Howell (2006). "The Kinning of Foreigners: Transnational Adoption in a Global Perspective." Berghahn Books, New York, p. 82.

151 D. Michielsen (2005). "Dochters van ver, belevenissen van een adoptiemoeder." Archipel, Amsterdam, p. 73.

152 I. Holla (2005). "Mijn droom van een kind, Waargebeurd verhaal van een vrouw die haar wens om moeder te worden niet opgeeft." Uitgeverij Sirene, Amsterdam, p. 102.

153 *Ibid.*, p. 156.

154 G. Bakker (2008). "Het Adoptieboek, Stap voor Stap, Stress Tijdens de Adoptie Periode." Uitgeverij Aspekt, Soesterberg, p. 175.

155 A. Wenzek-Grüneberg (2005). "Das Regenbogenkind, Die Geschichte einer Auslandsadoption." Books on Demand, Norderstedt, p. 97.

156 *Ibid.*, pp. 88-90.

was destined to meet.[157] The 'red thread' is a common trope among parents who adopted a child from China. It refers to the Chinese folktale about a matchmaker, the Old Man of the Moon, who arranges marriages by tying a red thread between prospective spouses the moment they are born. The legend's message is that husband and wife are tied to each other by fate which cannot be changed.[158] By mobilizing the trope of the 'red thread' adopters seek to bring out that they and their adopted children were destined to meet, "regardless of time, place, or circumstance".[159]

Not only narratives of 'fate' but also of 'love at first sight' recur often in adoption stories. They serve the adopters to transform a biologically unrelated child into their own child by suggesting that an undeniable love tie exists between the adopters and the child which, just like a blood tie, strongly links them together. Palm-Hensel describes how she and her husband immediately recognized the Indian girl assigned to them as 'their child' when they saw her photograph for the first time:

> There she was [...] in a pink dress, with frenetic curls on her head, looking at us with her big brown eyes! Our daughter was absolutely beautiful! We immediately fell in love with her. That was our child! We were crying for joy over our long-awaited child and proudly showed everybody her pictures.[160]

Also, Michaela, a woman who adopted a boy from Kenya, describes the strong feelings of love and affection she immediately had for her adoptive son when she saw him in the orphanage for the first time:

> It is an unbelievably beautiful feeling for me. I sense the positive energy and the love for this child. A warm shiver runs through my body. I realize how happy and pleased I am. We have arrived. This made up all our efforts. And for this boy, there is a happy ending. This child finally has parents who love him with no limits.[161]

Some adopters note that the love they feel for their prospective adoptive child could not be any stronger for a biological one, thereby assimilating adoptive and biological parent-

---

157 D. Michielsen (2005). "Dochters van ver, belevenissen van een adoptiemoeder." Archipel, Amsterdam, p. 68.

158 M. G. González and E. Wesseling (2013). "The Stories We Adopt By: Tracing" The Red Thread" in Contemporary Adoption Narratives." The Lion and the Unicorn, 37, 3, 257-276, pp. 260-261.

159 *Ibid.*, p. 261.

160 A. Palm-Hensel (2008). "Stella, Unser Stern aus Indien, Die Geschichte einer glücklichen Adoption." Kleine Schritte, Trier, p. 25.

161 A. Michaela (2014). "Neun Monate Sommer, Tagebuch einer Adoptionsschwangerschaft in Kenia." Tausendschlau Olga Bien, Munich, pp. 32-33.

hood.[162] One adoptive mother claims her parental status by comparing the first encounter with her adoptive son from Kenya with a conception:

> I took him out of his bed and held him close to me. Hard to believe that you hold your child that moment. Unreal to be aware that from this moment on the unstoppable urge to have him started and was no longer to be stopped. Unbelievable that it only happened just now, still so clear on the retina and engraved in the heart. The seed cell had met the egg and did not intend to undo the fertilization. I was pregnant, but at the same time, I could take a look at the uterus.[163]

The sentimental narratives of 'meant to be' and 'falling in love' do not only serve adopters to claim somebody else's child as 'their own child'. They also provide a forceful language to neutralize or deny the significance of money in the adoption process as well as to eliminate the weight of the adopters' selfish interests and the rational choices they have been making. The idea of God or fate bringing the adopters together with a particular child and of the love tie linking them with each other helps them to 'decommodify and renaturalize' the adoption process as a whole.[164] The concepts of the meant-to-be child and of the irrefutable emotional bond obscure the role that the adopters' superior status (as wealthy Westerners) has played in the process of finding the 'right child', and it imposes a natural and non-economic appearance on international adoption.

Homans, who has explored representations of adoption in literature, explains: "the language of romance [...] plays [the] role of justifying, naturalizing, and rendering inevitable or fated a relationship whose arbitrary beginnings in an economic transaction are intolerable to think about and must be obscured".[165] She furthermore notes: "the discourse of 'falling-in-love' and a quasi-religious discourse of 'miracle' and 'meant to be' enable writings by recent adoptive parents to finesse the conceptual and moral obstacles to seeing the market system of adoption, even as they sometimes indirectly acknowledge their participation in it. How can loved children be purchased objects or unpaid workers, if they are with us by magic and are the focus of so much love?"[166]

162 A. Wenzek-Grüneberg (2005). "Das Regenbogenkind, Die Geschichte einer Auslandsadoption." Books on Demand, Norderstedt, p. 129.
163 G. Bakker (2008). "Het Adoptieboek, Stap voor Stap, Stress Tijdens de Adoptie Periode." Uitgeverij Aspekt, Soesterberg, p. 59.
164 M. Sandelowski (1993). "With Child in Mind: Studies of the Personal Encounter With Infertility." University of Pennsylvania Press, p. 193.
165 M. Homans (2013). "The Imprint of Another Life: Adoption Narratives and Human Possibility." University of Michigan Press, p. 36.
166 *Ibid.*, pp. 55-56.

Some authors do voice critical thoughts about the intercountry adoption system as a whole and the role they play in it. For instance, Michielsen, a Dutch woman who adopted two girls from China, describes that she and her husband felt ashamed and guilty when they were confronted with the commercial and imperialistic nature of an intercountry adoption. In a hotel in Hefei, where they were waiting to meet their adoptive daughter for the first time, they saw a large group of American adopters having dinner with the Chinese baby girls they had received the day before:

> Auke and I looked at each other shocked. What inspired us to make all this effort here to take away Chinese daughters? Well, rationally considered, it was clear that the girls had better future perspectives in a Western family than here in a children's home – however, at the moment, it did not feel like that at all. [...] To make such a vulnerable child your own as you want a family suddenly seems to be the peak of egoism. And then to think that there were people complimenting us as for having the guts to do that.[167]

The day after, however, when the author saw the Chinese girl selected for her for the first time, feelings of love seem to brush aside the critical reflections about transnational adoption she and her husband had only a few days earlier. The rest of her book is dominated by tropes of 'love' and 'fate' which shift the emphasis from the adoption system back to the individuals, Michielsen and her 'own Lisa-Xiu',[168] whose undeniable bond of love draws a veil on the economic asymmetries, the adopters' privileged status and their money that made the adoption possible in the first place.

Later in her book, the author uses another powerful linguistic choice to naturalize the adoption process. She describes her daughter as being a gift from the country she adopted from: "China gave us our daughter as a present and for that, we will always be grateful to this country".[169] The rhetoric of the gift can also be found in other adoption stories. For example, after the couple van der Staaij received 'the call' from the agency offering a Colombian child for adoption, they performed a special ritual: "before we went to bed, we thanked God for the great gift that He was willing to give us".[170] The adoption announcement cards they sent out after they had returned to the Netherlands let family and friends know that: "God's hand connected our fates. This life was given in our hands as a precious

167 I. Holla (2005). "Mijn droom van een kind, Waargebeurd verhaal van een vrouw die haar wens om moeder te worden niet opgeeft." Uitgeverij Sirene, Amsterdam, p. 90.

168 D. Michielsen (2005). "Dochters van ver, belevenissen van een adoptiemoeder." Archipel, Amsterdam, p. 91.

169 *Ibid.*, p. 110.

170 M. K. Van der Staaij (2004). "Liefs uit Bogotá, Ons verhaal over adoptie." Uitgeverij Boekencentrum, Zoetermeer, p. 31.

gift".[171] Holla believes that she and her husband were chosen to fulfil the task of raising their adoptive daughter from Sri Lanka, a task which she understood as a 'gift from life'.[172]

Like the tropes of 'love' and 'fate', the trope of 'the gift' serves adopters as a forceful tool to 'decommercialize' the adoption process.[173] Since a child is traditionally considered 'inalienable by sale',[174] the authors creatively conceptualize the adoptee as a gift. The trope projects the 'system of associated commonplaces' which defines the concept of the gift onto the concept of the adoptee. A gift is conventionally considered as an item or service which is given out of affection, respect or generosity and without the expectation of payment or return, thereby causing gratitude and appreciation on the side of the recipient. Thus, metaphorically calling the adoptive child a gift implies that he or she was given freely out of love and care and it excludes the disturbing aspect of payments and rational choices that have been made by the privileged adopters. Conceptualizing adoption as the transfer of a gift – from God, the child's native country or from life to the adoptive parents – downplays the economics at play in intercountry adoption and obscures the violation of the ideology which separates parenthood from the economic sphere.

5.2 *Exhibiting Ownership*

Concepts of 'fate', 'love' and 'gift' serve the authors of the adoption narratives as emotional and intellectual tools to transubstantiate a biologically unrelated child selected for them into 'their own child'. From a legal perspective, however, the assigned child still belongs to the birth family and does not have any link to the prospective adoptive parents whatsoever. A court has yet to transfer the parental rights from the child's birth family to the adopters. In order to make visible (to others) the child's new belonging to the prospective adoptive family already before the official adoption act is rendered, the adopting parents engage in a number of symbolic rituals.

First, many authors rebaptize the child immediately after the matching. Holla, a Dutch adoptive mother, explains why she decided to name her prospective adoptive child Larissa: "We found Devika, her original name, too Sri Lankan and for me, it was important to give

171 *Ibid.*, p. 76.

172 I. Holla (2005). "Mijn droom van een kind, Waargebeurd verhaal van een vrouw die haar wens om moeder te worden niet opgeeft." Uitgeverij Sirene, Amsterdam, p. 152.

173 J. S. Modell (1999). "Freely Given - Open Adoption and the Rhetoric of the Gift." In L. L. Layne (ed), "Transformative Motherhood: On Giving and Getting in a Consumer Culture." New York University Press, 29-64, p. 49. L. L. Layne (1999). "The Child as Gift: New Directions in the Study of Euro-American Gift Exchange." In L. L. Layne (ed), "Transformative Motherhood: On Giving and Getting in a Consumer Culture." New York University Press, 1-27, p. 3.

174 M. J. Radin (1996). "Contested commodities." Harvard University Press, p. 18.

her a name chosen by us".[175] The new name relabelled the Sri Lankan girl, who still officially belonged to her birth family, as the Dutch adopters 'own child'. By renaming the adoptee, Holla erased one of the girl's most crucial symbolic links to her biological parents – the name chosen by the birth mother – and earmarked her as 'her daughter'.

Other adopters keep the child's original name as a tribute to the child's roots. For instance, Bakker decided to call the assigned Kenyan girl Mette (after Bakker's grandmother) Joanne (mingling the names of her and her husband's parents called Anne, Annet, and Johannes) Salomé (after the girl's birth mother). She explains: "All roots that she now has are contained in her name".[176] The Dutch names allow the woman to establish a visual connection between her family and the adoptee. The order of the girl's names thereby illustrates the priority of the (emotional) bond between the girl and her new adoptive family over the (blood) ties with her birth family.

Another symbolic ritual which exhibits the adopters' new status as parents of the prospective adoptee is that of consuming for the child. Right after a particular child has been assigned to the adopters, many go shopping and start furnishing a nursery for 'their child' – a process called 'nesting', which can also be observed with childbearing couples. Michielsen writes how glad she was when she could finally give in to her urges to purchase baby products after she learned that a Chinese girl was selected for her and her husband:

> I let all my breaks lose at several baby departments. Our virtual child finally was of flesh and blood! What a pleasure to shop clothes of size 74, to practice folding out and in the McLaren baby buggy and to flip open the chapters about caring for a 1 ½-year-old baby.[177]

When seeing the prospective adoptee for the first time, many adopters remove the child's clothes and equip him or her with a new outfit, toys or jewellery that they already purchased at home. One female author describes how she changed her future daughter's clothes when seeing her for the first time. Even though the child's birth mother, who had to recover from the delivery and could thus not be present, had not yet relinquished her parental rights and still had custody of her child, Holla put the baby girl in a shirt with long sleeves as "for her own taste she was dressed way too cold in her cotton dress".[178] She explains: "Such a vulnerable, small baby must be kept warm, thus I finally also put her in a sleeping

---

175 I. Holla (2005). "Mijn droom van een kind, Waargebeurd verhaal van een vrouw die haar wens om moeder te worden niet opgeeft." Uitgeverij Sirene, Amsterdam, p. 212.

176 G. Bakker (2008). "Het Adoptieboek, Stap voor Stap, Stress Tijdens de Adoptie Periode." Uitgeverij Aspekt, Soesterberg, p. 32.

177 D. Michielsen (2005). "Dochters van ver, belevenissen van een adoptiemoeder." Archipel, Amsterdam, p. 73.

178 I. Holla (2005). "Mijn droom van een kind, Waargebeurd verhaal van een vrouw die haar wens om moeder te worden niet opgeeft." Uitgeverij Sirene, Amsterdam, p. 104.

bag which we had brought with us".[179] After meeting up with the child's birth mother the following day, Holla gave her a bag with a "yellow dress, super small yellow socks, several pampers and a bottle of milk".[180]

The act of gift giving does not only convey the image of the Dutch woman as a better mother who, unlike the birth mother, is able to provide the child with material benefits, and thereby legitimizes the child's transfer from one woman to another woman. The material objects also served the female author as a tool to brand the child that still officially belongs to the Sri Lankan woman as 'her child'. Vollmer, a German adoptive mother, describes a similar ritual that she performed to relabel an Argentinian woman's baby girl that was just offered to her, as 'her daughter':

> That was Scarlett, my Scarlett, our Scarlett. Even if she had another birth name – Maria Belén [...] – we would call her Scarlett. [...] I took out the bracelet in which I had had the name engraved. I already have carried it around with me for so long, now finally my dream came true. I laid the little one on our bed and unwrapped her from the tattered woolen blanket that had kept her warm. [...] Then I took off the romper which needed to be washed badly. Finally, I freed her from the cotton cloth that had been wrapped around her waist as a diaper. From the way it looked and smelled, this must have been already hours ago. Scarlett wouldn't need her old clothes anymore. I brought along a complete layette.[181]

After having undressed the baby, the woman gave her a bath, the last step of the metamorphosis of transubstantiating a strange Argentinian woman's child into her 'own daughter' by erasing any signs of previous ownership. Again, the act of replacing the child's old 'tattered' and 'smelly' clothes with new ones does not only allow the author to 'earmark' the child as her 'property', it also presents the birth mother as incompetent and unfit to properly care for her baby and this tool thereby legitimizes the transfer of the child to Vollmer as the new mother.

5.3 *'Bringing Home My Child'*

After the adopters have been matched with a particular child, their language immediately changes. Their abstract wish 'to adopt a child somewhere out there' turns into the imperative 'to bring home their child' as soon as possible. For the adopters, the idea of fate and

179 *Ibid.*
180 *Ibid.*, p. 112.
181 R. Vollmer (2004). "Mein Kind aus der Fremde." Rowohlt, Reinbek bei Hamburg, p. 162.

of the inevitable connection of love has already transformed the assigned biologically unrelated child into their own child. The judicial adoption proceeding, which is still needed to legalize this effective bond, is often considered by adopters as a mere technicality, a bureaucratic obstacle that stands in the way of finally bringing home what they already consider to be theirs anyway. Bakker, a Dutch woman who compared the first meeting with her adoptive daughter to giving birth, writes: "Mette was our daughter! The delivery was a fact, we only had to wait, it appeared, until we can take her home".[182]

With the assignment of a particular child, the post-matching waiting period begins which many adopters experience as even more frustrating and stressful than the pre-assignment phase. After the matching, the prospective parents have a palpable image of their long-anticipated child onto which they project their emotions and expectations that they have accumulated over the past years. Palm-Hensel, for instance, describes her and her husband's growing longing for the assigned Indian girl, that they had not yet personally met but that they had already accepted as their own daughter, as the adoption proceedings were delayed due to strikes at the courts in New Delhi:

> We were doing our jobs, however, every free thought was with Grace in India. Our helplessness was racking our nerves. We woke up and went to bed thinking about our daughter.[183] [...] Harald and I missed our child in a distant country. [...] Every day without her seem to be a lost day for us.[184]

The adopting couples' longing becomes stronger after personally meeting the assigned child. Many authors spent weeks or even months in the child's native country, waiting for the adoption proceeding to be finalized. They visit the child care institution to feed, pamper and play with their prospective child and they seek to build a relationship of trust with him or her. During this time, the wish of having a child, of finally achieving parenthood becomes palpable for adopters and most cannot imagine giving up this identity. Holla who had already met her prospective adoptive daughter a couple of times writes: "I do not want and can't picture my life without her anymore".[185]

For many authors, the idea that a child that they came to accept as their own has to live in an orphanage and is being provided only with the barest necessities is unbearable. Moving the adoption process forward to rescue 'their child' from the immediate circumstances in the child care institution and to finally bring him or her 'home' becomes the

182 G. Bakker (2008). "Het Adoptieboek, Stap voor Stap, Stress Tijdens de Adoptie Periode." Uitgeverij Aspekt, Soesterberg, p. 40.

183 *Ibid.*, pp. 28-29.

184 *Ibid.*, p. 30.

185 I. Holla (2005). "Mijn droom van een kind, Waargebeurd verhaal van een vrouw die haar wens om moeder te worden niet opgeeft." Uitgeverij Sirene, Amsterdam, p. 180.

couples' primary mission. Again, the authors place the focus on the individual child's need for love and care, thereby sweeping aside possible critical thoughts about the adoption system as a whole. The child's precarious living conditions in the orphanage cast a cloud over the imperialistic and commercial nature of international adoption that some adopters might have felt uncomfortable with before. Schulz describes how leaving her crying daughter behind in an orphanage, as she temporarily had to go back to Germany, accelerated her adoption efforts:

> It is the saddest weeping of a child that I have ever heard – it is the weeping of my daughter.[186] [...] I became restless. Is there anybody pacifying her when she is weeping during the night? And if she is weeping during the day, is there anybody who hears her in the crying of all the other children? [...] As of tomorrow, I will do everything to advance the adoption. My intention is to get Indira away from the orphanage on her first birthday.[187]

Naturally, the adopting couples' mission to bring home 'their child' does not only lie in their own hands but is dependent on the actions of several stakeholders in the adoption system, including caseworkers, government officials and ultimately the court in the sending country. After the prospective parents are matched with a particular child, it often takes several weeks or even months before a court officially grants the adoption. Documents need to be issued and court decisions must be rendered before the adopting parents can finally take their assigned child home with them, and it is not unusual for complications to arise which cause additional delays in the adoption proceedings. For many adopters, the adoption process is overly bureaucratic and fails to take into the account their assigned children's individual needs. Schulz, for instance, describes the moment she had to leave her prospective adoptive daughter in the orphanage:

> I turned around and saw Indira rolling on her knees starting to rock her body, rhythmic and monotonous. I got panic. I starred at the long rows of cribs, the crying babies, the dark, barred windows and suddenly the slow bureaucracy of our adoption procedure seems intolerable lengthy and mind-numbing.[188]

Even though the assigned child still legally belongs to his or her birth mother, the authors claim full ownership. Right after Michielsen and her husband were matched with a Chinese girl, they flew to Hefei to pick her up. As the bus with the Chinese babies arrived at the

186 *Ibid.*

187 *Ibid.*, p. 106

188 B. Schulz (2005). "Tochter Indira, Die Geschichte einer Adoption aus Indien." Ullstein, Berlin, p. 103.

hotel were all the prospective adoptive parents were waiting, the couple could not repress their impatience. The author writes: "We immediately went there *[the room where the babies were brought to]*, ready to demand our daughter, if necessary with force".[189] Additionally, other authors use language which illustrates their sense of entitlement to the child that has been assigned to them. As the adoption procedure in Sri Lanka was delayed for several weeks and Holla's husband suggested to go back to the Netherlands without the child, she responded: "I won't leave without Kumudini. [...] She belongs to us, even if I still have to wait for months!".[190] The woman describes feelings of frustration as, after several weeks of waiting, she did still not have exclusive possession of her 'own child': "The sporadic short visits make me too desirous. I want Kumudini for real and not for a little while like a borrowed baby".[191]

Paradoxically, whereas many authors demand full possession of the assigned child as if he or she was a piece of property, they are disturbed by other people's language degrading 'their child' to a replaceable item of consumption. Gaedicke, for instance, who spent several weeks in the Russian child care institution taking care of her adoptive daughter was shocked at the director of the child care institution, when he offered her another, even younger, child after her adoption application was rejected by the court. She writes: "During the last weeks, Nina has become my daughter and I cannot just give her up". She explained to her lawyer who could not understand her problem: "Where the problem is? In my heart of course! I cannot just push Nina aside: make way for another child, because we cannot have you!".[192] As her lawyer later tried to calm her down by suggesting going to another child care institution where she could even choose the right child, she replied:

> "[...] and to make a choice? As a member of a desperate group I will be guided through the common rooms full with children; I will receive the inconspicuous hint that the blonde girl on the sofa or the boy with the plaid shirt in the corner is still available. And then – over a cup of coffee – the prospective parents will talk about the attractiveness of the offer and a fight will emerge among the applicants because two couples do want the same girl. What a grotesque idea."[193]

Even Vollmer, who paid their intermediaries inordinate sums of money to secure a child to adopt, who accepted that her name was being used as the biological mother's name on the child's birth certificate and who then smuggled the child to Germany (she denies having

189 D. Michielsen (2005). "Dochters van ver, belevenissen van een adoptiemoeder." Archipel, Amsterdam, p. 91.

190 I. Holla (2005). "Mijn droom van een kind, Waargebeurd verhaal van een vrouw die haar wens om moeder te worden niet opgeeft." Uitgeverij Sirene, Amsterdam, p. 183.

191 *Ibid.*

192 M. Gaedicke (2009). "Wunschkind, Geschichte einer Adoption." Hoffmann und Campe, Hamburg, p. 188.

193 *Ibid.*, pp. 234-235.

had any knowledge of the "illegal activities" of her private agent), was shocked that 'her daughter' was being objectified by the authorities. When she received a letter from an Argentinian authority requesting to bring the illegally obtained child back to her native country, she writes:

> Not with me! I would never give away my daughter! This is absolutely out of the question. How I hated those writs! This legal jargon with its sober formulations, as if it was all about a dead item! Who were those people who are negotiating with other people like about money?[194]

The adopters deny the commercial component in a transnational adoption and their role as consumers by repeatedly stressing that 'their child' is not a commodity, a 'dead item'. The language of the 'irreplaceable children' obscures the economics in a transnational adoption and draws the reader's attention to the fated emotional connection between the adopter and the child which cannot be removed offhandedly.

Adopters are aware that other people will ultimately decide on whether or not they can keep and take home 'their child'. Many authors describe feelings of extreme frustration due to the fact that they cannot actively influence the outcome of the adoption proceedings and that the future of their family life lays beyond their control. Like in the pre-assignment phase, they feel that they are being moved through a system which does not care about their emotions and in which they have no say whatsoever. Even do-it-yourself-adopters, taking a more active role in steering the adoption, come to realize that their scope of action reaches its limits at some point and that they, too, are reliant on somebody else's actions and decisions. Holla writes in this regard that: "It feels so powerless that we cannot do anything, that we have to leave the initiative to others and that we need to trust somebody else's expertise."[195] Gaedicke notes that she felt as if she was at the mercy of unknown government officials and judges who would not appreciate the strong emotional connection they and their child already had and for whom the system seems to be more important than the persons:

> Again we are at the mercy of other people, of their powers, their commitment, and their attitude towards our wish to become a family. Not only our desires and behaviour are decisive but others, often strangers, for who Nina and we are only a case file, the object of a process or a source of money.[196]

194 R. Vollmer (2004). "Mein Kind aus der Fremde." Rowohlt, Reinbek bei Hamburg, p. 188.

195 I. Holla (2005). "Mijn droom van een kind, Waargebeurd verhaal van een vrouw die haar wens om moeder te worden niet opgeeft." Uitgeverij Sirene, Amsterdam, p. 116.

196 M. Gaedicke (2009). "Wunschkind, Geschichte einer Adoption." Hoffmann und Campe, Hamburg, p. 32.

Again, the Western individualistic mindset prompts some adopters in the post-assignment phase to take active – sometimes irregular or even illegal – measures to accelerate the adoption process. One couple hoped that they could move forward the procedure with the help of the Sri Lankan minister of Public Health, whom they had met at a party.[197] Another adopting couple was tempted to pay some extra money in order to overcome the last obstacle that stood in their way of being united with the girl that they considered to be their daughter in any case. After Palm-Hensel and her husband received an email from the Indian orphanage informing them that the judge currently responsible for intercountry adoptions required an extra fee of €10,000 for each case, they contemplated paying the money:

> It simply cannot be the case that is up to one single person that Grace and us would not come together! In our desperation, we seriously thought about raising the money for the deposit and sending it to Delhi. We asked the orphanage if the judge accepted cash or if a bank guarantee on the required amount serving as a security sufficed.[198]

The idea that the child is supposed to be the adopters' child in any case and that an undeniable emotional bond links them together, legitimizes the taking of extraordinary measures or paying additional fees. They serve the adopters with a means to facilitate a greater good: 'bringing home their child' and finally providing him or her with the much-needed love and care. The rhetoric of 'fate' and 'love' obscures the irregularity or even illegality of their actions. After all, how can it be illegal if adopters take home a child that was meant to be theirs anyway and that they came to love so deeply?

6 Discussion and Conclusion

In contemporary Western societies, children are considered to be priceless and parenthood is understood to be separate from the market sphere. However, the narratives of the German and Dutch adopters analysed in the present study illustrate that seemingly contrary domains – parenthood and consumption, money and love – are complexly intertwined with each other and create a tension. Children are not only seen as human beings with unique needs and characteristics, worthy of dignity and respect, but they are also considered as objects of desire and consumption, serving adopters with a means to accomplish parenthood. In

197 I. Holla (2005). "Mijn droom van een kind, Waargebeurd verhaal van een vrouw die haar wens om moeder te worden niet opgeeft." Uitgeverij Sirene, Amsterdam, p. 118.

198 A. Palm-Hensel (2008). "Stella, Unser Stern aus Indien, Die Geschichte einer glücklichen Adoption." Kleine Schritte, Trier, p. 33.

an individualized capitalist society, where people are used to the idea that every goal can be achieved by one's own actions – so long as they have the necessary financial means – childlessness is typically understood as a condition that can be overcome. Almost all authors have spent large sums of money on reproductive treatments to achieve pregnancy. Only after they realize that these treatments failed to succeed, does international adoption offer a backup or last resort measure to embrace the identity of a parent. For the authors, intercountry adoption restores the freedom of choice which has been taken from them through their infertility. It should be kept in mind that it is not only infertile couples and individuals that pursue an international adoption. One author did not report any problems with producing biological children. For him and his wife, intercountry adoption did not serve as a means to embrace the identity as a parent, but rather the identity as a good Samaritan living according to the spirit of the Bible.

Despite the authors' selfish or self-centered motives, intercountry adoption is commonly portrayed as an altruistic deed aimed at 'saving' one of the many poor children who have to endure a miserable life in a child care institution. Dominant in the narratives that were analysed is the commonplace of an 'orphan crisis' in 'Third World' countries which serves adopters with the means to justify the decision to adopt internationally. However, the authors do not want to save just *any* child. They are looking for 'a suitable child', 'the right child'. In most cases, this means a healthy infant. The language that the authors employ to describe their preferences concerning the child and their expectations in the selection process strongly emphasizes the commercial aspect of intercountry adoption. As becomes apparent from the narratives, the adopters exercise a key market component: choice. Not only do they choose an international adoption as a means of having a child. They also make rational choices concerning the child's characteristics and native country. Those who want to exercise greater choice and autonomy over selecting the 'right child' might even choose to pursue a do-it-yourself or private adoption. In addition to the exercise of choice, the payment of money is a key component of the adoption market.

The fact that international adopters make choices and pay large sums of money for a child to love naturally clashes with the ideology that separates children and parenthood from the market sphere. To weave in the aspects of consumption into a plot which is based on the cultural belief that children are priceless, the authors of the narratives employ a number of linguistic persuasive strategies. Recurring in all adoption stories is the 'rhetoric of disavowal'. The adopters refuse to consider themselves as choosing 'the right child', claiming that it is, on the contrary, the child who selects the right adoptive parents. Furthermore, they deny and resignify the meaning of the payments that they have to make during the adoption process. Even though they spend considerable amounts of money, they emphasize that they are not technically purchasing a child. Financial transactions made in connection with the adoption – even irregular or even clearly illegal ones – are labelled as 'service costs', 'administrative fees', 'contributions', 'down payments', 'broker's fees', 'donations' or 'gifts': anything but the payment for a child.

Some adopters deny the existence of an international adoption marketplace by stressing that children are priceless and *ipso facto* beyond commerce. After all, how can children be bought if their value cannot be assessed in monetary terms? Others disavow the significance of money in an intercountry adoption by assimilating adoption with reproductive treatments, another costly means, they argue, of having a child. Some authors suppress the significant role that their payments and their rational choices play in becoming parents by comparing adoption to a pregnancy (some even refer to an 'adoption pregnancy'). Appropriating the metaphor of a pregnancy allows the adoptive parents to "renaturalize" and "decommodify" the international adoption process.

The rhetoric of disavowal also dominates the narratives describing the post-assignment phase. The assignment of a particular child, or in the case of a do-it-yourself adoption, the first meeting with the child selected for the adopters, is a crucial moment in the adoption process: it transforms the adopters' abstract wish for 'a suitable child' into a tangible subject of anticipation. The fact that the prospective parents now have a palpable image of their long-anticipated child is reflected in their use of language. Dominating in the adoption stories are narratives of fate and God bringing the adopters together with a particular child, as well as of an undeniable love tie linking them together. There is thus a flagrant contradiction between the language used in the pre- and post-assignment phase: whereas the former is governed by 'choice', the latter is governed by 'fate'. These two sets of linguistic choices sit at odds with each other.

The narratives of fate and God do not only allow the adopters to claim somebody else's child as 'their own child'. They also provide them with forceful language to downplay or deny the economics at play in intercountry adoption, as well as to eliminate the weight of the adopters' selfish interests and the rational choices they have been making during the adoption process. Moreover, the recurring trope of the child as a 'gift' serves this decommodifying function. By metaphorically labelling the adoptee a 'gift' – either from God, the child's native country or from life – the authors imply that the child was given freely out of love and care rather than in exchange for the money they paid.

After the adopters have been assigned a particular child, their abstract wish 'to adopt a child somewhere out there' transforms into the imperative 'to bring home their child' as soon as possible. Even though the assigned child still legally belongs to his or her birth mother, the authors claim full ownership of the child. By placing the focus on the individual child's need for love and care, the authors brush aside any critical thoughts about the adoption system, particularly its commercial and imperialistic nature. The language of the 'irreplaceable children' obscures the economics in a transnational adoption and draws the reader's attention to the fated emotional connection between the adopter and the child. Many describe feelings of extreme powerlessness due to the fact that they cannot influence the outcome of the adoption procedure and because their fate lies beyond their control. They feel they are at the mercy of decision makers who do not care about their emotions and who do not recognize the ordained, magical nature of the relationship between them and 'their child'. At this uncertain stage of the adoption process, the adopters' Western individualistic mindset surfaces again, prompting some to take active measures to accelerate the adoption process. Some even consider paying extra money to overcome the last obstacle that stands in the way of being united with the assigned child. Again, the narratives of 'meant to be' and 'fall in love' allow adopting parents to neutralize or deny the significance of money. How can they buy a child that was meant to be 'their child' and that they came to love so deeply? God's hand or fate that has brought them and the child together and the undeniable love that they have for each other transcends any economics in an international adoption, according to the adopters.

The denial that the authors – and probably other adopters as well as adoption advocates – engage in concerning the role of money in international adoption is undoubtedly harmful. By disavowing the significance of payments, the adopters' role as consumers and the instrumentalization of adoptees hinders an open and honest discussion about the intercountry adoption system's validity as a whole. It also facilitates the laundering of children in individual cases. Reframing money or goods that are offered to the child's birth mother as 'gifts' and payments made to private intermediaries sourcing a suitable child to adopt as 'down payments' or 'broker's commission' obfuscates the sometimes illegal nature of these transactions. The idea that 'fate' or 'God's hand' brought the child and the adopters together – rather than money and demand – and that an undeniable love tie links them with each other legitimizes and gives meaning to any 'irregularities' that may have occurred during the adoption process. The concept of destiny and transcending love even gives the adoption of a child, who actually was obtained illegally, a legitimate touch.

VIII Comparative Analysis, General Conclusions, and Recommendations

1 Introduction

The present study has aimed to identify the organization and operation of the illegal transnational adoption market in children from a criminological perspective and it has sought to outline the similarities and main differences, in terms of structure and functioning, between conventional forms of human trafficking (meaning human trafficking for the purpose of, for instance, sexual and labour exploitation) and child trafficking for adoption purposes. In addition, the study has sought to uncover and explain the criminogenic conditions in the German and Dutch adoption system that encourage and facilitate the trafficking of children into Germany and the Netherlands for the purposes of adoption. This Chapter summarizes the study's main findings and compares the German and Dutch intercountry adoption systems. Based on the general conclusions of this study, possible policy changes will be discussed.

2 The Transnational Illegal Adoption Market

2.1 Demand and Supply

Chapter II used the basic logic of Cohen and Felson's routine activity theory to conceptualize the adoption market and to identify its structural components: demand, supply and social control.[1] It follows that adopters and adoption agencies from wealthy Western countries constitute the demand component.[2] Whereas up until the 1970s, intercountry adoption was primarily perceived as a humanitarian deed intended to rescue children from war-torn countries, it has gradually become an attractive (and often last resort) alternative for many involuntary childless couples and individuals to form a family. Their demand for adoptable healthy babies exerts an inexorable pull on child-rich poor countries. The pressure on these countries does not only originate from the adoptive parents, but also from Western adoption agencies that have both an ideological and financial motivation to keep children from poor countries moving through the adoption system.

1 See Chapter II, section 2.
2 See Chapter II, section 2.2.

The large volume of poor families and orphanages caring for children in low income countries of the Global South (including post-communist Eastern Europe), particularly from China, Russia, and more recently several African states, constitute the supply component of the illegal adoption market.[3] Conflicts, extreme poverty, natural disasters and epidemics leave numerous children in these countries vulnerable and in need of protection. Yet, contrary to the common Western belief of a 'global orphan crisis',[4] only a small percentage of these children are deprived of their family environment, at least according to Article 20 of the UNCRC, and are therefore legitimately available for an intercountry adoption. And of those children that are in need of a family, only very few have the characteristics that the majority of international adopters are looking for: young and healthy. The latter can often be placed in (extended) families within their own countries and they are therefore not in need of intercountry adoption. The Western demand for adoptable young and healthy children is thus higher than the actual supply.

In order to meet the high Western demand for healthy babies, actors in the supply countries employ a variety of illegal methods to generate 'adoptees'. Children are purchased or abducted from their families, hospitals or orphanages. Vulnerable birth parents are coerced or provided with misleading information as to the consequence of an adoption in order to obtain their consent. The directors of child care institutions and government officials are paid to subvert the subsidiarity principle – pursuant to the Hague Convention and the UNCRC – in order to increase the supply of adoptable children.

2.2 *The Laundering Process*

For an illegal adoption market to be sustained, demand and illegal supply sources must be linked to each other, and this is organized differently than the conventional forms of human trafficking.[5] Whereas the purpose of conventional forms of human trafficking is illegal (e.g. sexual exploitation, organ removal, slavery), adopting a child is perfectly legal at the demand end of the system. This is also the reason why the trafficking of children for the purposes of adoption is not considered as a form of human trafficking according to most international legal instruments, most notably the 2000 Trafficking Protocol.[6] An adoption only becomes illegal when the child has been illegally obtained. Therefore, the illicit means by which children are obtained must be disguised: a laundering process is therefore crucial in this regard.

---

3 See Chapter II, section 2.3.
4 See Chapter III, section 5.3.
5 See Chapter II, section 2.4.
6 See Chapter II, section 3.

In basic parlance, there are two ways to launder a child. The first one involves the adopters who bypass the adoption system by taking the illegally obtained child home as their biological child after having falsified or fabricated the child's birth certificate. The second means of laundering an illegally obtained child is by passing him or her through the adoption system as a legally relinquished or abandoned child. This involves falsifying or fabricating birth certificates and other such documents that are necessary for an adoption (e.g. the parents' death certificates, relinquishment declarations). As a final step in this laundering process, an illegal adoption decision is rendered by a court that bears all the hallmarks of a perfectly legal adoption procedure. By the time the child arrives in the receiving country, all traces of the illegal adoption are usually wiped out and the adoptive parents and the adoption agencies can plausibly deny knowledge of the child's illegal origin.

The laundering process is usually facilitated by legitimate individuals and organizations from both the public and the private sector that actually ought to serve as guardians in the adoption system. The intercountry adoption system's integrity relies, to a large extent, on capable guardians in the form of regulatory institutions which are to monitor and control the adoption process and make sure that only children that are in need of international adoption enter the system. The drafters of 1993 Hague Convention on Protection and Cooperation in Respect of Intercountry Adoption believed that illegal and abusive adoption practices could best be prevented by increasing capable guardians in the form of regulatory institutions in the adoption system. Thus, the treaty obliges its Contracting States to designate a Central Authority which needs to act as a gatekeeper through which all intercountry adoptions must be channelled. The Central Authority must fulfil the tasks outlined in the Convention, some of which may be delegated to public authorities (e.g. youth welfare offices, family courts) or to private bodies that must be accredited by the state (e.g. child care institutions, adoption placement agencies).[7]

However, as the uncovered cases of illegal adoptions have shown, the individuals who are employed in these public-sector and private-sector organizations do not always serve as guardians in the adoption system, but rather they misuse their knowledge and status to pass the children through their organization. They create the necessary linkage between demand and illegal supply sources by transforming illegally obtained children into 'orphans' and then 'adoptees'. These institutions might not only serve to connect buyers and sellers, but they may also be involved in illegally sourcing children for adoption in the first place.

The foreign representatives and cooperation partners of the adoption placement agencies in the receiving states play a particularly crucial role at the demand-supply nexus.[8] They are often involved in the most crucial phase of the child placement process: the phase beginning with the abandonment or relinquishment of the child by his/her birth parents

7 See Chapter IV, section 3.5.
8 See Chapter II, section 2.4.2.

and concluding with the actual court-backed adoption, where most of the illegal and abusive practices typically occur. They are important 'cogs' in the intercountry adoption system because their working method, integrity as well as understanding of the child's best interests have a significant influence on the adoption process. On the one hand, they could – and actually should – serve as guardians that only let those children pass through the adoption system who are legitimately available for intercountry adoption. On the other hand, they may allow illegally obtained children to be laundered through the system. As uncovered cases of child trafficking have shown, adoption agencies' partners and representatives in the sending countries are sometimes involved in abusive adoption practices. They illegally secure children for intercountry adoption themselves, are involved in laundering illegally obtained children through the system or facilitate abusive practices by other individuals and organizations by simply looking the other way.

The limited effectiveness of regulatory institutions, which in essence facilitates the child laundering process, can be traced to widespread corruption and unwillingness to enforce existing laws. A high incidence of corruption in the sending countries is a significant reason for illicit practices within the intercountry adoption system. Public officials are accustomed to demanding and receiving payoffs to provide not only legitimate, but also illegitimate, approvals and services. And generous (by sending nations' standards) fees and payments from Western adopters and adoption agencies are conducive to creating an intercountry adoption system that is greased by bribery. Corruption is the lubricant which enables child laundering to flourish, as it protects the covert nature of illegal adoption practices, distorts the decision-making process and diverts law enforcement resources. Within the context of an adoption system often suffering from corruption through bribery and personal connections, the regulatory safeguards, which the Hague Convention obliges its Contracting States to establish, actually become opportunities for abuse.[9]

2.3 *Criminogenic Asymmetries*

The high demand for and the illegal supply of adoptable children are partly caused by demographic as well as economic asymmetries between the sending and the receiving countries.[10] Whereas the rich Western countries are struggling with low birth rates and decreasing numbers of children available for domestic adoption, birth rates are increasing in the poor countries of the Global South. These asymmetries shape the motivation of actors in the source countries to illegally obtain adoptable children. The large sums of money paid by adopters create an incentive for orphanage directors, government officials and others to illicitly source children for intercountry adoption. The criminogenic asym-

9 See Chapter IV, section 5.3.
10 See Chapter II, section 2.5.

metries have also reduced the ability or willingness of legal guardians to control the adoption system. Widespread corruption in the sending countries, which was both caused by and which further increases these existing asymmetries, has weakened official controls. Individuals and organizations from both the public and private sector, that ought to monitor and control the adoption system, essentially misuse their function to connect demand and illegal supply by laundering children through their organization.

2.4 *The Dimensions of Child Trafficking for Adoption Purposes*

Chapter II applied Henry and Lanier's prism of crime to analyse and explain the different dimensions of child trafficking for adoption purposes.[11] Just like crime in general, adoption trafficking can be conceptualized as a prism that is composed of multiple dimensions: harm, (in)visibility, extent of victimization, public agreement on seriousness and the probability of a severe social response. Shedding light on these dimensions helps us to better comprehend this social phenomenon.

Trafficking children for adoption purposes causes profound *harm*. For one, it creates individual harm to the illegally obtained children and their families, whose basic human rights are severely violated (most notably, the child's right to identity preservation,[12] to be cared for by his or her parents,[13] to know his or her origin and identity,[14] as well as the child's and the parents' right to family life[15]). Illegally obtaining children for adoption also causes indirect social harm by disrupting the local child protection and welfare system in the sending country. The large sums of money that are involved in the intercountry adoption system (be it in the form of 'adoption fees' or 'donations') make it more attractive for the stakeholders in the supply countries to send children abroad rather than considering or investing in domestic child care options.

The harm caused by child trafficking for adoption purposes often remains *invisible* for several reasons. First, the link between the payment of money or contributions (to the birth parents or the orphanage caring for the child) and their harmful effects is often obscured. Second, many victims either do not realize their victimization or do not have the means at their disposal to report it. The children are usually too young to realize the illegal circumstances of their placement and their parents often do not have the capacities to seek justice for the removal of their children. The birth parents' invisibility is further increased by the fact that intercountry adoptions commonly involve a clean break between the child and his or her family, whose identity is not disclosed. The practice of keeping the

11 See Chapter II, section 4.
12 Art. 8 UNCRC.
13 Art. 7(1), 9(1) UNCRC.
14 Art. 7(1) UNCRC.
15 Art. 16, 9(1) UNCRC.

adoptees' origin secret masks the illegal activity and protects the guilty. Finally, illegal adoption practices often remain invisible because they are embedded within the legitimate adoption system. The question of which adoption is legal and which not is compounded by the fact that the system's legal and illegal parts are so intertwined that, without specific information about the children, it is impossible to separate them from each other. Arguably, the Hague Convention works to further obscure illegal adoption practices. By raising the level of bureaucracy, the treaty provides adoptions from Hague countries with the appearance of legitimacy.

Given the hidden nature of illegal adoption practices, no official statistics are available on the incidence of child trafficking for adoption purposes. The actual *extent of victimization*, therefore, remains unknown. Prominent trafficking incidents that have been uncovered in numerous sending countries indicate the widespread existence of the trafficking within the adoption system. And there is much to suggest that these detected cases only represent the tip of a much larger iceberg.

There appears to be some *disagreement* on the extent and seriousness of the child trafficking issue. Whereas some experts (including the author of this book) believe that the uncovered cases of illegal adoption practices only constitute the visible part of a much large phenomenon, others insist that the extent of trafficking activities in the adoption system is greatly exaggerated. Some consider restrictions on foreign adoptions placed by sending countries that have experienced abuses as disproportional and irrational responses. Others minimize the injury suffered by children and their parents and deny the harm that the large sums of money involved in the adoption system cause. This, it was argued, might be due to the Western conception of the poor sending countries, from which children must be rescued, and of the view that intercountry adoption is an inherently humanitarian act that only serves and never harms children.

Even if cases of child trafficking are uncovered, the *probability of a severe social response* is usually low. The actors involved in illegal practices in the sending countries often go unpunished or are only convicted for relatively mild criminal offences, such as forgery of documents. Moreover, the adoption agencies in the receiving countries typically do not have to fear severe consequences in the receiving countries, especially if it turns out that an adoptee was illegally obtained. Usually, they can plausibly deny having had any actual knowledge of the child's illegal origin. And even if they moved children from a country or an orphanage where systemic abuses have become apparent for those willing to see, they are not held responsible if it transpires that one of the children they had placed was in the intercountry adoption system illegally.

3 The Criminogenic Conditions in the German and Dutch Adoption Systems

3.1 The Principle of the Child's Best Interests

The principle of the 'child's best interests' plays a key role in the intercountry adoption system. The UNCRC stipulates that in all decisions concerning a child, the child's best interests need to be taken into account as a primary consideration.[16] In adoption decisions, the child's best interests shall even be the *paramount* consideration,[17] meaning that the child's interests shall override the interests of all others that are involved in or affected by adoption (e.g. the child's parents and (extended) family, the local community, and the State). Also, the Hague Convention lays down that intercountry adoptions need to take place in the best interests of the child.[18]

The principle appears to be the primary safeguard in the intercountry adoption system, guaranteeing ethical and child-centered adoptions. However, in Chapter III it was explained that the principle might actually work to facilitate abusive adoption practices. The concept of the child's best interests does not have a universally agreed-upon definition. It was deliberately left undefined by the drafters of both the UNCRC and the Hague Convention so as to cover diverse individual situations and different socio-cultural contexts. Yet, this open-mindedness, which is considered by some as the principle's strength, might actually be its major weakness as it is susceptible to local conventions and understandings, as well as to the values of the individual decision-makers which will naturally change over time. What is considered to be in the best interests of the child in one society, by one judge or at one point in time, may be regarded as harmful in another society, by another decision maker or at another point in time time. It is exactly due to this subjectivity and bias that the concept of the child's best interests is susceptible to abuse. In the past, it has been used to motivate and justify practices that are now condemned as outright human rights abuses, such as the 'forced removal' of children from their indigenous families and unwed white mothers that took place in the 19th and 20th centuries in the United States, Canada, Australia and Europe, or the practice of 'forced migration' that resulted in about 150,000 British children being sent to Canada, Australia, New Zealand and other British colonies between the 1920s and 1970s.

In the present intercountry adoption system, the 'child's best interests' are often advanced by the stakeholders. As was explained in Chapter VII, the wish to 'save a child' from an underprivileged part of the world is a crucial motive behind many adopters'

16 Article 3(1) UNCRC.

17 Article 21 UNCRC.

18 Articles 1(a), 4(b), 16(1)(d), 21(1), and 24 Hague Convention.

decision to adopt internationally.[19] The present study has illustrated that the narrative of 'saving poor children' by way of adoption features strongly in the adoption stories that were written by German and Dutch adopters. This narrative is substantiated by the commonplace of an 'orphan crisis' in the 'Third World'. The countries the authors wish to adopt from are often conceptualized as a perpetual source of orphaned children that need to be provided with a family and who would otherwise endure a miserable life in an impoverished child care institution and then on the streets. The logic of rescuing one of the millions of orphaned children is not only advanced by infertile couples. As has been shown in the present study, it is also employed by adopters who wish to embrace the identity of a 'good Samaritan' living according to the spirit of the Bible.

Also, the Western adoption agencies' primary motivation is to serve the best interests of the child by finding loving homes for needy orphans.[20] Adoption agencies commonly portray themselves (and are generally perceived) as humanitarian organizations with the generous motive of saving unparented children from the intermediate circumstances in their native countries and providing them with loving families. The names the agencies use very often illustrate their philanthropic and altruistic identity. In addition, the information provided on their websites makes it clear that the agencies' primary mission is to serve the best interests of orphaned children.

The ideological conviction of 'saving children', which is often underpinned by the belief of a 'global orphan crisis',[21] might lead to harmful and unethical practices. Adopters might be motivated to pursue a speedier adoption without the involvement of state authorities, pay large sums of money to the orphanage they adopt from or bribe government officials to accelerate the adoption. Adoption agencies might continue moving children from a sending country in which systemic abuses have become apparent, or placing children from an orphanage that was involved in abusive adoption practices for the sake of rescuing orphans.[22]

The logic of 'saving a child' does not only serve as a motive in itself, but at the same time it is also used as a cloak for the adopters' own wishes and desires, as well as for adoption agencies' economic interests, and furthermore even as a justification for their harmful, unethical or clearly illegal practices.

Most international adopters are involuntarily childless individuals who have often already spent quite some effort, money and time on reproductive treatments in order to have a child of their own. In individualized Western societies, children fulfil important affective functions for their parents. They help to countervail the eroding chances of having a partner relationship that lasts, as well as to avoid loneliness in old age. Furthermore,

19 See Chapter VII, section 4.2.
20 See Chapter V, sections 5.2 and 7.2 and Chapter VI, section 5.2.
21 See Chapter III, section 5.3.
22 See Chapter V, section 7.2.

children serve their parents by helping them to build social and cultural capital. Parenting has been increasingly marked as a measure of value, self-worth and citizenship. Achieving parenthood is thus necessary in order to become a 'fully realized' citizen.[23] This is not only the case for heterosexual couples, but increasingly also for same-sex couples as well as singles who seek recognition within their own community. In an individualized capitalist society, where people are familiar with the idea that every goal one has set oneself can be achieved – provided the necessary financial means are available – childlessness is perceived as a condition that can be overcome. For many couples and individuals who are unable to have their own child, intercountry adoption is a last resort measure to accomplish parenthood. It restores the freedom of choice that has been taken away from them by their infertility. The logic of 'saving a child' from a poor country helps them to come to terms with their decision to form a family through adoption, as well as to downplay or justify any harmful practices that may arise.[24]

The logic of 'saving children' might also serve as a cloak for the adoption agencies' economic interests. Adoption agencies' placement activities do not only serve the best interests of the children, but also the interests of their staff members whose jobs are reliant on the number of intercountry adoptions.[25] As section 6 will address in more detail, adoption agencies in both Germany and the Netherlands face financial pressure to keep their business up and running.[26] This pressure might lead them to cut ethical corners, for instance, by placing children from a sending country in which abuses and irregularities occur on a regular basis or by holding on to a shady foreign cooperation partner or by accepting child proposals that do not include sufficient information about the child.[27] The appeal to the higher goal of serving the best interests of children by saving them from a life in an institution is a rationalization technique which allows the agency personnel to repel criticism, protect the agency from blame and to maintain their image as a child welfare organization abiding by ethical norms and obligations.[28]

Arguably, the vague concept of 'the child's best interests' is open to an interpretation that ultimately serves the desires and interests of the adopters and adoption agencies.[29] In industrialized Western societies, the child's interests are generally considered to be best served by policies and practices that encourage material prosperity and education. Furthermore, the concept of the 'child's best interests' is based on a liberal and individualistic notion of childhood. It implies that all children should be treated the same without regard to their different social backgrounds and that their interests are independent of those of

23 See Chapter VII, section 4.1.
24 See Chapter VII, section 4.2.
25 *Ibid.*
26 See Chapter V, section 5.. and Chapter VI, section 5.2.
27 See Chapter V, section 7.2.
28 See Chapter V, section 4.3.
29 See Chapter III, section 6.4.

their parents or wider community. Since the child's community or culture is often considered as unable to provide for their children, the imperative to 'save the child' therefore emerges. Against this backdrop, removing the child from his or her extended family appears to be natural and legitimate, even honorable.

The principle of the child's best interests constitutes a breeding ground for misconception and manipulation and it is a suitable device to justify and legitimize adoption practices that are harmful to children, most notably that of illegally obtaining children from their parents. Even worse, it might blind actors that are involved in intercountry adoption towards the harmful consequences of their practices.

The concept might not only encourage harmful adoption practices. As this study has shown (and as will be addressed in more detail in the following section), the principle of the best interests of the child is also often advanced by the German and Dutch courts to legitimize a private adoption.[30] And in the Netherlands, a family court even employed the principle to reject the request of an Indian couple, who claimed that their son had been stolen and then adopted by a Dutch couple, to conduct a DNA examination.[31]

3.2 *Private Adoptions in Germany and the Netherlands*

This study has explained that intercountry adoptions which are privately pursued are particularly prone to abusive practices.[32] The adoption placement procedure is not supervised and controlled by the adoption placement office and the authorities in the receiving countries whatsoever. The latter may only gain knowledge of the international adoption placement *after* the child has been transferred to Germany. Private adopters are often not sensitized to the risks that are involved in the intercountry adoption procedure. They might fall into the hands of shady adoption agents that promise a quick and unbureaucratic adoption placement procedure, who then directly contact the child's parents and be inclined to make donations to the family or the orphanage, unaware of the harm they create as a result.

Intercountry adoptions are privately pursued for a variety of reasons.[33] Some people are unaware of the fact that if they adopt internationally, then the regulations on intercountry adoption need to be complied with. This is particularly the case in intercountry kinship adoptions or in cases where couples or individuals adopt from their own country of origin. Yet, others maliciously bypass the adoption placement procedure as they find it too lengthy and cumbersome or because they do not fulfil the legal requirements (e.g. age requirements).

30 See Chapter V, section 4.3 and Chapter VI, section 4.3.
31 See Chapter III, section 6.4.
32 See Chapter V, section 4.1.
33 See Chapter V, section 4.2

The present study has shown that in both Germany and the Netherlands, intercountry adoptions that are pursued in circumvention of the official adoption placement procedure are, generally speaking, tolerated by the family courts.

In Germany, the law neither explicitly prohibits private adoptions nor does it provide for any negative consequences if one is pursued.[34] This has led to a generous case law on the recognition of private adoptions: a study from 2007 revealed that 90% of foreign decisions on an adoption that took place in circumvention of the official adoption placement procedure were recognized by the German courts. Arguably, a judgment by the German Supreme Court from 2014 could further encourage the German courts to recognize private intercountry adoptions. In its judgment, it dealt with the question as to whether a Californian court decision which declared a German homosexual couple as the legal parents of a surrogate child was contrary to German public policy. Even though surrogacy is illegal in Germany, the Supreme Court declared that the foreign decision had to be recognized, stating that the right to family life (Article 8 ECHR) and the principle of the child's best interests would generally preclude the refusal of a foreign decision only because this might prevent others to circumvent the ban on surrogacy agreements. Applying this consideration to intercountry adoptions, this implies that general preventive considerations, namely the consideration that the best interests of the children *in abstracto* can best be served by refusing the recognition and thereby preventing other adopters to bypass the official adoption placement procedure, cannot justify a violation of the rights and the best interests of the child *in concreto*. Considering the lack of a ban on private adoptions and the generous case law on their recognition, it will come as no surprise that in Germany, an estimated 50% of international adoptions are pursued without the involvement of a German adoption placement office.

Unlike in Germany, private adoptions are explicitly prohibited by law in the Netherlands and doing so constitutes a misdemeanour *(overtreding)*. Thus, adopters who circumvent the official adoption placement procedure are punishable with a fine of up to €8,200 (Article 28 WOBKA). Other than in the German adoption system, a foreign court decision on an adoption that was privately pursued cannot be recognized according to Dutch law.[35] In addition, the Dutch family court may place the illegally adopted child in an approved Dutch foster family or even send the child back to the country of origin. However, in practice, this last measure is rarely ordered. The best interests of the individual child, as well as the right to family life according to Article 8 ECHR, usually make it impossible for the Dutch courts to remove the child from the illegal adopters. In most cases, the Dutch court decides to leave the child with the private adopters and either grants an adoption or at least interim guardianship, if the adopters have engaged in particularly objectionable

34 See Chapter V, section 4.3.
35 See Chapter VI, section 4.3.

actions. Furthermore, adopters are rarely held liable for Article 28 WOBKA, as the deadline for prosecuting this misdemeanour is only three years. Even if they are convicted, the issued fines are considerably low. Illegal adopters may be held liable for criminal offences, such as forgery of documents or even human smuggling.[36] However, if adopters are convicted, all too often they are sentenced only to community work or imprisonment on probation. Whether such mild sentences have any deterrent effect on prospective adopters is therefore questionable.

Both the German and the Dutch case law on private intercountry adoptions can be considered as inviting prospective adopters to bypass the typically very time-consuming and tedious official adoption placement procedure and to pursue a more rapid and less bureaucratic independent adoption.

3.3 *Institutional Pressure of German and Dutch Adoption Agencies*

In both Germany and the Netherlands, private bodies need to meet high standards in order to be permitted as intercountry adoption agencies.[37] The agency personnel must be qualified as social workers, psychologists or pedagogues, they need to have the necessary personal competencies (such as empathy, professional integrity, reliability and trustworthiness) to carry out adoption placements and have experience in the field of intercountry adoption. In addition, German and Dutch adoption placement agencies must not pursue any profit objectives, meaning that they must not derive any improper financial or other gain by charging fees that are unreasonably high.

German and Dutch agencies routinely stress that they adhere to the standards and principles of the Hague Convention as well as the UNCRC.[38] On their websites and during the interviews that were conducted they claim that their mission is to serve the best interests of the child and to find parents for children, not children for parents. Many assert that they promote the subsidiarity principle by supporting aid projects in the sending states, which aim to help children grow up in their own ethnic and cultural environment. The agencies emphasize that they only place those unparented children who cannot be cared for in their native countries. Some stress that it is therefore not healthy infants they are placing up for adoption, but primarily children with special needs (e.g. with mental or physical diseases, or a social stigma) for whom no proper childcare solution can be found in their native country. They seem to have a realistic idea of the pitfalls and risks in the intercountry adoption system, for example they appear to be particularly well aware of the negative influences that Western money has in the intercountry adoption system. Hence,

36 See Chapter VI, section 8.1.

37 See Chapter V, section 5.1 and Chapter VI, section 5.1.

38 See Chapter V, section 5.2 and Chapter VI, section 5.2.

many (but not all!) refrain from providing donations to their foreign cooperation partners and from paying 'contingency fees' to their representatives in order to avoid encouraging illegal practices in the sending countries. It is thus fair to say that most adoption agencies in Germany and the Netherlands try hard to not actively or willingly encourage illegal practices in the sending countries.

However, it appears that German and Dutch agencies passively facilitate the trafficking of children by failing to closely scrutinize the adoption fees that their foreign partners determine and to strictly monitor their activities in the sending countries. Control, generally impeded by the geographical distance, is substituted by trust in the cooperation partner, the authorities in the countries of origin or even in their adopters.[39] Trust generally becomes problematic if it leads the agencies to ignore 'red flags' that suggest irregularities in the foreign adoption system.

On the one hand, adoption agencies are ideologically motivated to ignore or minimize signs of abusive practices. As section 4 already discussed, the primary motivation of the Western adoption agencies is to rescue orphans. This ideological conviction might lead agencies to keep children moving through the adoption system, notwithstanding credible allegations of systemic abuses in the foreign adoption system or illegal activities by its cooperation partner in the sending country.

On the other hand, adoption agencies also have a financial motivation to turn a blind eye to signs of irregularities in the sending countries. In both Germany and the Netherlands, adoption placement agencies experience financial strain.[40] Unlike adoption agencies in, for instance, Norway or Sweden, they do not receive any public funding but rather they have to exclusively finance themselves with the 'administration fees' that are paid by their adoption applicants. Hence, in order to keep their business up and running, they must handle a particular number of adoption placements per year. This financial dependency on adoption placements is problematic for two reasons. First, the adoption agencies might be inclined to accept more adoption applicants than they can find children for and thereby create expectant prospective adoptive parents, who put pressure on the agency personnel and on the sending countries by extension.

Second, they might be inclined to cut ethical corners regarding their cooperation with the sending countries. This study has shown that adoption agencies often readily accept the fees that their partners in the sending countries determine, without knowing exactly what they are used for.[41] And even if the costs are made transparent, the agencies would not check whether they are reasonable. They often trust that the foreign partners and representatives, who are familiar with the adoption process and the local conditions, have

39 See Chapter V, section 6.4 and Chapter VI, section 6.3.
40 See Chapter V, section 5.2 and Chapter VI, section 5.2.
41 See Chapter V, section 6.2 and Chapter VI, section 6.2.

a better overview of the costs that are incurred in an adoption procedure as well as a better understanding of their reasonableness.

The financial strain might also lead adoption agencies to continue moving children from a sending country despite clear signs of systemic irregularities in the foreign adoption system.[42] The case study that was conducted as part of this research described the abusive practices that were uncovered in the Ethiopian adoption system around 2009 and zoomed in on how a German adoption agency, moving children from Ethiopia, reacted to allegations of abuse by an orphanage it cooperated with. Although it became apparent that adoptions from Ethiopia were too risky and even though the orphanage that the German agency placed adoptees from was exposed to have engaged in illegally securing children for adoption, the agency decided to continue placing children from Ethiopia until the orphanage was finally closed down by the authorities. Such decisions are facilitated by both the German and the Dutch adoption system which do not hold adoption agencies accountable for the activities of their foreign cooperation partners.

The case study identified the narratives that the agency personnel advanced to resolve the tension between this decision, on the one hand, and the high standards of due diligence to which the German adoption agencies usually ascribe, on the other hand.[43] In order to protect the agency from blame and to maintain its image as a child welfare organization abiding by ethical norms and obligations, the agency personnel employed a number of rationalization techniques. They a) denied the extent and seriousness of the abusive practices abroad by insisting that they were incidental rather than systemic, b) emphasized the higher cause of saving children through adoption, c) denied their responsibility by claiming that they did not actively engage in illegal practices themselves (e.g. by bribing) and by minimizing their powerful role at the demand end of the adoption market and d) condemned critics for lacking the necessary know how to properly asses the incidences abroad and the media for misrepresenting and exaggerating the facts of individual cases. These narratives work to encourage child trafficking, as they free the agency personnel from the moral bind of their high ethical standards, allowing them to move children from a country in which abuses and irregularities are systemic.

Over the last couple of years, the financial strain on the German and Dutch adoption agencies has further increased as the number of intercountry adoptions has dramatically fallen in both countries, whereas the number of agencies continues to stay high, thereby resulting in high competition.[44] In the Netherlands, there are currently six accredited adoption agencies which carried out a total of 210 placements in 2017. In Germany, even

---

42 See Chapter V, section 7.
43 See Chapter V, section 7.3.
44 See Chapter V, section 2 and Chapter VI, section 2.

nine adoption agencies were accredited as of 2017, whereas the number of adoption placements decreased to 313.

In Germany, the competition among German adoption agencies and the resulting financial strain thereon is further exacerbated by the fact that the 12 Central Adoption Offices are also permitted to place children up for adoption.[45] Some refer adoption applicants to private agencies and only carry out international adoptions from Hague countries for which no agency has been authorized. Others, however, are very active adoption placement offices themselves.

The high requirements that German and Dutch adoption agencies must meet in order to be accredited and authorized to place intercountry adoptions does not necessarily guarantee the absence of illicit activities. Even the most benevolent adoption placement office might feel forced to turn a blind eye on signs of systemic abuses in the sending countries or of questionable practices of its foreign partners, particularly if it derives its funds exclusively from adoption placements. The lack of sufficient financial resources in the German and Dutch adoption system, combined with agency irresponsibility for the activities in the sending countries, can thus be considered as a major criminogenic condition in both adoption systems, encouraging the trafficking of children to Germany and the Netherlands.

3.4 *The Flow of Money into the Sending Countries*

As was explained in Chapter II, the Western money involved in the intercountry adoption system is the primary incentive for actors in the poor sending countries to illegally obtain children for adoption.[46] The Hague Convention, acknowledging the harmful role of money, thus provides that only costs and expenses that are reasonably high in relation to the services may be charged and paid for.[47]

The German and Dutch adoption agencies that were interviewed all adopt a laissez-faire approach with regard to the money they transfer to the states of origin. They either had difficulties or were unwilling to carefully itemize the fees they charged the adopters for their services abroad. Typically, they simply passed on the country fee that the foreign organizations required without knowing exactly as to which services it covered and if they were reasonably high for the standards in the sending country.

German law fails to establish financial limits on intercountry adoptions. It does not restrict the amount of money that German agencies are allowed to pay to their foreign cooperation partners, for instance, by providing guidelines for reasonable fees and remu-

45 See Chapter V, section 8.4.
46 See Chapter II, section 2.5.
47 See Chapter IV, section 4.4.

neration.[48] Moreover, the German Central Adoption Offices have not specified as to when adoption costs can be considered as 'reasonable'. They typically leave it up to the Central Authority of the sending countries to establish standards for fees and remunerations. German law also lacks specific provisions regulating donations and contributions to sending countries. Particularly, it does not explicitly prohibit adoption placement offices from donating money or material goods to the child care institutions they are cooperating with.[49] The German adoption system thus allows inordinate sums of money to be introduced into the international adoption system, which might then facilitate abusive practices.

Dutch law, by way of contrast, seeks to restrict the transfer of money to the sending countries by prohibiting Dutch adoption agencies from paying unreasonably high fees to their foreign partner organizations and representatives. The country fees that the adoption agencies transfer for the services rendered abroad must not be disproportionate compared to the average income in the sending country.[50] Dutch adoption agencies that violate this provision commit a misdemeanour which is punishable by a fine (Article 28 WOBKA) or – in case they act with motivations of profit – even a criminal offence (Article 27 WOBKA)[51] and they might have their accreditation withdrawn.

Yet, in practice some country fees that the Dutch agencies charge their adopters appear rather unreasonable, especially considering the average costs in the sending states. In some sending countries, the actors are reluctant to properly itemize the fees that foreign adopters are required to pay, making it difficult for the foreign adoption agencies to assess whether or not they are actually reasonable.[52] And considering the agencies' financial and ideological motivation to keep children moving through the adoption system, they might be reluctant to ask too many questions about the country fees that their establish partner organizations establish so as to prevent jeopardizing the cooperation.

The objective of the Dutch adoption law to prevent financial inducements by restricting the transfer of money to the sending countries is not consistent. First, Dutch law only prohibits adoption agencies from paying unreasonably high fees to their partner organizations and representatives, but it does not stipulate any provisions regulating donations or contributions.[53] Money or goods that foreign adoption agencies donate to child care institutions create inducements for the personnel to keep children moving for the purposes of intercountry adoption and could thus encourage them engaging in abusive practices. Also, contributions that are made to help finance the child welfare system of the sending country might have such a harmful effect. Second, the Dutch Central Authority tolerates

48 See Chapter V, section 6.2.
49 See Chapter V, section 6.3.
50 See Chapter VI, section 6.2.
51 See Chapter VI, section 8.2.
52 See Chapter VI, section 6.2.
53 *Ibid.*

'facilitation payments' to authorities in sending countries where bribes are customary. The Dutch provision prohibiting adoption agencies from paying unreasonably high fees for services abroad is thus annulled altogether by the fact that there are no regulations whatsoever with regard to donations and a high tolerance towards 'facilitation payments'.

3.5 *The Monitoring and Control System in Germany and the Netherlands*

In both Germany and the Netherlands, the monitoring and control of the adoption placement agencies is considerably tight. The state authorities have a good insight into the agencies' financial situation and activities in Germany and the Netherlands. The German and Dutch agencies need to have an accreditation in order to be allowed to carry out international adoption placements. In the accreditation procedure, the agencies are required to provide a great deal of information, including about their personnel, financial situation and the placement procedures.

In Germany, the Central Adoption Offices (the Central Authorities on state level) are responsible for accrediting the adoption placement agencies and for subsequently monitoring and controlling their activities. The agencies have several reporting obligations towards the Central Adoption Offices. And the latter may furthermore request information, inspect adoption files and other documents, or enter the premises of the adoption agencies at any time they wish.[54]

In the Netherlands, an accreditation is granted by the Dutch Ministry of Justice and Security (the Central Authority) and must be renewed every five years, which gives the Dutch authorities the opportunity to screen the agencies' organization and financial situation. In addition, the Dutch Ministry meets up with the personnel of the agencies on a regular basis to talk about the agencies placement activities. Also, the Dutch Youth Inspectorate is involved in monitoring the adoption agencies and is responsible for inspecting the agencies between the accreditation renewals, usually after irregularities have occurred. Finally, the Dutch agencies have several reporting obligations.[55]

Both the German and Dutch authorities have the power to intervene if necessary. They can withdraw an agency's authorization to cooperate with a specific sending country or even its accreditation if they find that it does not or can no longer meet the requirements thereof, or if it has violated legal provisions. In addition, they can issue directions to the agencies. Even though the agencies are not legally obliged to follow such directions, the authorities' power to withdraw their authorization or accreditation will generally motivate them to comply. Finally, the authorities can file criminal charges against the staff members of an adoption agency if they suspect them of being involved in illegal practices. In Ger-

54 See Chapter V, section 8.1.
55 See Chapter VI, section 7.1.

many, agency personnel can be held criminally liable for granting consideration to parents or legal guardians in exchange for their consent to the adoption of their child.[56] In the Netherlands, staff members of an agency can be held criminally responsible if they have violated the relevant provisions of the WOBKA.[57]

Whereas the German and Dutch authorities have a fair insight into the agencies activities in Germany and the Netherlands, their possibility to monitor the activities of the agencies' representatives or partner organizations in the sending countries is limited. They have no legal or regulatory control over what happens in another foreign nation and no legal authority over the actors involved in the foreign adoption system. All of that falls within the responsibility of the authorities in the sending country. The authorities in the receiving countries cannot investigate suspicious activities abroad or check the legitimacy of the adoptees' documents. Yet, they can and must closely observe the developments in the sending countries, place pressure on the foreign authorities to clarify allegations of abuses and ban intercountry adoptions from a country if they find them to be too risky. Compared to the Dutch adoption system, the German adoption system is particularly restricted in that regard, mainly due to two reasons.

For one, Germany's monitoring structure that has been established to control intercountry adoptions is too fragmented and cumbersome to effectively respond to allegations of illegal practices abroad.[58] In the course of ratifying the Hague Convention, the German legislator has not designated one, but 13 Central Authorities which have different tasks and responsibilities. The 12 Central Adoption Offices on state level are in charge of accrediting, approving and supervising the adoption agencies that are located in their jurisdiction. In practice, each Central Adoption Office decides itself as to how to control the agencies and how to respond to allegations or indications of adoption irregularities and abuses. In the past, they have often failed to engage in a concerted response to undesirable developments in the states of origin. The dispersion of responsibility has led to a situation whereby none of them seem to understand the big picture of the processes and possible pitfalls in the sending country's adoption systems. The Central Adoption Offices' lack of control and of a general overview of the activities in the states of origin appears to have been compensated by the trust placed in the competent authorities in the sending countries. This is particularly the case if they are States Parties to the Hague Convention (see section 3.6).

The Federal Central Office was established in order to prevent the diffusion of knowledge about irregularities and unfavourable developments in the sending countries. As a 'holding' of the Central Adoption Offices, it is responsible for collecting and distributing the necessary

56 See Chapter V, section 9.1.2.
57 See Chapter VI, section 8.2.
58 See Chapter V, section 8.3.

information and promoting cooperation among them. However, it often experiences difficulties in distributing the necessary information about the sending countries. Furthermore, the Federal Central Office does not have the authority to issue directions to the Central Adoption Offices. If it discovers irregularities or abuses in a particular sending country, it can only advise them to stop placing children from this state and to withdraw their agencies' authorizations. The Federal Central Office can significantly influence intercountry adoptions to Germany by proposing to raise an objection to a sending country's accession to the Hague Convention. This basically has the effect that adoptions from this state are blocked. Yet, this possibility to ban intercountry adoptions is only available with regard to states which were neither Member States of the Hague Conference at the time the Hague Convention was adopted nor participated in the drafting procedure and only at the time of the accession (and not afterwards).[59]

The monitoring and control system in the Netherlands, on the contrary, is centralized. There is only one Dutch Central Authority which is responsible for supervising all Dutch adoption agencies and monitoring the adoption placements to the Netherlands.[60] This centralized structure encourages the gathering and distribution of information among the Dutch adoption agencies and facilitates an immediate response to unfavourable developments in the sending countries.

It is not only the decentralized monitoring structure that is a limitation of the German adoption system, but also the fact that the Central Adoption Offices do not generally visit the states of origin.[61] They lack the resources to travel to the sending countries that the German agencies are cooperating with, in order to get a picture of their adoption system and the way the agencies' foreign representatives and partner organizations operate. The Central Adoption Offices can thus only make assessments regarding the integrity of the foreign adoption system on the basis of the information provided by the German adoption placement agencies during the authorization procedure and of the child proposals, which the agencies are required to present to them.

This is different in the Netherlands, where the Central Authority visits the countries of origin on a regular basis, particularly after irregular practices have been uncovered or are being suspected by a Dutch agency or embassy.[62] In the sending country, the Dutch Central Authority meets with the competent authorities, talks to international organizations, like UNICEF or other countries' embassies, visits the Dutch adoption agencies cooperation partners (orphanages) and it may look into adoption files in order to get an idea of the foreign adoption system's integrity. If it finds that the adoption procedures are not properly carried out, the Central Authority may put pressure on the sending countries to fulfil their

59 *Ibid.*
60 See Chapter VI, section 7.3.
61 See Chapter V, section 8.3.
62 See Chapter VI, section 7.3.

tasks and responsibilities properly or decide to suspend intercountry adoptions from this particular sending country. It has already done the latter with regard to Guatemala, Cambodia, Haiti and Uganda.[63]

Yet, even though the Dutch monitoring system goes much further than the one in Germany, it also has its limitations. First, the Dutch Central Authority might be reluctant to put pressure on the sending countries because of diplomatic or other interests that are at stake. Generally speaking, a receiving country's decision regarding the manner in which to respond to reports of irregular adoption practices in a sending country is not only based on the best interests of the children, but it also takes into account diplomatic interests as well as the interests of adoption agencies as well as (prospective) adopters. When the Dutch Ministry was confronted with reports of abusive practices in China, the important economic relationship between the Netherlands and China and the fact that China was the most significant supply country of children for Dutch couples may explain why the Ministry was reluctant to put pressure on the Chinese authorities or to discontinue adoptions from China altogether.[64] Second, with regard to adoptions from Hague sending countries, the Dutch monitoring system is restricted by the Ministry's interpretation of the concept of trust that has been created by the Hague Convention (see following section).

Finally, the Dutch and German immigration processes are not suited to prevent illegally obtained children from entering Germany and the Netherlands. In Germany, the embassies in the sending countries are responsible for processing a visa or Dutch passport for the child. In the Netherlands, the embassies in the states of origin only accept visa or passport applications which are then processed by the IND or the Ministry of Foreign Affairs, respectively. The German and Dutch authorities only assess whether all the documents required for a passport or visa were submitted and are in order, but it would never double-check the accuracy of their content.

The embassies may become askance if they notice a sudden increase in the number of 'abandoned' babies showing up in a particular child care institution or region. However, there is little they can do to actually prove irregular or abusive adoption practices in the sending country as they do generally not conduct investigations into the children's background. The authorities may only decline to process a passport or visa if the necessary documents are not complete or where inconsistent information about the children's origin or background has been provided. However, in those cases where the children were laundered 'properly', meaning where all the adoptees' documents appear to be in order, they cannot prevent them from entering Germany or the Netherlands, even if they suspect systemic abuses in the sending country's adoption system.

63 See Chapter VI, section 7.3.
64 See Chapter VI, section 7.4.

3.6 *Trust in the Hague Sending Countries*

The Hague Convention constitutes the most significant endeavour to tackle illegal and abusive practices in the intercountry adoption system. The Convention, its two Guides to Good Practices as well as numerous recommendations drawn up by the Permanent Bureau of the Hague Conference on Private International Law have set the standards for ethical and sustainable international adoptions which respect the rights of children and their birth parents.[65]

Nonetheless, incidences of child trafficking for adoption purposes have still been uncovered in sending countries that have ratified the treaty, suggesting that the convention is not a panacea for the abduction, sale and traffic in children. The drafters of the Convention believed that the intercountry adoption system would be best safeguarded against illegal and abusive practices by regulating and controlling it. To this end, the treaty provides a set of minimum standards and procedures for its Contracting States to follow. However, it leaves its Contracting State much latitude to define and regulate individually the specific aspects of international adoptions.[66] Hence, some terms of the treaty were left deliberately vague ('adoptable', the child's best interests', and 'contrary to public policy') so as to allow the states to create an adoption system as they see fit. In addition, the Hague Convention fails to address the structural root causes of the illegal adoption market: the economic and demographic asymmetries between the sending and the receiving states which have fuelled the demand for adoptable children, created the motivation of actors in the source countries to illegally obtain them and further increased the level of corruption (see section 2.3). In the end, the treaty is thus no more than a set of principles and procedures, which are only as good as their implementation.[67]

The Convention distributes the responsibility for fulfilling the requirements of an international adoption between the sending and the receiving countries.[68] The lion's share of responsibility is thereby placed upon the states of origin, whose competent authorities are in charge of determining the child's adoptability, ensuring that the necessary consent for an adoption have been given freely, fully informed, counselled, without any financial inducement and in the required form and determining that the subsidiarity principle is complied with. The states of origin are therefore responsible for the most delicate phase of the adoption procedure, in which most abusive or illegal practices commonly take place. The authorities in the receiving countries, on the other hand, are only required to examine the prospective adoptive parents' eligibility and suitability to adopt internationally, to

65 See Chapter IV, section 4.
66 See Chapter IV, section 5.2.
67 See Chapter IV, section 5.3.
68 See Chapter IV, section 3.5.

properly counsel them and to make sure that the child is allowed to enter and reside permanently in the receiving state.

This allocation of responsibility makes sense, as the competent authorities in the child's native country are in a better position than the foreign authorities to clarify the child's eligibility for adoption and to determine whether or not an intercountry adoption is in his or her best interests. However, some sending countries lack the sufficient resources to effectively meet the tasks and responsibilities assigned to them by the treaty.[69] In addition, many states of origin face high levels of corruption which can impair the proper implementation of the Convention's standards and procedures. They often have difficulties in properly determining the child's adoptability and in implementing the subsidiarity principle, which obliges them to establish a functioning child and family welfare system that assists families in keeping their families together. Furthermore, some states may not have the political will to change a system that not only saves them a lot of expense, but also generates large volumes of money. In essence, they ratify the Hague Convention, but establish a system which runs contrary to the treaty's objectives and principles.

The Hague Convention does not designate an overseeing body to ensure that the Contracting States' laws and practices are in compliance with its standards and procedures and that holds them accountable for any violations. Rather, it provides a system of self-regulation in which it is the duty of the Central Authorities to enforce compliance with the treaty's provisions. The sending countries can thus set up an adoption system in which abuses go unpunished.[70]

Many experts have criticized the Hague Convention for these pitfalls and weaknesses. Yet, as this study has shown, numerous stakeholders in Germany and the Netherlands trust that sending states, which have ratified the treaty, have established proper safeguards and procedures that would effectively prevent illegal and abusive adoption practices. Thus, in an interview, the director of a German adoption agency claimed that the (even to him) unreasonably high fees charged for an adoption in Haiti had to be considered as reasonable as the country had ratified the Hague Convention.[71] The head of a German Central Adoption Office explained that the Office's personnel is usually more suspicious of adoptions from non-Hague countries than of adoptions from states which have ratified the Hague Convention, as it is believed that the latter have given more attention to the issue of child trafficking.[72] And in her book, a German adoptive mother reassured prospective adopters that international adoptions from Kenya were safe and free from abuse, since the country had ratified the Hague Convention.[73]

---

69 See Chapter IV, section 5.3.
70 *Ibid.*
71 See Chapter V, section 6.2.
72 See Chapter V, section 8.3.
73 See Chapter IV, section 5.4.

The Dutch Central Authority stressed the concept of mutual trust on several occasions after illegal practices were uncovered in sending countries that Dutch adoption agencies were placing children from. The rhetoric of mutual trust and shared responsibility featured particularly strongly in the Ministry's letters to the Second Chamber and parliament speeches regarding the child trafficking incidences uncovered in China.[74] Adoptions from China, by far the most significant sending country for the Netherlands, were long assumed to be free from irregularities. Yet, as of 2005, reports about abusive adoption practices in the Chinese intercountry adoption system began to mount. Several studies, media investigations as well as an inquiry by *Wereldkinderen*, a Dutch adoption agency, highlighted systemic abuses in the Chinese adoption system. Yet, notwithstanding these reports, the Dutch Central Authority accepted quite uncritically the explanations and reassurances given by the Chinese authorities. Instead of putting pressure on the Chinese Central Authority to properly investigate the uncovered incidences of child trafficking and to disclose more information on the children sent to the Netherlands – if necessary by threatening to discontinue adoptions from China altogether – it stressed the principle of trust instead. In several statements, the Dutch Ministry of Justice and Security explained that the responsibility to control whether an adoption complies with the Convention's requirements rests with the country of origin and that the Netherlands needs to have trust in the foreign authorities' integrity and on the reliability of the information provided about the children.

The relationship of trust between the authorities in the sending country and the receiving country indeed forms the basis of the Hague Convention. One of the treaty's main objectives is to establish a system of close cooperation amongst the Contracting States which shall work together to prevent abuses and to ensure the protection of children. Such close cooperation should help to promote confidence between states.[75] Yet, despite the Convention's allocation of the most important duties to the sending countries and the idea of mutual trust between its Contacting States, the Convention's Guide to Good Practice No. 2 emphasizes a mandate of 'joint responsibility' or 'co-responsibility'. This mandate implies that the receiving nations are still required to make their own assessments regarding the integrity of the sending countries' intercountry adoption system and the reliability of the information provided about the children. Yet, apparently, the Ministry interpreted the treaty's allocation of duties as relieving the Netherlands from any responsibility for the adoption steps taken in the sending countries and seems to understand the idea of mutual trust as a mandate of deference or bar against scrutiny.[76]

The creation of mutual trust between the stakeholders in the sending and the receiving countries is probably the greatest pitfall of the Hague Convention. The treaty has created

74 See Chapter VI, section 7.4.2.
75 See Chapter IV, section 5.4.
76 See Chapter VI, section 7.4.2.

an appearance of legitimacy that might lead stakeholders in the reiving countries to assume the integrity of Hague countries' adoptions system carte blanche. They may be inclined to believe that international adoptions are safer or think that they must trust that the authorities in the states of origin actually comply with their tasks and responsibility simply because the country has ratified the Hague Convention. This trust is dangerous when it is placed in States Parties to the Convention that have failed to properly implement the treaty's regulations. With regard to these countries, the Convention might then work as a 'Trojan horse': the illegal placement of a child appears to be perfectly legal as it formally complies with the procedures of the treaty. That way, the treaty helps to facilitate and encourage the laundering of the paper orphan through the adoption system.

3.7 *Adopters' Denying the Role of Money in Intercountry Adoptions*

In contemporary Western societies, children are considered to be priceless who cannot and should not be paid for, and parenthood is understood to be separated from the market sphere and therefore to be non-economic in scope.[77] In an intercountry adoption, however, the interrelation between the economic and the intimate sphere is particularly visible considering the large sums of money that adopters are required to pay for a child to love. The autobiographic stories of the German and Dutch adopters that were analysed in this study have once again illustrated that in intercountry adoption seemingly contrary domains – parenthood and consumption, money and love – are complexly intertwined, thereby creating tension. Children are not only regarded as human beings worthy of dignity and respect. They are also treated as objects of desire and consumption that serve adopters to accomplish parenthood. The narrative analysis yielded that adopters do not only want to save 'any child' that is in need of an adoption, rather they are looking for 'a suitable child', 'the right child', which in most cases means a healthy baby. The language the adopters employ to describe their preferences concerning the child and their expectations in the selection process illustrates the commercial component of an adoption.[78]

In order to resolve the moral tension between the ideology that separates children and parenthood from the market sphere and the adopters making choices and paying money during the adoption process, the authors advanced a number of linguistic choices. Recurring in all their adoption stories is the 'rhetoric of disavowal'. The adopters refuse to consider themselves as choosing 'the right child', claiming that it is, on the contrary, the child who selects the right adoptive parents. Furthermore, they deny and resignify the meaning of the payments they have to make during the adoption process.[79] Financial transactions

77 See Chapter VII, section 2.
78 See Chapter VII, section 4.3.
79 See Chapter VII, section 4.4.

made in connection with the adoption – including irregular or even clearly illegal ones – are labelled as 'service costs', 'administrative fees', 'contributions', 'down payments', 'broker's fees', 'donations' or 'gifts': anything but the payment for a child. Some adopters deny the existence of an international adoption marketplace by stressing that children are priceless and *ipso facto* beyond commerce. Others disavow the significance of money in an intercountry adoption by aligning adoption with reproductive treatments, another costly means of having a child, or by comparing it to a pregnancy ('adoption pregnancy'). The rhetoric of denial also features in the books describing the phase after the assignment of a particular child.[80] Dominating in the adoption stories are narratives of 'fate' and 'God' bringing the adopters together with 'their' child as well as of an undeniable love tie linking them with each other. Also, the recurring trope of the child as a 'gift' allows adopters to deny the economics at play in an intercountry adoption and to eliminate the weighs of the adopters' own interests and their rational choices during the adoption process.

The denial that the authors – and probably other adopters as well as adoption advocates – engage in concerning the role of money in international adoption is harmful. Disavowing the significance of payments, the adopters' role as consumers and of the instrumentalization of adoptees works to facilitate the trafficking in children for adoption purposes. Reframing money or goods offered to the child's birth mother as 'gifts' and payments made to private intermediaries sourcing a suitable child to adopt as 'down payments' or 'broker's commission' obscures the sometimes illegal nature of these transactions. The idea that 'fate' or 'God's hand' brought the child and the adopters together – rather than money and demand – and that an undeniable love tie links them with each other legitimizes and gives meaning to any irregularities that might have occurred during the adoption process. The concept of destiny and transcending love even gives the adoption of a child, who was obtained illegally, legitimacy.

4 Recommendations

4.1 *Banning Intercountry Adoptions?*

In 2016, the *Raad voor Strafrechtstoepassing en Jeugdbescherming (RSJ)* recommended banning intercountry adoptions to the Netherlands altogether, arguing that the risks of illegal adoption practices were too high and difficult to remove.[81] The Netherlands is the first receiving country to seriously consider banning intercountry adoptions. The present

80 See Chapter VII, section 5.1.

81 *Bezinning op Interlandelijke Adoptie, Advies van de Afdeling advisering van de Raad voor Strafrechtstoepassing en Jeugdbescherming (RSJ), 16.11.2016, Kamerstukken II 2015-216, Nr. 60 839,* p. 43.

study has shown that the transnational adoption market is intrinsically criminogenic in its nature and that the weaknesses inherent in the intercountry adoption system are indeed difficult to resolve. A system that is based on inequalities between the sending and the receiving countries and in which large sums of money further facilitate the already existing high incidences of corruption, is difficult, if not impossible, to reform. Standards and regulations, like the ones laid down by the Hague Convention, may only mystify rather than remove these underlying realities that are conducive to illegal adoption practices. The debate revolving around the question as to whether or not to cease intercountry adoptions altogether is thus understandable and legitimate.

A couple of weeks after the *RSJ* issued its recommendations, the Dutch Ministry of Justice and Security announced that it would not prohibit intercountry adoptions, claiming that it should remain available for children that cannot be cared for in their home countries.[82] From a criminological perspective, this was probably the right decision. As the Ministry itself stressed, banning foreign adoptions would remove the legal channel to adopt a child from abroad. This might lead to the unwanted consequence that Dutch couples and individuals simply pursue an adoption via 'underground' means, which, as has been discussed with regard to private adoptions, is devoid of any control and supervision. By prohibiting intercountry adoptions, authorities would give up the already few opportunities that are at hand to supervise and control international adoptions. The question should thus rather center on how to reform the adoption system, both in the Netherlands and Germany, so as to at least lower the risk of child trafficking.

4.2 *Intercountry Adoptions carried out by the State?*

Both the German and the Dutch adoption systems have too many stakeholders, considering the low number of intercountry adoptions. A complex monitoring structure involving too many actors makes effective control difficult to achieve and the (in relation to the falling adoption numbers) high number of adoption agencies creates financial pressure which was identified as a criminogenic factor in the adoption system.

Thus, what if the system of accredited adoption agencies was abolished altogether and the state carried out adoption placements from abroad? This would not only be more cost-effective but might also make adoptions safer, as they would be carried out and controlled by one institution which does furthermore not have the financial motivation to move children for adoption purposes. Germany and the Netherlands might consider setting up a state institution or designate the already existing authorities (the German Federal Central Office and the Dutch Central Authority) to carry out the adoption placements. Adoptions

82 *Brief van de Staatssecretaris van Veiligheid en Justitie, 31.01.2017, Kamerstukken II 2016-2017, 31 265, Nr. 62*, p. 4.

would then be handled in cooperation with the foreign Central Authorities or other competent authorities which are responsible for doing the matching. The German and Dutch authorities would need to travel to the potential states of origin to check whether there are children are in need of intercountry adoption and to make their own assessments regarding the integrity of the foreign adoption system and the reliability of the information provided about the children before starting its cooperation with a sending country.

The embassies in the sending countries could be involved in the adoption placement procedure by assisting the adopters, closely observing the adoption process and, if necessary, conducting inquiries in cases where there are doubts regarding the child's origin. Increasing the involvement of the embassies in the sending countries might impede the laundering of children through the adoption system. By monitoring the developments in the sending countries more closely and double-checking the adoption documents in case of any suspicion, the embassies may be better placed to prevent children from entering Germany and the Netherlands in the first place.[83]

Having the state carrying out adoption placements would, however, not be without its risks. As has been shown, intercountry adoption is a highly political issue. The authorities in the receiving countries might be reluctant to scrutinize the foreign adoption system too closely or, in case of signs of irregular practices, put too much pressure on the foreign authorities in order to avoid jeopardizing good diplomatic relations with that state. In addition, the authorities might be politically motivated to keep children moving for adoption. As has been explained, in many receiving countries, pro-adoption lobby groups seek to exert influence on the relevant laws and policies on intercountry adoption. The current financial pressure might simply be replaced by a political pressure which, too, might work to facilitate the trafficking of children for adoption purposes.

It is probably rather unrealistic that Germany, the Netherlands, or any other receiving country for that matter, would place intercountry adoptions into the hand of the state authorities. Such a policy would essentially abolish the adoption system as it exists right now, forcing all accredited adoption agencies to shut down. In addition, it is questionable if the state was willing to carry out intercountry adoptions that are inherently risky and could involve children that were illegally obtained.[84] In the Netherlands, the government has recently come under increased pressure concerning its role in the adoption system. In

83 Inspectie Jeugdzorg (2009). "Interlandelijke Adoptie Knelpunten in het Stelsel." Available at http://www.aoo.nl/downloads/2010-01-14-MvJ-a.pdf.

84 In 2016, a report drawn up by the consultancy bureau Andersson Elffers Felix described such a model for an adoption system for the Netherlands in which the state authorities would carry out the intercountry adoption placements (Smits et al. (2016). "De Toekomst van de keten voor interlandelijke adoptie." 17.05.2016, GV349/conceptrapport, Andersson Elffers Felix, available at https://www.rijksoverheid.nl/documenten/rapporten/2016/05/17/de-toekomst-van-de-keten-voor-interlandelijke-adoptie, pp. 52-57). This scenario was, however, rejected by the Dutch Ministry of Justice and Security (*Brief van de Staatssecretaris van Veiligheid en Justitie, 31.01.2017, Kamerstukken II 2016-2017, 31 265, Nr. 62*, p. 4).

2017, the failure of the Dutch authorities to properly control international adoptions was brought to light after child trafficking incidences were uncovered in Sri Lanka in the 70s and 80s.[85] And in the same year, a number of interests groups requested the Dutch government to provide funds for investigating past adoptions from countries in which abuses were uncovered and already announced claims for reparations.[86] This might be one of the reasons why the current Minister of Justice, like his precedessor, recently rejected a state-run adoption system, but promised suggestions for reforming the adoption system.[87] But how can the adoption system as it exists right now be reformed?

4.3 *Accountability of Adoption Agencies*

Both the German and the Dutch adoption system only hold adoption agencies accountable for the activities of their representatives, but not for the actions of foreign governmental or accredited institutions that they work together with. They therefore usually escape legal responsibility for illegal practices in the sending countries, claiming that they have trusted the organizations they had cooperated with. For example, the Dutch adoption agency *Meiling,* which placed an Indian boy who later turned out to have been kidnapped by the orphanage it had worked with, maintained that it believed the information provided in the child reports, and ultimately did not face any regulatory consequences for the illegal activities of its cooperation partner.[88]

This lack of agency responsibility, coupled with the agency's ideological and financial motivation to keep children moving through the adoption system, creates an incentive for them to turn a blind eye to signs of irregular practices in the sending countries. A number of experts have therefore already suggested holding adoption agencies liable for the activities of the foreign organizations they work with, even if they are accredited or state institutions.[89] As experience has shown, the fact that adoption placements are carried out in cooperation with a licensed or governmental organization does not rule out their

85 *Brief van de Minister voor Rechtsbescherming, 26.04.2018, Kamerstukken II 2017-2018, 31 265, Nr. 65.*

86 See http://www.againstchildtrafficking.org/wp-content/uploads/UAI17.briefTK-AO.0112.EN_.pdf (last accessed on 07.08.2018).

87 *Verslag van een Algemeen Overleg, 15.02.2018, Kamerstukken II 2017-2018, 31 265, Nr. 64,* p. 21.

88 See Chapter VI, section 6.3.

89 See, for example, D. M. Smolin (2004). "The Two Faces of Intercountry Adoption: The Significance of the Indian Adoption Scandals." Seton Hall Law Review, 35, 403-493, pp. 490-493; D. M. Smolin (2006). "Child Laundering: How the Intercountry Adoption System Legitimizes and Incentivizes the Practices of Buying, Trafficking, Kidnapping, and Stealing Children." The Wayne Law Review, 52, 1, 113-200, pp. 197-200; E. J. Graff (2010). "The Baby Business." Democracy Journal, Summer No. 17, available at https://democracyjournal.org/magazine/17/the-baby-business/; K. S. Rotabi and J. L. Gibbons (2011). "Does the Hague Convention on Intercountry Adoption Adequately Protect Orphaned and Vulnerable Children and Their Families?" Journal of Child and Family Studies, 21, 1, 106-119, p. 111.

involvement in illegal practices.[90] In sending countries with high incidences of corruption, these institutions might be involved in laundering children.[91] The adoption placement agencies in the receiving countries can thus not blindly trust them.

German and Dutch adoption agencies should be obliged to assess the integrity of the cooperation partner and the foreign adoption system in general before beginning cooperation with a sending country, but also *in concreto*, thus on a case-by-case basis. This obligation must also be emphasized particularly with regard to adoptions from Hague countries that some adoption agencies consider to be safer. An agency should be held legally responsible for the illegal practices of the organizations it cooperates with if there were red flags suggesting structural deficiencies in the foreign adoption system that rendered adoptions risky in general, or, *in concreto*, if the information provided about the children was incomplete or inconsistent. It should not be accepted that adoption agencies continue placing children from a country despite signs of systemic abuses in the foreign adoption system and then assert that they are not responsible for the illegal practices of the foreign organizations as they could not control what was happening abroad. An agency's claim of irresponsibility for the activities in the sending countries should also not be possible if it had accepted a child proposal including incomplete and inconsistent information about a child that later turns out to be in the intercountry adoption system illegally. An adoption system should not reward those adoption agencies that willfully ignore signs of abuse abroad and that can, therefore, place more children than those which exercise due diligence and care. Rather, it must properly sanction an agency's knowledge of or apathy towards wrongdoing in the sending countries (the line between the two is consistently blurred).

Administrative sanctions, such as the withdrawal of licenses and the imposition of fines, should be used as a primary enforcement mechanism for agencies' failure to carry out proper assessments. They are considered to be faster, more effective and less expensive than criminal sanctions. The criminal law, on the other hand, should be used as an enforcement method of last resort for cases were the agency personnel did not only ignore wrongdoings abroad but were actively involved in illegally obtaining children for adoption purposes (e.g. by providing money or goods in exchange the orphanage's required consent, see section 4.7) or laundering them.

Agency responsibility would create an incentive for German and Dutch adoption agencies to choose their cooperation partners more carefully, to better investigate how their partners are finding adoptable children, and to stop placing children earlier if signs of irregularities become apparent. Thus, it would remove the blind trust that the agencies have in their cooperation partners which in turn facilitates the trafficking of children into Germany and the Netherlands.

90 See, Chapter IV, section 5.3, describing the child trafficking incidences in the Indian adoption system.

91 Chapter II, section 2.4.1.

4.4 *Regulating the Flow of Money into the Sending Countries*

The German and Dutch adoption agencies should be required to disclose more detailed information about the country fees that the adopters are required to pay for services in the sending countries. They should break the fees down into four categories that should themselves also be carefully itemized and explained: 1. costs for the administrative procedures (including fees for court hearings, translations and the legalisation of documents, visa applications etc.), 2. costs for the services of the agency's partner organization (including salaries, rent, office equipment etc.), 3. costs for childcare ('maintenance costs', medical costs etc.) and 4. monetary and material donations made to any organization in the sending country. It should not be accepted that adoption agencies only present an all-encompassing fee to the authorities and the adopters without being able to properly explain the items they include. If the institutions in the sending countries cannot or do not want to disclose the fees that the adopters are required to pay, the agencies should not be allowed to place children from that country.

The adoption agencies should also be obliged to sufficiently demonstrate that the country fees they charge are reasonably high in relation to the services rendered abroad. Thus, before starting a new cooperation, they should be required to conduct inquiries into the sending country's customary salaries and to check which fees are charged for court hearings, legal documents etc. in that state.

The Central Authorities in Germany and the Netherlands should not simply rely on the information provided by the adoption agencies, but they should also make their own assessments regarding the country fees that German and Dutch adopters have to pay. Furthermore, they should make the itemized country fees that the adoption agencies charge, as well as the reports in which the agencies explain why they consider them to be reasonable, publicly available. Right now, the countries fees are handled with great discretion, making it difficult for outsiders to understand exactly how they are calculated. Publicly sharing the costs that the Dutch and German agencies charge could instigate an open discussion about the reasonableness of the amounts of money that are being transferred to the sending countries, not only among stakeholders of the national adoption systems but among authorities and adopters from other sending countries.

The German and Dutch adoption system should explicitly prohibit adoption agencies from donating money or goods to the orphanage they move children from (see section 4.8) and they should not tolerate 'facilitation payments' that are made to secure necessary approvals for an adoption or to accelerate the adoption procedure, even when they are 'customary' in the sending countries. Anything else would frustrate the current provisions which proscribe the payment of unreasonably high fees. As has been explained, any extra contributions made to the individuals and organizations involved in the adoption procedure create an incentive for them to secure a steady supply of children for intercountry adoption.

4.5 Strengthening the Role of the German and the Dutch Central Authority

The German and Dutch authorities' should more closely monitor the developments in the sending countries and the activities of the organizations, the adoption agencies co-operate with, and be able to intervene if they suspect irregularities abroad. The German adoption system especially requires reform in that respect. The Federal Central Office, the German Central Authority at the federal level, can now best be described as a 'toothless tiger', which does not have any power to influence intercountry adoptions to Germany. Its role has to be substantially strengthened in order for it to function as an effective safeguard within the German adoption system. The Dutch adoption system, and particularly the role of the Dutch Central Authority, might inspire reform in Germany.

First, like in the Netherlands, it should be the responsibility of the Federal Central Office, and not of the adoption agencies, to approve the matches between a proposed child and the adopters (with regard to Hague adoptions, purusant to Article 17c of the Hague Convention). Thus, the adoption agencies should be required to present all child reports to the Federal Central Office and not, as is currently the case, to the Central Adoption Offices at the state level. That way the Federal Central Office would be provided the opportunity to check all child proposals, require clarification from the sending country if the information about the children's background is incomplete or inconsistent (as was explained, the foreign authorities are often more willing to communicate with the Central Authorities than with the adoption agencies), and reject them if necessary.

Second, like the Dutch Central Authority, the Federal Central Office should have the responsibility to grant the German adoption agencies the authorization to carry out adoptions from a particular country and to withdraw it if it finds that the foreign adoption system can no longer guarantee ethical adoptions. The Central Adoption Offices on state level can continue to be in charge for accrediting the adoption agencies and for monitoring their financial situation as well as their activities in Germany. However, the control of the adoption agencies' cooperation with the sending countries should be centralized in order to avoid the diffusion of information about the developments in the sending counties and to allow for a more rapid response to irregularities abroad.

The Federal Central Office should properly assess the integrity of the foreign adoption system before, but also after, granting authorization. To that end, it should be able to visit to the sending countries that the German adoption agencies (want to) place children from. Like its counterpart in the Netherlands, the German Federal Adoption Office should travel to the countries of origin on a regular basis and in any case before the adoption agency starts its cooperation, and if irregular practices have been uncovered or are suspected. In the sending country, the Federal Adoption Office would then meet the competent authorities, talk to the German embassies, visit the German adoption agencies' cooperation partners (orphanages) and perhaps also look into adoption files in order to get an understanding of the foreign adoption system's integrity.

Also, the role of the Dutch Central Authority can be improved. First, an authorization from the Central Authority should be required for adoptions from all sending countries and not only for placements from Hague states. Second, before granting an authorization, the Dutch Central Authority should properly assess the foreign adoption system by conducting fact finding missions in the sending countries. Currently, it authorizes adoption agencies to move children from abroad without having first closely checked whether the sending county's system complies with the standards and principles of the UNCRC and the Hague Convention. Hence, it only gets an idea of the foreign adoption system after having been presented the first child proposals.

The Central Adoption Offices in both Germany and the Netherlands should treat adoptions from Hague and non-Hague sending countries with the same level of 'mistrust'.[92] The fact that a country of origin has ratified the Hague Convention does not rule out irregularities in its adoption system. The German and Dutch authorities should thus not be blinded by 'Hague conformant' adoptions. Furthermore, they must not interpret the treay's allocation of duties between the sending and the receiving countries as alleviating themselves from any responsibility for the adoption steps taken abroad and they must not understand the concept of mutual trust as a mandate of deference against scrunity. Rather, they should acknowledge the mandate of 'joint responsibility' that is emphazised by the Convention's Guide to Good Practice No. 2 which requires them to make their own assessments regarding the intergrity of the sending countries' adoption system and the reliability of the information provided about the proposed children and to ultimately cease adoptions from a country that does not seem to be able to guarantee ethical adoptions.[93]

Finally, in order to avoid a conflict of interest, the German and Dutch Central Authority should be able to place a total ban on adoptions from countries with which Germany and the Netherlands have special diplomatic relations. The way the Dutch Central Authority responded to irregular adoption practices in China showed that political interests can be too detrimental to the best interests of children. Thus, the German and Dutch authorities should be able to refuse granting authorization for adoptions from countries, if they find that economic and other interests might impede a critical assessment of the foreign adoption system.

---

92 See also P. Vlaardingerbroek (2012). "Interlandelijke adoptie, bezien vanuit het perspectief van het vertrouwensbeginsel." Beleidsdoorlichting interlandelijke adoptie, 15.03.2012, *Kamerstukken II* 2011-2012, 33199, Nr. 1, Bijlage V, p. 25.

93 See Chapter IV, section 5.4.

4.6 *Designating the German and Dutch Immigration Authorities as Gatekeepers*

Germany and the Netherlands should consider integrating the immigration authorities more closely into their intercountry adoption systems in order to impede the trafficking of children for adoption purposes. The US immigration process for adoptees can be used as a model for reform in this regard. In the US adoption system, the Immigration Service is required to investigate the child's circumstances to see whether he or she is an orphan as defined by US immigration law before processing a visa.[94] If the officer reviewing the submitted documents believes that further investigation is necessary, additional interviews, documentation and a field investigation would be conducted so as to determine whether the child is eligible for adoption.[95] If the Immigration Service in the course of such an investigation determines that money or other consideration has been given as payment for the child or as an inducement to release the child, the visa must be denied.[96]

Moreover, the German and Dutch embassies in the sending countries should have the mandate to investigate a child's eligibility for adoption in case of doubt, before letting him or her enter Germany or the Netherlands. If a child's illegal origin is ever uncovered in Germany or the Netherlands, it will be too late to rescind the illegal adoption by sending the child back to the country of origin. This became apparent in the case involving the Indian adoptee Rahul who had been kidnapped and then adopted by a Dutch couple.[97] Once an illegally obtained child has been brought to the sending country and has lived with his or her new caretakers for a certain period of time, it is impossible to send the child back to the biological parents after having uncovered the illegal circumstances of the adoption placement. Designating the German and Dutch embassies as gatekeepers in the adoption system could help to prevent illegally obtained children from entering Germany or the Netherlands in the first place. Of course, this additional layer of safeguard can only be considered for visa-required sending countries.

4.7 *Criminalizing the Purchase of Children for Adoption*

Germany and the Netherlands should properly criminalize the purchase of children by adopters and adoption agencies. The present study explained the harmful effects that the

94 D. M. Smolin (2004). "The Two Faces of Intercountry Adoption: The Significance of the Indian Adoption Scandals." Seton Hall Law Review, 35, 403-493, pp. 419-426.

95 See http://www.passportsusa.com/family/adoption_i600.html (last accessed on 03.08.2018); C. Tribowski (2015). "Kinder kauft man nicht. Die politische Ökonomie von Auslandsadoptionen in Deutschland und den Vereinigten Staaten von Amerika." PhD Thesis, Universität zu Köln, pp. 238-239.

96 T. Maskew (2004). "Child Trafficking and Intercountry Adoption: The Cambodian Experience." Cumberland Law Review, 35, 619-638, p. 625.

97 See Chapter VI, section 6.3.

payment of the large sums of Western money has in the sending countries.[98] Some adopters provide money or gifts to the birth parents in order to enable them to properly care for the rest of the family. Moreover, adopters or adoption agencies often donate money or goods to the orphanage that provided the child for adoption in order to help them cover expenses and to improve the living conditions for the children 'left behind' that will never be adopted. For poor families small financial or material support that is conditioned on the relinquishment of their children will have the effect of actually inducing relinquishment. Even assistance that is provided after consent was given could be seen as the fulfilment of an expectation which induced the relinquishment. The difference between a donation and an actual payment for a child then only becomes a theoretical one. The same basically applies to monies and goods that are donated to childcare institutions. Monies or goods which are donated not independently, but which are linked to intercountry adoption create an incentive for childcare institutions to provide children for adoption in return.

The German Criminal Code criminalizes the sale and purchase of children.[99] Individuals that take another person's child into their homes for an indefinite period of time and grant consideration therefor are criminally liable according to § 236 StGB. This criminal legal provision also covers intermediaries that grant consideration to the birth, adoptive or foster parents or legal guardians in exchange for the required consent to the adoption of their child. Yet, § 236 StGB will usually not be applicable to situations where international adopters or adoption agencies purchase a child.[100] Adopters and adoption agencies that provide money or goods to the orphanage or the child's parents can, in most cases, not be held criminally liable according to § 236 StGB as they will argue that they and the child's parents or legal guardian acted in the best interests of the child which excludes their *mens rea*. They act in the best interests of the child if the child's birth parents or the orphanage caring for the child face extreme poverty and gave their consent to the adoption to provide the child with a better life. The German Criminal Code does thus not criminalize purchasing a child from parents and orphanages in poor countries which are most vulnerable to abuse and exploitation. The German legislator should fill this criminal liability loophole by criminalizing any sale and purchase of children, regardless of the financial situation of the child's parents or the legal guardian.

In the Netherlands, adoption agencies commit a misdemenour according to Article 20(3) WOBKA if they pay unreasonably high fees to their representatives and partner organizations in the sending countries, and a criminal offence according to Article 27 WOBKA in case they act with the objective to profit.[101] To avoid legal loopholes, the Dutch legislator should not only prohibit Dutch adoption agencies from paying unreasonably

98 See Chapter II, section 4.2.2.
99 See Chapter V, section 9.1.
100 See Chapter V, section 9.1.1.
101 See Chapter VI, section 6.2.

high fees but also to provide any forms of 'donations' to the orphanage they move children from (see section 4.4). Furthermore, he might consider a criminal legal provision similar to that of § 236 of the German Criminal Code, which criminalizes individuals that take another person's child into their homes for an indefinite period of time and grant consideration therefor. Currently, there exists no Dutch legal provision prohibiting adopters from paying money or goods to the child's parents or the orphanage.

For some, it might feel wrong to criminalize individuals that 'only wanted to help'. Arguably, this is because many consider adopters and adoption agencies as ultimate benefactors with the noble motive of saving children from the intermediate circumstances in their native countries and providing them with a loving family. The idea that the money or goods they provide to the child's birth parents and the orphanage to help them care for the rest of the deprived children that cannot saved might thus be counter-intuitive. Thus, in order to reform the adoption system as it exists right now in Germany and the Netherlands, we need to do more than simply change laws and policies on intercountry adoption. Rather, we must also try to alter the way we think about children and their families in poor countries, the role of adopters and adoption agencies in the intercountry adoptions system as well as of the large sums of Western money they are willing to pay in order 'to do good'. This will be explained in the following and last section of this book.

4.8 *Reconsidering the Way We Think about Intercountry Adoption*

The German and Dutch intercountry adoption system is strongly influenced by the way adopters and adoption agencies – or more generally (we) Western societies – perceive ourselves and the countries we adopt from, how we understand childhood and which meaning we attach to the concept of the 'child's best interests' (see section 3.1). It is also these values, beliefs and attitudes that work to encourage the trafficking in children for adoption purposes. Thus, to effectively reduce incidences of child trafficking, we must become aware of and try to remove our harmful perceptions and wrong beliefs about intercountry adoption. The present study can be an agent of change, because it explicates the adopters' implicit values and ideas that they unwittingly take for granted, by exposing recurrent tropes and commonplaces in their narratives about intercountry adoption.

First, we must be prepared to acknowledge that the number of children that is truly in need of intercountry adoption is much smaller than we intuitively think it is. Extreme poverty as well as natural and man-made disasters leave millions of children across the world extremely vulnerable. Yet, contrary to the popular Western belief, only a small percentage of these children are deprived of their family environment and an even smaller share have the characteristics that international adopters are looking for: young and healthy.[102] The majority of these children have at least one parent or are brought up in extended family arrangements, a common form of child care in many non-Western societies, which extend beyond the nuclear family, including relatives and close friends of the child's family.[103] They are thus not eligible for intercountry adoption according to the standards of the UNCRC and the Hague Convention. However, the Western myth of a 'global orphan crisis' leads many adopters and adoption agencies to queue up to save a child. Our false perception of a plight of millions of orphans feeds into the demand for children from poor countries and subsequently to illegal practices by locals to obtain them.

Second, adopters and adoption agencies must acknowledge their powerful role as consumers in the adoption market and the significance of their money in the intercountry adoption system. They must be aware that they constitute the demand side of the adoption market, whose desire for 'the right child' to love/save exerts a pull on the children from poor countries and that their money creates the motivation to illegally obtain them. Only then is an open and honest discussion about the intercountry adoption system possible, in which narratives of 'love', 'fate' and 'rescue' do not obscure the economics at play in international adoptions or legitimize and give meaning to any irregularities which might have occurred during the adoption process.

102 See Chapter III, section 5.3.
103 See Chapter III, section 4.1.

References

Books and Journal Articles

M. Ainsworth and D. Filmer (2006). "Inequalities in Children's Schooling: AIDS, Orphanhood, Poverty, and Gender." World Development, 34, 6, 1099-1128.

P. Alston (1994). "The Best Interests Principle: Towards a Reconciliation of Culture and Human Rights." International Journal of Law and the Family, 8, 1-25.

P. Alston and B. Gimour-Walsh (1996). "The Best Interests of the Child, Towards a Synthesis of Children's Right and Cultural Values." UNICEF, Innocenti Studies.

P. Alston and S. Parker (1992). "Children, Rights and The Law." Oxford University Press.

H. Altstein and R. J. Simon (1991). "Intercountry adoption: A multinational perspective." Praeger, New York.

A. An-Na'Im (1994). "Cultural Transformation and Normative Consensus on the Best Interests of the Child." International Journal of Law and the Family, 8, 62-81.

A. Anagnost (2000). "Scenes of Misrecognition: Maternal Citizenship in the Age of Transnational Adoption." Positions: East Asia cultures critique, 8, 2, 389-421.

A. Anagnost (2004). "Maternal Labor in a Transnational Circuit." In J. S. Taylor et al. (eds), "Consuming Motherhood." Rutgers University Press, New Brunswick, 139-167.

I. Andersson (2006). "Bloem van China, Dochter in Nederland." Free Musketeers, Woerden.

I. Andersson (2009). "Dochters van China, Zusjes in Nederland." Free Musketeers, Zoetermeer.

A. Ansah-Koi (2006). "Care of orphans: Fostering interventions for children whose parents die of AIDS in Ghana." Families in Society: The Journal of Contemporary Social Services, 87, 4, 555-564.

R. P. Bach (1986). "Gekaufte Kinder, Babyhandel mit der Dritten Welt." Rowohlt, Hamburg.

R. P. Bach (1988). “Daten und soziale Hintergründe der Adoption von Kindern aus der Dritten Welt. Eine Untersuchung der Gemeinsamen Zentralen Adoptionsstelle der vier norddeutschen Bundesländer in Hamburg.” Zentralblatt für Jugendrecht, 75, 328-333.

R. P. Bach (2002). “Internationaler Kinderhandel aus der Sicht des Aufnahmelandes Bundesrepublik Deutschland.” In K. Holm and U. Schulz (eds) “Kindheit in Armut weltweit.” Leske & Budrich, Opladen, 241-252.

A. Bainham (2003). “International adoption from Romania - why the moratorium should not be ended.” Child and Family Law Quarterly, 15, 3, 223-236.

N. C. Baker (1978). “Baby Selling: The Scandal of Black-Market Adoption.” The Vanguard Press, New York.

G. Bakker (2008). “Het Adoptieboek, Stap voor Stap, Stress Tijdens de Adoptie Periode.” Uitgeverij Aspekt, Soesterberg.

G. Barak (1995). “Media, Process, and the Social Construction of Crime: Studies in Newsmaking Criminology.” Garland, New York.

G. Barak (1998). “Integrating criminologies.” Allyn and Bacon, Boston.

E. Bartholet (1993). “Family Bonds. Adoption and the Politics of Parenting.” Houghton Mifflin, Boston.

E. Bartholet (2007). “International Adoption: Thoughts on the Human Rights Issue.” Buffalo Human Rights Law Review, 13, 151-203.

E. Bartholet (2007). “International Adoption: The Child’s Story.” Georgia State University Law Review, 24, 333-379.

E. Bartholet and D. M. Smolin (2012). “The Debate.” In J. L. Gibbons and K. Smith Rotabi (eds), “Intercountry Adoption: Policies, Practices, and Outcomes.” Ashgate, Farnham, 232-251.

Z. Bauman (2001). “The Individualized Society.” Polity Press, Cambridge.

U. Beck (2002). “Individualization: Institutionalized Individualism and Its Social and Political Consequences.” Sage, London.

U. Beck and E. Beck-Gernsheim (1995). "The Normal Chaos of Love." Polity Press, Cambridge.

U. Beck, et al. (1994). "Reflexive Modernization: Politics, Tradition and Aesthetics in the Modern Social Order." Stanford University Press.

R. Behrentin (ed) (2017). "Handbuch Adoptionsrecht." C. H. Beck, Muenchen.

V. L. Bengtson (2001). "The Burgess Award Lecture: Beyond the Nuclear Family: The Increasing Importance of Multigenerational Bond." Journal of Marriage and Family, 63, 1, 1-16.

S. Besson (2007). "Enforcing the Child's Right to know her Origins: Contrasting Approaches nnder the Convention on the Rights of the Child and the European Convention on Human Rights." International Journal of Law, Policy, and the Family, 21, 137-159.

D. Berger (1995). "Improving the Safety and Efficiency of Foreign Adoptions: US Domestic Adoption Programs and Adoption Programs in Other Countries Provide Lessons for INS Reform." Cornell Journal of Law and Public Policy, 5, 33-65.

K. J. S. Bergquist (2009). "Operation Babylift or Baby Abduction?: Implications of the Hague Convention on the Humanitarian Evacuation and 'Rescue' of Children." International Social Work, 52, 5, 621-633.

M. Beyer (2006). "Zur Frage der ordre public-Widrigkeit ausländischer Adoptionsentscheidungen wegen unzureichender Elterneignungs- und Kindeswohlprüfung." Das Jugendamt, 8, 329-332.

J. Bhabha (2004). "Moving Babies: Globalization, Markets and Transnational Adoption." The Fletcher Forum of World Affairs, 28, Summer, 181-198.

R. Bhaskaran and M. Balwant (2011). "Surviving the Streets: A Census of Street Children in Delhi." Institute for Human Development and Save the Children.

H. Bianchi (1956). "Position and Subject-Matter of Criminology: Inquiry Concerning Theoretical Criminology." North Holland, Amsterdam.

H. Bienentreu und M. Busch (2003). "Stiefkind- und Verwandtenadoptionen im Recht der internationalen Adoptionsvermittlung." Das Jugendamt, 6, 273-278.

H. Bienentreu (2008). "Grenzüberschreitende Adoptionen – Eine Bestandsaufnahme." Das Jugendamt, 2, 57-62.

H. Bienentreu (2017). "Einzelne Fragestellungen der internationalen Adoptionsvermittlung." In R. Behrentin (ed) "Handbuch für Adoptionen." C.H. Beck, München, 51-70.

S. M. Bisignaro (1994). "Intercountry Adoption Today and the Implications of the 1993 Hague Convention on Tomorrow." Dickinson Journal of International Law, 13, 1, 123-149.

M. Black (1955). "XII.—Metaphor." Proceedings of the Aristotelian Society, 55, 1, 273-294.

H. E. Bogard (1991). "Who are the Orphans?: Defining Orphan Status and the Need for an International Convention on Intercountry Adoption." Emory International Law Review, 5, 571-616.

P. Bos (2007). "Once a Mother: Relinquishment and Adoption From the Perspective of Unmarried Mothers in South India." Ph.D. thesis, University of Amsterdam.

E. Boucher (2014). "Empire's Children: Child Emigration, Welfare, and the Decline of the British World, 1869-1967." Cambridge University Press.

J. Braithwaite (1984). "Corporate Crime in the Pharmaceutical Industry." Routledge, London.

M. Breuning (2013). "Samaritans, Family Builders, and the Politics of Intercountry Adoption." International Studies Perspectives, 14, 4, 417-435.

M. Breuning and J. Ishiyama (2009). "The Politics of Intercountry Adoption: Explaining Variation in the Legal Requirements of Sub-Saharan African Countries." Perspectives on Politics 7, 1, 89-101.

L. Briggs (2003). "Mother, Child, Race, Nation: The Visual Iconography of Rescue and the Politics of Transnational and Transracial Adoption." Gender & History, 15, 2, 179-200.

E. Briscoe (2009). "Comment, The Hague Convention on Protection of Children and Co-operation in Respect of Intercountry Adoption: Are Its Benefits Overshadowed by Its Shortcomings?" Journal of the American Academy of Matrimonial Lawyers, 22, 437-460.

B. Broad (2007). "Kinship Care: Providing Positive and Safe Care for Children Living Away from Home." Save the Children UK.

P. Brooks (1992). "Reading for the Plot: Design and Intention in Narrative." Harvard University Press, London.

A. D. Brown et al. (2008). "Making Sense of Sensemaking Narratives." Human Relations, 61, 8, 1035-1062.

T. W. Brown and J. Roby (2016). "Exploitation of Intercoumtry Adoption: Toward a Common Understanding and Action." Adoption Quarterly, 19, 2, 63-80.

A. Cardarello (2009). "The Movement of the Mothers of the Courthouse Square: "Legal Child Trafficking," Adoption and Poverty in Brazil." Journal of Latin American and Caribbean Anthropology, 14, 1, 140-161.

A. Cardarello (2012). "The Right to have a Family: 'Legal Trafficking of Children', Adoption and Birth Control in Brazil." Anthropology & Medicine, 19, 2, 225-240.

L. K. Carlberg (2007). "The Agreement Between The United States and Vietnam Regarding Cooperation on the Adoption of Children: A More Effective and Efficient Solution to the Implementation of the Hague Convention on Intercountry Adoption or Just Another Road to Nowhere Paved With Good Intentions?" Indiana International & Comparative Law Review, 17, 1, 119-153.

R. R. Carlson (1994). "The Emerging Law of Introductory Adoptions: An Analysis of the Hague Conference on Intercountry Adoption." Tulsa Law Journal, 30, 243-304.

D. Carr (1986). "Time, narrative, and history." Indiana University Press, Bloomington.

J. L. Carro (1994). "Regulation of Intercountry Adoption: Can the Abuses Come to an End?" Hastings International & Comparative Law Review, 18, 121-155.

K. A. Chadwick (1999). "The Politics and Economics of Intercountry Adoption in Eastern Europe." Journal of International Legal Studies, 5, 113-144.

K. E. Cheney (2014). "'Giving Children a Better Life?' Reconsidering Social Reproduction, Humanitarianism and Development in Intercountry Adoption." The European Journal of Development Research, 26, 2, 247-263.

K. E. Cheney (2014). "Conflicting Protectionist and Participation Models of Children's Rights: Their Consequences for Uganda's Orphans and Vulnerable Children." In A. Twum-Danso and N. Ansell (eds) "Children's Lives in an Era of Children's Rights: The Progress of the Convention on the Rights of the Child in Africa." Routledge, New York, 17-33.

K. E. Cheney (2016). "Preventing Exploitation, Promoting Equity: Findings from the International Forum on Intercountry Adoption and Global Surrogacy 2014." Adoption & Fostering, 40, 1, 6-19.

K. E. Cheney and K. S. Rotabi (2015). "Addicted to Orphans: How the Global Orphan Industrial Complex Jeopardizes Local Child Protection Systems." In C. Harker et al. (eds) "Conflict, Violence and Peace." Springer, Singapore, 89-107.

W. C. Chirwa (2002). "Social Exclusion and Inclusion: Challenges to Orphan Care in Malawi." Nordic Journal of African Studies, 11, 1, 93-113.

J. A. M. Cobbah (1987). "African Values and the Human Rights Debate: An African Perspective." Human Rights Quarterly, 9, 309-331.

L. E. Cohen and M. Felson (1979). "Social Change and Crime Rate Trends: A Routine Activity Approach." American Sociological Review, 44, 4, 588-608.

S. Cohen (1993). "Human Rights and Crimes of the State: The Culture of Denial." Australian and New Zealand Journal of Criminology, 26, 2, 97-115.

I. Curry-Sumner and M. Vonk (2008). "Ontwikkelingen op het gebied van internationale adoptie." Familie- en Jeugdrecht, 108.

M. A. Davis (2011). "Intercountry Adoption Flows from Africa to the U.S.: A Fifth Wave of Intercountry Adoptions?" International Migration Review, 45, 4, 784-811.

S. Detrick (1999). "A Commentary on the United Nations Convention on the Rights of the Child." Martinus Nijhoff Publishers, Leiden.

J. Dickens (2002). "The paradox of inter-country adoption: analysing Romania's experience as a sending country." International Journal of Social Welfare, 11, 1, 76-83.

J. Dickens (2009). "Social policy approaches to intercountry adoption." International Social Work, 52, 5, 595-607.

S. Dillon (2003). "Making Legal Regimes for Intercountry Adoption Reflect Human Rights Principles: Transforming the United Nations Convention on the Rights of the Child with the Hague Convention on Intercountry Adoption." Boston University International Law Journal, 21, 179-257.

A. Dohle (2008). "Inside Story of an Adoption Scandal." Cumberland Law Review, 39, 131-185.

P. Dorhout (2008). "Baby Donna, waar ging het mis?" Familie- en Jeugdrecht 2008, 70.

S. K. Dorow (2002). ""China 'R' Us?": Care, Consumption, and Transnationally Adopted Children." In D. T. Cook (ed), "Symbolic Childhood." Peter Lang, New York, 149-168.

F. J. Earls (2011). "The child as a citizen." SAGE, Los Angeles.

B. Ehrenreich and A. R. Hochschild (2002). "Global Woman: Nannies, Maids, and Sex Workers in the New Economy." Henry Holt, New York.

D. L. Eng (2006). "Political Economics of Passion: Transnational Adoption and Global Woman, Roundtable on Global Woman." Studies in Gender and Sexuality, 7, 1, 49–59.

A. Eser und J. Eisele (2014). "§ 236 Kinderhandel." In Eser et al. (eds), "Strafgesetzbuch Kommentar." 29. Edition, C.H. Beck, München.

H. A. Faberman (1975). "A Criminogenic Market Structure: the Automobile Industry." The Sociological Quarterly, 16, 438-457.

M. Farid (2012). "International Adoption: The Economics of the Baby Industry." Whittier Journal of Child and Family Advocacy, 12, 1, 81-103.

T. Feltes and R. Hofmann (2016). "Transnational Organised Crime and its Impacts on States and Societies." In P. Hauck and S. Peterke (eds), "International Law and Transnational Organised Crime." Oxford University Press, 42-62.

A. Fleisher (2003). "The Decline of Domestic Adoption: Intercountry Adoption as a Response to Local Adoption Laws and Proposals to Foster Domestic Adoption." Review of Law and Women's Studies, 13, 1, 171-197.

B. Flyvbjerg (2006). "Five Misunderstanding about Case-Study Research." Qualitative Inquiry, 12, 2, 219-245.

C. Fonseca (2009). "Transnational Connections and Dissenting Views, The Evolution of Child Placement Policies in Brazil." In D. Marre and L. Briggs (eds), "International Adoption: Global Inequalities and the Circulation of Children." New York University Press, 154-173.

M. Freundlich (2000). "Adoption and Ethics: The Market Forces in Adoption." Child Welfare League of America, Washington DC.

C. Friesendorf (2007). "Pathologies of Security Governance: Efforts Against Human Trafficking in Europe." Security Dialogue, 38, 3, 379-402.

P. Fronek and D. Cuthbert (2012). "History Repeating...Disaster-Related Intercountry Adoption and the Psychosocial Care of Children." Social Policy and Society, 11, 3, 429-442.

M. Gaedicke (2009). "Wunschkind, Geschichte einer Adoption." Hoffmann und Campe, Hamburg.

A. Gallagher, T. (2010). "The International Law of Human Trafficking." Cambridge University Press.

C. Geertz (1973). "The Interpretation of Cultures." Basic Books, New York.

Gibbons and K. Smith Rotabi (eds) (2012). "Intercountry Adoption: Policies, Practices, and Outcomes." Ashgate, Farnham.

A. Giddens (1991). "Modernity and Self-Identity, Self and Society in the Late Modern Age." Stanford University Press.

A. Giddens (1999). "Risk and Responsibility." The Modern Law Review, 62, 1, 1-10.

E. Goffman (2009). "Stigma: Notes on the Management of Spoiled Identity." Simon and Schuster, London.

M. G. González and E. Wesseling (2013). "The Stories We Adopt By: Tracing" The Red Thread" in Contemporary Adoption Narratives." The Lion and the Unicorn, 37, 3, 257-276.

M. Goodwin (2010). "Baby Markets: Money and the New Politics of Creating Families." Cambridge University Press.

N. B. Graff (2000). "Intercountry Adoption and the Convention on the Rights of the Child: Can the Free Market in Children be Controlled?" Syracuse Journal of International Law & Commerce, 27, 405-430.

R. Göpfert (1999). "Der jüdische Kindertransport von Deutschland nach England 1938/39. Geschichte und Erinnerung." Campus, Frankfurt.

C. Grünewald and T. Nunez (2017). "Zentralbehörden nach dem HAÜ und deren Aufgaben." In R. Behrentin (ed), "Handbuch Adoptionsrecht." C.H. Beck, München, 76-87.

M. Guelich (2006). "Adoptionen aus dem nicht-europäischen Ausland." BIS-Verlag der Carl-von-Ossietzky-Universität.

E. T. Hall (1989). "Beyond Culture." Anchor Books, New York.

A. Harrison (2007). "Globalization and Poverty." University of Chicago Press.

V. Haskins and M. D. Jacobs (2002). "Stolen Generation and Vanishing Indians: The Removal of Indigenous Children as a Weapon of War in the United States and Australia." In J. Marten (ed), "Children and War: A historical anthropology." New York University Press, 227-241.

P. Hayes (2011). "The Legality and Ethics of Independent Intercountry Adoption Under the Hague Convention." International Journal of Law, Policy and the Family, 25, 3, 288-317.

J. de Heer (2016). "Wet opneming buitenlandse pleegkinderen ter adoptie. "In M. J. C. Koens and A. P. M. J. Vonken (eds) "Personen- en familierecht, Tekst & Commentaar." Wolters Kluwer, Deventer, 2697-2741.

J. de Heer (2016). “Besluit opneming buitenlandse kinderen ter adoptie. “In M. J. C. Koens and A. P. M. J. Vonken (eds) “Personen- en familierecht, Tekst & Commentaar.” Wolters Kluwer, Deventer, 2743-2752.

J. de Heer (2016). “Besluit in zake het onderzoek naar buitenlandse contacten van aspirant-adoptiefouders. “In M. J. C. Koens and A. P. M. J. Vonken (eds) “Personen- en familierecht, Tekst & Commentaar.” Wolters Kluwer, Deventer, 2753-2756.

Heiderhoff (2017). “Art. 23 EGBGB.” In Bamberger et al. (eds) “Kommentar zum Bürgerlichen Gesetzbuch.” 45. edition, C.H Beck, München.

T. Helms (2018). “Art. 23 EGBGB.” In Säcker et al. (eds) “Münchner Kommentar zum Bürgerlichen Gesetzbuch.” 7. Edition, C.H. Beck, München.

S. Henry and M. M. Lanier (1998). “The Prism of Crime: Arguments for an Integrated Definition of Crime.” Justice Quarterly, 15, 4, 609-627.

S. Henry and M. Lanier (2001). “The Prism of Crime: Toward an Integrated Definition of Crime.” In S. Henry and M. Lanier (eds), “What is Crime? Controversies over the Nature of Crime and What to Do about It.” Rowman & Littlefield Publishers, Lanham, 227-243.

J. R Herbert and I. S. Rubin (2012). “Qualitative Interviewing, The Art of Hearing Data.” (3rd ed.) Sage, London.

K. Herrmann (2010). “Reestablishing the humanitarian approach to adoption: The legal and social change necessary to end the commodification of children.” Family Law Quarterly, 44, 3, 409-428.

L. Hertsig (2005). “Adoptie van buitenlandse kinderen door Nederlandse adoptiefouders.” Familie- en Jeugdrecht, 9.

S. Hoelgaard (1998). “Cultural Determinants of Adoption Policy: A Colombian Case Study.” International Journal of Law, Policy and the Family, 12, 202-241.

D. M. Hoffman (2011). “Saving children, saving Haiti? Child vulnerability and narratives of the nation.” Childhood, 1-14.

R. Högbacka (2008). “The quest for a child of one’s own: Parents, markets and transnational adoption.” Journal of Comparative Family Studies, 39, 3, 311-330.

R. Högbacka (2011). "Exclusivity and Inclusivity in Transnational Adoption." In R. Jallinoja and E. D. Widmer (eds), "Families and Kinship in Contemporary Europe: Rules and Practices of Relatedness." Palgrave MacMillan, Basingstoke, 129–144.

R. A. C. Hoksbergen et al. (1979). "Adoptie van Kinderen Uit Verre Landen." Van Loghum Slaterus, Deventer.

R. A. C. Hoksbergen (1991). "Intercountry Adoption Coming of Age in The Netherlands: Basic Issues, Trends, and Developments." In H. Altstein and R. J. Simon (eds), "Intercountry Adoption: A Multinational Perspective." Praeger, New York, 141-158.

R. A. C. Hoksbergen (1998). "Changes in Motivation for Adoption, Value Orientations and Behavior in Three Generations of Adoptive Parents." Adoption Quarterly, 2, 2, 37-55.

R. A. C. Hoksbergen (2011). "Kinderen die niet konden blijven: zestig jaar adoptie in beeld." Aspekt, Soesterberg.

I. Holla (2005). "Mijn droom van een kind, Waargebeurd verhaal van een vrouw die haar wens om moeder te worden niet opgeeft." Uitgeverij Sirene, Amsterdam.

M. I. Holt (1992). "The Orphan Trains: Placing Out In America." University Of Nebraska Press, Lincoln and London.

M. Homans (2013). "The Imprint of Another Life: Adoption Narratives and Human Possibility." University of Michigan Press, Ann Arbor.

S. Howell (2006). "The Kinning of Foreigners: Transnational Adoption in a Global Perspective." Berghahn Books, New York.

T. Hübinette (2006). "From Orphan Trains to Babylifts: Colonial Trafficking, Empire Building, and Social Engineering." In J. J. Trenka et al. (eds), "Outsiders Within: Writing on Transracial Adoption." South End Press, Cambridge, 139-149.

I. Iusmen (2013). "The EU and International Adoption from Romania." International Journal of Law, Policy and the Family, 27, 1, 1-27.

M. D. Jacobs (2014). "A Generation Removed, The Fostering & Adoption of Indigenous Children in the Postwar World." University of Nebraska Press, Lincoln and London.

W. Jacoby, et al. (2009). "Success in Slow Motion: The Europeanization of Romanian Child Policy." Review of International Organizations, 4, 111-133.

K. Johnson (2002). "Politics of International and Domestic Adoption in China." Law & Society Review, 36, 2, 379-396.

K. A. Johnson (2004). "Wanting a Daugther, Needing a Son." Yeong & Yeong, Minneapolis.

K. Joyce (2013). "The Child Catchers: Rescue, Trafficking, and the New Gospel of Adoption." Public Affairs, New York.

F. Juffer et al. (2008). "Adoptie als interventie (1)." Kind en Adolescent, 29, 1, 17-30.

F. Juffer et al. (2008). "Adoptie als interventie (2)." Kind en Adolescent, 29, 1, 31-49.

E. B. Kapstein (2003). "The baby trade." Foreign Affairs, 82, 6, 115-125.

L. M. Katz (1995). "A Modest Proposal? The Convention on Protection of Children and Cooperation in Respect of Intercountry Adoption." Emory International Law Review, 9, 283-328.

B. Katz Rothman (2004). "Motherhood under Capitalism." In J. S. Taylor et al. (eds), "Consuming Motherhood." Rutgers University Press, London, 19-30.

B. Katz Rothman (2004). "Caught in the Current." In J. S. Taylor et al. (eds), "Consuming Motherhood." Rutgers University Press, London, 279-288.

H. C. Kennard (1993). "Curtailing the Sale and Trafficking of Children: A Discussion of the Hague Conference Convention in Respect to Intercountry Adoptions." University of Pennsylvania Journal of International Business Law, 14, 4, 623-649.

C. E. Kimball (2005). "Barriers to the Successful Implementation of the Hague Convention on Protection of Children and Co-Operation in Respect of Intercountry Adoption." Denver Journal of International Law and Policy, 33, 4, 561-584.

S. King (2008). "Challenging Monohumanism: An Argument for Changing the Way We Think About Intercountry Adoption." Michigan Journal of International Law, 30, 413-470.

S. King (2012). "Owning Laura Silsby's Shame: How the Haitian Child Trafficking Scheme Embodies the Western Disregard for the Integrity of Poor Families." Harvard Human Rights Journal, 25, 1-47.

E. L. Kleiman (1996). "Caring for our own: why American adoption law and policy must change." Columbia Journal of Law and Social Problems, 30, 327-368.

M. Kline (1992). "Child Welfare Law, "Best Interests of the Child" Ideology, and First Nations." Osgoode Hall Law Journal, 30, 2, 376-425.

M. J. C. Koens and A. P. M. J. Vonken (eds) (2016). "Personen- en familierecht, Tekst & Commentaar." Wolters Kluwer, Deventer.

M. & I. Koolen (2009). "Moeders mooiste, vaders trots, Een bijzonder verslag van de lange weg naar adoptie." The house of books, Antwerpen.

I. Kopytoff (1986). "The Cultural Biography of Things: Commoditization as Process." In A. Appadurai (ed), "The Social Life of Things: Commodities in Cultural Perspective." Cambridge University Press, New York, 64-91.

I. Kopytoff (2004). "Commoditizing Kinship in America." In J. S. Taylor et al. (ed), "Consuming Motherhood." Rutgers University Press, London, 271-279.

P. Kunkel et al. (2006). "Adoptionsverfahren und Verwaltungsrecht." In H. Paulitz and R. P. Bach (eds), "Adoption: Positionen, Impulse, Perspektiven." (2nd edition) C. H. Beck, München, 181-241.

S. Kvale (2007). "Doing Interviews." In U. Flick (ed) "The SAGE Qualitative Research Kit." Sage, London.

I. Lammerant and M. Hofstetter (2008). "Adoption: at what cost? For an ethical responsibility of receiving countries in intercountry adoption." Terre des hommes, Lausanne.

D. C. Lane, et al. (2008). "Time Crime: The Transnational Organization of Art and Antiquities Theft." Journal of Contemporary Criminal Justice, 24, 3, 243-262.

G. Lange (2003). "Auslandsadoption: Wissenswertes zu einem aktuellen Thema." Schulz-Kirchner, Idstein.

L. L. Layne (1999). "The Child as Gift: New Directions in the Study of Euro-American Gift Exchange." In L. L. Layne (ed), "Transformative Motherhood: On Giving and Getting in a Consumer Culture." New York University Press, 1-27.

L. L. Layne (1999). "Transformative Motherhood: On Giving and Getting in a Consumer Culture." New York University Press, New York.

F. L. Leeuw and H. Schmeets (2016). "Empirical Legal Research, A Guidance Book for Lawyers, Legislators and Regulators." Edward Elgar, Cheltenham.

Y.-C. Lemke Muniz de Faria (2003). "Germany's 'Brown Babies' Must Be Helped! Will You?: US Adoption Plans for Afro-German Children, 1950-1955." Callaloo 26, 2, 342-362.

W. N. Leonard and M. G. Weber (1970). "Automakers and Dealers: A Study of Criminogenic Market Forces." Law & Society Review, 4, 407-424.

G. Lilienthal (1993). "Der "Lebensborn e.V." Ein Instrument nationalsozialistischer Rassenpolitik." Fischer, Frankfurt.

R. Lilith (2000). "Buying a Wife but Saving a Child: A Deconstruction of Popular Rhetoric and Legal Analysis of Mail-Order Brides and Intercountry Adoptions." Buffalo Women's Law Journal, 9, 225-262.

J. M. Lippold (1995). "Transnational Adoption from an American Perspective: The Need for Universal Uniformity." Case Western Reserve Journal of International Law, 27, 465-503.

M. Liu (1994). "International Adoptions: An Overview." Temple International & Comparative Law Journal, 8, 187-213.

E. Loibl (2016). "Crime in the Intercountry Adoption Industry: Towards a Broader Definition of Child Trafficking." in R. Moerland and H. Nelen, "Denialism and Human Rights." Intersentia, Cambridge, 119-134.

E. Loibl (forthcoming). "Trafficking in Children for Adoption Purposes: A Criminological Analysis of the Illegal Adoption Market." In J.A. Winterdyk and J. Jones (eds), "The Palgrave International Handbook of Human Trafficking." Palgrave Macmillan, London.

E. Loibl and C. Tribowski (2017). "Internationaler Adoptionskinderhandel und die Kontrollfunktionen von Landesjugendämtern: Kritik und Reformen in vier Thesen." Das Jugendamt, 2, 58.

K. Lovelock (2000). "Intercountry Adoptions as a Migratory Practice: A Comparative Analysis of Intercountry Adoption and Immigration Policy and Practice in the United States, Canada and New Zealand in the Post W.W. II Period. "International Migration Review, 34, 3, 907-949.

N. Luo and D. M. Smolin (2004). "Intercountry Adoption and China: Emerging Questions and Developing Chinese Perspectives." Cumberland Law Review, 35, 3, 597-618.

T. O. Mahmoud and C. Trebesch (2010). "The economics of human trafficking and labour migration: Micro-evidence from Eastern Europe." Journal of Comparative Economics, 38, 2, 173-188.

Majer (2015). "Die Anerkennung ausländischer Adoptionsentscheidungen." Neue Zeitschrift für Familienrecht, 1138-1142.

S. Marijnen and J. Doomernik (2015). "Baby Migration." AEMI Journal, 13, 133-149.

G. Marquez (2000). "Transnational Adoption: The Creation and Ill Effects of an International Black Market Baby Trade." Journal of Juvenile Law, 21, 25-39.

D. Marre and L. Briggs (2009). "International Adoption: Global Inequalities and the Circulation of Children." New York University Press.

M. S. Marx (2007). "Whose best interests does it really serve? A critical examination of Romania's recent self-serving international adoption policies." Emory International Law Review, 21, 373-412.

T. Maskew (2004). "Child Trafficking and Intercountry Adoption: The Cambodian Experience." Cumberland Law Review, 35, 619-638.

R. Matthews and A. M. Matthews (1986). "Infertility and involuntary childlessness: The transition to nonparenthood." Journal of Marriage and the Family, 48, 641-649.

D. Matza and G. M. Sykes (1961). "Juvenile Delinquency and Subterranean Values." American Journal of Sociology, 26, 712-719.

R. May (1975). "Values, myths, and symbols." The American journal of psychiatry, 132, 703-706.

D. McGoldrick (1991). "The United Nations Convention on the Rights of the Child." International Journal of Law and the Family, 5, 132-169.

L. McKinney (2007). "International Adoption and the Hague Convention: Does Implementation of the Convention Protect the Best Interests of Children?" Whittier Journal of Child & Family Advocacy, 6, 2, 361-412.

M. A. C. McMillan (1993). "International Adoption: A Step Towards a Uniform Process." Pace International Law Review, 5, 1, 137-164.

J. McQuillan et al. (2003). "Frustrated Fertility: Infertility and Psychological Distress Among Women." Journal of Marriage and Family, 65, 1007-1018.

P. J. Meier (2008). "Small commodities: How child traffickers exploit children and families in intercountry adoption and what the United States must do to stop them." The Journal of Gender, Race & Justice, 12, 185-224.

P. J. Meier and Z. Xiaole (2008). "Sold into Adoption: The Hunan Baby Trafficking Scandal Exposes Vulnerabilities in the Chinese Adoptions to the United States." Cumberland Law Review, 39, 1, 87-130.

A. Mens (2009). "Interlandelijke adoptie, Is deelbemiddeling in verdragslanden mogelijk?" Familie- en Jeugdrecht, 67.

R. K. Merton (1938). "Social Structure and Anomie." American Sociological Review, 3, 672-682.

B. D. Mezmur (2008). "Intercountry Adoption as a Measure of Last Resort in Africa: Advancing the Rights of a Child rather than a Right to a Child." International Journal of Human Rights, 6, 10, 82-103.

A. Michaela (2014). "Neun Monate Sommer, Tagebuch einer Adoptionsschwangerschaft in Kenia." Tausendschlau Olga Bien, Munich.

R. J. Michalowski (1985). "Order, Law, and Crime: An Introduction to Criminology." Random House, New York.

D. Michielsen (2005). "Dochters van ver, belevenissen van een adoptiemoeder." Archipel, Amsterdam.

F. Miro (2014). "Routine Activity Theory." In J. M. Miller (ed), "The Encyclopedia of Theoretical Criminology." Whiley Blackwell, Oxford, 735-742.

J. S. Modell (1994). "Kinship with Strangers: Adoption and Interpretations of Kinship in American Culture." University of California Press, Berkley.

J. S. Modell (1999). "Freely Given - Open Adoption and the Rhetoric of the Gift." In L. L. Layne (ed), "Transformative Motherhood: On Giving and Getting in a Consumer Culture." New York University Press, 29-64.

R. Monasch and J. T. Boerma (2004). "Orphanhood and childcare patterns in sub-Saharan Africa: an analysis of national surveys from 40 countries." AIDS, 18, 2, 55-65.

M. L. Needleman and C. Needleman (1979). "Organizational Crime: Two Models of Criminogenesis." The Sociological Quarterly, 20, 517-528.

H. Nelen and L. Ritzen (2013). "How They Still Try to get Away With It: Crime in the Dutch Real Estate Sector Before and After The Crisis." In S. Will et al. (eds), "How They Got Away With It: White Collar Criminals and The Financial Meltdown." Colombia University Press, New York, 223-245.

C. A. Nelson et al. (2007). "Cognitive Recovery in Socially Deprived Young Children: The Bucharest Early Intervention Project." Science, 318, 1937-1940.

K. P. Nelson (2006). "Shopping for children in the international marketplace." In J. J. Trenka et al. (eds), "Outsiders Within: Writing on transracial adoption." South End Press, Cambridge, 89-104.

L.B. Nielsen (2010). "The Need for Multi-Method Approaches in Empirical Legal Research." In P. Cane and H.M. Kritzer (eds) "The Oxford Handbook of Empirical Legal Research." Oxford University Press, Oxford.

B. C. Oude Breuil, et al. (2011). "Human Trafficking Revisited: Legal, Enforcement and Ethnographic Narratives on Sex Trafficking to Western Europe." Trends in Organized Crime, 14, 1, 30-46.

S. S. Padilla (1993). "Adoption of Alien Orphan Children: How United States Immigration Law Defines Family." Georgetown Immigration Law Journal, 7, 817-844.

A. Palm-Hensel (2008). "Stella, Unser Stern aus Indien, Die Geschichte einer glücklichen Adoption." Kleine Schritte, Trier.

R. Parker (2010). "Uprooted: The shipment of poor children to Canada, 1867-1917." Policy Press, Bristol.

S. Parker (1994). "The Best Interests of the Child - Principles and Problems." International Journal of Law and the Family, 8, 26-41.

N. Passas (1990). "Anomie and Corporate Deviance." Contemporary Crises, 14, 157-178.

N. Passas (1999). "Globalization, Criminogenic Asymmetries and Economic Crime." European Journal of Law Reform, 1, 4, 399-423.

N. Passas (2000). "Global Anomie, Dysnomie, and Economic Crime: Hidden Consequences of Neoliberalism and Globalization in Russia and Around the World." Social Justice, 27, 2, 16-44.

N. Passas (2002). "Cross-border crime and the interface between legal and illegal actors." In P. van Duyne et al. (eds.), "Upperworld and underworl in cross-border crime." Wolf Legal Publishers, Nijmegen, 11-41.

N. Passas and B. Bowman Proulx (2011). "Overview of Crimes and Antiquities." In S. Manacorda and D. Chappell (eds), "Crime in the Art and Antiquities World, Illegal Trafficking in Cultural Property." Springer, New York, 51-67.

H. Paulitz et al. (eds) (2000). "Adoption: Positionen, Impulse, Perspektiven." C. H. Beck, München.

H. Paulitz, et al. (2000). "Interstaatliche Adoptionsvermittlungsstellen in Deutschland, Vermittlungspraxis, Kinderhandel." In H. Paulitz et al. (eds), "Adoption: Positionen, Impulse, Perspektiven." C. H. Beck, München, 185-231.

H. Paulitz et al. (2006). "Adoption: Positionen, Impulse, Perspektiven." (2nd edition) C. H. Beck, München.

T. L. Perry (1998). "Transracial and International Adoption: Mothers, Hierarchy, Race, and Feminist Legal Theory." Yale Journal of Law and Feminism, 10, 101-164.

J. Peters (2014). "Kindheit im Strafrecht: Eine Untersuchung des materiellen Strafrechts mit besonderem Schwerpunkt auf dem Kind als Opfer und Täter." Herbert Utz Verlag, München.

P. Pfund (1993). "Hague Convention on Intercountry Adoption." Women Lawyers Journal, 79, 3, 6-8.

P. Pfund (1994). "Intercountry Adoption: The 1993 Hague Convention: Its Purpose, Implementation, and Promise." Family Law Quarterly, 28, 1, 53-88.

M. Pöcker (2018). "BGB § 1741 Zulässigkeit der Annahme." In Bamberger et al. (eds) "Kommentar zum Bürgerlichen Gesetzbuch." 46. edition, C.H Beck, München.

D. E. Polkinghorne (1991). "Narrative and Self-Concept." Journal of Narrative and Life History, 1, 2 & 3, 135-153.

E. Poncz (2007). "China's Proposed International Adoption Law: The Likely Impact on Single U.S. Citizens Seeking to Adopt from China and the Available Alternatives." Harvard International Law Journal, 48, 74-82.

R. Post (2007). "Romania–for Export Only: The Untold Story of the Romanian 'Orphans'." Netherlands: EuroComment Diffusion.

R. Post (2008). "De perverse effecten van het Haags Adoptieverdrag." Justitiële Verkenningen, 7, 25-37.

M. Quartly et al. (2013). "The Market In Babies: Stories of Australian Adoption." Monash University Publishing, Clayton.

M. J. Radin (1996). "Contested commodities." Harvard University Press.

J. Raymond (2002). "The New UN Trafficking Protocol." Women's Studies International Forum, 25, 5, 491-502.

J. Reinhardt (2006). "Gewollt oder nicht? Die private Adoption von Kindern aus dem Ausland." Zeitschrift für Rechtspolitik, 8, 241-272.

J. Reinhardt (2006). "Die Praxis der Anerkennung ausländischer Adoptionsentscheidungen aus der Sicht der Adoptionsvermittlung." Das Jugendamt, 8, 325-329.

J. Reinhardt (2017). "Adoptionsvermittlungsgesetz." 4. edition, Nomos Bundesrecht Erläuterungen.

R. Reinhardt (2017). "§ 2a AdVermiG." In J. Reinhardt (ed) "Adoptionsvermittlungsgesetz." 4. edition, Nomos Bundesrecht, Erläuterungen.

R. Reinhardt (2017). "§ 3 AdVermiG." In J. Reinhardt (ed) "Adoptionsvermittlungsgesetz." 4. edition, Nomos Bundesrecht, Erläuterungen.

R. Reinhardt (2017). "§ 4 AdVermiG." In J. Reinhardt (ed) "Adoptionsvermittlungsgesetz." 4. edition, Nomos Bundesrecht, Erläuterungen.

R. Reinhardt (2017). "§ 5 AdVermiG." In J. Reinhardt (ed) "Adoptionsvermittlungsgesetz." 4. edition, Nomos Bundesrecht, Erläuterungen.

R. Reinhardt (2017). "§ 11 AdVermiG." In J. Reinhardt (ed) "Adoptionsvermittlungsgesetz." 4. edition, Nomos Bundesrecht, Erläuterungen.

R. Rios-Kohn (1998). "Intercountry adoption: An international perspective on the practice and standards." Adoption Quarterly, 1, 4, 3-32.

R. Rios-Kohn (1998). "The Convention on the Rights of the Child: Progress and Challenges." Georgetown Journal on Fighting Poverty, 5, 2, 139-160.

J. L. Roby (2004). "Understanding Sending Country's Traditions and Policies In International Adoptions: Avoiding Legal and Cultural Pitfalls." Journal of Law & Family Studies, 6, 2, 303-322.

J. L. Roby (2007). "From Rhetoric to Best Practice: Children's Rights in Intercountry Adoption." Children's Legal Rights Journal, 27, 3, 48-71.

J. L. Roby and J. Ife (2009). "Human rights, politics and intercountry adoption: An examination of two sending countries." International Social Work, 52, 5, 661-671.

J. L. Roby and T. Maskew (2012). "Human Rights Considerations in Intercountry Adoption: The Children and Families of Cambodia and Marshall Islands." In Gibbons and K. Smith

Rotabi (eds), "Intercountry Adoption: Policies, Practices, and Outcomes." Ashgate, Farnham, 55-66.

K. S. Rotabi and N. F. Bromfield (2012). "The Decline in Intercountry Adoptions and New Practices of Global Surrogacy: Global Exploitation and Human Rights Concerns." Affilia: Journal of Women and Social Work, 27, 2, 129-141.

K. S. Rotabi and J. L. Gibbons (2011). "Does the Hague Convention on Intercountry Adoption Adequately Protect Orphaned and Vulnerable Children and Their Families?" Journal of Child and Family Studies, 21, 1, 106-119.

S. W. E. Rutten and K. J. Saarloos (2007). "De erkenning van de kafala in het IPR en het vreemdelingenrecht." Tijdschrift voor Familie- en Jeugdrecht, 125.

B. Rwezaura (1994). "The Concept of the Child's Best Interests in the Changing Economic and Social Context of Sub-Saharan Africa." International Journal of Law and the Family, 8, 82-114.

E. J. Ryan (2006). "For the Best Interests of the Children: Why the Hague Convention of Intercountry Adoption Needs to Go Farther, as Evidenced by Implementation in Romania and the United States." Boston College International and Comparative Law Review, 29, 2, 353-383.

E. W. Said (1979). "Orientalism." Vintage, New York.

E. W. Said (1993). "Culture and imperialism." Vintage, New York.

M. J. Sandel (2012). "What money can't buy, The Moral Limits of Markets." Farrar, Straus and Giroux, New York.

M. Sandelowski (1991). "Telling Stories: Narrative Approaches in Qualitative Research." Image: Journal of Nursing Scholarship, 23, 3, 161-166.

M. Sandelowski (1993). "With Child in Mind: Studies of the Personal Encounter With Infertility." University of Pennsylvania Press.

R. Scherman et al. (2016). "Global commercial surrogacy and international adoption: parallels and differences." Adoption & Fostering, 40, 1, 20-35.

S. Schlauss (2007). "Die Anerkennung von Auslandsadoptionen in der vormundschaftsgerichtlichen Praxis." FamRZ, 20, 1699-1702.

C. Schoenmaker et al. (2014). "From infancy to young adulthood: The Leiden longitudinal adoption study." Leiden University, available at https://openaccess.leidenuniv.nl/bitstream/handle/1887/25253/04.pdf?sequence=8 (last accessed on 07.08.2018).

B. Schulz (2005). "Tochter Indira, Die Geschichte einer Adoption aus Indien." Ullstein, Berlin.

T. Schumann (2012). "Faith - Adoption in Kenia, Ein Vater erzählt." Norderstedt, Books on Demand.

T. Schumann (2014). "Hope - Adoption in Haiti, Ein Vater erzählt." Books on Demand, Norderstedt.

H. Schwendinger and J. Schwendinger (1970). "Defenders of Order or Guardians of Human Rights?" Issues in Criminology, 5, 2, 123-157.

S. A. Scritchfield (1995). "The social construction of infertility: From private matter to social concern." In J. Best (ed), "Images of issues: Typifying contemporary social problems." (2nd edition) Aldine de Gruyter, Hawthorne, 131-146.

T. E. G. Seedorf (2006). "Interlandelijke adoptie; jurisprudentie voor aspirant-adoptiefouders zonder beginseltoestemming?" Familie- en Jeugdrecht, 2, 17.

P. Selman (2002). "Intercountry adoption in the new millennium; the "quiet migration" revisited." Population Research and Policy Review, 21, 3, 205-225.

P. Selman (2006). "Trends in intercountry adoption: Analysis of data from 20 receiving countries, 1998-2004." Journal of Population Research, 23, 2, 183-204.

P. Selman (2009). "The rise and fall of intercountry adoption in the 21st century." International Social Work, 52, 5, 575-594.

P. Selman (2011). "Intercountry adoption after the Haiti earthquake: Rescue or robbery?" Adoption & Fostering, 35, 4, 41-49.

P. Selman (2012). "The Global Decline of Intercountry Adoption: What Lies Ahead?" Social Policy and Society, 11, 03, 381-397.

P. Selman (2016). "The Rise and Fall of Intercountry Adoption in the 21st Century: Global Trends from 2001 to 2010." In J. L. Gibbons and K. S. Rotabi (eds), "Intercountry Adoption: Policies, Practices and Outcomes." Ashgate, Farnham, 2-27.

A. Shankar et al. (2009). "Identity, Consumption and Narratives of Socialization." Marketing Theory, 9, 1, 75-94.

R. Shome (2011). ""Global Motherhood": The Transnational Intimacies of White Femininity." Critical Studies in Media Communication, 28, 5, 388-406.

J. B. Singer (1992). "The Privatization of Family Law." Wisconsin Law Review, 1444-1567.

K. Smith Rotabi (2012). "Fraud in Intercountry Adoption: Child Sales and Abduction in Vietnam, Cambodia, and Guatemala." In J. L. Gibbons and K. Smith Rotabi, "Intercountry Adoption: Policies, Practices, and Outcomes." Ashgate, Farnham, 67-66.

D. M. Smolin (2004). "Intercountry adoption as child trafficking." Valparasio University Law Review, 39, 2, 281-325.

D. M. Smolin (2004). "The Two Faces of Intercountry Adoption: The Significance of the Indian Adoption Scandals." Seton Hall Law Review, 35, 403-493.

D. M. Smolin (2006). "Child Laundering: How the Intercountry Adoption System Legitimizes and Incentivizes the Practices of Buying, Trafficking, Kidnapping, and Stealing Children." The Wayne Law Review, 52, 1, 113-200.

D. M. Smolin (2007). "Child laundering as exploitation: applying anti-trafficking norms to intercountry adoption under the coming Hague regime." Vermont Law Review, 32, 1-55.

D. M. Smolin (2007). "Intercountry Adoption and Poverty: A Human Rights Analysis." Capital University Law Review, 36, 413-453.

D. M. Smolin (2010). "Child Laundering and the Hague Convention on Intercountry Adoption: The Future and Past of Intercountry Adoption." University of Louisville Law Review, 48, 441-498.

D. M. Smolin (2011). "The Missing Girls of China: Population, Policy, Culture, Gender, Abortion, Abandonment, and Adoption in East-Asian Perspective." available at https://works.bepress.com/david_smolin/9/ (last accessed on 19.07.2018).

D. M. Smolin (2013). "The Corrupting Influence of the United States on a Vulnerable Intercountry Adoption System: A Guide for Stakeholders, Hague and Non-Hague Nations, NGOs, and Concerned Parties." Utah Law Review, Journal of Law & Family Studies, 15, 81-209.

R. Snow and K. Covell (2006). "Adoption and the Best Interests of the Child: The Dilemma of Cultural Interpretations." The International Journal of Children's Rights, 14, 109-117.

B. R. Sonnen (2017). "§ 236 Kinderhandel." In U. Kindhäuser et al. (eds) "Nomoskommentar zum Strafgesetzbuch." 5. edition, Nomos, Baden-Baden.

D. L. Spar (2006). "The baby business: How money, science, and politics drive the commerce of conception." Harvard Business School Press, Boston.

T. Steiger (2002). "Das neue Recht der internationalen Adoption und Adoptionsvermittlung: Einführung-Erläuterung-Materialien." Bundesanzeiger-Verlag.

J. G. Stein (2001). "A Call to End Baby Selling: Why the Hague Convention on Intercountry Adoption Should be Modified to Include the Consent Provisions of the Uniform Adoption Act." Thomas Jefferson Law Review, 24, 39-82.

B. H. Stuy (2014). "Open Secret: Cash and Coercion in China's International Adoption Programm." Cumberland Law Review, 44, 3, 355-422.

E. H. Sutherland (1940). "White-Collar Criminality." American Sociological Review, 5, 1, 1-12.

G. M. Sykes and D. Matza (1957). "Techniques of Neutralization: A Theory of Delinquency." American Sociological Review, 22, 664-670.

V. Tadler (2010). "Child Trafficking for the Purpose of Inter-country Adoption, With a Case Study on Guatemala." PhD Thesis, University of Vienna.

P. Tappan (1947). "Who is the Criminal?" American Sociological Review, 12, 1, 96-102.

J. S. Taylor et al. (eds) (2004). "Consuming Motherhood." Rutgers University Press, New Brunswick.

Te Velde E. et al. (2012). "The effect of postponement of first motherhood on permanent involuntary childlessness and total fertility rate in six European countries since the 1970s." Human Reproduction, 27, 4, 1179-1183.

M. R. Textor (1991). "International Adoption in West Germany: A Private Affair." In H. Altstein and R. J. Simon (eds), "Intercountry Adoption: A Multinational Perspective." Praeger, New York, 109-126.

N. S. Thompson (2004). "Hague is Enough?: A Call for More Protective, Uniform Law Guiding International Adoptions." Wisconsin International Law Journal, 22, 2, 441-469.

J. J. Trenka et al. (eds) (2006). "Outsiders Within: Writing on transracial adoption." South End Press.

C. Tribowski (2015). "Kinder kauft man nicht. Die politische Ökonomie von Auslandsadoptionen in Deutschland und den Vereinigten Staaten von Amerika." PhD Thesis, Universität zu Köln.

J. Triseliotis (2000). "Intercountry adoption: Global trade or global gift?" Adoption and Fostering, 24, 2, 45-54.

M. Ulrich and A. Weatherall (2000). "Motherhood and Infertility: Viewing Motherhood through the Lens of Infertility." Feminism & Psychology, 10, 3, 323-336.

G. Van Bueren (1998). "The International Law on the Rights of the Child." Martinus Nijhoff Publishers, The Hague.

P. P. J. Van der Meij (2016). "Commentaar op art. 278 Sr." In C.P.M. Cleiren et al. (eds), "Strafrecht, Tekst en Commentaar." Wolters Kluwer, Deventer.

M. K. Van der Staaij (2004). "Liefs uit Bogotá, Ons verhaal over adoptie." Uitgeverij Boekencentrum, Zoetermeer.

M. Van IJzendoorn et al. (2008). "IQ of Children Growing Up in Children's Homes: A Meta-Analysis on IQ Delays in Orphanages." Merrill-Palmer Quarterly, 54, 3, 341–366.

M. Van Leeuwen (1999). "The Politics of Adoptions Across Borders: Whose Interests are Served? (A Look at the Emerging Market of Infants from China)." Pacific Rim Law & Policy Journal, 8, 1, 189-218.

Van den Dries et al. (2009). "Fostering security? A meta-analysis of attachment in adopted children." Children and Youth Services Review, 31, 3, 410-421.

R. Vollmer (2004). "Mein Kind aus der Fremde." Rowohlt, Reinbek bei Hamburg,

A. von Hirsch and N. Jareborg (1991). "Gauging Criminal Harm: A Living-Standard Analysis." Oxford Journal of Legal Studies, 11, 1, 1-38.

B. Wacker et al. (2006). "Interstaatliche Adoptionsvermittlungsstellen in Deutschland, Vermittlungspraxis, Kinderhandel." In H. Paulitz et al. (eds), "Adoption: Positionen, Impulse, Perspektiven." (2nd edition) C. H. Beck, München, 327-344.

L. D. Wardle (2005). "Parentlessness: Adoption Problems, Paradigms, Policies, and Parameters." Whittier Journal of Child & Family Advocacy, 4, 2, 323-373.

L. Webley (2010). "Qualitative Approaches to Empirical Legal Research." In P. Cane and H.M. Kritzer (eds), "The Oxford Handbook of Empirical Legal Research." Oxford University Press, Oxford, 926-950.

E. M. Weinwurm (1976). "Mutter-Kind-Interaktion bei asiatischen Kindern in Deutschen Adoptivfamilien. Begleitende Verhaltsbeobachtung von Terre des Hommes Kindern hinsichtlich des Deprivationssyndroms." PhD thesis, Universität Münster.

W. Weitzel (2006). "Anerkennung einer Auslandsadoption nach deutschem Recht trotz schwerwiegender Mängel der ausländischen Entscheidung?" Das Jugendamt, 8, 333-336.

W. Weitzel et al. (2006). "Rechtslage und Verfahrensgang bei Auslandsadoptionen." In H. Paulitz et al. (eds) "Adoption: Positionen, Impulse, Perspektiven." C. H. Beck, München, 271-326.

W. Weitzel (2013). "Adoptionswirkungsgesetz." 2. edition, Nomos Bundesrecht Erläuterungen.

J. A. Welsh et al. (2008). "Ready to Adopt: Characteristics and Expectations of Preadoptive Families Pursuing International Adoptions." Adoption Quarterly, 11, 3, 176-203.

Wenzek-Grüneberg (2005). "Das Regenbogenkind, Die Geschichte einer Auslandsadoption." Books on Demand, Norderstedt.

E. Wesseling (ed) (2016). "The Child Savage, 1890-2010: From Comics to Games." Routledge, New York.

Wieck-Noodt (2017). "§ 236 Kinderhandel." In W. Joecks et al. (eds) "Münchener Kommentar zum StGB." 3. edition, C.H. Beck, München.

I. Willing et al. (2012). "Review of sociological literature on intercountry adoption." Social Policy and Society, 11, 03, 465-479.

A. Wilson (2012). "Intimacy: A Useful Category of Transnational Analysis." In G. Pratt (ed), "The Global and the Intimate: Feminism in Our Time." Columbia University Press, New York, 31-56.

J. Winterdyk et al. (2010). "Introduction to Special Issue: Human Trafficking." European Journal of Criminology, 7, 1, 5-10.

R. Worthington (2009). "The Road to Parentless Children is Paved with Good Intentions: How the Hague Convention and recent Intercountry Adoption Rules are Affecting Potential Parents and the Best Interests of Children." Duke Journal of Comparative & International Law, 19, 559-586.

G. Wuttke (1996). "Ein Kind um jeden Preis? Eine Studie zum Adoptionskinderhandel." Terre des hommes Deutschland e.V., Osnabrück.

R. Yin (2003). "Case Study Research: Design and Methods." Sage, London.

A. Young (2012). "Developments in intercountry adoption - From humanitarian aid to market-driven policy and beyond." Adoption and Fostering, 36, 2, 67-78.

C. H. Zeanah et al. (2005). "Attachment in Institutionalized and Community Children in Romania." Child Development, 76, 5, 1015-1028.

V. A. Zelizer (1981). "The Price and Value of Children: The Case of Children's Insurance." American Journal of Sociology, 86, 5, 1036-1056.

V. A. Zelizer (1985). "Pricing the Priceless Child: The Changing Social Value of Children." Princeton University Press.

Media Reports

ABC documentary (2010). "Fly Away Home." 15.03.2010, available at https://documentaries.io/film/fly-away-home/ (last accessed on 14.07.2018).

Aravamudan, G. (2017) "Child trafficking, 'manufactured orphans': The dark underbelly of inter-country adoption in India." Firstpost, 03.09.2017, available at http://www.firstpost.com/india/child-trafficking-manufactured-orphans-the-dark-underbelly-of-inter-country-adoption-in-india-4000837.html (last accessed on 14.07.2018).

P. Black and A. Eshchenko (2014). "Russia enacts anti-gay adoption ban." CNN, 14.2.2014, available at https://edition.cnn.com/2014/02/13/world/europe/russia-same-sex-marriage-adoption-ban/index.html (last accessed on 25.07.2018).

S. Bom and H. Van Zon (2017). "Sri Lanka erkent handel in sjoemelbaby's." Algemeen Dagblad, 20.09.2017, available at https://www.ad.nl/buitenland/sri-lanka-erkent-handel-in-sjoemelbaby-s~a5687b0c/ (last accessed on 14.07.2018).

K. Bos (2016). "Baby? Dat gaat niet meer gebeuren. "NRC, 14.05.2016, available at https://www.nrc.nl/nieuws/2016/05/14/baby-dat-gaat-niet-meer-gebeuren-1620805-a325064 (last accessed on 14.07.2018).

Brandpunt (2011). "Kinderen te koop." 11.01.2011, available at https://brandpunt.kro-ncrv.nl/brandpunt/broadcasts/segment/68/ (last accessed on 14.07.2018).

Brandpunt (2013). "Kinderen te koop." 24.02.2013, available at https://www.npo.nl/brandpunt/04-08-2017/WO_KRO_795126 (last accessed on 14.07.2018).

Brandpunt (2015). "De Bulgaarse adoptie-industrie." 18.10.2015, available at https://www.npo.nl/brandpunt-reporter/18-10-2015/KN_1673048 (last accessed on 14,07.2018).

B. Demick (2009). "Some Chinese parents say their babies were stolen for adoption." LA Times, 20.09.2009, available at http://articles.latimes.com/2009/sep/20Hoksbergen (2000)./world/fg-china-adopt20 (last accessed on 14.07.2018).

B. Demick (2010). "A family in China made babies their business." LA Times, 24.01.2010, available at http://articles.latimes.com/2010/jan/24/world/la-fg-china-adopt24-2010jan24 (last accessed on 14.07.2018).

B. Demick (2009). "A young Chinese girl pines for her twin." LA Times, 20.09.2009, available at http://articles.latimes.com/2009/sep/20/world/fg-china-twins20 (last accessed on 14.07.2018).

P. S. Goodman (2006). "Stealing Babies for Adoption." Washington Post, 12.03.2006, available at http://www.washingtonpost.com/wp-dyn/content/article/2006/03/11/AR2006 031100942.html (last accessed on 14.07.2018).

E. J. Graff (2008). "The lie we love." Foreign Policy, November/December, 58-66, available at http://www.brandeis.edu/investigate/adoption/docs/FPFinalTheLieWeLove.pdf (last accessed on 23.07.2018).

E. J. Graff (2010). "The Baby Business." Democracy Journal, Summer No. 17, available at https://democracyjournal.org/magazine/17/the-baby-business/ (last accessed on 31.07.2018).

E. J. Graff (2010). "Anatomy of an Adoption Crisis." Foreign Policy, 12.09.2010, available at https://foreignpolicy.com/2010/09/12/anatomy-of-an-adoption-crisis/ (last accessed on 23.07.2018).

E. J. Graff (2014). "They Steal Babies, Don't They?" Pacific Standard, 24.11.2014, available at https://psmag.com/news/they-steal-babies-dont-they-international-adoption-schuster-institute-95027 (last accessed on 14.07.2018).

F. Harm (2014). "Wat doet China in Nederland?" NOS, 22.03.2014, available at https://nos.nl/artikel/626521-wat-doet-china-in-nederland.html (last accessed on 14.07.2018).

M. Holz (2005). "Die Situation in den Herkunftsländern, Auslandsadoptionen bei terre des hommes Deutschland e.V." Forum für Politik, Gesellschaft und Kultur, Nr. 247, 35-38, available at https://www.forum.lu/wp-content/uploads/2015/11/5308_247_248_Holz.pdf (last accessed on 04.08.2018).

K. Joyce (2016). "The Trouble With the Christian Adoption Movement." New Republic, 11.01.2016, available at https://newrepublic.com/article/127311/trouble-christian-adoption-movement (last accessed on 15.07.2018).

F. Klenk. "Die verlorene Tochter." Zeit Online, 08.01.2008, available at http://www.zeit.de/online/2008/02/adoptionen/komplettansicht (last accessed on 15.07.2018).

M. Lipman (2012). "What's behind the Russian Adoption Ban?" The New Yorker, 21.12.2012, available at https://www.newyorker.com/news/news-desk/whats-behind-the-russian-adoption-ban (last accessed on 15.07.2018).

B. Loyd (2008). "China's lost children." ABC News, 12.05.2008, available at http://abc-news.go.com/International/story?id=4774224 (last accessed on 15.07.2018).

Netwerk (2009). "Directeur adoptieorganisatie stapt op na intimidatie Netwerk." 18.08.2009, available at https://www.youtube.com/watch?v=rKzle3UQFoI (last accessed on 19.07.2018).

Netwerk (2007). "India eist gestolen adoptiekind uit Nederland terug." 22.05.2007, available at http://www.uitzendinggemist.net/aflevering/86316/Netwerk_eo_Ncrv.html (last accessed on 19.07.0218).

I. Pronk (2008). "Weer ophef rond adoptie uit China." Trouw, 11.03.2998, available at https://www.trouw.nl/home/weer-ophef-rond-adoptie-uit-china~af540f5a/) (last accessed on 19.07.0218).

A. Rexer (2009). "Adoptionsskandal um äthiopische Kinder: Zwei äthiopische Kinder Mütter klagen an." Profil, 20.01.2009, available at http://www.profil.at/home/adoption-sskandal-kinder-zwei-kinder-muetter-231092 (last accessed on 19.07.2018).

M. Roessingh (2009). "Weer adoptieschandaal China." Trouw, 03.07.2009, available at https://www.trouw.nl/home/weer-adoptieschandaal-china~a0620ea0/ (last accessed on 19.07.2018).

G. Taubert and B. Reuter (2010). "Der verlorene Sohn." TAZ, 15.05.2010, available at http://www.taz.de/!435381/ (last accessed on 19.07.2018).

P. Tumwebaze (2017). "Govt lifts ban on foreign adoption of Rwandan kids." The New Times, 21.09.2017, available at http://www.newtimes.co.rw/section/read/220313/ (last accessed on 03.08.2018).

Zembla (2017). "Adoptiebedrog." 17.05.2017, available at https://www.npo.nl/zembla/17-05-2017/VARA_101382216 (last accessed on 19.07.2018).

Zembla (2017). "Adoptiebedrog (2)." 20.09.2017, available at http://www.uitzendinggemist.net/aflevering/406615/Zembla.html (last accessed on 19.07.2018).

Zemble (2018). "Adoptiebedrog (3)." 12.07.2018, availabe at https://tvblik.nl/zembla/adoptiebedrog-iii (last accessed on 06.08.2018).

International Legal Instruments

Council of Europe, European Convention for the Protection of Human Rights and Fundamental Freedoms, as amended by Protocols Nos. 11 and 14, 4 November 1950, ETS 5.

Council of Europe, European Convention on the Adoption of Children, 24 April 1967, ETS 058.

Council of Europe, Council of Europe Convention on Action Against Trafficking in Human Beings, 16 May 2005, CETS 197.

Council of Europe, European Convention on the Adoption of Children (revised), 27 November 2008, ETS No.202.

Council of the European Union, Directive 2011/36/EU of the European Parliament and of the Council of 5 April 2011 on preventing and combating trafficking in human beings and protecting its victims, and replacing Council Framework Decision 2002/629/JHA, 15 April 2011, OJ L. 101/1-101/11; 15.4.2011, 2011/36/EU.

UN Economic and Social Council (ECOSOC), Supplementary Convention on the Abolition of Slavery, the Slave Trade, and Institutions and Practices Similar to Slavery, 7 September 1956, Res. 608(XXI).

UN General Assembly, Universal Declaration of Human Rights, 10 December 1948, 217 A (III).

UN General Assembly, Declaration of the Rights of the Child, 20 November 1959, A/RES/1386(XIV).

UN General Assembly, International Covenant on Civil and Political Rights, 16 December 1966, United Nations, Treaty Series, vol. 999, p. 171.

UN General Assembly, Declaration on Social and Legal Principles relating to the Protection and Welfare of Children, with Special Reference to Foster Placement and Adoption Nationally and Internationally, 3 December 1986, A/RES/41/85.

UN General Assembly, Convention on the Rights of the Child, 20 November 1989, Res. 44/25.

UN General Assembly, Protocol to Prevent, Suppress and Punish Trafficking in Persons, Especially Women and Children, Supplementing the United Nations Convention against Transnational Organized Crime, 15 November 2000, A/RES/55/25.

UN General Assembly, Optional Protocol to the Convention on the Rights of the Child on the Sale of Children, Child Prostitution and Child Pornography, 16 March 2001, A/RES/54/263.

UN General Assembly, International Convention for the Protection of All Persons from Enforced Disappearance, 20 December 2006, A/RES/61/177.

The Hague Conference on Private International Law, The Hague Convention on Jurisdiction, Applicable Law and Recognition of Decrees Relating to Adoption, 15 November 1965.

The Hague Conference on Private International Law, The Hague Convention on the Protection of Children and Co-operation in Respect of Intercountry Adoption, 29 May 1993, 32 I.L.M. 1134.

National Legal Instruments

Germany

Adoptionsübereinkommens-Ausführungsgesetz vom 5. November 2001 (BGBl. I S. 2950), das zuletzt durch Artikel 4 Absatz 17 des Gesetzes vom 17. Dezember 2006 (BGBl. I S. 3171) geändert worden ist.

Aufenthaltsverordnung vom 25. November 2004 (BGBl. I S. 2945), die zuletzt durch Artikel 1 der Verordnung vom 1. August 2017 (BGBl. I S. 3066) geändert worden ist.

Bürgerliches Gesetzbuch in der Fassung der Bekanntmachung vom 2. Januar 2002 (BGBl. I S. 42, 2909; 2003 I S. 738), das zuletzt durch Artikel 1 des Gesetzes vom 20. Juli 2017 (BGBl. I S. 2787) geändert worden ist.

Einführungsgesetz zum Bürgerlichen Gesetzbuche in der Fassung der Bekanntmachung vom 21. September 1994 (BGBl. I S. 2494; 1997 I S. 1061), das zuletzt durch Artikel 2 Absatz 4 des Gesetzes vom 20. Juli 2017 (BGBl. I S. 2787) geändert worden ist.

Gesetz zur Regelung von Rechtsfragen auf dem Gebiet der internationalen Adoption und zur Weiterentwicklung des Adoptionsvermittlungsrechts vom 5. November 2001 (BGBl. I S. 2950).

Gesetz über Wirkungen der Annahme als Kind nach ausländischem Recht vom 5.11.2001 (BGBl. I S. 2950, 2953), zuletzt durch Artikel 22 des Gesetzes vom 20.11.2015 (BGBl. I S. 2010) geändert worden ist.

Gesetz über die Vermittlung der Annahme als Kind und über das Verbot der Vermittlung von Ersatzmüttern in der Fassung der Bekanntmachung vom 22. Dezember 2001 (BGBl. 2002 I S. 354), das zuletzt durch Artikel 21 des Gesetzes vom 20. November 2015 (BGBl. I S. 2010) geändert worden ist.

Gesetz über das Verfahren in Familiensachen und in den Angelegenheiten der freiwilligen Gerichtsbarkeit vom 17. Dezember 2008 (BGBl. I S. 2586, 2587), das zuletzt durch Artikel 7 des Gesetzes vom 20. Juli 2017 (BGBl. I S. 2780) geändert worden ist.

Gesetz über den Aufenthalt, die Erwerbstätigkeit und die Integration von Ausländern im Bundesgebiet, in der Fassung der Bekanntmachung vom 25.02.2008 (BGBl. I S. 162), das zuletzt durch Gesetz vom 08.03.2018 (BGBl. I S. 342) geändert worden ist.

Gesetz über die Angelegenheiten der freiwilligen Gerichtsbarkeit vom 12. März 2009 (BGBl. I S. 470), außer Kraft getreten am 01.09.2009 aufgrund Gesetzes vom 17. Dezember 2008 (BGBl. I S. 2586).

Strafgesetzbuch in der Fassung der Bekanntmachung vom 13. November 1998 (BGBl. I S. 3322), das zuletzt durch Artikel 1 des Gesetzes vom 30. Oktober 2017 (BGBl. I S. 3618) geändert worden ist.

Staatsangehörigkeitsgesetz in der im Bundesgesetzblatt Teil III, Gliederungsnummer 102-1, veröffentlichten bereinigten Fassung, das zuletzt durch Artikel 3 des Gesetzes vom 11. Oktober 2016 (BGBl. I S. 2218) geändert worden ist.

The Netherlands

Besluit van 4 juli 1989, houdende vaststelling van het Besluit opneming buitenlandse pleegkinderen en wijziging van het Uitvoeringsbesluit Kinderbescherming (Besluit opneming buitenlandse kinderen ter adoptie), Stb. 1989, 262, zoals laatstelijk gewijzigd op 25 october 2011, Stb. 2011, 480.

Besluit van 18 mei 1995, houdende vaststelling van maatstaven die bij het in artikel 7a, eerste lid, van de Wet opneming buitenlandse pleegkinderen bedoelde onderzoek dienen te worden gehanteerd (Besluit inzake het onderzoek naar buitenlandse contacten van aspirant-adoptiefouders), Stb. 1995, 275, zoals laatstelijk gewijzigd op 30 juni 1998, Stb. 1998, 388.

Besluit van 13 maart 2000, houdende regels ter uitvoering van artikel 24a van de Wet opneming buitenlandse kinderen ter adoptie alsmede inwerkingtreding van dat artikel (Besluit klachtencommissie vergunninghouders interlandelijke adoptie), Stb. 2000,120, zoals laatstelijk gewijzigd op 5 juli 2005, Stb. 2005, 435.

Besluit van 23 november 2000 tot uitvoering van de Vreemdelingenwet 2000 (Vreemdelingenbesluit 2000), Stb. 2000, 497, zoals laatstelijk gewijzigd op 9 April 2018, Stb. 2018, 107.

Besluit van de Staatsecretaris van Justitie en Veiligheid van 21 juni 2018, nummer WBV 2018/4, houdende wijziging van de Vreemdelingencirculaire 2000, Stcrt. 2018, 36067.

Burgerlijk Wetboek Boek 1, inwerkingtreding 1 januari 1970, zoals laatstelijk gewijzigd met Stb. 2017, 245.

Burgerlijk Wetboek Boek 10, inwerkingtreding 1 januari 2012, Stb. 2011, 272, zoals laatstelijk gewijzigd met Stb. 2016, 290.

Protocol van 25 september 1995 inzake onderzoek naar buitenlandse contacten en deelbemiddeling bij interlandelijke adoptie, 25 september 1995/Nr. 516934/95/PJR.

Regeling van 17 augustus 1998 (Regeling gegevens buitenlandse betrekkingen vergunninghouder interlandelijke adoptie), Stcrt. 1998, 171.

Regeling van 17 augustus 1998 (Regeling aanvraag vergunning bemiddeling interlandelijke adoptie), Stcrt. 1998, 171.

Richtlijnen van 10 november 2000 (Richtlijnen opneming buitenlandse kinderen ter adoptie), Stcrt. 2000, 234, zoals laatstelijk gewijzigd op 29 september 2010, Stb. 2010, 15596.

Rijkswet van 19 december 1984, houdende vaststelling van nieuwe, algemene bepalingen omtrent het Nederlanderschap ter vervanging van de Wet van 12 december 1892, Stb. 268 op het Nederlanderschap en het ingezetenschap, zoals laatstelijk gewijzigd op1 maart 2017, Stb. 2017, 52, 53.

Rijkswet van 26 september 1991, houdende het stellen van regelen betreffende de verstrekking van reisdocumenten, Stb. 1991, 498, zoals laatstelijk gewijzigd op 17 mei 2017, Stb. 2017, 217.

Wetboek van Strafrecht van 30 januari 1886, zoals laatstelijk gewijzigd met Stb. 2017, 317.

Wet van 8 december 1988, houdende regelen inzake de opneming in Nederland van buitenlandse pleegkinderen met het oog op adoptie (Wet opneming buitenlandse kinderen ter adoptie), Stb. 1988, 566, zoals laatstelijk gewijzigd op 15 november 2014, Stb. 2014, 442.

Wet van 14 mei 1998 inzake de uitvoering van het op 29 mei 1993 tot stand gekomen verdrag inzake de bescherming van kinderen en samenwerking op het gebied van interlandelijke adoptie en, in verband daarmee, wijziging van de Wet opneming buitenlandse pleegkinderen en enige andere wetten (Uitvoeringswet Verdrag inzake de bescherming van kinderen en de samenwerking op het gebied van de interlandelijke adoptie), Stb. 1998, 302, zoals laatstelijk gewijzigd op 13 juli 2016, Stb. 2016, 290.

Judgments

Germany

Amtsgericht Düsseldorf, 02.10.2009, 98 XVI 16/08.

Amtsgericht Hamm, 17.04.2006, XVI 44/05.

Amtsgericht Hamm, 30.12.2009, XVI 82/09.

Amtsgericht Hamm, 26.04.2010, XV I 15/09.

Bundesgerichtshof, 14.12.1988, Iva ZR 231/87.

Bundesgerichtshof, 10.12.2014, XII ZB 463/13.

Bundesverwaltungsgerichtshof, 26.10.2010, 1 C 16.09.

Oberlandesgericht Brandenburg, 28.04.2016, 15 UF 184/15.

Oberlandesgericht Celle, 12.10.2011, 17 UF 98/11.

Oberlandesgericht Celle, 20.02.2017, 17 UF 131/16.

Oberlandesgericht Düsseldorf, 22.06.2010, 25 Wx 15/10.

Oberlandesgericht Düsseldorf, 18.01.2011, I-25 Wx 28/10.

Oberlandesgericht Düsseldorf, 27.07.2012, II-1 UF 82/11.

Oberlandesgericht Frankfurt, 19.01.2012, 20 W 93/11.

Oberlandesgericht Hamm, 21.01.2014, 11 UF 127/13.

Oberlandesgericht Hamm, 17/02.2015, 11 UF 222/14.

Oberlandesgericht Köln, 29.05.2009, 16 Wx 16/09.

Oberlandesgericht Köln, 29.05.2009, 16 Wx 251/08.

Oberverwaltungsgericht Hamburg, 18.10.2006, 4 Bs 224/06.

Oberlandesgericht Karlsruhe, 08.07.2010, 11 Wx 113/09.

Landesgericht Potsdam, 11.11.2010, 5 T 447/10.

Verwaltungsgerichtshof Hamburg, 12.7.2006, 13 E 2153/06.

Verwaltungsgerichtshof München, 24.4.2010, M 18 K 09.4652.

The Netherlands

Gerechtshof Amsterdam, 16.03.2000, 439/99, ECLI:NL:GHAMS:2000:AA5155.

Gerechtshof Amsterdam, 05.04.2004, 1288/2003, ECLI:NL:GHAMS:2004:AP0522.

Gerechtshof Arnhem, 12.11.2002, 21-21000804-02, ECLI:NL:GHARN:2002:AF4646.

Gerechtshof Arnhem, 18.11.2002, 21-000799-02, ECLI:NL:GHARN:2002:AF4646.

Gerechtshof Leeuwarden, 08.04.2010, 24-002474-09, ECLI:NL:GHLEE:2010:BM0459.

Gerechtshof Leeuwarden, 02.12.2010, 200.069.042, ECLI:NL:GHLEE:2010:BP0604.

Gerechtshof 's-Gravenhage, 13.04.2011, 200.068.764-01, ECLI:NL:GHSGR:2011:BQ2937.

Gerechtshof 's-Gravenhage, 21.03.2012, 200.093.249-01, ECLI:NL:GHSGR:2012:BX0126.

Gerechtshof Zwolle-Lelystad, 07.400176-09, ECLI:NL:RBZLY:2011:BR1615.

Hoge Raad, 01.12.2000, HR2000AA8715, ECLI:NL:PHR:2000:AA8715.

Hoge Raad, 20.11. 2001, 00460/00, ECLI:NL:HR:2001:AB2809.

Hoge Raad, 31.01.2012, S 10/01756, ECLI:NL:HR:2012:BU6921.

Hoge Raad, 19.04.2013, 12/02994, ECLI:NL:HR:2013:BZ7948.

Rechtbank Almelo, 21.06.2005, 08/005134-04, ECLI:NL:RBALM:2005:AT7809.

Rechtbank Den Haag, 05.07.2017, C/09/515621 / HA ZA 16-893, ECLI:NL:RBDHA:2017:6711.

Rechtbank Leeuwarden, 29.09.2009, 17/885166-09 VEV, ECLI:NL:RBLEE:2009:BJ8794.

Rechtbank Middelburg, 08.11.2012, 12/708507-08[P], ECLI:NL:RBMID:2012:BY2679.

Rechtbank Oost-Brabant, 12.02.2013, 01-810049-07 en 01-810050-07, ECLI:NL:RBOBR:2013:BZ1186.

Rechtbank Rotterdam, 26.09.2011, 371367/F2RK11-133 en 370919/F2RK11-104, ECLI:NL:RBROT:2011:BT8220.

Rechtbank Rotterdam, 20.03 2012, 10/700428-11, ECLI:NL:RBROT:2012:BV9975.

Rechtbank Rotterdam, 20.03.2012, 10/700429-11, ECLI:NL:RBROT:2012:BV9978.

Rechtbank 's-Gravenhage, 08.06.2011, 376129-FARK10-7586, ECLI:NL:RBSGR:2011:BQ8583.

Rechtbank 's-Gravenhage, 11.03.2010, 334600 / 09-2668, ECLI:NL:RBSGR:2010:BM2880.

Rechtbank Utrecht, 24.07.2002, 137028/FARK01-5441, ECLI:NL:RBUTR:2002:AN9168.

Rechtbank Utrecht, 26.10.2005, 197521/FA RK 05-3560, ECLI:NL:RBUTR:2005:AU4934.

Rechtbank Zwolle-Lelystad, 12.01.2006, 107814/FARK05-1186, ECLI:NL:RBZLY:2006:AV4706.

Rechtbank Zwolle-Lelystad, 27.11.2008, 151779 / JZ RK 08-908, ECLI:NL:RBZLY:2008:BG5827.

Rechtbank Zwolle-Lelystad, 12.02.2010, 07.400121-08, ECLI:NL:RBZLY:2010: BL4061.

Rechtbank Zwolle-Lelystad, 16.02.2010, 07.400121-08 and 07.400120-08, ECLI:NL:RBZLY:2010:BL4062.

Rechtbank Zwolle-Lelystad, 04.03.2011, 170085 / FA RK 10-1401, ECLI:NL:RBZLY:2011:BP6936.

Rechtbank Zwolle-Lelystad, 14.07.2011, 07.400176-09, ECLI:NL:RBZLY:2011: BR1615.

ECtHR

Akin vs. The Netherlands, 01.07.1998, No. 34986/97.

Di Lazzaro vs. Italy, 10.07.1997, No. 31924/96.

Jäggi vs. Switzerland, 13.07.2007, No. 58757/00.

Odièvre vs. France, 13.02.2003, No. 42326/98.

Pini and Others vs. Romania, 22.06.2004, No. 78028/01 and 78030/01.

X, Y and Z vs. the United Kingdom, No. 21830/93.

REPORTS AND WORKING PAPERS

J. van den Braak et al. (2004). "Evaluatieonderzoek Wobka, Een evaluatieonderzoek naar de Wet opneming buitenlandse kinderen ter adoptie." WODC, Adviesbureau Van Montfoort, Woerden.

H. Bochéat et al. (2012). "Investigating the Grey Zones of Intercountry Adoption." International Social Service.

K. Boele-Woelki, et al. (2011). "Draagmoederschap en illegale opneming van kinderen." WODC, Ministerie van Veiligheid & Justitie.

L. Bosch (2016). "Promising Practice: Legal Paths to Justice in the Netherlands." In International Social Service (2016). "Responding to Illegal Adoptions: A Professional Handbook." Available at https://fiom.nl/sites/default/files/responding-to-illegal-adoptions-a-professional-handbook-iss-april-2016.pdf, 40-44.

K. Browne (2009). "The Risk of Harm to Young Children in Institutional Care." Save the Children UK.

Bundesarbeitsgemeinschaft Landesjugendaemter (2014). "Empfehlungen zur Adoptionsvermittlung - 7., neu bearbeitete Fassung." 117. Arbeitstagung der Bundesarbeitsgemeinschaft Landesjugendaemter, available at http://www.bagljae.de/downloads/120_empfehlungen-zur-adoptionsvermittlung_2014.pdf (last accessed on 21.07.2018).

Bundeszentralstelle für Auslandsadoption (2018). "Gesamtsumme - 2002-2017." Bonn (on file with author).

N. Cantwell (2003). "Intercountry Adoption. A Comment on the Number of "Adoptable" Children and the Number of Persons Seeking to Adopt Internationally." The Hague Conference on Private International Law, International Child Protection, The Judges' Newsletter, V.

N. Cantwell (2005). "Is intercountry adoption linked with trafficking for exploitation?" International Social Service, Nr. 11-12.

N. Cantwell (2014). "The Best Interests of the Child in Intercountry Adoption." UNICEF, Office of Research, Florence.

K. E. Cheney (2014). "Executive Summary of the International Forum on Intercountry Adoption and Global Surrogacy 11-13 August 2014." Working Paper No. 596, International Institute of Social Studies.

M. Dambach and C. Baglietto (2010). ""Expediting" intercountry adoptions in the aftermath of a natural disaster...preventing future harm." International Social Service.

Defence for Children International, Terre des Hommes, International Social Service (1991). "Preliminary Findings of a Joint Investigation on Independent Intercountry Adoptions." (on file with author).

Gezamenlijke vergunninghouders interlandelijke adoptie (2013). "Kwaliteitskader Vergunninghouders Interlandelijke Adoptie." 2nd version (on file with author).

R. Hodgkin and P. Newell (2007). "Implementation Handbook for the Convention on the Rights of the Child." UNICEF (3rd edition).

R. Högbacka (2014). "Intercountry Adoption, Countries of Origin, and Biological Families, Report for Thematic Area 2 International Forum on Intercountry Adoption and Global Surrogacy 11-13 August 2014." Working Paper No. 598, International Institute of Social Studies.

R. A. C. Hoksbergen (2000). "Vijftig Jaar Adoptie in Nederland, Een historisch-statistische beschouwing." Utrecht, available at http://www.vijfeeuwenmigratie.nl/sites/default/files/bronnen/VIJFTIG%20JAAR%20ADOPTIE.pdf (last accessed on 07.08.2018).

M. Holz et al. (2013). ""Wir suchen Eltern für Kinder" Die Geschichte der Adoptionsarbeit von terre des hommes." Terre des hommes e.V., Osnabrück, available at https://www.tdh.de/fileadmin/user_upload/inhalte/04_Was_wir_tun/Themen/Weitere_Themen/Ado/2013-05_Geschichte-der-Adoptionsarbeit.pdf (last accessed on 04.08.2018).

Human Rights and Equal Opportunity Commission (1997). "Report of the National Inquiry into the Separation of Aboriginal and Torres Strait Islander Children from Their Families." Sydney.

I. Hut (2009). "Bevindingen met betrekking tot Interlandelijke Adoptie t.b.v. het Algemeen Overleg Adoptie op 6 oktober 2009." 01.10.2009, available at http://poundpuplegacy.org/files/Reactie%20Ina%20HR%20Hut%20ivm%20AO%206%20okt%202009.pdf (last accessed on 15.07.2018).

Inspectie Jeugdzorg (2009). "Interlandelijke Adoptie Knelpunten in het Stelsel." Available at http://www.aoo.nl/downloads/2010-01-14-MvJ-a.pdf (last accessed on 15.07.2018).

Institut für Demoskopie Allensbach (2007). "Unfreiwillige Kinderlosigkeit." Nr. 11, available at https://www.ifd-allensbach.de/uploads/tx_reportsndocs/prd_0711.pdf (last accessed on 15.07.2018).

International Social Service (2005). "Benefits of compulsory participation of adoption accredited bodies in the receiving countries under the supervision of the Central Authorities." Geneva, Nr. 70, September.

International Social Service (2005). "In the spirit of article 29 of THC-1993, any contact between prospective adoptive parents (PAPs) and the child's parents or carer, should be prohibited until the matching decision." Geneva, Nr. 6.

International Social Service (2005). "The principle of subsidiarity and the extended family as caregivers." Geneva, Nr. 3.

International Social Service (2007). "Adoption 'on holiday'." Geneva, Nr. 1.

International Social Service (2007). "From respite care abroad... to adoption?" Geneva, Nr. 2.

International Social Service (2008). "Diversification of countries of origin and an increase in the age of adopted children against a background of inter-country adoption that continues to be tense." Geneva, Nr. 7-8.

International Social Service (2008). "Exposing myths about the number of adoptable children and the need for more precision when defining who is adoptable." Geneva, Nr. 10.

International Social Service (2013). "Are the best interests of the child always best?" Geneva, Nr. 1.

International Social Service (2014). "The concept of 'family': The challenge of protecting children in and out of families." Geneva, Nr. 187 November – December.

International Social Service (2016). "Responding to Illegal Adoptions: A Professional Handbook." Available at https://fiom.nl/sites/default/files/responding-to-illegal-adoptions-a-professional-handbook-iss-april-2016.pdf (last accessed on 03.08.2018).

N. A. Kalsbeek et al. (2008). "Report on Intercountry Adoption - "All things of value are defenceless"." Committee on Lesbian Parenthood and Intercountry Adoption, available at http://poundpuplegacy.org/files/10866_Interlandelijke-Adoptie_tcm34-137684.pdf (last accessed on 03.08.2018).

P. L. A. Ken (2007). "Children without Parental Care in the Caribbean Systems of Protection." UNICEF, available at https://www.unicef.org/easterncaribbean/cao_resources_children_without_parental_care.pdf (last accessed on 15.07.2018).

E. C. Kimelman (1985). "No quiet place: final report to the Honourable Muriel Smith, Minister of Community Services." Review Committee on Indian and Métis Adoptions and Placements, Manitoba.

Kommunalverband für Jugend und Soziales Baden-Württemberg (KVJS) (2014). "Auslandsadoptionen: Beratung, Unterstützung und Vermittlung durch den KVJS." Stuttgart, available at https://www.kvjs.de/fileadmin/publikationen/spezial/Spezial-Adoption.pdf (last accessed on 15.07.2018).

Latin American Institute for Education and Communication (ILPEC) (2000). "Adoption and the Rights of the Child in Guatemala." Available at http://poundpuplegacy.org/files/Guatemala-UNICEFILPECENG.pdf (last accessed on 03.08.2018).

L. Méndez Pérez (2008). "Situation faced by institutionalized children and adolescents in shelters in Guatemala." SBS, La Secretaría de Bienestar Social de la Presidencia de la República, Charcas.

Ministerie van Justitie en Veiligheid (2007). "Statistische gegevens betreffende de opneming in gezinnen in Nederland van buitenlandse adoptiekinderen in de jaren 2002-2006."

Available at https://adoptie.nl/wp-content/uploads/2017/03/Statistieken.pdf (last accessed on 03.08.2018).

Ministerie van Justitie en Veiligheid (2010). "Adoptie, Trends en Analyse, Statistisch overzicht interlandelijke adoptie over de jaren 2005 tot en met 2009." (on file with author).

Ministerie van Justitie en Veiligheid (2013). "Adoptie, Trends en Analyse, Statistisch overzicht interlandelijke adoptie over de jaren 2008 tot en met 2012." Available at https://adoptie.nl/wp-content/uploads/2017/03/Adoptie_trends_en_analyse_2013.pdf (last accessed on 03.08.2018).

Ministerie van Justitie en Veiligheid (2016). "Adoptie, Trends en Analyse, Statistisch overzicht interlandelijke adoptie over de jaren 2011 tot en met 2015." Available at https://adoptie.nl/wp-content/uploads/2017/03/2011_tm_2015_Trends_en_analyse_interlandelijke_adoptie.pdf (last accessed on 03.08.2018).

Ministerie van Justitie en Veiligheid (2017). "Adoptie, Trends en Analyse, Statistisch overzicht interlandelijke adoptie over de jaren 2012 tot en met 2016." Available https://adoptie.nl/wp-content/uploads/2017/03/2012-2016-Trends-en-analyse-interlandelijke-adoptie.pdf (last accessed on 03.08.2018).

Ministerie van Justitie en Veiligheid (2018). "Adoptie, Trends en Analyse, Statistisch overzicht interlandelijke adoptie over de jaren 2013 tot en met 2017." Available https://www.rijksoverheid.nl/documenten/rapporten/2018/03/07/adoptie-trends-en-analyse (last accessed on 03.08.2018).

Nederlandse Adoptie Stichting (2015). "Jaarverslag 2014." Available at http://www.nederlandseadoptiestichting.nl/documents/NAS_Jaarverslag2014.pdf (last accessed on 29.07.2018).

G. Parra-Aranguren (1994). "Explanatory Report on the Convention on Protection of Children and Co-operation in Respect of Intercountry Adoption." The Hague Conference on Private International Law.

The Permanent Bureau of the Hague Conference on Private International Law (1994). "Report of the Special Commission on the Implementation of the Hague Convention of 29 May 1993 on Protection of Children and Co-operation in Respect of Intercountry Adoption." The Hague.

The Permanent Bureau of the Hague Conference on Private International Law (2000). "Report and Conclusions of the Special Commission on the practical operation of the Hague Intercountry Adoption Convention of 29 May 1993 on Protection of Children and Co-operation in Respect of Intercountry Adoption 28 November-1 December 2000." The Hague

The Permanent Bureau of the Hague Conference on International Private Law (2005). "Conclusions and Recommendations of the Second Meeting of the Special Commission on the Practical Operation of the Hague Convention of 29 May 1993 on Protection of Children and Co-operation in Respect of Intercountry Adoption (17-23 September 2005)." The Hague.

The Permanent Bureau of the Hague Conference on Private International Law (2008). "The Implementation and Operation of the 1993 Hague Intercountry Adoption Convention: Guide to Good Practice No. 1." The Hague.

The Permanent Bureau of the Hague Conference on Private International Law (2010). "Conclusions and Recommendations and Report of the Special Commission on the Practical Operation of the 1003 Hague Intercountry Adoption Convention (17-25 June 2010)". The Hague.

The Permanent Bureau of the Hague Conference on International Private Law (2012). "Accreditation and Adoption Accredited Bodies: Guide to Good Practice No. 2." The Hague

The Permanent Bureau of the Hague Conference on Private International Law (2015). "20 Years of the 1993 Hague Convention: Assessing the Impact of the Convention on Laws and Practices Relating to Intercountry Adoption and the Protection of Children." The Hague.

The Permanent Bureau of the Hague Conference on Private International Law (2015). "Conclusions and Recommendations adopted by the Fourth Meeting of the Special Commission on the practical operation of the 1993 Hague Intercountry Adoption Convention." The Hague.

K. S. Rotabi (2010). "From Guatemala to Ethiopia: Shifts in Intercountry Adoption Leaves Ethiopia Vulnerable for Child Sales and Other Unethical Practices." The Social Work and Society Online News Magazine, available at https://www.uni-vechta.de/fileadmin/user_upload/Soziale_Arbeit/Dokumenten/Kutscher/Socmag_Archiv/June2010/June2010-

Rotabi__Kara_Smith-_From_Guatemala_to_Ethiopia__Shifts_in_intercountry_adoption_leaves_ethopia_vunerable_for_child_sales_and_other_unethical_practies.pdf (last accessed on 22.07.2018).

M. Rupprecht (2012). "Intercountry Adoption: ensuring that the best interests of the child are upheld." Parlamentary Assembly of the Council of Europe, Committee on Social Affairs, Health and Sustainable Development, 19.10.2012, Doc. 12597.

P. Selman (2015). "AFRICA: The 'new frontier' in international adoption." Paper Presented at 2015 SPA Conference, Belfast, available at http://www.adoptionhoksbergen.com/index.php/nl/2-algemeen/87-africa-the-new-frontier-in-international-adoption (last accessed on 27.07.2018).

P. Selman (2018). "Global Statistics for Intercountry Adoption: Receiving States and States of Origin 2004-2016." 03.05.2018, The Hague Conference on Private International Law.

R. Siewert et al. (2012). "Commonwealth Contribution to Former Forced Adoption Policies and Practices." Community Affairs References Committee Australia, Canberra.

Stichting Kind en Toekomst (2016). "Jaarverslag 2015." (on file with author).

Stichting Meiling (2015). "Annual Report 2014." (on file with author).

Smits et al. (2016). "De Toekomst van de keten voor interlandelijke adoptie." 17.05.2016, GV349/conceptrapport, Andersson Elffers Felix, available at https://www.rijksoverheid.nl/documenten/rapporten/2016/05/17/de-toekomst-van-de-keten-voor-interlandelijke-adoptie (last accessed on 30.07.2018).

D. Tolfree (2006). "A Sense of Belonging: Case studies in positive care options for children." Save the Children UK.

UK Parliament Selection Committee on Health. "The Welfare of Former British Child Migrants." 23.07.1998, 3rd report, available at https://publications.parliament.uk/pa/cm199798/cmselect/cmhealth/755/75502.htm (last accessed on 29.07.2018).

UN Commission on Human Rights (1981). "Report of the Working Group on a Draft Convention on the Rights of the Child." 17.02.1981, UN Doc. E/CN.4/L.1575.

UN Commission on Human Rights (1988). "CCPR General Comment No. 16: Article 17 (Right to Privacy), The Right to Respect of Privacy, Family, Home and Correspondence, and Protection of Honour and Reputation." Adopted at the 32nd Session of the Human Rights Committee on 08.04.1988.

UN Commission on Human Rights (1989). "Report of the Working Group on a Draft Convention on the Rights of the Child." 02.03.1989, E/CN. 4/1989/48.

UN Commission on Human Rights (2000). "Report of the Special Rapporteur on the Sale of Children, Child Prostitution and Child Pornography." 27.01.2000, E/CN.4/2000/73/Add.2.

UN Committee on the Rights of the Child (1994). "Report on the 5th Session." 08.03.1994, CRC/C/24.

UN Committee on the Rights of the Child (2000). "Report on the 24th Session: Concluding Observations on Kyrgyzstan." 09.08.2000, CRC/C/15/Add. 127.

UN Committee on the Rights of the Child (2000). "Report on the 25th Session." 14.11.2000, CRC/C/100.

UN Committee on the Rights of the Child (2003). "General Comment No. 5: General Measures of Implementation of the Convention on the Rights of the Child (arts. 4, 42 and 44, para. 6)." 27.11.2003, CRC/GC/2003/5.

UN Committee on the Rights of the Child (2006). "Report on the 40th session." 17.03.2006, CRC/C/153.

UN Committee on the Rights of the Child (2007). "Report on the 44th session: Concluding Observations on Malaysia." 25.06.2007, CRC/C/MYS/CO/1.

UN Committee on the Rights of the Child (2009). "Report on the 50th session: Concluding observations on the Democratic Republic of Congo." 10.02.2009, CRC/C/COD/CO/2.

UN Committee on the Rights of the Child (2009). "Report on the 50th session: Concluding observations on the Republic of Moldova." 20.02.2009, CRC/C/MDA/CO/3.

UN Committee on the Rights of the Children (2013). "General Comment No. 14 on the right of the child to have his or her interests taken as a primary consideration (art. 3, para. 1)." 29.05.2013, CRC/C/GB/14.

UNICEF International Child Development Centre (1998). "Intercountry adoption." UNICEF, Florence (Innocenti Digest no. 4).

UNICEF (2002). "The State of the World's Children 2003." Available at https://www.unicef.org/publications/index_4810.html (last accessed on 03.08.2018).

UNICEF (2006). "Excluded and Invisible, The State of the World's Children 2006." Available at https://www.unicef.org/sowc06/pdfs/sowc06_fullreport.pdf (last accessed on 03.08.2018).

UNICEF (2006). "Alternative Care for Children in Without Primary caregivers in Tsunami-affected countries: Indonesia, Malaysia, Myanmar and Thailand." Available at https://www.unicef.org/eapro/Alternative_care_for_children.pdf (last accessed on 03.08.2018).

UNICEF (2009). "Guidance Note on Intercountry Adoption in the CEE/CIS Region." (on file with author).

UNICEF (2009). "Progress for Children: A Report Card on Child Protection." Available at https://www.unicef.org/publications/files/Progress_for_Children-No.8_EN_081309.pdf (last accessed on 03.08.2018).

UNICEF and International Social Service (2004). "Improving Protection for Children Without Parental Care - Kinship Care, An Issue for International Standards." Available at https://bettercarenetwork.org/sites/default/files/Improving%20Protection%20for%20Children%20Without%20Parental%20Care%20-%20Kinship%20Care%20-%20An%20Issue%20for%20International%20Standards.pdf (last accessed on 03.08.2018).

UNICEF and Terre des Hommes (2008). "Adopting the Rights of the Child, A Study on Intercountry Adoption and Its Influence on Child Protection in Nepal." Available at http://www.bettercarenetwork.org/sites/default/files/attachments/Adopting%20the%20Rights%20of%20the%20Child.pdf (last accessed on 23.07.2018).

UNODC (2006). "Travaux Préparatoires of the negotiations for the elaboration of the United Nations Convention against Transnational Organized Crime and the Protocols thereto." New York.

UNODC (2015). "Issue Paper, The Concept of "Exploitation" in the Trafficking in Person Protocol." Available at http://www.unodc.org/documents/human-trafficking/2015/UNODC_IP_Exploitation_2015.pdf (last accessed on 03.08.2018).

USAID and UNICEF (2008). "The evidence base for programming for children affected by HIV/AIDS in low prevalence and concentrated epidemic countries." Available at https://www.unicef.org/aids/files/OVC_final.pdf (last accessed on 03.08.2018).

J. H. A. Van Loon (1990). "Report on Intercountry Adoption." The Hague Conference on Private International Law, April 1990, Prel. Doc. No. 1.

J. H A Van Loon (1993). "International Co-operation and Protection of Children with Regard to Intercountry Adoption." 244 Recueil des cours, 195-456.

J. H. A. Van Loon (2007). "Statement on the Occasion of the Deposit of the Instrument of Ratification of the Hague Convention of 29 May 1993 on Protection of Children and Co-operation in Respect of Intercountry Adoption, by the United States of America." 12.12.2007, The Hague Conference on Private International Law.

P. Vlaardingerbroek (2012). "Interlandelijke adoptie, bezien vanuit het perspectief van het vertrouwensbeginsel." Beleidsdoorlichting interlandelijke adoptie, 15.03.2012, Kamerstukken II 2011-2012, 33199, Nr. 1, Bijlage V.

B. Wacker (1999). "Qualitätssicherung der Auslandsadoption - genügt die Haager Konvention? Dokumentation einer Fachtagung veranstaltet von terre des hommes Deutschland e.V. am 10.September 1998 in Köln." Terre des hommes Deutschland e.V., Osnabrück.

B. Wacker (2000). "Verbrechen und andere Kleinigkeiten, Der Fall "pro infante. action: kind in not e.v." und seine Konsequenzen." Terre des hommes Deutschland e.V., Osnabrück.

Wereldkinderen (2016). "Annual report 2015 Wereldkinderen." Available at https://www.wereldkinderen.nl/websites/implementatie/mediadepot/1443483d20c4.pdf (last accessed on 26.07.2018).

Wereldkinderen and Against Child Trafficking (2009). "Fruits of Ethiopia. Intercountry Adoption: The Rights of the Child, or the "Harvesting" of Children? A Study on Intercountry Adoption in Ethiopia." Available at http://www.againstchildtrafficking.org/wp-content/uploads/Second-Interim-Report-FINAL-redacted-for-distribution+annexures.pdf (last accessed on 22.07.2018).

The World Bank (2013). "World Development Indicators." Available at http://databank.worldbank.org/data/download/wdi-2013-ebook.pdf (last accessed on 03.08.2018).

The World Bank (2016). "Gross national income per capita 2015, Atlas method and PPP." Available at https://astrofizyka.files.wordpress.com/2016/09/pnb-na-gc582owc499-wg-ppp-2015.pdf (last accessed on 03.08.2018).

J. Zermatten (2010). "The Best Interests of the Child: Literal Analysis, Function and Implementation." Institute International Des Droits De L'Enfant.

Parliamentary Documents

Germany

Antwort der Bundesregierung auf die Kleine Anfrage der Abgeordneten Cornelia Pieper, Ina Lenke, Klaus Haupt, weiterer Abgeordneter und der Fraktion der FDP vom 19.11.2014, Deutscher Bundestag, 15. Wahlperiode, Drucksache 15/4240.

Begründung des Entwurfs eines Gesetzes zur Regelung von Rechtsfragen auf dem Gebiet der internationalen Adoption und zur Weiterentwicklung des Adoptionsvermittlungsrechts vom 10.05.2001, Deutscher Bundestag, 14. Wahlperiode, Drucksache 14/6011.

Beschlußempfehlung und Bericht des Rechtsausschusses (6. Ausschuß) vom 12.09.1997, Deutscher Bundestag, 13. Wahleriode, Bundesdrucksache 13/8511.

Entwurf eines Sechsten Gesetzes zur Reform des Strafrechts (6.StRG), Deutscher Bundestag, 13. Wahleriode, Drucksache 13/8587.

Entwurf eines Gesetzes zur Stärkung eines aktiven Schutzes von Kindern und Jugendlichen vom 22.06.2011, Deutscher Bundestag, 17. Wahlperiode, Drucksache 17/6256.

The Netherlands

Achtergrond Onbekend? Onderzoek naar het Handelen van Twee Vergunninghouders bij de Interlandelijke Adoptie van Zeven Chinese Kinderen, 13.01.2010, Kamerstukken II, 2009-2010, 31. 265, Nr. 29.

Beleidsdoorlichting Interlandelijke Adoptie, 15.03.2012, Kamerstukken II, 2011-2012, 33 199, Nr. 1.

Bezinning op Interlandelijke Adoptie, Advies van de Afdeling advisering van de Raad voor Strafrechtstoepassing en Jeugdbescherming (RSJ), 16.11.2016, Kamerstukken II 2015-216, Nr. 60 839.

Brief van de Minister van Justitie, 18.04.2001, Kamerstukken II 2001-2002, just000339.

Brief van de Minister van Justitie, 07.11.2007, Kamerstukken II 2007-2008, 31 265, Nr. 1.

Brief van de Minister van Justitie, 14.03.2008, Kamerstukken II 2007-2008, 31 265, Nr. 3.

Brief van de Minister van Justitie, 03.06.2008, Kamerstukken II 2007-2008, 31 265, Nr. 7.

Brief van de Minister van Justitie, 10.09.2008, Kamerstukken II 2007-2008, 31 265, Nr. 9.

Brief van de Minister van Justitie, 20.01.2010, Kamerstukken II 2009-2010, 31 265, Nr. 30.

Brief van de Minister van Justitie, 15.02.2010, Kamerstukken II 2009-2010, 31 265, Nr. 31.

Brief van de Minister van Justitie, 18.02.2010, Kamerstukken II 2009-2010, 31 265, Nr. 33.

Brief van de Minister van Justitie, 23.07.2010, Kamerstukken II 2009-2010, 31 265 Nr. 35.

Brief van de Minister voor Rechtsbescherming, 10.01.2018, Kamerstukken II 2017-2018, 31 265, Nr. 63.

Brief van de Minister voor Rechtsbescherming, 26.04.2018, Kamerstukken II 2017-2018, 31 265, Nr. 65.

Brief van de Staatssecretaris van Veiligheid en Justitie, 10.12.2010, Kamerstukken II 2010-2011, 31 265, Nr. 36.

Brief van de Staatssecretaris van Veiligheid en Justitie, 11.06.2012, Kamerstukken II 2011-2012, 31 265, Nr. 43.

Brief van de Staatssecretaris van Veiligheid en Justitie, 04.10.2012, Kamerstukken II 2012-2013, 31265, Nr. 44.

Brief van de Staatssecretaris van Veiligheid en Justitie, 31.01.2017, Kamerstukken II 2016-2017, 31 265, Nr. 62.

Kamerstukken II, 20 046, Nr. 6.

Meiling en adoptie uit India; Onderzoek naar het handelen van vergunninghouder interlandelijke adoptie Meiling in de periode 1995 t/m 2002 naar aanleiding van signalen over mogelijke misstanden in India, 09.11.2007, Kamerstukken II 2007-2008, 31 265, Nr. 1

Ministerie van Justitie, Antwoorden kamervragen over gestolen Chinese adoptiekinderen, 04.08.2009, Kamerstukken II 2009-2010, 5610670/09/DJJ.

Verslag van een Algemeen Overleg, 17.09.2003, Kamerstukken II 2003-2004, 28 457, Nr. 7.

Verslag van een Algemeen Overleg, 30.05.2001, Kamerstukken II 2000-2001, 27 256, Nr. 8.

Verslag van een Algemeen Overleg, 12.02.2009, Kamerstukken II 2008-2009, 31 265, Nr. 11.

Verslag van een Algemeen Overleg, 06.10.2009, Kamerstukken II 2009-2010, 31 265 Nr. 28.

Verslag van een Algemeen Overleg, 13.12.2012, Kamerstukken II 2012-2013, 31 265, Nr. 45.

Verslag van een Algemeen Overleg, 15.02.2018, Kamerstukken II 2017-2018, 31 265, Nr. 64.

Vragen gesteld door de leden der kamer, met de daarop door de regering gegeven antwoorden, 02.09.2009, Kamerstukken II 2008-2009, 2009Z14923.

Printed by Libri Plureos GmbH in Hamburg,
Germany

9 789462 369160